Frontpiece. Lloyd George with Derby on a visit to the Liverpool Docks

In memory of Jo Cassar Anto

Lloyd George at War

Lloyd George at War, 1916–1918

GEORGE H. CASSAR

ANTHEM PRESS
LONDON · NEW YORK · DELHI

Anthem Press
An imprint of Wimbledon Publishing Company
www.anthempress.com

This edition first published in UK and USA 2011
by ANTHEM PRESS
75-76 Blackfriars Road, London SE1 8HA, UK
or PO Box 9779, London SW19 7ZG, UK
and
244 Madison Ave. #116, New York, NY 10016, USA

Copyright © George H. Cassar 2011

The author asserts the moral right to be identified as the author of this work.

All rights reserved. Without limiting the rights under copyright reserved above,
no part of this publication may be reproduced, stored or introduced into
a retrieval system, or transmitted, in any form or by any means
(electronic, mechanical, photocopying, recording or otherwise),
without the prior written permission of both the copyright
owner and the above publisher of this book.

British Library Cataloguing in Publication Data
A catalogue record for this book is available from the British Library.

Library of Congress Cataloging in Publication Data
The Library of Congress has cataloged the hardcover edition as follows:
Cassar, George H.
Lloyd George at war, 1916–1918/George H. Cassar.
p. cm.
Includes bibliographical references.
ISBN-13: 978-1-84331-793-7 (hardcover : alk. paper)
ISBN-10: 1-84331-793-1 (hardcover : alk. paper)
1. Lloyd George, David, 1863–1945. 2. World War, 1914–1918—Great Britain.
3. Great Britain—Politics and government—1910–1936. I. Title.
DA566.9.L5C37 2009
940.3'1—dc22
2009021994

ISBN-13: 978 0 85728 392 4 (Pbk)
ISBN-10: 0 85728 392 8 (Pbk)

This title is also available as an eBook.

TABLE OF CONTENTS

List of Illustrations   ix

Maps   xi

Preface   xix

Acknowledgements   xxi

Abbreviations   xxiii

1. Setting the Stage   1

Part I: The Home Front

2. The Search for a Manpower Policy   21
3. The Challenge of Labor   39
4. Controlling Shipping and Food   57

Part II: Strategy and the War

5. The First Attempt at a Unified Command   77
6. Facing the Submarine Menace   101
7. Prelude to Catastrophe   111
8. The Horror of Passchendaele   127
9. The Peripheral War   139
10. The Quest for a Negotiated Peace   155

Illustrations Insert

11. The Creation of the Supreme War Council   171
12. The Plans for 1918   191

13.	Before the Storm	219
14.	Crisis on the Western Front	245
15.	The Maurice Affair	261
16.	The Origins of Intervention in Russia	273
17.	The German Advance Halted	297
18.	The Turn of the Tide	311
19.	The Road to the Armistice	325

Conclusion   343
Notes   353
Bibliography   399
Index   409

LIST OF ILLUSTRATIONS

Frontpiece. Lloyd George with Derby on a visit to the Liverpool Docks

1. Lloyd George in 1916, shortly before he became prime minister (National Army Museum)
2. Lloyd George in 1917 (U.S. Army Military Institute)
3. Cartoon showing Lloyd George's optimism in the face of the nation's war-time shortages (from *Punch*, September 5, 1917)
4. Lloyd George, Milner and Kerr walking near Walton Heath (Parliamentary Archives)
5. Robertson (U.S. Army Military Institute)
6. Haig (U.S. Army Military Institute)
7. Lloyd George with Briand in 1917 (author's collection)
8. Foch (Library of Congress)
9. Pétain (Library of Congress)
10. Clemenceau (Library of Congress)
11. Pershing (Library of Congress)
12. Woodrow Wilson (Library of Congress)
13. Cartoon showing Wilson mystified as to why the belligerents are not attracted to the concept of peace without victory implied in his Fourteen Points (from *Punch*, January 31, 1917)
14. Robertson (far left) and Lloyd George (seated on far right) are enjoying a picnic with their French hosts near Beauvais (from Frances Lloyd George, 1918, *The Years That Are Past*)
15. Lloyd George with his wife, daughter Megan and Hughes, leaving the Abbey after the service (National Army Museum)
16. Lloyd George, Wilson and Foch en route to the Supreme Allied War Council, 1918 (Parliamentary Archives)

17. Lloyd George, Smuts and Hankey in Paris, November 1918 (from Stephen Roskill, *Hankey: Man of Secrets*)
18. Lloyd George and Clemenceau taken during the discussion of the peace treaty (from Lloyd George, *War Memoirs*)

MAPS

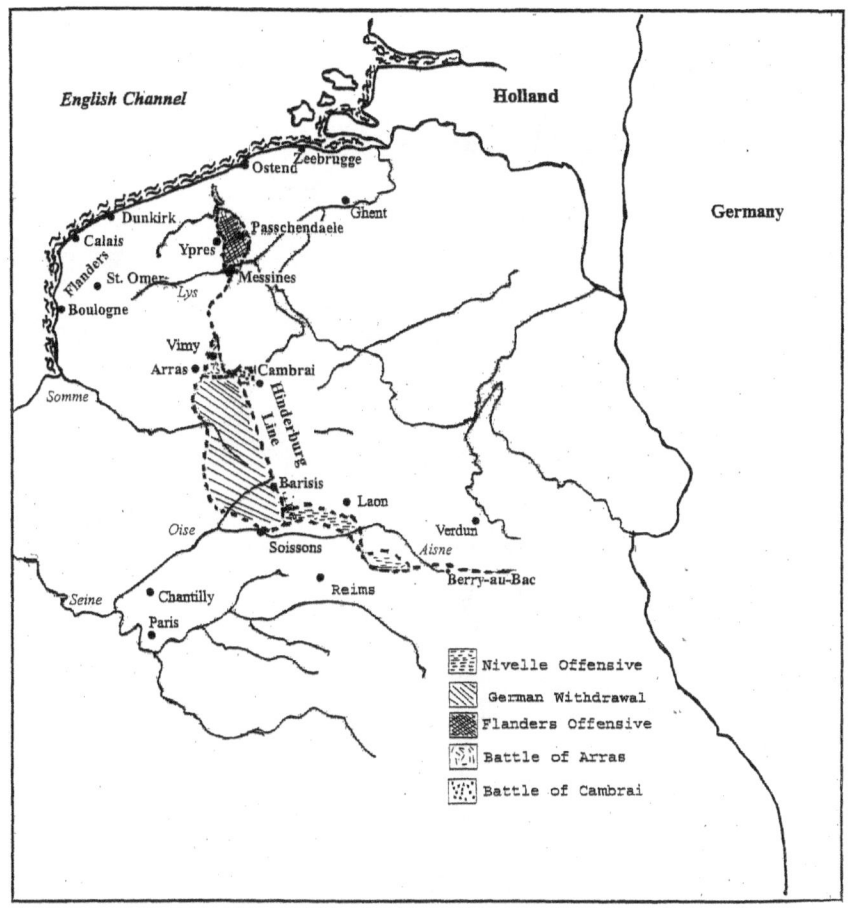

Map 1. The western front in 1917: Northern France and Belgium

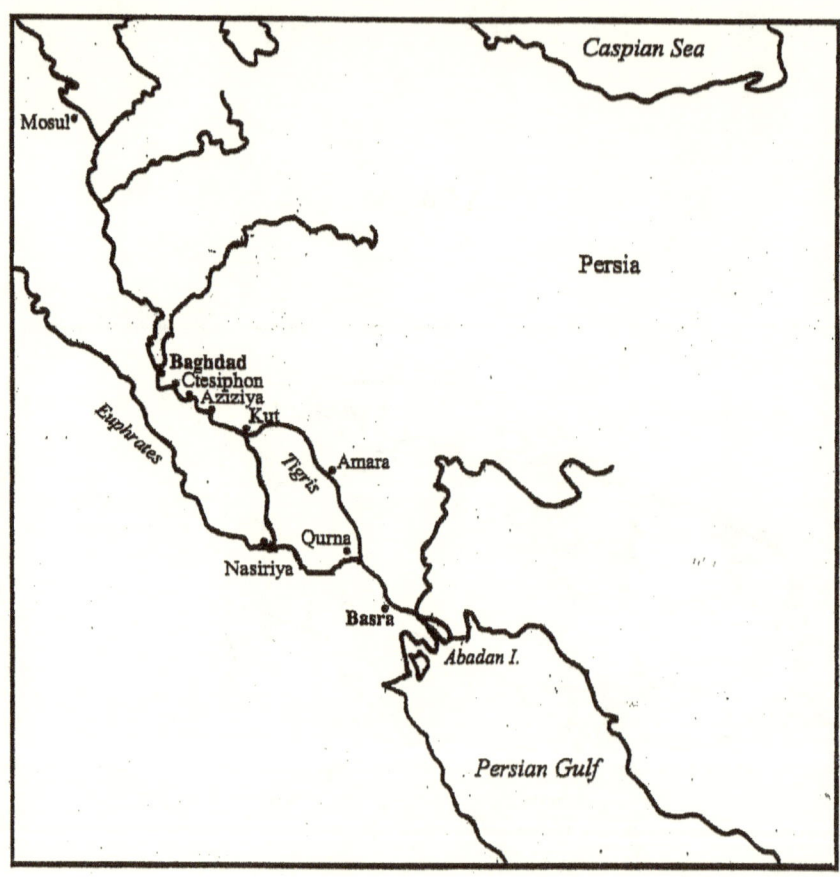

Map 2. Mesopotamia

Map 3. The Balkans

Map 4. Palestine and Syria

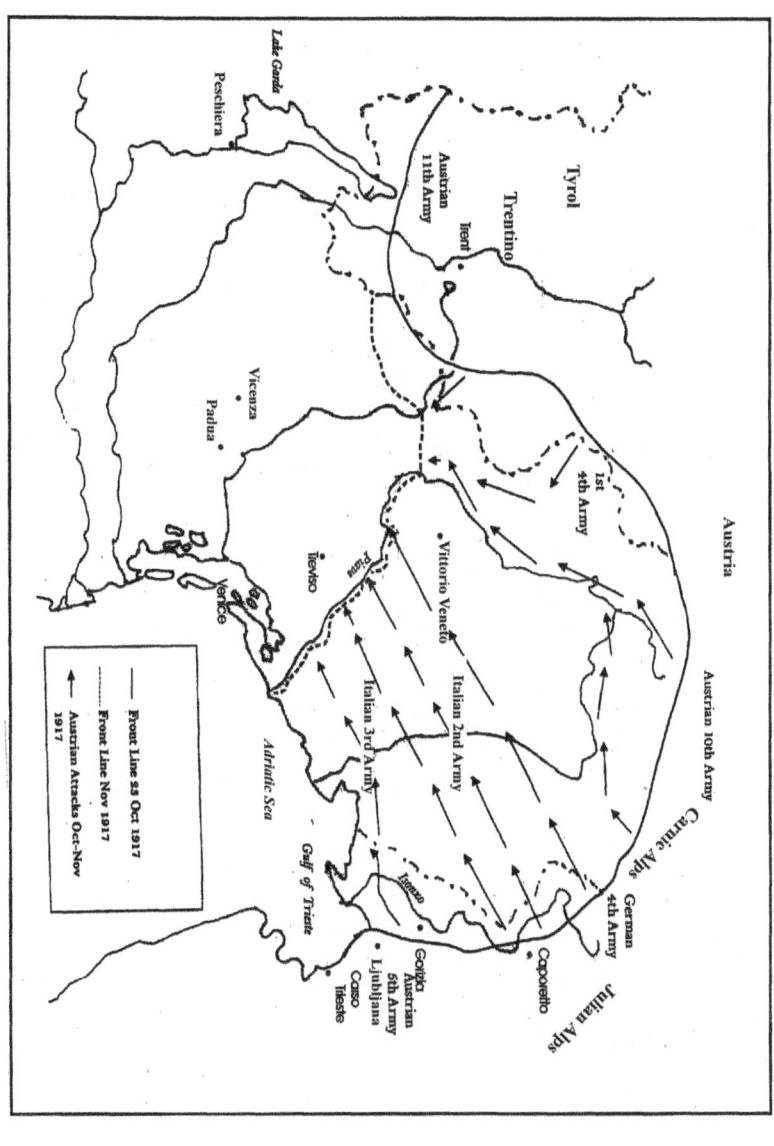

Map 5. Caporetto and the Retreat to the Piave

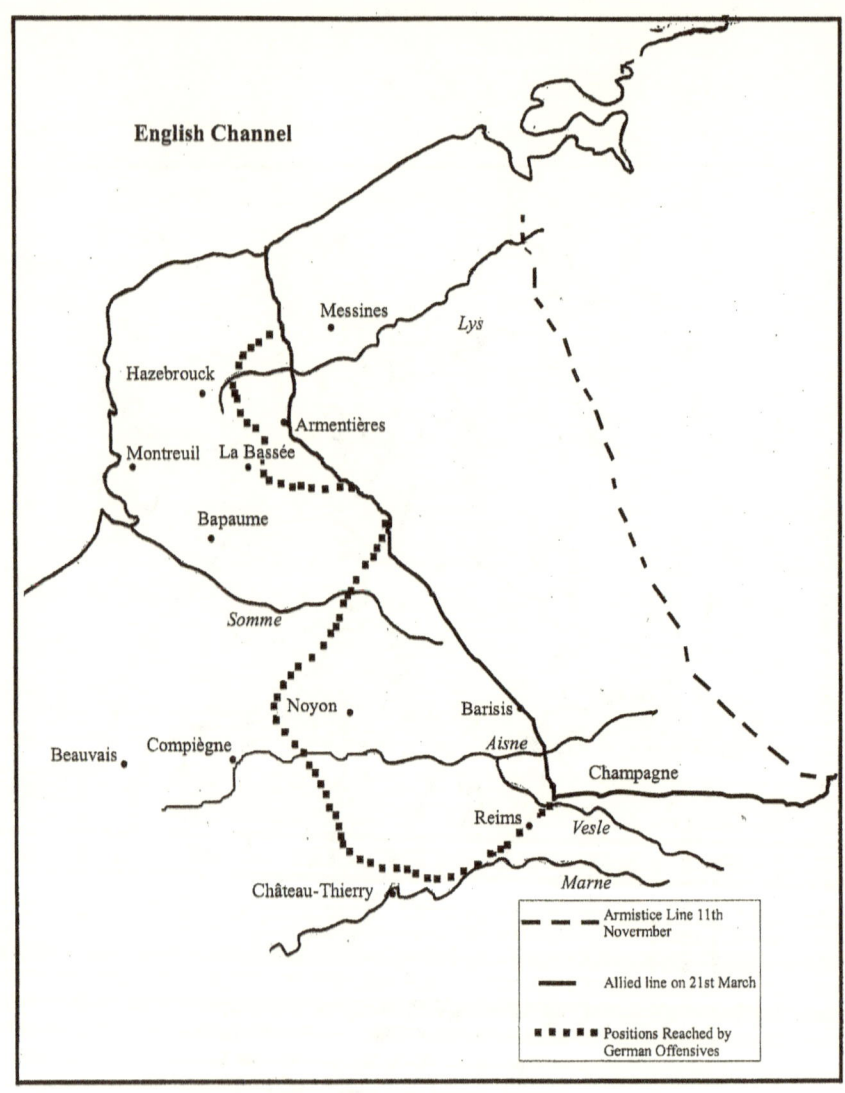

Map 6. The German and Allied Offensives, 1918

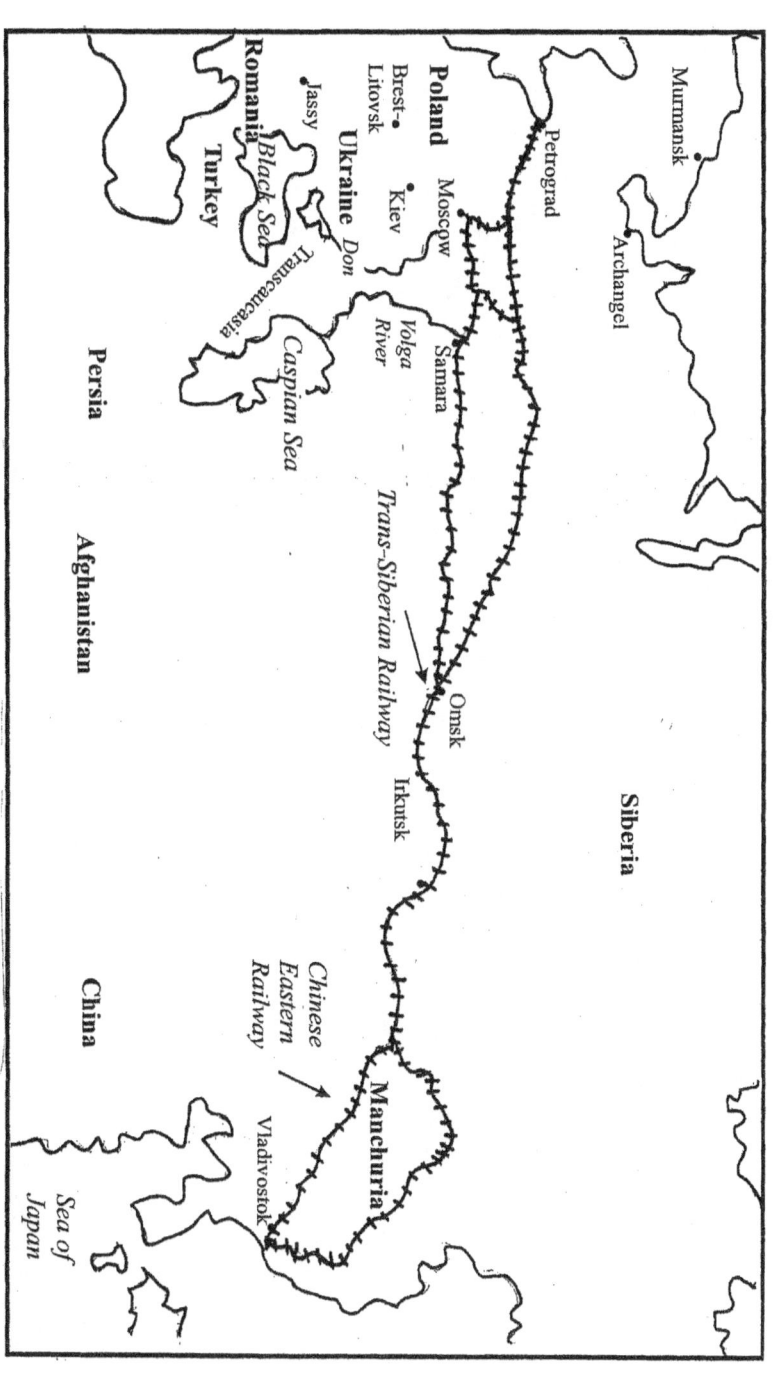

Map 7. Russia and the Ukraine

PREFACE

The only Welshman to occupy 10 Downing Street, David Lloyd George, stood well above his contemporaries as the most dominant figure in British politics in the first quarter of the twentieth century. He was unconventional in behavior for he did not fit in any obvious category. One biographer described him as a "rogue elephant among British prime ministers" and there was undoubtedly a highly adventuresome, almost buccaneering quality about him.[1] He seemed larger than life, with political abilities that entranced and dazzled as well as deep failings that aroused controversy and outrage. No one, it seems, can be entirely neutral on the subject of Lloyd George. He is, as sometimes happens, a historical character who polarizes opinion. Regardless of how he is viewed, he is undeniably one of the most interesting and colorful politicians of the last century. In comparing the two best-known war leaders of his era, Lord Beaverbrook remarked that "Churchill was perhaps the greater man but Lloyd George was more fun."[2]

The length, diversity and controversial nature of Lloyd George's political career explains why he continues to be the object of scrutiny and review. The number of biographies or monographs dealing with aspects of his political career are so numerous that they would easily fill a volume. Yet, curiously enough, his work between 1916 and 1918, although invariably praised by recent scholars, has generally received only superficial investigation. In fact, only the late John Grigg's last study (which was not quite finished when he died) covers the years of his war leadership in detail. Because Lloyd George remains a remarkably elusive figure, surely there is room for another book on the most critical period of his career.

My study differs from that of Grigg in several respects. I have chosen to treat my subject's activities quasi-thematically rather than in strict chronological order. Such an approach will make it easier for the reader to follow and to evaluate Lloyd George's handling of a complex issue than if the information were scattered piecemeal throughout the text. Secondly, I have tried to maintain the focus on Lloyd George and the War Cabinet, omitting any mention of his private life (except in the introductory chapter) and including only such references to domestic politics and marginal characters and incidents as are necessary to make the story intelligible. Finally, and most importantly, I have been especially critical of Lloyd George's war strategy. As a keen student of the Great War for over 40 years, it always seemed to me that Lloyd George was vastly overrated as a war leader. My research for this book reinforced the unfavorable view of Lloyd George that I had previously held.

Grigg is among a host of recent scholars who have elevated Lloyd George almost to the status of cult figure, revered as "the man who had won the war," and very favorably contrasted with the man he had deposed. While I liked Grigg personally and admired his scholarship, it seemed to me that he was inspired, to a large extent, by a devotion to the political tradition, if not to the party, with which the "Welsh Wizard" was identified. To be sure, Grigg could not be accused of whitewashing Lloyd George's political deviousness or pulling punches over his moral lapses. Still, he rarely disagreed with Lloyd George's domestic and war policies and adopted the line that his achievements, when measured against the dimensions of the problems he faced, were exceptional, greatly overshadowing his faults and few failures. I view matters differently. In his conduct of the war, Lloyd George did more harm than good. His work on the home front was, on the whole, good, but not so spectacular as to preclude other talented individuals from obtaining similar results or nearly so. When the final tally is taken, it is difficult to rank Lloyd George alongside Pitt the younger and Churchill as a great war leader.

George H. Cassar
Ypsilanti, Michigan

ACKNOWLEDGEMENTS

In a book that has taken me five years to research and write, my intellectual debts are beyond numbering. To cite every individual and institution that assisted me during my lengthy research would be impossible. That said, a number of individuals and librarians cannot justly go unnoted. I must begin by acknowledging my gratitude to Dr. David Marshall, who cast a friendly but critical eye over my manuscript. His comments saved me from some embarrassing gaffes and made me think harder about some of the issues discussed in this book. I am equally grateful to Dr. Paul Halpern, who read the chapter on the submarine menace and gave me the benefit of his unrivalled knowledge of the Admiralty and naval organization during the Great War. My colleagues Dr. Robert Citino, Dr. Phil Schmitz, Dr. Walter Moss and Dr. Ron Delph helped me at various points during this project, with everything from critiquing parts of the work in progress to the more mundane, but no less vital, task of offering much needed advice on editorial matters as well as researching and identifying remote places for the maps. Once again, the members of the Michigan War Studies Group, especially Dr. John Shy, Dr. Jonathan Marwil, Dr. James Holoka and Major Stephen Gregory, provided much needed encouragement as I thought and talked my way through numerous problems of organization and interpretation that I found perplexing. My cartographer, Miss Kelly Parrish, deserves high praise for turning my rough sketches into excellent maps. I am no less appreciative of the history department secretarial staff of Eastern Michigan University, particularly Mrs. Claudia Cullin, for attending to my many requests. It goes without saying that I alone bear the responsibility for what appears in this book.

It would have been impossible to write this book without the help and courtesy of numerous archivist and librarians. I would especially like to thank the following: Patricia Methven, archivist at the Liddell Hart Centre for Military Archives; Mr. Andrew Powers, library assistant at the Halle Library at Eastern Michigan University; Mr. William Spencer, senior reader advisor at the National Archives; Mr. R. W. A. Suddaby, keeper of the Department of Documents at the Imperial War Museum; and the staffs at the British Library, the Liverpool Record Office, Churchill College at Cambridge, the National Library of Scotland, the Scottish Record Office, the Birmingham University Library, the Department of western Manuscripts of the Bodleian Library, the Parliamentary Archives; and the Hatcher Library at the University of Michigan.

For permission to quote from materials for which they hold the copyright I would like to thank the following institutions and individuals: the Trustees of the Liddell Hart Centre for Military Archives; the Trustees of the Imperial War Museum; the Masters and Fellows of Churchill College, Cambridge; the Wardens and Scholars of New College, Oxford; the Clerk of the Records, Parliamentary Archives; the Trustees of the National Library of Scotland; Lord Haig; the Earl of Derby; Lord Hankey, Lord Robertson; and Lord Esher. Crowncopyright material in the National Archives is reproduced by kind permission of the Controller of Her Majesty's Stationary Office. I made every effort to contact copyright holders, but if I unwittingly overlooked any individual or institution, I offer my sincere apologies.

An undertaking such as the present study can seldom be completed without relief from teaching responsibilities and outside financial help. I am grateful to Eastern Michigan University for awarding me a sabbatical, which allowed me to complete all my research in the United Kingdom, and to the former dean of the Graduate School, Dr. Robert Holkeboer, for providing me with a modest stipend to help cover the costs. Above all, I am grateful to my wife Mary, who not only endured my absences and tolerated my preoccupation, but collected many of the illustrations that appear in this book.

ABBREVIATIONS

ADC	Aide-De-Camp
AEF	American Expeditionary Force
ASE	Amalgamated Society of Engineers
BEF	British Expeditionary Force
CAB	Cabinet
CIGS	Chief of the Imperial General Staff
C-in-C	Commander-in-Chief
C of S	Chief of Staff
CUP	Committee of Union and Progress
DMO	Director of Military Operations
DORA	Defence of the Realm Act
EEF	Egyptian Expeditionary Force
FO	Foreign Office
GHQ	General Headquarters (British)
GOC	General Officer Commanding
GQG	*Grand Quartier-Général* (French Army Headquarters)
HMSO	His Majesty's Stationary Office
MCWR	Military Correspondence of Sir William Robertson
MEF	Mesopotamian Expeditionary Force
OHL	*Oberste Heeresleitung* (German Army Headquarters)
PPDH	Private Papers of Douglas Haig
PWW	Papers of Woodrow Wilson
PRO	Public Record Office
SWC	Supreme War Council
TUC	Trade Union Congress

Lloyd George at War

Chapter 1

SETTING THE STAGE

David Lloyd George was born near Manchester on January 17, 1863, an irony, to be sure, for the most famous Welshman in recent memory. His father William George, originally from Pembrokeshire in Wales, had become headmaster of an elementary school in Manchester. Failing health forced William George to abandon teaching and to return to Pembrokeshire where he died of pneumonia in June 1864, leaving behind two small children and a wife (Elizabeth) who was expecting a third. Left practically penniless, Elizabeth was forced to move in with her brother Richard and her mother in Llanystumdwy, not far from Criccieth. Richard Lloyd was a lifelong bachelor and, to his credit, looked after his sister's family as if it were his own. He was an unpaid Baptist preacher, self-educated, highly intelligent, passionate about Welsh culture and history, and a die-hard Liberal. He made a comfortable living carrying on a shoemaking business, so that young David and his siblings grew up without enduring privation in a stable and loving environment. At school it was clear that David was bright, with a phenomenal memory and he excelled in mathematics, history and geography.[1] His formal education came to an end in 1878 when, thanks to uncle Lloyd's connections, a post was found for him in a leading law firm in nearby Portmadoc and the following year he was articled to the junior partner for a period of five years. In 1884 David did just enough to pass his law examination, but rather than remain with the firm, set up his own practice in Criccieth.

The early months were difficult for Lloyd George, as they normally are for any new attorney in private practice, and he had to content himself with whatever small cases came his way – debt collecting and defending clients accused of poaching, breach of promise and assault. Tentative in the beginning, he lost more cases than he won, but as he gained in experience and knowledge of the law, his performance improved dramatically.[2] He was a compelling orator, a skill he had developed preaching in chapels and in local debating societies, and soon acquired a reputation for preparing his briefs carefully, skillfully arguing cases in court, and being ready to stand up to magistrates to defend the rights of the small man.[3] As a result, his practice prospered and he subsequently opened offices in several nearby towns.[4]

During the first year of his law practice, Lloyd George began courting Margaret Owen, daughter of Richard Owen, a prosperous farmer.[5] Eventually, the romance blossomed and they married in January 1888. Although the couple had five children, two boys and three girls, and outwardly seemed happy, it was only because of Margaret's almost saintly forbearance that the relationship endured. It was not long before Lloyd George found married life confining and a bit tedious and began a pattern of conduct that would lead him into one adulterous affair after another. It was impossible for Margaret not to hear rumors of her husband's affairs and, while there were heated quarrels between them, she eventually became reconciled to that side of his nature.[6] Regard for her husband's position prevented her from making more of a fuss, but there was probably a more poignant reason why she tolerated her husband's philandering: she still loved him.

Lloyd George had warned Margaret before their marriage that he had high ambitions and that to attain them he was prepared to sacrifice everything, "even love itself under the wheels of my Juggernaut" if it obstructed the way.[7] Drawn to politics while still a teenager, Lloyd George gained local prominence through his work as a Liberal activist, many speeches and articles for various causes and as secretary to the Anti-Tithe League in south Caernarvonshire. These activities not only kindled his political ambition, but also advanced his prospects. An opportunity opened up when the sitting MP representing Caernarvon Boroughs died suddenly, precipitating a by-election. Lloyd George was chosen as the Liberal candidate and, in a hard-fought campaign, defeated his Tory rival by a mere 18 votes. Twenty-seven years old when he entered parliament in 1890, he would hold the seat through thirteen general elections over the next fifty-five years.[8]

Although single-minded and eager to make his mark in national politics, Lloyd George was bound up with issues mainly of local or Welsh interest during his early years at Westminster.[9] As a backbencher, he was actively involved in supporting Welsh Home Rule, financial assistance for Welsh education, and the disestablishment of the Welsh Church. His stinging and hard-hitting speeches, together with his habit of placing Welsh goals above all else, annoyed the Liberal leadership as much as the rival Tory party. During the ten years of Conservative ascendancy he became the leading spokesman for the Welsh Liberals and the recognized champion of Welsh nonconformity. Nevertheless, outside of Wales he remained an unknown public figure until the Boer War, which broke out in 1899.

The Liberal party was divided over the war and Lloyd George associated himself with the radical left of the party, which regarded it as morally insupportable. From the start he battled to counteract the jingoistic hysteria whipped up by the government, exposing himself to considerable danger, both politically and personally. His blistering attacks on the government, accusing it of waging a war for the benefit of gold-mining syndicates without any consideration for the suffering of the Boer women and children herded in concentration camps, caused riots and counterdemonstrations and made him the most unpopular man in the country. The best known incident, one which brought him within peril of his life, occurred at a meeting in Birmingham, fortress of Joseph Chamberlain, the colonial secretary. An angry mob of rioters, waving Union Jacks and blowing trumpets, surged into the hall and all efforts by the police to drive them out proved unsuccessful. Before Lloyd George made his speech, a huge melee broke out and he was whisked off the platform and safely smuggled out of the building disguised as a policeman.[10]

Lloyd George reignited his political career after the end of the Boer War by broadening his horizon and acting as a spokesman for the British as a whole, and not just the Welsh. Shedding his image as a Welsh extremist and rabble-rouser, he worked hard and diligently to establish himself within the broad center of British Liberalism. When the Liberals returned to power in 1906 under Sir Henry Campbell-Bannerman, Lloyd George became president of the Board of Trade. In his first ministerial post, Lloyd George proved that he was a firm and competent minister, steering a number of bills through parliament.[11] He was responsible for the Merchant Shipping Bill in 1906, which, apart from raising the standard of safety for ships, improved the pay, working conditions and accommodations of merchant sailors. Furthermore, he showed himself to be a skillful negotiator in the handling of labor, especially in averting a railroad strike in 1907. During the two years that he served at the board of trade, he compiled a solid if not spectacular record, confirming the growing impression in political circles that his wild and rabble-rousing days were a thing of the past and that he had now become a moderate and diligent statesman.

In 1908 Lloyd George became chancellor of the exchequer, an office vacated when H. H. Asquith succeeded the dying Campbell-Bannerman as prime minister. As such, he provided a powerful stimulus to the social policies of the Liberal government. He emerged as the leader of the radical wing of the Liberal party, determined to use the power of the state to improve conditions for the poor and the suffering. His first major task was to introduce the outgoing chancellor's budget, which, among other things, allotted pensions to those over 70 years of age. When he prepared his own budget for the following year, he required to find additional revenue in order to finance the construction of new dreadnoughts, as well as to cover the costs of old-age pensions and other social services. His solution was to raise death duties sharply (inheritance taxes on estates) and impose a super tax on incomes over £5,000, a land tax amounting to a 20 percent levy on any increase in the value of land (to be paid whenever it was sold) and an annual duty on the undeveloped land of large estates. Introduced in 1909, the so-called people's budget announced the intention of the government to tax the rich to promote a limited redistribution of the national income through social programs for the poor. It was a revolutionary principle and created a firestorm of controversy. It was heatedly debated in the House of Commons, session after session, and delayed other legislation for the rest of the year. Only after the general elections of 1910, when the Liberals were reelected by a narrow margin, was the budget issue finally settled.

Another of Lloyd George's cherished causes requiring navigation through rocky waters was the National Insurance Act of 1911, the capstone to the body of social legislation the Liberals began five years earlier with free school meals for children. The general plan provided for insurance against sickness and disability for manual workers, as well as unemployment benefits, though limited to industries in which employment was seasonal. It was to be a contributory scheme with the employer, employee and the state sharing the costs. The bill aroused widespread opposition and Lloyd George had to call upon all his reserves of charm and skill before it was carried into law.

After years of hard work and impressive political achievements, Lloyd George faced a major threat to his career in the form of the Marconi scandal.[12] In the spring of 1912 Lloyd George, who was always looking for a windfall to alleviate his financial worries, unwisely bought 1,000 shares in the American Marconi Company at £2 each. He had acted on the advice of his colleague, Rufus Issacs (later the Marquess of Reading), the attorney general, whose brother was head of the English Marconi Company and a director of the American Marconi Company. The purchase had taken place at a time when the English Marconi Company was about to enter into a very lucrative contract with the British Government to construct a chain of wireless stations between Britain and its Empire. It was not very long before the shares were selling for £4 on the open market and Lloyd George immediately recovered his investment by selling half of his holdings. When his activities were revealed in the press in the summer there was a clear suspicion that he had benefited from insider trading to line his pockets. The opposition accused him of corruption and hypocrisy and it was only because of Asquith's indulgence and robust defense in the Commons that he survived.[13]

Although Lloyd George would remain under a cloud for some time, he was still a central figure in the cabinet and indispensable to Asquith. He was the chief spokesman for the radical wing of the Liberal party. He was on intimate terms with labor and instrumental in settling a railroad strike in 1912. Furthermore, he was sent to Ireland to try to bring the opposing factions together. In early 1914 he devised a plan that called for the temporary suspension of the application of

Irish Home Rule to the six counties of Ulster. Asquith proposed to Sir Edward Carson, leader of the Ulster backbenchers in parliament, that the six counties could remain separate from Dublin for six years after which the public, through general elections, could decide their fate. Carson rejected the compromise. At that critical juncture external events intervened.

The long spell of peace in Europe was shattered on July 28, 1914, when Austria attacked Serbia, holding it responsible for plotting the assassination of the Archduke Franz Ferdinand, presumptive heir to the Austrian throne, at Sarajevo a month earlier. Within a few days other powers became involved, with Germany lining up behind Austria, and Russia and France rallying to Serbia's side. As late as August 2 the British cabinet was divided over whether to enter the war in support of France. As a man on the left, opposed in the past to heavy defense spending and foreign entanglements, Lloyd George stood alongside the ministerial group that opposed intervention. What was missing was the usual combativeness and fierce passion that accompanied his defense of a cause to which he was committed. When the Germans invaded Belgium, prompting the British cabinet to declare war, Lloyd George, after much soul-searching, opted not to resign. "In the final analysis," Michael Fry concluded, Lloyd George "had sat too long with Asquith and Grey to walk away from power and responsibility."[14] A champion of international peace in his earlier career, the war would transform him into a belligerent nationalist, in which stance he would frequently call, at least publicly, for a decisive victory over the enemy.

The Liberal cabinet's pre-1914 strategic doctrine did not represent any radical departure from the manner in which Britain had fought its wars over the past two centuries. The idea was to leave Russia and France to carry the main burden of fighting on land. Britain would provide money and supplies to its allies, send a token military force to the Continent and use the Royal Navy to keep the sea lanes open and impose a blockade of Germany.[15] In a matter of a few months Britain would ensure Germany's defeat and preserve the balance of power without serious dislocation to its economy and trade. Lloyd George shared his colleagues' expectation that the war would be brief and one of limited liability for Britain. He told his wife on August 11, "We are keeping the sea for France – that ought to suffice here for the moment especially as we are sending 100,000 men to help her to bear the first brunt of the attack. That is all that counts for Russia will come in soon."[16] Fortunately, Lord Kitchener, who was brought in by Asquith as secretary of state for war to give the cabinet the benefit of his military experience, had the foresight to see that the war would last at least three years and set about immediately to recruit a million-man army.

Lloyd George's most immediate concern in the opening days of August was to deal with the monetary panic that began as soon as the war appeared imminent. The bank holiday on August 3 was extended an additional three days while he sought advice from experts and implemented various measures to restore the credit system and bolster confidence. When the banks reopened on August 7, they reported that business was proceeding as usual. The financial crisis had passed. Leading economists, long suspicious of Lloyd George's ability to handle public finance, now praised him for his skill and courage in saving the economy from ruin.

Lloyd George's next challenge (when the politicians realized that the conflict would not be over by Christmas) was to provide the financial means to carry on a major war of undetermined duration. In November he submitted his first wartime budget in which he raised direct taxes and increased duties on tea and beer. On the whole, the budget was well received and further enhanced his reputation.

Lloyd George played a central role in the events leading to the creation of the coalition government. In mid-May 1915 the conjuncture of two controversies, one a military setback attributed supposedly to a shell shortage and the other to the abrupt resignation of the impetuous and headstrong First Sea Lord, Lord Fisher, after a volcanic dispute with Churchill, occasioned the change. On May 17 the Unionist chief, Bonar Law, called on Lloyd George at 11 Downing Street and told him that, owing to the recent revelations, he could no longer hold his backbenchers in check. Lloyd George agreed with him that the only way to maintain a spirit of unity in the Commons was to broaden the government to include the Unionists. Lloyd George then went straight next door to see Asquith and impressed on him the need to forestall a renewal of party conflict, which would damage the war effort. Lloyd George's arguments in favor of a coalition won the day.[17] When the government was reconstructed under Asquith's leadership a week later, Lloyd George left the Treasury to take charge of the newly created Ministry of Munitions.

Lloyd George worked at a relentless pace from the moment he undertook his new task. Large orders were place with foreign firms, new national factories were built, men were recruited from industry to carry out policy or act as administrators, controls were imposed on the supply of raw materials, technical innovations were made and production was speeded up by relaxation of trade union rules. Although Lloyd George, in his memoirs, exaggerated the obstacles that he had to overcome and gave no credit whatsoever to what Kitchener and the War Office had accomplished in very difficult circumstances, there is no denying that his stay at the Ministry of Munitions was a success and that his contribution in stimulating armament production was substantial.[18]

As 1915 wore on, Lloyd George became increasingly involved in shaping military policy in the inner councils of war. In late summer, with Serbia threatened from two directions, he was instrumental in persuading his colleagues to join the French in sending an expedition to the Balkans.[19] The catastrophe that befell the Dardanelles campaign in the spring and summer of 1915 should have made the British politicians wary about leaping into a new adventure without examining the potential pitfalls, defining the objectives and adopting a sound plan. It would not be an exaggeration to say that it was one of the worst strategic mistakes made by the British authorities during the war. Anglo–French forces landed at Salonica during the first week in October and immediately advanced north, but the numerically superior Bulgarian army drove them back. The maneuver to save Serbia having failed, logic dictated that the Allies liquidate that disastrous venture; but Lloyd George, together with the French, thwarted every effort. The number of Allied troops would eventually swell to over 600,000 and include five nationalities – Russian, Serbian and Italian in addition to French and British. This army, held at bay by Bulgarians and a scratch force of Germans, served no purpose. It did not drive Bulgaria to seek peace, provided no help to the beleaguered Russians, posed no threat to Turkey and failed to draw significant German troops from the western front. German journalists were not far off the mark when they jeeringly referred to the massive number of soldiers locked up around Salonica as "the greatest Allied internment camp."

Another issue that absorbed Lloyd George's attention in 1915–1916 was conscription, over which the cabinet was split, mainly, but not entirely, on party lines.[20] The response to Kitchener's appeal for recruits to serve in the new armies had been phenomenal and by Christmas 1914 over a million men had enlisted. The removal of large numbers of men with irreplaceable skills from civilian work at a time when there was a sharp increase in the demand for war-related goods could not help but impede output. The introduction of compulsory service would have allowed manpower resources to be allocated between military and civilian needs, but it would have meant a break with tradition and Asquith feared it would be strenuously opposed by the trade unions. As long as enough men rushed to the colors there was no pressure on Asquith to act, but in the summer of 1915 enlistments began to fall off, just when the necessity for greatly increased forces became necessary. When National Registration in August showed that at least two million more men were immediately available, some members of the cabinet, anxious that the war effort be kept in high gear, urged the speedy introduction of compulsion.

The vast majority of Liberals opposed a system of national military service on the grounds that it was contrary to democratic principles. The Conservatives, almost to a man, saw it as the only effective and fair way to meet the needs of the army and the economy and they were soon joined by Lloyd George. Over the next six months Asquith took a series of half-measures, including the drafting of bachelors, to appease the proconscription ministers and save his government.[21] Matters came to a head in April 1916 when the British army's requirements for more men could be met only by extending conscription to married men as well. Lloyd George took the line that general conscription was necessary and that Asquith ought to be resolute in leading the way. Pushed hard by Lloyd George and the Conservatives, Asquith gave in lest his coalition break up. In May 1916 a bill cleared parliament extending compulsion to all British subjects between the ages of 18 and 41, married as well as single. Labor accepted the bill grudgingly, for to have done otherwise would have furnished proof to the world that Britain was not united in its determination to see the war through.

Although the conscription issue drove a wedge between Lloyd George and his Liberal colleagues, his skill as a troubleshooter made him an invaluable asset to the government. Asquith was worried that the continuing troubles in Ireland would adversely affect public opinion in the United States and so he asked Lloyd George to find a formula that would see them through the war. Lloyd George agreed to undertake the task. For three weeks he carried on delicate negotiations privately with Sir Edward Carson and John Redmond, leader of the moderate Irish Nationalist party, and when it was over, he seemed on the verge of an astonishing triumph. The agreement unraveled, however, when both Asquith and Bonar Law proved reluctant to throw their weight behind it. Failure to push the deal through weakened Redmond's Nationalist party, which had been committed to achieving Irish independence through the parliamentary process.

Before the talks over the Irish issue collapsed, there was a dramatic shift in the political landscape. On June 5 Kitchener met a tragic death when the cruiser HMS *Hampshire*, on which he was traveling to Russia, hit a mine in stormy seas and went down off the Orkneys. Asquith weighed the claims of several Conservatives before appointing Lloyd George to the vacant post.[22] Lloyd George spent five unproductive months at the War Office where he frequently found himself at loggerheads with the military hierarchy over the way the war was being fought. Still, he gave every sign in public that he was united with the generals in his determination to win the war. On September 26 he gave his so-called "knockout" interview to Roy Howard, an American reporter, in a bid to throw cold water on President Wilson's anticipated peace initiative. It was reproduced in the *Times* next day. Lloyd George essentially made public, admittedly in an undiplomatic tone, the Cabinet's policy, which was to discourage American mediation for a negotiated peace.[23] He insisted that "the fight must be to the finish – to a knockout," however long and whatever the cost, and he warned that Britain would not tolerate the intervention of any state, including neutrals with the highest purposes and the best of motives.[24]

Lloyd George's unhappiness at the War Office deepened in the autumn of 1916. The war was going badly for the Allies and his efforts to circumvent the obstructionism of the military hierarchy had failed. He could see no ray of light ahead. Pondering on how to achieve greater civilian control of the generals, he could think of no other way than to remove the higher conduct of the war from Asquith's hands.

Lloyd George admired Asquith's intellectual qualities, his unique skills as a parliamentarian and the resourcefulness that he had shown as prime minister in times of peace. Indeed, during the prewar era Lloyd George had acted as a creative spark for the Liberal social program and someone on whom Asquith could depend, and the two, however different temperamentally, had formed a very effective team. But tensions in their relationship began to appear in the summer of 1915 owing to their differences over conscription. In the months that followed, the gap between the two became more acute as Lloyd George grew increasingly disillusioned with, and critical of, Asquith's inefficient and leisurely management of the war. Not only did Asquith defer to his generals, but he insisted on preserving the cabinet's executive authority. This meant that all major rulings in the War Council and its successors, the Dardanelles Committee and the War Committee, were referred to the full cabinet, where, too often, issues that provoked disagreement were shelved rather than decided on one way or another. Lloyd George reflected his discontent with the dilatory war methods in a speech in the Commons on December 20, 1915:

> Too late in moving here! Too late in arriving there! Too late in coming to this decision! Too late in starting with enterprises! Too late in preparing! In this war the footsteps of the Allies have been dogged by the mocking spectre of "Too Late," and unless we quicken our movements, damnation will fall on the sacred cause for which so much gallant blood has flowed.[25]

As Lloyd George put more and more distance between him and Asquith, he forged new links with a number of prominent Unionists. As a group, the Conservatives also wanted greater efficiency and speed in decision-making. They distrusted Lloyd George, however, regarding him as a Welsh radical who in previous years had been a fierce critic of the Boer War. Still, they were impressed by his driving force and by his determined approach to waging war, regardless of infringements on individual liberty. In the final analysis, they saw Lloyd George as a lesser evil than Asquith.

The press joined restive Conservatives to clamor for reform of the executive. The *Morning Post* summed up the frustration felt by many with Asquith's ministry when it wrote on December 1, 1916, "Nothing is foreseen, every decision is postponed. The war is not really directed – it directs itself." There were demands that Asquith be replaced as prime minister by Lloyd George, who seemed better fitted to play the part of a war leader. In short, the country as a whole wanted a change, a livelier organizer of victory, a new Pitt.

On December 1, 1916 Lloyd George, with Bonar Law's backing, presented Asquith with a plan that would reconstruct the system for prosecuting the war. This involved delegating executive authority to a small committee consisting of three or four ministers free of departmental responsibilities, and under the chairmanship of Lloyd George. Asquith would be excluded from the new body, but would remain prime minister. After some modification, Asquith accepted the arrangement. On December 4, a leading article in the *Times* attacked Asquith personally and implied that he had been reduced to a subordinate position in his own cabinet. The piece was clearly written by someone with good inside information. It appears that Carson was the informant, but Asquith suspected Lloyd George, who was known to have friendly relations with Lord Northcliffe, owner of the *Times*. His pride injured, Asquith repudiated his earlier agreement with Lloyd George, determined to fight. Lloyd George's response was to resign. Asquith could have weathered Lloyd George's defection, but confronted by the loss of all, or nearly all, of the Conservatives in the cabinet, he had no option but to resign. The king immediately sent for Bonar Law, the most obvious choice to succeed Asquith. Bonar Law declined the offer when Asquith made it clear that he would not serve under him. Thereupon the king turned to Lloyd George and invited him to form a government. Lloyd George accepted and between December 7 and 9 garnered enough support from the Conservative and Labour parties as well as Liberal sympathizers to form a government. His longstanding ambition to succeed Asquith had been achieved, not so much by intrigue as by accident.[26]

Lloyd George was 54 years old when he moved to 10 Downing Street. Although his formal education was limited and his reading as an adult was confined mostly to novels and newspapers (he refused to wade through complicated and lengthy documents preferring to ask leading questions from those who had done so[27]), there were few men in public life who could match his intelligence and perception. He had a prodigious memory, even if he could never remember the birthdays of his wife or any of his children.[28] He radiated an air of extraordinary strength and authority that people in his presence had encountered in no other politician. If he wanted something badly, he was indefatigable and, if one line of approach failed, he would drop it and take another. He was skillful at overcoming colleagues who doubted or resisted his policies, and rare were those who did not succumb to his genuine, unforced charm. He had a lifelong fascination with the press, understanding more than most its capacity to mold public opinion, and was extremely adroit in manipulating it. He employed a press secretary – the first prime minister to do so – to shield him from correspondents while cultivating close relations with press barons, providing them with inside information in return for support.

Bored with details, Lloyd George preferred to concentrate on the direction or conception of policy. A. J. Sylvester, his former secretary, wrote in hindsight, "Lloyd George never liked matters of detail. His strength lay in his ability to conceive, direct and drive."[29] He surrounded himself with all types of experts whom he consulted regularly. He was an eager listener, drawing into his mind the opinions and experiences of others. Possessing superabundant energy, he radically increased the amount and pace of government activity and even after leaving his office in the early evening, remained restless and found it difficult to avoid mixing business with pleasure.[30] At a party or dining with political associates, small talk would often take a serious turn. One person after another would be sent for, and what was a social gathering had turned into a political conference at which important decisions were taken.[31] Off duty, when his mind was briefly not on work, he enjoyed singing Welsh hymns around the piano, taking walks if he happened to be in the country, or playing golf, by all accounts more enthusiastically than skillfully.

Much of Lloyd George's success was attributable to his outstanding skill as an orator, which was unmatched by any of his contemporaries with the possible exception of Asquith. He would spend many days, sometimes several weeks, in preparing for an important speech. Because of his reluctance to read anything that he did not have to, he mastered his subject mostly by delegating the research to his staff and by picking the brains of experts. From the notes that he and others had taken, he would dictate a draft of what he intended to say, and, after committing it to memory, would reduce it to a skeletonized outline so as to give the impression that he was speaking off the cuff. He was careful in the manner that he delivered his speeches, judiciously marshalling facts and concentrating on his strong points while glossing over the weak ones. As a rule, he would begin his speeches softly in order to capture the audience's attention and his voice would gradually rise in volume as he built up to an emotional climax. He always seemed to sense the mood of an audience and could project himself as if he was speaking personally to each man and woman. Like all gifted orators, his timing of dramatic pauses or hand and head gestures was perfect. By combining power and passion, often in the style of a lay preacher, he could move an audience to tears.[32]

There was a dark and disturbing side to Lloyd George's character. According to his son, he was cruel to his wife and pursued women with the mad passion of a Casanova,[33] although, as prime minister, his extramarital activities were confined mostly to one woman, his secretary Frances Stevenson.

But adultery was not the least of his failings. Indeed, his deceitful behavior, even by political standards, stood out so conspicuously that one would be hard pressed to identify another prime minister in the last century who inspired as much distrust as he did. He put political ambition before anything else and, to that end, was unencumbered by fixed principle or party loyalty. As Lord Beaverbrook, a close friend, put it, to "Lloyd George no policy was permanent, no pledge final," and "like a trick rider at the circus," leaped "from one back to another."[34] Lloyd George personalized politics to an unusual degree and was relentless in persecuting those he disliked. He was ruthlessly cold, and had no compunction about discarding loyal subordinates when they no longer served his interests.[35] Few who knew him, even close colleagues, had anything kind to say about his ethical conduct. John Maynard Keynes's damning indictment was that he was "rooted in nothing", that he was "void and without content."[36] Clementine Churchill so distrusted him that she once described him as a "direct descendant of Judas Iscariot."[37] The first Labour prime minister, Ramsay MacDonald, had a similar view of Lloyd George, noting in his diary that he was "a colleague who was ever disloyal," that "he never used a partner, but for his own ends and sacrificed everyone who trusted him."[38] The late A. J. P. Taylor was not far off the mark when he wrote that Lloyd George "had no friends and did not deserve any."[39]

A severe handicap facing Lloyd George when he assumed office was that he did not have a secure party base. He could count on the support of about half the members of his own party. Only minor Liberal figures agreed to join his government. All the Liberal ministers in the 1915–1916 cabinet were so appalled at his disloyalty that they would have nothing to do with him, preferring instead to follow Asquith into political exile.[40]

From the very beginning Lloyd George knew only too well that his fate rested in the hands of the Unionists. Conscious of the precariousness of his position, Lloyd George could not shake his nagging fear that he might be deserted by his allies or that Asquith would find a way to turn the tables on him and sweep him out of office. These fears proved groundless. Although the Tories were aware of his personal and professional shortcomings, or at least most of them, they could see no alternative to his vigorous leadership. Nor did Asquith pose any threat. The former prime minister might have been expected to use his position as the leader of the opposition to lash out at his usurper on the slightest pretext. It is not unfair to suggest that Lloyd George would have done so if the circumstances had been reversed. Asquith, however, avoided even the normal opposition role lest he be accused of disloyalty and being motivated by personal bitterness.[41] He showed restraint and encouraged his followers in parliament to do the same.

The late administration had been dominated by Liberals who filled fourteen of the twenty-five seats. The Lloyd George cabinet consisted of fourteen

Unionists, seven Liberals, one Labourite and three who were not at the time members of either House. The figures reflected the shift in the balance of political power with the Tories occupying all the major places in the government except 10 Downing Street. Arthur Balfour was put in charge of the Foreign Office. A former prime minister, cunning and a skillful negotiator, Balfour's early connection with foreign affairs and service on the Committee of Imperial Defence and various war councils had made him well qualified for the task, at least on paper. Approaching seventy and in ill health, he concentrated on high policy, leaving career officials to do the routine work. Robert Cecil (minister of blockade) deputized for him when he was confined to his sickbed. Balfour's frequent absences from work meant that British foreign policy lacked consistency and vigor, and, more often than not, reflected the wishes of Lloyd George.[42]

Lloyd George worried less about Balfour than the men he selected to head the service departments. The Earl of Derby went to the War Office, partly to compensate him for siding with those who had rebelled against Asquith and partly to assure the generals that the new administration would not seek to remove control of strategy from their hands. Lloyd George did not have a high regard for Derby's ability. "As to the size of Derby's brain," he once told Lord Bertie, the British ambassador in Paris, "you must have long ago realized what it is."[43] He frequently made similar disparaging remarks about Derby to others as well. Derby was a great Tory magnate, with a reputation based more on who he was than on what he did. He was a corpulent, unimpressive-looking man, without strength of character or ambition, but honest, well-meaning, and reasonably sensible. He saw his role as shielding the military leaders against the intrusions of politicians.[44]

Installed at the Admiralty, Sir Edward Carson, the leader of the Ulster Unionists, was a brilliant speaker, courageous, hard working and energetic. But he had no administrative experience and he was the first to concede that he knew nothing about the technical side of the navy. Hence, he saw his function not as framing policy, but, like Derby, as protecting "his professional advisers against political attacks."[45]

Lloyd George, moreover, recruited new men, mostly with special skills or a business background, to fill ministerial jobs. H. A. L. Fisher, vice-chancellor of Sheffield University, took over at the Board of Education.[46] Sir Albert Stanley, a director of the London Underground Railway, was made responsible at the Board of Trade. R. E. Prothero, a Tory who sat for Oxford University, became president of the Board of Agriculture. Lloyd George sent Lord Rhondda, a successful businessman and parliamentarian, to the Local Government Board.

To cope with problems generated by the war, Lloyd George created a number of new ministries, beginning at once with Pensions, Labour, Shipping,

Food Control and National Service. Here, too, he turned to individuals outside traditional political circles. For the ministries of Labour and Pensions, Lloyd George brought in John Hodge and George Barnes, respectively.[47] They were two highly respected trade union leaders and thus judged to be ideal to preside over areas of working-class sensitivity. Lloyd George could not have made a better choice to head the Ministry of Shipping than Sir Joseph Maclay, a wealthy Glasgow ship owner. He would play a pivotal role in defeating the U-boat menace. Lloyd George selected Lord Davenport to assume the duties of food controller. He had been a large food distributor before embarking in politics and seemingly was amply qualified for the new post. However, he did not live up to expectations anymore than did Neville Chamberlain, who abandoned his work as lord mayor of Birmingham, to become the first director of the Department of National Service.[48]

An important and original feature of the Second Coalition was the creation of a small flexible body invested with supreme executive responsibility. Under the Asquith administration, all conclusions reached by the War Council and its successor bodies had been tentative and required the full cabinet's final approval. The decision-making process was thus slow and chaotic. Lloyd George's remedy was to create a War Cabinet, in the place of the full cabinet and the War Committee, originally composed of himself (as chairman), Arthur Henderson, Bonar Law, Lord Milner and Lord Curzon. Only Bonar Law, as chancellor of the exchequer, carried any departmental responsibilities. The rest were ministers without portfolio, free to devote their full time to the wider aspects of war policy. Ministers outside the War Cabinet were confined to departmental affairs and played no role in shaping war policy. The Chief of the Imperial General Staff (CIGS) although not a member, was on hand at the start of most of the sessions to provide military information and answer questions.[49] Lloyd George's determination to avoid the obstructionism of the services led him to exclude Derby and Carson. This decision had unfortunate consequences. Without close supervision the civilian heads of the services, owing to their insecurity, allowed their professional advisers to set policy to which the War Cabinet often objected, provoking head-on collisions that could not help but hinder the war effort.

Political considerations, rather than administrative ability, determined Lloyd George's choices for the War Cabinet. Henderson, leader of the Labour Party, was a talented administrator but unacquainted with even the basic elements of strategy. Lloyd George did not hold him in high regard, but his inclusion had been in exchange for Labour's support of the new government. Henderson's chief value was that he served as a spokesman and, as a reassuring figure, for the labor movement. He was treated politely, occasionally given roving commissions or asked for his opinion on the likely effects certain measures would have on the working classes, but in reality, was unwanted and out of his depth in the War Cabinet.[50]

As leader of the Unionists, Bonar Law's support was indispensable to Lloyd George's survival. If Lloyd George hoped to devote all of his time to the daily management of the war, which he considered essential under his new centralized system, he required to be relieved of the arduous task of leading the Commons. To that end, he deputed the responsibility to Bonar Law, on top of his work at the exchequer. By divesting himself of the bulk of parliamentary business, Lloyd George did not have to worry about answering tough questions or being dragged into heated debates. He appeared in the Commons only on special occasions, when it was vital that he address its members in person.

Not brilliant, but of appreciable ability, Bonar Law was modest, clear-headed and unselfish, with simple habits and a reputation for honesty and integrity. Temperamentally, no two men could have been more dissimilar than Bonar Law and Lloyd George. Yet, the two worked well together, no doubt because Bonar Law was content to be the junior partner. The Unionist chief understood that the new administration rested, more than the previous ones, on the shoulders of one man. In a letter to a colleague he wrote, "This is essentially George's Government and my own intention ... is to back him to the fullest extent I can. There is, I think, no alternative." He was confident that Lloyd George could provide the dynamism the previous administrations had lacked. The two men met practically every day and Lloyd George made it a point to use him as a sounding board before advancing any major proposal to the War Cabinet. The Commons occupied most of Bonar Law's time and, whenever he managed to attend a War Cabinet meeting, sat silently, puffing on his pipe and occasionally nodding in agreement.[51]

Curzon, a former viceroy of India and staunch imperialist, owed his accession essentially to his standing as an elder statesman in the Unionist party. His rare intellectual qualities, inexhaustible industry and encyclopedic knowledge of the Empire were a great asset to the War Cabinet. Lloyd George used him for many purposes, including the chairmanship of many subcommittees. For all his qualities and impressive record of accomplishments, Curzon was curiously handicapped by self-doubt and irresolution. While he could identify and clearly explain complex problems, he lacked the confidence to work toward finding solutions for them.[52]

The most formidable figure was Milner, ex-high commissioner for South Africa, whose selection had been totally unexpected.[53] Lloyd George had been a harsh critic of Milner during the Boer War and since then the two men had rarely spoken. Milner was the darling of a clique of young Tory intellectuals and much admired in right-wing political circles. Lloyd George chose Milner to remove him from the camp of the generals and to gain the backing of two separate but influential groups, the Tory intelligentsia and the Tory diehards (who wanted to win the war at any cost). But he also gained a brilliant minister. Grateful to return to high political office after a dozen years in the wilderness, Milner later became Lloyd George's most stalwart supporter against the generals and certainly the most creative administrator in the government.

None of the four men selected was expected to seriously challenge Lloyd George on war matters. Contemporary observers were fond of referring to the prime minister as a dictator. It is true that Lloyd George dominated the War Cabinet to an unusual degree, but to suggest that he was a dictator, or behaved like one, is an exaggeration. H. A. L. Fisher wrote in his autobiography, "Lloyd George was far too skilled in his management of men to ride roughshod over his colleagues. On more than one important occasion he allowed his Cabinet to adopt a course of which he did not approve."[54]

The War Cabinet inherited from its predecessor the nucleus of a secretariat presided over by Lieutenant Colonel Maurice Hankey, an administrator of exceptional ability. Hankey occupied a position of considerable influence in the government. He saw the prime minister practically every day and, if asked for his opinion or advice, had no hesitation about responding orally or in writing. His memoranda on broad strategic matters were informative, imaginative and cogently expressed. Given that he possessed more than the usual allotment of tact, he was often called upon to mediate between warring parties. His discretion, upright character and amazing capacity for work earned him the complete trust of Lloyd George, as they had his predecessor.[55]

Hankey, provided with four assistants, built the secretariat into a considerable instrument of power. It prepared the agenda and determined the priority of business for the War Cabinet. It summoned ministers and experts whose opinions were relevant to items under discussion. It kept minutes of cabinet meetings, a major innovation.[56] Previously cabinets had operated without minutes and it was not uncommon for ministers to leave meetings without a clear idea of what, if any, decisions had been reached. The only formal record of cabinet proceedings was the prime minister's letter to the Sovereign, which was subjective and sketchy.

Since the War Cabinet lacked a staff, Lloyd George set up a personal secretariat, known as the "Garden Suburb," so called because it was initially housed in the garden of 10 Downing Street.[57] Lloyd George became the first prime minister to employ a "brain trust" of highly talented men to provide him with information and advice on a on a wide range of issues. The group was headed by an Oxford don, Professor W. G. S. Adams, of whom Lloyd George recalled in later life that he "found his knowledge and sagacity of great service."[58] Another figure Lloyd George added to his personal staff was Philip Kerr, a disciple of Milner, and a man of even temper, charm, sincerity and brilliance.

His expertise was in foreign policy.[59] Like the president of the United States, Lloyd George frequently relied more on his unofficial advisors than on his ministers. This naturally generated resentment in the established departments, which saw the Garden Suburb as encroaching on their functions.[60]

The War Cabinet was less fractious and more decisive than its predecessor. Its reduced size was a factor but there were other more important considerations. The second wartime coalition did not have to grapple with contentious issues, such as Gallipoli and conscription, that had racked the first. Then, too, there was the personality of Lloyd George. He did not hesitate to bypass parliament, or bring pressure to bear on his colleagues in an effort to reach a quick decision. Moreover, his willingness to lead reduced the chances of divisions and counteracted the emergence of a rival to lead malcontents and pose a threat to his leadership.

Lloyd George appeared to have shaken the government from top to bottom by the institutional changes that he had introduced, but in fact, there was much continuity between his administration and that of his predecessor. The real differences were of style rather than substance. Lloyd George was responding to the changing nature of the war and it is doubtful that there was much difference between his administration and that of Asquith's. It would appear as if Lloyd George's system was stronger in some areas, but weaker or the same in others.[61]

Lloyd George had expected the War Cabinet to enhance the speed and efficiency of the central government. But the delays inherent in the late administration's conduct of business were caused not so much by institutional flaws as by clashes of personalities and by his own disruptive behavior. Sir William Robertson, the CIGS, and Kitchener had sat on the War Committee, but none of the members of the War Cabinet had any army experience or much, if any, understanding of the deeper issues of strategy. Like Asquith's inner councils, it grew progressively larger. Balfour, the foreign secretary, had the option of attending meetings whenever he wanted to. Other ministers and departmental experts were called in when matters of their special concerns were under discussion. If a highly controversial issue was on the agenda, it was not unusual for as many as twenty nonmembers to be in attendance.

Lloyd George's impulsive nature and dislike of convention made him approach his work in an intuitive rather than in a systematic manner. He infuriated his aides when he gave an order only to cancel it later, changed transportation plans at the eleventh hour, arbitrarily altered his day's schedule and summoned meetings whenever it suited him, usually without adequate notice. Hankey was exasperated by Lloyd George's "horribly unbusinesslike methods," which "render organization almost impossible."[62] Although the War Cabinet met on nearly every day of the week, frequently twice on the same day and occasionally even on Sundays and national holidays, Lloyd George's tendency to expatiate on his latest idea, rather than keeping discussion centered on the agenda, meant that items awaiting the War Cabinet's decision mounted and mounted. "The War Cabinet has met every day this week, but ... [t]hey never discuss their Agenda paper at all," Hankey complained. "Consequently all the work is dreadfully congested – far worse than it ever was under the so-called "Wait and See Government."[63]

Adding to the logjam was the extra work caused by interdepartmental disputes. The complex system which Lloyd George created, with the multiplication of new ministries and overlapping responsibilities, often caused interdepartmental squabbles over policy issues.[64] A major portion of the War Cabinet's time and energy was devoted to resolving differences among recalcitrant departments. Early in 1917 Lloyd George began the practice of delegating work to subcommittees, usually chaired by departmental ministers or War Cabinet members. With the number of standing and ad hoc committees multiplying rapidly, the War Cabinet found itself acting as a sort of supreme court, supervising their decisions, rather than as a plenary body making decisions itself.

Lloyd George's method of conducting war may not have been ideal, but no system is perfect. A good operator can overcome institutional flaws, and ultimately the nation's fate would hinge more on Lloyd George's leadership than on his complex system of government. What, then, were the challenges that Lloyd George faced? John Ehrman correctly observed that a prime minister engaged in total war was required to carry out three vital tasks: mobilize the home front, devise a coherent strategy and keep up the nation's fighting spirit.[65] It remained to be seen whether Lloyd George had the wherewithal to respond effectively, or reasonably so, to the exigencies both at home and on the battlefield.

Part One
THE HOME FRONT

Chapter 2

THE SEARCH FOR A MANPOWER POLICY

Lloyd George's displacement of Asquith in December 1916 gave the nation hope that the war would be pursued on a more energetic and creative level. But the deficiency in manpower organization was one vital area of the war effort in which Lloyd George was dilatory in taking firm action. His interest in manpower came gradually, necessitated as it was by the new elements affecting traditional warfare. The massive casualties resulting from technological changes and the scale of land battles led the High Command to make inordinate demands for recruits to keep its divisions at full establishment. At the same time, the unprecedented demands for munitions, for ships to replace those lost at sea and for the creation of an aircraft industry required the retention of more and more men in vital war production. It was not until the end of 1917 that Lloyd George showed the resolve to devise a coherent manpower plan defining the interrelationship of military operations and industrial production. For almost a year he met the growing manpower crisis with a patchwork of ad hoc measures reminiscent of his predecessor.[1]

At the outset of the war, the public's general opposition to conscription made it impossible for the government to devise a policy that would allocate manpower between military and civilian needs. As a rapid enlargement of a field force was the nation's highest priority, Kitchener achieved phenomenal success through the voluntary system, but at the cost of dislocating the economy. Recruiting was quite indiscriminate, pulling in, among the tens of thousands that rushed to the colors, far too many competent and skilled workers. By the end of 1914 the supply of skilled labor was beginning to hamper the war effort.[2] Consequently, a system evolved to provide badges to workers, signifying that they were involved in production vital to the war and should not be asked to enlist – there was considerable moral pressure to do so. In the fall of 1915 a more systematic approach was taken to exempt men in certain industries from military service.[3] Occupations receiving the greatest protection were engineering, mining, armaments and agriculture. The introduction of appeal tribunals towards the end of 1915 completed the exemption process. These military courts were empowered to decide the cases of men who were not in protected industries but had requested exemptions for other reasons such as ill heath or family obligations.[4]

The number of exemptions increased considerably after conscription became law in the spring of 1916. More workers were required for the new factories and for expanding production in existing firms that were engaged in fulfilling government orders. At the same time, the British army suffered severe casualties at the battle of the Somme and the intake of recruits was insufficient to keep its divisions at full strength. There was a feeling among War Office authorities that too many exemptions were given to men working in trades that were not of national importance. Their concern resonated with some members of the War Committee, which sought to find more men for the army by initiating a process of "debadging." In August 1916 the Asquith government set up the Manpower Distribution Board which was charged with "combing out" fit young men from key workshops to make them available for military service, as well as adjudicating the competing demands among government departments for labor.[5] A dispute arising from the Board's preliminary report calling for a two-week moratorium on badging workmen while it prepared a comprehensive plan led to a strike among skilled workers at the Vickers munitions factory in Sheffield. The workers claimed that the government had violated a pledge that skilled men would not be recruited for military service. Acting on the advice of Henderson, the Asquith government worked out a plan with the trade unions, allowing them to decide which skilled men would serve in the army.[6] The so-called Trade Card Agreement was a failure because the trade unions were torn between deciding whether a man should be retained in civil life or turned over to the army. Since they tended to hold back men whose skills were questionable, they were unable to deliver recruits in sufficient numbers to meet the army's needs.

The Manpower Distribution Board was no more successful. It lacked executive authority and, as its proposals encountered strong opposition from interested agencies, recommended the creation of a department to control national service. The old War Committee accepted the suggestion in principle and commissioned a subcommittee under Edwin Montagu to draft the bill. It had just completed its task when Asquith fell from power.[7]

A comprehensive and coherent system of national service was high on the priority list of the new administration, which took office during the second week of December 1916. The Director of Recruiting, Auckland Geddes, submitted a memorandum, dated December 12, in which he observed that there were 1,226,000 men in nonvital occupations. It was his opinion that most of these workers, approximately 1,000,000, should be transferred by voluntary or compulsory means to essential industries to release the men required for the army. He saw no other way to maintain the army at full strength.[8]

Montagu's plan was taken off the shelf and aired in the War Cabinet on December 14 in the absence of Lloyd George, who was ill. Using it as a basis, the members provisionally agreed to the following points: that a Director of National Service should be put in charge of both military and civilian compulsory national service; that the director keep the military and civilian sides separate, appointing, to serve under him, a civilian director and a military director, with a clear line of demarcation between them; and that the functions of the Ministry of Labor and the Director of National Service should be carefully defined and clearly set apart. Opinion was unanimous that Montagu should be the man to undertake the duties of director.[9]

The War Cabinet, with the prime minister in the chair, learned at its session on December 19 that there was an insurmountable barrier to the draft bill. Henderson, along with the Labor Minister, John Hodge, had met with trade union leaders and found them vehemently opposed to civil compulsion, which they saw as meaning the subordination of labor to the state and the loss of privileges they had fought so hard to attain. As the War Cabinet wished to avoid an open confrontation with industrial workers, it found it necessary "to proceed, in the first instance, on the lines of voluntary enrollment and the transferal of labour without a Bill."[10]

The other matter involved finding a substitute for Montagu, who had declined to join the new coalition out of loyalty to Asquith. Probably the best choice would have been Henderson, given his association with labor and his unique talents as an organizer. As it was, only one candidate, Neville Chamberlain, drew all the attention. A day or two earlier, Austen Chamberlain, the secretary of state for India, had collared Curzon and pressed for the appointment of his half-brother, Neville. Curzon now brought out Neville's name, which was enthusiastically endorsed by Milner.[11] Lloyd George had never seen Neville Chamberlain nor knew anything about him other than he had built a fine reputation as lord mayor of Birmingham. In the afternoon, the prime minister interviewed Chamberlain and offered him the job, giving him ten minutes to make up his mind – as he wished to make an announcement of the appointment that same evening to the House of Commons before it adjourned for the Christmas holidays. Pausing for a few minutes, Chamberlain accepted the post, although with considerable reluctance. It was a decision that he would soon regret.

Chamberlain had been led to believe that military recruiting and civilian labor, hitherto separate entities, would come under the control of his department. As it happened, the terms of his office were never that broad. He was given responsibility only for civilian labor, not the recruiting machine, which remained distinct and under the aegis of the War Office.[12]

The relationship between the two men was unhappy from the start, and Lloyd George later admitted that Chamberlain "was not one of my successful selections."[13] It may be that the prime minister did not appreciate the extent to which the civil departments, already controlling most of the labor, would be unwilling to surrender their power. The fact nevertheless remains that Chamberlain was faced with a Herculean, if not impossible, task of trying to establish a system that would redistribute labor on a voluntary basis.

Tall, gaunt, and somber, the forty-eight-year-old Neville Chamberlain had pursued a successful career in business, before immersing himself in local politics, where he had proved himself a diligent and competent administrator. Notwithstanding his family's tradition, he had never stood for parliament and, while people had heard of him, few perceived him as a statesman of national stature. In truth, he lacked the initiative and dynamic vigor of his father, Joseph, and the negotiating skill of his brother, assets he would need in full measure if he was to tackle the extremely difficult task he was assigned. Quite apart from personal shortcomings, he never received the kind of assistance he had a right to expect from the prime minister. His authority was ill-defined despite several interviews with Lloyd George. Chamberlain seemed to be under the impression that his role consisted chiefly of finding recruits for the army by combing out protected industries. Lloyd George, on the other hand, wanted him to concentrate on enrolling civilians into a volunteer labor force that could be sent, as warranted, to different parts of the country to replace workers taken from essential occupations. Whenever disputes arose with heads of civil departments, Lloyd George never interceded on his behalf. A seat was not found for him in the House, a serious handicap, as he was not directly answerable to parliamentarians for the work of his department. His standing was further diminished because Lloyd George did not bother to make him a privy counselor to which he was entitled as head of a department.

Still, Chamberlain must take some of the responsibility for his brief and ill-fated foray into national politics. Rather than choosing experienced assistants from other ministries, he insisted on bringing down his own officials from Birmingham, officials unversed in the ways of Whitehall. He failed to put his foot down when other departments ignored his requests or impinged on his own responsibilities. Most important of all, he made the mistake of waiting for the overburdened prime minister to define the area of initiative instead of devising a realistic plan and insisting that he be given the means to carry it out or he would resign.[14]

In announcing Chamberlain's appointment to the Commons, Lloyd George anticipated a huge flow of volunteers, raising expectations that no one could fulfill.[15] He noted that the director's task was to produce a system that would control and direct, in the most efficient manner, the whole manpower of the country. He implied that voluntary enlistment would be tried at first, but if that should prove unsatisfactory, the government would extend compulsion to the industrial sector. Thus, to obtain the needed recruits for the army, exhortations and appeals would be tried before the Directorate of National Service was given the powers to enforce compulsion. To create the maximum impact, the prime minister promoted the idea of equality of sacrifice. He paid tribute to the courage and resolution of the men fighting on the western front and urged workers to be no less patriotic in serving their country, reminding them that conditions at home were far better than in the trenches.[16]

On January 12, 1917 Lloyd George tried to provide Chamberlain with a good start by arranging a conference at which he could consult the other ministers concerned with labor. Chamberlain created a bad impression on everyone present. The prime minister was upset because, as he complained to Hankey, Chamberlain did not appear to have made any progress in working out his scheme. Chamberlain was instructed to prepare a blueprint post haste, recommending the organization that would be required to obtain and enroll National Service volunteers, the method by which labor would be allocated to vital war work and the measures contemplated to provide the army with the necessary recruits.[17]

Chamberlain's first report, put together after many weary hours with his collaborators, was examined closely in the War Cabinet on January 19. It was divided into two parts. The first proposed the means to meet the army's demands for recruits and the second dealt with the machinery to attract and allocate labor where it was most needed. The report's answer for the army's pressing demands for 450,000 men by the end of March was to cancel all exemptions issued to men between the ages of 18 and 22, except in rare circumstances. Simultaneously, a patriotic appeal for recruits, known as the "industrial army," would be launched to replace the mass of men withdrawn from essential industries. The second section involved the inspection of farms, shipyards and industrial works to ensure that workers were properly employed.[18]

The report was given rough treatment in the War Cabinet, running, as it did, into conflict, not only with the Trade Card Agreement, but also with key civilian departments whose needs for manpower were as great as those of the army. There was a consensus that Chamberlain's plan would make more men available to the army, but at the expense of seriously undermining vital sectors of the economy. The upshot was that the War Cabinet accepted the principle of canceling exemptions, but excluded men in occupations covered by the Trade Card Agreement and employed in shipyards, mines, agriculture, munitions work, transportation and the production of steel.[19]

To the British military authorities, the shortage of drafts was of serious concern since they believed that the German army, with at least 55 more divisions than in the previous year, would unleash a major attack in the summer of 1917.[20] During the first week in February the Army Council submitted a memorandum to the War Cabinet, emphasizing that the recent measures introduced to provide more recruits "have proven to be quite inadequate." It noted that 50,000 men were raised for general service in January, whereas the minimum required was 100,000. As there was no evidence that recruiting under the current conditions would be materially better in the months ahead, it predicted dire consequences unless drastic action was taken at once. The Army Council was convinced that the shortage of recruits was not so much due to the lack of men of military age as to the want of an organization for utilizing them to the best advantage. It urged that legal powers should be obtained to cancel all existing exemptions by successive age groups and to compel all men up to the age of 55 or 60 to engage in work of national importance where and when required.[21]

The War Cabinet took the army's desperate call for additional manpower in stride and showed no sense of urgency. At the same meeting on February 5 it moved on to examine Chamberlain's second report. Chamberlain admitted that the restrictive guidelines imposed by the War Cabinet had ruled out any chance that enough men could be transferred from industry to the army. He recommended the gradual cancellation of all exemptions from military service for men up to the age of 31. He was convinced that the removal of fit men of military age would not hamper output, providing a little time were given to their replacements for adaptation to the new conditions. He thought that many employers and trade unions would welcome sweeping away the present restrictions that protected certain individuals while leaving others, equally deserving, to risk their lives for the common cause. Under his plan, he estimated that 590,000 men would be released for the army by June 1917.[22] Unfortunately for Chamberlain, stiff resistance from the civilian departments, in particular Munitions and Labour, doomed the adoption of his scheme.

By now, Lloyd George had concluded that the nation would not accept conscription of the workplace. Since he was committed to the present voluntary methods, he was unwilling to risk the collapse of certain sectors of the economy simply to pile men into France who would be frittered away in Somme-like offensives. The prime minister explained his position to Colonel Repington, military correspondent for the *Times*, during lunch at 10 Downing Street on February 9. A fervent defender of the generals, Repington could scarcely believe what he heard. He preserved a record of their conversation in his diary:

> He seemed to me to be influenced by sentiment and prejudice, rather than by a reasoned view of the military necessities of the case, and although he had been the head and front of the demand for men under the Asquith leadership, he now seemed to me to be adopting an attitude

which threatened danger for the success of our arms. He said that he was "not prepared to accept the position of a butcher's boy driving cattle to the slaughter and that he would not do it." ... I said that I thought we might be faced in the West with almost an equality of forces, and that ... I saw no reason on military grounds why he should expect a decisive victory in the West this year. We seemed to me, I said, to be preparing, at the best, for 1918. The P.M. said that the country could not spare the men that the Army wanted, and that we could not denude the shipyards, the farms, and other essential national industries.[23]

On February 6 Chamberlain launched his National Service campaign with a speech outlining his proposals at the Central Hall, Westminster. A number of dignitaries and cabinet ministers, including the prime minister, were on hand to encourage men, physically unfit for military service or engaged in nonessential trades, to volunteer to work in vital industries as substitutes for those who would then be drafted into the army.[24] Early indications were disappointing, revealing that the number of enrollments would fall far short of those set by Chamberlain's department. With a little over three weeks to go before the cutoff date of March 31, only 114,000 had enrolled out of a projected target of 500,000, to the prime minister's dismay.[25] To make matters worse, of those who had volunteered, many were either unsuitable or already engaged in work of national importance. It was apparent that Chamberlain's volunteer scheme was not the answer to the army's manpower shortage.

Lloyd George was disappointed that Chamberlain had failed to produce instant and effective results. He thought that the director lacked drive, and that he had not held nearly enough rallies, or shown the creative talent to stir public interest in his campaign to pull in industrial volunteers in large numbers. His unsteady performance led Lloyd George to conclude that he was not up to the task.[26] Although the prime minister made no effort to remove him from office, he asked Lord Rhondda, president of the Local Government Board, to investigate the manpower issue and to recommend a policy.[27]

Lloyd George was well aware that the success of the National Service Department in mining the patriotic good will of the nation would strengthen the assumption that his appointment as prime minister guaranteed that the war would be prosecuted more effectively. Alternately, the failure of Chamberlain to fulfill his mission would damage the credibility of his government. The activities of the National Service Department were closely scrutinized in the press, which called for industrial compulsion and did not miss an opportunity to ridicule the administrative glitches that are inevitable in any new and large organization. Concluding that the National Service plan could use more favorable publicity, Lloyd George approached Chamberlain about hiring Kennedy Jones, a reputable journalist, as his deputy. Lloyd George deliberately omitted to tell him of Jones's conditions. Chamberlain discovered, during an interview with Jones, that he would come only if allowed to run the operation. Chamberlain naturally rejected his appointment.[28] The incident would have a lasting adverse impact on his relations with Lloyd George. In a conversation with Bonar Law three years later, Chamberlain showed that the anger aroused at the time had not in any way subsided:

> I could not forget nor forgive Ll.G.'s treatment of me in deliberately concealing from me K. J.'s conditions when he tried to get me to accept him.... [W]hat I could not stand was the attempt to push me into a trap, an attempt actually continued in face of K. J.'s frank admission that he would only come on condition that he ran the show.[29]

During the third week in March the Rhondda committee reported its findings. It offered a number of options but doubted that adequate numbers for the army would be forthcoming without the adoption of compulsion, which would permit workers to be transferred from nonessential to vital industries. Still, the committee recognized that, given the government's pledge to the unions, any measure of conscription would at present be impractical and thus it supported the plan of national service volunteers advanced by the director and a modified version in which substitute volunteers would replace men released from essential work for military service. It proposed directing the appeals to trades likely to yield the kind of men required, and that they ought to be made through local committees representing workers and employers. If, after a limited period, this method was shown to be inadequate, the case for compulsion would undoubtedly command overwhelming general assent. The committee further recommended that the Trade Card scheme "be superseded by a schedule of occupations with age limits."[30]

The Rhondda committee's report was favorably received by the War Cabinet when it was considered on March 23. But there was general agreement that the strong feeling in the country against industrial conscription precluded its adoption, at least until it was shown that voluntary enrollments and substitute volunteers to replace men in essential industries proved incapable of yielding the required recruits for the army. Similarly, it was decided to cancel the Trade Card Agreement, thereby regaining the state's power to determine the exemptions from army service.[31]

The War Cabinet appointed Milner and Henderson to determine which men could be released from certain protected industries. The two men made a careful survey and concluded that 215,000 men should be set free. The War Cabinet notified the departments concerned to make the men available.

The order was ignored, however, and the prime minister apparently did nothing to enforce its application. Robertson recalled with some bitterness in later years that "up to May 25, two months after the order was given, the Army had received, of the allotted number, one man."[32] Derby was convinced, as he would tell Lloyd George, that the only satisfactory way of dealing with the issue was the "clean cut"; that is, taking men on the basis of age, not occupation, beginning at the age of nineteen and gradually working up.[33] Again, there was no movement on the part of the prime minister. In despair, Derby and Robertson went over to 10 Downing Street to confer with the prime minister. They were told that "the time had now arrived when we must face the fact that we could not expect to get any large number of men in the future, but only scraps." Lloyd George explained that this was because of labor unrest in the country as well as the inordinate demand for men for shipbuilding and food production.[34]

The War Office reacted angrily to the War Cabinet's feeble effort to remove the impediments responsible for the army's manpower shortage. Haig needed to know whether he could count on the requested reinforcements so that he could frame his future plans. In a memorandum dated May 31 the author, Lieutenant General Sir Nevil Macready (Adjutant General) raged against the tribunals for providing exemptions in excess of what were required in the protected occupations. He accused government departments of encouraging that practice on the grounds that the men shielded would be more useful in vital civilian work than in the army. He claimed there were adequate numbers of men in the country to keep the army up to strength without affecting industrial production. Macready's solution, hardly a novel one, called for raising the age of military service from 45 to 50 years, enacting legislation that would restrict the power of the tribunals, and adopting a policy that would conscript men based not on occupation, but on the "clean cut," beginning with the youngest class.[35]

The paper received scant attention by the War Cabinet. Nor did Chamberlain's latest initiative fare any better. Troubled that his mandate to resolve the manpower dilemma was slipping increasingly out of his hands, he returned to the charge on June 22 with a familiar theme. He recalled his previous two reports in which he had recommended that all exemptions be cancelled and that men for military service be called up by age groups. He remained convinced that his suggested policy was the only answer to the challenge providing the men required for the army. Short of the War Cabinet's adoption of his proposals, he saw no reason for the continued existence of his department.[36]

While Chamberlain waited for the War Cabinet to make the next move, he read in the morning paper on June 29 that Cecil Beck would be replacing

Stephen Walsh as the parliamentary secretary to the National Service Department. Chamberlain was dumbfounded by the announcement. He had not been informed, let alone consulted, about the change. Immediately, the director poured out his wrath in a note to Lloyd George, accusing him "of an exhibition of discourtesy so extraordinary that I have difficulty in believing it to be unintentional," and asking to be told as quickly as possible whether this signified a want of confidence in his leadership.[37] Replying four days later, Lloyd George maintained that the discourtesy was inadvertent, caused by the rush to announce the appointment, and he expressed deep apologies.[38] Chamberlain professed to accept the lame excuse and he assured the prime minister that he considered the incident closed.[39] Privately, he told his sister that he thought Lloyd George's explanation rang hollow.[40]

As the weeks passed with still no word from the War Cabinet, a frustrated Chamberlain sought to bring matters to a head. With the support of Derby, Rhondda (now Food Controller), Walter Long (Colonial Secretary) and William Hayes Fisher (president of the Local Government Board), Chamberlain submitted a memorandum to the War Cabinet on July 18, presenting practical arguments for the adoption of his program.[41] When the subject was not raised in the War Cabinet the next day, Chamberlain could no longer contain his anger. He wrote a sharp letter to the prime minister that he and his staff were despondent over the sense that they were wasting their time, the lack of help from the government and the frequent and obviously inspired press attacks. He considered that his position had become hopeless and warned that unless the War Cabinet adopted his report at once, "I must ask you to accept my resignation ... and to allow me to state publicly my reasons for relinquishing my office."[42] Lloyd George asked Chamberlain to reconsider, at least until Auckland Geddes's report, which suggested a different basis for recruiting, was discussed in the War Cabinet.[43] Chamberlain reluctantly agreed.[44]

Geddes, in his paper, made no mention of civilian compulsion, which he considered the most efficient and equitable system, but, like Lloyd George, understood that it was unenforceable because of labor's opposition. The core of his argument was that the criterion for the combing-out process should be based on occupations rather than on age. Notwithstanding Geddes's assertion, his plan was not substantially different from Chamberlain's, which, as a practical matter, had recognized leaving indispensable men in civilian occupations. Geddes, moreover, recommended bringing all questions of manpower under one head.[45] The prime minister was sympathetic to Geddes's call for a coherent system and to his reasoned arguments. On August 1 he established a Committee on Manpower under the chairmanship of Milner to consider a recruiting authority and a manpower policy. Milner held talks with Geddes on August 4 and agreed with his view that restructuring the

National Service Department "was the only course of action which would encourage public opinion, and particularly the trade unions, to be more favorably disposed towards the military demand for men."[46] On August 8 the Milner committee met and concluded that a centralized organization was needed and specified that the National Service Department should combine the functions of recruiting men for the services and civilian work. There was no question of inviting Chamberlain to preside over the new department as he had lost the confidence of the prime minister and had been publicly discredited by a steady stream of press criticism. Nor was Chamberlain anxious to take on the expanded responsibilities.[47] On the advice of Milner, who privately wanted him to go, he submitted his resignation and listed his reasons for doing so.[48] The prime minister disputed some of the charges, but accepted his resignation.[49] Chamberlain returned to Birmingham with an intense and enduring contempt for Lloyd George, whom he blamed for the callous and humiliating treatment he had endured for eight months.[50]

Lloyd George first approached Edward Shortt, a Liberal backbencher, as a possible successor to Chamberlain. Shortt was unfamiliar with the details of the recruiting process, an operation he estimated would take him at least four months to understand. Wisely, he declined the offer.[51] The prime minister turned next to Auckland Geddes, whom Derby had recommended as an excellent alternative. As Director of Recruiting, Geddes had shown a genius for administration. Geddes had no intention of repeating his predecessor's unfortunate experience. He accepted the appointment on condition that his role was clearly defined.[52] He was designated "minister," provided with a seat in the Commons, appointed a privy counselor, and allowed to refer intricate questions to Milner's Manpower Committee, which had the support of the War Cabinet.[53] Conferred with substantially more power than that which Chamberlain had received, Geddes's position was further strengthened after the second half of 1917, when casualties in the British Army rose dramatically and compelled the War Cabinet to yield to the demand for more efficient allocation of manpower.

Geddes defined the functions of his department, now known as the Ministry of National Service, which were approved by Milner's Manpower Committee and further confirmed by the War Cabinet on September 12. These included the following: to review the whole field of manpower, to arrange the transfer of labor from nonessential occupations to urgent national work, to determine the relative importance of civil work and periodically prepare lists of reserved occupations, and to secure men for the army in numbers laid down by the War Cabinet without detriment to essential public services.[54]

Geddes's first assignment was to undertake a general survey of available manpower in the country. His report, dated October 13, maintained that of the 3,600,000 men of military age in civil life, only a small percentage, slightly over a quarter of a million, were eligible for Category A; that is, suitable for overseas duty. The rest were either unfit or engaged in vital occupations. Geddes noted that additional manpower could be found from two untapped sources: one, the pool of men over 41, and the other, Ireland. By raising the age from 41 to 50, Geddes estimated that 150,000 recruits could be obtained. Approximately the same number of men could be found by extending the Military Service Act (compulsion) to Ireland. Women would be the main source to replace the men taken from industry. Only by exercising economy in human power, Geddes cautioned, could the demands of the army be met without hampering industrial production.[55] The stark reality of the memo was disheartening, but the prime minister was impressed by Geddes's presentation of the statistical data and independent assessment.

For Geddes and the War Cabinet, the already difficult chore of forging a policy that would balance the needs of the army and the civilian workplace was exacerbated by the unparalleled horror endured by the British Expeditionary Force (BEF) during its four months of futile slogging at Passchendaele. Both sides had sustained heavy losses, but the Allies were in a far less favorable position to absorb them than the Germans. The French Army had not recovered from outbreaks of mutiny in the spring, the Italians had been routed at Caporetto, Russia had collapsed, and the prospect of large-scale American help was a distant one. By repeating the bloodletting that had occurred at the Somme a year earlier, Haig was depleting Britain's precious reserve of manpower at a perilous moment in the war.

During the last week of November, while the prime minister was away in France, the War Cabinet discussed how the nation could survive until the Americans entered the fray in great strength and redressed the military imbalance. There was a consensus that in allocating manpower, shipbuilding should receive the highest priority, even over the army. This was because the transport of the American troops depended largely on British ships. The War Cabinet also considered the proposals contained in Geddes's memorandum of October 13. The members doubted that parliament would consent to raise the age for military service beyond 41 or allow an extensive comb-out of workers in essential industries. They advised, moreover, against the application of conscription in Ireland even in extreme circumstances.[56]

Manpower remained the central issue at the War Cabinet meeting on December 3 and again three days later. By then, military intelligence indicated that the enemy was planning to launch a decisive attack in the west early in 1918. It was estimated that if the Germans withdrew troops from the Italian and eastern fronts, they would enjoy a numerical advantage in the west by some 200,000 troops. Consequently, Sir Douglas Haig, commander of the BEF wanted an additional 600,000 men over the next twelve months to keep his armies up to strength. The Army Council looked to Geddes to offer suggestions as to how the army's professed needs, however exacting under the circumstances, could be met.

Geddes had submitted a memorandum to the War Cabinet in which he gave detailed sets of figures showing that the nation was approaching the limit of its manpower reserves. The greatest number of men that could be collected was estimated to be less than 300,000, roughly half of what General Headquarters (GHQ) had requested. Even then it would necessitate the cancellation of promises made to trade unions and reductions of either food production or essential industrial output. Viewed from any direction, the prospects were somber.[57]

Curzon reminded his colleagues that in the past, the War Cabinet, when confronted with a grave decision, had set up a subcommittee to examine the evidence and to recommend a course of action. He suggested that such a subcommittee be appointed at this critical juncture and report its findings to the War Cabinet at the earliest possible date. His motion carried, subject to the concurrence of the prime minister – who was still absent.[58]

Thus far, no national policy exerting political control over the nation's manpower resources had been developed. The Lloyd George coalition had simply adopted ad hoc responses to the problem of manpower allocation. The lack of political will and administrative expertise had inhibited the establishment of a system that would effectively distribute men between industry and the armed forces. Indeed, it would not be an exaggeration to say that Lloyd George's management of manpower in 1917 was not any better than that of his predecessor.[59]

Back in the chair at the War Cabinet meeting on December 10, Lloyd George brought up the subject of manpower, which he regarded as "most pressing." He noted that he had received figures furnished by the Director of Military Intelligence at the War Office (Lieutenant General Sir George Macdonogh), which indicated that on the western front, the British and the French together had 400,000 more rifles than the Germans. Even if the Germans were to transfer all their serviceable divisions from the eastern front, some thirty-two divisions, an approximate total of 300,000 men, they would still be at a numerical disadvantage in the west. In these circumstances he was unable to understand the alarmist tone exhibited by General Headquarters that was causing unnecessary distress among the public.[60]

Nevertheless, Lloyd George accepted the War Cabinet's recommendation and set up a special committee, which included himself as chairman, to sort out the conflicting claims of industry and the services. The work of the Manpower Committee will be chronicled in greater detail in a later chapter and only a bare outline is warranted here. In carrying out its task, the committee was guided by two considerations: a determination to avoid attacks on the scale of the Somme and Passchendaele, and an assumption that the war would not end in 1918. The immediate objective was to limit losses by inducing Haig to adopt a defensive strategy and to wait for the Americans to array their full force in France. Once the Allies had built up a preponderance of military might, they would be able to finish off the Germans in 1919 or 1920. In the interim, attention had to be paid to the general maintenance of national life in addition to war production.

Having engaged in the most thorough inquiry yet into the nation's manpower resources and how they could best be allocated, the committee gave the requirements of the navy and air force, shipbuilding, the construction of tanks and airplanes, food production and even timber-felling, higher priority than the army. Its official rationale was that a lesser number would be required because the High Command in France would be pursuing a defensive strategy and therefore suffering fewer losses than if engaged in offensive action. Of the 600,000 men requested for 1918 by General Headquarters, no more than 150,000 were to be withdrawn from civil life. The Army Council was mortified and fought hard to reverse the Committee's recommendations, but to no avail.

Once the War Cabinet endorsed the Committee's report, it became Auckland Geddes's responsibility to identify and channel men for the services in relation to maintaining essential war production. To preserve peace on the home front, Geddes conducted negotiations with the various trade unions to obtain their cooperation. The Amalgamated Society of Engineers (ASE), the most important union in the munitions industry, lodged strong objections and refused to attend the meetings of the engineering group, insisting there was no justification for recruiting skilled men until all the "dilutees" (unskilled and semi-skilled workers) been taken from industry.[61] Nevertheless, the government hurried through parliament a new Military Service Act, which gained the Royal assent on February 6, 1918. By its terms, the Ministry of National Service was empowered to cancel exemptions granted on occupational grounds and to call up men based on occupation, age and marital status. A few days before the law went into effect, Geddes's department issued a revised Schedule of Protected Occupations in which 23 was the minimum age of exemption.[62] At long last, ad hoc solutions had been replaced by a policy setting out priorities with a comb-out procedure that permitted recruitment from among the youngest men in not-too-essential industries.

The Military Service Act, while part of the law of the land, had not been fully implemented when the long-awaited German offensive struck with unprecedented force on March 21, rolling back the British armies towards the line of the Somme. From March 21 to March 30, British casualties totaled 122,000 men with the daily wastage projected at 20,000 during heavy fighting.

It seemed obvious that the British army would not survive without a heavy influx of reinforcements. In these circumstances, Macready requested 282,000 men and urged the adoption of a principle that would reserve all fit men in the country for military service. Lloyd George was not ready to yield to such drastic measures, although he intervened at the War Office to temporarily suspend the War Cabinet's decision to limit the flow of reinforcements to Haig. For two weeks after March 21, the manpower issue dominated discussions in the War Cabinet. Measures adopted included returning troops on leave to France, withdrawing men from munitions, coal mines and dockyards, lowering medical standards and sending lads of eighteen-and a-half to the front. Even so, Geddes warned that finding the necessary men without disrupting munitions output could be achieved only by applying conscription to Ireland and by extending the age limits for military service. Geddes maintained that by raising the age limit to 45, an additional 50,000 men would be available for military service; and if another five years were added to the age of liability the number would total 110,000. Similarly the extension of compulsion to Ireland would provide an estimated 150,000 men for the army. The War Cabinet could think of no other options that would bring in as many recruits. Thus, on March 25 it instructed Geddes to draft a Military Service Bill embodying both measures.[63] The War Cabinet had acted in haste, without adequate information or a careful analysis of the political implications.

The draft bill, given its brevity, was ready for distribution to the War Cabinet the following day. It called for lowering the minimum age of military service to 17 while raising the maximum age to 55. Geddes hinted that the drastic age extensions proposed were in response to the improbability that the War Cabinet would enforce compulsion in Ireland. His remaining recommendation was for the abolition of the tribunal system. Instead, as a means to eliminate exemptions, he wanted the creation of advisory committees whose authority would be limited only to delaying induction of individuals.[64]

The bill was bound to arouse widespread opposition in parliament, among labor, and in Ireland. There was something unseemly about sending men approaching old age and youths under 19 to the western front. A troubled Barnes wrote to Lloyd George about the proposed bill: "I hope you won't commit yourself to it. Seventeen is too low and fifty-five is too high."[65] The threat of industrial action, resulting from labor's unconcealed aversion to the abolition of the tribunal system and to cancellation of existing exemptions, could not be ignored. Lloyd George had worked long and hard to induce labor to yield to the government's requests and he did not think that they would be receptive to making further concessions without corresponding sacrifices from Ireland.[66] It was questionable, however, whether conscription could be imposed on Ireland without turmoil.

No expert on Ireland, Lloyd George solicited the opinion of a number of British officials on the scene, including Lord Wimborne (Lord Lieutenant of Ireland), H. E. Duke (Chief Secretary for Ireland), General Sir Bryan Mahon (Commander In Chief) in Ireland and Brigadier Sir Joseph Byrne (Head of the Royal Irish Constabulary). Wimborne, Duke and Mahon thought it would be a serious mistake, and that the Irish would use violence to resist compulsion. Byrne was not as adamant as the other three, but neither was he as optimistic as Lloyd George seemed to think. He did state that conscription could be enforced, but only "with the greatest difficulty." He went on to say that bitter resistance was likely to come from the clergy and Nationalists and that he anticipated organized strikes that would dislocate the life of the country.[67] Sir John French, on the other hand, was one of the few dissenting voices. French flattered himself into thinking that his Irish background gave him a special insight into understanding the people of his native land. A recent three-day tour of the island had persuaded him that, properly handled, the Irish would accept the inevitability of conscription. He was confident that with a slight increase in the British garrison, law and order could be maintained.[68]

Lloyd George was relieved to hear a contrary opinion. Somehow, he convinced himself that conscription was possible in Ireland, though, unlike French, he anticipated that its unpopularity would lead to bloodshed. In the end he was worried less by Irish disturbances than by defeat in the war. The question which he never seriously addressed was whether Ireland would yield anywhere near the number of recruits Geddes had predicted to compensate for an increase in the number of British troops there to contain the disorders that were certain to occur.

Malcolm Thompson (Lloyd George's official biographer) writes that the issue of conscription, to which his subject "had given a forced and inattentive consent" owing to his preoccupation with the cataclysmic events in France in the spring of 1918, "proved to be a deplorable blunder with no mitigating feature."[69] The author's subtle efforts to lessen Lloyd George's culpability requires a response. For one thing, Lloyd George was not forced, but chose, to give his consent. For another, he failed to use good judgment to compensate for his preoccupation with the war crisis. The logical approach would have been to pay heed to the warnings of men such as Wimborne, Duke and Mahon, who were versed in Irish affairs. Instead he chose to overrule them.[70]

The diversity of opinion from various departments over Geddes's draft, prompted Lloyd George on March 29 to set up a committee under the Home Secretary, Sir George Cave, to review all clauses of the Military Service Bill.[71] The Cave committee's recommendations came before the War Cabinet on April 5 and 6.[72] The lower age limit was left unchanged at 18 to avoid possible parliamentary objections, but the upper limit was raised to 50 and, in cases of men in particular occupations like medical doctors, higher still. It was further decided not to dissolve the tribunal system on account of expected labor resistance. Cancellations of exemptions could be achieved through an Order-in-Council, as an emergency measure, without reference to the tribunals.

The prime minister introduced the amended Military Service Bill in the Commons on April 9 with a speech judged by most listeners to have been ineffective.[73] The Irish MPs, unswayed by a vague promise of Home Rule, walked out of the chamber after venting their anger.[74] But there was less opposition from trade unions and the Labor party than had been expected. The continuing bad news from the front silenced most critics of the manpower bill, which passed its third reading on April 16 and received the Royal assent two days later.

The provisions of the bill confined to Ireland were never really enforced. Fierce popular resistance compelled the War Cabinet to retreat and announce that conscription would be suspended if enlistments were adequate. A half-baked policy resembling the Derby scheme went into force,[75] drawing a mere 9,000 enlistments by the end of the war.[76] In the interim, the number of British troops in Ireland rose from 25,000 in March to 100,000 in June "with virtually no Irish recruits to offset them or replace the losses in France."[77]

The rest of the bill strengthened the authority of the National Service Ministry by weakening the authority of tribunals, limiting the right of appeal and laying down common rules for exemption from military service. Furthermore, the bill allowed Geddes to implement a "clean cut" in protected occupations, which cancelled exemptions for males up to the age of 23, and above this age limit if necessary. The War Cabinet temporarily revised the priority list compiled the previous autumn in response to the military crisis in France. Until the end of the war, Geddes played a key role in the equitable distribution of manpower in accordance with the changing character of the war. The main sources of supplying the army came not only from the protected industries, but also from the Home Army and men in category Bi – described by the Chief of the Inperial Staff (CIGS) as "nearly-A men." The number of drafts sent to France from March 21 until July 13 totaled 351,824 men.[78] The recognition by Haig that the state was approaching the limit of its manpower resources made him much more conscious than in the past of avoiding unnecessary casualties. Had the war extended into 1919, the need to maintain war production and civilian services almost certainly would have compelled the government to reduce the size of the British army.

Chapter 3

THE CHALLENGE OF LABOR

Lloyd George observed in his *War Memoirs* that trying to keep labor unrest within manageable limits was probably the most delicate and perilous task the British government faced on the home front during the Great War.[1] The need to organize the nation's industrial resources for modern warfare transformed the state's relations with labor. It meant that the government was required to pay more attention to workshop conditions, seek to control wages, invite the advice of key trade unions such as the Trade Union Congress (TUC) and take a more active role in settling labor disputes. Prowar Labour Party leaders were brought into the government in the expectation that they could induce trade unions to forgo strike action.

As the conflict dragged on with no end in sight, war production became nearly as important as the fighting itself. This meant that the labor force had to be augmented and deployed effectively. At the commencement of the war the government had two options. First, to impose general conscription, both combatant and industrial, with every man of suitable age and health called up for national service and assigned to whatever task the government deemed appropriate. Soldier and civilian would stand on substantially the same footing with the latter regarded as a temporary exempted combatant and subject to the same discipline and obligation as the former. In this way, the government would exert control over the worker's movements and bind him to the job if it so wished. The second option was military conscription with a limited measure of industrial regulation. The first course would have been preferable, but the traditional antagonism of the nation to conscription prevented its adoption. By default, the second course was chosen and workers were left with a substantial measure of freedom and governed only by such regulations as were required for the national interest.[2]

The war broke out at the peak of industrial tension. Although in a strong bargaining position, labor leaders showed their patriotism by declaring an immediate truce and vowing not to use the strike as an instrument of policy. While prewar issues receded into the background, new sources of friction soon developed, not the least of which were the long hours, conditions of work in the factories, low pay, resentment against excessive profits of employers who were at least partially responsible for the high inflation, and opposition to the dilution of labor. Still, for the first six months of the war there were practically no strikes in such vital trades as metal, engineering and shipbuilding.

To meet the growing needs of the armed services, the government examined ways of expanding the supply and productivity of labor in war-related industries. Lloyd George was Asquith's chief troubleshooter and he was especially effective in dealing with labor because of his negotiating skill and his prewar reputation as a social reformer and an enemy of the privileged.[3] It was not an easy task to extract from labor certain rights they had won, after many years of hard bargaining, from their employers. In March 1915, however, Lloyd George persuaded union leaders in the so-called Treasury Agreement to suspend practices and restrictions that might hamper national output. In July 1915 the Munitions of War Act gave force of law to the Treasury Agreement. Strikes and lockouts were prohibited in war industries, the settlement of disputes was to be left to compulsory arbitration, resisting the dilution of labor in state-owned factories was declared illegal, and workers were not permitted to seek jobs elsewhere unless their employer gave them a "leaving certificate." Labor leaders were assured that traditional practices would be restored without prejudice at the end of the war.[4]

As it turned out, official trade union compliance did not always act as a government conduit to the rank-and-file in the workplace. There were sporadic disorders and strikes in 1915 and 1916, particularly in the engineering and munitions plants. As a rule, the workers' demands were reasonable enough, although they were frequently portrayed as unpatriotic in the press. Lloyd George had outgrown his dislike of the privileged classes and acquired a healthy respect for captains of industry and large corporations as essential to the nation's economic progress. He still had compassion for the poor and recognized that many working-class grievances were genuine, but he was unsympathetic to strike action. He considered that even if laborers had to endure hardships in their workplace and were underpaid, they were still far better off than the men in the trenches.[5] Yet, labor provided a service in essential industries and transport that was so vital to the war effort that authorities could not afford to let a dispute run its course, that is, to take a tough line until the exhaustion of funds compelled strikers to yield.

It is interesting to note that industrial unrest was inspired not by union leaders, but by shop stewards, a new force on the labor scene. Before the war, shop stewards were union officials charged with minor local administrative duties. They assumed an important role during the war because, with the trade union leaders pledged to industrial peace, disgruntled workers turned to them to act as their spokesmen. Consequently, their numbers increased enormously and employers, who hitherto had ignored them, found it necessary to recognize and work through them. For the most part the shop stewards were mainly concerned with rectifying sectional labor grievances, although some, imbued with syndicalist ideas of workers' control of industry, were antagonistic to employers and to the trade union hierarchy and on their own initiative, organized strikes to advance their own objective. Their propaganda activities found a receptive audience among an important segment of workers, particularly in the engineering trade, as well as a wing of the British Socialist Party and the Independent Labour Party, which were opposed to the war. As prime agitators in strikes and lockouts in industry, militant shop stewards added significantly to the government's difficulties.[6]

The comparative peace on the domestic labor scene ended at the close of 1916. Labor's mounting unrest was caused by pressure for greater productivity in the workshops, long hours, failure of wages to keep up with the sharp rise in the cost of living, food shortages and bad housing. Resentment was aggravated by "combing out" fit young men in less-skilled occupations, efforts to extend dilution, state control of industries and the restrictions imposed by the Munitions of War Act. Lloyd George came to power at a time when the accumulation of workers' concerns made it highly unlikely that they could be kept in check for the remainder of the war.

As prime minister, Lloyd George's central concern was naturally with the general direction of the war. Consequently, his role with labor changed and he became less involved. Except in emergencies, he left other officials in the government to undertake negotiations with unions and employers. Although Lloyd George created a new Ministry of Labour, headed at first by John Hodge, industrial matters continued to be handled by other departments – such as the Ministry of Munitions and Admiralty – as well. In difficult circumstances the prime minister did not hesitate to call upon Arthur Henderson, and later, his Labour successor in the War Cabinet, George Barnes, to supervise industrial negotiations.[7] He assumed, incorrectly as it turned out, that he could win the support of labor by buying the principal voices of trade unionism with an office, just as he would a troublesome politician.

Lloyd George's industrial policy, while at times short on social justice, was clearly a success. He took pains to keep the workers' movement divided, splitting labor officials and moderates from militants. Given that war priorities were a pressing consideration, the patriotic support of most of the working class made it easier for the government to resist unreasonable demands by strikers. His determination to deal only with official leadership checked the authority of the radical shop stewards who often provoked strikes to achieve their political ends. During strike action, he concentrated on enlisting the sympathy of the press and public so as to gain an edge in the negotiations with the labor unions.

Lloyd George tried, with less than scintillating results, to foster a spirit of cooperation between labor and capital. He might have had better luck if he had been evenhanded in his dealings with industry and labor. More often than not he was on the side of large business. He allowed the free market to set prices, and took no steps to limit war profiteering or insist on equality of sacrifice.[8] By contrast, he made demands of labor for concessions, but opposed wage increases in spite of rapidly rising prices. In so doing he angered workers and occasionally provoked strikes.

The first major strike in 1917 broke out on March 21 and was triggered by engineers engaged in munitions work at Barrow. The executive council of the Amalgamated Society of Engineers (ASE) ordered the men back to work at once, pending arbitration of their grievances. At a mass meeting, the rank and file rejected their leaders' advice and, subsequently, all efforts on the part of the Ministry of Labour to reach a settlement proved unsuccessful. Lloyd George lost patience with the strikers and opted to take strong measures. At a War Cabinet meeting on April 2 it was decided to issue a proclamation, ordering the men to return to work within twenty-four hours. Failure to do so would result in the arrest of their shop stewards, who had instigated the strike, for hampering the production of war matériel – a breach of the Defence of the Realm Acts (DORA).[9] It was further stated that the government would not address the Barrow workers' claims unless they had first resumed work.[10] The strikers agreed to the condition and, in the negotiations that followed, the issues in dispute were duly resolved. The work stoppage had lasted a fortnight and naturally affected munitions output.[11]

Far more damaging were the outbreaks of engineering strikes in late April and May. It all started when the directors of a private Rochdale firm hired women to engage in skilled work without securing an agreement from the unions. It was bad enough that they ignored a warning from the Ministry of Labour that their action had been improper, but their next move was to sack a number of male employees for refusing to train the women for their new jobs. Acting on behalf of the locked-out men, the leadership of the powerful ASE called on the government to prosecute the firm.[12] Had the Ministry of Munitions intervened immediately, it might have averted the ensuing crisis. But its head, Christopher Addison, hesitated to act, hoping that he could persuade the directors to give ground by appealing to their good nature and common sense. He made an unfortunate miscalculation. Lloyd George described the directors as stubborn, arrogant and autocratic; men who, in response to the Ministry of Munitions, made it clear that they did not intend to alter their methods and, in fact, would prefer to close the firm rather than yield to the trade unions.

In the meantime the strike spread, first to other parts of Lancashire, then to many outside centers, including Sheffield, Rotherham, Derby, Crayford,

Erith, Woolwich and London. While the initial strike in Rochdale was caused by opposition to the dilution of labor in nongovernment work, similar action elsewhere was, for the most part, in reaction to the government's proposal to abolish the Trade Card scheme – a step noted in the previous chapter. Lloyd George had always regarded the Trade Card scheme as an inadvisable concession by Asquith, but his push to cancel it at a time when trade unions were already seething over the extension of dilution to private establishments was in itself a serious mistake, leading to the biggest conflict with labor in the war.[13] At their peak, the strikes involved shops in forty-eight towns and cities and idled nearly 200,000 workers.[14]

Lloyd George was wary of labor unions, viewing them more of a potential threat to the state than the subversive propaganda spread by left-wing ideologues. He had hoped that they could be controlled through the TUC and men like Henderson and Hodge, but soon discovered that, under the sway of shop stewards, they were immune to the influences of their local and national leaders. Given that organized labor was fragmented, he avoided dealing with unofficial bodies and tried to isolate them from trade union leadership.[15] During the strikes, he sought to gain public support by adopting a moderate position and agreeing to rectify the legitimate grievances of workers.

Addison was selected to lead the negotiations with union executives. His opposite number was J. T. Brownlie, President of the ASE, who had nothing but contempt for the strike ringleaders for defying edicts from their own union leadership. More ominously, they were threatening to wrest control of the working-class movement from the elected officials of the trade unions. To end their mischief, however, Brownlie required concessions from the government. The issues were complex and, therefore, the negotiations were arduous for the men involved. Lloyd George kept abreast of developments and authorized major decisions.

Faced with continuing escalating strikes, the War Cabinet was driven to take drastic action. On May 17, with the prime minister giving the lead, it issued warrants for the arrest of ten of the most violent troublemakers. Next day, seven of the ten wanted men were arrested and locked up in Bristol jail. The other three went into hiding. The arrests delighted the ASE executives to a man.[16]

Several days earlier, representatives of a hundred unofficial strike committees gathered at Walworth sent a ten-man deputation to discuss with Addison terms of a settlement of the strike. Addison, with the full backing of the War Cabinet, refused to receive them behind the backs of the constituted authority of the trade unions.[17] Thereupon, the Walworth delegates consulted with the ASE executive, and the parties reached a decision to hold joint talks with Addison. The tripartite meeting was held at the Ministry of

Munitions on May 19. Addison was conciliatory in laying out the government's case. Intimidated by the arrests of most of the leading militants, the Walworth delegates stated their grievances and withdrew, leaving the ASE to settle the strike.[18]

That afternoon, Addison and the ASE executive reached the outline of a settlement, which was approved by the prime minister. The shop stewards were to urge the men to return to work and to promise to refrain from taking unconstitutional action in the future. In return, the prime minister agreed to release the arrested men on condition that they agree to honor the agreement. It is interesting to note that the settlement made no mention of the issues that had provoked the strike.[19]

The industrial strike, which had cost the country 1,500,000 working days, was over. Addison had tackled his task with a judicious blend of firmness and flexibility and achieved a notable triumph. Besides ending the strike, his strategy had gone far towards reestablishing the authority of union officials. He was therefore astonished when it was widely reported in the press that the settlement had been reached at 10 Downing Street under the watchful eye of the prime minister. The doctored version implied that Addison had so mishandled the negotiations that Lloyd George had to step in at the eleventh hour to clear up the mess. Addison described the bombshell "as horrible an experience as ever I have had in my life." While he hated the idea of trying to advertise his achievements, he felt the need to redeem the reputation of the Ministry as well as that of his own. He confronted Lloyd George and insisted that he make a statement in the House to repair the damage. The prime minister professed to be as angry as Addison, adding that if the facts had been misrepresented, his press secretary, William Sutherland, would be fired. For a man known to read several newspapers daily, the intimation that the published reports of the settlement had escaped his attention is, of course, preposterous. Nevertheless, in answer to a question in the House on May 21, the prime minister acknowledged that the agreement with the unions had been reached on Addison's initiative, and he extended his congratulations for the skillful manner his colleague had conducted the negotiations. This statement, Addison lamented, received scant publicity in the press as compared to the misleading account that had appeared earlier.[20]

Addison could not bring himself to believe that the man with whom he had enjoyed "years of close friendship and association" was behind the colored press release. He recognized that Lloyd George had shown a lack of scruples in toppling Asquith, but for him to act dishonorably "at the serious cost of damaging one of his colleagues in a case like this is not only beastly, but silly."[21] If Lloyd George had turned against the very man (Asquith) who had saved his political career on at least two occasions, what made Addison think that he would not do something as simple as rob him of his of accomplishment? Addison knew Lloyd George as well as anybody. He and Lloyd George first collaborated during the passage of the National Insurance Act in 1911 and since then they had built up a close relationship.[22] In short, Addison ought to have known better than to trust Lloyd George. Did he honestly believe that Sutherland had acted on his own initiative? What would have been his purpose? Was Addison not aware that Lloyd George was a habitual liar? Did he not know that Lloyd George was obsessive about his image and that he had a propensity to claim credit for the achievements of others? Did he not think it was curious that for all of Lloyd George's bluster, Sutherland was not removed from his job? Addison was certainly no fool. He was a physician and had been a former professor of anatomy before embarking on a political career. He had risen rapidly through Liberal ranks to become Minister of Munitions where he had done admirable work. How an enlightened and seasoned politician could be so naïve defies explanation. At any rate, the row over the press release was soon forgotten and the relations between the two men remained strong until their final break in 1921.[23]

As the laborers returned to work, Lloyd George set up eight regional commissions to investigate the causes of the industrial unrest. The commissions, each of which had a separate chairman and included an employer and a representative of labor, were asked to submit their findings within a month.[24] Before the reports came in, the prime minister, anticipating one of the major grievances, announced a new policy of subsidies to keep food prices down. He followed this program up by taking immediate steps to increase the domestic production of food. To that end, the War Cabinet decided in the latter part of June not to withdraw any more men from agriculture for the army.

Lloyd George and his colleagues carried out other reforms in response to the commissions' reports, which were submitted on July 17. Pension claims, resulting from the war, were to be treated in a more generous manner. A government study showed that such claims, rejected at a rate of about 2,000 a month before April, had fallen to less than 100 by October. The want of sufficient housing accommodations in congested areas, however, was one important issue that the government addressed only superficially. Given the premium on resources, particularly manpower, it resolved to deal only with extreme cases of overcrowding. The Munitions of War Act was unpopular with workers and its amendment was seen as a matter of great urgency. Foremost among their complaints was the barrier against switching jobs without a leaving certificate from their employer – which could not be readily obtained. The authorities feared that abolishing leaving certificates would open the door for many skilled workers to leave for higher paying semiskilled jobs, seriously affecting war production. While the government felt compelled to abolish leaving certificates, it adopted measures, including hiking the skilled workers' hourly pay rates, to encourage them to remain in their current work. Finally the authorities quietly dropped the proposal to extend dilution to private firms in view of the continuing hostility of trade unions. The wide publicity given to the government's concessions to redress labor's grievances, and its promise of more changes, eased tensions and led to an improved atmosphere in the workplace.[25]

As industrial unrest diminished, events in Russia, which brought a "democratic" regime to power in March 1917, served to release some of the pent-up energies of British working-class activists. Belligerent trade unionists pointed out that workers in Russia were much more powerful than their peers in Britain; they were a prominent force in the government, in the military and in the shaping of legislation. There was no reason why British workers could not follow the Russian example. In the spring of 1917 militant leftists sought to generate a national movement among the rank and file of labor in order to establish a radical system on the Russian model. Accordingly, they called for a conference at Leeds in early June to which peace groups, trade unions and other labor organizations were invited to send representatives. There was uneasiness in some government circles about the possible disturbing effects of such a gathering. Lloyd George was urged to ban it, but he declined to do so on the grounds that "it would be a serious mistake to take it too seriously."[26] The War Cabinet endorsed Lloyd George's stand, judging that it "would be undesirable to take any steps to suppress further advertisement or to prohibit the meeting itself, though it was of such a revolutionary character." The only restraint it imposed was to forbid soldiers in uniform from attending the conference.[27]

All major unions such as the TUC as well as the Labour party boycotted the conference. Many of the delegates attending it, as Lloyd George observed, "were individual enthusiasts who came without authority or instructions from any organized bodies; their votes bound no one but themselves."[28] Speakers hailed the Russian revolution and talked wildly about the imminence of a revolution and a dictatorship of the proletariat. Resolutions, passed by sweeping majorities, called for the formation of workers' and soldiers' councils as in Russia and urged the British authorities to end wartime conscription and adopt war aims in harmony with the Russian formula.[29] The denunciations and positions taken at the conference had little impact on mainstream labor. As one labor leader put it, the Leeds conference "did not represent working-class opinion and was rigged by a middle-class element more mischievous than important."[30]

Still, the Labour party and most trade unions welcomed the new order in Russia, since it could now justly be claimed that their side was fighting to make the world safe for democracy. The troubling question was whether the Provisional Government would be able to keep Russia in the war in the face of internal opposition, food shortages and war weariness. All sections of labor urged the Allies to offer encouragement and assistance to the Russian government to prevent it from signing a separate peace treaty.

Working at opposite ends was the Socialist International. Stirred by news from Russia, in April a joint Dutch–Scandinavian committee called for a socialist and labor conference to be held in Stockholm, at which delegates from all the belligerents, as well as neutrals, were invited to attend. The object of the gathering was to formulate a possible basis for peace. Antiwar socialists in Britain and elsewhere argued that putting an end to the military stalemate was the only way to save the Russian revolution.[31]

The announcement of a forthcoming socialist conference hardly caused a murmur in London. Lloyd George dismissed any thought that either side would seriously consider peace terms dictated by an international socialist conference. He was confident that the majority of socialists in Britain and in other Allied countries continued to support the war. On May 11 Henderson told the War Cabinet that the executive of the Labour Party had decided to reject the invitation to attend the Stockholm conference. Instead, it proposed to send him and several others on a mission to Petrograd with the object of urging Russian socialists to continue to support their government in carrying on the war. The War Cabinet had no objections to the mission, but was reluctant to allow Henderson to leave the country in view of the industrial unrest.[32]

The matter was taken up again after the Petrograd Soviet of Workers' and Soldiers' Deputies,[33] usually simply called the Petrograd Soviet, expressed hope that the Allied governments would allow representatives of majority and minority socialist groups to journey to Russia for discussions with its leaders.[34] The Petrograd Soviet was eager to "unite all forces of the international proletariat to obtain a peace without annexations and indemnities, on the basis of the right of self-determination."[35] Lloyd George and his colleagues were hesitant to comply until they had some idea of who wanted to go and what was the objective of the proposed conference. Yet they refrained from issuing a blunt refusal lest it irritate Russian extremists and discourage the moderates. Before issuing a reply, they sounded out the Allied governments.[36] On May 16 Henderson informed the War Cabinet that the Labour Party had put off sending a delegation pending receipt of further information from the Russian socialists "as to the nature of their proposals."[37]

Information received in London suggested that the Germans were planning to send a socialist delegation to Stockholm. The matter was discussed at a War Cabinet meeting on May 21. Acting on behalf of the Foreign Office, Cecil thought that it was vital for the British government to send a strong delegation to counteract German influence should a conference take place.[38] The prime minister was concerned about Germans fraternizing with Russians in view of the growing antiwar sentiment in Russia. It was a matter of utmost urgency that Russia remain in the war to prevent the Germans from transferring their troops in the east to the western front. On May 23 the War Cabinet adopted two resolutions. The first was to send Henderson to Petrograd to consult with the Russian government and, if he deemed it best, to replace Sir George Buchanan, the British Ambassador. The rap against Buchanan was not that he was imperceptive and his advice frequently unsound, but that he might be viewed with suspicion and mistrust by the Provisional Government. What was needed was someone calculated to exercise a strong influence on labor and socialist elements that dominated the Russian government.

The second ruling sanctioned the granting of passports to a party of minority socialists, headed by Ramsay MacDonald, a well-known member of the antiwar movement and treasurer of the Labour Party. Accepting the Petrograd Soviet's invitation, they planned to visit Russia via Stockholm.[39] The idea that peace activists would go to Stockholm and take part in a conference that included enemy agents sparked a firestorm of criticism at home and in Allied countries, particularly in France. The War Cabinet could not revoke the passports of the delegation of minority socialists without offending the Russian socialists. But as a result of the attitude of the British public and the French, Lloyd George made it clear to MacDonald that his activities in Stockholm were to be confined to establishing cordial relations with the Russian socialists and doing his utmost to steer them away from all thoughts of a separate peace. There was a chance, Lloyd George thought, that MacDonald's visit might actually do some good. If he presented Allied aims regarding Belgium and France in their proper light, it was possible that the more radical socialists would turn against the Germans.[40] As it happened, MacDonald's journey ended at the port of embarkation because members of the Seaman's Union (bitter and angry over the loss of coworkers at the hands of German U-boats) refused to transport him to his destination.

Henderson arrived in Russia on June 1. It was not long before he came to the conclusion that Buchanan had developed excellent relations with the Provisional Government and that he was better suited to carry out the wide-ranging and difficult task facing the British ambassador. Although Henderson was an excellent political organizer, hard working and alert, he had the good sense to realize that the job of British ambassador required assets, including knowledge of the Russian language, which he did not possess. More dramatic was his change of heart over the value of the Stockholm conference, which he had opposed before going to Russia. He, along with the new French Ambassador, Albert Thomas, had tried to dissuade the Petrograd Soviet from sending delegates to the conference. When that proved unsuccessful, the alternative was either to attend the international socialist gathering and attempt to guide it, or leave the Russians exposed to unchecked German influence. Whether Henderson had made up his mind then is unclear, but he may have been leaning towards the former option. Besides counteracting the potential damage of German agents, he hoped that Stockholm would "help clarify British war aims and thereby refute Bolshevik propaganda about the imperialistic nature of the War."[41]

Henderson returned to Britain during the third week in July, just as the results of the ill-fated Kerensky offensive (named after the prime minister of the Provisional Government) became known. The event further discredited the tottering Provisional Government. Henderson became convinced that a revision of Allied war aims (in response to the Reichstag's recent resolution against annexations), which he would spell out at Stockholm, would strengthen the Provisional Government and keep Russia in the war. Although a weak reed, Kerensky's moderate regime was at least sympathetic to the Allies and infinitely better than the alternative, a Russia ruled by Bolsheviks committed to a separate peace. On July 25 Henderson met with members of the Labour Party's Executive Committee and requested that they call a special party conference, at which he would recommend that a delegation be sent to Stockholm. The party executive acceded to his wishes and decided that he and MacDonald should go to Paris to consult the French socialists who had declared their intention to join the conference.[42]

Henderson had acted without conferring with his War Cabinet colleagues. From the moment he accepted ministerial office, he faced the problem of divided loyalties. Still, in the past he had taken the government's side in the introduction of dilution, conscription and other industrial innovations that the Labour party had opposed. Now it seemed that he was inclined to act less as a team player in the War Cabinet and more as a detached and independent spokesman of the Labour Party.

While the rapidly deteriorating condition of Russia had converted Henderson to the usefulness of the Stockholm conference, they had, oddly enough, the opposite effect on Lloyd George and the other members of the War Cabinet.[43] The failure of the Kerensky offensive had been accompanied by a breakdown in army discipline, leading Lloyd George to write off Russia as a viable partner for the remainder of the war. There were other reasons for the War Cabinet's shift in attitude. There was a danger in adopting a line at variance with Britain's European allies, who expected the Stockholm conference to call into question the legitimacy of their war aims. Lastly the War Cabinet feared that the Stockholm conference would boost the power of the left, which had already demonstrated its ability to exploit the discontent in the country by masterminding the May strikes.

Henderson failed to make an appearance at the War Cabinet meetings on July 25 and 26, and it was only after the Labour Party applied to the Foreign Office for passports for its delegates that his colleagues became aware of his proposed visit to Paris. Understandably perturbed, they called him in, seeking an explanation. The meeting was held in the evening on the 26th with Bonar Law in the chair (as the prime minister was in Paris attending an inter-Allied conference). The members of the War Cabinet expressed disapproval with Henderson's plan to visit Paris, but did not press the issue after he offered to resign.[44]

Lloyd George was indignant on learning of Henderson's visit to Paris, which he characterized in his *War Memoirs*, with some justification, as "a profound blunder." He went on to say:

> As a Member of the British War Cabinet he had no right to go off to Paris without even consulting his colleagues in the Cabinet, arm in arm with Ramsay MacDonald, who was openly opposed to the War, and to all measures for its effective prosecution, and had been organizing pacifist propaganda, to talk over with French Socialists the arrangements for an International Conference of which his own Government did not approve, and to which our Allies the French, the Italians and the Americans were strongly opposed.[45]

As soon as Lloyd George heard that Henderson was back from Paris, he summoned him to 10 Downing Street where he reprimanded him for placing the government in an awkward predicament. What else passed between them is not known, but before the interview ended Lloyd George asked Henderson to return at 4:30 in the afternoon to discuss the matter with the rest of the War Cabinet.[46] But when Henderson arrived he was told to wait in another room. No slight had been intended; Lloyd George had wanted to spare his feelings while his colleagues pondered his fate. Still, Henderson deeply resented the humiliation of being left on the "doormat" like a mischievous schoolboy waiting to be called into the principal's office. An hour later when he was admitted, he defended his action vigorously, saying that the object of his trip to Paris had been to do his utmost to postpone the Stockholm conference as long as possible and to ensure that it was a consultative assembly, not one at which binding decisions should be taken. Although challenged by French and Russian socialists at the Paris gathering, he had secured the adoption of his goals. He was evasive when asked if he would join the Labour delegation if invited, although he understood that he would not be able to proceed to Stockholm as a member of the War Cabinet.[47]

The ministers were incensed with Henderson, considering his action a breach of collective responsibility. Indeed, at a meeting held on the morning of August 1 (before Lloyd George interviewed Henderson) the animated discussion centered on his possible removal from the War Cabinet. The consensus was that he had gravely compromised the government's position on the Stockholm conference. His support of the conference had implied, even to members of the Labour Party's executive, consent on the part of the government. Consequently, there was a real danger that opinion among the trade unionists might shift in a direction contrary to the views of the government.[48]

There was a strong feeling among some of the ministers that to correct the public's misimpression, the government required to issue a formal statement opposing the attendance of a British delegation to the Stockholm conference. Milner told Curzon that there were enough labor members who disliked the idea or were uncertain about the purpose of the Stockholm conference that if they could get a lead from the government, there was a good chance that they could turn opinion in their party against it. He was critical of the prime minister for failing to take a clear and definitive line, observing "that he was either in favor of or not very opposed to British representation at Stockholm." He went on to say that while the prime minister was dragging his feet, "one member of the Cabinet is busy trying to bring the thing about and has already swung a good number of Labour men in his direction." If this state of affairs was permitted to continue, Milner warned, "we shall very shortly find the whole Labour Party committed to it – and where shall we be then?"[49]

Carson was of the same mind as Milner. Taking the bull by the horns, he wrote to Lloyd George to tell him pointedly that it was a mistake for the government to refrain from making its position known. In the first place, he thought it was illegal for Britons to be holding talks at a conference with the king's enemies. Additionally he found that his unionist friends were very disgruntled and it "takes a good deal of argument to persuade them that the [g]overnment was not behind Henderson in his visit."[50] Failing to receive an answer, he wrote another letter to the prime minister three days later to remind him that the labor unions had a right to know the views of the government before their conference in a few days.[51]

Lloyd George heard from several other members of the government as well. Of those, Leo Amery, the Assistant Secretary of the War Cabinet, was perhaps the most emphatic. His letter to the prime minister was followed by a memorandum that was circulated to the members of the War Cabinet. He maintained that even if the conference itself caused no great harm, "it would be the beginning of a claim on the part of a sectional organization to be consulted at every step affecting the conclusion of peace, which might end by leading us into an intolerable situation." He thought that the government should tell labor leaders that while it had initially regarded attendance at the conference as an open question, it was now convinced, given the legal opinion of the attorney general (who confirmed Carson's suspicions), together with the strong sentiment of the Allies, that British delegates ought not to go and urge them to vote against participation.[52]

Lloyd George, however, was leery about taking any action that might precipitate Henderson's ejection from the government. His desire to keep his relationship with Henderson intact was based not on personal attachment, but on practical reasons. Henderson was the leading prowar Labour figure as well as an invaluable asset in the government's dealings with organized labor. Then, too, his departure might lead to a break with the Labour Party, which would undermine Lloyd George's political position. Finally the danger existed that an alienated Labour Party would move leftward and embrace pacifism.[53] Lloyd George looked to labor itself to solve his dilemma. Information filtering in, perhaps from Labour ministers, made him cautiously optimistic that the Labour Party would refuse to participate in the Stockholm Conference.[54]

The matter regarding the Stockholm Conference was finally aired at a meeting of the War Cabinet on August 8. There was general agreement that in May, the War Cabinet's main object for favoring the conference had been to sustain the Russian government, but since then, decisive changes had taken place. It was now clear that the influence of the Soviets in the Kerensky government had been substantially reduced and thus attendance of British socialists in Stockholm was far less critical. The decision was taken not to allow a British delegation to go to Stockholm, but to refrain from making the announcement publicly until after the Labour Conference had been held. It was felt it would be more conducive to maintaining good relations with the workers if they themselves refused to attend, rather than if the government should make the decision for them and thus appear to be dictating to the Labour Party. During the discussion, Henderson, to the satisfaction of the prime minister, gave the impression that he no longer favored sending a British delegation to Stockholm and would convey that view to the Labour Conference.[55]

Henderson apparently had second thoughts and on the appointed day took the lead in urging that the Labour party reverse its previous decision and send a delegation to Stockholm. Given his considerable standing in the party, the resolution to accept the invitation passed by a three-to-one majority.[56] Henderson had not only gone back on his word, but was also acting against the policy of the government of which he was still a member. The country was opposed to pacifism in any form and Henderson came under blistering attacks in parliament and in the press. A stunned Lloyd George bristled with rage. He immediately sent for Henderson and rebuked him sharply for his disloyalty. Henderson had come to realize that he could no longer maintain his dual position as a member of the War Cabinet and a leading Labour official.[57] He submitted his resignation on August 11. Henderson remained committed to supporting the war, although he resented bitterly his perceived mistreatment by Lloyd George.

Lloyd George's fears that Henderson's departure might occasion a political change or undermine the war effort proved groundless. Although the prime minister's handling of the incident caused considerable resentment in trade union circles, the Labour Party continued to participate in the government with George Barnes replacing Henderson.[58] The Labour delegation to Stockholm, denied passports, never left the shores of Britain. It can be argued that Lloyd George overestimated the effects pacific propaganda emanating from the Stockholm conference would have had on the trade unions, but, in view of the attitude of Britain's allies, he could hardly have acted otherwise.

Relieved of War Cabinet responsibilities, Henderson was free to turn to matters of interest, one of which was to formulate an independent program of war aims for Labour in association with Ramsay MacDonald and Sidney Webb, a prominent socialist and member of the party executive. Henderson's views on the war differed widely from those of MacDonald and Webb, but all three came together to produce a moderate declaration. The draft was circulated and discussed among party officials and endorsed by a special Labour conference in Central Hall, Westminster, on December 28. Labour's statement was designed to boost democratic institutions and end war as an instrument of policy. To that end, it called for the following: the democratization of all governments, the abandonment of compulsory military service, limitation on all armaments, an end to secret diplomacy, the establishment of a league of nations to mediate disputes among states, territorial adjustments based on the principle of self-determination, indemnification by the Germans and a full judicial investigation into alleged war crimes.[59]

Labour's idealistic vision and repudiation of Old Diplomacy received wide publicity and brought immediate results. The prime minister readily granted an interview to a deputation from the trade unions, eager as he was to retain labor's cooperation. He subsequently reported to the War Cabinet that the talks were amicable and that he was relieved to learn that the party's concrete aims were in line with those of the government.[60] At the time, the War Cabinet was grappling with the vexatious problem of manpower. As the British army was carrying the burden of the fighting on the western front – owing to the exhaustion of France, the exit of Russia from the war, and the absence of Americans in large numbers – it was in desperate need of reinforcements to fill its depleted ranks. Consequently, the government looked to comb out industry, but to do so it required to be released by organized labor from earlier promises not to recruit skilled workers. Labor unions were not likely to give up such a concession unless the government guaranteed that it would not prolong the war simply to fulfill imperialistic ends. War weariness had begun to take hold in the country and the government became alarmed at the influence pacifist propaganda was having on labor union members. The government's prospects of a settlement on its own terms would have been potentially fatal if organized labor had demanded an immediate armistice and peace negotiations, and used the threat of a general strike to gain its objective. Thus, as the year came to a close Lloyd George recognized the need to pay attention to Labour's views on the war and to bend every effort to stop, or at least weaken the growth of, the peace movement.

On January 5, 1918 Lloyd George delivered his first official pronouncement on war aims. It is interesting to note that he spoke not to the House of Commons or to a public gathering, but to a conference of trade unionists. The contents of his address will be described and analyzed in a subsequent chapter, but for our purpose here it is sufficient to say that labor leaders enthusiastically welcomed his moderation and apparent agreement with their own major proposals. They could now use the prime minister's speech as a device to contain the peace movement and to unite the right and left against revolutionary elements in their ranks.[61]

The great German offensive in March 1918 led the government to extend the Munitions of War Act, under which it adopted measures amounting to industrial conscription in all but name. Men up to the age of 23 were to be withdrawn from industry, regardless of occupation. The stringent comb-out of industry made it necessary to make the best use of remaining skilled labor. Consequently, skilled workers, surplus to requirements in their current place of employment, were subject to relocation to other shops. At the same time, another proposal to economize skilled workers went into effect. By invoking the Defence of the Realm Act, restrictions were imposed on employers with a disproportionate quantity of skilled workers. The effect of these regulations, in particular the labor embargo, triggered a brief but serious strike late in July 1918, breaking out first at Coventry and then spreading to munitions plants in Birmingham.[62] The War Cabinet met on July 24 to decide what measures to take. Winston Churchill, now Minister of Munitions, indicated that the reports coming in seem to suggest that the men were hesitant, as if "they were not quite certain of their power." He observed that the War Cabinet had to decide whether to delay taking action or act at once before the movement became stronger. He was prepared to advise that the War Cabinet should act immediately by issuing a notice that the men on strike would have their exemption certificate withdrawn.

Lloyd George did not want to see the strike extended, but he thought it was more important for the government to face down the unofficially led trade unions. If putting men in the army would help the state to win, then he was all in favor of using the Military Service Act. But he did not want the government to be burdened with unnecessary difficulties. It was most desirable that the bulk of the workers should be on the side of the state and that no provocative action should be taken that would throw them into the opposite camp. He was of the opinion that the government ought to wait to see how the strike developed before deciding the nature of its action.

The Minister of Labour, G. H. Roberts, understood that the strikes had occurred in defiance of official union instructions. Thus, he thought that it was important to allow the strikers time so that they could seize the implications of their conduct. He was not sure whether the patriotic elements among the workmen had grasped the character of the strike in which they were asked to join. He suggested that Churchill should consult the Trade Union Advisory Committee before taking drastic steps. Other members expressed similar sentiments. Churchill said he was quite prepared to meet with Advisory Committee members and invite them to settle the strike, which was as much against them as it was against the state. He was to warn the strikers that unless they returned to work, the government would have no choice but to withdraw their exemptions from military service. The War Cabinet authorized Churchill to go ahead with the meeting.[63]

Churchill's confab with the Advisory Committee the next day did not produce the results that he and the War Cabinet had hoped for. In fact, the labor crisis deepened. On July 26 the employees at Birmingham Electric Supply Company and at munitions plants in Leeds threatened to walk off their jobs in four days' time. The news prompted Lloyd George to intervene that same day. He issued a statement warning the men to return to work by July 29 or they would be called up for military service.[64] There was no need to enforce the threat as the strikers returned to work. Both Churchill and Lloyd George were praised in the press for the firm manner in which they had handled the potentially serious strike. The domestic scene was relatively free of labor disturbances for the remainder of the war.

Lloyd George's hold on organized labor was fragile during the last two years of the war. His reputation as a social reformer and man of the people had stood him in good stead at the start of the conflict, but the later emergency measures alienated important segments of the working class. There were other less critical instances in which he made mistakes in his dealings with labor. Still, the success of his overall policy cannot be denied. Although industrial stoppages had occurred in 1917 and 1918, the wonder is, given the strength of labor, that there were not more.

Chapter 4

CONTROLLING SHIPPING AND FOOD

During the first year of the war there was nothing to suggest that Britain, the world's main carrier, would experience a shipping shortage of critical proportions. But by the end of 1915 the cumulative effect of factors associated with the enlarged scale of the conflict had begun to strain merchant shipping. In the first place, British merchant ships were requisitioned to transport troops, animals and stores to the various theaters of war. As many continental ports were closed to British traffic, it became necessary to travel longer distances to fetch food and raw materials. To make matters worse, much of Britain's overseas imports went to supply the requirements of its allies who were cut off from their prewar sources – Italy from countries now at war with it, and France from its own provinces now held by the enemy. Then, too, the submarine menace had not only reduced available tonnage, but required ships to take circuitous routes to avoid the danger zones. Finally, ships were often immobilized for long periods owing to congestion in the ports.[1]

As the months passed, the exigencies of the war required increased imported supplies, while the number of ships to transport them diminished. In January 1916 the Asquith government appointed a Shipping Control Committee under Curzon to advise on allocating the requisitioned tonnage with the essential needs of the country. After a general survey showed a 25 percent shortfall in tonnage, the Curzon Committee recommended a temporary prohibition of all nonessential imports, amounting to an annual reduction of 13,000,000 tons. The Board of Trade, however, was unwilling to accept such a drastic reduction of imports and in the end, the final agreed figure was 4,000,000 tons. The shipping shortage grew more acute as the year wore on. Between January and October 1916 British merchant shipping lost to enemy mines and submarines amounted to 877,413 tons, more than twice the output of the nation's shipyards during this period. In November 1916 Lloyd George urged the appointment of a Shipping Controller with the authority to control the distribution of tonnage. Asquith, however, dragged his feet, reluctant as he was to overrule the Board of Trade, which was unwilling to accede to the diminution of its authority. His time ran out several weeks later when he was compelled to leave 10 Downing Street.[2]

One of Lloyd George's first acts as prime minister was to create a Ministry of Shipping with broad but undefined powers. The duties of the new ministry became more precise as its organization was built up and included, among other things, the direction of merchant shipbuilding, control of port facilities and allocation of tonnage to meet the requirements of government services.[3] The man Lloyd George selected to head the new department was Sir Joseph Maclay, a Glasgow shipowner. The prime minister had never met Maclay, who had been highly recommended by Bonar Law. When he tried contacting him by telephone, the line was so bad that neither could hear what the other was saying. An interview was arranged whereupon Maclay took the night express and met Lloyd George the next morning at the War Office. Maclay initially declined the post on the grounds that he lacked the requisite experience and influence, but under heavy pressure from both the prime minister and Bonar Law, reluctantly acceded. Maclay had sold himself short, for by all accounts he possessed wide knowledge and great technical experience and was industrious, unencumbered by precedent, and easy to work with. Lloyd George was not exaggerating when he wrote nearly two decades later that "no minister ever served his country more effectively in an emergency."[4]

Although Maclay was uncertain whether he was equal to the gigantic task that lay ahead, he did not wait until the ministry was officially constituted (on December 22) before rolling up his sleeves. After leaving Lloyd George, he invited two of the nation's leading shipbuilders to his hotel and arranged with them for an immediate meeting of the Shipbuilders' Association. The nation faced a crisis. The destruction of British shipping for November 1916 exceeded by far the total recorded for any previous month. There was no letup at the start of December.[5] Maclay was alert enough to understand that the nation risked almost certain defeat unless a way could be found to create new tonnage at a faster pace than the Germans could destroy it. Maclay also persuaded three of the most able shipowners to sit on a new Shipping Committee to assist him in his work and provide him with advice.[6]

With only half of the country's merchant marine under public control, Lloyd George pledged, when he addressed the House of Commons as prime minister for the first time on December 19, that "shipping would be nationalized in the real sense of the term" for the duration of the war.[7] It has been argued by a recent biographer that the phrase was open to interpretation and that Lloyd George was not necessarily calling for a socialist formula.[8] He alludes to a preceding phrase by Lloyd George who indicated that he intended to place shipping on practically the same footing as the railways (which were still in private hands). His assumption, however, is at odds with what Lloyd George himself wrote in his memoirs, namely, that the state of affairs was such that he was driven "to bring our shipping under

[g]overnment control," implying that he favored transferring it from private ownership altogether.[9] In any case, it would appear that Lloyd George, from his representation to the Commons, was motivated by a desire to clamp down on the high cost of freight and excessive profits. The relevant excerpt ran as follows:

> The prodigious profits which were made out of freights were contributing in no small measure to the high cost of commodities, and I always found not only that, but that they were making it difficult for us in our task with labour. Whenever I met organized labour under any conditions where I would persuade them to give up privileges, I always had hurled at me phrases about the undue and extravagant profits of shipping. This is intolerable in wartime, when so many are making so great sacrifices for the State.[10]

Maclay, however, was adamantly against nationalization of the merchant fleet and not necessarily because he was a shipowner. He offered sound and convincing arguments:

> You retain all the advantages of the experience of practical men who know their business, and also, as far as possible all the elaborate system built up by private enterprise and pay nothing for it, and there is the further certainty that, after the War, owners would be able without loss of time, to resume their regular services.

Maclay was equally convinced that limiting war profits, as suggested by the prime minister, would be counterproductive. He noted that to impose severe taxes on excessive profits would rob shipowners of all incentive to economize and "to exert themselves to the utmost." While he agreed that huge profits should be taxed, he suggested one of two options: average the profits of two years before 1914, plus an allowance to cover wartime costs; or use the machinery currently in force to confiscate all profits beyond a certain level. Personally he favored the former course.[11]

The issues of nationalization of shipping and shipowners' profits were considered in the War Cabinet on February 12, 1917. At the end of a long debate, the War Cabinet accepted both of Maclay's recommendations. It was further decided that whenever requisitioning tonnage for government service, the shipping controller should apply Blue Book rates (so called because they were published in a blue book), that is, standard scales of rates for different classes of vessels. Only exceptional circumstances would justify circumventing Blue Book rates. The shipping controller was asked to give periodic reports on the progress made in carrying out these decisions.[12] He did so on April 10 and again a week later. He pointed out that virtually all the mercantile fleet of the country was under requisition (but remained in private hands) at Blue Book rates. On another matter, he calculated that the average profit of shipowners for the five years preceding the war was just over ten percent. The War Cabinet decided that a formula to limit profits be worked out between the chancellor of the exchequer and Henderson, in consultation with the shipping controller.[13]

It was not until the enemy unleashed its policy of unrestricted submarine warfare at the start of 1917 that Lloyd George's government adopted a five-point program as a remedy to ease the shipping shortage. The various arrangements, as in other sectors of the economy, proceeded piecemeal, sometimes as a reluctant response to events. They may be summarized as follows: (1) the convoy system; (2) speeding up the construction of merchant ships; (3) maximizing the carrying capacity of available tonnage; (4) reducing material imports so as to free ships for war purposes; (5) increasing home-grown supply of food and imposing controls on consumption.

The most effective weapon in combating U-boats, and one that Lloyd George perhaps undeservedly claimed credit for its introduction, was the convoy system. As will be shown in a subsequent chapter, the Admiralty at first resisted employing the convoy system and the prime minister, much as he favored the adoption of such a course, was reluctant to force the issue. But the U-boat campaign was taking a frightful toll on Allied and neutral shipping. February and March 1917 saw 232 British ships sent to the bottom of the seas, mostly by submarines, and the loss of cargo totaled 666,956 tons. British losses reached their peak in April, during which 169 ships were sunk, all but 14 by submarines, and the tonnage figure added up to 545,282.[14] Only when it became apparent that Britain was in danger of losing the war was the convoy system put into force. Consequently, between July and December the number of attacks on merchant ships was reduced by nearly one-third and the loss of tonnage fell from 358,000 to 173,452. Still, the delay in applying the convoy system meant that "its real impact only began to be felt in the second half of the year," thus reducing its effectiveness in thwarting Germany's plans to starve Britain into surrendering.[15]

The British naval building output required to be accelerated considerably to replace the shipping that was being destroyed after the start of February 1917. Shipbuilding remained in the hands of the shipping controller until May 1917 when it was turned over to the Admiralty. Maclay got off to a quick start. In January 1917 he obtained exemptions from military service for all men employed in shipbuilding and engineering shops. He expedited work on vessels already under construction, ransacked ports for old tonnage, approved designs for four standard types of cargo ships and placed orders for an additional 112 ships totaling 1,280,000 tons. As the building program received top priority, "it was carried out at the expense of suspending work on three battle cruisers and five light cruisers."[16] Still, the results of the first quarter of 1917 were disappointing, as new tonnage produced amounted to 246,000 tons, well below the 820,630 tons sunk by the enemy.[17] Maclay sounded the alarm at the end of May, observing that the 1,718,058 tons of merchant tonnage under construction was wholly inadequate in view of the estimated 4,500,000 tons that Britain would lose in the course of 1917. He urged that the shipping program be expanded so that the country would be able to launch new tonnage equivalent to 3,000,000 tons by the end of the year.[18]

Maclay's recommendation resonated with Sir Eric Geddes, the man Lloyd George had appointed as controller at the Admiralty to take charge of the shipbuilding program. In July Geddes produced a memorandum in which he promised to lay the groundwork for a great program that would yield over 3,000,000 shipping tons by the end of 1918.[19] The object of both Maclay and Geddes was to ensure not only that imports did not fall sharply below vital needs, but also that in the postwar period Britain retain its domination of world trade.[20]

The total mercantile tonnage produced and acquired in 1917 came to a little under a million-and-a-half tons, a substantial improvement over 1916. But it was not nearly enough to make good the 3,729,785 tons lost at sea.[21] Impeding the production of greater British tonnage were factors over which Maclay and Geddes had no control. There were mounting demands on British shipping, shortages of steel, allocation of insufficient labor, strikes and endless calls to repair ships that had broken down or subjected to enemy action. Moreover, large orders placed abroad were not always filled. When the United States entered the war, ships under construction for Britain were confiscated by the Wilson government. As a result, in November Geddes lowered his 1918 production estimates for British yards from 2,300,000 tons to 1,800,000. The actual tonnage completed in 1918 was 1,310,000 tons, sufficient to replace only about two-thirds of the 1,924,000 sunk. The gap between output and loss narrowed, but it was never completely closed.[22]

In the short run, when things looked bleak, the impact of government's efforts to extend the carrying capacity of existing tonnage proved to be invaluable. An investigation by Sir Leo Chiozza Money, Parliamentary Secretary to the Ministry of Shipping, concluded that nearly all of Britain's vital commodities could be brought over from Canada and the United States, instead of from distant places requiring sea voyages two or three times as long.[23] The concentration of ships on the North American routes, quite apart from economizing precious cargo space, would provide a higher degree of protection than if they had been dispersed all over the seaways of the world and, as an added benefit, lightened the Admiralty's task. The drawback was that in the postwar period, Britain might not be able to restore economic ties with its old customers. Led by Maclay and the First Sea Lord, Sir John Jellicoe, a committee set up to look into the matter, recommended the North Atlantic route as an immediate solution to the shipping crisis. The War Cabinet had no alternative but to go along, for the risk of defeat outweighed all other considerations.[24] According to Fayle, it was "one of the most important decisions of the war."[25]

Equally telling were the steps taken to reduce congestion at British ports so that ships could unload their cargo and set out on their next trips without excessive delay. A Transport Worker's battalion – servicemen engaged in dock labor – organized in 1916, was sent where there was special need. Numbering 600 at the start, it rose to 10,000 by April 1917. Although falling far short of demand, trains and lorries were diverted to relieve bottlenecks in and out of ports, and inland waterways were used whenever possible.

The Admiralty had its own ideas of how to deal with the tonnage problem and reduce the rate of loss. Jellicoe pointed out that the amount of transport to maintain two-and-a-quarter million troops overseas was placing an intolerable burden on its shipping resources. In a series of memos, he pleaded for a reduction of commitment in the distant theaters to free not only merchant vessels to bring in essential goods, but also naval craft needed for escort duty.[26] He strengthened his case by emphasizing that the need to supply armies in the east militated against the rapid transit of American troops to France. Time and time again he supported the position of the CIGS, Sir William Robertson – although for a different reason – that British resources should be concentrated in France with the armies in the east adopting a defensive strategy.

Another measure to conserve tonnage was to place drastic limits on the amount of material imports. Non-vital trade was practically eliminated and even freight required for the war effort was reduced to the lowest practical limits. The greatest single saving was in timber, which averaged 11.6 percent of Britain's total imports between 1909 and 1913. The amount brought into the country in 1913 was slightly over 11,500,000 tons and, notwithstanding the war demands, that figure had fallen to 2,875,000 in 1917. Part of the reduction was due to strict economy. Then, too, the army in France was able to exploit the forests of France. At home the output of timber more than tripled – from the prewar level of 900,000 tons to 3,000,000 in 1917 – at the expense of stripping the land of many of its trees.[27]

A central element to a successful war effort was the formulation of a coherent and equitable food policy. Required to import about 60 percent of its total food supply in 1914, Britain was more vulnerable to starvation than any of the other belligerents. During the first two years of the war, the

Asquith government saw no reason to interfere with private trading and the normal process of food supply and distribution. The government's policy was shaped by its confidence in the free play of private enterprise, the ability of the Royal Navy to keep the sea lanes open and abundant food sources. But the outlook changed in the latter part of 1916. Crop failures in the Americas and at home, together with the sudden escalation of the submarine campaign, gave rise to official concern about the future supply of food.[28]

The fear of uncontrollable discontent caused by food shortages troubled Lloyd George from the beginning of his tenure.[29] He had long favored some form of state control over agriculture, regarding food, like munitions, a vital instrument of war. Consequently, he wasted no time in pushing ahead vigorously with work already begun or contemplated under his predecessor's watch. There were two aspects of Lloyd George's food program: one was to increase home production to lessen the impact of lost tonnage, and the other to provide for an equitable distribution. The Board of Agriculture was responsible for the former and the food controller for the latter. Lloyd George selected R. E. Prothero (later Lord Ernle) as president of the Board of Agriculture and Lord Devonport as food controller.

Although Prothero's administrative experience was limited, he turned out to be an excellent choice. Practical, independent-minded, tactful, persuasive and with a sound knowledge of agriculture and rural life, he did not allow precedent or his close association with landed interests to influence his judgment.[30] He faced a daunting task. Rural output had declined steadily because of the following reasons: the requisitioning of horses for the military; serious deficiencies in agricultural machines and implements, transport, and fertilizers; and a considerable segment of the labor force had been taken by the army or lost to higher-paying jobs in industry. From the beginning, Prothero had a clear idea of what needed to be done to boost food production at home. As an agricultural expert, he had been appointed to serve on Milner's food committee in 1915, which had been set up to advise on measures for the increase in production. Its recommendations, set aside by Asquith as contrary to the principle of noninterference with the machinery of private enterprise, could now be given practical effect. Prothero knew that he could count on the support of Milner, an old friend since their undergraduate days at Balliol College, Oxford, and more importantly, on that of the prime minister. Indeed, Prothero gave Lloyd George much of the credit for his accomplishment:

> When, early in December 1916, I accepted the Presidency of the Board I had asked the Prime Minister whether he was in favor of a vigorous effort to maintain and, if possible, increase food production at home. "Most certainly," he replied; "it is an essential plank in my platform."

From that statement he never swerved; throughout the food production campaign, he gave me his unfailing support.[31]

Prothero prepared the ground for his new policy by speaking at a meeting of the Federation of War Agricultural Committees on December 20 and, in the same month, followed with two circular letters sent to each of the counties.[32] Dubbed the "plow policy," it was closely based on Milner's Committee report. There were three components to Prothero's controversial policy: an increase in the area of arable land, powers to enforce cultivation, and decentralization.[33]

The main object of the first part was to restore to food production much of the land that had been set aside for animal husbandry. To encourage farmers to alter land usage, the state would provide them with long-range financial security by guaranteeing minimum prices for their produce. Similarly, farm laborers, many of whom were underpaid, would receive a boost in salary for a standard work week. The second part gave the government the necessary authority to carry out its measures. Regulations were added to DORA that permitted the government to commandeer land if the occupier resisted orders to cultivate derelict land or to plow up pasture for gain crops. The impossibility of supervising some 300,000 farms directly from Whitehall introduced the third part. Powers were delegated to County Executive Committees, which were directed to take all steps necessary to raise agricultural production and to ensure that the Board's policy was implemented. Each committee was to send weekly reports of its activities to the Board. The sixty-one committees were grouped into 21 districts, at the head of each was a commissioner appointed by the Board.[34] To oversee this structure, the Food Production Department, a subdivision of the Board of Agriculture, was created on January 1, 1917, with T. H. Middleton, a senior civil servant, as its first director.[35]

The following month the Food Production Department was reorganized and given separate status in all but name only with Arthur Lee, replacing Middleton as director. Middleton remained in the Food Production Department as Lee's deputy. A sinister figure, Lee owed his appointment to Lloyd George.[36] He was unpopular with his Tory colleagues because of his unconcealed ambition, lack of humor, ruthlessness and abrasiveness, but, as undersecretary at the Ministry of Munitions during the Asquith Coalition, he had impressed his master, Lloyd George, by his bullying and shoving to achieve the desired results.[37] Prothero, although strong on policy, was a weak administrator. He welcomed Lee and did not interfere with his activities, and, as a consequence, the two men worked well together.

The Lloyd George administration laid down the gist of its food policy in the early weeks of its existence. As a first step, it left the president of the Board of Agriculture and food controller to define their respective responsibilities.

That done, both men were empowered to incur the expenses necessary to stimulate agricultural production. Prices for the 1917 crops were to be fixed under DORA Regulations. The president of the Board of Agriculture was to concert with the War Office measures to form work parties for agriculture out of men not fit for military service.[38] New provisions were subsequently added and the revised program was contained in a Corn Production Bill that was introduced in April 1917. The measure was not really necessary and provoked heated debates before it passed into law on August 21.[39]

The government program was not particularly popular with tenant farmers or landowners. The former worried about the need to adapt to new farming methods, how compensation would be calculated if the average market price of grain fell below the guaranteed rate and whether the government's commitment to agriculture was temporary or would last for the remainder of the war. The latter resented the increased cost of labor and government interference in the management of their estates. But no one wanted to seem selfish and unpatriotic, and there was little resistance to the program. To give effect to the dictates of the County Executive Committees, however, required the allocation of labor, machinery, horses and fertilizer, all of which were in short supply.[40]

Any increase in food production was contingent on finding extra men to work on the land or, at the very least, retaining those already there. To the astonishment of Prothero, the War Office announced in January 1917 that it would be calling up 30,000 men from agriculture in England and Wales. Lloyd George urged Derby to scale down his demands. He told Derby pointedly, "Unless we are able to increase the food supplies in this country, we shall be beaten by starvation."[41] Derby softened the blow by promising to provide, as substitutes, soldiers unsuited to overseas service. He made a further concession when he agreed to release, on furlough from the Home Forces, 30,000 men for the planting season. Unfortunately, most were inexperienced and it reflected in their work. Thus, on June 17 the government announced that no man who had been a full-time employee on a farm as of June 1 could be conscripted for military service without the consent of the Agricultural Executive Committee.[42] Agriculture became a protected occupation, as in the case of such industries as munitions and shipbuilding, and would remain so for the next nine months. The new arrangement was broken when the "clean cut" policy was introduced in April 1918, in response to the massive German offensive of the previous month.[43] Fortunately, the 30,000 men claimed by the army came at a time when preparation for the 1918 harvest was nearly completed.[44]

The Board of Agriculture found unconventional sources to supplement labor on land. One was to secure the services of schoolboys for the hay and corn harvests. Another was to use prisoners of war, a program that succeeded in putting 30,000 to work by the autumn of 1918. Still another was the recruitment of women for farm work. A women's branch of the Board formed a 12,000-strong Women's Land Army whose members could be sent wherever they were needed. Its greatest contribution was to enroll some 210,000 female village workers, though about 80 percent were part-timers.[45]

The Food Department hoped that dependency on manpower would be lessened if more reliance were placed on machines. Lee, having received carte blanche from Lloyd George, placed orders for 10,000 tractors from Ford, but by the end of August 1917 only 929 had been delivered. It turned out that tractors, although practical for the "vast plains of America," were "frequently inoperable on the sloping fields and differing soil conditions of the United Kingdom."[46] Tractors were new to most farmers and, when the machines broke down, few firms in the country were able to repair them. As a rule, tractors were not a significant factor in food production and the farmer's best tool continued to be the horse-drawn plow. Although horses had been requisitioned by the army, an arrangement was worked out allowing farmers to obtain horses from military camps during plowing season.

None of the steps taken to increase food production would have had much of an impact without an adequate supply of fertilizers. The poor harvest of 1916 had been attributed, at least in part, to a shortage of fertilizers "caused by the loss of potash imports from Germany and the diversion of other chemicals from agriculture to munitions." The Food Production Department encouraged the use of sulphate of ammonia as a substitute for potash and, as such, contributed immensely to the big harvest of 1918.[47]

The results of the food production campaign, contrary to the glowing accounts left by Lee and Middleton, were not overly impressive. Prothero began a little late to achieve significant increases in food supply in 1917. Wheat, an autumn crop, had already been sown and showed only a slight increase. Instead, the authorities wanted farmers to concentrate on producing more spring-sown staple crops by reclaiming grassland. The overall target for extra tillage in England and Wales was about 3 million acres with 0.8 million in 1917 and 2.2 million in 1918. But the new arable land tilled in 1917 amounted to some 0.9 million for the entire United Kingdom, of which Ireland accounted for 0.6 million. This fell short of the desired goal. While the increased output of potatoes and oats was substantial, it was achieved at the expense of a reduction in meat and dairy products. Total food production in 1917 was below prewar levels, but 6 percent higher than in the previous year. At least the decline in the food supply, in danger of deepening, had been halted and reversed.

The Food Department's aim for 1918 was unrealistic, with Lee proposing to break up 3 million acres of grassland. In a speech at Guildhall in

April 1917, an ebullient Lloyd George rashly predicted that the program for the forthcoming year would make Britain self-sufficient.[48] Since the high-water mark had been reached in Ireland and Scotland, it meant that England and Wales would have to contribute practically all the new tillage area. In June the Food Department, blaming the delay in arranging military furloughs for substitute agricultural labor, scaled down the increase of arable land in England and Wales to 2.6 million acres.[49] The revised goal was still ambitious, calling as it did for a 31 percent increase beyond the 1916 tillage area in one year.[50] The dry, mild weather in November 1917 aided plowing and sowing, leading authorities in the Food Department to grossly overestimate the increase in food production. Indeed, Lee informed Lloyd George in April 1918 that the original goal of taking 3 million acres of grassland had been surpassed and he, along with senior officials in his department, predicted that the total would probably approach 4 million acres.[51] If true, it meant that the harvest would provide at least forty weeks of the year's supply of grain.

As it happened, the final figures of 1,999,000 acres of new arable land in the United Kingdom in 1918 fell short of even the revised target. Still, it was a notable achievement. Grain for the United Kingdom increased by 65 percent over the average prewar level (that is, between 1904 and 1914) and the yields of oats and potatoes showed similar spectacular gains. But balanced against this were losses in other agricultural sectors such as meat, milk and fruit.[52] Total home-grown food was higher than in the prewar years, but by how much cannot be answered with certainty. It was nowhere near self-sufficiency as had been promised. One independent study shows an 8 percent gain over prewar figures while another claims that it was a mere 1 percent.[53] The government's food production policy did not solve the wartime food problem, but it did make the country less dependent on imported food.

Alongside the Board of Agriculture, Lloyd George created the Ministry of Food to deal with the other area of the food problem, that is, control of price and distribution. Lloyd George's first appointee as Food Controller, Lord Devonport, was an astute businessman who had made a fortune by founding a retail grocery chain. He also had considerable experience as a public administrator. He had been a Liberal MP between 1892 and 1910 and in 1905 became parliamentary secretary to Lloyd George at the Board of Trade.[54] Here he impressed Lloyd George by his "clear-headedness and businesslike and masterly handling of every problem" left to his charge.[55] The press was lavish in praising his appointment as food controller.[56] The *Times* judged it to be "an appointment of distinction," while the *Observer* claimed "that there could hardly be a better choice."[57] But as a junior minister his powers had been defined, whereas in his new capacity he was expected, like Prothero, to come in and lay down the line on which he proposed to operate.

But he had no precedents to guide him and he assumed that his task would entail carrying out the policy dictated by the War Cabinet. In the absence of clear guidelines from the War Cabinet, he was reluctant to press forward with measures that, although justified by necessity, were complex and deemed by many to be economically unsound.

From conversations with Lloyd George, Devonport appeared to be under the impression that his new ministry would be staffed by businessmen. Instead, the top administrative positions were filled by civil-service personnel transferred from the Boards of Trade and Agriculture. Typical were Sir Henry Rex, ex-Assistant Secretary of the Board of Agriculture, who became permanent secretary and William Beveridge, the former head of the Board of Trade's Food Department, who, as second secretary, accepted a junior position in the new ministry. Devonport was highly suspicious of civil servants, describing them as "molluscus" (invertebrates), and tended to treat them not as highly trained professionals, but as "office boys." Instead, he chose to do much of the work himself, even dealing personally with trifling matters.[58]

During the early months of 1917 relations between Devonport and leading civil servants became strained, if not stormy. Beveridge and others tried in vain to persuade Devonport to allow them to implement the machinery for compulsory rationing. But a system of outright food control was alien not only to his free marketing instincts, but to the government as well. Striving to maintain the existing channels of trade, he resorted to such futile measures as meatless days, prescribing the size of bread rolls and rules against hoarding.[59] Thus, the food controller scurried about without settling on a policy, relying on exhortations and symbolic gestures.[60] Yet, the fault for delaying the implementation of a rationing system appears to lie more on the government than on Devonport.

Lloyd George admitted that shortly after taking office, Devonport (notwithstanding his free-marketing bias) had set up a committee to study in depth the question of compulsory food rationing. Within three weeks the committee had prepared such a plan but the government opted not to press ahead with its implementation. Lloyd George justified the decision on the grounds that the general public, in particular the working class, were empathically opposed to a rationing system. Before taking the matter in hand, the best course, as he saw it, was to exhaust the possibilities of voluntary control, just "as had previously been done with compulsory service."[61] It is ironic that the man who derided his predecessor for procrastinating before introducing military conscription should consider such behavior appropriate on the matter of food control.

Beveridge did not share Lloyd George's cautious approach. He recognized, in the final analysis, that Devonport, for all personal shortcomings, was merely an instrument of the government, which refused to acknowledge that the days of voluntary appeals were over. He wrote as follows:

> The new Government, though they had threatened drastic control of food and had made weakness in relation to food one ground for overthrowing their predecessors, were not themselves prepared for strong measures. ... In retrospect, it seems clear that the public would have been ready for compulsory rationing of sugar and of other articles, as need arose, at any time after the end of 1916.[62]

Recent studies have shown that Devonport's work was made harder because of the government's reluctance to commit to a practical plan. A leading authority on the subject noted: "Time and again measures were taken up for consideration and put aside without any final verdict being made, schemes were continually being drafted that were never used and orders were issued that were rescinded within a few weeks."[63] Consequently, Devonport had little to show for the first six months that he served in office. Public anger against shortages and rising prices mounted. The government became increasingly concerned when rising food prices was cited as one of the principal grievances for the wave of strikes in May. Devonport was pilloried in parliament and in the press for his timid policies. A cartoon in *Punch*, expressing public resentment, depicted the food controller, in response to a question if this was the place where they control food, uttering the words, "Well, Sir, 'control' is perhaps a strong word. But we give hints to householders and we issue 'grave warnings.'"[64] Lloyd George pondered about what to do with Devonport, who had become something of a laughingstock. Northcliffe warned him that unless the food issue was resolved, his government would collapse.[65] The prime minister was not in the habit of tolerating for long an associate who had outlived his usefulness, regardless of personal feelings. He was immensely relieved when Devonport resigned on May 30, supposedly on account of ill health.

Lloyd George hunted far and wide to find a replacement. He offered the post to Robert Smillie, president of the Miners' Federation, who turned it down, partly because he lacked the qualifications for the difficult task and partly because he considered that his proper place was to serve the miners.[66] He then approached Addison, only to be told that he preferred to stay at the Ministry of Munitions.[67] Finally Lord Rhondda, president of the Local Government Board, accepted the job "with very great reluctance" and only after Lloyd George pledged to give him a free hand and to take early steps to establish a new Ministry of Health.[68]

Rhondda had little in common with his predecessor other than they were both successful businessmen. While his experience in food distribution was negligible, he was a good administrator and possessed a strong grasp of practical economics. He assembled an excellent staff and brought in businessmen to fill some of the executive posts. A man of moral rectitude, wide vision and considerable charm, he developed a close rapport with businessmen and civil servants in his department, fusing them into a loyal and effective team. As his health was frail, he did not concern himself with the day-to-day affairs and readily delegated to subordinates wide discretionary and policy-making powers.[69]

Rhondda disliked state control as much as Devonport, but considered it a necessary evil in wartime. His foremost responsibility, as he saw it, was to be an advocate for the consumer. At a private meeting with heads of government, he reportedly told them that he did not care whose interests suffered "if I can make this job of the Ministry of Food a success for the consumer."[70] He listened to expert advice, made himself readily accessible to journalists and his ministry held meetings and conferences to invite discussion and critique of its policies. Rhondda approached each individual case with meticulous care, studying all the relevant information before reaching a decision.[71] As challenging as his task was, he benefited from two factors: the peak of shipping losses had passed, and much of his program had been drafted under his predecessor's watch.

As promised, Rhondda received wide powers – unlike Devonport – so that he could frame an ambitious economic policy. Foremost among his concerns was the need to control rising food prices, which had risen 102 percent above their level in July 1914, well above the general inflation figure. The steadily mounting prices, one of the principal causes of industrial unrest, was hampering the output of war matériel. Further industrial action was threatened by workers' organizations on the grounds that their members required an increase in wages to keep up with the higher cost of living. Rhondda's objective was to fix the price of articles by controlling all stages from producer to consumer, thereby checking speculation and eliminating the middlemen in the link of the chain.[72] But he could not do so without bringing under his ministry control of the food supply. As matters stood, there were a number of agencies, including the Board of Trade, Ministry of Munitions, War Office and Admiralty, that imported food, often without reference to one another. By using the authority obtained from the War Cabinet, Rhondda assumed responsibility for most of the purchases abroad – only the resistance of the War Office prevented a complete takeover.

The key to supervising rationing and price control was a large measure of decentralization similar to that used by Prothero at the Board of Agriculture. The country was broken up into regions, each headed by a commissioner with experience, standing and his own administrative staff. To assist the commissioners, local food control committees were set up in their areas. These committees ultimately numbered nearly 2,000 and their membership consisted of a cross-section of the community.[73]

With the administrative machinery in place, Rhondda could begin the process of controlling food prices. His highest priority was to ensure that bread, the prime article of mass consumption, was available and at a reasonable price. The price of a four-pound loaf had risen from 5.5 pennies in 1914 to 1 shilling by the spring of 1917 and was about to climb still higher. One option was to ration bread, but the War Cabinet abandoned the idea for fear of social repercussions. A state subsidy was proposed as an answer, but reducing the price of bread would increase demand and make it more difficult to maintain supplies. There were also strenuous objections from the chancellor of the exchequer, who was already weighed down by an acute financial crisis. But, unwilling to risk popular riots, the War Cabinet in the end voted to subsidize bread. In the closing days of June the prime minister announced that as of September 17 the price of a four-pound loaf of bread would be reduced to 9 pennies. The cost to the Treasury amounted to about £50 million a year.[74] Rhondda had succeeded in winning a major political victory and in the process eliminated a potential cause of working-class unrest. As it turned out, adequate imports and increased home production of wheat ensured an unlimited supply of bread for the remainder of the war.

The food controller fixed the maximum prices for most of the food consumed in Great Britain. He had the authority to requisition food and, except in rare instances, set prices at both wholesale and retail levels. The prices of certain fruits – e.g., plums, pears and raspberries – were fixed only at the wholesale level, while maximum retail prices were imposed only on some minor foodstuffs like beans, rice and chocolate. The price of such major foodstuffs as meat, cheese, sugar, condensed milk and imported bacon, was controlled at every stage between producer or manufacturer and the corner store. Whenever possible, Rhondda maintained the normal methods of trade. Articles free of price control accounted for no more than 10 percent of the nation's food. Falling into this category were such commodities as biscuits, shellfish, spices, salt and wine.[75]

Because cargo space aboard ships was reserved for wheat, imports of other commodities necessarily had to be reduced. A case in point was meat. Before the war, it was estimated that 40 percent of the total supply that reached the butcher's shop was imported, but three years later that figure had fallen to 12.5 percent, nearly all of which was requisitioned for the army.[76] Another example was sugar, which was purchased entirely from abroad. Its consumption was second only to that of bread and, owing to shipping losses, demand quickly outstripped supply. While the annual consumption per man for bread rose by one-half pound over the prewar level, that of sugar declined by roughly one-third. Given that certain items were in short supply, abuses were inevitable.

The only sure way to ensure an equitable distribution was to implement a thoroughgoing system of rationing. In May Devonport had submitted a proposal for compulsory rationing to the War Cabinet, arguing that although "we might carry on for a few months with the present stocks and rate of consumption under the existing system, it would not be possible to carry on for a year without control of distribution."[77] He won approval in principle, but after his resignation, the War Cabinet had been reluctant to commit itself to a rationing plan. There were several factors that dissuaded Lloyd George and his colleagues from pressing ahead. One was a statement from Henderson claiming that it was apt to provoke working-class unrest.[78] Another was the knowledge that rationing in Germany had bred fraudulent practices and failed utterly.[79] As a result, the War Cabinet opted for less drastic control to assist distribution by requiring householders to register with a local retailer.

War Cabinet hopes that general rationing could be avoided were blasted when diversion of merchant shipping to transport American troops to France again caused food shortages in the last quarter of 1917. Retailers were unable to purchase sufficient popular commodities, such as butter, tea and bacon, to meet their customer's demands. Unrestricted prices rose sharply. When it became apparent that supplies were limited, the public panicked and in many parts of the country long lines formed outside the shops.[80] It was not unusual for a person to wait six or even eight hours before being attended to, only to find the shelves empty of the desired items.[81] Husbands sometimes left their work early to take the place of their wives in the food lines. The resentment of the industrial classes over the lines was intensified by a feeling that families with deep pockets were not affected by the food shortages. At a Trade Union Congress on December 29, 1917 labor leaders protested that the government was causing unnecessary suffering by failing to arrange for an equitable distribution of food. A resolution was passed calling for compulsory rationing so that essential foods would be distributed equally to all classes and not according to the purchasing power of the wealthy.[82] On July 26 50,000 miners in Lanarkshire, angered by high food prices, walked off the job and not long afterwards the Shipbuilding Engineering and Allied Trades Federation threatened to call a general strike unless the government took firm action.[83] Equally ominous was the effect food shortages at home were having on the men in the trenches. As a result of rumors, very much exaggerated, of starvation in Great Britain, mass meetings were held in which speakers demanded to know why, while men risked their lives for their country, it "could not even manage to feed their wives and children at home."[84]

The prime minister and his War Cabinet colleagues presented a brave front throughout these difficult months, but privately they were worried about the impact of food shortages on the whole war effort. Adding to their woes were the rising revolutionary feelings among a segment of the working class that was being fed by the events in Russia after the Bolshevik takeover. It did not set their minds at ease when London dailies linked long food lines in Petrograd to the start of the Russian revolution. On February 22, 1918 Lloyd George, accompanied by Bonar Law and the Quartermaster-General of the Army, Sir John Cowans, went over to the Ministry of Food to get some answers from Rhondda. It was a painful interview for Rhondda, who sat uneasily in his chair while his visitors expressed their anxiety about the social unrest and badgered him about his plans to end the lines.[85]

With Rhondda's reputation sinking, there were calls from all sides, particularly from the labor press, for his dismissal. Lloyd George was also feeling the heat, and rightly so. He certainly deserved a good part of the blame for resisting the practical enforcement of rationing when it was initially proposed. His dithering could not have been occasioned by political obstacles. But, as usual, he targeted others for his mistakes. His remedy was to restructure the food control system. Concluding that the task was too large for one man to handle, he fastened on a scheme to remove control of supplies out of the hands of the food controller, leaving him with only rationing.[86] Lloyd George was evidently thinking of duplicating the arrangement between Prothero and Lee at the Board of Agriculture, which operated smoothly and without a hitch. But it was a faulty analogy. While Rhondda and Prothero were admirable on policy, only the former was a talented administrator as well.[87] In short, Lloyd George's proposal to divide executive responsibility at the ministry was unnecessary and might have made matters worse.

Rhondda was hopeful that he and his staff could surmount the food crisis and so he put off appointing a new man for the job. Already on shaky grounds because of the chaos in food administration, Rhondda's delaying tactics further deepened Lloyd George's despair. Indeed, the prime minister told Hankey on February 24, 1918 that he was thinking of sacking Rhondda.[88] The idea, fortunately, never went beyond the verbal stage.

For Rhondda, things could not have looked much bleaker. His health was deteriorating rapidly, caused in large part by the strain of his work and the intense hammering from all sides to which he was subjected practically on a daily basis. It gnawed at him that he was in danger of ending his career in government, not in a blaze of glory as he had hoped, but "as an even greater failure than Devonport." There were rumors circulating in the corridors of Whitehall that he would resign rather than accept a demotion.[89]

As events played out, Rhondda's new plan, which was set in place piecemeal, met the latest challenge and rescued him from his dilemma. The irony was that Rhondda had not been a great advocate of rationing.[90] Heavy pressure from different segments of society, rather than from Rhondda himself, induced the War Cabinet to take unprecedented action. Before the close of 1917 it directed Rhondda to introduce rationing without delay. Compulsory rationing began at the local level in November 1917 and applied to only a few commodities such as sugar. By July 1918 it had developed into a nationwide scheme covering all major items except bread. The impact on food distribution was swift. In the London area the number of people standing in food lines in the latter part of February 1918 was 1,339,392, but a week later that figure had fallen to 208,115. By the start of May food lines had practically vanished.[91] The press, which had attacked Rhondda mercilessly, now hailed him as a hero. The honors that he had dreamed of thankfully arrived shortly before his death in July 1918.

The rationing and distribution system worked well in Britain, generally much better than in most of the countries where it was introduced. This was due to several factors. There was less strain on the system because bread was abundant and even the supply of rationed food was greater than in most of the European countries. The bulk of the supplies were purchased abroad and, on arrival at the ports, came under the control of the food controller who could distribute them as he chose. There was, moreover, the right balance between centralized and decentralized responsibility. The national system was uniform and implemented by local officials who were familiar with the needs of the neighborhood.[92]

Despite the losses at sea and the diversion of merchant ships to transport troops from America, the population of Britain was never in real danger of starvation or even malnutrition – as was the case in Germany and Austria. There was a decline in the availability of certain foods, in particular meat, milk, butter and sugar. On the other hand, bread could be purchased in unlimited quantities and such commodities as potatoes, bacon, ham, flour and margarine increased during the war and compensated for some of the shortages. The food supply crisis was largely psychological and could have been averted if a rationing plan had been in place earlier. It is interesting to note that Lloyd George, before taking office, had often cried "too late" in reproaching Asquith for failing to take timely action on vital issues.[93] He might have applied the same expression to describe his own behavior regarding food distribution.

Part Two

STRATEGY AND THE WAR

Chapter 5

THE FIRST ATTEMPT AT A UNIFIED COMMAND

As the conflict entered its third winter, an Allied victory appeared remote and uncertain. The bloody four-month Battle of the Somme had sputtered out in the cold and rain of November with negligible gains. Despite strenuous efforts, the Italian offensives along the Isonzo River in 1916 had not succeeded in denting the Austrian line or pushing it back significantly. Hopes that Romania, which joined the Entente on August 17, 1916, would become a factor in the war had been quickly dashed when it was overrun by the Central Powers four months later. In June 1916 Russian armies under General Brusilov attacked the Austrians along a wide front, but their advance, which began with such promise, was thrown back when the Germans rushed troops to support their ally. When the fighting ended, the Russians had lost another million men and their army was practically finished. On the seas, German U-boats were taking an increasing toll on Allied and neutral shipping. Sir John Jellicoe, then C-in-C of the Grand Fleet, found it necessary to warn the cabinet that shipping losses on the present scale might drive the Allies out of the war by the early summer of 1917.[1] Adding to this somber picture was the cost of the war, which had risen to about £5,000,000 a day. In the autumn of 1916 the Treasury revealed that Britain's reserves of gold and convertible securities were nearly exhausted and that soon it would have to finance the war with US loans.[2]

Such was the situation when Lloyd George came to power in December 1916. The country as a whole counted on him to break through the inertia of the previous administration and turn the tide in 1917. Although he could expect a short period of grace, he realized that he would have to produce tangible victories, not only for his own political survival, but to boost the morale of the war-weary British public.

Lloyd George understood that the only way to win the war was to defeat the German armies in France. He feared, however, that the exact opposite would happen if he permitted the nation's manpower reserves to be drained through costly attritional battles such as had occurred at the Somme and later at Passchendaele. To save the British army from destruction, he aimed to pursue peripheral campaigns and shift the main burden of fighting the Germans to Britain's allies – Russia, France and, after April 1917, the United States. As he saw it, attacking the weakest members of the Central Powers would avoid heavy casualties and so weaken Germany as to bring about its collapse. By adopting a long-term but less costly strategy, Lloyd George hoped that at the conclusion of the fighting Britain would emerge as the strongest of all the belligerents and be able to dictate peace terms to enemies and allies alike. But there were fatal flaws in this line of thought. In the first place, it was Germany that propped up its allies, not vice versa. Secondly, fighting the war along principles of limited liability was unrealistic. With France and Russia fading and the United States unprepared for war, Britain required to deploy the bulk of its armies on the western front to avoid defeat.

In laying down military policy, it would have been immensely helpful if Lloyd George had tried to educate himself in the ways of conducting war. He had no army experience, and prior to the war had shown no interest in the study of warfare. During the years between 1914 and 1916 when he was a key member in the inner councils of war, in addition to serving briefly as minister of war, he made little effort to add to his meager military knowledge. As prime minister, whenever he went to France, he never bothered to visit the front (unlike Georges Clemenceau after he became French prime minister in 1917) where he could have questioned army commanders and gained a better insight into trench warfare. He might have found out that there were alternatives to the High Command's methods of fighting such as the more prudent "bite and hold" strategy favored by some generals,[3] not to mention that he might have been able to identify a potential replacement for Haig.

Alas, Lloyd George did not realize "the depths of his own ignorance," as Arthur Balfour (who had devoted much time to the study of war[4]) accurately surmised, and approached strategy "as an essentially simple subject that had been unnecessarily complicated by the professionals."[5] As a military novice, he failed to comprehend that the course of war does not follow any preconceived scenario, however well reasoned, that it is unpredictable and the first requirement in planning strategy is attention to detail and provision for all conceivable contingencies.

Lloyd George had inherited from Asquith, as the government's chief military advisor, a first-rate soldier in Sir William Robertson. Incredibly enough, Robertson, had started out as a private and rose to the highest rank in the army as a result of innate shrewdness, immense energy and obsessive devotion to his profession. Robertson abhorred the prime minister's peripheral strategy, which to him made no military sense and did nothing to hasten Germany's defeat. Dominated by short-term concerns, he wanted all resources concentrated in France so that pressure could be maintained on the German army. His markedly different approach to the war was bound to affect his relationship with the prime minister, which was bad from the start and grew progressively worse.[6]

Robertson and Sir Douglas Haig, the supreme army commander, were never close friends but they formed what David Woodward describes as "the most important and influential military partnership in British history."[7] Both shared a common disdain of politicians and, although they did not always see eye to eye at the operational level, were united in their belief that the war could only be won on the western front. On the other hand, their social backgrounds and personalities were vastly different. Of humble origins with limited formal education, Robertson never overcame the pedestrian habit of dropping his aitches. He was blunt, graceless, and prone to emotional outbursts when upset. Haig came from a prominent family that had not only made a fortune distilling whiskey, but could actually trace its lineage back to the twelfth century. Being a gentleman, he was courteous, dignified, reserved, self-contained, with emotions kept tightly in check.

Time and time again Haig would induce Robertson to bend to his will. One can only speculate why someone as tough-minded and opinionated as Robertson would habitually defer to Haig. The reason, it would seem, was not because Robertson was awed or felt socially inferior, but because he was convinced that any split between the two would be exploited by the politicians to further their own agendas.[8]

Haig was fifty-five years old when he succeeded Sir John French as C-in-C of the BEF in December 1915. With graying hair, handsome features, neatly trimmed moustache and well-tailored uniform, he looked the part of a commanding general. He was an excellent defensive general, as he showed during the First Battle of Ypres, but he was rather unimaginative in his approach to modern offensive warfare, guided as he was by principles he had learned as a student at Camberley – the Staff College emphasized learning by rote rather than encourage its students to take more than a routine approach to problems that required new ideas. Still, few today would call into question Haig's overall perception of the war. He understood that the western front was the decisive theater and that the German army could only be defeated after the depletion of its material and human resources. If he was to win the war, he had no alternative but to pursue a policy of attrition and accept heavy casualties.

What is in dispute, however, is not Haig's concept of attrition, but his approach to it. In common with other leading generals of the conflict, he did not fully appreciate the changes that had occurred in military technology. He was obstinate in adhering to fixed plans regardless of the facts and was unreceptive to new ideas. At the Somme and again at Passchendaele, the

British army suffered horrendous casualties because of his pursuit of objectives that were unattainable. There are critics who believe that Haig would have been better served if he had adopted the doctrine of "bite and hold" rather than attempt a breakthrough. Haig, however, has his share of defenders. They maintain passionately that Haig's wearing out battles brought heavy losses, but carried within them the price of victory. There is no argument that the great battles fought in 1916 and 1917 took a huge toll on the German army and contributed to its defeat, but it is an open question whether another commander, with more imagination and flexibility, could have achieved the same results at less cost.[9]

Lloyd George's relations with Haig were just as stormy as they were with Robertson. Given his lack of military knowledge, it would have served the interests of the country if he could have relied on the judgment of the army chief. But he regarded Haig as rigid, unimaginative and delusional, with no idea of how to win the war other than to charge like a bull at the enemy's impregnable front. The most obvious remedy was to replace Haig, but that option was unavailable to Lloyd George at the beginning of his tenure. The Tories had made Haig's retention a condition for their participation in his government. Forced to coexist with an army chief he distrusted, Lloyd George was determined to seize control of the war and steer British military policy in a new direction.

The first order of business facing the War Cabinet in December 1916 was to consider Berlin's offer of peace communicated through the American government.[10] Britain had entered the war in August 1914 to preserve the balance of power in Europe, although Germany's breach of Belgian neutrality provided the moral justification for doing so. Under the Pact of London signed on September 5, 1914, the Entente partners agreed not to conclude a separate settlement or even to consider any peace offer without previous consultations. Asquith studiously avoided defining Britain's overall war aims, lest it lead to serious quarrels with France and Russia – although the three powers had reached agreements over the partition of the Ottoman Empire. Thus, public statements tended to be vague and at times emotional, combining the need to destroy Prussian militarism with the liberation of Belgium and the evacuation of northeast France.[11]

Although confident of holding a psychological advantage in the wake of their capture of Bucharest on December 6, 1916, the Germans could not have chosen a more inopportune moment to deliver their note. Lloyd George's accession to power reflected the nation's repudiation of Asquith's "wait-and-see policy" and a desire for a more ruthless and forceful prosecution of the war. As a member of the Asquith government, Lloyd George had not shied from using bellicose language in public to flog Germany, and he reinforced it by contemptuously dismissing any proposal for peace short of victory.[12] If Lloyd George was publicly committed to total victory, in private and with colleagues he had been more ambivalent. He spoke out against President Wilson's initiative in February 16, 1916, but at a crucial meeting on March 21 remained conspicuously silent when the issue was discussed. In November he repudiated Lord Lansdowne's memorandum calling for a negotiated settlement and subsequently asked Robertson to issue a reply.[13] While in the process of forming a government in December, he met with a delegation of socialist and Labour leaders. Asked whether he favored continuing the war until victory had been achieved, he responded that he would consider any peace proposals put forward by neutrals or the enemy that were reasonable, but before entering into negotiations he had to know Berlin's terms.[14] It can be argued that Lloyd George's remarks were disingenuous, calculated solely to enlist the support of Labour and the socialists, but, as he changed his mind frequently, it also may have accurately reflected his outlook at the time.

At any rate, Lloyd George was not encouraged by the German peace initiative in December 1916. The note was truculent and boastful in tone, implied that the Allies were responsible for the war and, while offering to negotiate, lacked concrete terms. The prime minister rejected the move towards peace in principle, but, as he would tell the Commons, he did not intend to enter into negotiations without knowledge of Berlin's terms, for to do so was tantamount to putting "our heads into a noose with the rope end in the hands of Germany."[15] As the Germans made no effort to define their war aims, Lloyd George drew the inevitable conclusion that they were not interested in a compromise peace, suspecting that their proposal had been intended as a propaganda ploy and possibly to divide the Entente. Nevertheless, to avoid offending neutral opinion, he opposed any reply that implied an unequivocal refusal to negotiate. At a War Cabinet meeting on December 18 it was agreed that it would be best for the Allies to concert an identical reply to the German note, signed in Paris by their representatives.[16] When consulted, Britain's allies were equally convinced that the Germans were engaged in a sham and that it was a waste of time to ask Berlin for a more definite statement. Before the Allies were able to frame their reply to Berlin, President Wilson, operating independently, asked the belligerents on December 20 to state the terms on which they would be willing to conclude the war. In his preliminary remarks, President Wilson offended the Allies by observing that the objects of the belligerents were virtually the same, namely that each "side desires to make the rights and privileges of weak peoples and small states as secure against aggression or denial in the future as the rights and privileges of the great and powerful states now at war."[17] Still the Allies, mindful that their blockade of Germany had strained their normally good relations with Washington, could not afford to further annoy President Wilson by an outright rejection. They counted heavily on American aid. A Foreign Office memo pointed out that if the president so chose, he could prevent "the raising of Allied loans in the United States, not to speak of interference with the export of munitions and other necessities."[18]

Lloyd George knew that, with Germany in possession of a large part of Allied territory, it held most of the trump cards. In any negotiations the Allies could not hope to gain what they wanted in Europe, much less satisfy their imperial ambitions abroad. Germany was bound to emerge from any peace settlement stronger than it had been in August 1914. In the eyes of Lloyd George such a prospect would be analogous to defeat. Britain was approaching the apex of its military power and until it had exerted greater efforts it made no sense to settle for an arrangement that would leave it less secure in the future. In short, it seemed to the prime minister a bad idea to attempt to negotiate peace from a weak position. The members of the War Cabinet were united in expressing similar sentiments.

The French did not even want to hear German terms, they were so committed against entering into peace negotiations. At an Anglo–French conference held in London between December 26 and 28, a text was drafted in reply to the German and American notes. Approved by all the Allied Powers, it was handed to the American ambassador in Paris on December 30. In the note, the Allies, having denied President Wilson's suggestion that the aims of the belligerents on both sides were similar, outlined their conditions for peace. They included, among other things, German evacuation of invaded territory, the liberation of subject peoples and the return of Alsace-Lorraine to France.[19] These terms were such that they would never have been acceptable to the Central Powers as long as their strength was unimpaired. The Germans, like the British, were not interested in ending the conflict except on their own terms. When that seemed unlikely, they decided to carry out a policy of unrestricted submarine warfare on which they believed that their best hope of victory rested.

Of more immediate concern to Lloyd George than President Wilson's noble but futile pursuit of peace, was to find a way to reorient Allied war policy more in line with his strategic vision. In November 1916 Allied military leaders, meeting at Chantilly to consider the strategy for 1917, had devised a plan that closely paralleled the one taken at the same location a year earlier. It had been agreed that the Allies would again mount large-scale offensives on their own front and that they would begin simultaneously at a date to be determined later.[20] Lloyd George was not keen on a plan that promised to repeat the horrors of the Somme. Instead, he preferred to strike where the enemy could be dealt a crippling blow on the cheap. In considering any scheme, he tended to disregard the obstacles involved because, as one who knew him well wrote, "he is not a man of detail."[21] One possibility, as he saw it, was to make a concerted effort in the Balkans where the Allied armies had achieved little since landing at Salonica in the fall of 1915.

The situation in Greece was anomalous, with Allied troops installed in a portion of a country that was neutral and whose king, Constantine I, was the Kaiser's brother-in-law and understandably sympathetic to the Central Powers. Except on rare occasions, the Allied or Eastern Army under a French general, Maurice Sarrail, was inactive, though it continued to grow in size. King Constantine grew more antagonistic towards it the longer it remained in his country and Sarrail did not help matters by meddling in Greek politics.

In the fall of 1916, Sarrail, in search of a more compliant regime, encouraged and aided Eleutherios Venizelos, the pro-Entente former prime minister, to lead a revolt against Constantine. Venizelos proclaimed a provisional government, which was established at Salonica. His government formally declared war on Germany and Bulgaria on November 23, 1916 and immediately began to recruit an army to take the field alongside the Allies. Greece was now a country divided against itself.

When royal troops began to concentrate at Larissa on the left rear of the Eastern Army, Sarrail feared that Constantine was on the verge of joining the Central Powers. His solution was to undertake an immediate offensive against Larissa to avoid the possibility of being trapped between Bulgar–German troops in the north and by Greek royalist troops in the south. The French government supported Sarrail's proposal. It arranged to send two divisions to Salonica and requested that the British do likewise.

Robertson had no use for sideshows – least of all the one in the Balkans, which he considered a waste of resources. His formula for winning the war, as already noted, was to concentrate troops where they could kill the most Germans and in the Balkans the principal enemy was the Bulgarian army. His theoretical stance was fortified by practical experience. In 1906 he had toured the Balkans and, in his view, the difficult mountainous terrain and poor communications, made it unlikely that offensive operations could be carried out successfully.[22] Robertson stated his objections to Sarrail's plan at the first War Cabinet meeting on December 9 and subsequently circulated two memos to strengthen his case. He pointed out that he had no confidence in Sarrail, that the number of Allied troops approached nearly half a million and should be able to turn back any attack against them, and that, given the state of British shipping, the two divisions could not be properly maintained. He doubted that the Germans had the resources to enter Greece, but that even if they did, the two British divisions could not arrive in time to help ward off the attack. Believing that the Allies were overextended, he recommended that they fall back and shorten their line of defense, which would enable them to hold their own against a simultaneous attack if and when it occurred.[23]

The War Cabinet still hoped that Constantine could be persuaded to follow a policy of benevolent neutrality. There was a disinclination to give Sarrail a free hand lest it lead to a war with Greece and unite that country at a moment when Venizelos' movement was steadily gaining ground. One of the chief architects of the Salonica expedition, Lloyd George does not appear to have participated in the discussion. Presumably he was exhausted by the events that had propelled him to power and he had no wish at this time to challenge Robertson.

French Prime Minister Aristide Briand sent a delegation to London during the last week in December in the hope of persuading the British government to reverse its stand. The three-day conference, at which the French were represented by Alexandre Ribot, Jules Cambon and Albert Thomas, was held at 10 Downing Street. Privately, Lloyd George favored sending two more divisions to Salonica, not to enable Sarrail to undertake a campaign against royalist forces, but in anticipation of a future offensive or simply to secure the line now occupied. However, he concealed his true beliefs in his discussion with the French. He remarked that the question of time had to be taken into consideration. If it required three months for the troops to arrive, as the Admiralty maintained, was it of any use to send them at all? By then the crisis would be over. Thomas replied that if the Germans attacked Sarrail the reinforcements would still be useful. The battle would not be over in one or two days and possibly the climax might occur in two or three months when the reinforcements would be of the greatest value. Robertson felt that withdrawing troops from the western front for a theater that promised no benefits would be playing into Germany's hands. He maintained that Sarrail had enough troops to meet any attack if steps were taken beforehand to prepare suitable defensive positions. Robertson was convinced that the French attachment to the campaign was based not on military factors, but on a desire to dominate Greece in the postwar period. He distrusted Sarrail and feared he might use reinforcements to overthrow Constantine. His suspicions seemed confirmed when Cambon admitted that Sarrail's proposal might lead to war with Greece. Jellicoe was equally averse to enlarging the British garrison in the Balkans. He noted that given the alarming increase of enemy submarine activity in the Mediterranean, he could not spare escorts for the safe arrival of additional transports and store ships.

From time to time Lloyd George joined in the talks, but he did not tip his hand one way or the other. He was anxious to avoid a breach with either the French or Robertson. The deadlock that ensued allowed him to come up with an ingenious solution to his predicament. He brought up the idea of an inter-Allied conference to reach an understanding on the future role of the Eastern

Army as well as on a general plan for 1917. The prime minister proposed Rome as the site of the gathering so that Sarrail would be able to attend. He stressed that the French general was unknown to the British and that meeting him personally was likely to be beneficial. Ribot was noncommittal, but indicated he would raise the matter with the cabinet on his return to Paris.[24]

As the prospects in the Balkans appeared dim, Lloyd George scanned other secondary theaters that offered more immediate benefits. The more he thought about it, the more he became convinced that the Allies ought to concentrate on defeating the enemy's weakest link, Austria–Hungary, and that the far eastern end of the Italian line was the most inviting area from which to launch a major offensive. He envisaged breaking through the Austrian position on the Isonzo Front with British, French and Italian troops and driving northeast towards Trieste and ultimately Vienna.[25] Once Austria–Hungry capitulated, he believed that Germany, economically weakened and demoralized, would probably abandon the struggle. But Lloyd George's optimism was misplaced. The common frontier between Austria and Italy, from the Tyrol in the West to the Julian Alps to the East, some 375 miles in length, formed a tangle of high ridges and precipitous crags. The Austrians held the crests everywhere. The only avenue of advance was on the extreme Italian right flank where the Isonzo River cuts through a curtain of mountains. But an offensive along this narrow corridor was exposed to flank and enfilading fire from the Austrians who occupied the higher ground.[26] Since entering the war, the Italians had tried and failed nine times to reach Trieste, beyond which lay Ljubljana Gap and the plain of the Danube river. In the process the Italian army had suffered over 600,000 casualties.[27]

Nevertheless, Lloyd George believed that previous Italian setbacks were due to indifferent tactics and particularly to a lack of sufficient artillery and ammunition. He stated his case in his memoirs:

> It never occurred to the two rigid minds of the two GHQs [British and French Military Headquarters] that a kind of attack was possible on the Italian Front that would have taken the Austrians completely unawares and achieved a real break-through and not impossibly a break-up, before the Germans could come in sufficient numbers to the succour of their routed allies. ... The Italians had a definite numerical superiority over the Austrians. Had they been equipped with a corresponding superiority in heavy guns and ammunition, the Austrians might have been overwhelmed. They certainly would have been taken completely by surprise. Their soldiers had no experience on any front of that kind of bombardment and it would have completely unnerved them for some time.[28]

Lloyd George made no secret that he abhorred the policy recommended by the Chantilly conference, notwithstanding his predecessor's approval of it. To his colleagues he openly restated his distrust of Haig and criticized his conduct of the Somme operation, stressing that the losses were out of all proportion to the results achieved. On receiving notice that the French and the Italians were in favor of an Allied conference, it remained for Lloyd George to persuade them that his indirect approach to winning the war was preferable than the ineffective and costly offensives against the well-entrenched enemy on the western front. On December 30 the War Cabinet authorized Lloyd George to make whatever arrangements he deemed necessary in Rome.[29] Some of its members like Curzon and Milner understood the importance of the western front, but after the Somme, they saw merit in husbanding the nation's resources and turning to other fields of action where British imperial interests could be advanced.

On New Year's Day, Lloyd George, along with other members of the British delegation, left London to attend the Allied conference in Rome. Here Lloyd George put forward a paper that called for a combined British–French–Italian offensive through the Julian Alps that would end with the capture of Vienna.[30] It was a proposal that surprised everyone, including Robertson, who was furious that he had not been consulted or apprised beforehand, quite apart from his opposition to concentrating resources elsewhere than on the western front. The idea that knocking Austria out of the war in 1917 ought to be the centerpiece of Allied strategy for that year also was repugnant to Britain's allies. The French did not want to be drawn into secondary theaters that would disrupt plans for the forthcoming offensive on the western front. Then, too, the Italians, recognizing that Britain and France would have their hands full with their joint attack, feared embarking on a large campaign with the prospect of receiving little assistance. Both adopted the line that Allied military plans could not be changed at the eleventh hour, particularly since no reference had been made to the responsible military chiefs.

At the very minimum, Lloyd George hoped to loan the Italian army 250–300 British guns from the western front and a similar number from the French, if it resumed its drive towards Trieste. Knowing that Robertson was hostile to the move, he sent Hankey to enlist the support of General Luigi Cadorna, the Italian C-in-C. Robertson had already lobbied Cadorna, so Hankey's mission was unsuccessful.[31] Cadorna's stated excuse for turning down the guns was that they could not be returned to the western front in time for the spring offensive. The real reason was that he did not wish to provoke the Germans into attacking his front in strength. In the end, the conference decided to turn over Lloyd George's memorandum to the General Staffs of the three Allied governments for further study, thus giving it a quiet burial.[32]

Similarly, the conference failed to reach an agreement in the matter of reinforcements to Salonica. Lloyd George had indicated in his paper that a grave transportation shortage precluded Britain from sending two more divisions to the Balkans. He suggested instead that Italy provide the necessary reinforcements since it had much to lose from the collapse of the Balkan front. He also noted that the sea route from Italy to the Balkans was comparatively short and well protected. There was no reaction from the Italian delegation.

The French prime minister, Aristide Briand, countered with a long and impassionate speech, described by Lloyd George as the finest piece of oratory "I have ever heard at any conference."[33] Briand refused to believe that it was impossible for the British government to find the ships to transport two or three divisions. His logic clouded by wishful thinking, he asserted that with three more divisions, victory on the Balkan front was a certainty, but to leave Sarrail without adequate reserves was a prescription for disaster.[34] After the conference adjourned for the day, Robertson approached Lloyd George and expressed the hope that the prime minister would resist the pressure to send additional forces to the Balkans. Lloyd George gave an evasive answer. This prompted an already angry Robertson to send Lloyd George a sharp note: "I don't know what effect Mr. Briand's oratory may have upon you in regard to the wretched Salonika business, but it seems only right and fair ... that I should tell you *now* that I could never bring myself to sign an order for the dispatch of further British Divisions to Salonika."[35] The prime minister was rather annoyed over the veiled threat, but there is no evidence that he had been tempted to fall in step with the French.

Before the session opened on the third day, Lloyd George interviewed Sarrail at the British Embassy. He had been led to believe that Sarrail was a flamboyant adventurer, a political general whose accomplishments had not justified his elevation to the position of supreme commander. The prime minister was pleasantly surprised with Sarrail, finding him charismatic, thoughtful, fascinating and, although impulsive, amenable to rational argument. Sarrail requested that he be given a free hand to take preemptive action against the Greek royalist forces. Lloyd George refused to sanction any such move, pointing out that it would drive Constantine in the arms of the Germans, to say nothing of the impact it would have on neutral nations. Although he recognized the danger to the Allies, he was confident that differences with Constantine could be resolved diplomatically.[36] Friendly exchanges continued and then Lloyd George said, "Look here. I promise you that whatever happens in the Balkans, I and my colleagues will see that you get fair play." Sarrail replied "Done," and he gave his word that he would not move southward without British permission. The bargain was sealed with a handshake.[37]

When the conference reassembled, Lloyd George announced that if eloquence alone could carry two divisions to Salonica, Briand's speech on the previous day would have accomplished the task. Unfortunately, ships were needed and the British had none to spare.[38] Of course, as Briand had clearly maintained, the ships could have been found if the British had been inclined to do so. But they had determined that Sarrail (whose Eastern Army at the time numbered twenty-three divisions) had more than enough troops for defensive purposes. On the other hand, if he tried to simultaneously engage the forces of Constantine and the Central Powers he would need more than the four divisions he had requested. And neither the British nor the Italians were prepared to send massive reinforcements to the Balkans.

The Rome conference ended without an agreement on a unified military strategy for 1917. Consequently, the blueprint drawn up at Chantilly in December 1916 remained in force. As Lloyd George journeyed back home, he received a message that General Robert Nivelle, the new C-in-C of the French army, wished to see him during his brief stop in Paris.[39] Nivelle wanted to outline his plan for an offensive based on the novel methods he had used successfully in earlier operations. But Lloyd George, thinking that Nivelle wanted to discuss the extension of the British line on the western front, declined to meet him in the absence of Haig. Instead, he invited him to come to London to meet with Haig and the members of the War Cabinet.

In mid January Nivelle arrived in London to sell his plan to the British government. Nivelle, who had succeeded General Joseph Joffre in December 1916, had built his reputation at Verdun where his two set-piece operations had recaptured several forts and a good deal of ground at comparatively low costs. Backed by massive artillery support, both attacks had been conducted on narrow fronts and broken off when the objectives were reached. Nivelle attributed his success to the introduction of new assault tactics and scientific use of artillery.

Nivelle appeared before the War Cabinet on January 15. Accustomed to dealing with their tongue-tied generals, the ministers were surprised to hear Nivelle speaking lucid and impeccable English (his mother's native tongue). Nivelle proposed a gigantic assault on the great German salient on either side of the Somme, with the French delivering the main blow between Soissons and Reims in the south and the British carrying out a diversionary strike near Arras in the north. He was adamant that what had worked well at Verdun could be carried out with equal success on a much larger front and bring the war to a sudden end. To his captive audience, he explained what his unorthodox approach entailed – a shattering and simultaneous preliminary bombardment of forward and rear German lines, followed by infantry waves sweeping forward in one great rush under a creeping barrage, circumventing surviving pockets of resistance and passing unopposed into open country. Instead of attritional battles lasting weeks or months, he indicated that the operation would be a short, violent affair, designed to smash through the entire depth of the German front in one bound. If the desired results were not achieved within forty-eight hours he would call off the attack.[40] "Nivelle is much too loud in his hopes of success," Robertson told Lord Esher, a British observer in Paris. "It is quite right to be confident, but for a man in his place he should keep his confidence to himself and his troops."[41]

It is difficult to know what Nivelle's excessive confidence was based on, other than perhaps a cover for his insecurity. Beginning the war as a colonel in the artillery, he had risen quickly in rank, eventually receiving command of the Second Army in May 1916. As an artillerist he was innovative and able to coordinate infantry and artillery as well as anyone, but he lacked attributes necessary for a commander-in-chief. "With the outcome of the war at stake," Robert Doughty wrote, "French political leaders had placed all their bets on an officer with no experience as a strategist, little understanding of how to work with allies and only six month's experience as an army commander."[42]

Hesitant at first, Lloyd George was quickly won over, dazzled by the self-assured and smooth-talking Nivelle. He found the French General unassuming and personally agreeable, was impressed by his spectacular success at Verdun and believed him to be highly imaginative, with a much better grip on modern warfare than Haig. He was attracted to Nivelle's plan for a number of reasons: it was bold, emphasizing surprise, massive force and novel use of artillery; since the British were assigned only a supporting role, he anticipated that casualties would be kept to a minimum; and it would be apparent quickly if the offensive failed, so there would be plenty of time to try something else.[43]

On the morning of January 15, in advance of the main meeting with Nivelle, Lloyd George had called in Robertson and Haig and made blunt and unfavorable comparisons between the accomplishments of the two armies during the past summer, concluding "that the French army was better all-around, and was able to gain success at less cost of life."[44] He chose to treat the future direction of Anglo–French operations as though it were contest between Haig and Nivelle, with the latter enjoying his unqualified support.

Haig did not share Nivelle's unbridled optimism, but agreed to the plan on condition that if a breakthrough did not occur immediately, the attack would be broken off.[45] Haig did not want Nivelle's operations to drag on and derail his own pet scheme for an offensive in Flanders, intended for late in the spring of 1917. Its object was to clear the Belgian coast of enemy naval bases and to remove the German threat to the Low Countries. Such an operation, quite apart from its attractive aims, would allow the British to fight for the first time on a battlefield of their choosing.

Robertson had even stronger reservations about the Nivelle plan than Haig. He was correct in stressing that it was a fallacy to believe that the Verdun formula could be applied successfully on an operation of this scope. He noted that the front was too wide and the enemy's defenses too deep to meet the expectations of a breakthrough within the promised forty-eight hours. Nor was it feasible to assume that a battle could be terminated arbitrarily, for such a move would depend on circumstances that could not be foreseen. Although the British armies would be acting in a subsidiary capacity, they were expected to make a great effort and it was erroneous to assume that heavy losses could be avoided. Lastly, he maintained that the expenditure in men and material incurred in the fighting might jeopardize Haig's Flanders project.[46]

On the evening of January 15 the members of the War Cabinet deliberated among themselves for several hours and the next day conferred with Robertson and Haig before summoning Nivelle. Overriding their generals on all key points, they endorsed Nivelle's scheme. Lloyd George and his colleagues had every right to set military policy, but in view of the skepticism of Robertson and Haig, it behooved them to pause and undertake a careful scrutiny of Nivelle's plan to ensure that the advantages claimed were attainable and not the product of wishful thinking. Put simply, it was reckless for men without any experience in the study of warfare to have ignored the government's military advisors and taken it upon themselves to commit the British army to a hazardous operation. A cursory investigation would have shown that the French Minister of War, General Hubert Lyautey, was open in his contempt of the scheme – indeed, he had described it as "a plan for the Grand Duchess of Gerolstein" – and even considered sacking Nivelle before realizing – or being told – that it would have an unsettling effect on the army and public.[47]

At the conclusion of the meeting on January 16 the War Cabinet directed Haig to comply with Nivelle's schedule of attacking no later than April 1, ignoring his recommendation that the offensive be delayed until May when the weather would permit the Italians and the Russians to apply pressure on their fronts. It further ordered him to accede to Nivelle's request to take over an additional twenty-mile stretch of the line in order to free French troops for the offensive.[48]

Haig's reluctance to extend his front and his wish that the attack be delayed until the spring aroused Lloyd George's suspicion that he was looking for a way to avoid supporting Nivelle. His distrust of Haig was heightened by information from French sources. It was pointed out that Nivelle was "very disturbed about Sir Douglas Haig," finding him rigid, inflexible and unaccommodating. "L.G. would like to get rid of Haig," Hankey noted in his diary, "but cannot find an excuse."[49] Undoubtedly at the urging of Lloyd

George, the War Cabinet took the rather unusual step of instructing Haig (through Robertson) to carry out both the letter and spirit of its agreement with Nivelle, warning him that on "no account must the French have to wait for us owing to our arrangements not being complete."[50]

Whatever his misgivings, Haig was too loyal an officer not to fulfill his brief, but over the next few weeks the lack of transportation facilities in France hampered his military preparations. Nivelle complained to London that Haig was tardy in occupying the new stretch of front that had been assigned to him. Haig argued that the delay sprang from severe shortcomings in the French rail system. This was confirmed by Sir Eric Geddes, Director-General of Transport with the BEF and a Lloyd George appointee. Lloyd George, however, suspected that Haig was dragging his feet.[51]

The incident could not have come at a worse time for Haig, who had just given an interview to a group of French journalists, predicting an imminent end to the war. The interview included a brief reference to a shortage of big guns, the kind of peace that the Allies would accept, and hinted at the lack of resolve of the men in public life. It struck the right chord with a segment of the press. "Sir Douglas Haig is the reverse of a talking General," wrote the *Evening Standard*. "When he declares that 'we shall most certainly break the German front, and severely, and at many points,' he means exactly what he says."[52] Other dailies expressed similar sentiments. On the other hand, the article provoked a highly adverse reaction among the politicians who resented that their patriotism had been called into question. A member in Parliament asked whether Haig's comments had been approved by the home authorities. Caught off guard, the government was compelled to issue a statement to the press in which it squashed any hope that the war would be concluded in the near future.[53] The fallout from the interview, not to mention the inference that a lack of guns might have hindered operations and the type of peace the Allies were likely to accept, fueled Lloyd George's resentment towards Haig. As he began to consider ways to bring Haig to heel, he fastened on the idea of a unified command in the west. Such an arrangement had previously existed between French and British commanders in Gallipoli and Salonica and Lloyd George saw no reason why Haig could not be subordinated to Nivelle.[54] Before proceeding, he evidently needed to obtain the authority of the War Cabinet.

On February 15 Lloyd George went over to see Hankey and, on entering his office, saw him chatting with Commandant Bertier de Sauvigny, the French liaison officer at the War Office. Interrupting the conversation, the prime minister laid down a plan by which he hoped to gain his objective. He claimed that Nivelle had made a great impression on him and the War Cabinet and he was convinced that he was the only man capable of bringing the war to a successful conclusion by year's end. To do so he would require to make use of all the forces operating on the western front, his own as well as those of the British. The prime minister maintained that Haig's popularity with the public and the British army ruled out placing him directly under the authority of Nivelle. However, if the War Cabinet was persuaded that putting the British army under Nivelle's orders was the key to success, it would not hesitate to sanction the measure even if it entailed Haig's resignation. Lloyd George counted on the French authorities to bring the necessary pressure on London to achieve their common goal.[55]

The idea of a unified command was undoubtedly sound but to make it workable required goodwill on both sides. The way Lloyd George went about promoting it was devious and calculated to engender maximum antagonism and opposition. Moreover, the conditions were not right. Yet, here was a prime minister, barely two months in office and without the knowledge of his generals or authorization of the War Cabinet, prepared to place the British army under an overconfident and untested foreign commander, responsible only to his government.

Although the French leaders would never have ventured to suggest it, the proposal of tying the large British army to their own declining troop strength was indeed welcome news. An Anglo–French Conference was arranged to be held in Calais on February 26. Here Lloyd George proposed to anoint Nivelle as commander of the British army. To pave the way he requested through the French Ambassador in London that Nivelle submit a scheme at the upcoming conference, stressing that Haig's subordination to him was indispensable to victory.

If the plot was to succeed, Lloyd George realized that both Robertson and Haig had to be kept in the dark until the last moment, before they could rally their supporters. On the eve of the conference, the War Cabinet held an important meeting with neither Robertson nor Derby in attendance. The War Cabinet minutes are brief, merely stating that it was decided to empower the prime minister to "ensure unity of command both in the preparatory stages of and during the operations."[56] Hankey's diary, normally detailed on important matters, barely adds anything. It reads as follows: "Much discussion about Haig and Nivelle's merits. [?] Eventual conclusion that Haig is the best man we have, but that is not saying much and that, as between Haig and Nivelle, Ll. G. should support the latter."[57] However, Curzon, in a conversation with Lord Stamfordham, the king's private secretary, laid down Lloyd George's case in support of Nivelle: the French had nearly twice as many troops as the British on the western front; recent French tactics showed that the French General Staff was superior to that of its British counterpart; Nivelle was more clever than Haig; and since the French would be assuming the main responsibility for carrying out the attack, it was vital to leave them no possible grounds for claiming that any failure was due to the British.[58] With no War Office authority present to contest Lloyd George's arguments, it is not surprising that they carried the day. Conforming to the prime minister's wishes, Hankey delayed circulating the minutes of the proceedings. Robertson was unaware of what had transpired at the War Cabinet meeting when he left for Calais with Lloyd George and the other British delegates.

Shortly before the start of the Calais conference, Lloyd George met privately with Aristide Briand, the French prime minister. There is no record of their conversation but, in light of what later occurred, Lloyd George apparently suggested it would be preferable if Nivelle introduced the idea of a unified command, which he would then greet with surprise and delight.[59] The Anglo–French Conference got under way at 3:30 p.m. on February 26 in a bleak room at the railroad station hotel. Besides Lloyd George and Robertson, the British delegation consisted of Haig, Hankey and the usual compliment of advisers and assistants. The first session was devoted to the railroad question and when the two sides reassembled at 5:30 p.m., discussion centered on plans for the offensive. Observing that much depended on the forthcoming attack, Lloyd George asked Nivelle whether anything further could be done to render British cooperation more effective. Briand chimed in and prodded Nivelle to speak frankly if he had any disagreements with Haig. Nivelle does not appear to have been a willing participant in the plot.[60] That may explain why his face turned red and he was slow to take the cue. For someone so verbally adept, Nivelle hesitated and stammered without coming to the point. He praised Haig, with whom he claimed he had been in perfect agreement, and wished to thank him for his cooperation. Although he did not anticipate any difficulties with Haig, he thought there must be certain rules guiding the relations of the two generals and should be binding on their successors "if either one of them disappeared." Growing impatient, Lloyd George asked Nivelle to be more precise and to put his views in writing before the next session.[61]

After taking a stroll, Lloyd George returned to his room where he was joined by Briand, Nivelle and Lyautey. He was given the requested document, which had actually been drafted a week earlier at Nivelle's headquarters.[62] Simply put, the proposal would have incorporated Britain's forces into the French army and reduced Haig to the equivalent of an adjutant general, with control over personnel and discipline only. Lloyd George liked the scheme even though it went further than the War Cabinet had contemplated.

When Hankey was shown the document, he was horrified, but, as always, retained a passive exterior.[63] The British public was certain to be inflamed at what he perceived was a dangerous and flawed command arrangement. Nivelle was requesting that the British army surrender its independence and essentially accept the same status as the Foreign Legion and that its commander be excluded from having a say whatsoever in matters connected with the operations. To make matters worse, while Nivelle would exercise executive authority over the British army, he would be responsible only to his own government. It was apparent to Hankey that the prime minister had not understood the implications of the French proposal. There was a world of difference between placing Haig under Nivelle and handing the BEF over to the French lock, stock and barrel. "It seemed incredible that the greatest army we had ever sent abroad," lamented Lieutenant Colonel Edward Spiers (later changed the spelling of his surname to Spears), Head of the British Military Mission to Paris, "now at the height of its power and absolutely confident of its superiority over the enemy, should be confronted with terms such as might be imposed on a vassal state."[64]

Robertson was handed a translated copy of the French document just as he was finishing his dinner. Spiers described what followed: "Wully's face went the colour of mahogany, his eyes became perfectly round, his eyebrows slanted outwards like a forest of bayonets held at the charge – in fact he showed every sign of having a fit." Turning to his ADC he shouted, "Get 'aig."[65]

Haig was shown the note when he arrived and, like Robertson, was stunned. The two soldiers hurried over to Lloyd George's room and found him closeted with Hankey. A terrible row ensued. Robertson did most of the talking. He went over every paragraph in the document, raising one objection after another. Lloyd George replied that he was acting on the War Cabinet's authority, thus revealing that he had known all along what was coming and that he had deliberately concealed it from his military associates. This only fanned the generals' anger. Haig insisted that the plan was unworkable and that, in his opinion, British troops would not fight under French leadership. The atmosphere in the room became charged as Lloyd George found himself fighting a rear guard action. Eventually driven into a corner, his combative instinct was to strike back, even if it meant landing blows well below the belt. With his temper out of control, he turned on Haig and unleashed a crude tirade, insinuating that he would have to resign if he did not fall in step. Robertson and Haig departed in disgust, ready to resign rather than to betray the British army.[66] Lloyd George evidently did not realize the consequences of his brinkmanship, which threatened to break up not only the conference, but, more importantly, his fragile coalition.

The ever-astute Hankey, by contrast, saw that the prime minister was on dangerously thin ice. The next day he saved Lloyd George from his self-made predicament by finding a way around the impasse. He produced a counterproposal that was acceptable to all parties. Under the compromise formula, Haig would be subordinated to Nivelle, but only for the forthcoming campaign. Haig was free to direct the operations within his sector as he saw fit and had the right of appeal to the War Cabinet if he believed that Nivelle's instructions endangered the safety of his army or prejudiced the chances of an Allied victory.[67]

Back in London, Lloyd George gave the War Cabinet a distorted version of the negotiations that had led to the Anglo–French agreement at Calais. Robertson, who was in attendance, may have exploded inside, but held his tongue. On leaving the meeting he wrote to Haig: "He [Lloyd George] is an awful liar. His story to the War Cabinet gave quite a wrong impression this morning. He accused the French of putting forward a monstrous proposal, and yet you and I know that he was at the bottom of it. ... I cannot believe that a man such as he can for long remain head of any government."[68] Details of Lloyd George's deceit quickly spread around Whitehall. Bonar Law admitted to Hankey that he "didn't much like" the Calais arrangements, but refrained from saying so to Lloyd George out of loyalty.[69] Others were not as charitable. Derby was among an influential group of Conservatives who reproached Lloyd George for subordinating the British army to a French commander and for the manner in which he did it.[70] The king, who disliked Lloyd George for his impudent attitude towards the monarchy,[71] weighed in, admonishing him sternly for placing his army under foreign control without his knowledge.[72] Even the War Cabinet backpedaled and, as a rebuke to Lloyd George, sent a letter to Haig expressing its utmost confidence in his leadership.[73]

Lloyd George faced further difficulties when Haig, backed by Robertson, resisted implementing the Calais agreement. Haig, already irritated at the commanding tone Nivelle adopted towards him,[74] learned that the Germans had withdrawn to a newly constructed line running between Arras and Soissons. This line, known to the Allies as the Hindenburg line, was a formidable defensive barrier, shortening the front by some twenty-five miles and releasing between 15 to 20 German divisions, as well as flattening out much of the great salient against which Nivelle intended to strike. The German retreat made it less likely that Nivelle's chances for a complete and rapid breakthrough would be realized.[75] Haig feared that the Germans would use the reserves they had amassed to attack the northern part of his line around Ypres and cut off the BEF's communications with the coast.[76] In these circumstances, he warned the War Cabinet that the inviolability of his line would be jeopardized if he committed part of his force to assist the French offensive. Nivelle was furious when he read Haig's memo and wrote back at once. He dismissed the likelihood of a German counteroffensive in Flanders or anywhere else, made it clear that his plan would go forward with only minor alterations, and insisted that the

British attack "must not be reduced by a single man or gun."[77] Simultaneously, the French general sent an arrogant communication to Lloyd George, decrying Haig's behavior and suggesting that he be replaced by Sir Hubert Gough, commander of the Fifth Army.[78] The French government followed up by sending an intemperate telegram to London, accusing Haig of trying to evade the decisions reached at Calais and demanding that he conform to Nivelle's instructions.[79] The French had no qualms about crossing the line of diplomatic propriety, because they were certain that Lloyd George's views coincided with their own.[80]

However, there were limits to Lloyd George's capacity to hold back the rising tide of dissent in London. Since returning from France, Robertson had been relentless in trying to drive a wedge between Lloyd George and the other members of the War Cabinet. Speaking to them singly, he told them exactly what had occurred in Calais, reproached them for their decision on February 24, made while he had been deliberately kept away, and asked them whether they were prepared to endanger the BEF in an unsound French offensive and ignore Haig's warning of a German threat to the Channel ports. In a memorandum prepared for the policy makers on March 2, Robertson poured scorn on the Calais agreement, which he insisted he had signed only because their assent had left him no alternative.[81] Robertson's onslaught had the effect of changing the mood in the War Cabinet.[82]

Although the handwriting on the wall was plain enough for Lloyd George to see, he remained defiant, convinced that Haig's fear of a counteroffensive was merely a smokescreen to evade the Calais agreement and regain full control over the BEF. He considered replacing Haig or forcing his resignation, but he was worried that such a move would prompt Robertson and Derby to leave their posts. Given the public's trust in its military leaders, their sudden disappearance might spell the end for his ministry.[83] Uncertain about what to do, he turned to Hankey for advice. Hankey discreetly sounded out the members of the War Cabinet and found that Bonar Law alone would sanction the dismissal of Haig, though not out of conviction. Hankey reported to Lloyd George that, if Haig were dismissed, the government would probably fall. He recommended retaining Haig whom he believed was right and Nivelle wrong.[84] Any thoughts Lloyd George entertained about holding his ground were dispelled by the War Cabinet, which rallied behind Haig. On March 8 the ministers insisted on another Anglo–French conference to resolve the differences between the two commanders and on the following day instructed Lloyd George to tell the French government that Haig had their full confidence.[85]

Another Anglo–French Conference was held, this time in London, on March 12 and 13. The soldiers welcomed its results, which took some of the sting out of the earlier settlement at Calais. Under pressure from his colleagues, Lloyd George executed an abrupt volte-face. He handled the preliminaries with his usual dexterity and resource. He saw Haig and Nivelle separately and prepared the way for the two to reach an agreement about the operational conduct of the offensive. During the conference, he pointed out that Haig enjoyed the complete confidence of the War Cabinet and removed the threat of making the BEF a contingent in the French army by forbidding the amalgam of the two armies. He rebuked Nivelle for couching his instructions to Haig in a manner of a general addressing a subordinate rather than the commander-in chief of the greatest army Britain had ever put in the field. The conference addressed all the contentious issues, most of which were resolved in Britain's favor.[86] The French, however, retained strategic control of the BEF.

As Nivelle's most enthusiastic champion, Lloyd George had a good deal riding on the outcome of the forthcoming offensive. But before the operation began, great events radically altered the strategic and political scene. A spontaneous revolution broke out in Petrograd on March 8 and spread quickly to other cities. The Tsar abdicated on March 15 and was replaced by a social democratic government that opted to continue the war despite the war weariness of the Russian people. Although there were signs that conditions in Russia were deteriorating rapidly, the revolution had happened so quickly that it caught Lloyd George and the other members of the War Cabinet by surprise. While there was no indication that Russia under a new administration would drop out of the war, any nation that had undergone so violent an upheaval was not likely to be in a position to exert significant pressure on its front for some time. This was confirmed later in March by the Russian commander who doubted that he would be able to mount a large-scale offensive before the summer and hinted that the Anglo–French command should reconsider its plans.[87] For their part, the Italians, worried about an Austro–German attack, either in the Trentino or on the Isonzo Front, were requesting help and certainly could not be counted on to assist in the Anglo–French operations.[88] The elimination of Russia and Italy as important elements in the coming battle would have justified a postponement of Nivelle's plan.

To further complicate matters, the French government fell on March 19. The minister of war, General Lyautey, who was a brilliant colonial administrator but a political novice, resigned abruptly on March 15 after being shouted down in the Chamber of Deputies.[89] The departure of this popular soldier made it impossible for the ministry to continue. Briand resigned and was succeeded by the octogenarian Alexandre Ribot with Paul Painlevé as minister of war. Painlevé, perhaps the most powerful man in the government, was skeptical about Nivelle's offensive, which he feared would only further deplete the war-weary French army. His anxiety deepened when he privately sounded out the army group commanders (Louis Franchet d'Esperey, Philippe Pétain and Joseph Micheler) and learned that they also had no faith in Nivelle's plan. But there were political risks in arbitrarily canceling the offensive, particularly in view of Britain's strong support of it.[90] Painlevé tried to persuade Nivelle to scale down his offensive, but to no avail. Nivelle even threatened to resign, confident that the government would not dare replace a newly appointed commander because of the effect it would have on French public opinion and on the morale of the army. Concerned that Nivelle's departure might spell the downfall of the Ribot government, Painlevé allowed the offensive to proceed.[91]

After bad weather caused a brief delay, Haig opened his attack north of Arras on April 9, with the object of tying down German reserves before the French launched their massive drive on the Aisne a week later. Caught by surprise, the Germans were thrown into disorder, enabling the Canadians to storm Vimy Ridge in a feat of arms that surpassed anything the British had thus far achieved on the western front. Haig was eager to exploit his victory, but bad weather, as well as lack of reinforcements and artillery support, enabled the Germans to patch up their lines. Although he had achieved a local success, in addition to absorbing German reserves, the cost had been heavy. By end of the first week in May he had incurred 110,000 casualties, a huge number for a subsidiary operation – in fact the government was so worried by the public's reaction to the losses that it withheld the figures from the press.[92]

On the French front, Nivelle's much-heralded offensive got under way on April 16. The Germans had received ample advance warning of the offensive. Nivelle had been incredibly indiscreet in revealing his blueprint to politicians outside of official circles and even to the press. During March, German parties had raided French trenches and uncovered documents providing details of the impending attack. Thus, the German High Command had shifted its reserves and strengthened defenses in the targeted area. The French made initial gains but there was no breakthough. French losses, about 120,000, had been no higher nor mistakes greater than in some of the earlier battles, but this was supposed to be a quick and decisive victory. Since expectations had been raised so high, the failure of Nivelle's offensive had a devastating effect on the spirits of the French soldiers. A wave of disturbances, some amounting to outright mutinies, swept through nearly half the French divisions, with the protesters essentially limiting their actions to refusing to obey orders to attack. Nivelle was hastily replaced by General Pétain, an officer with an aversion to unnecessary casualties and rash adventures.[93]

For Lloyd George there was a high price to pay for betting on the wrong horse. His tortuous machinations in placing Haig under Nivelle permanently soured relations between him and his senior generals, driving Robertson and Haig, by no means always in agreement at the operational level, to close ranks to prevent further political interference, setting back the cause of a unified command on the western front for many months, weakening his political support and undermining his credibility in military affairs. It also meant that the British army, with France so seriously weakened, would have to shoulder the major burden of the fighting in the west, at least for the remainder of 1917.

Chapter 6

FACING THE SUBMARINE MENACE

During the early months of the war, Britain employed its naval superiority to keep the sea-lanes open and impose an economic blockade of the Central Powers.[1] The German Navy could not break the blockade, but it could damage Britain's sea-borne trade with a new weapon, the submarine, or U-boat. To cope with the growing submarine menace, the Admiralty relied on a series of countermeasures. It organized naval patrols to hunt for submarines and detailed destroyers and small craft to guard the routes used by merchant ships; it armed merchantmen, employed nets and mines, and introduced depth charges and detecting instruments known as hydrophones.[2] But for the whole of 1916 the British navy managed to sink only 15 U-boats, small inroads into a force that had increased to 140 by year's end. At the same time, German submarines were sinking merchant ships at a rate faster than the capacity of British shipyards to provide replacements.[3] Walter Runciman, president of the Board of Trade, warned the War Committee on November 9, 1916 that if losses continued at the present pace, there would be a complete breakdown in shipping.[4]

The lack of success against submarines cast doubt on the whole conduct of naval affairs and led to changes at the Admiralty during the last month of the Asquith administration, with Jellicoe leaving the Grand Fleet to take over the duties of First Sea Lord.[5] Although Jellicoe was intellectually gifted, excelled as a sailor and handler of ships and was held in high esteem by all ranks in the navy, he was poorly suited for his new position. His health had deteriorated under the strain of wartime command and overwork, due in part to his reluctance to delegate authority. He was, moreover, inclined to be overcautious, undoubtedly because he realized that if he made a wrong decision he could lose the war. During the crisis of the submarine war, the country required a first sea lord who was bold and innovative, rather than cautious and filled with misgivings.[6]

The new administration had no new ideas and flatly rejected suggestions made by Lloyd George and Bonar Law in the War Committee on November 2, 1916, about the feasibility of using a convoy system[7] – merchant ships sailing in organized groups, protected by two or more destroyers. It was not as if the concept was novel. The convoying of merchantmen, protected by warships, had long been a traditional British practice in time of strained relations and of war.[8] In fact, it can be traced back to the thirteenth century and was used repeatedly since then, most recently during the Napoleonic wars. Its efficacy was unquestioned, but in the pre-1914 generation, a new doctrine had emerged that stressed naval activism, that is, using men-o'-war to hunt, rather than to protect merchantmen. In keeping with this principle, the Admiralty considered convoy work as defensive, whereas the proper role for destroyers was to act offensively, to hunt in areas submarines were known to be operating.[9]

The prevailing naval doctrine undoubtedly colored the outlook of Admiralty leaders even if no mention of it was made in the arguments they brought forward in the succeeding months: that it would be difficult, if not impossible, to keep cargo ships together and in close station to enable a few destroyers to screen them; that confusion would arise at night or in the event of a fog; that a convoy offered too big a target; that ships in a convoy could not zigzag; that valuable time was wasted as the speed of the convoy was determined by the slowest ship; and that, at any rate, there were not enough destroyers to act as escorts.[10] Naval leaders insisted that single ships, following recommended routes, stood a better chance of reaching their destination than if they formed part of a convoy.

On February 1, 1917 Germany, throwing caution to the wind, announced that it would resume a policy of unrestricted submarine warfare, threatening to sink without notice every merchant ship, whether Allied or neutral, in certain areas, including the waters around the British Isles. The thinking was that the destruction of about 600,000 tons of Allied (but largely British) shipping a month, combined with a reduction of neutral traffic of as high as forty percent that would be frightened away, would starve Britain into submission within six months.[11] In adopting this course, German leaders had no illusions about the probable reaction of the United States. But the Allied blockade was causing severe shortages of food and other materials and they had concluded that Germany could not afford the continuation of the military stalemate. They were confident that, since the United States was unprepared for war, its troops could not reach Europe in time and in sufficient numbers to affect the outcome.

At first, the submarine campaign met and even exceeded the expectations of its planners. U-boats claimed a total of 540,006 tons (Allied and neutral) of shipping in February, slightly more in March, and with the advent of longer days and better weather, sent another 881,027 tons to the bottom in April. By the third month of the campaign, a quarter of the ships leaving British ports never returned home.[12]

The Admiralty could offer no remedy to avert the disastrous losses other than the intensification of the current methods of protection and submarine hunting. Jellicoe was adamant that there was no single answer to the submarine menace, that the cumulative effect of all the measures in place would solve the problem. But these were proving inadequate, sinking U-boats at the rate of only one or two a month. Arming merchantmen had limited value since U-boats normally struck from beneath the sea; depth charges were useful only when submarines were located, and the hydrophone could not detect a U-boat beyond several hundred yards. As the hemorrhaging continued, Britain was in danger of losing the war. Jellicoe was doleful from the very outset and his pessimism worsened after the unrestricted U-boat campaign got under way. "Is there no solution for the problem?" asked Rear Admiral William S. Sims, sent over by Washington (several days before its declaration of war against Germany) to act as liaison officer between the US Navy and the Admiralty.[13] "Absolutely none that we can see now," was Jellicoe's reply.[14]

Day after day, in an atmosphere of unrelieved gloom, Jellicoe announced the list of sinkings to the War Cabinet without offering hope that effective countermeasures would soon be put in place. His pessimism did not sit well with Lloyd George who came to regard him as a liability. After Jellicoe finished his daily tale of woe, the prime minister was known to make cynical remarks about the navy's shortcomings or treat him with studied rudeness.

From the moment he took over at the Admiralty, Carson had never wavered in his support of Jellicoe. He held Jellicoe in the highest esteem, personally and professionally, and looked to him for advice and guidance. "He was in my opinion," Carson insisted, "the best man at his job that I met with in the whole course of the war for knowledge, calmness, straightness and the confidence he inspired in his officers."[15] Carson had to reassure Jellicoe that he had absolute confidence in his leadership each time the admiral, dejected by the prime minister's attitude towards him, asked that his resignation be accepted. Carson ignored Lloyd George's often-voiced recommendation that he make sweeping changes in his department and bring in "fresh men with sea experience." Tired of hearing the prime minister dwell on the same theme, he answered with mordancy one day, "I must be under a strange hallucination, Mr. Prime Minister, for I thought that Admiral Jellicoe had just come from the sea."[16] Carson also resisted Lloyd George's plea to give convoys a trial. It was not that Carson was averse in principle to experimenting with convoys, only that he found no support for such an idea from any of the naval experts at the Admiralty.[17] In a speech delivered at a luncheon on May 8, 1917 he warned civilian authority, presumably Lloyd George, not to interfere in naval matters:

> I advise the country to pay no attention to amateur strategists, who are always impatient and always ready for a gamble. We cannot afford to gamble with our fleet. As long as I am at the Admiralty the sailors will

have full scope. They will not be interfered with by me and I will not let anyone interfere with them.[18]

Although Lloyd George had lost confidence in the navy's ability to cope with the submarine menace, he did almost nothing to push along the use of convoys, to hasten to bring them into effect. Instead, it was Hankey who prevented the matter from drifting indefinitely. Troubled by the litany of sinkings that was causing him sleepless nights, he too was convinced that the Admiralty's antisubmarine arrangements were insufficient.[19] Accordingly, he prepared a memorandum for the prime minister, listing objections to the current Admiralty policy and arguing forcibly for the adoption of convoys as the only effective answer to the U-boat menace.[20]

Lloyd George was sufficiently swayed by the paper to at once summon Jellicoe, Carson and Admiral Sir Alexander Duff (Head of the Anti-Submarine Department) to 10 Downing Street on February 13. After the memo was read to them, he asked for their thoughts. Hankey was on hand to further expound on his ideas and to answer questions. A former lieutenant colonel of marines, Hankey possessed enough naval knowledge to hold his own with the Admirals, but Lloyd George was at a serious disadvantage when pitting his amateur views against theirs on technical matters. Jellicoe and Duff acknowledged that, as a statement of strategic principle, they found no fault with Hankey's paper. From a practical measure, however, it left unanswered the question of how more escort ships were to be obtained for the task.[21]

The breakfast lasted two hours and ended without a commitment from Jellicoe. Carson was more favorably disposed towards convoys, but he was reluctant to press his case. Nevertheless, Lloyd George derived some comfort from Carson's promise to seek the opinions of merchant ship captains on the practicability of the convoy system and to be guided by the results of two experiments in "controlled sailings" (term used for convoys) that had recently been initiated – one involving ships in the Scandinavian trade and the other, vessels carrying coal to France.[22] It would, of course, require time before a proper assessment of the second measure could be made. Ten days later, Carson held a conference at the Admiralty with ten sea captains whose ships lay in the London docks. The assembled mercantile skippers were adamant that station-keeping was impossible and all expressed a preference to sail alone rather than as part of a convoy. There is no record of Lloyd George's initial reaction to the report, although in his *War Memoirs* he dismissed it as a contrived survey, insisting that Sir Joseph Maclay "had not been consulted as to either the names or class of ship that ought to be represented at the gathering, and that the officers of the smaller tramp were not deemed fit for so exalted a conclave."[23]

What is indisputable was that Lloyd George took no further action for about six weeks. Why did it take him so long to enforce a measure that he had supported all along? Hankey speculates that Lloyd George, already at loggerheads with Robertson and Haig, would have invited wide press and parliamentary criticism if he had clashed with the Admiralty chiefs. He also observes that Lloyd George lacked the technical expertise to refute the Admiralty's arguments.[24] Grigg reminds us that Hankey omitted the Carson factor. The prime minister could not have imposed a naval policy without crossing swords with Carson who stood solidly behind his professional advisers.[25] Already unhappy at being excluded from the War Cabinet, Carson had shown in the past that he would not hesitate to give up a cabinet post on a matter of principle and that once in Opposition, was capable of creating immense mischief. Nor could Lloyd George forget that Carson's good will and support was vital if he hoped to achieve a settlement in Ireland.

It is never a good idea for amateurs to ignore the advice of technicians of warfare. But there were a host of senior admirals, including David Beatty, C. F. Thursby (Vice Admiral Commanding East Mediterranean) and R. E. Wemyss (C-in-C East Indies), who disagreed with Admiralty policy, and from early in 1917 had urged the adoption of convoys.[26] Still, overruling Admiralty leaders would have entailed political risks. But set against this was the nation's survival. The stocks of wheat and other foodstuffs were declining rapidly and there was every likelihood that they would dwindle even further. Common sense dictated that more than the old methods were needed to deal with the U-boats. Yet, the prime minister kept dragging his feet. There are two plausible explanations for his conduct: either he did not think that the problem was sufficiently urgent to warrant negotiating through a political minefield, or that delay would render the danger more acute so that there would be no political repercussions when he decided to act.

Hankey, meanwhile, fretted over the rising shipping losses and Lloyd George's inattention to the subject. Try as he might, he was unable to awaken Lloyd George to the deepening crisis. On April 22 he was told bluntly, "Oh, well, I have never regarded that matter so seriously as you have." Lloyd George's statement defies comprehension in view of the staggering British losses – 545,282 tons out of a total of 881,027 – that were the highest on record that month. Hankey wrote in his diary:

> Personally I am much worried about the shipping outlook owing to submarines and the inability of the Admiralty to deal with it, and their general ineptitude as indicated by their stickiness towards any new proposal. I have many ideas on the matter, but cannot get at Lloyd George in regard to it as he is so full of politics. I am oppressed by the

fear I have always had that, while moderately successful on land, we may yet be beaten at sea.[27]

Hankey, to his credit, refused to give up. During the third week in April he wrote a memo, placing all the facts before the prime minister and stressing the need to address the submarine campaign.[28] As shipping losses became more alarming week after week, Hankey was not the only one expressing concern over the prime minister's rather complaisant attitude. During the War Cabinet meeting on April 20, from which the prime minister was absent, Curzon felt that something had to be done to cope with the submarine threat. There followed a long discussion during which several options were considered, including the possibility of abandoning the Salonica campaign in order to ease merchant shipping. The one thing all agreed on was that the matter required to be brought to the attention of the prime minister immediately after his return.[29] That same day Robertson wrote to Curzon:

> I was very glad you raised today the submarine question. It ought to be faced, not merely discussed, and the necessary action taken. We know quite enough already to feel that it is serious, and we should at once cut down all unnecessary shipping. I have had many talks on the subject with the First Sea Lord, and also with the Food Controller, and if we do not do something at once, serious trouble may be in store for us.[30]

Milner was also of the opinion that the prime minister could no longer delay taking a hard look at the antisubmarine campaign.[31] Feeling the heat from the War Cabinet, Jellicoe felt compelled to again present arguments to justify his stand. In a memorandum entitled "The Submarine Menace and Food Supply," he proposed no changes, confident that the various antisubmarine measures already in effect would eventually pay dividends.[32]

Jellicoe's reassurance did not resonate with Lloyd George, who had shaken off, seemingly overnight, his indifference to the growing crisis. His refocus stemmed from a number of factors besides Hankey's latest memorandum. He was under considerable pressure from Maclay who was adamant that the country could not continue to sustain shipping losses on the present scale and that an ocean convoy system should be introduced, at least on a trial basis. In April mercantile tonnage losses were four times as great as those in January 1917.

Then, too, with his faith in Jellicoe gone, Lloyd George had turned to junior naval officers for advice. Among his key informants were Captain Herbert Richmond and Commander R. G. Henderson, both of whom were at odds with the trade protection thinking and methods of their seniors at the Admiralty.[33] During the early months of 1917 Henderson made a surprising discovery that had profound implications. As the officer in charge of organizing the controlled sailings in the French coal trade, he was in regular contact with authorities in the Ministry of Shipping. From one in particular (Norman Leslie), he received information showing that Admiralty statistics of vessels arriving and leaving British shores were grossly misleading. The alleged total of some 2,500 voyages a week each way, Henderson realized, consisted mostly of small coastal craft, ships moving from port to port, and cross-Channel steamers. The actual figure of weekly sailings of oceangoing ships was between 120 and 140.[34] That being the case, the number of escorts required to implement a full convoy system was far less than the Admiralty had assumed. It was no longer an insurmountable problem for the navy to provide destroyers for the oceangoing trade, especially since more would be available from across the Atlantic now that the United States had entered the war. Feeding information to Lloyd George through the back door, they produced figures and arguments demolishing the anticonvoy case. The conduct of Henderson and other junior officers violated strict naval code and, if discovered, would have been grounds for instant dismissal. Be that as it may, their revelation was the catalyst that drove Lloyd George to intervene.

At a War Cabinet meeting on April 23 the prime minister raised the possibility of adopting the convoy system, which he claimed had been advocated by Admirals Beatty and Sims. Jellicoe stated that the issue was under consideration but that one of the chief obstacles to adopting such a scheme was the shortage of torpedo-boat destroyers. He thought that there was some prospect of obtaining the help of American destroyers and, in fact, six had already been ordered to sail for Britain. Nevertheless, a much larger number would be necessary before any convoy system could be instituted. He mentioned that the experiment of controlled sailings on the Scandinavian route had not been altogether successful, as two vessels in separate convoys had been torpedoed and sunk. He undertook to make a further report on the matter to the War Cabinet.[35]

By now, Lloyd George had become thoroughly disenchanted with the Admiralty. He considered its opposition to convoys as incomprehensible, the product of preconceived notions, ill-founded theories and blind obstinacy. He described the Admirals as hidebound, unimaginative and "stunned by pessimism." Although Lloyd George had good reason to fault the laggardness and conservatism of Jellicoe and his advisers, his generally withering language when referring to them was scornful, excessive and vengeful.[36]

On the morning of April 25 Lloyd George saw Carson briefly to inform him that he intended to take peremptory action on the question of convoys. Accordingly, he received authorization from the War Cabinet later in the day to visit the Admiralty to investigate all the means presently being used in antisubmarine warfare.[37] A message was sent to the Admiralty that Lloyd George would be coming over for a visit on April 30. "At last Ll G has set himself to tackle the submarine problem seriously – when it is almost too late," a relieved Hankey wrote in his diary.[38]

In the course of the next few days, the Admiralty's attitude toward the convoys underwent a complete change. On April 26 Duff handed Jellicoe an important memorandum in which he suggested the introduction of a comprehensive system of convoys. His recommendations were based on the large increase of daily losses of merchant ships, the success of the convoys carrying coal to France and the prospect of obtaining escort craft from the United States.[39] Left unsaid, but obvious to all who read the memo, was the discovery of the mistakes in the shipping figures. All these factors combined to immediately convince Jellicoe that the North Sea and Channel experiments should be extended to the Atlantic.[40] Scarcely had this decision been made, then orders went out (April 28) to arrange an experimental convoy from Gibraltar. It reached Britain on May 10 without mishap. Thereafter, the Admiralty introduced convoys in stages to all ocean sailings with the result that losses began to decline. By September 1917 it was apparent that the tide had turned, although until August of the following year, the sinkings would remain higher than they had been before unrestricted warfare was inaugurated. The convoy had reversed the fatal trend, but like the Second World War, it was not any single measure that had mastered the U-boat.

The leading sailors were already committed to the convoys when Lloyd George descended upon the Admiralty on April 30. His visit turned out to be anticlimatic, although it has often been overly dramatized in published works. Scholars, with few exceptions, have relied almost exclusively on Lloyd George's account of the episode. It ran as follows:

> Apparently the prospect of being overruled in their own sanctuary galvanised the Admiralty into a fresh inquisition, and by way of anticipating the inevitable they further examined the plans and figures which Commander Henderson had prepared in consultation with Mr. Norman Leslie of the Ministry of Shipping. They then for the first time began to realise the fact which had been ignored by them since August, 1914, that the figures upon which they had based their strategy were ludicrous, and that therefore protection for a convoy system was within the compass of their resources. Accordingly when I arrived at the Admiralty I found the Board in a chastened mood. We discussed the whole matter in detail. We agreed to conclusions which I thus reported to the Cabinet.[41]

Lloyd George is not subtle about claiming that the introduction of convoys was due to his own initiative. He argues that it was the threat of his impending intervention that drove the Admirals to make a complete somersault rather than risk dismissal. His recollection of the incident was challenged by more than one of his contemporaries. Carson did not mince his words when he told a reporter from a leading London daily, "It is the biggest lie ever was told."[42] Duff emphatically denied that his memorandum was a face-saving device. He noted that he had no way of knowing that Lloyd George's visit was intended to compel the Admiralty to adopt the convoy system. It might also be added that the memorandum, given its length and importance, could not have been thrown together in a few hours. A. J. Marder concludes, after a careful investigation, that Duff's conversion was due, not to Lloyd George's coming visit, but to the factors identified in his memorandum.[43]

Indeed, it is more appropriate to hold Lloyd George accountable for what he failed to do. He had good reason to act immediately after receiving Hankey's original memorandum on February 11 suggesting the adoption of convoys. If Jellicoe and Carson deserve to be reprimanded for their implacable and prolonged resistance, is there any reason why Lloyd George should escape criticism for allowing matters to drift for six weeks? We have seen that as late as the start of the third week in April the prime minister was on record as saying that he did not consider the submarine menace to be as serious as Hankey perceived it. The long-held view that Lloyd George rescued the country from the brink of disaster is a gross distortion. Actually Hankey, who, unlike Lloyd George, refrained from beating his own breast, deserves more credit than any other single individual. At any rate, the adoption of the convoy system, which reduced the number of sinkings to tolerable levels, ranks high among the decisive events of the war.

Chapter 7

PRELUDE TO CATASTROPHE

Allied military plans to win the war in 1917 were derailed by a distracted Russia and by a breakdown of discipline in the ranks of the French army in the wake of Nivelle's debacle. The waning effectiveness of the Russian and French armies made Britain the mainstay of the anti-German coalition. The numerical advantage on which the Entente had counted to wear down the Germans was nullified, at least for the foreseeable future. Britain faced two dangerous choices. If it took on the Germans with only limited help from its European allies, it would bleed to death and be unable to sustain the struggle in the final stages.

The other option was to remain inactive until American forces could be thrown into the scale. But the United States was unprepared to fight in a major war.[1] Both the British and French governments had tried unsuccessfully to urge Washington to permit and encourage the massive enlistment of Americans in their respective armies. For the immediate future, American assistance would be limited to one division. The best estimate in London was that American troops would not be able to assume a large burden of fighting in the land war until late in 1918 or even 1919. Thus, if the Allies remained quiescent in the west, there existed the possibility that the Germans would seize the initiative and finish off Russia or Italy or both, forcing Britain to accept a peace settlement that would deprive it of much of its empire and its status as a first-class power.

The debate over a strategic policy dominated the proceedings in the War Cabinet in the spring and summer of 1917. During this period, the belief crystallized in the mind of the prime minister that it was no longer possible to inflict a defeat on Germany in the traditional sense, by military means. His best hope – his definition of victory – was to gain an advantage on the battlefield, leading to a settlement under which Britain's principal war aims in Europe and overseas would be fulfilled and the German threat reduced. Since the prime minister had no faith that military gains could be achieved on the western front, he sought to redirect British strategy eastwards. Handicapping the prime minister was the lack of support from his colleagues. The imperialist members of the War Cabinet were anxious to add certain areas of the Middle East to the British Empire, but not at the expense of imperiling the western front.

It was not Lloyd George's nature to give up easily, and by persisting he again came into conflict with the High Command. Haig was one of the few leading Britons who never for a moment doubted that an outright military victory was attainable on the western front if he was provided with the requisite resources.[2] Now that he had fulfilled his commitment to cooperate in the disastrous Nivelle offensive, he was eager to carry out a plan that he had been contemplating since be first became commander-in-chief. His aim was to break out of the Ypres salient and drive his force towards the Belgian coast, capturing bases, threatening vital railway communications and perhaps forcing a German retirement from Belgium.[3] Grossly optimistic reports from Brigadier General John Charteris, the chief of intelligence at General Headquarters, had persuaded Haig that the German army was on its last legs.[4]

The information that Robertson was receiving from his own intelligence contradicted Charteris's fanciful calculations. Robertson would have preferred more cautious and deliberate tactics, but he made no impression on Haig, whose mind remained fixed on distant objectives in Flanders.[5] Still, Robertson did not think it was his place to impose his views on Haig. He was convinced that if he wavered in his support of Haig, Lloyd George would eagerly take the war to the Austrians or to the Turks. Although he was clearly uneasy about Haig's grand designs, he preferred an operation on the western front to any sideshow in some distant theater. For Robertson, a successful campaign was not contingent on a distant advance. What he hoped for in Flanders was an attritional battle in which the Germans would suffer more casualties than the British, who had a growing artillery superiority.[6]

The ultimate decision as to whether Haig would be allowed to move forward with his plan rested, of course, with the War Cabinet. Lloyd George wanted to avoid a ghastly repetition of the Somme. Since he assumed that the war would extend into 1918 or longer, he thought it essential that Britain conserve its manpower resources. But his reputation and judgment had been seriously damaged because of his unstinting support of Nivelle. As a result, he no longer felt strong enough or confident enough to openly challenge his generals, especially in view of Haig's latest publicly acclaimed success.[7] Instead, he resorted to playing a double game. While he pretended to back Haig's massive attack in the west, he worked tortuously behind the scenes to secure the adoption of a different strategy.

Chastened by Nivelle's defeat in the west, Lloyd George returned to the idea of knocking away Germany's props. What seemed like a wonderful opportunity to induce Austria to leave the war presented itself in the spring of 1917. Acting behind Germany's back, Karl, the new Emperor of Austria–Hungary, sent a message to the French president through Prince Sixte, his Bourbon brother-in-law (who was serving in the Belgian army), announcing his ardent desire for peace.⁸ Lloyd George was shown the letter during a meeting with Alexandre Ribot, the French prime minister, at Folkestone on April 11. Pouring over its contents, he became convinced that Austria desperately wanted a separate peace. In his excitement, however, he underrated the political and logistical difficulties of achieving this objective. In the note Karl promised to grant Serbia access to the Adriatic Sea on condition that it abandon its support of groups seeking to bring about the disintegration of the Hapsburg Empire; and he promised to exert his influence on Berlin to ensure that Alsace–Lorraine was turned over to France and that Belgian independence was restored. Conspicuously absent in Karl's terms was an offer to concede territory to Italy. Playing off one side against the other, Italy had entered the war in April 1915 to liberate its nationals still subject to Austrian rule, in addition to wanting to extend its interests along the Adriatic and elsewhere. But Lloyd George felt confident that he could persuade the Italians to renounce their Adriatic claims in exchange for concessions in Turkey. To that end, he wanted to bring Italy into the negotiations, but Ribot objected, as it would have involved betraying the Austrian emperor's confidence. As a compromise, it was agreed that the matter could be discussed in general terms, without revealing the existence of Karl's letter. Ribot was not sure that the Austrian offer was worth pursuing. He was attracted by the proposed return of Alsace and Lorraine but he had no confidence that the Austrians carried enough weight to persuade the Germans to give them up. Although Ribot did not reveal his private thoughts to Lloyd George, he agreed to set up a meeting with Baron Sidney Sonnino, Italy's foreign minister and the strongest figure in its cabinet.⁹

Lloyd George did not report the central feature of his talk to the War Cabinet, but did let Hankey in on the secret while they were traveling together to attend the inter-Allied conference.¹⁰ Shortly after arriving in Paris, Lloyd George was driven to the Hotel Crillon for a highly secret meeting with Prince Sixte. They had a pleasant conversation. Lloyd George stressed that it was vital for the Italians to be informed about the Austrian overtures so that peace terms might be negotiated. But Sixte was adamant that they should not be told. He feared that if the Germans happened to hear about the peace initiative they would exact reprisals against the Emperor. Karl had made no mention of the Italians in the deal because he doubted he could meet their extravagant demands. Lloyd George assured him that he would do his best to sound out Sonnino without betraying the Emperor's confidence.¹¹

The Anglo–French–Italian Allied Conference took place in a railroad carriage in St. Jean de Maurienne on April 19. Lloyd George could not have been more disappointed with its results. When the subject of peace terms with Austria was raised in a general way, Ribot said little, preferring to let Sonnino crush Lloyd George's hopes. Sonnino had no desire to see a separate peace with Austria concluded. He had engineered Italy's entry into the war for the sole object of acquiring large blocks of territory in Europe as well as in Asia Minor. He knew that Italy's war aims could not be realized unless the Central Powers were decisively defeated. As Lloyd George saw it, Sonnino alone stood in the way of a separate peace with Austria. Consequently, he did not conceal his displeasure, bluntly telling the foreign minister that Italy's efforts in the war hardly justified its inordinate demands.[12]

On the way back from the conference on April 20, Lloyd George stopped in Paris and again held talks with Sixte at the Hotel Crillon. He reported that difficulties with Sonnino had been exacerbated by the prohibition to acquaint him with the Emperor's concrete proposal. "What did Italy demand?" the prince inquired. Lloyd George replied that in his opinion, it would insist on the Trentino, Dalmatia and perhaps Trieste as the minimum price for peace with Austria. Sixte doubted that Austria would make such concessions to an enemy with a poor record of achievements in the field. The prime minister emphasized that it would be best for Austria to make an offer that would placate Italy, otherwise it might have to pay more dearly at a later stage. He hoped that the Emperor would take into consideration that the Allies were in a position, now that they had acquired the backing of the United States, to fight on as long as it was necessary to win a victory.[13]

Lloyd George's desire for a peace settlement with Austria were revived a month later when Prince Sixte visited London, dangling an attractive bait. He hinted that in return for peace, Austria was willing to part with Trentino, but not Trieste – which ranked higher than any other item among Italy's ambitious Adriatic aims. Lloyd George "was impressed by the idea that if only Trieste could be captured, Austria would resign herself to its permanent loss while Italy would abandon her ambitions farther down the Dalmatian coast."[14] Lloyd George was additionally encouraged by reports suggesting that Austria–Hungary was approaching the end of its will to fight and would not require much of a stimulus to abandon the war. To Lloyd George, this was an ideal moment to implement the plan he had urged in January 1917 at the Rome conference for a major assault on the Italian front against Austria. All that remained for him was to devise a blueprint to surmount the British High Command's objections to his project.

Lloyd George's ploy to bring the War Cabinet in line with his way of thinking backfired. He asked General Smuts, the much-respected South African soldier-statesman who had come to London to attend a conference of Dominion prime ministers, to provide the War Cabinet with a report of "your views on the general strategic and military situation, as well as with the impressions you gained from your visit to the western front".[15] He assumed that Smuts, bringing a civilian's perspective to a military issue, would recommend a course that differed from that of the British Imperial General Staff. Robertson, as the government's chief adviser on military matters, might have objected to being bypassed if he had not been aware of Smuts's outlook. Back from visiting General Headquarters and frequently in contact with Robertson, Smuts had been subjected to a steady dose of the standard western line. But it would be probably inaccurate to suggest that he had been brainwashed by the soldiers. Smuts was a perceptive soldier, understood clearly what was at stake, and it is more likely that their views paralleled his own. He rejected adventures in outlying theatres and endorsed an attritional policy to exhaust and break the will of the enemy. Given Britain's considerable military, economic and naval contributions to the Entente, he was incensed at France's domination of strategy in the west. He endorsed the Flanders operation, both because it ruled out French interference and it served Britain's best interests. While he doubted that a breakthrough was possible, he thought that with France and Russia wavering, Britain had no option but to keep the pressure on the enemy.[16] A memo by Robertson on April 30 warmly endorsed Smuts's recommendations.[17]

The two documents were considered at the War Cabinet meeting on May 1. Although Lloyd George did not openly criticize Haig's plan, it was obvious that his sentiments lay elsewhere. He observed that the French, recognizing that no help from Russia would be forthcoming in the near future, were in no mood to entertain big and costly attacks on the western front until American power could be brought to bear. He noted that they currently favored an active-defense policy and it was his feeling that they were likely to advocate that the Entente's surplus strength should be employed elsewhere, to eliminate Turkey, Bulgaria or even Austria. He warned that if Britain took on Germany single-handedly, its army would be bled white and compelled to seek a compromise peace. But Lloyd George was a lone voice in the wilderness. Smuts, who was in attendance, played a pivotal role in persuading the other members of the War Cabinet to reject the French idea of an active-defense, which he characterized as equivalent to a defensive policy. He asserted that to relinquish the initiative in the third year of the war would be fatal, generating pessimism and despair among the Allies, while allowing the Germans to recover their spirits. He did not believe that the German line could be broken, but added that relentless pounding might ultimately drive the enemy to accept a peace settlement. The War Cabinet decided to sanction Haig's attack and to request that the French army cooperate actively, as well as to reoccupy the trenches recently taken over by British forces.[18]

Lloyd George was bound to carry out the War Cabinet's instructions at the forthcoming inter-Allied conference scheduled to meet in Paris on May 4, but it was not an assignment that he relished. He could ill afford to oppose his generals as he had done at Calais. Crossing the Channel the day before the start of the conference, he went out of his way to make peace with Haig, whom he had treated abominably in the past. Haig recorded in his diary that Lloyd George said that he was ready "to press whatever plan Robertson and I decided on."[19] The prime minister may have given the impression that he was in step with his generals, but in reality he remained unalterably opposed to another slogging match on the model of the Somme.

On the morning of May 4 French and British military leaders met at the War Ministry in Paris to consider future military strategy on the western front. The soldiers ruled out any attempt at a breakthrough and instead agreed that relentless attacks with limited objectives should be resumed to wear down and exhaust the enemy's resistance.[20] Robertson, who acted as chairman, presented a brief report of the meeting to the plenary session of the conference in the afternoon. Lloyd George fully supported the generals' conclusions, emphasizing that the Allies "must go on hitting and hitting with all our strength until the German ended, as he always did, by cracking." Ribot appeared to be wavering, cautioning against attacks that risked incurring excessive losses. Lloyd George repeated that his government was prepared to use the entire strength of the British army to pursue an offensive strategy, but saw no purpose in doing so unless the French did the same. Painlevé replied that the French government was in complete accord with Lloyd George's opinion and there was wide agreement that it should be left up to the generals to determine the time and place of the attacks.[21] Important results emerged from the conference: it marked the moment at which military predominance passed to the British, it formally ended British obligations under the Calais agreement and it left Haig free to pursue his offensive in Flanders.

It is a safe bet that Lloyd George would have strenuously opposed the Flanders operation if he had known the true state of the French army. The Ribot government had managed to conceal the extent of the mutinies in the French army from their allies and, more surprisingly, from the enemy as well.[22] When Lloyd George returned to London he was more worried about Russia's possible defection than anything else. Hope that the revolution would reenergize Russia's war effort had been quickly dashed. British observers in Russia gave alarming reports of the growing chaotic conditions in the country and of the disintegration of the Russian army, which by most accounts was likely finished as an effective instrument in applying pressure either in Europe or Asia.[23] A note of pessimism began to seep into the ranks of British policy makers. Sir Henry Wilson (then the chief British liaison officer with French Headquarters) who was in attendance at the first meeting of the War Cabinet on May 1, was struck by the defeatist attitude of several ministers, in particular Lord Cecil.[24] It appeared that Cecil was the most vocal of a small group that considered the loss of a major ally sufficient cause to open, or at least consider, peace talks with the enemy. Lloyd George remained steadfast, according to Wilson, but, as will be shown below, made an about-face at a subsequent meeting on the same day. Derby conveyed his apprehension to Haig, describing the unrest spawned by the revolution as "dangerous," and observing that he would not be surprised if Britain followed Russia out of the war.[25]

Lloyd George added to the somber atmosphere at a second meeting of the War Cabinet on May 1 and at another gathering on the 9th when he expressed doubts that the war was winnable. Russia's defection, he pointed out, would transform the entire military picture to the detriment of the Allies. One effect would be to practically neutralize the British blockade, since the Central Powers would be able to take possession of Russia's boundless stocks of wheat, oil and minerals once they organized the necessary means of transportation. Another would allow the Germans to bring together virtually all their forces in France. In these circumstances, Britain required to strengthen its bargaining position in preparation for peace talks with Germany. What was the best course of action to balance Russia's collapse? The prime minister maintained it would be a terrible mistake to sacrifice hundreds of thousands of lives to engage in more attacks on the western front where the chances of success were nonexistent. Instead, he was adamant that the Allies ought to try to induce Austria to make a separate peace or undertake a campaign to force Turkey out of the war.[26]

Robertson, who was much better at marshalling his arguments on paper – though Maurice was often entrusted with the task of putting everything together in coherent form – than in debate, challenged the prime minister's Eastern strategy in a memo. He claimed that Russia's near collapse made it unlikely that either Turkey or Austria could be defeated and that Britain, with its limited resources, did not have the capacity to conduct operations on multiple fronts. As Britain could not count on immediate American aid, it was necessary that it concentrate its military power on the western front to prevent France from suffering the same fate as Russia.[27] Smuts, Milner and Curzon were all ardent imperialists and they shared Lloyd George's interest in peripheral operations, particularly in the conquest of Mesopotamia, which was seen as vital to the security of Egypt and India. Nevertheless, they stood firmly behind Robertson because they understood that if France collapsed, the war would be lost.[28]

Robertson may have felt that the only road to victory lay through France, but he was less than enthusiastic about Haig's plan to sweep across the Flanders plain. He was leery of distant objectives and, furthermore, his intelligence service at the War Office had convinced him that Haig, fed unrealistic reports by Charteris, was wrong in thinking that the German army was as good as done for. In view of the shortage of British manpower, he worried about the possibility of heavy casualties, and he was equally concerned about French war weariness. On May 11 Robertson received a note from Lord Esher, a British official whose finger was on the pulse in Paris, warning him not to rely on the commitments the French had recently agreed to. The French, according to Esher, habitually say "Yes" in order to be pleasant and avoid a scene, but then "proceed to procrastinate or to forget." Robertson turned the letter over to Lloyd George, who asked that a message be delivered to Haig reminding him that the War Cabinet had laid down as a condition for its support full French participation in the offensive. Haig was to be told to keep this in mind during his talks with Pétain. The prime minister wanted to make it abundantly clear that the War Cabinet "could never agree to our incurring heavy losses with comparatively small gains, which would obviously be the result unless the French cooperate wholeheartedly."[29]

Although in the presence of the British, the French approved of Haig's proposed attack and promised to assist it to the best of their ability, they thought differently about it in private. Pétain told Wilson that Haig's efforts to clear the coast was hopeless and doomed to fail. He claimed that, as he was already holding a line that was far too long, he could not undertake a major operation. He indicated that he would make three or four small attacks and, once the limited objectives had been reached, the fighting would cease.[30] Foch, the eternal optimist, was no more encouraging. He thought that Haig's plan to "march through the inundations of Ostend and Zeebrugge" was "futile, fantastic and dangerous."[31] He made no effort to convey his concerns to Haig or suggest an alternative. Neither Pétain nor Foch questioned the need for a British attack, only the choice of Flanders as the theater.

Pétain was more forthcoming a fortnight later (June 2) about the state of the French army. He sent his Chief of Staff, General Eugène Debeney, to inform Haig that, owing to the breakdown of discipline in the French army, he would be unable to keep his promise to attack in support on June 10. Debeney pointed out that the dissatisfaction had been sparked by the men's exhaustion, compelling Pétain to grant leave on a large scale.[32] He did, however, assure Haig that the French army would cooperate in the later Flanders offensive as arranged. Haig now faced a dilemma. His attack at Messines, a necessary preliminary to the main offensive in the north, was only five days away. If he reported what he knew about the condition of the French army, it was a virtual certainty that he would be ordered to call off his own attack at Messines. Confident that the attack would succeed, he kept Debeney's revelation to himself. But the War Cabinet was bound to find out what had taken place, as it would six days later through Wilson, who had seen Debeney's notes of the meeting.³³ By going ahead with the knowledge that he would essentially be acting alone, Haig went against the instructions of the War Cabinet, putting Robertson in an awkward situation and increasing Lloyd George's distrust of him.

Haig assigned the Second Army, under General Sir Herbert Plumer, to storm the heavily fortified Messines Ridge, which dominated the Ypres salient. On June 7 the Second Army successfully carried off one of the most brilliant limited-objective operations of the war. For two years the British had tunneled deep under the German front line and laid twenty-one huge mines filled with over a million pounds of explosives. The blast, heard as far away as London, was followed by a creeping barrage of crushing intensity as nine infantry divisions surged forward, reinforced by 72 tanks. The surviving defenders were too dazed to offer much resistance and by June 9 the British had taken possession of the entire ridge with negligible casualties. At one blow, Haig had swept the Germans from the southern flank of the Ypres salient, clearing the way for his attack further north.³⁴

Even before Haig's attack at Messines, rumors began to circulate in London that there was something wrong with the French army. The first intimation came from Spiers, who apprised the CIGS's office on June 4 and 5 that there were significant disturbances, amounting to mutinies, in a number of French regiments.³⁵ On June 6 he wrote that the present difficulties "might easily become very serious," likening them to a slow-burning fire, "which might easily be fanned into flame."³⁶ Two days later, Henry Wilson told the War Cabinet that Pétain had gone back on his promise to attack on June 10 and that he doubted whether the British could count on the continued resistance of the French army. He went so far as to suggest that France was likely to make peace unless the Allies scored a major military or diplomatic victory before long. Hankey recorded the prime minister's reaction to Wilson's report:

> It was clear from General Wilson's statement that the French were finding it difficult to go on ... Until quite recently ... General Wilson had always taken a hopeful view; at times he had perhaps been ultra-sanguine; it was very significant that he now took a dejected view, and the War Cabinet must take this very seriously into consideration.³⁷

Wilson's ominous disclosures reinforced a paper written by Milner on the previous day in which he suggested that in view of the important changes on the Continental scene, the time had come to review Britain's policy as a whole and frame fresh plans.³⁸ It was a suggestion that Lloyd George put forward at the meeting and gave it his hearty endorsement. He claimed that hitherto, the government had based its war policy on the advice of its experts, who often had been proved wrong, conveniently omitting any reference to his own decisive role in the Nivelle affair. At his urging it was decided to set up a small committee, named the War Policy Committee, to undertake a comprehensive investigation of the nation's war policy and its prospects. The new committee consisted of Lloyd George, Milner, Curzon and Smuts, now a permanent member of the War Cabinet, with Hankey as its secretary. The War Policy Committee convened sixteen times between June 11 and July 20, in the course of which it interviewed a number of witnesses, before submitting its report to the full War Cabinet.[39]

The investigation boiled down to whether Haig should be permitted to continue with his preparations for an offensive in Flanders or if large British resources should be shifted to the Italian front. Haig crossed the channel on June 17 to testify before the War Policy Committee. Meeting beforehand with Robertson, who was astutely aware of political subtleties, he was advised what to say. Accompanied by Robertson, Haig attended five meetings in the span of a week, beginning on June 19. He repeated familiar arguments, reinforced by new ones, as to why he should be allowed to move forward with his operation and revealed for the first time details of his plan and objectives, immediate and long-range.[40] Brimming with confidence, he believed that he could sweep across the Belgian coast by a series of limited attacks following so fast on each other that the Germans would have no time to recover.

Robertson was not nearly as optimistic as Haig. He foresaw difficulties in the ambitious operation, partly because the level of French assistance was likely to be limited, but mostly because he was highly dubious of Haig's inflated estimates of Germany's declining troop strength. He had conveyed some of his concerns to Haig on June 9 only to be sternly rebuked.[41] Thereafter he kept his doubts to himself, wishing to present a united front. Any expression of skepticism on his part would open the way for Lloyd George to take the war to the Austrians. Although the prospects of success appeared to him dim, he consoled himself into thinking that the Flanders plan would at least have the effect of wearing down Germany's ability to continue fighting. When interrogated by Lloyd George, an uneasy Robertson was nevertheless unswerving in his support of Haig's scheme.[42] His behavior was inexcusable. As military adviser to the government, it was his duty to share with the politicians his differences with Haig, not act as his accomplice.

Lloyd George was tired of hearing the generals promise much but deliver nothing except a huge butcher's bill. It is no wonder that he subjected Haig and Robertson to rigorous cross-examination. He indicated, with justification, that when he had agreed in Paris to the idea of a vigorous offensive, he did not think that the British would have to fight the Germans practically single-handed. As he pointed out, the Americans would not be in the field for months and French help was uncertain, but even if forthcoming, Allied superiority in men and artillery would only be marginal, insufficient by all accounts to dislodge the Germans from their formidable defenses.

The prime minister believed it was necessary to prevent Haig from expending the strength of the British army in a futile attack, for its depleted ranks could no longer be easily filled. He tried to emphasize the repercussions of a failed strategy on the domestic scene and on the peace process. Each time the government had "combed out" protected industries to obtain more men for the army, it had faced resistance from trade unions or had provoked strikes. The March events in Russia "had a very unsettling effect in all countries and there was a good deal of talk of revolution everywhere." The prime minister reminded the generals that given the state of the French army and the slowness with which the United States was developing its resources, Britain was sustaining the whole burden of the war on the Allied side. He was afraid of being drawn into a great military venture before Britain was ready. The object was not only to defeat Germany, but to ensure that Britain did not exhaust itself in the process and lose the peace. He felt that the British High Command ought to hold its hand until 1918 when the French army had been resuscitated and the Americans could play a leading role.

As he was immensely concerned about the staying power of the British army, Lloyd George wanted to adopt less wasteful tactics. He returned to his own plan of assisting the Italians in mounting a large-scale assault on the Austrians, with Trieste as its objective. He observed that Austria was war-weary and anxious for peace. He claimed that a severe defeat, involving the loss of Trieste and accompanied by heavy casualties, might provide the inducement necessary to drive Vienna to break with Germany and consent to peace terms acceptable to the Allies. In such an event, the prime minister contended that the consequences might be decisive. He proceeded to sketch a rosy scenario. With the opening of a sea route to the Black Sea, the Allies could provide relief to Russia and increase the chances of keeping it in the war. Isolated and cut off from vital German war supplies, Bulgaria and Turkey would probably sue for peace as well. British troops would be released from Egypt, Mesopotamia and the Balkans for concentration against Germany.[43] In sum, Lloyd George's plea was that the Allies should husband resources, hold the Germans in the west, concentrate on forcing Austria out of the war, and postpone the climatic battle until 1918 when the Americans would be present in force.

Haig, backed by Robertson, remained unwavering during the debates. He claimed that some British action on the western front was necessary to prevent Germany from regaining the initiative and finishing off France. Added to this was his insistence that the German army was exhausted and demoralized and that keeping it under constant attack would guarantee final victory, perhaps before the end of the year. Haig was probably disingenuous when he went on to say that he was confident that he could count on French collaboration. He claimed that they seemed to be recovering from their latest trouble and he had every reason to believe that they would participate fully in the attack as promised. He assured the Committee that he was sensitive to the need to conserve manpower and that his plan had been devised to limit the advance at each stage of the projected campaign so as to minimize casualties. Both he and Robertson promised that the attack would be broken off if it became clear that it had no chance of succeeding.

Haig received an unexpected boost from Jellicoe, who warned that Britain's future security depended on the conquest of the Belgian coast. Jellicoe insisted that Germany's destroyers, rather than its U-boats, were the main threat to breaking Britain's Channel links with the Continent. Hitherto they had conducted only desultory raids but they would be in a position to inflict incalculable damage if they attacked in mass. As the Royal Navy had taken on the duties of protecting convoys, it was already overstretched and would be unable to control the Channel. Thus, the war would be lost unless the army took possession of the Belgian ports. Jellicoe had a reputation for being pessimistic and it is not surprising that Lloyd George indignantly challenged his dire warnings. But Jellicoe stuck to his guns and, given that Haig relied heavily on cross-Channel supplies, probably strengthened the case for persisting with the Flanders offensive.[44]

No one confronted Haig on his flawed logic. The German army could not have been on the verge of collapse and conduct a powerful offensive against France at the same time. In the course of the lengthy meetings some of the members talked randomly and inconsistently, occasionally coming down in support of the Flanders operation and at other times seeming to prefer concentration on another front. None offered a clear-headed alternative to Haig's proposal within the context of a western strategy. Lloyd George did suggest that Haig ought to abandon the big offensive in favor of waging a series of limited operations, "a punch here and a punch there," as a less costly means of eroding the strength of the German army.[45] But Lloyd George mentioned this option almost casually, without attempting to marshal strong arguments in favor of it – perhaps because he had not grasped the principles that underlay the concept of bite and hold. Instead he clung passionately to his Italian scheme, which would leave the fighting to the Italian army with the British providing heavy guns and some troops. However, it was not in his power to set such a campaign in motion.

Robertson identified further drawbacks to Lloyd George's preference for concentrating on the Italian front. The Germans, enjoying interior lines and anxious to keep Austria in the war, could easily match any reinforcements the Allies sent to Italy. The Italians, it was well known, were terrified of the Germans, and their commander, General Cadorna, would not fight them unless he received strong reinforcements from Britain. Would the British government repeat the same mistake it had earlier in the year when it entrusted the fate of its armies to a foreign commander who had shown no marked ability in the war? The enemy's defenses in Italy were much more formidable than in Flanders, making any progress unlikely. Finally, Robertson believed that sending heavy guns and reinforcements to Italy would invite the Germans to attack France in force or transfer more troops to the Russian front.[46]

At the tenth meeting of the War Policy Committee on June 21, in which all the arguments were thoroughly reviewed, the members found it difficult to come to a decision. Since there was much at stake, Lloyd George begged Haig and Robertson to reconsider their plan.[47] There was no change in their outlook when they returned four days later.[48] On the other hand, there was a divergence of opinion among the politicians taking part in the debates. Lloyd George was absolutely convinced that the proposed undertaking in Flanders had not the remotest chance of success and he was generally supported by Milner and Bonar Law. Smuts and, to a lesser degree, Curzon, felt that Haig should be allowed to go ahead. Still the last word rested with Lloyd George. Had he been adamant about stopping the Flanders operation, it is unlikely that his colleagues would have tried to overrule him. But after the Nivelle fiasco, he was reluctant to impose his strategic views on the army. If he had done so, he reasoned that he would almost certainly have faced an outcry in parliament and in the press that might have spelled his doom. Thus, against his better judgment, he deferred to the soldiers. On June 25 the War Policy Committee authorized Haig to continue his preparations for the battle, but a final decision was postponed until consultations could be carried out with the French to ensure that they made a simultaneous attack further south.[49]

Professor David Woodward has speculated that if Asquith had still held the reins of power, and if the same scenario had played out, Lloyd George would certainly have blasted him for abdicating to the military. He wrote that Lloyd George "would have been contemptuous of the argument that the civilians could not overrule the generals on strategic questions when life and limb of tens of thousands of soldiers from Britain and the Empire were at stake."[50] Few would challenge Woodward's observation.

Although Lloyd George and Haig were at loggerheads over military strategy, they shared the belief that drastic changes were required at the Admiralty. During his stay in London, Haig had seen Eric Geddes, controller at the Admiralty and formerly his director of transport in France. Geddes revealed that he was frustrated with his job because of the chaotic state of affairs at the Admiralty. Haig penned the following comments in his diary: "The First Lord (Carson), has recently married, is very tired, and leaves everything [to] a number of incompetent sailors! Jellicoe, he says, is feeble to a degree and vacillating."[51]

On June 26 Haig and Geddes breakfasted with Lloyd George at 10 Downing Street and the state of the Admiralty was one of the issues they discussed. Lloyd George agreed with them that Admiralty leadership was inept and immediately sent for Milner, who was both a close friend and a critic of Carson, to join their deliberations.[52] Lloyd George considered Jellicoe a defeatist and had long desired to replace him but was reluctant to make the move as long as Carson, who protected him, was in office. Therefore, to send Jellicoe packing, Lloyd George first had to remove Carson from the Admiralty. Robertson's name came up as a possible replacement for Carson. Who made the suggestion and how seriously it was taken is unknown. The prospect of killing two birds with one stone makes it likely that Lloyd George would have been drawn to the idea. The Admiralty needed to be shaken up and Robertson was known as a firm and talented administrator, but more importantly for Lloyd George, his departure from the War Office would have broken up the military's strategic dictatorship without political repercussions. What is more difficult to surmise is why Haig would become involved in a movement to dispose his staunchest defender in London. He may have sensed that Robertson was not sufficiently committed to the Flanders offensive, believing that he could bend his successor to his will. Haig was indeed fortunate that Roberson turned down the proposal on the grounds that he had no desire to become a politician.[53] Without Robertson's unflinching support month after month, Haig would almost certainly have been dismissed before the end of the war.

Lloyd George briefly toyed with the idea of sending Hankey to the Admiralty,[54] before accepting Milner's suggestion that Eric Geddes be appointed as first lord and that Carson be brought into the War Cabinet.[55] Lloyd George feared offending Carson, who could be potentially troublesome on the backbenches. On July 6 Lloyd George formally invited Carson to join the War Cabinet, stressing that its central direction of the war would be immensely enhanced by "your insight, courage and judgment." It was obvious to Carson why the offer was made. He replied the following morning, saying that he was quite prepared to resign his position at the Admiralty if it was the prime minister's wish, but as to joining the War Cabinet he wanted time to think it over.[56] The last thing that Lloyd George wanted was a breach with Carson who hinted that he might leave the government altogether if pressed to give up the Admiralty. Lloyd George's resolve failed him and he hasted to send a conciliatory message to Carson, explaining that his previous letter had been misunderstood. The members of the War Cabinet were anxious for his help, but if he preferred to remain at the Admiralty "then the suggestion falls to the ground."[57] Milner sought to assist the prime minister by writing a personal letter to Carson, encouraging him to switch jobs. "He and I are such old friends," Milner told Lloyd George, "that I thought it might influence him to some extent to know that I felt strongly – as I really do – that he could be of the most use to the Government and the country in the Cabinet."[58] Milner's entreaty apparently made no impression on the first lord.

Carson did not respond immediately to the prime minister, leaving him to stew in his juices. However much he may have been irritated, Lloyd George did not feel secure enough politically to force the issue. For ten days he dallied, consulted his principal colleagues and invited their suggestions until Milner intervened and urged him to move forward.[59] The next day Lloyd George announced to the newspapers that Carson would be elevated to the War Cabinet and that Geddes would replace him as first lord. Carson grudgingly consented to the changes but indignantly refused to sack Jellicoe before leaving the Admiralty, as Geddes had requested. Geddes did not want to do the job himself lest he begin his tenure by sparking a national outcry.[60] The new first lord made his presence felt as soon as he had settled in at the Admiralty. A man of exceptional ability, single-minded and resourceful, there was a marked improvement in the conduct of naval affairs under his stewardship.

The business at the Admiralty resolved, Lloyd George could no longer delay sanctioning Haig's operation in Flanders. Thus far, the intended conference with the French had not occurred because the War Cabinet had been mired in heated debates day after day over the controversial Mesopotamia Commission Report.[61] In view of the approaching date for the commencement of the battle, the War Policy Committee met at 10 Downing Street on July 16 to take a final decision. Once again the members went over familiar ground. Although they were unaware of the extent of the unrest in the French army, they were fairly certain that Haig would receive only minimal help from his allies to the south. In these circumstances, such assistance as Pétain was able to render would be insufficient to draw away German reserves from Flanders, leaving Haig to face the bulk of the enemy on his front.[62] Nevertheless, there were other factors that tipped the scales in Haig's favor: to ensure that the Belgian ports did not fall into German hands; and, more importantly, the fear that, if the British did not attack, France might seek release from the war.[63] The committee's decision was ratified by the War Cabinet on July 20. The ministers did stipulate, however, that if the attack degenerated into an indecisive and costly affair, it would be brought to a halt and British resources would then be transferred to the Italian front.[64]

Lloyd George and his colleagues seemed to think that the battle was like a water spigot that "could be turned off as quickly as it was turned on."[65] They assumed that the offensive could be stopped "if the results are not commensurate with the effort made and the losses incurred."[66] Although desperate to avoid a repetition of the futile massacres of the Somme, there was a flaw in their reasoning. As amateurs and removed from the scene, they could not judge whether Haig's attack was close to victory or had stalled. If they had intervened prematurely, they would have been accused of interfering in military matters and preventing the British army from ending the war in 1917. Haig had not promised a decisive breakthrough, so if he encountered more resistance than anticipated, he could justify continuing the attack by claiming that German losses were greater than his own and that he was making progress. The problem was that there was no way to verify casualty figures until long after the battle had ended. In the final analysis, only Haig could abandon the offensive once it had begun, and given his unbridled optimism, that was not going to happen.

Chapter 8

THE HORROR OF PASSCHENDAELE

No sooner had the War Cabinet given reluctant and conditional assent to the Flanders operation, than Lloyd George tried different means to prevent Haig from carrying it out, lobbying instead for his Italian scheme. His big opportunity came when he crossed the Channel on July 22, along with Robertson and several members of the War Cabinet, to attend an inter-Allied conference in Paris. Before the start of the conference, he visited Painlevé and dined with his old friend, Albert Thomas.[1] He advanced his case for concentration on the Italian front and, while they were attentive and sympathetic, they remained noncommittal.

Robertson, for his part, had no idea that Lloyd George was planning to rally the French authorities to his peripheral strategy. His first intimation of Lloyd George's machinations came when he, Foch, Pétain and Cadorna were asked to advise on the feasibility of sending assistance to Italy. By now, nothing that Lloyd George did should have surprised Robertson. At the gathering, Robertson persuaded the generals that it was folly to flip from one war plan to another and that the only sensible thing to do was to allow the existing arrangements to stand. It was agreed by all that the dispatch of Anglo–French troops to the Italian front should be considered only after the battle in Flanders was over and its results assessed. Their attitude was to some extent influenced by the desperate military situation on the eastern front and the possibility that Russia might opt out of the war.[2] In these circumstances the Germans were likely to bring maximum pressure on the western front before the arrival of the main body of Americans. Judging that the danger period for the Entente in 1918 would be between March and August, there was a consensus that the western front be rendered as strong as possible. It was therefore recommended that a passive attitude be adopted in distant theaters and that troops from there be withdrawn and concentrated in the west.[3]

On the other hand, it was conceivable that after finishing off the Russians, the Germans would choose to transfer a significant number of divisions in the east to Italy. If that should happen, the Italian army would be unable to hold on in the absence of outside help. Lloyd George had long urged that at the very least, plans should be prepared to reinforce Cadorna with British and

French troops in the event of an emergency. It was another issue that the Allied generals addressed at their meeting, agreeing that a scheme "for the dispatch, concentration, and maintenance of French and British divisions should at once be worked out by the respective General Staffs in combination with the Italians."[4]

The Allied conference on July 26 opened with Foch reading a prepared statement recommending the policy that should be adopted in case Russia was driven to make a separate peace. Lloyd George scoffed at the suggestion that the Allies should fall back on the defensive in secondary theaters, calling this an act of despair. He observed that, even if Russia collapsed, a long time must elapse before the Germans and Austrians could remove all their forces from the eastern front. Instead of waiting for the Germans to deliver a blow, why not strike first against their wavering allies, Turkey and Austria? To do otherwise was to invite disaster.

Lloyd George's frustration mounted each time a speaker commented fatuously or questioned his alternative proposal. Sonnino stated that an argument could be made for doing something along the lines suggested by the British prime minister, but at the same time admitted that he was not really qualified to express an opinion on technical military matters. He regretted that Cadorna was not present to assess the military prospects on the Italian front. The French were more conclusive. Foch doubted that sufficient pressure could be brought to bear on the Turks to force them out of the war. He was no more encouraging about a strike against the Austrians. The only way to achieve decisive results, in his opinion, was by a combined attack, one from the Russo–Romanian side and the other from the Italian front. A double attack in the foreseeable future, however, was out of the question. Thomas followed up by strengthening Foch's arguments. He drew attention to the technical difficulties, particularly the shortage of shipping, in mounting operations against Turkey. He also pointed out that with the British and French about to start a very large offensive, it seemed to him illogical, especially in view of the general war weariness in France, of sustaining a further action in cooperation with the Italians.[5]

Emerging empty-handed from the conference, Lloyd George was in a dejected mood on his return journey. But once in London, he had no time to fret about his personal setback. The news from Russia continued to be grim and it was generally assumed that the end could not be far off. At a secret session of the War Cabinet on July 31 the discussion centered on the consequences of Russia's defection. Thus far American's entry in the war had not eased the burden of the anti-German coalition and it was doubtful whether the British army could sustain the alliance for another six months or so without exhausting itself in the process. Notwithstanding the probable heavy cost to Britain and its

Empire, the War Cabinet was determined to fight on and agreed with Smuts that "the issues at stake are too vast for us to ever ... contemplate a peace which will in effect mean a defeat."[6]

Hours before the War Cabinet met, Haig's long-awaited attack in Flanders, known officially as the Third Battle of Ypres, but more often referred to as Passchendaele, began with twelve divisions climbing over the top on an eleven-mile front. The Germans, having received ample warning of the impending British assault, had brought up reinforcements and replaced the old rigid defensive line with a flexible defense-in-depth system.[7] Worse still, the steady rains and the destruction of the intricate drainage system after a fortnight of uninterrupted British preliminary artillery fire had reduced the ground to a morass of mud with watery craters that neutralized the effectiveness of the tanks. After four days of infantry attacks, Haig's forces had suffered 31,000 casualties and were still less than halfway to reaching the objectives set for them on the first day. The chances for a tactical success appeared to fade.[8]

Haig, seeking to put the best possible spin on the early action, told the War Cabinet that his men were overcoming heavy artillery fire and ejecting the enemy from their positions and doing so without suffering undue losses. He had no doubt that but for the torrential downpour, his advance would have reached all of its objectives. He claimed that the Germans had sustained heavy casualties, probably twice as high as his own. "Summarising the results of the battle, I regard them as most satisfactory," was Haig's conclusion.[9] Haig was miserly about providing the War Cabinet with concrete information and there was no way to verify what little he had divulged. Robertson approved of filtering the news from the battlefield. He told Sir Lancelot Kiggell, Haig's chief of staff, that all he needed was a few lines about the progress of the operation now and then, stressing that secrets be withheld from him so that he would not have to pass them on to the War Cabinet.[10] Lloyd George suspected that he was being misled and that the offensive was turning out to be a failure. When another inter-Allied conference was held in London on August 7 and 8, he saw an opportunity to exploit the split between Robertson and Foch who appeared to be wavering in his support of Haig's offensive. In conversation with Wilson and others, Foch saw no useful purpose in continuing attacks on the western front and instead recommended that the Anglo–French army should concentrate on Germany's allies.[11]

Foch was not the only one whose views had undergone a change in the last fortnight. At the conference Sonnino raised the possibility of a massive Allied thrust on the Italian front. He noted that Italian intelligence had reported that the enemy's position on the Carso Plateau was weak and, in his opinion, it was one place where a strong attack might produce decisive results. An Italian offensive was about to begin shortly, but, even if it started well, Cadorna was not strong enough to achieve anything significant. He thought that if reinforced with 400 artillery pieces and a modest force, the Italian army could dispose of Austria. Lloyd George inquired whether Cadorna could delay his attack, set to begin in a week, until the end of September, when it would be possible to supply him with the guns and men he deemed essential for victory. General Alberico Albricci, who accompanied Sonnino as Cadorna's representative, replied that climatic conditions made it impractical to attack the Carso Plateau after the end of August. Lloyd George thought that the weather in September was generally good, but Albricci remarked that preparations were too far advanced to delay till then and that the chances of rainy weather were too great.

Lloyd George had a difficult time keeping his temper under control. He observed that the best policy for the Allies was to try to crush Austria. He had initially made the proposal in Rome and it was then considered too early. He made it now and it was apparently considered too late. He wondered why the Allies could not pool their resources and deliver a smashing blow. Sonnino, seeking to smooth Lloyd George's ruffled feathers, suggested that it should be put to Cadorna to decide whether he would consider it worthwhile to postpone his offensive if the British and the French committed to send him a certain number of guns and troops by September. He recommended that in any case, it might be possible to begin to send ammunition now and the guns later when they would be free. Lloyd George thought that their military advisers should consider the various proposals advanced and recommend which one should be accepted.[12]

If Lloyd George was relying on Foch to stand firm in support of his position, he was in for a rude shock. Foch did sound out Robertson about the wisdom of continuing to pound away on the Belgian front, but he was rebuked in forthright terms and quickly retreated to the safe haven of western orthodoxy. The two soldiers reaffirmed the conclusions they had reached at Paris a fortnight earlier. They noted that Britain and France had sent to Italy all the heavy artillery and ammunition they were able to spare. They pointed out, furthermore, that with the operations now in progress, it was impossible to supply Cadorna with ten Anglo–French divisions and 400 heavy guns that he considered essential to defeating Austria. As a sop to Lloyd George, the generals indicated that once Haig's offensive was over, it might be possible to place at Cadorna's disposal the forces necessary to enable him to compel Austria's surrender. They concluded by saying that in their opinion it was too late to attempt to change the military plans for 1917.[13]

The politicians reassembled at 3:30 p.m. on August 8. The conference opened with Lloyd George asking Foch whether the Central Powers could be defeated without Russia's participation. Foch, trying to avoid alienating either Lloyd George or Robertson, evaded the question and confined his answer to identifying the difficulties confronting the Allies in the west and in the alternative theaters under discussion. Lloyd George maintained that something more than holding the enemy in check was needed. The peoples of Britain, France and Italy had shown great tenacity, but war weariness was setting in and if they concluded that victory was no longer in sight, they would refuse to go on with the war. He held no hope that any progress could be made in the west. As matters stood, Haig's offensive had stalled owing to the steady downpour and he would require ten days of dry weather for a further advance. Given the likelihood of a lengthy delay, Haig would practically have to start all over again, which would further reduce his chances of reaching his objectives. Lloyd George asserted "that we had put our money on the wrong horse, and that we ought to have supported General Cadorna, as this might have won us the war." He maintained that policy ought to be laid down by the cabinet, not the soldiers, whose responsibility should be confined to determining how to carry out the plans.

Sonnino agreed with Lloyd George's central point, namely, that if no other offensive was likely to produce the desired results "we ought to deliver a strong blow on the Italian front." Albricci reminded the gathering that no major operation on the Italian front could take place before the spring of 1918. Ribot chimed in by saying that whatever might be contemplated later on, nothing should be done to interrupt Haig's offensive. Future Allied strategy must hinge on the fate of Russia. In a fortnight or three weeks the picture might become clearer. He added, "Everything was in suspense, and it was difficult to form any definite plans at the moment." That seemed to be the attitude of most of the assembled delegates. The conference ended by directing the three general staffs to consider, during the winter months, a plan of operation where substantial results could be achieved.[14]

Both Lloyd George and Robertson were unhappy over the outcome of the conference, although for different reasons. Lloyd George's struggle to switch the main Allied effort to the Italian front had once again been stymied. Robertson was troubled by what he perceived was a plot orchestrated by Lloyd George to take strategic control out of his hands. During talks in and outside the conference, Foch had urged that an Allied military staff be set up in Paris to coordinate strategy. Although the idea had not been pursued, Robertson was convinced that he had not heard the last of it.[15] He told Haig on August 9:

> As the French keep rubbing in that it is necessary to have a Central Staff at Paris I can see Lloyd George in the future wanting to agree to some such organization so as to put the matter in French hands and to take it out of mine. However we shall see about this. His game is to put up ... Foch against me as he did Nivelle against you in the spring. He is a real bad 'un.[16]

Robertson did not have to wait long for his next clash with Lloyd George. Suspicion and hostility between the two began anew after Haig resumed his drive on August 16. Progress was limited owing to the swampy condition of the battlefield, as well as to the enemy's heavy shelling and determined counterattacks. Haig's reports to London during this period gave no hint of the level of enemy resistance or the natural obstacles his men faced at Passchendaele. On the contrary, they were euphoric, praising the accomplishments of his men and stressing that the Germans were on the ropes and on the verge of collapse.[17]

All the same, Robertson knew that the fighting was not going according to plan. His belief that the British army's artillery superiority would exact a deadly toll on the enemy had not been borne out. The torrent of high-explosive shells used by Haig, together with the incessant rain, had turned the broken terrain into a treacherous bog of slime, with conditions growing worse every day. The chances of achieving appreciable results, which would have been difficult in the best of circumstances, now seemed to vanish. Robertson understood the dilemma facing General Headquarters, remarking to Kiggell that "unless we use a great deal of artillery fire we cannot get on, and if we do use it the ground is destroyed."[18] But Robertson did not reveal his misgivings to the War Cabinet, for he could not bring himself either to break ranks with Haig or risk seeing the main military effort diverted to another front.

Robertson's own reports to the War Cabinet in certain instances played up moderate advances, but in others masked lack of progress by large and questionable promises. Not everyone was lulled by his attempts to put the best possible face on the events at Passchendaele.[19] By mid-August it was becoming increasingly evident to Hankey that Haig's offensive was incurring heavy losses without the likelihood of achieving commensurate gains. He approached Lloyd George with the suggestion that the time had come to review and perhaps terminate the operation. To his dismay, Lloyd George was unresponsive.[20] As Haig's operation continued amid horrifying conditions with little or no progress, Milner begged Lloyd George to intervene, but to no avail. Reflecting on the operation a year later, Milner confided the following to Curzon:

> It is quite true that we agreed to that d - - - d offensive, but it is also true that ... we laid it down expressly that we should watch the course of the offensive and *call it off,* if the results seemed incommensurate to the sacrifice. If we had done this, we should have been all right, but the P.M. is just as much responsible as anyone for the fact that it was not done. When ... the attempt was evidently hopeless, I tried in vain to get him to intervene. Of course I ought to have tried harder. But we have all got to share the blame.[21]

It was not as if Lloyd George was unconcerned about what was evolving into a grizzly replay of the Somme.[22] But he had his reasons for refusing to call off the operation. He was uncertain of support in the War Cabinet and he feared the political consequences.[23] In dealing with a controversial issue, it was not in Lloyd George's nature to engage in a frontal attack if there was a way around.[24]

Putting his fertile mind to work, Lloyd George fastened on the idea of creating a military triumvirate, composed of Henry Wilson, Sir John French and another general, to scrutinize plans submitted by the general staff. The names of Wilson and French came to him instantly, because they had no more use for the Haig–Robertson monolith than he did. Currently out of work, Wilson, by his own admission, was out to create mischief.[25] Both Robertson and Haig distrusted and disliked him because of his love of intrigue and close association with politicians. French was in charge of the Home Forces, although he began the war as C-in-C of the BEF, a position for which he was conspicuously inadequate. French hated Haig, whom he believed had engineered his removal.

Lloyd George broached his scheme to French who seemed to approve of it. On August 17 French saw Wilson and reported his conversation with the prime minister. Wilson thought that the arrangement was unworkable and instead put forward his own blueprint, which had been germinating in his mind for two-and-a-half years, of an inter-Allied war council charged with supervising the various fronts. The council, made up of the prime ministers of Britain, France and Italy, plus three soldiers, would reign over all the CIGSs and work on developing plans for the 1918 campaign.[26] Lloyd George, who was enjoying a few days' rest at Riddell's home near Hurstpierpoint in Sussex, got wind of Wilson's proposal. As he wanted to learn more about it, he invited him and French to lunch on August 23. Here the prime minister spent the better part of the morning berating Robertson and Haig, accusing them of having a parochial outlook and only able to suggest a repeat of past mistakes. He admitted that he did not have the knowledge to conceive of alternative plans and feared that even if he tried to take some sort of action, he would be attacked in the press for overruling the soldiers.

The conversation then shifted to the main item. Lloyd George listened to what Wilson had in mind and periodically asked questions. In the end, he determined that Wilson's plan was better than his own. He suggested that Wilson see other members of the War Cabinet to convince them of the merits of his concept.[27] After his guests left, Lloyd George told Riddell that in the current war he considered Sir John French "the biggest soldier we have yet produced."[28] It is incomprehensible how he could pay such tribute to a hopeless incompetent like French.

In keeping with the prime minister's wishes, Wilson sounded out Milner, Bonar Law and Carson and generally found them receptive to his proposition.[29] Although Lloyd George had a mandate to act, developments elsewhere intervened before he could approach the French government.

On August 19 Cadorna mounted an attack – the eleventh – on the Izonzo, which was heavier than in previous battles. The early reports from the British ambassador in Rome, Sir James Rennell Rodd, suggested that the Italian army was on the verge of a major victory. The news of Cadorna's success (exaggerated, as it turned out) excited Lloyd George, who was still at Riddell's home. Hankey found the prime minister, when he came over for lunch on August 26, engulfed in a wave of optimism and anxious to provide Cadorna with enough guns and men to keep him going. During the afternoon the two discussed the events on the Italian front and the likely consequences that would flow from them. Lloyd George was in such a euphoric mood that he asked Hankey to stay for the night. After dinner Lloyd George "chanted Welsh hymns, which started a regular 'sing-song' of old-fashion songs."[30] Around 11:00 p.m. Lloyd George suddenly decided to write a letter to Robertson, suggesting that Britain and France make up the Italian army's deficiencies so as to enable it to convert the Austrian retreat into a rout.[31] What Lloyd George did not reveal to Robertson was that he intended to propose to the War Cabinet that operations on the western front be suspended and that a number of divisions and 300 guns be sent to Italy.[32] At the same time, Lloyd George wrote to Bonar Law, emphasizing that without prompt action, they would be forfeiting a golden opportunity to eliminate Austria and urged him to bring pressure on Robertson to soften his attitude.[33]

Robertson was astute enough to see that the kind of military assistance Cadorna required could only be provided by halting Haig's attack. At the War Cabinet meeting on August 28, from which Lloyd George was absent, a weary Robertson released his pent-up frustration with the policymakers, accusing them of changing their minds every week and warning that no plan could succeed unless carried out with confidence and resolution. He claimed that it would be unsound strategy to close down the Flanders offensive in order to send Cadorna aid that could not reach him in time to be effective.[34] Cecil, who was present, wrote to Balfour the next day, saying that both he and Carson "were very much impressed and would have liked to say that we quite agree," but "B. L. [Bonar Law] and Milner would not let us."[35]

Robertson followed his angry tirade in the War Cabinet by motoring to Riddell's home the next day for a face-to-face confrontation with Lloyd George. Robertson arrived with the Director of Military Operations (DMO), General Sir Frederick Maurice, shortly before midday. To put the CIGS in a good frame of mind, apple pudding, his favorite sweet, was served at the end of the main course.³⁶ Whether the stratagem had the desired effect was problematical, but at least lunch was a success. Robertson had two generous servings of apple pudding and sent the cook his compliments.³⁷ The talks after lunch were conducted in a cordial atmosphere and produced an agreement. A telegram would be sent to Rome, promising Cadorna substantial help at the expense of breaking off the Flanders offensive if he could guarantee a decisive victory over Austria. Hankey believed that Robertson's acquiescence was based on his conviction that no such assurance would be forthcoming from Cadorna.³⁸ He may have been right.

The amicable arrangement reached between the two antagonists began to unravel almost immediately. The CIGS had second thoughts after returning to London, perhaps because he worried that he might have displeased Haig. In a note to Maurice, he claimed that it was the War Cabinet's decision, not his, to offer assistance to Italy.³⁹ Matters were further complicated when the French government wired London on September 3, expressing a wish to send 100 guns to Italy and requesting that they be withdrawn from the First French Army, at the time cooperating with Haig's forces at Ypres. Foch was on his way to discuss the issue with Robertson.⁴⁰ In the past, the French had opposed any help to Italy and Robertson suspected that their sudden change of heart had been inspired by Lloyd George, who had entertained Albert Thomas at Riddell's home the previous week.⁴¹ That same day, Robertson notified Haig of the contents of the French note and suggested that he be present for the conference with Foch.⁴²

On the morning of September 4 Haig, Robertson and Foch held a military conference at the War Office. Foch's position was that withdrawing 100 guns from the First French Army would not impede the Flanders operations, but would make all the difference on the Italian front. Haig countered by saying it would upset his plans, not the least of which would be to weaken the force protecting his left flank. The two soldiers were unable to settle their differences.⁴³

The War Cabinet convened after lunch and heard Haig give a report of his talk with Foch. An animated discussion followed. Lloyd George stood practically alone in supporting Foch over the British High Command. On the other side, Carson and Smuts insisted that Haig ought to have the last word, and Cecil, acting on behalf of the Foreign Office, was even more adamant. In the face of their opposition, Lloyd George pulled back, though later he took Haig aside and begged him to reconsider, exclaiming, "We must not give the French the power of saying that *they wanted* to send 100 guns, but the British would not let them go." Eventually, a compromise was worked out. Haig consented to release 50 guns on condition that Pétain did the same.⁴⁴ Lloyd George had pried far fewer guns from the soldiers than the 300 or so he really wanted. Obviously disappointed, Hankey grumbled that "Lloyd George had been very truculent about the idea of overruling the soldiers, but when he came to the point, he funked it." Still, Lloyd George had sensed, probably correctly, that this was not "the moment for a row with the soldiers."[45] Had he taken a tougher line with the military authorities he would have almost certainly provoked a political storm. According to Lord Hardinge (Permanent Under-Secretary at the Foreign Office), if Lloyd George had tried to impose his will over Haig, Robertson, Derby and Cecil would have resigned.[46]

At 4:00 p.m. the members of the War Cabinet held a conference with Foch at 10 Downing Street. The prime minister spoke on behalf of the War Cabinet. He explained that he had just learned that the guns that the French government proposed to remove from the First French Army were assisting in protecting the left of the BEF. He wished to say that after he and his colleagues had given the matter their most careful and sympathetic consideration, they had concluded that to take away so many guns from the French section of the British front, where heavy fighting was currently going on, would compromise Haig's operation. At the same time, the prime minister continued, the War Cabinet desired to assist General Cadorna in order to enable him to achieve a decisive victory. In these circumstances he proposed a meeting between Field Marshal Haig and General Pétain to consider whether the guns in question could be collected from different parts of the Allied line.

Foch saw no harm in withdrawing guns from the First French Army, which had been inactive since July 31. But he doubted that Pétain would consent to the removal of guns from other parts of the French line. Lloyd George pointed out that as much as the War Cabinet wanted to support Cadorna, it could not do so at the expense of weakening Haig's attack. As a compromise, the prime minister would ask Haig if he could spare 50 guns from the French First Army on condition that Pétain agree to make an equal sacrifice. In the end it was decided to arrange a military conference between Haig and Pétain as soon as possible, with a view to scrapping 100 guns from the British and French front to support Cadorna's attack.[47]

A meeting between Haig and Pétain at Amiens three days later produced the guns. Contrary to what Foch had implied, there was no hesitation on the part of Pétain. He indicated that he had reorganized his artillery in such a way as to give him a reserve of guns to be employed as circumstances warranted.[48]

After all the fuss to get the guns, by the time they reached Cadorna the situation on the Isonzo had been transformed. Cadorna's earlier attack, begun with promise, had stalled after Austrian resistance stiffened. For Cadorna the concentration on his front of additional Austrian divisions, with more likely to come now that the Russian army was falling apart, meant that the enemy was preparing to deliver a counterattack. This consideration, coupled with the heavy losses his army had sustained in the just-concluded offensive, induced him to abandon the idea of attacking again in 1917. He proposed to wait for the Austrians to make their move and, in the meantime, devise plans for an offensive in the spring of 1918. Lloyd George was stunned by Rome's announcement on September 20, and all of his subsequent efforts to pressure Cadorna to reconsider went for naught.[49]

As Lloyd George's hope, however unrealistic, of knocking out Austria foundered, the War Cabinet once again set its sights on Flanders where the last phase of Passchendaele was underway. Persistent rain had converted the sodden battlefield into a mud porridge that was so thick that the infantry was often reduced to crawling into battle. Progress was painfully slow. Finally, on October 26 Canadian forces slogged forward towards the crest of the ridge and on November 10 took what was left of Passchendaele village.[50] Haig now mercifully terminated the offensive, partly because the treacherous condition of the terrain made a further advance unlikely and partly because, as we shall see in a later chapter, he had to part with some of his divisions.

After months of desperate fighting, Haig's final conquest had been an objective he had expected to reach on the first day. British losses were officially put at 244,897,[51] but some observers contend that the figure was much higher. Although the British had suffered fewer casualties than at the Somme, the results were no better. Haig, quite apart from underestimating the difficulties of attacking in Flanders during the rainy season, does not appear to have grasped the lessons of the Somme. If he had, he would have known that there was no way, other than by applying new methods and weapons, to break through a fortified position defended by artillery and machine guns.

It is difficult to rationalize the need for the Flanders offensive. It had not, as we shall see, prevented a final Russian collapse or the Germans from sending troops to help Austria inflict a crushing defeat on the Italian army at Caporetto. If action on the western front was required to save the French army from imminent destruction during its morale breakdown, a feasible alternative to Passchendaele was available. There should have been no reason why a series of limited attacks, properly organized and coordinated and backed by massive artillery fire, could not have served the same purpose at a much-reduced cost in British manpower. No less serious was Haig's persistence in continuing the attack long after it should have been apparent that his lofty objectives could not be attained. It weakened his army and left him without the reserves needed to exploit his subsequent success at Cambrai and, more critically, to stem the tide of the German onslaught in the spring of 1918.

There are others who cannot escape responsibility for the bloodletting at Passchendaele. Robertson deserves to be censured for his conduct. It was his duty to provide the War Cabinet with impartial military advice, not to behave throughout as Haig's advocate and conceal from it data relevant to the planned offensive. Lloyd George is equally, if not more so, at fault. He had been derelict in gaining a better understanding of the technical side of the war, as a result of which he had caved in and allowed the generals to assert their control over policy. During the debates he showed his ignorance by focusing only on the Italian plan as the one meaningful alternative to Flanders. There was another obvious course: undertaking limited operations of the Messines type while awaiting for full concentration of American forces. If at the outset he had possessed the knowledge and courage to lay down such a policy, the generals would have gone along, particularly Robertson, as the fighting would have occurred on the western front rather than in another theater. Then, having given his lukewarm consent to the Flanders operation, Lloyd George compounded his error by devising means to delay it, giving the Germans more time to prepare and preventing Haig from initiating action during the good weather of July. Finally, he refused to step in and order Haig to break off the operation when there was evidence that it was turning into a bloodbath.

The effects of Passchendaele were quickly felt on the higher direction of the war. The relationship between Robertson and Haig began to cool because of their divergent views during the planning stages of the operation. Distrust deepened between Lloyd George on one hand and Robertson and Haig on the other. Lloyd George felt that his doubts about the offensive had been corroborated and he no longer placed any faith in the professional judgment of Haig and Robertson. The other members of the War Cabinet were equally disillusioned by the meager results of the Flanders offensive and some were troubled by Robertson's reluctance to call for an early halt to the battle.[52] As everyone was concerned with the staying power of the British army, sentiment shied away from more wearing-down operations in the west, instead turning increasingly towards distant theatres where political and military benefits could be achieved at much reduced cost.

Chapter 9

THE PERIPHERAL WAR

Apart from the desultory action in German East Africa,[1] Britain was involved in three subsidiary campaigns in the east when Lloyd George became prime minister in December 1916: Mesopotamia, the Balkans and Egypt. Of the three eastern theaters, Mesopotamia was the most badly managed and the most inhospitable. After the surrender of a British-led army (made up largely of Indian troops) at Kut in April 1916, direction of the front passed from the military authorities in Delhi to the War Office. Robertson, despite his hatred of sideshows, understood that for the sake of Britain's prestige and the security of India, a withdrawal was out of the question.[2] But he wanted operations conducted at minimal costs so that troops would not be diverted from Haig's army in large numbers. Under his stewardship there was a dramatic improvement in communications, supplies and administration as well as an increase in forces. In the second week in December 1916 General Sir Stanley Maude, the British commander, was authorized to organize an advance, though no grand objectives were set. By then Maude had received reinforcements to the point where he held an advantage of roughly three to one in manpower (150,000 as against 48,000) over the Turks and possessed far more artillery. He began a slow, methodical advance and over the course of the next three months, ejected the Turks from their positions along the Tigris, culminating in the recovery of Kut on February 24, 1917. The remnant of the defeated army fled in disorder toward Baghdad.[3]

When news of the Turkish rout reached London, Lloyd George could not suppress his excitement. "Will Maude get to Baghdad?" he asked Robertson. Cautious as usual, the CIGS replied that it would depend on the state of Maude's transport and supply services. The prime minister urged Robertson to give Maude the green light if at all possible, stressing that for months the public had experienced nothing but disappointments and that it was necessary to produce a victory that would catch their fancy and boost their morale. Robertson promised he would do his best to meet the prime minister's wishes.[4]

With the outcome of the campaign no longer in doubt, Lloyd George and his colleagues began looking ahead to postwar annexations in the east that would ensure British ascendancy in that region. As a treaty was already in existence for the eventual partition of the Ottoman Empire,[5] Lloyd George wanted Maude to occupy the Baghdad vilayet as soon as possible.

On February 28 the matter was discussed fully in the War Cabinet. Robertson had reservations about continuing the advance, and not because of the feasibility of reaching Baghdad, which was a foregone conclusion. But to hold Baghdad it would be necessary to push the front some fifty miles to the north to block the three approaches to the city. This would inevitably require more troops and further extend the already long lines of communication. Lloyd George, however, saw things differently. He felt there was no risk. A competent general was in charge and he had given his assurance that he could take Baghdad without difficulty; in addition, there were general staff reports that the Turkish army on the Tigris was heavily outnumbered and all but beaten. He stressed that acquiring a prize like Baghdad would wipe out the shame of Kut and leave a tremendous impression on British and world opinion.[6]

Robertson, knowing when to retreat, asked whether it was the War Cabinet's desire to establish British influence in the Baghdad vilayet, subject to the security of the force and the capacity of its communications. Told that it was, the CIGS was directed to convey instructions to Maude in that sense and to urge him to exploit his recent success to the fullest possible extent.[7] On the same day, Robertson telegraphed Maude to give him his new orders. He advised waiting until his action could be coordinated with the Russians, who were expected, as soon as climatic conditions would allow, to move through Persia and on to Mosul. But in a separate telegram he warned Maude that he was not to let the Russians reach Baghdad first.[8]

Maude resumed the advance on March 5 and drove the Turks out of their last position before entering Baghdad unopposed.[9] He proceeded quickly to occupy the surrounding area. Lloyd George had hoped that the Russian Army of the Caucasus would link with Maude north of Baghdad and together they would conquer the outlying Ottoman territories and compel the Turks to surrender. He anticipated that Bulgaria would follow suit as a consequence and the end of the war would then be in sight. He was extremely disappointed when the promised Russian aid failed to materialize. The Russian revolution had resulted in a rapid breakdown of discipline in the Army of the Caucasus, just as it had in Russian forces on other fronts. Indeed, the Army of the Caucasus, except for an isolated detachment, did not advance beyond the frontiers of Mesopotamia and before long withdrew by stages from land they had won. Without Russian cooperation, a British move beyond the Baghdad vilayet would have been imprudent. Reinforced by troops released from the Russian front, there were reports that the Turks might be able to bring together an army of some 120,000 men and 300 guns in a bid to recapture Baghdad.[10] It was felt that Maude, with about 50,000 men and 200 guns in the Baghdad neighborhood, would probably require two additional divisions before continuing his march. Consequently, Maude confined his activities to the immediate area north of the city when the intense summer heat brought campaigning to a temporary halt.

The scenario in Mesopotamia in which the British suffered casualties at the cost, not to Germany, but to one of its allies, was repeated in the Balkans. As we saw earlier, the conference in Rome in January 1917 had ended without resolving two basic questions: no agreement had been reached regarding the issue of reinforcements for the Balkans and the future role of the Eastern Army had not been defined. Back in Salonica, Sarrail received his instructions for the new year from the French minister of war, General Lyautey. With the Nivelle offensive about to begin, Sarrail was told to be sufficiently active to prevent German troops in Macedonia from being transferred to the western front. Lyautey requested that Sarrail submit a plan of operation for his approval. If deemed satisfactory, it would be forwarded to London for the British government's scrutiny.[11] Sarrail's first plan, which aimed at Sofia, was rejected as being too bold, but the second one was in keeping with Lyautey's admonition that the purpose of his operations was to contain the enemy in the Balkans.

Sarrail's two plans were discussed by representatives of the British and French governments meeting at Calais on February 26 and 27. Lloyd George's enthusiasm for his brainchild had begun to diminish and he no longer pushed for an ever-larger commitment to the Balkans. After months of self-deception, he had to admit that the Balkan campaign was not yielding results commensurate with the expenditure of men and equipment that it entailed. Although the prime minister and Robertson rarely saw eye to eye, the gap between the two on this issue had narrowed significantly.

The conference dealt initially with other matters before turning to the Balkans. Briand went over Sarrail's two plans and recommended the adoption of the less ambitious one as more in accordance with the size of Sarrail's forces. Robertson responded that both he and the British prime minister were in agreement that the scope of the Eastern Army's mission must be clearly defined before any action was sanctioned. It seemed to the ever-suspicious Robertson that Sarrail's smaller operation was meant to set the stage for a march on Sofia. He reminded the delegates that expert opinion had always maintained that an advance on Sofia must be accompanied by an offensive from the north by Russians and Romanians. He then proposed that, since Russia and Romania could not be counted on at present to render assistance, "the decisive defeat of the Bulgarian army is not a practical objective, and that the mission of the Allied forces at Salonica is to keep on their front the enemy forces now there." Briand concurred in the main with Robertson's formula and suggested adding the following words at the end: "and to take advantage of striking the enemy if opportunity offers."

Lyautey thought there was nothing wrong in Sarrail's proposal that the final objective should be Sofia. He admitted that there was no sense in undertaking a large operation without a strong advance from the north, but added that Sarrail ought to get the most out of his army. He pointed to the fine results that had been achieved in Mesopotamia with moderate efforts and saw no reason why it could not be repeated in the Balkans. Lloyd George stated that he was in full agreement with Lyautey. What Robertson was proposing was similar to the instructions he had given General Maude, in which there was no mention of Baghdad. Still, the prime minister would not have wanted to exclude the possibility that Maude could advance to Baghdad if events favored him. In the end, Robertson's resolution, as amended, carried without dissent.[12]

Robertson had been pleased by the prime minister's role at the conference and it encouraged him to believe that he might accept a reduction in the size of the Balkan force – a move that could lead to the liquidation of the enterprise. In pleading his case he knew that he could rely on Jellicoe, who favored abandoning the Balkan adventure because of the submarine danger in the Mediterranean.[13] In late March Robertson argued in the War Cabinet that the shortage of shipping made it increasingly difficult to provide the tonnage required for the maintenance of troops and he suggested that the force at Salonica be reduced. His comments struck a responsive cord in the War Cabinet. Besides appreciation of the shipping crisis, there was general agreement that the absence of effective military activity did not justify tying down so large a force.[14] Lloyd George indicated that he would discuss the matter with Painlevé, the new French minister of war.[15]

On April 18 Lloyd George set off to attend an inter-Allied conference in St. Jean de Maurienne. Arriving in Paris around 6:00 p.m., he held a private meeting with Painlevé, during which he warned him that unless Sarrail's forthcoming offensive resulted in considerable success, Britain would reduce its contingent in the Balkans. At the Allied conference on the following day, Lloyd George repeated that the Eastern Army had one last chance to justify its existence. To strengthen his position he distributed a paper, dated April 17, which Jellicoe had written for the benefit of the War Cabinet. Pessimistic as always, the first sea lord insisted that the strain on shipping was such that he would not be able to supply the British force beyond 1917 unless it was drastically reduced in size.[16] Ribot and Painlevé showed less opposition to the British declaration than Lloyd George had anticipated, but as the discussion wore on, it became evident that they were looking for something in return. What they wanted was British assistance in clearing up the troubling situation in Greece, including, if necessary, the removal of Constantine from the throne.

The prime minister was inclined to accept a bargain struck along those lines as a quid quo pro for the reduction of British manpower in the Balkans. It was eventually decided to reconsider the whole question at another conference to be held in Paris in two weeks' time.[17]

At the War Cabinet on May 1 Robertson suggested the desirability of considering the Balkan question before the approaching Paris conference. For over a year he had tried every conceivable means to liquidate or scale back the scope of the operations in the Balkans, only to be told each time that any lessening of British commitment in that theater would cause the collapse of the reigning French government and might propel to power Joseph Caillaux, who was committed to a compromise peace. Robertson refused to believe the claim by the current French government (as well as previous ones) of the intense feeling its public attached to the fate of the Balkan expedition.[18] For the first time, he saw an opportunity to remove some, if not all, British troops. He suggested that at the next Allied conference the French leaders should be informed that Britain could not possibly continue to keep its present forces at Salonica and that it intended to bring away two brigades of mounted troops and one division immediately, to be followed by the whole or greater part of the remainder as soon as shipping was made available. Lloyd George indicated that he proposed to include Jellicoe in the British delegation so that he could impress upon the French the seriousness of Britain's shipping shortage.[19]

Lloyd George and his colleagues dominated the proceedings of the Anglo-French conference in Paris on May 4 and 5. The prime minister observed that he had been in favor of the Balkan campaign from the very start, but that owing to the unendurable strain on the nation's shipping resources, he had concluded that the British force should be reduced to the level required to hold an entrenched camp in front of Salonica. He announced that the withdrawal of one division and two mounted brigades would begin on June 1, but that he would reconsider his decision if Sarrail drove Bulgaria to seek peace terms by the end of May. The French delegates grudgingly assented, pending the approval of their cabinet.[20]

All of a sudden Lloyd George had unilaterally altered Sarrail's mission from an operation designed to tie down enemy divisions in the Balkans to one calling for a march on Sofia. He knew that Sarrail did not possess the necessary means to inflict a fatal defeat on the Bulgarians and had said so on previous occasions. But Sarrail's failure to reach the new objective set for him would make it easier for the British to reduce their commitment in the Balkans.

Sarrail did not help himself when his spring operation failed to achieve a tactical victory. The attacks were poorly coordinated and easily repulsed. The offensive, halted on May 21, was considered a major disappointment and further tarnished Sarrail's military reputation. Although it had prevented enemy troops from being dispatched to the main front, it had cost 14,000 casualties and produced no territorial gains.[21] British losses had been disproportionately high, and once again questions were raised in the War Cabinet whether more troops should be withdrawn, in addition to those already announced.

Lloyd George and his colleagues suspected that France clung tenaciously to the Salonica-based operation principally as a means to further its imperial designs in the Balkans in the postwar period. But the British, like the French, wanted to maintain and strengthen their empire as much as they wanted to win the war. They considered most of the Middle East – Mesopotamia, Syria and Palestine – vital to their imperial strategy.[22] To protect the route to India it was necessary to dominate the region either through direct or indirect rule. This meant revising the Sykes–Picot Agreement of 1916 that had placed much of Palestine under international control and laid the framework for the division of Ottoman lands, with the British accorded control in southern Mesopotamia and a sphere of influence over the Hejaz, and the French an area extending from the north Syrian coast to the upper Tigris Valley and including the mineral-rich district of Mosul. Neither power wanted the other close to, or impinging on, its future zone of influence. Since the British had begun to advance into Palestine, the French worried that without their physical presence, they might lose control of their promised territory. They preferred to keep British forces in the Balkans, "where they did little and suffered from endemic malaria and paratyphoid," rather than see them diverted to Palestine. As Chaim Weizmann, the Zionist leader in Britain pointed out, "French policy in Greece was partly dictated by the desire to prevent our reinforcing the Palestinian front so as to prevent Britain gaining a foothold in Palestine."[23]

Thus, the French would not go beyond what had been agreed upon at the last Anglo–French conference. At the War Cabinet on May 23 Derby, just back from a visit to Paris, reported his conversation with Painlevé and a subsequent one with Ribot, who essentially took the same position. Painlevé informed him that the French cabinet had acquiesced in the withdrawal of one British division and two cavalry brigades, but opposed the departure of more troops. He argued that weakening the Eastern Army would compel it to fall back to the fortified lines around Salonica and, in his opinion, encourage Constantine to join hands with the Germans. In such an event, Greek harbors would become bases for German submarines, threatening the communications of the Allied force and possibly forcing its surrender. To avoid such a contingency, Painlevé proposed that Sarrail be allowed to march on Thessaly and occupy Athens with a view to depose Constantine and in his place install a government headed by E. Venizelos – a former prime minister who was sympathetic to the Entente.[24]

The War Cabinet proceeded to discuss the desirability of a Greek coup as contemplated by the French. Derby noted that Ribot had insisted that popular sentiment in France was such that his government could not survive unless drastic action along the recommended lines was taken. It was pointed out that the French had used the same argument ever since October 1915 when they had induced the British authorities to support their Balkan policy. There was a consensus that London was under no obligation to prop up the current French ministry. The War Cabinet agreed that transport limitations precluded the British government from modifying its declared policy of reducing British forces at Salonica.

Left undecided, however, was whether the British ought to acquiesce in the French proposal to unseat Constantine.[25] Robertson opposed military action against Greece, fearful it might lead to a long war against the royalists and thus make it unlikely, if not impossible, to bring away the British troops in the Balkans.[26] Lloyd George's position was not recorded in the minutes, but according to Frances Stevenson, he was "inclined to side with the French," and unlike the military, had no desire to close the front at Salonica. She added, "A good deal depends on the outcome of this conference, not only from a military, but I think also from a political point of view."[27]

The British and French governments, which had agreed to meet again at the close of their conference in Paris on May 5, did so in London during the last week of the month. Ribot, invited to open the proceedings, had known for several days of the War Cabinet's decision. In arguing the French case, he said nothing that the British had not already heard before. Other speakers followed, including Jellicoe and Robertson, before Lloyd George took his turn. He recapitulated the arguments advanced by his service leaders, namely that the shipping was unavailable for broadening the Allied commitment in the Balkans. He shared the French dislike of Constantine, whom he considered had become a threat to the security of the Eastern Army. He stressed, however, that the British government wanted steps taken against him, but carried out in as friendly a manner as possible so as not to provoke the Greeks.[28] What Lloyd George had in mind was contained in a memorandum that was distributed to the French delegation at the conclusion of the morning session. Rather than use force to overthrow Constantine, the British preferred a plan hatched by Cecil that would achieve the same purpose by purchasing the Thessalian harvest and threatening to starve Athens into submission.[29]

The French provided a written reply to the British suggestion when the conference reconvened later in the day. They urged that to forestall organized resistance, it was necessary at the outset of the Thessaly operation to impose a blockade and take military action against royalist troops, and that there be no further reduction of the forces at Salonica until a friendly regime had been installed at Athens.³⁰ The War Cabinet discussed the French note immediately after the conference adjourned and continued early the next morning. As a good-will gesture, the members relented somewhat and reached the following decisions: that as soon as the military posts in Thessaly had been established, the demand for Constantine's abdication would be made; that if the king declined to step down, Greece should be blockaded by sea and supplies from Thessaly denied to the royalist faction; that if the king tried to take military action against the Allies, Sarrail should immediately land a force on the Isthmus of Corinth; and finally, there was to be no further reduction of British troops for six weeks, when another conference would be held between the two governments to consider this question.³¹

The French were delighted with the sudden shift in the British position. Lloyd George urged that Sarrail be given explicit instructions that the operation was to be carried out peacefully and with as little provocation as possible. Ribot gave assurances that he would. At Lloyd George's suggestion, the conference agreed that a small British force should go with the French contingent if it became necessary to occupy the Isthmus of Corinth.³² On that note the conference broke up.

Lloyd George was satisfied with the outcome of the Anglo–French gathering, in contrast to Robertson. There is the following entry in Francis Stevenson's diary:

> The French departed today, and D. is very pleased with the result of the Conference. They have decided to depose Tino [Constantine] and establish a republic in Greece – this much against the will of our military people, but D. overruled them. R. was inclined to be nasty, but D. turned on him roughly. "We are entitled to your military advice General Robertson," he said sternly, [but] "the policy is ours." D. said he crumpled up, and was as meek as a lamb for the rest of the Conference.³³

Lloyd George felt there were political and military advantages to keeping British troops in the Balkans, even though he was determined to bring some away for other purposes. He was convinced that by keeping the pressure up in the Balkans, the Austrians, who seemed exhausted and anxious for peace, might ultimately break with Germany. He did not want more troops piled on the western front, which he was certain Haig would only fritter away in senseless assaults. An equally significant factor in his thinking was that the British force in the Balkans was close to Constantinople and part of it would be available to race ahead of its allies to strengthen London's claims to Ottoman territory. In May he had declared that "the postwar zones of influence in Asia Minor would be determined by whichever country made the greatest wartime contribution to the defeat of Turkey."[34] Robertson, in the belief that he was close to putting an end to that wretched Balkan theater (as he often referred to it) once and for all, was livid at the prime minister's apparent *volte-face* and the prospect that the campaign would be prolonged indefinitely, consuming resources badly needed elsewhere.

The one thing that Lloyd George and Robertson could agree on was that Sarrail had outlived his usefulness. At the War Cabinet on June 5 Robertson maintained that all reports received from the Allied commanders on the spot – British, Russian, Italian and Serb – pointed to Sarrail's mismanagement of the recent offensive in the Balkans and the consensus of opinion was that he was more concerned with fomenting a revolution in Athens than in fighting the Bulgarians. From the information received, Robertson concluded that whatever instructions Sarrail received from the French government, he could not be relied on to implement Allied policy in Greece in a conciliatory manner. Lloyd George had been impressed by Sarrail when he met him in Rome, but subsequent events led him to believe that a more tactful general might have avoided driving Constantine into open hostility. In view of the damning evidence, the War Cabinet authorized the prime minister to ask Ribot on its behalf to replace Sarrail without delay.[35]

The next day Lloyd George wrote to Ribot questioning Sarrail's fitness to remain in command of the Allied troops. He explained that reports received from British representatives on the scene indicated that Sarrail had lost the confidence of the officers and troops under his command. It was felt that a great opportunity to deal the enemy a serious blow had been missed because of his faulty leadership. Although he had been an admirer of Sarrail and defended him on more than one occasion so that he would have the chance to carry out the policy agreed upon, the reports he had read led him to concur entirely with the War Cabinet that "we should not be justified in leaving the British forces in the Balkans under the supreme command of General Sarrail."[36]

Ribot had his own doubts about Sarrail and was tempted to recall him once the Thessaly operation was completed, but in the French council of war on February 7 Painlevé rose to his defense, dwelling on the difficulties of commanding troops of different nationalities.[37] Replying to Lloyd George, the French prime minister observed that it was politically impractical to supersede Sarrail at the very moment when Allied policy in Greece was about to be applied.[38] Ribot's plea was aided by Painlevé, who cautioned London through unofficial channels that Sarrail's removal would cause a political crisis, possibly resulting in the fall of the French government.[39] It was best to wait, he advised, until the situation in Greece was stabilized so that Sarrail could be brought back home not in disgrace, but as having accomplished his mission.[40]

The War Cabinet agreed that the transfer of Sarrail should be postponed until "after the present critical phase of the military situation in Greece had passed."[41] Over the next few days the French, following their own agenda, kept the War Cabinet in the dark about the true state of affairs in Athens and fed it only reassuring information. News received directly from Athens was sketchy and contradicted by the French if it suited their purpose. Consequently, Lloyd George and his colleagues, apart from not knowing for sure what was happening in Athens, were receiving mixed signals about whether a landing was about to take place.[42] Fortunately, the negotiations with Constantine went more smoothly than might have been expected and on June 11 he abdicated in favor of his son, Alexander.[43] A fortnight later the new king appointed Venizelos prime minister of a united Greece, committed to the Entente.

The War Cabinet was so elated by the recent diplomatic coup, which Sarrail had consistently recommended, that it decided not to press the French government to have him transferred to another sphere of activity.[44] Now that Greece had been converted from a questionable neutral to an active ally, there was no longer any need to entertain a policy of withdrawing to an entrenched camp surrounding Salonica, as Robertson had often urged. But the question being asked was whether anything meaningful could be accomplished in the Balkans to justify the presence of so large an Allied force.[45] Accordingly, the War Cabinet's War Policy Committee was asked to conduct an in-depth investigation. Robertson, trying to sway Curzon, one of its members, sent him a letter telling him that contrary to the thinking of the prime minister "that there is a single range of hills between the Salonica Force and Sofia," the whole country was, in fact, "a mass of mountains" and very favorable to the defense. He claimed that there was no chance of achieving military success in the Balkans unless the Russians struck in force from the north, a prospect that at the present time seemed remote.[46]

The report of the War Policy Committee on July 19 basically agreed with Robertson. It advocated that the British government's policy in the Balkans should aim at the gradual withdrawal of its divisions from the fighting line in order to form a reserve that could be used in some other theater.[47] The next day the War Cabinet adopted the Committee's recommendations and, as a preliminary move, called for the immediate withdrawal of one division from Salonica in order to reinforce the British Expeditionary Force in Egypt.[48]

At long last the British government had adopted a policy for the Balkans, but whether it could be implemented remained to be seen. Five days later at a conference in Paris, attended by representatives of numerous Allied countries, there was a prolonged discussion on the matter of the immediate withdrawal of one British division from Salonica. What was the purpose, Lloyd George asked rhetorically, of locking up forces far in excess of what was required for defense when there was no prospect of an offensive. He made it clear that as more Greek divisions took the field, British forces would be reduced even further. He assured the Allied delegates that Britain had no intention of withdrawing completely from Salonica.

The British objective provoked a hostile reaction from the French and, to a lesser extent, from the other representatives (Italians, Greeks, Russians, Romanians and Serbs). The withdrawal of the British division, so the main line of argument went, would be a sure sign that the Allies did not intend to attack, enabling the Bulgarians to withdraw forces from the Balkan front and concentrate them against the Russians, who were in a most critical condition. As there seemed no likelihood of breaking the deadlock, it was decided to resume the discussion at the next conference set to be held in London.[49]

At the London conference on August 7 and 8 both sides restated their arguments. Lloyd George noted that the question had been so thoroughly thrashed out that there seemed no prospect of one side convincing the other. Persuaded that the British would not budge this time, Ribot modified his position. He indicated that he would accept a British commitment not to withdraw any more divisions from Salonica beyond the one presently under consideration. Lloyd George took the concession. The conference agreed to his resolution that the British government would not withdraw any additional units without further consultation with its allies, and then only if unexpected events occurred.[50] The British had gotten their division, but at the expense of effectively keeping their remaining forces in the Balkan theater until the end of the war.

As no meaningful action was likely to occur in the Balkans, Lloyd George transferred his interest to another distant theater. He had struck a bargain with Robertson that the troops released from the Balkans would be sent not to the western front, but to Palestine to assist in the fight against the Turks. As much as Robertson hated sideshows, he consoled himself with the thought that by going to Palestine, these troops would at least be making more of a contribution to winning the war than as part of the futile Eastern Army, not to mention that they would be under British control.[51]

The campaign in Palestine began as an extension of the Egyptian front. In the opening months of the war, Britain had amassed a large force in Egypt to protect the Suez Canal, a vital link to the oil fields of the Persian Gulf and through which passed convoys bringing imperial contingents from India and elsewhere to Europe. Early in 1916 the British commander, General Archibald Murray, in order to provide a belt of protection for the canal, pushed his perimeter eastward into the Sinai Desert and at the close of the year took El-Arish without a fight.[52]

Lloyd George, who assumed power shortly before the fall of El-Arish, thirsted for a resounding victory somewhere to raise national morale and offset recent Allied losses. Lloyd George had in mind an advance into Palestine, but Robertson, who wanted to limit operations in Murray's theater, asked if the prime minister would settle for the capture of the Turkish stronghold of Beersheba. Lloyd George demurred, preferring the holy city of Jerusalem as more likely to stir the public's imagination.[53]

Robertson had favored using what resources were necessary to defend Egypt and the Suez Canal, but his mood changed when the Egyptian Expeditionary Force's operations became offensive in character and absorbed men that he felt were desperately need on the western front where the struggle was approaching a climatic stage.[54] But in the beginning, he tried to give effect to the prime minister's wishes without weakening the main effort in France. Accordingly, he wired Murray, asking him to submit plans for an advance beyond El-Arish and to state what additional troops he would require for the task. Murray replied the next day, recommending an advance along the coast and requesting two more divisions, which would bring his total to six. Robertson estimated that Murray would require an additional three divisions, not two. The dispatch of so many troops from France could not be implemented if plans for Haig's summer offensive were carried out. Backpedaling, Robertson wired Murray that, notwithstanding the previous instructions sent to him, the primary mission of the EEF was still confined to the defense of Egypt and that he would be "informed if and when the War Cabinet changes this policy."[55] Murray went ahead with the forces at his disposal and on December 23 captured Magdhaba, clearing the Sinai peninsula of Turks and reaching the frontier of Palestine.[56]

Robertson persuaded the War Cabinet that the strain on shipping, logistical difficulties and lack of troops made an invasion of Palestine impractical during the winter and summer seasons. He suggested delaying the campaign in Palestine until the autumn when operations in France would be winding down. In the interim, Murray would be given such troops as were available and instructed to make preparations for an offensive at a later date.[57] Far from receiving reinforcements, Murray was instructed on January 17, 1917 to release a division for service in France.[58] The French wanted Haig to extend his front to free French soldiers for Nivelle's offensive, and this meant finding another division.

At the War Cabinet meeting on January 30 Lloyd George asked Robertson to report on the progress of the preparations being made for the Palestinian campaign. Robertson indicated that there was no certainty that the operation would take place, as it was impossible to say if it would prove to be practical in eight or nine months. In short, Robertson seemed to be telling the ministers that Murray would be given a chance only if there was no significant progress in France during the summer.[59]

Although gaining the War Cabinet's approval for a defensive policy, Robertson had given Murray discretion to engage in some activity in southern Palestine. Murray, with only three infantry divisions under his command, decided to attack Gaza, which commanded the coastal road into Palestine. Robertson did not object when Murray informed him of his plans. The operation against Gaza on March 26 was skillfully planned, but its execution was marred by poor staff work with the result that the British troops were repulsed. Murray rashly sent London a misleading account of the battle. He understated his own casualties, greatly exaggerated those of the enemy, and described the operation "as most successful."[60]

Murray's apparent victory aroused the hopes of Lloyd George and the War Cabinet, following the British capture of Baghdad on March 11, as well as other Allied successes against the Turks – Russian pressure had compelled the Turks to withdraw from Persia and the Arab revolt in the Hejaz was gaining strength. Lloyd George and his colleagues were convinced that the Ottoman Empire was on the verge of collapse. They welcomed Robertson's recommendation that Murray's role should change from active defense to offensive.[61] To that end, Robertson urged Murray to exploit his (alleged) success and to take every opportunity to defeat the forces opposed to him with the object of taking Jerusalem.[62]

Trapped by his own deceit, Murray had no option but to renew the assault against Gaza. The Second Battle of Gaza was fought between April 17 and 19 and the outcome was a total failure. Murray lacked the artillery required to help his men overcome an enemy that had been reinforced and its defenses improved. Murray called off the attack after suffering losses that were heavier than on the previous occasion.

Murray's defeat "coincided with an abrupt downturn in Allied fortunes." Nivelle's offensive had not yet produced the promised breakthrough. Germany's submarines in April were sinking an average of thirteen British ships a day, leading to speculation in London of a possible pullback of imperial operations. News from Russia was equally grim. The effects of the revolution in Russia were being felt in the army. Unrest among Russian soldiers in Persia and the Caucasus had surfaced, ruling out further advances on the Turkish front.[63]

Lloyd George resisted Robertson's desire to impose a passive policy on the imperial fronts. Disillusioned with the prospects in France and unable to shift the main effort to the Italian front, he continued to pin his hopes on an advance in southern Palestine that would end triumphantly in the seizure of Jerusalem. But he had lost confidence in Murray, particularly after learning that he had deceived the War Cabinet about the First Battle of Gaza. The prime minister claimed that Murray was timid and lacked the dash of someone like Maude to bring the campaign to successful conclusion. He reminded his colleagues that the only reason that Murray had been sent to Egypt was because it was necessary to find him another post after Robertson had taken his place as CIGS at the end of 1915. He demanded that Murray be relieved of his command.[64] Even Robertson, a close friend of Murray, realized that a change was desirable.

Lloyd George's first choice to succeed Murray was Jan Smuts, who had been asked to remain in Britain. Smuts had wide experience as a field commander, was resourceful and energetic with a reputation for getting things done. But he turned down the command after Robertson refused to promise him the men and material he deemed necessary for a decisive victory.[65] Although Lloyd George was disappointed, he sought to utilize his qualities in another capacity, appointing him a member of the War Cabinet.

Lloyd George then turned to Robertson to suggest a suitable replacement for Murray. Robertson recommended General Sir Edmund Allenby, a classmate at the Staff College two decades earlier. A cavalryman, the 56-year-old Allenby had commanded troops at the Somme and Arras with mixed results. His relations with Haig were known to be strained. A tall man with a large powerful frame, he had a forbidding manner and an explosive temper. But he was open-minded, imaginative, dynamic and popular with his troops, and, unlike many of his fellow commanders, stayed close to the front. The wily Robertson had his own reasons for selecting Allenby. He not only gave Lloyd George a fighting general, but in addition, relieved Haig of an unwanted subordinate and put in charge of the campaign a "Westerner" who was "extremely unlikely to make excessive demands for men and resources needed in France."[66]

Lloyd George was satisfied with Allenby. He had met Allenby in France and had been impressed by his strength of character and his reputation as a dashing cavalry officer. He believed the cavalry would be a key weapon in the vast open spaces and that Allenby was the right man to breathe new life into the moribund campaign.[67] The War Cabinet confirmed the appointment on June 5 and on the same day Robertson communicated the news to Haig and asked him to send Allenby to London at once.

Allenby was unhappy with his new assignment. He regarded it as a demotion and a virtual end to his career, but his spirits picked up after his interview with the prime minister in London.[68] Here Lloyd George unveiled his plans for Palestine, promised Allenby considerable freedom and all the reinforcements and supplies that he would need and gave assurances that no policy would be set until he had time to make an appreciation on the spot. In return, Lloyd George told him that the War Cabinet expected "Jerusalem before Christmas."[69]

The change in command led to a reassessment in the War Cabinet of the future of the campaign in Palestine. In general, the members were not all that optimistic. For one thing, the Russians could not be counted on to be active in the Caucasus. For another, the possibility existed that the Turks would abandon Mesopotamia, in which case they were likely to concentrate more forces in Palestine at a time when Robertson warned that because of the Russian revolution, he could not promise to send Allenby all the reinforcements he required to undertake a major offensive drive.[70]

Lloyd George tried a different approach to overcome his colleagues' reluctance to sanction a campaign in Palestine. At meetings of the War Cabinet on May 1 and 9, as we have already seen, he gave a bleak appreciation of Allied chances of victory in light of Russia's probable collapse. To strengthen its bargaining position in preparation for peace talks with Germany, he concluded that the conquest of Mesopotamia and Syria was a matter of urgency.[71] The Allies had already made significant strides towards breaking up Turkey – Russia currently occupied Armenia, the British were well on their way to conquering Mesopotamia and they were also on the borders of Palestine. To continue the process of releasing subject peoples from Ottoman rule would pay dividends in the end.[72]

Bearing in mind that the prime minister had established himself as the nation's prime exponent of total victory over Germany, what are we to make of his counsel of despair? As students of the period know only too well, Lloyd George did not always mean what he said. A cynic might be tempted to believe that Lloyd George had concocted a plausible line of argument simply to rally his colleagues behind his Eastern policy. As it happened, it represented his real assessment of the Entente's prospects at the time.

Chapter 10

THE QUEST FOR A NEGOTIATED PEACE

In the spring of 1917 Lloyd George underwent a change of heart and toyed with the idea of a negotiated settlement with Germany. He could see no dramatic changes immediately ahead, nothing to stimulate hope or signal an approaching climax. Gradually, the idea took root in his mind that the defeat of the German army might be either impossible or prohibitively costly to Britain. He began to backpedal from his announced policy of continuing the war until a knockout blow had been delivered. Strangely enough, his interest in considering peace negotiations came only after the United States had entered the fray. But he was told by the experts that the United States would not be able to place significant military forces in the west for at least a year. The unfitness of the French army for further action in 1917, Britain's shrinking manpower, the deadly toll exacted by the enemy's submarine campaign and the precipitous decline of Russia all combined to make it uncertain that the Entente could hold the Germans at bay until the following year.

Anticipating that in the near future his government might be confronted with an instant demand for peace, Lloyd George felt that some attention should be given to defining the nation's war aims. Accordingly, he prepared a statement that he intended to deliver at the initial meeting of the Imperial War Cabinet. This body had been created to induce India and the Dominions to increase their already considerable military effort by pretending to associate them with the higher direction of the war. Lloyd George may also have wanted to use it to rein in Robertson and Haig. As a last resort, he could argue that he was responding to decisions reached by an executive body dominated by representatives of India and the Dominions, whose contingents were forming an increasingly important part of a shrinking British army. In any case, it was supposed to handle administrative problems, decide war policy, and consider peace terms. There was, of course, already a less wieldy system in place – the War Cabinet – to deal with such issues. Hankey found it amusing that the Dominion prime ministers had been invited to give their views on "questions of great urgency," when in fact they did not have the slightest "notion of what they are to discuss." Bonar Law nursed similar sentiments, bluntly telling the prime minister, "When they are here, you will wish to goodness you could get rid of them."[1]

Predictably, the Imperial War Cabinet was not much more than a public relations ploy. Its work was redundant and time-consuming, and brought few tangible benefits. From March 20 until it adjourned on May 2 the Imperial War Cabinet held fourteen sessions, usually meeting three times a week. Chaired by Lloyd George, its members included the rest of the War Cabinet, the Dominion prime ministers and representatives of India.[2]

The prime minister opened the conference on March 20 by blaming Germany for the war and disclosing the agenda for the upcoming meetings. High on his priority list was a frank discussion of peace terms. In stating the obvious, he noted it was essential that the representatives at the peace conference should have a clear comprehension of what Britain and its empire hoped to achieve. He emphasized that it was too early to lay down rigid terms, for Germany had more troops in the field than ever, was in possession of thousands of square miles of Allied territory and was still a formidable foe. Nevertheless, there were certain objectives he considered indispensable for an acceptable peace. First and foremost, Germany was required to surrender all of its territorial gains and compensate the countries it had occupied and ravaged. The map of Europe had to be redrawn to take into consideration the aspirations of subject nationalities. He called for an organization to keep the peace, an end to autocracy, and the breakup of the Ottoman Empire. He did not refer to the French demand for the return of Alsace–Lorraine, which, it should be noted, he did not officially endorse until later in the year. Finally, he made no recommendation about the fate of the German colonies, merely saying that they had to be dealt with as only one of the many problems of the war.[3]

At the second session on March 22 two subcommittees were set up: one under Curzon, was to tackle territorial aims, and the other, presided over by Milner, was to consider nonterritorial issues, in particular, reparations, arms limitation and the creation of a league of nations. The Curzon committee, meeting on April 17, 18 and 19 recommended that Britain retain its German and Turkish conquests on grounds of national or imperial security – annexation sentiment was especially strong among the Dominion representatives. The one aim deemed vital to British interests was the liberation of Belgium. The committee showed less concern for other objectives, such as French ambition to recover Alsace–Lorraine, the principle of national self-determination for the peoples of the Austro–Hungarian Empire and Poland and ways to reduce German power.[4] The Milner committee also reported back within a fortnight, but it failed to decide anything of substance, influenced as it was by the likelihood of Russia's withdrawal from the war and the possibility of having to accept an unsatisfactory peace.[5]

Both reports were debated at length in the full Imperial War Cabinet on April 26 and May 1. Lloyd George was disappointed with the Curzon report, which seemed to have lost sight of why the war was being fought. As he had stated recently, Britain's primary objective was to break the militarists' grip over Germany, restore the balance of power in Europe and set up democratic governments wherever possible. The acquisition of overseas territory was therefore of secondary importance. That was apparent when he urged that the government scale down its territorial objectives so as not to deny the French and the Russians – both of whom had suffered heavily in the war – a fair share of the spoils. Faced with incessant annexationist demands, Lloyd George found himself in a quandary. After all his fanfare of promising to heed to the voices of the Dominions, he could hardly turn his back on their advice. His only escape from his dilemma was to gain freedom of maneuver. Calling upon his formidable forensic skills, he amended the Curzon committee's conclusions with a proviso that they serve as guidelines, rather than definitive instructions, to the British delegation at the peace conference that would be required to correlate the demands of His Majesty's Government with those of its allies. The resolution passed with Henderson casting the only dissenting vote.

Lloyd George was equally unhappy with the work of the Milner committee, not the least because it shrugged off the idea of a league of nations and had not dealt at all with the question of disarmament or the limitation of armaments. He wrote in his memoirs, "I thought that there would be great disappointment if it were thought that at the end of the War nothing could be done in these directions."[6] The prime minister read a statement that was designed to cover both aspects of the terms of peace – which the Milner and Curzon's Committees had attempted to deal with. After some discussion, the Imperial War Cabinet reached the conclusion that the policy of the British Empire should have the following ends in view:

- The re-establishment of liberty and public right in Europe and on the high seas, the settlement of the political boundaries of Europe in accordance with the wishes of its people, and the liberation of the oppressed nationalities of the Turkish Empire from the Turkish yoke.
- The security and integrity of the Empire and of the nations of which it is composed.
- The framing of measures for the preservation of lasting peace in concert with our Allies.[7]

It was apparent from the discussions and reports that the prime minister and the other members of the War Cabinet disagreed among themselves as to what Britain should strive to achieve in the war. Still, all would have agreed that the war aims they advocated were not of equal importance. Professor Brock Millman has placed Britain's war aims essentially in three categories that he identifies as "permanent," "conditional" and "contingent." A permanent war aim was one considered essential. Failure to attain, say, the liberation of Belgium, would have been akin to a British defeat. Acquiring a conditional objective, such the creation of a Polish state, would have been welcomed, but not considered vital. A contingent war aim was something that could be used as a bargaining chip at the peace conference. That noted, it should be pointed out that war aims were not etched in stone and tended to change depending on how the war was apt to end. If a decisive victory was anticipated, the list of conditional aims was extensive. On the other hand, if there was cause for a negotiated peace, such as was currently contemplated by the prime minister, these aims required clarification and reduction. Lastly, when there was a distinct possibility of a military defeat, even permanent war aims were consigned to the conditional category.[8]

Lloyd George worried that the differences between Britain's desire for overseas territories and President Wilson's distaste for imperialism would be a barrier to close Anglo–American cooperation. Wilson's objectives were not the same as those of the Allies. Earlier, as we have seen, he sought a compromise peace that would have left Germany in a strong position and able, if it so chose, to resume the war at a later date. As might be expected, his views underwent a change after America became a belligerent. He now took a hard line against Germany, accusing it of trying to extend a wide swath "of military power and political control across the very center of Europe and beyond the Mediterranean into the heart of Asia." He warned that German expansionism must be stopped, otherwise "America will fall within the menace." He went on to say, "We and all the rest of the world must remain armed, as they will remain, and must make ready for the next step in their aggression."[9]

Although President Wilson shared Britain's abhorrence of Prussian militarism, he was intent on imposing freedom of the seas, was unconcerned about restoring the balance of power in Europe and had no sympathy whatsoever for the Entente's territorial ambitions. Wilson's announced policy was that the United States was fighting the war not for conquest or domination, but to make the world safe for democracy. As if to underline that America was in the war for its own reasons, he refrained from signing the Pact of London (under which France, Russia and Britain pledged not to make a separate peace) and was adamant that his country would act as an associate, not as an ally, of the Entente. Unencumbered by formal diplomatic ties, Wilson was free to set his own conditions, which the Allies could not flaunt without jeopardizing the flow of United States assistance. Indeed, under the right circumstances Wilson might well have risked a rupture with the Allies. In his speeches he made it clear that the United States did not seek punitive damages and that a fair settlement was open to Germany if its people overthrew their military masters, renounced wars of conquest and withdrew from occupied territories. According to Arthur S. Link, had moderate forces in the Reichstag gained the ascendancy, "Wilson almost certainly would have responded eagerly, even if Allied refusal to cooperate had resulted in a separate peace between Germany and the United States."[10]

For Lloyd George, the challenge was to find the right balancing act, one that would satisfy the annexationists at home and in the Dominions without appearing to bear the stamp of selfish imperialism and incurring a costly American reception. The first tentative steps were taken by Balfour while he was on a mission to Washington. He met Wilson and his trusted confidante, Colonel Edward House, in the closing days of April and together they discussed peace terms at length. Balfour disclosed British objectives in Europe and the Near East in a general way, as well as details of the secret territorial arrangements the Allies had made among themselves. He made no mention, however, of the "British Empire's interest in the conquered German colonies, a matter not covered in the secret treaties."[11]

Although President Wilson did not consider the United States bound by the secret treaties, he did not raise objections to the annexationist aims of the Allies. He never thought of using the matter of American support as a club to force a revision of these treaties. He understood that any attempt on his part to modify the Entente's war aims would be divisive and seriously weaken the anti-German coalition. As he saw it, the most immediate goal was to defeat Germany, by which time America's ever-growing military power would allow him to dominate peace negotiations and impose his liberal program on the vanquished as well as on the victors. Wilson felt he could afford to bide his time. His indifferent response to the secret treaties came as welcomed news to the War Cabinet.

Lloyd George, however, found it more difficult to reconcile territorial differences with Paris. The British invasion of Palestine had aroused French fears that they might lose the rights to Syria that they had established under the Sykes–Picot Agreement. Just as London began to lay plans to erect a permanent structure of British power in Mesopotamia after the fall of Baghdad, so it desired a similar arrangement for Palestine once Jerusalem was occupied.[12] Lloyd George was concerned that if the war should end in a *status quo* peace, Germany, rumored to be tightening its hold over Turkey, would be well positioned to threaten Britain's eastern empire. To head off such a contingency, he was determined that Britain should acquire Palestine as a secure bulwark for Egypt. Sir Francis Bertie (British ambassador in Paris) reminded Lloyd George during one of his visits to Paris, of the influence France exerted in greater Syria and that Ribot, although a Protestant, was certain to be under pressure from nationalists and the Catholic Church to resist the establishment of a British Protectorate over Palestine. To which Lloyd George replied, "We shall be there by right of conquest and shall remain, we being of no particular faith and the only power fit to rule Mohammedans, Jews, Roman Catholics, and all religions."[13]

When Lloyd George sent Mark Sykes, a recognized expert on the Middle East, to act as General Murray's chief political officer, he warned him not to enter into any commitments that would stand in the way of Britain's acquisition of Palestine.[14] But a necessary component of the prime minister's design was to renegotiate the Sykes–Picot Agreement, which had called for Palestine to be placed under an international administration. The War Cabinet discussed the issue on April 25 and, not surprisingly, the consensus was that Palestine, instead of being internationalized, ought to come under British control. Lloyd George pointed out that at the last conference with the French, his hint at such an arrangement had met a cold reception. The War Cabinet concluded that the provision in Sykes–Picot Agreement relating to Palestine might have to be abrogated but that no action should be taken for the time being.[15]

The ministers had good reason to believe that there was no hurry to reach an accommodation with the French. In Palestine the British drive had been halted at Gaza and it was understood that further operations would be difficult. With the Russian army no longer able to apply pressure in the Caucasus, the British in the east would be facing the entire Turkish army, estimated at half a million men. Robertson was better disposed towards Palestine than any of the other sideshows, but he was not willing to send over the divisions required to defeat the Turks, and the War Cabinet, contrary to Lloyd George's pleas, refused to overrule military advice.

British prospects in Mesopotamia were only slightly better. Maude's men had captured Baghdad, but owing to the summer heat, had temporarily suspended operations. Further progress was not a forgone conclusion, however, as they would soon be facing an enemy strengthened by the addition of troops from the Russian front. Fueling British anxiety were repeated warnings from a variety of sources that the Turks were assembling a large army for an attack on Baghdad in the autumn.[16] As in Palestine, Robertson was prepared to provide Maude with just enough additional manpower to allow him to hold his own. Given the uncertain outlook in the two theaters, Lloyd George was slowly being driven to the idea of negotiations with the Turks, in which case the British would be required to scale down their claims in the Middle East.

The impetus for a separate peace with Turkey came mostly from the Foreign Office. Taking for granted the demise of the Straits Agreement, senior officials felt that it was possible to end the war in the east by making symbolic concessions to the Turks. They had been encouraged by the outcome of informal talks held between Aubrey Herbert and certain Turkish elements,[17] one of whom was a close friend of the Grand Vizier (prime minister). Herbert reported that according to his informants, the Turkish authorities would be willing to make peace if the Allies abandoned some of their annexationist aims. The implementation of only part of the Sykes–Picot Agreement seemed a small price to pay for an end to Turkish belligerency.[18]

Lloyd George shuddered at the prospect of allowing the Turks to continue as a ruling race in view of their barbaric policy to exterminate the Armenian population and their abhorrent treatment of prisoners. Set against this consideration was that neither Turkey nor Germany showed signs of wilting and there was no certainty that both could be defeated. But peace with Turkey, no matter how odious, would relieve Britain of a heavy military, naval and financial drain and bring fresh resources to bear against other members of the Central Powers. As it turned out, Lloyd George did not have a say in the matter. Foreign Office efforts to draw the Turks to the negotiating table went unanswered. Apparently, the Turkish authorities were divided as to whether they should seek a separate peace.[19]

All this talk of a compromise peace, spurred on by the imminent defection of Russia, dismayed some War Cabinet members who did not share Lloyd George's pessimism. To Smuts, in particular, a settlement short of victory was the same as a defeat. He conceded that Russia's infirmity was a serious blow and even suspected that the nadir of the Entente's fortunes had not yet been reached. He did not exclude the possibility that France would leave the war if Germany offered to return Alsace–Lorraine in part or in whole. But in his view, even if that should happen, "we shall continue to hold very strong cards and should under no circumstances contemplate a disastrous peace." He claimed that Britain's world leadership in trade and communications, combined with the incomparable resources in matériel and manpower of America, "should enable us in the end to bring Germany to terms favorable to us."[20]

The War Cabinet held a long secret meeting at 10 Downing Street on July 31 to discuss future Allied prospects. Most of the members, like Smuts, remained steadfast, even though the signs were not hopeful. It was pointed out that the elimination of Russia would give the Central Powers a substantial numerical advantage on the western front and all but rule out an Allied victory. A suggestion was made that the Allies might consider reducing the number of their adversaries through negotiations so that they could concentrate all their resources against Germany. Such an option would require a readjustment of claims by some Allied nations and even abandonment of them by others. The possibility of detaching one or more of Germany's allies in exchange for only modest political concessions appealed to both Curzon and Robertson. There was a general feeling, however, that modification of war aims by itself would be insufficient and that if Germany's allies were to be induced to make a separate peace, it would be necessary, before opening the talks, to inflict a military defeat on them.[21]

The War Cabinet meeting broke up without a decision to revise war aims or enter into serious peace negotiations. In fact, it deliberately avoided doing so. Haig's much-anticipated offensive at Passchendaele had been launched just hours before the meeting. The War Cabinet did not intend to take a position until the outcome of the battle were known.

As the first phase of the campaign approached its end without coming near to accomplishing any of Haig's larger objectives, Pope Benedict XV made another appeal to the heads of the belligerent states, offering his mediation in a quest to end the process of mutual self-destruction.[22] Early discussion in the War Cabinet centered on whether the Allies ought to again make a public declaration of their war aims. There was little support for that option. It was pointed out that the Entente's reply to President Wilson's peace initiative in December 1916 had been used by the Central Powers to prove that their enemies' war aims were imperialistic and grasping. Nor did the idea of convening a conference to revise the secret treaties gain any traction. The reasoning was that the moment a particular ally was asked to reduce its war aims, there was a danger that it would relax its efforts. The War Cabinet decided to sit tight and wait for the Germans to reply to the Pope's note. If their terms included the evacuation of Belgium, it would mark an advance on their part towards a settlement. If, on the contrary, they showed no such intention, "it would prove that no basis whatsoever for discussion existed."[23]

There was a sense, quite erroneously, that the Vatican was not striving to be neutral and that its proposals had been inspired, directly or indirectly, by the Central Powers.[24] That aside, there was not much enthusiasm for a patched-up peace that would have left the militarist clique more firmly in control of the German government than ever. In the back of everybody's mind was the feeling that they really had no choice but to fight on, even though victory was far from assured. Lloyd George likened the Pope's proposals to a sort of a truce, "a slightly more lasting peace of Amiens,[25] with the war to be renewed on the first pretext when nations had rested and re-equipped."[26] On the whole, the War Cabinet was not optimistic that the Pope's plan would form a good basis for negotiation, since it was unlikely to meet the expectations of the belligerents.

On August 21 Balfour informed the Vatican that as a precondition for peace negotiations, Germany had to clearly define its war aims, particularly its intention to liberate Belgium as well as to compensate it for damages caused by the war. The British note was passed on to Berlin where it was interpreted as a cautious peace feeler. The German foreign minister, Richard von Kühlmann, concluded that while the question of Alsace–Lorraine precluded an agreement with France, a compromise with Britain might succeed. He deluded himself into believing that if Germany promised to liberate Belgium, Britain, in turn, was likely to press France to renounce its claim to the lost provinces. At the very least, Kühlmann hoped to drive a wedge between the two Allied powers.[27]

While the German reply to the Pope's initiative was courteous but evasive, Kühlmann decided, with the approval of the German chancellor, Georg Michaelis, to open a new neutral channel to sound out the British government. He selected as an intermediary with London, an old friend from earlier days and a highly respected diplomat, the Marquis de Villalobar, Spanish ambassador to Brussels.[28]

The German peace initiative came as a bombshell in London. On September 20 Balfour prepared a memorandum for the prime minister on the subject. Although suspicious of German motives, he opposed an outright rejection on the following grounds: that it would unite Germans in favor of the war and, conversely, have an adverse effect on public opinion at home, which would resent what seemed like "an unreasonable determination to fight for fighting's sake." He advised against secret bilateral conversations with the Germans lest Britain's allies suspect that the Lloyd George government was prepared to abandon them. To avoid any misconceptions, he requested authorization to call together the Allied ambassadors to inform them of the German peace approach.[29]

Lloyd George was in Criccieth in North Wales for a brief spell of rest when he learned of the latest diplomatic development on September 22. He raced back to London the next day and conferred with Balfour, who explained that the Germans, parallel with their overtures to London, had informally approached the ex-French premier, Aristide Briand, with a promise to return Alsace–Lorraine if guaranteed negotiations on favorable terms. Oscar von der Lancken, head of the German political section in Brussels, had contacted Briand through intermediaries and suggested that he should meet with a high-level German representative in Switzerland to discuss peace possibilities. Ribot immediately notified London about the Lancken feeler and suggested that it be rejected.[30] As Paul Cambon, the French ambassador to London, handed Balfour the letter meant for Lloyd George, he discussed its contents. Unknown to the French, the German offer did not have official roots. Lancken had acted on his own initiative, without authorization from either Kühlmann or Michaelis.[31]

The German approach came at a time when the war was not going well for the Entente. The Passchendaele offensive, still in progress, was costing the

British army dearly and had yet to produce tangible gains. Early in September, General L. G. Kornilov had tried unsuccessfully to overthrow the Kerensky government, which he blamed for the breakdown of discipline in the Russian army. For many in Britain, Kornilov's counterrevolutionary movement had represented the last chance to save Russia. In view of the darkening military situation, Lloyd George was highly attracted to what was apparently a generous peace feeler from Berlin.

The War Cabinet met on September 24 to discuss the German peace initiative. Balfour gave an account of the German offers made to both the British and French governments. He thought that the Germans presented conditions that were so favorable to the French and British that he could not help but be suspicious of their motives. Their suggested terms included the following: return of Alsace–Lorraine to France, evacuation of Belgium and Serbia, territorial compensation to Italy and colonial concessions to Britain.

Conspicuously absent was any reference to Russia. It was difficult to avoid the conclusion that the Germans were offering the western Allies generous peace terms in return for a free hand in the east. A long discussion followed Balfour's opening statement. There was disagreement among the members as to whether Britain should inform its allies about Germany's proffered terms. Bonar Law suggested that a decision on this point should be postponed until the French had been consulted. He argued that Britain could not afford to ignore the German peace feeler in view of Russia's possible withdrawal from the war. Lloyd George thought that Robertson should be asked to investigate whether Britain, with Russia out of the war, would be able to achieve its objective by means of the blockade. If the War Cabinet determined that the prospects of success would be destroyed by a Russian collapse, then, in his opinion, they should consider the terms offered to the French. He was convinced that Germany wanted to acquire Courland (in Latvia) and Lithuania and "to make some arrangement in regard to Poland as her spoils of war." Until it could be ascertained what the Germans intended to propose, he favored no communication with Britain's allies.

Milner and Balfour thought that Britain would be accused of perfidy if it became known that it carried on peace discussions without consulting its allies. Lloyd George, evidently recognizing the merit of their arguments, retreated slightly and suggested taking Italy, promised territorial concessions (when it joined the Entente), into their confidence. But he adamantly opposed notifying the Russians, who were certain to object to any settlement at their expense. It was incongruous, he insisted, to bring in Russia at a time when important sections of the country were discussing the possibility of a separate peace. Curzon supported Balfour's position that all the Allies were entitled to be told of the German peace proposal, prompting Lloyd George to return to the charge. He pointed out that it was no use regarding the present conditions as the same as when France and Britain entered into agreements with Russia, implying that it had to pay a price for letting "us down."

Milner warned that any compromise settlement would leave Germany more powerful than when it entered the war, with the result that there would be another conflict in ten years' time. That observation made an impression on Bonar Law and George Barnes (who had replaced Henderson as the Labour representative), both of whom opted for continuing the war if there was a reasonable chance of success. Lloyd George endorsed their views on condition that the CIGS gave assurances "that we could smash Germany, with Russia out of the war and the blockade gone." Before the meeting broke up, it was decided to withhold any communication with Britain's allies pending the result of the prime minister's upcoming talks with Painlevé.[32]

The meeting had revealed that a fundamental split existed between the prime minister and his foreign minister. Balfour held the hope that Russia would be able to muddle through, and thus continue to tie down a sizeable segment of the German army. His plea that Moscow should be informed of all communications with Germany was driven more by pragmatic reasons than by concern of a peace at Russia's expense. He thought that Germany's main war aims lay in the west, not the east, and that it was certain to inform Moscow of any Anglo–French overtures to Berlin, provoking Russia into leaving the war in disgust. If that should occur, Germany would be able to concentrate all of its forces in the west for a smashing blow.

On the other hand, Lloyd George saw an opportunity to end the war on terms that would satisfy his government, with Russia paying the price. The alternative was "defeat or an unbroken stalemate that sapped the treasure and manpower of Britain and the Empire." But any negotiations with the Germans also carried immense political and military risks. Balfour had already pointed out the hazard that would flow from a breakup of the alliance, and there were pitfalls at home as well. Lloyd George had many political enemies waiting to attack him the moment he made a slip. He had been brought to power because of his commitment to total victory. If the public learned that he was not fulfilling his mandate, the ensuing uproar might topple his government.[33]

That evening Lloyd George crossed the Channel and the following day held a private conversation with Painlevé at Boulogne. Painlevé told Lloyd George that he was uncertain of what Berlin was prepared to offer, because Briand had fluctuated in his account of its terms. One moment he claimed that Germany was prepared to give up Belgium and Alsace–Lorraine, and the next that it was merely willing to discuss their future. Painlevé was inclined to think that the offer was genuine and for that reason, he and the other French ministers were unwilling to enter into any peace negotiations at this stage.

They feared that that the war-weary French people would not continue to fight if it were known that Alsace–Lorraine could be recovered by peaceful means.[34] Lloyd George expressed similar fears about his countrymen and claimed to fully share Painlevé's decision to disregard the German peace feeler. But in professing to adopt a hard line towards Germany, Lloyd George was being disingenuous. In fact, he did not want to rule out peace talks, preferring to follow the Lancken–Briand channel, as the unofficial probe would have meant acting in concert only with the French. What he did not know was that the French government intended to prevent Briand from conferring with Lancken in Switzerland.

The French were not the only ones who objected to a compromise peace. In Britain, the king, much of the British press, Unionist backbenchers and Asquithian Liberals, opposed any settlement that would have left intact the autocratic faction that ruled Germany. In fact, even in the War Cabinet, Lloyd George stood practically alone. But it was not in Lloyd George's nature to give up easily. While on a visit to France, he sought to redress the balance by eliciting the support of Haig and Robertson, the two soldiers whose views he normally held in utter contempt.

Accompanied by Robertson and Hankey, Lloyd George drove to Haig's headquarters near St. Omer on September 26. The prime minister outlined Berlin's terms and while admitting that it would leave the German Empire stronger, doubted that the British people would "fight to win for Russia, what she herself was unwilling to fight for." He asked the C-in-C for his views. Haig dismissed the thought that Britain should desert Russia. Buoyed by a recent attack (during the later phase of the slogging match at Passchendaele) that had achieved its modest objective without sustaining heavy casualties, Haig claimed that the Germans were worn out and reduced to keeping men of inferior quality in the fighting line. His advice was to continue pounding them until they cracked. Robertson was not as sanguine. As he was beginning to have doubts that the war against Germany could be carried to a successful conclusion, he adopted the same line as the prime minister.[35] He thought that if Russia succumbed, the chances of winning were practically gone. He emphasized that in view of the inactivity of the Russians, French and Italians, the British army could not single-handedly defeat the Germans. Before leaving, Lloyd George obtained Haig's consent to submit a memorandum assessing Britain's prospects in the event of a Russian collapse.[36] Exactly what Lloyd George's deeper purpose was must remain a matter of conjecture, but on the surface it made no sense to request in writing what he already knew.[37]

When Lloyd George returned to London he learned, to his horror, that Asquith had declared, during a speech in Leeds, that he assumed, as a matter of course, that Britain's war aims included the enemy's evacuation of the occupied territories of France and Russia.[38] "If Germany is asked to surrender all her gains on the East as well as to retrocede Alsace–Lorraine," Lloyd George lamented to C. P. Scott, editor of the *Manchester Guardian*, "she will fight on for years and, with access to the cornfields of Russia, she can do it."[39] Lloyd George's distrust of Asquith bordered on paranoia, scenting in his every irregular activity, a plot to oust him from 10 Downing Street. Shortly before his speech on war aims, Asquith had crossed over to France and taken the time to visit Haig, with whom he was on excellent terms. The proximity of the two events led Lloyd George to suspect that Asquith, in collusion with Haig, was laying the groundwork for a push to replace him in case he should retreat from the his announced policy of total victory.[40] What he did not realize was that the Foreign Office had instigated the affair to undercut any negotiations with Berlin. Sir Eric Drummond, Balfour's private secretary, had informed Asquith of Lloyd George's train of thought and encouraged him to make the speech at Leeds.[41] Drummond, a good friend and former secretary of Asquith, had presumably acted at the behest of Balfour, who had joined hands with Paul Cambon, French ambassador to London, to frustrate Lloyd George's designs .[42]

At the War Cabinet on September 27, Lloyd George reported the gist of his conversation with Painlevé and then proceeded to denounce Asquith for what he considered were injudicious remarks in Leeds. He had ascertained during his trip that the French were not making much of an effort to help Haig and he was certain that they would not be prepared "to go on fighting for Russia, if the Russians would not fight for themselves." He pointed out that at Haig's headquarters on the previous day, Robertson had said outright that if Russia succumbed, "we could not inflict a military defeat on Germany." The prime minister did not reveal Haig's views, stating simply that he had asked the field marshal "to send his considered opinion on the subject." Try as he might, Lloyd George could not rouse much interest among his colleagues for a compromise peace with Germany. Only Carson gave him (lukewarm) support. Balfour led the opposition. The main counterarguments were: that the danger of Russia dropping out of the war would no longer be in doubt if it found out that Britain and France were prepared to make peace at its expense, and that the British people would not accept a peace settlement that left Germany in a powerful position and able to launch another war at a later date.[43]

The setback Lloyd George encountered in the War Cabinet was followed by a damaging article in an influential conservative daily, the *Morning Post*, whose editor evidently had received inside information about the German peace approach. Under the provocative headline, "PEACE OR VICTORY," it issued a clear warning to the government: "The business of our statesmen and of the nation is to see that the blood of our soldiers is not wasted nor their courage betrayed. ... If our politicians were now to make peace with an undefeated enemy, it would make our captains sick, and our dead would turn in their serried graves."[44] The decisive blow, however, came from Balfour, who had been adamant that talks with Germany should not take place except in concert with the Allies.[45] On October 4 he informed Washington of the German peace proposals and two days later summoned the Entente representatives in London to the Foreign Office where he repeated the news and asked them whether they approved of his reply via Madrid that the British government would listen to any German communication on peace and discuss it with its allies. No one dissented.[46]

Berlin did not respond to the British note. Even if the British had agreed to independent talks, Kühlmann could not have met their precondition. He had been forbidden by the German government to make a declaration guaranteeing the integrity of Belgium. The overpowering team of Hindenburg and Ludendorff was prepared to renounce the coast of Belgium, but not its hinterland.[47] On October 9 Kühlmann slammed the peace door shut when he delivered an angry speech to the Reichstag. He categorically refused to make any concessions on Alsace–Lorraine, and was unclear about German intentions on the question of Belgium.[48] In hindsight, it is apparent that Germany, confident in its military leaders and in the invincibility of its armies, was in no mood to surrender part of its territory and valued conquests as the price for peace. Kühlmann had used deception to prolong the life of the peace move in an attempt to promote suspicion and create dissention among the Allied powers. The British had acted properly by refusing to take the bait. Lloyd George had misjudged the willingness of Germany's leaders to negotiate a settlement based on British terms.

Since neither peace nor peace talks were in the offing, Lloyd George saw no alternative but to pursue the war energetically. The outlook was not promising. The Entente had not won a great victory since the Marne and its fortunes were currently at a low ebb. Germany, although experiencing mounting internal difficulties, still possessed a powerful army and its population was stubborn and resilient. Lloyd George did not expect the Allies to be able to deliver a single knockout blow, but felt that a combination of factors might erode Germany's strength and compel it to submit. The Entente was in a position to attack not only Germany, but its allies as well. The blockade continued to seal off Germany from acquiring imports and the shortage of food was affecting its civilian morale. By using their various weapons, the Allies might apply sufficient pressure to induce the Germans to come to terms. Lloyd George did not expect that this objective could be reached before 1919. Time was needed to permit the Americans to concentrate sizeable detachments in the field, to restore the morale of the French army and perhaps to revitalize the Russian army.

Lloyd George had no wish to see the United States emerge as the strongest military power at the end of the war. To that end, he was determined to do whatever was necessary to prevent the British army from being bled white in futile attacks. What he had in mind was a series of set-piece operations that would wear down and immobilize the Germans in the west, forestalling them from finishing off the Russians. The application of limited objectives, the so-called Pétain's tactics,[49] would pay dividends without the huge loss of life involved in Haig's ambitious operations. At the same time, every effort would be made to detach or defeat Germany's allies. With Germany's strength being sapped steadily, the Entente would be ready in 1919 for an all-out push that would win the war, though perhaps not by a knockout.[50]

1. Lloyd George in 1916, shortly before he became prime minister (National Army Museum)

2. Lloyd George in 1917 (U.S. Army Military Institute)

3. Cartoon showing Lloyd George's optimism in the face of the nation's war-time shortages (from *Punch*, September 5, 1917)

4. Lloyd George, Milner and Kerr walking near Walton Heath
(Parliamentary Archives)

5. Robertson (U.S. Army Military Institute)

6. Haig (U.S. Army Military Institute)

7. Lloyd George with Briand in 1917 (author's collection)

8. Foch (Library of Congress)

9. Pétain (Library of Congress)

10. Clemenceau (Library of Congress)

11. Pershing (Library of Congress)

12. Woodrow Wilson (Library of Congress)

13. Cartoon showing Wilson mystified as to why the belligerents are not attracted to the concept of peace without victory implied in his Fourteen Points (from *Punch*, January 31, 1917)

14. Robertson (far left) and Lloyd George (seated on far right) are enjoying a picnic with their French hosts near Beauvais (from Frances Lloyd George, 1918, *The Years That Are Past*)

15. Lloyd George with his wife, daughter Megan and Hughes, leaving the Abbey after the service (National Army Museum)

16. Lloyd George, Wilson and Foch en route to the Supreme Allied War Council, 1918 (Parliamentary Archives)

17. Lloyd George, Smuts and Hankey in Paris, November 1918
(from Stephen Roskill, *Hankey: Man of Secrets*)

18. Lloyd George and Clemenceau taken during the discussion of the peace treaty (from Lloyd George, *War Memoirs*)

Chapter 11

THE CREATION OF THE SUPREME WAR COUNCIL

With the fortunes of the Entente growing bleaker as 1917 wore on, Lloyd George was too shrewd a politician to take popular feeling for granted. He acted as his own minister of morale. Quite apart from adopting measures designed to pacify labor and maintain the amenities of everyday life, he assiduously heeded Bonar Law's dictum that "in war it is necessary not only to be active but to seem active."[1] During the Second World War, Churchill's voice could reach practically every British household and so his leadership became more personal, but twenty-five years earlier films were silent and the radio was not readily available to the public. The means that Lloyd George used to project an image of a dynamic man of action, single-mindedly committed to winning the war, were not novel, but it is doubtful if anyone else could have combined them to greater effect. With indefatigable energy, he dashed from place to place, addressing crowds, visiting British General Headquarters and attending inter-Allied conferences. Wherever he went, he made certain that a bevy of reporters and photographers were on hand to tout and record his activities. While there were occasions in the darkest of days when he spoke confidentially to his associates that the war was unwinnable, he never gave the least hint of discouragement in public. His vitality and buoyancy were contagious, imbuing the public with determination and confidence in ultimate victory.

During the fall of 1917 Lloyd George became more determined than ever to alter the lines along which the war was being fought. To that end, he surveyed other options and concluded that a supreme effort should be made to knock Turkey out of the war. The success of such an operation would not end the war, but it would boost morale at home, protect Britain's imperial interests in the Middle and Far East and strengthen the government's hand in the event that the war ended inconclusively. Lloyd George had in mind a landing at Alexandretta in conjunction with British drives from Mesopotamia and Palestine.

The scheme to isolate Turkey from its forces in Mesopotamia and Palestine by a thrust from Alexandretta was not novel. It had first been contemplated in December 1914, but was laid aside when the Dardanelles operation got under way.[2] The idea was revived in the fall of 1915 as a means to cushion the political impact of the Allied withdrawal from the Dardanelles, but quickly rejected by the General Staff as almost certain to face strong Turkish opposition.[3] Since then, the number of Turkish troops that could be brought to the area in a timely fashion had declined, but they were undefeated and still capable of resistance. Additionally, there were other factors that rendered the plan unsound. Enemy submarines, practically nonexistent in the Mediterranean during the first year of the war, now infested these waters. According to War Office estimates, the amphibious operation would require about eight divisions and even if these could be scrapped together, it would have been impossible for the Admiralty to transport them all at once to their destination when it was currently at its wits' end to find ships for the thousands of American soldiers waiting to cross the Atlantic, as well as to supply British troops in France and in distant theaters. Lastly, there was no guarantee that anything of significance could be achieved. Had the landing force been unable to break out of its beachhead, it ran the risk of uselessly draining resources, just like the Allied army at Salonica.[4]

Disregarding all but the obvious difficulties, Lloyd George considered the plan feasible. As far as he was concerned, only two obstacles had to be overcome: one was manpower and the other was transportation. Accordingly, he turned to the War Policy Committee, which he reconvened on September 24. Robertson's views about sideshows were well known and so he confined his remarks to the operation itself. He claimed that British troops would have to land quickly – not necessarily because of initial resistance, since intelligence had revealed that there was only one enemy division in the immediate vicinity – as the Turks could bring 70,000 to 80,000 troops to the region within a fortnight. Naval experts argued that they could not provide the ships to land all eight divisions simultaneously at Alexandretta, but they could arrange to carry them in stages. The question of manpower proved more difficult to resolve. Lloyd George doubted that the Turks, with fronts in Mesopotamia and Palestine, could put 70,000 to 80,000 men in the field to oppose an Allied landing. He felt certain that the French, determined to protect their interests in the Levant, would be more than willing to participate, possibly with as many as eight divisions.[5]

Once again, Lloyd George was guilty of tunnel vision. He overlooked the fact that the French, given the state of their army and already being engaged at Salonica and on the western front, might refuse to take on another military commitment. He received a rude shock at the Anglo–French conference on

September 25 when he invited Foch to speak about the prospects in the Turkish theater. The French general claimed to find seductive the idea of British forces driving forward simultaneously in Palestine and Mesopotamia and finishing off the Turkish army by a thrust from Alexandretta. However, he doubted that under the circumstances the ambitious operation could succeed. The British army in Mesopotamia could not advance towards Mosul owing to the quiescence of the Russians in the Caucasus. The one in Palestine might eventually reach Jerusalem but it could not push forward rapidly because of insufficient railroads and manpower. That being the case, the Turks would be able to concentrate a powerful army to oppose any landing on the coast. As a sop to Lloyd George, he would not rule out the operation at a later date, possibly for the summer of 1918, if conditions were favorable. Lloyd George asked whether the moment would not be opportune for an attack at Alexandretta in the event the Turks were seriously embroiled in Mesopotamia and facing a British assault from the south. Foch replied that if the forces in Palestine were to advance and those in Mesopotamia were to hold their own in a big engagement, and if there was some activity on the Russian front, it might be worthwhile to land troops at Alexandretta on the understanding that they were intended to exploit a success and not fight a fresh battle.[6] The many qualifications Foch laid down amounted to a veto of France's participation in the projected operation.

The French were undoubtedly hoping that their lack of support would deter the British from moving ahead with plans to land at Alexandretta. Quite apart from the troops that would be diverted from the western front to the Middle East, they had no wish to see the British occupy the whole area, even though under the Sykes–Picot Agreement they had been promised Greater Syria (present day Syria and Lebanon).[7] They knew only too well that physical possession mattered a great deal and their realization that the British wanted to renegotiate the inter-Allied arrangement seemed to confirm their worst fears.

As already noted, the War Cabinet was eager to bring Palestine, a vital strategic asset in safeguarding the approaches to Egypt, under British control. The Sykes–Picot Agreement had also granted the British southern Mesopotamia and a stretch of Palestine's coastline, including Haifa and Jaffa, but Jerusalem and the rest of Palestine were to be placed under an international administration. Much had changed in the war against Turkey since the Sykes–Picot Agreement had been signed, and as a result, Lloyd George no longer felt bound by its terms. The problem was that the French refused to even consider renegotiating the previous arrangement.[8] Lloyd George's challenge was to find a way to undo the troubling features of the Sykes–Picot treaty without breaking faith with the French. In these circumstances, he became committed to a Zionist proposal that the British government should make a public commitment to support a homeland for the Jewish people in Palestine.

Lloyd George was introduced to Zionism in 1903 when, as an attorney, he represented the movement as it sought to define itself under its founder, Dr. Theodore Herzl.[9] As far as we know, he had no personal interest in Zionism during its formative stage. Nor is there evidence that he held any special feelings for Jews, one way or the other. In common with others of his class and time, he occasionally made pejorative references about Jews that by today's standards would be labeled racist. But passing jibes in conversation or correspondence about any ethic group should not be taken too seriously and it can be stated without qualification that he was not an anti-Semite. Indeed, as a Welsh nationalist reared on the bible, the vision of Zionism tended to appeal to his romanticism.[10]

Turkey's belligerency at the start of November 1914 gave an extra impulse to the Zionist goal of reuniting the Jews with the land of their forefathers. On the assumption that the Turks would be defeated, the Asquith cabinet had committed itself to the revolutionary path of partitioning their Empire at the end of the war. Early in 1915 Herbert Samuel, the first Jew to sit in a British cabinet, urged the development of a Jewish homeland in Palestine under British auspices. Lloyd George found the idea attractive, less on philosophical grounds than on the belief that it would serve the strategic interests of the British Empire.[11] But neither Asquith nor Grey, the foreign secretary, favored adding more territory to the British Empire and so the Zionist project occupied no place on the British cabinet's agenda for the next two years, until after Lloyd George came to power.

Undaunted by the attitude of the Asquith cabinet, Zionists concentrated on trying to win over individual ministers to their cause. While at the Ministry of Munitions, Lloyd George had reason to be grateful to Dr. Chaim Weizmann, a brilliant scientist who discovered a cheap process to obtain acetone, a vital ingredient in the production of high explosives. In declining rewards for his own services, Weizmann, a fervent Zionist, pleaded that Lloyd George do something for his people. Years later Lloyd George wrote that his sponsorship of a Jewish national home in the Middle East was in gratitude for Weizmann's war work.[12] Weizmann's contributions were undeniable, but Lloyd George's claim was a piece of fiction.[13] In fact, Lloyd George had no clear policy in regard to Palestine until events forced him to make a choice.[14]

Lloyd George intended to retain possession of Palestine for Britain as soon as the fighting was over, calculating that the French would have no option but to accept this as a fait accompli. However, in the final days of winter and spring of 1917 two external developments compelled Lloyd George to seek a new line of approach. The March Revolution in Russia had created considerable optimism in the west that the Provisional Government would prosecute the war with renewed vigor. But it was not long before Russia was plunged into chaos and confusion and the possibility that Petrograd might seek a negotiated settlement could not be discounted. The British were under the impression that the Zionist movement in Russia, where half of the twelve million Jews in Europe lived, wielded great influence in political circles. As it happened, the Zionist movement in Russia was large enough – about 200,000 members – but it was disorganized and of no political consequence. It was more concerned with acquiring equal rights for Jews, a long persecuted minority, than with the idea of returning to a homeland in Palestine. Sir George Buchanan, the British ambassador in Petrograd, was right on the mark when he reported that the Jewish community was weak and could not possibly affect government policy.[15] But Foreign Office leaders discounted his observations. Encouraged by Weizmann and his group, they persisted in believing that a pro-Zionist declaration would rally the Russian Jews to the Allied camp and effectively block the faction agitating for a separate peace with Germany.

Similarly, it was felt in British governmental circles that an expression of sympathy for Zionist aspirations would unite American Jews, many of whom were indifferent about the outcome of the war or inclined towards Germany, and give them a stake in the Entente's victory. It was taken for granted in London that President Wilson, in keeping with his anti-imperialist policy, would oppose British annexation of Palestine. The Zionist movement in the United States was strong and its leader, Louis D. Brandeis, a lawyer of outstanding ability, was on intimate terms with the president. Allowed to use British channels, Zionists in London were in frequent contact with Brandeis, who assured them that Wilson would actively assist in the establishment of a Jewish state. The Lloyd George government hoped that Jews close to Wilson would lean on him to accept British presence in a postwar Palestine as a necessary step towards Jewish self-determination. The idea was "to provide a cloak under which Britain could appear free from any annexationist taint" and at the same time remain in control of Palestine.[16]

There remained the possibility that the French would upset the applecart by claiming that they had as much right to Palestine as the British. Mark Sykes, who had negotiated with Georges Picot the partition of much of the Ottoman Empire, had now converted to the idea that Palestine, far from being placed under international control, should be taken over by the British. With Lloyd George's blessing, he undertook diplomatic missions to Paris to lobby for French recognition of Zionist aims. The French were receptive to the argument that it would encourage Russian Jews to press the Provisional Government to remain in the war. Still, they were reluctant to commit to the proposed arrangement for the Jews, because they feared it amounted to abandoning Palestine to the

British. In negotiations with the Quai d'Orsay (French Foreign Office), Zionist leaders made no mention of the eventual suzerain power in Palestine. On the assumption that Jews were neutral on the issue, French officials relented. In June 1917 the Quai d'Orsay promised British Zionist leaders that its government would support the historic right of the Jewish people to Palestine.[17]

French assurance was followed by President Wilson's approval of the Zionist formula in mid-October. It only remained for the British government to issue its own declaration. Although the principal figures in the administration were pro-Zionists, there were several ministers who opposed the creation of a Jewish Palestine. The most vocal anti-Zionist was Edwin Montagu, an influential member of the Jewish community and secretary of state for India. Interestingly enough, he spoke for the majority of British Jews. He argued with a sense of anguish that the existence of a Jewish state would compromise the position of assimilated Jews in countries where they had established themselves as citizens. He insisted that Judaism was a religion, not a distinct nationality, and it pained him to think that the country his family fought for and that he had served since leaving the university was telling him that his natural home was Palestine.[18] "I have been striving all my life to escape from the Ghetto," he lamented to Lord Morley, a former Liberal cabinet minister.[19] Now Lloyd George, among others, wanted to force him back there. Montagu had a close ally in Curzon, who was concerned, not by the dispute between Zionist and anti-Zionist, but whether it was appropriate for the British government to raise hopes that could not be realized. How, he asked, could a desolate land without natural wealth sustain a large Jewish population? Moreover, what was to be done with the Muslims already living there?[20] Bonar Law, for his part, counseled delay in the belief that the moment was not propitious for a consideration of the Zionist program.

The opposing side was led by Balfour, the minister most committed to promoting Zionist interests. Balfour conceded that some rich Jews in Britain were opposed to the idea of a Jewish homeland. Nevertheless, it commanded the support of a majority of Jews in the United States and Russia and possibly in other countries as well. He warned that the Germans were endeavoring to capture the sympathy of the Zionist movement so as to provide themselves with a useful political instrument, particularly inside Russia. The statement was based on faulty evidence. Balfour stressed that it was vital that the British government preempt the Germans by acting without delay. Finally, in reply to Montagu's principal concern, the foreign secretary saw nothing inconsistent between the establishment of a Jewish state and the complete assimilation and absorption of Jews into the nationality of other countries.[21] Lining solidly behind Balfour were Lloyd George, Smuts and Milner. On October 31, 1917 the War Cabinet overrode the objections of Montagu and Curzon and approved a draft, known as the Balfour Declaration, in which the British government formally endorsed the establishment of a Jewish commonwealth in Palestine.[22] The Zionist experiment that Lloyd George sponsored for anticipated benefits to the Alliance and Empire would have fateful consequences. Zionist Jews reaped priceless benefits. Rootless, persecuted and the object of discrimination for centuries, they had at last acquired a national homeland, which eventually became the state of Israel. By contrast, it would prove an unmitigated disaster for the British and no less so for Palestinian Arabs. Of course, Lloyd George had no way of knowing that the route ahead was tortuous and strewn with pitfalls.

The British could not lose sight of the fact that they had to beat the Turks before they could achieve their aims with regard to the Ottoman Empire. Lloyd George's frustration with France's unwillingness to contribute troops to fight in the Middle East did not deflect him from his goal. When future strategy was discussed in the War Policy Committee on October 3, Lloyd George stated that every effort should be made to knock out Germany's allies, beginning with Turkey. He acknowledged that at present they had no such policy, but in his view the only way to win the war was to isolate Germany from its allies. He thought that a combination of diplomatic and military success might induce the Turks to negotiate a separate peace, particularly if the terms dangled were attractive. He favored offering the Turks a loan for reconstruction and protectorate status that would place Syria, Palestine and Mesopotamia under the nominal suzerainty of the sultan. Milner maintained that the best approach was to beat the Turks before offering them generous peace terms. He doubted, however, that the British public would stand for the return of Palestine and Mesopotamia to Turkey. The prime minister changed track, remarking that an impression must be made on the Turks in one place or another and that it was just as well to attack in Palestine as in Mesopotamia. Curzon favored a push in Mesopotamia where progress supposedly would be easier, but recommended that any action against the Turks be delayed until the following year. Lloyd George produced a paper by Lieutenant General Sir George Macdonogh, chief of intelligence at the War Office, which claimed that Turkish reserves were exhausted. The prime minister urged the necessity of attacking at once, before the Turks improved their railway communications. To clinch his argument, he gave a distorted version of his recent interview with Foch, whom he inferred believed that the Alexandretta enterprise was eminently feasible. The committee put off making a decision until the CIGS could be consulted.[23]

Robertson was in attendance when the War Policy Committee met again on October 5. The CIGS worried that Allenby might be tempted to push northward deep into Syria and become bogged down in a protracted campaign that absorbed precious reserves badly needed in France. Instead, he preferred that Allenby follow a prudent course and advance slowly, consolidating his position before taking the next step. Such a piecemeal advance did not appeal to Lloyd George who wanted quick results.

As Hankey was at home with a cold, unfortunately no minutes were taken. Milner saw Hankey the next day and told him that an ugly exchange had taken place between Lloyd George and Robertson. Apparently, Robertson had changed his mind and challenged the committee's earlier decision to send two divisions from France to Egypt as a reserve for either Maude or Allenby. This provoked an angry outburst from Lloyd George, who raked Robertson over the coals, dwelling on his past military advice, which he claimed had been uniformly unsound.[24] Robertson had reason to reverse himself. At Boulogne he not been able to prevent Lloyd George from agreeing in principle to the French request that the British army extend its front.[25] Haig, who was not consulted beforehand, was furious and felt that Robertson had let him down.[26] Robertson sought to assuage Haig by assuring him that "I have never yet given in on important matters and never shall. In any case, whatever happens, you and I must stand solid together."[27] The CIGS had no wish to further alienate Haig by removing two divisions from his command and risk jeopardizing his plans for next spring.

The tug-of-war between Lloyd George and Robertson over the Palestine campaign showed no signs of abating in the ensuing days. Jellicoe and Haig added their customary argument in support of Robertson. The first sea lord maintained that reinforcing secondary theaters would place an intolerable strain on Britain's dwindling shipping capacity.[28] Haig's memorandum dated October 8 amounted to an indictment of Lloyd George's war leadership and a defense of his western strategy. He was confident that if the government fulfilled his military requirements, he could defeat the Germans, regardless of whether the Russians stayed in the war. To concentrate every available man and gun in the west, he emphasized, required cutting down Britain's commitments in all other theaters to the minimum.[29]

The General Staff at the War Office had information that the Germans might move thirty divisions from Russia to the western front, making the opposing armies there almost equal numerically. Milner wondered how Haig, who thus far had made little headway, could expect to overwhelm an army reinforced by thirty divisions.[30] Lloyd George did not need to be prodded to pour venom on Haig. But it was rather disingenuous on his part to feign astonishment at what he called "this inebriated document."[31] Lloyd George must have known what to expect when he asked Haig to submit his views in writing while visiting General Headquarters a fortnight earlier – as discussed in the previous chapter. Predictably, Robertson had an opposite reaction and considered Haig's paper "splendid."[32]

At the next War Policy Committee meeting on October 8, Robertson brought along Major General Arthur Lynden-Bell, former chief of staff of the EEF under Murray, to explain why it was unlikely that Allenby could advance beyond the Jaffa–Jerusalem line. Lynden-Bell's testimony may be summarized as follows: that in view of the limitations of water and transport, the difficulties of sea communications, the absence of harbors and the dangers from submarines, little more than what was now being done was possible.[33] The next day Robertson followed up by submitting two memoranda. In the first, entitled "Future Military Policy," he claimed that Britain, fighting practically alone, did not have the resources to seek a decision on two fronts simultaneously. The first rule of war was to concentrate all available forces in the main theater. Any departure from this basic practice was a gamble that might prove fatal. The best chance of victory was to act on the defensive in the east and hammer away at the German army in France.[34] In the second paper, he laid out several alternate scenarios that the Turks might be expected to follow to counteract the British advance, and gave an estimate of the forces Allenby would require to occupy the Jaffa–Jerusalem line. He anticipated that Allenby could not rupture the Gaza–Beersheba front without a fierce engagement and then "he may have to fight at least two more such battles before Jerusalem is captured." He thought that Allenby could advance without reinforcements, but that once in Jerusalem he would need three divisions to relieve his battle-weary men. He did not exclude the possibility that he might have to send over an additional two divisions in case Allenby faced a potential threat. Robertson thought that the Turks could bring a force of about 120,000 men against Allenby, more if they abandoned Mesopotamia. He warned that it would be inviting disaster to take five divisions from the western front, not to mention the improbability of being able to supply Allenby's enlarged force. He concluded that a winter campaign, even resulting in the capture of Jerusalem, would accomplish little beyond boosting the nation's morale.[35]

Robertson's inflated assessment of the needs of EEF paled in comparison with Allenby's absurd demands. Robertson had written privately to Allenby and impressed on him that, in view of "many uncertain factors," he should not minimize his difficulties when submitting his requirements for an advance on Jerusalem. Allenby did as he was told, and in painting a troubling picture in which he might have to face practically the entire Turkish army, requested thirteen divisions in addition to his existing force of seven divisions and three cavalry divisions. The call for so many divisions could not be met, even in the unlikely event that Haig could be persuaded to remain on the defensive. Well might Robertson assure Haig that "the Palestine thing will not come off."[36]

Robertson ought to have known better than to underestimate Lloyd George's resolve. Fed up with both Haig and Robertson, the prime minister considered setting up an inter-Allied War Council as a means to end their dominance over strategy. He had secretly approached Painlevé at Boulogne on September 25 and found him receptive to the idea.[37] Before the plan could be implemented, however, there were political obstacles that needed to be overcome and the public and press had to be prepared. In the interim, Lloyd George adopted another expedient, which he unfurled in the War Cabinet on October 10.

The general view expressed at the meeting was that Haig, in his memorandum on October 8, did not provide a convincing argument that he could inflict a fatal defeat on the German army, particularly if Russia bow out of the war. The discussion centered on the relative merits of remaining on the defensive in the west in order to reinforce Allenby. It was pointed out that "a success in Palestine might lead to the elimination of Turkey from the war, bringing with it the release of great forces for service on the western front, and the opening up of direct communications through the Dardanelles and Bosphorus with Russia and Roumania." The ministers recognized, however, that any large-scale operations in the peripheral theaters must await settlement of a policy for the western front. It was then that Lloyd George proposed summoning a Council of War, as Asquith had done in August 1914.[38] Its object would be to give the War Cabinet different options from which to choose for 1918. There was a suggestion that Robertson, who was absent, was likely to be offended by the move. In reply, Lloyd George reminded the ministers that neither Sir Charles Douglas, then the CIGS, nor Sir John French, the C-in-C-designate of the BEF, had resented the Council of War that was held at the start of the conflict. The list of senior officers he proposed to invite included French and Wilson, known critics of the current military leadership. Lloyd George undoubtedly calculated that since the War Cabinet would be called upon to break the deadlock, it would be able to impose policy at long last. After the prime minister gave assurances that he would explain the matter fully to Robertson, the War Cabinet acceded to his wishes.[39]

As promised, Lloyd George called in Robertson, but the meeting ended on a sour note. Robertson regarded the summoning of a Council of War not only a breach of his compact with Kitchener, but also a vote of no confidence. He was so upset at Lloyd George's blatant maneuver to undercut him that he offered his resignation. Derby refused to accept it, explaining that the War Cabinet still possessed full confidence in his judgment. Curzon told Hankey that if Robertson's resignation took effect, he, Balfour, Cecil, Derby and Carson probably would leave as well, which would then lead to the collapse of the government. Hankey passed on Curzon's warning to Lloyd George, who "took the hint very quickly," evidently recognizing that saving his ministry was more important than forcing Robertson's resignation.[40]

At the Council of War meeting on October 11 Robertson was in attendance, as were French and Wilson. Lloyd George explained that summoning a Council of War was to assist the War Cabinet in reaching decisions on important military questions and in no way reflected a loss of confidence in the CIGS. He claimed that there were four considerations that had caused the War Cabinet the most anxiety: the military collapse of Russia; the French army, which had been reduced to such a state that it was incapable of any sustained effort; the inability of the Italian army to resume the offensive because it lacked the drafts to replace wastage; and the likelihood that American troops would not arrive in great numbers until 1918. Among the Allies, Britain was the only country involved in any major fighting. Thus, the British were within their right to decide what course to pursue and to impose it on its allies. It was for this reason, so the prime minister insisted, that he had decided to follow the precedent set by Asquith in August 1914.

Lloyd George then proceeded to outline the alternative policies open to the government. The first of these was to concentrate the entire force on the western front, reducing the number of troops in secondary theaters to the lowest figure consistent with their safety. The second was to concentrate mainly on the western front, but to utilize the forces now in the various overseas theaters in active operations. The third was to recognize that until Russia recovered and the United States was in a position to supply enough men to ensure superiority in the west, Britain ought to concentrate on economic warfare and carrying out a succession of minor attacks. The fourth policy was to isolate Germany by depriving it of its allies. This could be achieved by a combination of military operations and diplomatic negotiations directed first against Turkey. The idea was to inflict a heavy military defeat on the Turks and then offer terms to buy them out. A similar approach would be taken in the case of Bulgaria and Austria, with negotiations to follow major Allied victories. No attack on Germany would be contemplated until large numbers of troops had been released from secondary theaters and substantial American units had been concentrated in France. But until that moment arrived it was his view, based on (a loose interpretation of) remarks made by Allenby, that an offensive on the western front could not succeed as long as the opposing forces were approximately equal.[41] French and Wilson were asked to comment in writing on the alternative strategies discussed, keeping in mind the likelihood of a Russian collapse.[42] As the post of CIGS was the only channel through which communications were supposed to reach the War Cabinet, Robertson requested that the papers be submitted directly to him.

Lloyd George spent the weekend of October 12–14 at Chequers, which one of his most fervent acolytes, Arthur Lee, had donated to the nation as a country residence for its prime ministers. As was his custom, Lloyd George could not help mixing business with pleasure, having invited a French delegation that included Foch and Henri Franklin-Bouillion, the minister of propaganda in the new cabinet headed by Painlevé, as well as Smuts, Balfour and Hankey. In the course of his discussion, he urged the creation of an inter-Allied council with a permanent general staff in Paris to study the war as a whole and suggest the strategy that should be adopted. He pointed out that the current system was flawed, because each commander was interested in his own front and there was an absence of real cooperation among them. Franklin-Bouillon became excited and remarked that the French government had always favored setting up such an institution. Balfour chimed in with a suggestion that if an inter-Allied staff was established, its responsibility should initially be limited to the western front and thus consist of only French and British generals. Later, it might extend its scope and include officers from other nations concerned. Franklin-Bouillon agreed with Balfour and requested that the inter-Allied staff be appointed within a week, hoping, no doubt, that it would serve to induce Haig to further extend his line. The prime minister explained that immediate action was quite impossible, as he had not yet consulted his other colleagues on the subject. He had merely wanted to ascertain how the French would respond if the proposal were formally made.

Franklin-Bouillon implored the British to take over 100 kilometers (62 miles) of the French front, so as to set free some 200,000 men, supposedly to bring in the crop in the fields. He warned that unless these men were released from the colors, France would face starvation. Lloyd George, who earlier had gone along with the French request, reversed gears after encountering extreme resistance from Haig. He now told his French visitors that Haig could not possibly spare the men required while his offensive was in progress or, for that matter, even after it had come to an end. As the field marshal was anxious to renew his attack at the earliest possible moment next year, it was necessary to give his men leave and rest. The discussion ended with both the French and British agreeing that a meeting between the two prime ministers and their commanders should take place at once to settle the burning question.[43]

Hankey thought that Lloyd George had acted rashly by committing himself, even if only informally, to the creation of a supreme war council before a decision had been taken in the War Cabinet.[44] It also seemed to him that the prime minister was taking a big gamble by going over Robertson's head and seeking advice from Wilson and French. He knew that Robertson, if pushed too far, would not hesitate to resign, an act that was likely to bring down the government. Much would depend on how the War Cabinet responded to what French and Wilson produced.

On October 20 both Wilson and French submitted their paper to Hankey, rather than to the CIGS as they had been charged to do. Hankey, uncertain of how he should proceed, sent them to the secretary of war after consulting Lloyd George. Derby sat on the memos for several days, as he was reluctant to hand them over to Robertson in their original form. He talked the matter over with Hankey and the prime minister. It was agreed that some of French's passages needed to be softened to make them less offensive to Robertson. Hankey and Wilson met with French for about an hour on October 24 and helped him make the changes. Thereupon, both French's revised document and Wilson's report were forwarded to Robertson, who read them and circulated them to the War Cabinet, along with his reply.[45]

It must be remembered that both French and Wilson had their own agendas, the former, out of sheer bitterness, making no secret of his desire to bring down the Robertson-Haig combination, and the latter seeing in the conflict between the prime minister and the CIGS an opportunity to advance his career. The first part of French's paper was a lengthy, hard-hitting assault on the leadership of Haig and Robertson. French argued that Haig's confidence in his strategy had been misplaced, that the results of his efforts had fallen far below expectations, that there was no evidence to sustain the claim that the German army had been reduced to the breaking point by the recent hammering, and he cited figures showing that Britain's operations between July 1, 1916 and October 1, 1917 had cost over a million casualties, implying that they were greater than those suffered by the enemy. He categorically opposed a renewal of the offensive on the western front, which he described would be more of a gamble "than anything else we have undertaken." He was no less critical of Robertson, essentially accusing him of being Haig's agent, instead of providing the government with sound, independent advice. In the second part of his paper, French carefully examined the options opened to the British. He thought that as attacks in the west were fraught with difficulties, the British should have sought a decision in Palestine. But it was now too late in the year and, in his opinion, the only feasible course was to await the arrival of large forces from the United States and in the meantime adopt an active-defense strategy in the west. He was further convinced in the necessity of a supreme war council that alone "could thoroughly examine a joint scheme of action in all its bearings."[46]

Wilson's paper was less anti-Haig in tone and its arguments were cogent and lucidly expressed. He acknowledged that he was still a "westerner," because it was in France that the bulk of the enemy's forces were deployed. He attributed the poor results in the past to an absence of coordination between commanders who concentrated on their own front without reference to the others. Wilson advised against trying to knock out the Turks and, also like French, pressed for the establishment of an inter-Allied war council to concert strategic policy and ensure unfettered action.[47]

The fact that neither French nor Wilson favored operations outside the western front made it easier for Robertson to tolerate the harsh criticism directed at Haig and himself for past military policy. In reply, the CIGS adopted a restrained tone. He said little about the idea of a supreme war council and confined his comments to the other issues raised by his antagonists. He argued that there were risks to standing on the defensive and waiting for the concentration of American forces in the west. He thought that if they could pass over the next eighteen months and resume the war under present conditions and with a rejuvenated France and the addition of a million well-trained American troops, then there would be no question as to the best policy. But, as he did not believe in miracles, he had to consider whether the Entente would not be much weaker rather than stronger in 1919, in spite of American assistance. As for the campaign in Palestine, it was not a question of being too late, but of altered conditions. He noted that the General Staff had initially approved of the project, which at the time seemed feasible and promising. Since then the whole situation in Asiatic Turkey had been changed by the collapse of Russia and the acute shipping crisis. These factors and others had led the General Staff to advise against the campaign.[48]

On the same day that Robertson submitted his paper, he struck a bargain with the prime minister during a private interview. According to Derby, as reported by Hankey, Robertson had asked the prime minister "not to decide either for or against a big offensive next year owing to the military uncertainty in Italy and Russia, but to be prepared for either." Lloyd George not only agreed, but also promised to try to set up the supreme war council in London, which would allow Robertson to control the British delegation to it.[49] The truce had barely gone into effect when news arrived in London of a major disaster on the Italian front.

During the eleventh battle of the Isonzo (August 19–September 12), the Italians had pushed the Austrians back some eight kilometers, but inadequate supply lines and exhaustion had forced them to halt. After the battle, the Austrian High Command, doubtful that its badly shaken forces could withstand another such attack, appealed to the Germans for help. As a result, the OHL (*Oberste Heeresleitung*, German Army Headquarters) arranged to create a new army, the Fourteenth, with six of its fifteen divisions being German, as was most of its artillery. This mixed force, under the command of a first-rate German general, Otto von Below, was to be used to spearhead a counteroffensive on the Isonzo. To avoid detection, Below moved his men forward at night to well-camouflaged jumping-off positions.

At 2:00 a.m. on October 24 the Fourteenth army's assault in mist and rain, following a short, intense bombardment that included gas and smoke shells, achieved complete surprise and broke through the front at Caporetto almost immediately. The combined force raced forward up to fifteen miles in places at the end of the day by adopting infiltration tactics and exploiting breeches in the Italian lines. Rumors of a breakthrough undermined the will of the Italian army to resist and before long the entire front had dissolved with thousands of soldiers streaming down from the mountains in headlong flight southward.[50]

The magnitude of the debacle was not known in London until October 27 when a French liaison officer informed Hankey, adding that his government was prepared to send the Italians immediate help. Hankey drove down to Walton Heath to convey the news to Lloyd George and found him at the local golf club house.[51] The prime minister's dismay quickly gave way to rage as he blamed Robertson for scuttling his earlier plan to reinforce the Italian front, which he felt would have allowed the Italians to take the initiative and preempt the enemy's breakthrough at Caporetto. "The Germans have struck at the weak link," Hankey wrote in his diary, just as Lloyd George "himself wanted to do on (almost) the very same spot."[52] But the prime minister was guilty of wishful thinking. It is unlikely that even a well-coordinated operation against the Austrians would have succeeded. If forced back from their fortifications in the mountains, the Austrians could have counted on the Germans to bail them out, as in the past. Then, too, the prime minister did not consider what the consequences would have been if the Austrians, backed by the Germans, had struck first and broken through the Izonzo front (as they did at Caporetto) or from the Trentino (between Vicenza and Verona). In either case, the British troops would have been caught in a panic withdrawal and with no way out, would have been forced either to surrender or fight to the finish.[53]

If Lloyd George's earlier plan to send troops to the Izonzo front was highly questionable, his response to the disaster was courageous and would pay far greater dividends than he, or anyone else, could have imagined. Lloyd George was ready to do what was necessary to retrieve Italy's position. He could not, for political and military reasons, allow Italy to suffer the same fate as Serbia, Romania and Russia. To do so would have further undermined the prestige of the Entente and, more seriously, opened another front in the south of France.[54]

When Robertson arrived at Walton Heath on October 28, Lloyd George had calmed down sufficiently and the two came together in a rare instance of unity. Robertson had already alerted Haig to be ready to send two divisions from his command to Italy. These two divisions would be supplemented by four from France. Robertson suggested that he should proceed to Italy to assess the conditions for himself so as to determine if further assistance was required. Lloyd George readily gave his consent and the next day Robertson hurriedly left London.[55]

At the War Cabinet on October 29 Lloyd George's wrath and frustration resurfaced as he let loose a vicious tirade against the absent CIGS that Derby found so offensive he would have resigned on the spot had he not been restrained by Hankey.[56] But the prime minister's dissatisfaction with Robertson was not confined simply to critical remarks. Seeking to wrest control of the war from Robertson, he proposed to set up a system that would provide him with an alternate source of military advice, which he naturally anticipated would be more to his liking. He wisely chose to act while Robertson was out of the way and he was riding high because his recent military recommendations had been overridden to the apparent detriment of the Entente. The enemy breakthrough at Caporetto, on a front he had struggled in vain to reinforce, together with the costly stalemate at Passchendaele, an operation he had opposed from the outset, had restored his credibility and gave him an opportunity to bring his scheme to fruition.

The prime minister convened the War Cabinet at noon on October 30 and discussed the idea of a supreme Allied council with an advisory general staff. He maintained that recent Entente setbacks had been due to the absence of a single plan to which all could subscribe. As matters stood, each power carried out its own plans without reference to its allies. What was needed, he insisted, was an inter-Allied general staff to survey the war as a whole and prepare a joint plan of campaign for 1918. It was essential that such a body be entirely independent, without any input from the national general staffs. Lloyd George's arguments made a deep impression on the War Cabinet, which granted his request that he be allowed to put his proposal before Painlevé.[57]

Lloyd George turned to Sir Frederick Maurice, who represented Robertson on the War Cabinet while he was away, to draft a constitution for a supreme war council.[58] Caught off guard, Maurice could hardly refuse the prime minister's request. It was a crafty move on the part of Lloyd George, who ordinarily would have assigned the task to Hankey. Bringing Maurice into the picture was tantamount to receiving the stamp of approval from the General Staff.

On the morning of October 31 Lloyd George met Painlevé and the French delegation that had come over to London to discuss the question of aid to Italy. Lloyd George used the occasion to introduce his concept of a permanent military staff to study the war as a whole and to make policy recommendations to the heads of government. It probably was unnecessary, but Lloyd George resorted to a form of blackmail to ensure that the French premier gave him the needed support. In a letter sent to Painlevé on the previous day, Lloyd George made it clear that the British army would not take over more of the line in France until plans for 1918, based on the recommendations of an inter-Allied general staff, had been settled.[59]

At the War Cabinet meeting on November 1, Lloyd George went over Maurice's draft for a proposed supreme war council. Derby, troubled that a new tier of command would diminish Robertson's authority, suggested that the document serve only as a basis for discussion. His expressed reason was that it had been drawn up at short notice and could not possibly represent considered military opinion. But his efforts to protect Robertson did not garner much support.[60]

The next day Lloyd George had breakfast with a French delegation (which consisted of Painlevé, Franklin-Bouillon and Pétain) at 10 Downing Street. The topic of conversation centered on the seriousness of the present situation in Italy. Pétain was under the impression that the Italian army no longer existed. If it did, it was probably only in the form of individual units, not as an army. There was general agreement that they should proceed to Rome to confer with the Italian authorities.[61]

That evening, the War Cabinet assembled and approved in principle a scheme for an inter-Allied war council and, at the urging of Lloyd George, designated Wilson as Britain's representative on the body's permanent general staff.[62] The prime minister then forwarded to Painlevé a copy of the draft Maurice had prepared, with a note that they could make the final adjustments on their way to Italy.[63]

On November 3 the prime minister set out for Italy, accompanied by Hankey, Smuts, Maurice and Wilson. They stopped in Paris for a day, during which Lloyd George conferred with French leaders. The next day the prime minister and his associates continued their journey, arriving at Rapallo, the site of the conference, late on the afternoon of November 5.[64] Lloyd George had been so overwhelmed with work during the past ten days that he had scarcely paid attention to the change of ministry in Italy. The first head to roll after Caporetto had been the aged prime minister, Paolo Boselli. He was replaced by Vittorio Orlando, a younger and more energetic politician, committed to defending the country at all costs. Sonnino retained his post of foreign secretary in the new ministry of national unity.[65]

Robertson was already waiting in Rapallo, having completed his fact-finding mission. He was in a surly mood. Maurice had secretly cabled him earlier of what Lloyd George had done in his absence. Robertson regarded a supreme war council a device hatched by the prime minister to marginalize him and ultimately remove him from office. That certainly was a goal of the prime minister, but not the only one. He firmly believed that victory depended on the establishment of a centralized system to coordinate strategic direction.

In preparation for the conference, the French and British delegations met at the New Casino Hotel on the evening of November 5. Foch pointed out that the Second Army, which had borne the brunt of the Austro–German attack, was completely broken, but that the remaining three Italian armies, some thirty-five divisions, were intact and retiring on the line of the Piave, where he felt they should have no difficulty in halting the invaders. Lloyd George inquired whether there was anyone capable of taking charge. Foch surmised that a change in the Higher Command would likely occur. Lloyd George suggested that as a condition of sending Italy further reinforcements, they should insist that the Italian government dismiss Cadorna.[66]

The issue was raised on the first day of the conference on November 6 when discussion centered on the extreme military crisis and the state of the Italian army. Orlando was confident that the Italian army could hold the line along the Piave if reinforced by fifteen Anglo–French divisions. Lloyd George pointed out that four French divisions were already on their way to Italy and that two British divisions were about to leave. He intended to send two more, which would bring the total of British and French divisions to eight. Allied assistance, however, was contingent on assurance of effective Italian leadership, without which "British and French divisions might find themselves left in the lurch." From inquiries he had made, he was convinced that "at present the leadership of the Italian armies was not such as to justify entrusting to it the British and French divisions." Painlevé agreed with Lloyd George that it was necessary to have a good and reliable high command. When the delegates reconvened after lunch, Orlando announced that his government, subject to the king's approval, proposed to relieve Cadorna of his command and appoint him to the inter-Allied general staff. Their condition met, Lloyd George and Painlevé promised Italy ample help.

In the evening, Smuts and Franklin-Bouillon met to resolve the differences between their respective governments over the draft of an inter-Allied supreme council.[67] The document was introduced at the first session the following morning and, except for minor amendments here and there, was quickly accepted by all three delegations.[68] There was uncertainty about the role the United States would play, and Russia was written off, as it was deemed likely to drop out of the war.

As constituted, the Supreme War Council (SWC) was empowered to watch over the general conduct of the war and to ensure the coordination of military action. It consisted of two representatives from each of the powers, the prime minister and another member of the government, who were expected to meet at least once a month to confer with the military experts. Each power selected a military representative to the permanent inter-Allied general staff, whose functions included offering technical advice to the

SWC as well as recommending action for consideration by the governments concerned. It was understood that the general staffs and the commanders of the armies of each power were to remain responsible to their respective government, but they were under obligation to submit their plans to the SWC, which had the authority to review and, if necessary, to alter them.[69] In theory, the SWC was only an advisory body, but in practice it held enough sway to influence the course of the war.

Lloyd George had a difference of opinion with the French over two related issues. The first was the choice of Paris as the site for the SWC. This, he feared, would make the council a tool of the French government. He would have preferred a town close to the British front, but as the Italians supported the French, ultimately settled for Versailles. For the same reason, he objected when the French wanted to select Foch to serve as their permanent military representative on the Allied general staff while retaining his current army post. Here Lloyd George stood firm and compelled Painlevé to release Foch from his duties as chief of the French general staff. In keeping with the War Cabinet's wishes, Lloyd George selected Wilson to be the British representative.[70]

Robertson struck the only discordant note by refusing to be a party to the formation of an institution he resented. During the proceedings he rose from his chair and walked towards the door, stopping only to tell Hankey, "I wash my hands of this business."[71] Robertson would have been amenable to the idea of a supreme war council if it had been restricted to inter-Allied consultation. As he saw it, there were benefits to establishing such an institution that would have brought together heads of state on a regular basis and helped to coordinate national policies. But he had concerns about the way the SWC was designed. The council was a committee of politicians, not soldiers, and in his view, was unqualified to plan and coordinate military operations. Then, too, the principle that technical experts were independent from their national general staffs would have created a dual and competing system of military advice.[72]

The close of the conference was followed by the first session of the SWC on November 7. Not much business was transacted. Apart from ironing out details related to the council, the military representatives were instructed to conduct an investigation to advise on the amount of Anglo–French assistance Italy would require.[73]

The Rapollo Conference was a personal triumph for Lloyd George, who had dominated the proceedings and gained his main goals. He could now circumvent Robertson in favor of Wilson, whose military outlook was more in line with his own. He had imposed a machinery for inter-Allied cooperation that Britain, given that it was shouldering the bulk of the fighting, was in a position to use to its advantage. He had pressured the Italian government to replace Cadorna, opening the way for a rescue operation. Thanks to plans already prepared for such a contingency, there were no serious hitches and the Anglo-French troops were quickly transported to Italy. Their presence put fresh heart into the Italians, who were able to establish a new line along the Piave. It is to Lloyd George's credit that he had done everything within his powers to keep Italy in the war.

Chapter 12

THE PLANS FOR 1918

When the Rapollo conference broke up, it only remained for the Italian king, Victor Emmanuel, to approve the decisions that his government had taken. Accordingly, the three delegations left by special train for Peschiera on Lake Garda, where the king had established his military headquarters. The British were surprised at his diminutive size, described as being not much taller than a dwarf (actually he was 4 feet 11 inches) and "rather a pathetic figure with his country tumbling about his ears."[1] But they liked him because he seemed sincere, resolute, plucky and good-hearted. He readily consented to the removal of Cadorna, but he was less accommodating over the choice of his successor. Foch and Robertson wanted the Duke of Aosta, Italy's most accomplished soldier, but the king, never very secure, was jealous of his charismatic and popular cousin and deemed him unacceptable. Instead, he appointed General Armando Diaz, a fifty-five-year-old officer who had been a corps commander for only three months. Very little was known about him and the fact that he had spent most of his career on staffs did not exactly inspire confidence among the British and French delegations. But while his résumé was not overly impressive, he proved to be an excellent choice. He was sensible, courageous, concerned about the welfare of his troops, possessed combat experience and was tactically astute.[2]

Lloyd George broke his homebound journey by spending a few days in Paris. He went to see Georges Clemenceau, a hard-bitten old politician and a strident critic of the French government, to ask him to support the SWC in his newspaper, *L'Homme enchaîné*. He came away pleased, according to Hankey. Next he dined with Painlevé and tried to persuade him to form a stable government, similar to his own, with Thomas as minister of war and Briand duplicating the role of Bonar Law in the Chamber. Painlevé politely turned down the suggestion on the grounds that the Chamber would never accept Thomas as minister of war.[3]

During a luncheon on November 12 to which all French deputies and senators had been invited, Lloyd George followed Painlevé's announcement of the creation of a SWC with a carefully prepared speech. He maintained that the absence of unity had resulted in painful experiences, the last being at Caporetto. He and the other Allied leaders had come to recognize that unity was the only pathway to victory. For that reason, they had scrapped the practice of periodic conferences, which had served no tangible purpose, in favor of setting up a permanent machinery to survey the whole field of battle and decide where Allied resources could be most effectively employed. His explanation for the council's necessity was broadened into a blistering attack on the British High Command's conduct of the war. He unfavorably compared Haig's fruitless and costly operation in Flanders with the Austro–German success at Caporetto.[4] The prime minister sought to use his platform to strike another blow against the military command before Robertson, who was back in London, could "reorganize his broken front."[5] He was confident that momentum had swung in his direction, in large measure because of the Italian defeat at Caporetto, the Rapollo agreement and Passchendaele. Further boosting his stock was the recent progress made in Palestine, where Allenby, although still without reinforcements, had attacked and driven the Turks from the Gaza–Beersheba line. The road to Jerusalem now lay open.

By coming down hard on the generals in his Paris speech, Lloyd George had overplayed his hand and created a firestorm back home. The public, its perception shaped by the press, which had hyped even minimal progress at Passchendaele as a great victory, continued to place its faith in Haig and Robertson.[6] Newspapers with close ties to the government, like the *Manchester Guardian*, the *Observer* and *Daily Chronicle*, remained loyal to Lloyd George, interpreting his speech as a criticism of certain generals and Passchendaele as an ill-advised campaign that, for a few miles of worthless territory, had left the British army badly battered. The Harmsworth press, which included the *Times*, fearful that Asquith would return to 10 Downing Street if Lloyd George fell, was restrained in its comments, approving of the SWC in principle, but advising against using it to hamstring the British High Command and as a vehicle for armchair strategists. But pro-Asquith dailies , led by the *Westminster Gazette*, and particularly the conservative press, such as the *Morning Post*, the *Globe*, and the *Daily News*, assailed Lloyd George for his reckless behavior and for insulting the British army, warning him not to meddle in the generals' conduct of strategic policy. Two popular weeklies, the *Spectator* and the *Nation*, were equally condemnatory, with the former declaring that Lloyd George was unfit to be prime minister and suggesting that he be replaced by either Eric Geddes, the First Lord of the Admiralty, or Lord Cecil.[7] The early fissure between Lloyd George and a large segment of the press would widen in succeeding months.

On top of the press attacks, ill feelings against Lloyd George mounted in political circles. Sensing his own vulnerability in the wake of Caporetto, the CIGS had been busy, working up not only the press, but habitual political allies as well. In the War Cabinet, Derby pushed for acceptance of the Army Council's proposal that the British military representative, like all military officers, be subject to its authority.[8] Lloyd George initially wavered, a position that was reflected in the contradictory resolution adopted by the War Cabinet on November 16. While it did not question that the British military representative was subject to the orders of the Army Council, it went on to say that "he will have unfettered discretion as to the advice he offers."[9] But the resolution only deepened the Army Council's suspicions about Lloyd George's intentions. There were rumors, later confirmed, that the military members of the Army Council were prepared to resign *en bloc* unless assured that Robertson's powers would not be divided. Derby did not think that Lloyd George would be able to survive the resignation of the entire Army Council, particularly if it were followed by his own.[10]

Pressure on Lloyd George continued to build up over the next few days. Back from spending a week at the front, Austen Chamberlain, a prominent Unionist, told Curzon that many members of his party would withdraw their support of the coalition government if the British generals were any way superseded. On November 18 Curzon reported the conversation to Lloyd George and urged him to meet and come to terms with Robertson before the parliamentary debate the next day.[11] With the survival of his government in jeopardy, Lloyd George felt compelled to retreat. He called Derby over to 10 Downing Street and the two worked out an arrangement. To avoid any misunderstanding, Derby recorded the main points of their agreement, which he sent to Lloyd George the following day for his confirmation. It was understood that all proposals to be discussed at the SWC would be initiated by the War Cabinet after hearing the opinion of the CIGS. Furthermore, the CIGS would be permitted to attend all meetings of the SWC along with Wilson.[12] Curiously enough, the powers and responsibilities of the British military representative remained undefined. Still, the talks had been conducted in an amicable atmosphere, and when Derby left, he was satisfied that he had erected "a sufficient safeguard against any wildcat scheme."[13]

In the midst of his troubles, Lloyd George invited Colonel House, President Wilson's close advisor and special emissary, to dine with him at 10 Downing Street on November 13. The prime minister told House that it was imperative that the United States be represented in the SWC because of the moral effect it would have in Britain. At length, he was able to extract a promise from House that he would advise President Wilson to appoint General Tasker H. Bliss as the US military representative on the SWC.[14]

Since the late summer of 1917, Lloyd George had tried to forge closer ties with Washington as a means to win support for his indirect strategy. In the first week in September he stated his case in a long personal letter to President Wilson. He painted a grim portrait of the Allied military position, which he attributed to a lack of unified leadership. Allied strategy, he went on to say, had been unimaginative, confined to headlong assaults against the German army's impenetrable defenses. The war had taken the form of a siege and, in these circumstances, it seemed to him that the soundest tactics to adopt was to strike the enemy at its weakest point, not at its strongest. By concentrating against Germany's allies, a satisfactory peace might be gained "without the bloody sacrifice required to destroy the German army through a frontal assault."[15]

Lloyd George then brought up the question of America's participation in Allied councils. He understood that the American people might object to being drawn into the complexities of European politics but, at the same time, stressed that there were compelling reasons why they should be represented at Allied conferences. He wrote:

> I believe that the presence at the deliberations of the Allies of independent minds, bringing fresh views, unbiased by previous methods and previous opinions, might be of immense value in helping us to free ourselves from the ruts of the past, and to avoid having our armies drawn into a strategy which is bound to be immensely costly, and which may not be that calculated to give us the best results.

Another reason, Lloyd George advanced, was to help Britain maintain unity in the anti-German coalition. The desire for peace in some quarters was growing, fed by the daily suffering and carnage. Nations had mobilized their resources to the utmost without making a decisive impression on the enemy's position, and people were beginning to ask whether victory was obtainable at all. Although in his view victory was within reach, it would come only if the Allies exhibited greater moral unity and tenacity than the Central Powers in the last desperate days. He observed that their allies, having fought as valiantly as they could, were, consciously or unconsciously, relying on the British and Americans to "supply that additional effort which is necessary in order to make certain of a just, liberal and lasting peace." After attributing the recent boost in morale in Entente countries, particularly in France, to the appearance of the vanguard of the American army, he played up to President Wilson in the following way:

> I would ask you to consider, therefore, whether it is not of the utmost importance that the purpose and ideals as well as the wisdom of America should be manifested in the Council Chambers as well as on the battlefield, if we are to preserve unshaken during this difficult winter season the resolution of the Allies to go with the war until Prussian military despotism over Germany and her allies is broken, by revolution from within or defeat from without.[16]

Lloyd George's attempt to forge a close alignment on war policy between the English-speaking democracies met a cool reception in Washington. Wilson was no strategist, but like Lloyd George, he appreciated that reckless attrition on the western front could not continue indefinitely and that it was essential to find new ways to fight the war. Nevertheless, the idealistic Wilson had sharp differences with the British. In his moralistic crusade to strive for a new and better order out of the ashes of the conflict, he held, as absolute values, national freedom and self-determination – evidently exempting the past behavior of the United States.[17] He was scornful of the British government's conservative bent and, while he respected men like Sir Edward Grey, the former foreign secretary, and Balfour, he considered Lloyd George unprincipled and unsavory. Then, too, House had warned him that there was a link between Lloyd George's peripheral strategy and Britain's postwar territorial ambitions: "The English naturally want the road to Egypt and India blocked, and Lloyd George is not above using us to further this plan," House observed. "He is not of the Grey–Balfour type and in dealing with him it is well to bear this in mind."[18] In short, Wilson did not intend to be a full partner with his European co-belligerents, limiting America's participation in their activities.

Over the next few weeks, President Wilson's position underwent a change, due at least in part to the urging of Sir William Wiseman, head of British intelligence in the United States. Wilson was reluctant to carry on negotiations with the British Ambassador, Sir Cecil Spring-Rice, both because of his occasional breaches of diplomatic protocol and his warm friendship with Teddy Roosevelt, the former Republican president.[19] To the benefit of both governments, a new channel of communication opened, thanks to an arrangement worked out between House and Wiseman. House found Wiseman to be knowledgeable, astute and engaging, and the two formed a close personal relationship. Since Wiseman had access to the Foreign Office, House could bypass the British ambassador and still retain the link he required.[20] Wiseman's intimate rapport with House paid dividends. On October 13 he wrote to Eric Drummond, Balfour's private secretary, that President Wilson had changed his mind about membership in the various inter-Allied bodies.[21] This was confirmed when Wilson told an inquiring House that he had already decided that the US should be represented in the SWC: "Please take the position that we not only accede to the plan for a single war council, but insist on it, but think it does not go far enough."[22] What he meant by the last phrase is not clear. He may have been referring to unity of command, which he was known to favor. In any case, Wilson designated Bliss as the American military representative at Versailles, but made no comparable appointment at the political level. House did not immediately deliver Wilson's note to Lloyd George to prevent him from using it in the upcoming House of Commons debate. He did not wish to give the appearance that the American President was taking sides in a matter involving British domestic politics.[23]

The Prime Minister was in splendid form when he made a rare appearance in the Commons on November 19 to fight for the life of his government. He faced the loyal Opposition headed by Asquith, known to be sympathetic to the military party, and many disgruntled Tory backbenchers, whose revolt likely would have proven fatal. Asquith opened the debate in what was his first opportunity to attack Lloyd George's leadership. Normally a brilliant speaker, he gave a lackluster performance on this occasion and disappointed his supporters. He made no telling points. He denied that the High Command was as inept as Lloyd George had claimed. He tried to show that Allied coordination, to the extent that it was useful, had been achieved during his administration and saw no purpose in a formal body such as the SWC. A surprised Lloyd George later admitted that Asquith "was not as censorious as those who supplied his brief would have wished."[24]

Lloyd George made better use of his rhetorical skills and gave a classic example of shadow boxing. His speech bore no relation to what he had in mind or, for that matter, to his statements in Paris, and he had no compunction about lying or twisting the facts to suit his purpose of appeasing a potentially hostile House. He pointed out that in the SWC he was resurrecting an idea first advanced by Kitchener in 1915. What he did not say was that Kitchener's conception of an inter-Allied war council was markedly different from his own. Kitchener planned to use it to control Allied strategy and not as a source of advice to civilian policymakers.

Lloyd George insisted that the SWC would have no executive authority, denied that he regarded the British military representative as a rival to the CIGS, and as a means to assuage the fears of those who suspected that unity of military action might develop into unity of command, claimed to oppose the appointment of a generalissimo – an idea, it should be underlined, he had approved in his talk with Painlevé in August.[25] He gave assurances that he had no intention of interfering in military strategy, that he had the utmost confidence in the army's leaders, and that the SWC was designed solely to coordinate Allied plans, not impinge on Robertson's authority. He made no mention of how the new council would work with the existing Imperial General Staff nor attempted to define the functions of the British military representative. He sat down amid a storm of cheers, having scored a great personal victory.[26] In the span of a month, Lloyd George, by sheer drive and will power, had converted his plan into reality. His selfish motives notwithstanding, this was an act of superb statesmanship.

Robertson was generally satisfied with the outcome of his latest row with Lloyd George. Although unable to prevent the SWC from taking form, he had been promised oversight over the British military representative at Versailles. Robertson delighted in telling Haig that while Lloyd George had told his audience in Paris that the SWC would have real power, he had been compelled to back down and concede "that it would have practically no power at all."[27] Lloyd George, moreover, showed no signs that he would renege on his deal with Derby. Replying to the secretary for war on November 26, he declared that he was in "substantial agreement" with the points in his letter, but was ambivalent about whether the CIGS would be allowed to vet the views of the British military representative.[28] Political necessity had dictated Lloyd George's concessions to Robertson, but he probably found it more palatable to do so because of the unexpected good news from the western front.

Haig followed up his offensive at Passchendaele with another one farther south in an area near Cambrai, a town behind a thinly held section of the Hindenburg line. Haig aimed at a local success, not a breakthrough. He hoped to end the year on a winning note and compensate somewhat for the dismal outcome at Passchendaele. The attack was to be spearheaded by over 350 tanks, followed by six infantry divisions and backed by a thousand guns. Surprise was crucial to success. Accordingly, it was decided to forego the customary preliminary bombardment so as not to alert the enemy of the impending offensive. The artillery would wait until the offensive actually began before laying down a short but intense bombardment, and then shift to a rolling barrage well ahead of the advancing tanks. GHQ anticipated that the element of surprise, along with the shock provided by the large concentration of tanks, would break open the Hindenburg line.

Everything went according to plan after the attack began at 6:20 a.m. on November 20. Stunned by the intense bombardment and frightened at the sight of dense columns of tanks rolling forward, many of the surviving defenders threw away their weapons and fled to the rear. On the first day of the battle, the British had advanced, in some cases, to a depth of four miles, at comparatively low cost of casualties. In Britain, church bells rang in celebration, the first time they had sounded since the start of the war.

Haig had given advance notice of his attack to Robertson, but not to the War Cabinet. Robertson had chosen to remain silent, rather than share the information with the prime minister and his colleagues. It was not until November 21, after the British assault had scored an immediate success, that the CIGS broke the news to the War Cabinet.[29] Lloyd George was elated at the promise of a great triumph, one badly needed to boost public morale after the bleak events of the past year. As it turned out, the jubilation in the country proved to be premature. The massive losses at Passchendaele, coupled with the dispatch of five divisions to Italy (an additional one had been added to the four already promised) had left Haig with insufficient reserves to throw into the gap to exploit his initial break-in. Once again Charteris had discounted reports by intelligence officers and provided Haig with misleading information about the availability of enemy reserves.[30] As the Germans brought up reinforcements to the targeted area to stiffen their defense, Haig's offensive lost momentum and sputtered to a halt. On November 30 the Germans staged a surprise counterattack, pushing the British back, in some places beyond their original line.

Given the wide publicity accorded to his spectacular beginning, Haig was embarrassed and thus reluctant to admit defeat.[31] It was only by degrees that the War Cabinet extracted from GHQ an admission that the tables had been turned. At the War Cabinet on December 5 Robertson was giving a sanitized version of the latest events at Cambrai when attention was drawn to a dispatch by the special correspondent of the *Daily Telegraph*, suggesting that the German counterattack had come as a complete surprise to the British. Derby pointed out that it appeared that a British division had been overwhelmed, but he thought that Haig was probably ignorant of the causes of this reverse. Robertson joined Derby in expressing confidence that "there had been no intention of minimizing the extent of the reverse suffered."[32] A livid Lloyd George asserted that GHQ had deliberately kept the War Cabinet in the dark and he suspected that Haig had connived to suppress the bad news. He wanted to know how the German attack could have come as a surprise to the British troops if regular aerial reconnaissance had been carried out and if there had been proper defensive arrangements. The next day Robertson wrote to Haig:

> There was a long discussion in Cabinet and, as you can imagine, L. G. was well on the warpath and seemed to think they ought to have heard more details already. Nothing that I could say, and I said a good deal, could in any way convince him of the difficulty of getting information in such circumstances. He was in one of his abominable moods.[33]

Barely emerging from an inhumanly long and bloody struggle at Passchendaele, Haig ought to have given his depleted army a rest instead of fighting another battle. Cambrai cost the British about 50,000 casualties and nothing of strategic value was gained. The disappointing results belied Haig's claim that the German army had been seriously degraded over the previous months of fighting. German losses were about equal or slightly less than those of the British. With little prospect of receiving adequate replacements, Haig could not afford a further reduction of manpower, but the Germans, in the short run, could make good their losses by bringing back divisions from the inactive eastern front.

For Lloyd George, Cambrai was the last straw, convincing him that the army could no longer afford Haig's profligacy. The result of the battle had shown the hollowness of Haig's argument – as justification for his prolonged attritional campaigns in Flanders – that the German army was on the point of collapse. Lloyd George felt certain that the British army was being mismanaged and that unless a change was made, it would be drastically undermanned in the final phase of the struggle. He dearly wanted Robertson's head as well. His grievances against the CIGS had piled up over the months and the latest, as we shall see immediately below, was one that he found difficult to stomach.

On December 10 Lloyd George was astonished to learn from the most recent intelligence reports that Allenby had nearly a five-to-one advantage over the Turks in the Palestine theater, 95,812 as against 21,000.[34] Yet he could scarcely forget that in October Allenby had requested thirteen additional divisions on the grounds that the Turks could counter his thrust towards Jerusalem by bringing together as many as twenty divisions. The next day word arrived in London that Allenby had captured Jerusalem without any of the reinforcements he had requested. It was apparent to Lloyd George that the earlier estimates of Turkish strength had been deliberately inflated to thwart his scheme for the conquest of Palestine so that more manpower would be available for Haig to engage in Passchendaele-like operations.[35] Robertson could only offer a weak excuse for his faulty assessment, in effect saying that that Allenby's rapid advance had "made it impossible for the Turks to bring up the anticipated reinforcements."[36]

On December 11 Lloyd George tried to persuade Derby of the need to remove both Haig and Robertson from their posts. He suggested for Haig the same fate that had befallen Joffre in France, namely, that he should be appointed to the ceremonial post of generalissimo of all the British forces. Robertson would be similarly kicked upstairs and given a high-sounding sinecure.

Lloyd George was now in a stronger position to make a change in the leadership of the BEF than he had ever been. A number of newspapers, restless in the wake of Passchendaele, were demanding an investigation into the failure at Cambrai. The *Times*, hitherto solidly behind Haig, urged the removal of "every blunderer."[37] Derby, however, was not receptive to Lloyd George's formula to replace Haig and Robertson and hinted that he might resign unless the matter was dropped. Alas, the prime minister's courage failed him and he allowed political expediency to triumph over his better judgment. He drew back and accepted Derby's suggestion that Haig be pressured into shaking up his headquarters staff. Robertson concurred that drastic changes among Haig's sycophantic staff were long overdue. Haig resisted at first, but with almost everyone on the other side, his instinct for survival overrode his loyalty to subordinates. The principal officers purged included Charteris, Kiggell, the chief of staff, and General R. C. Maxwell, the quartermaster-general.[38] In the end Haig escaped the guillotine. So had Robertson, but his reprieve was only temporary.

Lloyd George's frustration over his inability, or so he believed, to sack Haig and Robertson was partially relieved when he managed to rid himself of

Jellicoe, whom he had long regarded as pessimistic, unimaginative and timid. Lloyd George's faith in Jellicoe had been shaken by his opposition to the introduction of convoys, even after the Germans had adopted unrestricted submarine warfare early in 1917. Lloyd George could not help but further resent Jellicoe for vigorously supporting Haig's disastrous Flander's plan.[39] The prime minister might have forgiven Jellicoe if the navy had notched the occasional glorious victory to offset the blood and disappointment of the land war and bring some comfort to the British public. But the senior service could not boast of even one major victory in 1917. It is true that the U-boat campaign was gradually being won, but the campaign was unspectacular and shipping losses remained high. The naval blockade of the enemy's coast would ultimately pay enormous dividends, but at the time, attracted even less publicity. In an important segment of the press there was a swelling chorus of dissatisfaction with the leadership at the Admiralty, which was accused of being too passive and of failing to think ahead and prepare future naval operations.[40]

In the summer the moment seemed propitious to make a change at the Admiralty. By making Carson a member of the War Cabinet, Lloyd George assumed that the way would be clear for him to send Jellicoe packing, but his plan was disrupted by the new First Lord, Sir Eric Geddes. When Geddes agreed to succeed Carson at the Admiralty, he did so on the understanding that Jellicoe be allowed to retain his post.[41] It was sensible for Geddes to avoid stirring a hornet's nest, but he had another, practical reason for not wanting to part with Jellicoe. Geddes was an excellent administrator but his experience was in railway management and he knew little about the Admiralty and even less about the navy.[42] Recognizing his limitations, he understood that it would be to his benefit to have Jellicoe, with his experience and high standing among senior naval officers, at his side.[43] Relations between Geddes and Jellicoe, however, quickly deteriorated. The crux of the problem was that vital matters were neglected, because Jellicoe, although overwhelmed with work, refused to delegate executive authority to his subordinates.[44] This was apparent when a convoy from Norway was lost in October to German surface-level craft. An inquiry concluded that Jellicoe had neglected to act on receiving information from a secret but highly reliable source warning of the likelihood of an attack on the convoy.[45]

On October 26, 1917 Geddes met with Lloyd George and his two predecessors at the Admiralty, Balfour and Carson, to discuss the desirability of superceding Jellicoe.[46] No minutes were kept, but with Carson in attendance it is probable that a decision was postponed. Lloyd George's preoccupation in the land war and in establishing a SWC distracted him from coming to grips with the issue. But an unsuccessful naval attempt to trap German minesweepers and their covering force in Heligoland Blight on November 17, followed by the destruction of a second Norwegian convoy on December 12, convinced the prime minister that he should take advantage of a new wave of anti-Jellicoe criticism in the press – much of which, it was alleged, he inspired – to make his move. What sealed Jellicoe's fate was his support of Admiral Sir Reginald Bacon (head of the Dover Patrol) who was accused by some high naval officials, among them, Sir Rosslyn Wemyss, now deputy first sea lord, of failing to adopt more stringent methods – besides nets and barriers – to sink U-boats trying to pass through the Straits of Dover. Wemyss wanted to replace Bacon, but Jellicoe insisted that he was the best man for the job. Caught between the opposing views of his two principal naval advisers, Geddes came down on Wemyss's side.[47] Although Geddes was convinced that Jellicoe was not the right man for the job, he was reluctant to sack him because of the strong adverse reaction he anticipated from the Admiralty board. Indeed, Geddes hoped to avoid discharging this unpalatable task by returning to his railway work in France. Under pressure from Lloyd George, however, he agreed to remain at the Admiralty and to move forward on the Jellicoe case. The question of removing Jellicoe was not put to the War Cabinet where Carson was certain to lead a fight against it.

Jellicoe may have been miscast as first sea lord, but few men had to confront the crushing responsibilities he had borne for more than three years in the service of his country, and at the very least, he was entitled to leave with dignity. But not even part-time staff deserved the kind of treatment meted out to Jellicoe. Instead of breaking the news to him personally and at a more appropriate time, Geddes chose to notify him by special messenger on Christmas eve. The tactless and brutal manner in which it was done bore all the imprint of Lloyd George.

Geddes's missive had been timed to make it easier for Lloyd George to contain the political fall out from Jellicoe's removal. At this late hour, Jellicoe could not consult the sea lords, all of whom, with the exception of Weymss, probably would have resigned. Public debate and comment would be less acute, because no newspapers would appear for two days. Parliament had just gone into recess, and by the time it reconvened, the event would have become an irreversible fait accompli.[48] Still, there were later troubles, serious if not critical, with both Parliament and the Admiralty board, but the outcry died down after a week or so. Nothing, however, could mollify an enraged Carson. He resigned from the War Cabinet towards the end of January 1918, but cited as reason for going, his dissatisfaction with the government's handling of Irish affairs.[49]

The new First Sea Lord, Admiral Weymss, was much different from his predecessor in temperament and outlook. He was neither a reformer nor a great intellect and he did not enjoy Jellicoe's lofty prestige in the navy. Nevertheless, the change was probably for the best. Weymss was a good organizer, receptive to new ideas, optimistic and unafraid of delegating authority. Equally important, he was outgoing and got along well with people, in particular Geddes, and would see the navy through until the end of the war.[50]

Geddes maintained at the time that he had acted independently in determining that new leadership was needed and that the prime minister had not attempted to influence his judgment. It is absurd for Geddes to have made such a claim. It is true that he had been the one to make the direct assault on Jellicoe, but surely Lloyd George had pulled the strings in the background. Even John Grigg concedes that "it is surely inconceivable that Geddes would have taken a step which was bound to have serious political repercussions without consulting the Prime Minister and securing his support."[51] The day after dropping the bombshell, Geddes telephoned Lloyd George to tell him that Jellicoe had gone quietly. With one less troublesome issue to worry about, the prime minister exclaimed exultantly, "It's a good thing."[52]

While Lloyd George was orchestrating the removal of Jellicoe, he was deeply involved in trying to map out a strategy for 1918. Looking at the course of the war over the past twelve months, he could not have been optimistic about the Entente's prospects. U-boats, although hampered by the convoy system, continued to exact a high toll of merchant ships. The Entente had suffered major setbacks on the western front and the French army, rocked by a great mutiny, had not fully regained its offensive power. The Italian army was all but broken at Caporetto in one of the most shattering defeats suffered by an Allied power since the opening weeks of the conflict. Propped up by eleven Anglo–French divisions, the Italian army would need nursing for many months to recover from the catastrophe. To the east, Russia's will to fight, declining rapidly since the summer, evaporated completely in late autumn. A second revolution in November brought the Bolsheviks under Vladimir Lenin to power, and as they were eager for peace, immediately opened separate negotiations with the Central Powers. The loss of Russia was bound to dramatically alter the strategic balance. It meant that significant German troops in the east would be available to reinforce those on the western front, opening the way for the Germans to gain a numerical advantage they had not enjoyed since the start of the war; it would provide the Germans with an opportunity to neutralize the British blockade by drawing upon Russia's vast mineral and food resources; and it would allow the Turks to concentrate exclusively on the British in Palestine and Mesopotamia. The one ray of light was the entry of the United States in the war, but the expansion of its army was proceeding at a leisurely pace, giving rise to speculation in Allied capitals that it would not be a major factor until 1919.

The declining physical and moral strength of the Entente, plus the slow arrival of American troops, convinced Lloyd George that Germany could not be defeated in 1918. In the first eleven months of 1917 Haig had suffered gigantic losses, nearly 780,000 casualties in hopeless battles.[53] If Britain expected to play the leading role in the decisive campaign in 1919, it needed to husband its dwindling manpower reserves. To Lloyd George, the ideal solution would be for the British army to adopt an active-defense on the western front, while waiting for the buildup of American forces in France. In the interim, troops above and beyond those required to hold the line in France should be sent to Palestine to ensure that Allenby achieved propaganda victories needed to fortify the civilian population's resolve to fight on to a successful conclusion. Before his program could be implemented, Lloyd George had to convince, first the War Cabinet, and then Britain's partners, of its merits.[54]

The most strenuous opposition to a defensive strategy on the western front obviously came from Robertson and Haig. On November 19 Robertson submitted a memorandum to the War Cabinet warning that Britain could not afford to wait for the Americans and defer its main effort until 1919, because the Germans were likely to try to reach a decision in 1918. The proper course for the Entente was to retain the initiative so as to disrupt enemy preparations and forestall attacks.[55] Robertson's advice did not resonate with Lloyd George any more than it had on previous occasions. The prime minister calculated that without a preponderate advantage in rifles, it would be the height of folly for the Entente to launch massive attacks in 1918. The War Cabinet, reluctant to override the views of either the General Staff or the prime minister, referred the question to the SWC.[56]

Toward the end of November a British delegation headed by Lloyd George crossed the Channel and made its way to Versailles. A new government in Paris had taken charge since Lloyd George's last visit to France. Painlevé had fallen from power and been replaced by the seventy-six-year-old Georges Clemenceau. During his inaugural speech, "the Tiger," as Clemenceau was often called, left no doubt about the policy he intended to follow: "Neither treason nor half-treason: war, nothing but war."[57] A die-hard patriot, fierce-tempered, and highly obstinate, Clemenceau cracked down on defeatists of all kinds and injected a new spirit in the country, stiffening morale just in time to meet Germany's onslaught in the spring of 1918.

Lloyd George had met Clemenceau several times in the past and considered him opinionated, disagreeable and bad-tempered.[58] Research by his aides confirmed his earlier impressions and he recognized that the old man would be a tough customer to deal with. Clemenceau, for his part, did not have an opinion about Lloyd George at the start but, as the months passed, developed a dislike of him that bordered on contempt.[59] Thus, because of temperamental differences and divergent national interests, the relationship between the two men was never close and was punctuated by sharp clashes in which violent language was used during their exchanges. If there was no love lost between the two on a personal level, they at least made an effort to get along as working partners. In time, Lloyd George developed a grudging admiration for Clemenceau's exceptional qualities, particularly his courage, single-mindedness, unbending will to win and ability to infect others with his own combativeness and optimism. Lloyd George paid high tribute to Clemenceau's war leadership in his memoirs, but he was disingenuous when he went to pains to emphasize that their clashes amounted to little more than good-humored bantering. It is equally difficult to believe that he enjoyed the company of Clemenceau, a man who, by some accounts, intimidated him just as he did everyone else. Indeed, according to Spiers, whenever there was a difference of opinion between the two prime ministers, Lloyd George went through a sort of ritual to steel himself for combat.[60] A day after arriving in Paris but before the Allied conference got underway, Lloyd George locked horns with the French prime minister for the first time.

It started well enough with the two leaders exchanging polite greetings and engaging in small talk. They touched briefly on the Sarrail affair. As we have seen, the British government was dissatisfied with Sarrail, but had not pressed for his removal out of consideration for Painlevé. When Painlevé fell, Robertson urged that the moment was ripe to renew the British government's demand that Sarrail be recalled. The War Cabinet concurred and Lloyd George was asked to turn over to Clemenceau a copy of the letter that he had sent to Ribot on June 6 requesting that Sarrail be recalled.[61] Clemenceau had no attachment to Sarrail, who was a frequent cause of friction between London and Paris, and he assured Lloyd George that he would take care of the matter. He was true to his word.

The cordial atmosphere dissipated when the next subject was discussed. Clemenceau was not enthusiastic about the idea of an SWC because he saw it as a threat to his authority. What compounded his dislike of the body was his innate distrust of generals. Since he could not fail to honor a firm commitment made by his predecessor, he proposed to use the body as a tool of French policy. To that end, he tried during informal talks to modify an arrangement concluded at Rapollo by appointing Foch chief of staff in addition to his assignment as permanent military representative. This contravened Lloyd George's principle that the permanent military representative should be independent of the national general staffs. An enraged Lloyd George reacted by threatening to return immediately to London unless Foch gave up one of his positions. Clemenceau gave way, agreeing to send General Maxime Weygand to Versailles as the French permanent military representative while retaining Foch for the more important job of chief of staff. It was not much of a concession. Foch once said of Weygand, "He is my doormat. I use him to wipe my boots on."[62] To say that Weygand could be counted on to act as the mouthpiece of the French General Staff would be an understatement. In fact, both the Italian and American representatives at Versailles were also extensions of their respective general staffs. Cadorna was the former Italian army commander and General Bliss had just retired as the chief of staff of the US army. Henry Wilson was the only permanent military representative expected to act independently of his nation's general staff. These were the conditions Lloyd George was willing to accept to keep Robertson and Haig on a short leash.

The second meeting of the SWC opened at 11:00 a.m. on December 1 with Clemenceau in the chair. The French premier gave a brief introductory speech which he had crafted in consultation with Lloyd George. As a sop to Lloyd George, he inserted a piece at the end to remind the technical advisers of their duty. They were expected to act, not as representatives of their own countries, but as a single body, studying the problems before them from the point of view of the Allies as a whole and submitting their findings to the SWC. Very little business was transacted at the meeting. The permanent military representatives were instructed to study and recommend a policy for 1918 as well as to draw up reports, particularly on the situation in Italy and the Balkans.[63]

Since no answer could be expected for several weeks, British policymakers, on their return home, turned to the long overdue matter of manpower. For weeks Haig had cried for more recruits to fill the ranks of his existing formations depleted by his bloody bludgeoning in Flanders. Whatever reproach Haig may have invited by his inept handling of military operations, even bitter critics recognized that it was essential to reinforce the BEF if it hoped to resist a great enemy attack that was certain to come in the spring of 1918. But in London it was becoming apparent that the recruiting apparatus was no longer able to replace the army's horrendous losses in view of the growing competition for manpower from the navy and merchant fleet, shipbuilding, munitions, mines, agriculture, transportation and other vital occupations. To determine the distribution of available fit young men between the armed services and industry, the War Cabinet, as we have already seen, set up a Manpower Committee composed of Lloyd George, Smuts, Curzon, Carson and George Barnes with the indefatigable and indispensable Hankey as secretary.[64] Although several members of the General Staff and other military authorities were called to give evidence, the War Office was not represented on the committee. Much has been made about this omission, but the problem before the committee was not one that the soldiers could solve. With the nation's manpower pool near the bottom of the barrel, the committee's superhuman task, as Hankey accurately perceived, "was to avert a military catastrophe without plunging us into an economic catastrophe equally fatal to the cause of the Allies."[65]

Lloyd George presided over the first meeting at 10 Downing Street on December 10, as he would on the remaining five that followed. The Prime

Minister was determined to deny Haig any more men than was required to hold the line lest he squander them in more Passchendaele-like battles. Nor did he think that his action risked leaving Haig so weak that he would be unable to hold his own. War Office information provided to the Manpower Committee showed that the Allies had a superiority of 18.5 divisions on the western front.[66] If in the past the Allies had failed to achieve a breakthrough, the odds were no better that the German army, numerically inferior, at least for the time being, would succeed in doing so. There was a risk, however, that with reinforcements from the east, the German army would gain a preponderance on the western front, allowing it a last gamble's throw for victory in the spring of 1918 before American power could be brought to bear. If that should happen, the prime minister was confident that with the arrival of more and more American divisions the margin of German superiority would not be enough to permit it to rupture the Allied line.

Above all, Lloyd George wanted to protect trade and vital war industries so that Britain could fight on into 1919 or even 1920. The cost of the war to Britain, which was also providing financial help to its allies, was placing inordinate stress on its economy. To avert an economic collapse, Britain's export industries had to be maintained. More ships needed to be built to secure maritime communications and to bring American troops over to Europe. In addition, attention had to be given to the production of food, munitions, artillery, gas, airplanes and tanks. Thus, in the prime minister's view, the needs of the economy came before those of the army. By contrast, the high command thought only in terms of maintaining the army's military strength.

Lloyd George's case was unwittingly strengthened by the War Office, which presented misleading evidence. After scrutinizing the facts and figures of the military authorities, Hankey noted in his diary that they were "utterly unreliable," because they were "twisted to support their arguments."[67] The War Office had requested 600,000 category A (physically fit) men in 1918 to help stem the tide of a massive enemy attack expected in the spring of 1918. It could offer no plausible explanation to reconcile its exorbitant demands for recruits with Haig's smooth assurances before and during Passchendaele that the German army was at the end of its tether.

The committee's report was consistent with Lloyd George's thinking, emphasizing as it did the importance of maintaining Britain's staying power until American numbers in the field could swing the scales. In allocating manpower, it gave top priority to the navy while ranking the army last, below shipbuilding, the construction of tank and aircraft, food production and timber-felling. The army was promised between 100,000 and 150,000 new recruits compared to the 600,000 it had requested. The committee urged the army to employ its existing resources to greater effect, including using the cavalry in dismounted work and reducing the size of the divisions from twelve to nine battalions so as to create a divisional reserve.[68]

The Army Council protested strongly against the recommendations of the committee, warning that, in view of German preparations for an attack, it was imperiling the BEF and unnecessarily taking a grave risk of losing the war.[69] Whatever effect the Army Council's memorandum might have had on the committee was vitiated by Haig when he appeared before the War Cabinet on January 7, 1918 in connection with the extension of the British army's front. In the course of the discussion, Bonar Law suddenly asked him a direct question: "If you were a German Commander, would you think there was a sufficient chance of a smashing offensive to justify incurring the losses which would be entailed." Haig doubted that the Germans would make such an attempt, because if they failed, their position would become critical owing to the growing strength of the Allies in the last half of 1918. It seemed to him that the Germans would embrace a policy of limited attacks to avoid depleting their army.[70] Haig evidently would have given a different answer if he had seen a copy of the committee's draft report. Robertson and Derby, both of whom were in attendance, were horrified by Haig's response. For weeks the General Staff had warned that the Germans would mount an all-out assault on the western front in the spring of 1918 to gain a decision before the concentration of a powerful American army. Now the British commander, the greatest authority on the military situation in the west, had contradicted the General Staff's judgment. Several members of the War Cabinet seized upon Haig's comments to develop the argument that, since a major enemy attack was not expected, there was no urgency to bring the army to full establishment. On the way out, Robertson bluntly told Haig that, given his testimony, it would be impossible for the War Office to obtain the necessary drafts he required.[71] Haig tried to repair the damage by at once submitting a written statement to the War Cabinet, but it was too late.[72] On reading the note, Lloyd George contemptuously threw it aside, asking rhetorically how much stock should be placed in a man whose opinion differed from one day to the next.[73]

Lloyd George expected that with fewer recruits crossing over to France, Haig would be compelled to change methods, abandoning costly and fruitless attacks in favor of the Pétain tactics. Allenby's capture of Jerusalem on December 11 gave Lloyd George a new opportunity to change the focus of British strategy. Allenby's triumph, widely celebrated and played up in the press, had helped to dispel some of the war weariness that was creeping over the country. The event acquired historical and religious significance in English-speaking countries, with the press drawing parallels to the Crusades and acclaiming the capture of the city containing the sacred shrines of Christendom. Caught up in the euphoria, Lloyd George wanted Allenby to follow up his victory with a push northwards, convinced that with the loss of Jerusalem, the Ottoman Empire was on the verge of collapse.

The rapid pace of Allenby's march, five weeks instead of the anticipated six months, raised the question about the reliability of British intelligence in assessing Ottoman power and the probable level of opposition. "It is quite clear that the information which has been given to us about the number of Turkish troops available in that theatre was utterly wrong," Lloyd George exclaimed to Robertson.[74] The matter was debated in the War Cabinet the next day and the intelligence service came under severe criticism for overrating the combat strength of the Turkish forces.[75] While Lloyd George was right in accusing both the War Office and Allenby of overestimating the Turks' power of resistance, he was wrong in thinking that an advance into Syria would compel Constantinople to sue for peace. In fact, there was little to commend such an operation. It is true that the Turkish army had suffered heavy losses in recent months, but its military power was far from shattered. If necessary, the Turks would have been able to supply their forces in northern Mesopotamia from an area in eastern Anatolia evacuated by the Russians. Then, too, Syria was not, anymore than Palestine, pivotal to Ottoman strategy. This was confirmed after the EEF advanced to Aleppo in October 1918, but "this push did little or nothing to bring about the surrender of the Ottoman Empire." Finally, unlike Jerusalem, no city in Syria held any special meaning for the English public.[76]

Lloyd George felt that if Allenby did not have the resources to carry out his strategy, he would settle for the conquest and defense of the whole of Palestine. Following the War Cabinet meeting on December 12, both Allenby and the General Staff were asked for their estimate of the force required to successfully accomplish each of these options as well as the course to pursue in Palestine.[77]

Allenby's reply was cautious. He indicated that he could occupy Palestine with his present force providing local Turkish strength did not rise beyond 60,000 troops. On the other hand, if he was required to advance an extra 250 miles to Aleppo, he would need another eight to ten divisions, more than doubling the number of divisions he then possessed.[78]

Robertson was troubled by Allenby's assessment that Palestine could be subjugated and defended without additional reinforcements. As mentioned earlier, it was in October that the GOC in Egypt had "asked for an additional thirteen divisions just to conquer and hold southern Palestine, the Jaffa–Jerusalem line."[79] That fact was not lost on Lloyd George. He had long maintained that Robertson, in collusion with Allenby, was deliberately overrating the power of Ottoman resistance so as to discourage deeper involvement in Palestine. As a consequence, he noted in his memoirs, valuable time had been lost and it had taken Allenby "nine or ten months to accomplish what could have been achieved in two or three."[80]

Looking back, it can be seen that the tug-of-war between Lloyd George and Robertson over the campaign in the Turkish theater was having a debilitating effect upon the war. Quite apart from the time both consumed in attempting to outflank the other, it had led to delays or adoption of half-measures.

Fed up with Robertson, Lloyd George proposed to bypass him by referring all military and strategic questions relating to Turkey to the inter-Allied staff in Versailles. There, Lloyd George felt that he could count on Wilson to persuade the other permanent military representatives to support his agenda for 1918. Lloyd George's confidence in Wilson to do his bidding was not misplaced. The soldiers at Versailles maintained that the western front would be safe as long as the British and the French armies were supplied with the drafts necessary to keep their divisions up to strength and if, as expected, they were reinforced by at least two American divisions a month. They advised that the Allies should confine their efforts to local operations (to maintain the morale of the troops) until 1919, when the presence of Americans would be felt in France. In the interim, it was seen as unwise to remain relatively idle everywhere. There was not much likelihood of reaching a decision in the Balkans because of the enemy's superior lines of communication and the strength of its homogenous forces. On the other hand, they claimed, Turkey was on its last legs. Its armies, numbering no more than 250,000, were exhausted and scattered in three widely separated theaters with inferior communications linking them. The permanent military representatives calculated that the existing Allied forces in Mesopotamia and Palestine, reinforced perhaps by troops from India and East Africa, where fighting was dying down, would be sufficient to pound the Turks into submission. They saw no need to shift Allied troops from France to the Turkish theaters, a move that was not only unnecessary, but dangerous, in the face of an expected German attack.[81] The report, known as Joint Note No. 12, could not have pleased the prime minister more if he had written it himself.

Robertson was enraged that the prime minister was conspiring with Wilson to deny him a voice in deciding future military operations in Palestine. In a memorandum dated December 26 he mustered a host of technical arguments to show the War Cabinet that any significant extension of the campaign in Palestine was inadvisable and fraught with danger. He confined his remarks to the less ambitious of the two projects advanced earlier, explaining that with the Mesopotamian front locked in a stalemate and Russia out of the war, the Turks could concentrate a force of some 180,000 combatants in Syria and Palestine. It was conceivable that Allenby, with a force that would total 145,000 combatants after the addition of a division from Mesopotamia, could complete the conquest of Palestine but at the anticipated cost of 57,000 casualties, not counting the 20,000 or so that would be put out of action due to illness. The tens of thousands of replacements required to fill the manpower gaps could only be provided at the expense of Haig's army, a highly precarious step in view of the probable enemy attempt to seek a decision in the spring of 1918. To further strengthen his argument, Robertson pointed out that the conquest of the whole of Palestine, with the inevitable heavy casualties and the diversion of large forces from the western front, might still not produce the expected far-reaching results. Robertson reminded the War Cabinet that the Germans were in control of the Ottoman army and that, even if Constantinople wanted to bow out of the war, it was unlikely to be able to do so.[82] Robertson had undoubtedly inflated the level of Turkish resistance that the EEF was likely to encounter, but he was right in trying to restrict an advance beyond Jerusalem that would have drained resources needed elsewhere and brought no strategic or moral benefits.[83]

Robertson's memo made no impression on the War Cabinet, which went ahead with plans to prosecute the war more forcefully against the Turks. Lloyd George knew that Robertson, even with his influence slipping, would not abandon his efforts to impose a passive role on the British forces in the Middle East theaters. Taking advantage of parliament's recess during the holiday season, he summoned Wilson from Versailles to offer him Robertson's post. The two had a long talk about Britain's future military policy at the end of which Lloyd George was satisfied that Wilson's views coincided closely with his own. But Wilson was reluctant to go to the War Office under the prevailing circumstances and suggested instead that he be given more authority at Robertson's expense.[84]

By now, Lloyd George was more determined than ever to take control of the war away from the western bloc. While he searched for another way to drive Robertson out of the War Office, he also tried to identify a competent soldier to replace Haig. Robertson had assured the War Cabinet on December 19 that Haig fully realized that "we must act on the defence for some time to come, and he had no offensive plans in mind at present."[85] Haig contradicted that statement when he attended a meeting of the War Cabinet on January 7, 1918. He thought it was possible that the Germans would attack both the French and the BEF in the spring of 1918, holding their reserves in hand to exploit any break in the line. In such an event he expected the French to ask him for help, either in the form of British reserves or an extension of his front. He went on to say:

> In either case the British front would be weakened. In my opinion the best defence would be to continue our offensive in Flanders, because we would retain the initiative and attract the German Reserves against us. It is doubtful whether the French Army can withstand for long, a resolute and continued offensive on the part of the enemy.[86]

How the German army could sustain a full scale offensive against either of its foes when it was supposedly approaching collapse was a question that Lloyd

George failed to pose to Haig. Still, he and the other members of the War Cabinet were in no mood to see the slaughter in the Flanders mud repeated. It was the final straw for Lloyd George and he made up his mind to try to remove Haig before he destroyed the fighting strength of the BEF. On January 18 the prime minister invited Smuts to lunch and, during their conversation, asked him to undertake an extensive inspection of the western front and along the way to talk to the leading officers in the British army. The intent of the mission, as recorded by Hankey, who was present, was "to find out who are the rising men, and to see the new defences they are making to meet the forthcoming German offensive." When Smuts agreed to go at once, Lloyd George turned to Hankey and said, "I think you had better go, too."[87] It is not absolutely clear whether Smuts and Hankey were aware of the true purpose of their trip. In conversation with Haig, they were friendly and pledged their support and, from all appearances, gave no hint that Lloyd George wished to replace him.[88] In short, they were either somewhat naïve or hypocrites – the latter alternative seems unlikely.

On the day that the pair left for France, Lovat Fraser of the *Daily Mail* wrote a controversial article under the heading "Things Hidden" in which he ripped the General Staff for squandering Britain's manpower by pursuing an archaic strategy. It was as if Lloyd George had written the piece himself, but whether he was behind it is anybody's guess. Professor Woodward exonerates Lloyd George on the grounds that the last thing he "wanted was any suggestion that he was at the beck and call of Northcliffe, who inspired hatred in many quarters because of his often clumsy and megalomaniacal attempts to manipulate public opinion."[89] In any case, Fraser's blast backfired, generating heated condemnations in parliament and prompting the Unionist War Committee, a body representing Conservative backbenchers, to pass a resolution in support of Haig and Robertson and demanding that the government repudiate the press attack against them. The furor inhibited Lloyd George from making any change in the military leadership. The bitter pill was easier for him to swallow when Smuts and Hankey reported that the only promising general they encountered was Claude Jacob, a relatively obscure officer who commanded the Second Corps.[90] It had not been a very extensive survey, it should be added.

Robertson had no doubts that Lloyd George had inspired the article in the *Daily Mail* with one purpose in mind. With great bitterness, he wrote to H. A. Gwynne, editor of the Conservative *Morning Post* and outspoken opponent of civilian interference in military affairs: "What a d. ... d disgraceful position for a government to be in, to have to resort to such vile and unmanly tactics to get rid of those they don't like!"[91] The tortured CIGS was at the nadir of his fortunes, with his authority on the wane and subject to continuing direct and indirect attacks from the prime minister. His contempt for Lloyd George knew no bounds. The gap between the two men was so wide that no compromise was possible. "They can't pull together and the conduct of the war suffers accordingly," observed Maurice.[92] The vicious infighting could not continue indefinitely, and insiders recognized that ultimately the country would have to choose between the CIGS and Lloyd George. Although losing ground fast, Robertson still had plenty of fight left in him. This was evident at the SWC, which opened its deliberations on January 30, 1918.

The meeting of the SWC had been called to address several outstanding issues between Paris and London. Things were rather chaotic on the first day, owing mostly to indifferent planning on the part of Lloyd George. Hankey, called upon to write reports at the eleventh hour or, when taking minutes, forced to make sense out of confused testimony, painted an unflattering portrait of Lloyd George's methods in his diary on January 31:

> We are in a most frightful muddle – largely due to Ll. George. As usual he insisted on bringing over everyone he could think of. The result was that at yesterday's meeting we had present no less than three sets of military advisers – the Permanent Military Advisers on the Supreme War Council, the Chiefs of Staff, and the Commander-in-Chief. They all gave different advice, and the meeting got into a worst state of chaos than I have ever known in my wide experience.[93]

The first major order of business was to consider the conclusions contained in Joint Note No. 12. As noted previously, there was general agreement that since the Allies did not have the forces available for any large-scale operations in 1918, they ought to adopt an essentially defensive policy. Foch provoked an angry reaction from Lloyd George when he accused the British government of failing to call up enough men for military service, as if to suggest that Britain was not pulling its weight in the fight against the Germans. Lloyd George pointed out that Britain was making great naval, maritime and industrial efforts, not only for itself, but also for its allies, and for which a large supply of manpower was indispensable. He emphasized that beginning with the battle at the Somme, BEF losses had been greater than those of any of the Allies. He made it clear that the disposal of British manpower was the business of his government, not that of the French. Clemenceau interjected to cool tempers by stressing that Foch was drawing deductions from the actual drafts available and his remarks should not be interpreted as criticism of an ally.

The discussion turned to consider whether an all-out effort against Turkey, as recommended by the permanent military representatives, should take place. The French had no desire to see the level of British involvement in the Middle

East grow. Quite apart from the likelihood that their postwar territorial ambitions in that region would suffer, they worried that Lloyd George might be tempted to divert troops from the western front. Clemenceau did not conceal his displeasure with the Eastern venture, insisting that the security of the western front overrode all other considerations. With more and more German troops arriving on the western front and three French provinces under the heels of German invaders, it was difficult for him to approve of the dispatch of Entente troops to fight the Turks in another continent. He noted that the inter-Allied General Staff had recommended a campaign against the Turks, but only if the effectives on the western front were maintained. Since this condition could not be met, the proposal was automatically cancelled.

Lloyd George rejected Clemenceau's logic, claiming that the Germans, with a numerical inferiority of two to three and a half, had experienced no difficulty in maintaining their front in the west. He was no longer hopeful, as he had once been, that the Germans could be driven back to the Rhine. That being the case, the only option was to force the capitulation of one of Germany's allies. To that end, he would not abandon territory gained in Mesopotamia and Palestine in order to bring back the troops to bolster the western front, which had always been "overinsured".

The lively debate between Clemenceau and Lloyd George carried over the next day with the latter, more often than not, finding himself on the defensive. Robertson derived a good deal of satisfaction from watching Clemenceau pummel Lloyd George. "The P.M was very badly mauled and I never saw him look more knocked out," he subsequently wrote to Derby.[94] At the morning session on February 1 Lloyd George agreed to a compromise to win over a reluctant Clemenceau. An offensive against Turkey was accepted on condition that the British government take no steps to divert forces from, or relax its efforts on, the western front. Before the resolution passed, Clemenceau asked Robertson, who had remained silent during the discussions, for his opinion. The French prime minister was counting on the CIGS to condemn a plan that both he and Foch disliked. He was not disappointed. Unequivocal in favoring a defensive posture in all secondary theaters, Robertson was no less adamant in declaring that the proposed campaign in Palestine was impractical and that to attempt it would "be very dangerous and detrimental to our prospects of winning the war."[95] Robertson had committed the unpardonable sin of speaking out against his prime minister before a council of foreign delegates. He apologized to Lloyd George after the meeting, explaining that to have acted otherwise might have been interpreted as compliance with the plan. He noted that he was "afraid of being left in the same position as Fisher[96] over the Dardanelles affair."[97] But the prime minister was not appeased and, in fact, gave Robertson a piece of his mind. He told Robertson that having already made his views known to the War Cabinet, there was no need to repeat them before the SWC. Reflecting on the incident years later Robertson questioned Lloyd George's double standard:

> This [Lloyd George's blunt reply] I may observe was quite a different attitude from the one he had taken up when giving evidence before the Dardanelles Commission a year or so earlier.[98] He then agreed with the Commissioners that if naval and military advisers present at Ministerial Councils did not express dissent it was legitimate to assume that they agreed with what was being done.[99]

The plans for 1918 having been decided, the council turned its attention to the idea of creating a General Reserve, as proposed by the inter-Allied General Staff in a separate report identified as Joint Note No.14. Recent intelligence confirmed the likelihood that the Germans were beginning to shift some of their divisions from Russia to the west. Consequently, the Allies had to consider creating a central Strategic Reserve to be thrown, as required, against the Germans when they chose to attack, presumably in the next few months. But where would the necessary divisions come from? The three army commanders – Haig, Pétain and Diaz – expressed no opposition in principle to the establishment of a General Reserve, but none wanted to part with any troops at their immediate disposal. The second serious problem was to determine who would be in charge of the central mobile reserve. Seeking to bypass Wilson and the other permanent military representatives, Robertson collaborated with Foch to propose that the allocation of reserves should be controlled by the French and British chiefs of staff with Italy, the United States and Belgium to be represented in some capacity. Lloyd George objected at once, since control of the General Reserve would impact Allied strategy. He tactfully pointed out that Robertson had the duty of advising the War Cabinet in London and would not always be able to leave his post in case of an emergency. Robertson's blueprint for the new organization was rejected when both Clemenceau and Orlando spoke out against it as well. There was no support for the other schemes introduced and so the issue remained unresolved when the conference adjourned until the following day.[100]

Robertson was so troubled by the prospect that he might be denied any role in the management of the Strategic Reserve that he sent the prime minister a note after returning to his room:

> I do not quite see how a British Commander-in-Chief can be made, constitutionally, to obey the orders of an Allied body, or indeed of anyone except the Army Council and the Secretary of State for War – a Minister

of the Crown. If the CIGS were made a Member of the Versailles body, as is proposed in the case of General Foch, this difficulty could be more easily surmounted perhaps.[101]

Robertson's plea had no effect on Lloyd George. The prime minister remained committed to excluding the CIGS from any body supervising the General Reserve, although he was unable to produce a plan on his own to that end. At breakfast on the morning of February 2 Wilson came to the rescue of the prime minister. He proposed a formula calling for a board composed of permanent military members with his close friend Foch, who would replace Weygand, serving as chairman. Lloyd George hesitated to give Foch, known to be offensive-minded and with whom he had just crossed swords, the authority to influence strategy. But the compromise, which he came around to accepting, did offer two precious advantages from his point of view: it would eliminate Robertson from having a voice and be "a giant step" towards creating the post of generalissimo that he "had long argued was essential to the efficient conduct of the war."[102]

To pave the way for the passage of Wilson's plan, Lloyd George met privately with Orlando and Clemenceau, with the former expressing concern before reluctantly accepting it. In defending it in the full council, Lloyd George's skillful and impassionate arguments, according to Hankey, brought tears to the eyes of Foch, Clemenceau and Orlando.[103] Haig and Robertson, on the other hand, simmered with indignation. Haig broke his silence by observing that under the constitution, the British Commander-in-Chief received his orders through the intermediary of the CIGS. Since it would involve a change in constitutional procedure, he asked the following question, "By what channel am I to receive my orders from this new body?" Lloyd George replied that orders would come directly from the permanent military representatives. Given the importance of the matter, Haig probed further, only to be cut off by Lloyd George, who remarked brusquely that he was acting with the full authority of the War Cabinet.[104] When the session broke up, Robertson, who allowed his bitterness to boil over, "remained sitting alone in his place, motionless, his head resting on his hand, glaring silently in front of him."[105] Haig, although sharing Robertson's sentiments, was more philosophical and less vehement in his opposition to something he was powerless to change. In any case, he doubted that his plans would be affected by the General Reserve since he had no intentions to hand over to it any divisions under his control. He could justify his stand by claiming that as the government had not met his request for reinforcements, he could not part with any of his troops for reasons of safety. Haig told his wife that if the Allied prime ministers wanted to create a General Reserve, the necessary troops would have to come from Italy, Salonica or some other secondary theater.[106]

The new body, known as the Executive War Board, was invested with much of the powers hitherto reserved for the chiefs of staff and the ministers of war. Consisting of Foch (as chairman), Wilson, Cadorna and Bliss, it was to provide a General Reserve for the western, Italian and Balkan fronts. It was to determine the size of the General Reserve, the contribution of each national army to it, and the areas of concentration. It would decide when and where the reserves would be used before handing them over to the relevant commander-in-chief.

The appointment of Foch as head of the Executive Board facilitated the settlement of the troublesome question dealing with the adjustment of the British and French lines. At the Boulogne Conference in September 1917 the principle that the British line should be extended was accepted, but it was left to the two Allied commanders to fix the distance. Haig met Pétain at Amiens in mid October and arranged to extend his front as far as Barisis, thus relieving half a dozen French divisions. Haig, however, was compelled to delay implementing the agreement because of the heavy German counterattack at Cambrai and the dispatch of five of his divisions to help shore up the beleaguered Italians. Worried about the safety of the French front, Clemenceau warned London that he would resign unless the British extended their line all the way to Berry-au-Bac, thirty-seven miles beyond Barisis. The British balked, but succeeded in persuading Clemenceau to refer the matter to the inter-Allied General Staff. On January 10 the permanent military representatives put forth their report (labeled as Joint Note No. 10), which amounted to a compromise. They recommended that the British extend their line some fourteen miles beyond Barisis, the exact point of junction to be settled by the two commanders.[107] By the time the opening meeting of the Supreme War Council began on January 30, Haig had fulfilled his promise and assumed control of the French front as far as Barisis.

Haig objected to the inter-Allied General Staff's recommendations for an extension of the British front beyond Barisis but he did so in a restrained manner. He recalled many instances when he had willingly complied with requests to take over more of the French line, at times without reference to his own government. His position as regards manpower was critical in view of the heavy casualties sustained in recent fighting, the dispatch of divisions to Italy and the lack of replacements from home. If, as was possible, the enemy attacked in force, his losses could reach half a million, in which case the number of his divisions would be reduced from fifty-seven to thirty-five. As much as he would like to help the French, it was impossible for him, with the forces at his disposal, to lengthen his front any further.

Lloyd George followed up, emphasizing the danger of overruling the field marshal after he had stated that he could not be responsible for the safety of the line beyond Barisis. He reminded the French that the British army had borne the brunt of the fighting for many months and, as a result, its divisions were depleted and required rest and its fortifications were badly in need of repair. In search of a compromise, the British accepted in principle the recommendations of Joint Note No. 10, with the proviso that it be left to Haig and Pétain to arrange the point of contact between the British and French armies.[108] In private, Pétain told Haig not to fret, for he would not press him to carry out the extension.[109] As it happened, the two commanders never bothered to meet again to discuss pushing the British line beyond Barisis.

Lloyd George had good reason to be satisfied over the outcome of the Versailles conference, which he had thoroughly dominated. He had been able to outflank Robertson and Haig through the creation of the Executive Board, which would control the General Reserve and exercise a good deal of influence over Entente strategy. He had succeeded in redirecting Britain's military effort against Turkey and persuading Britain's allies to adopt an active-defense on the western front in 1918. Russia's collapse, the weakness of the French army, and the slow arrival of the Americans in the fighting line, convinced him that victory on the western front in 1918 was unattainable, or would prove so costly as to prevent Britain from dominating the peace settlement. He preferred to delay the final decision in the west until 1919 when the French army had recovered and significant American assistance was on hand. In the interim Britain would defeat Turkey, providing both a moral boost to encourage the British public to sustain another campaign and a greater measure of security for the nation's Asiatic empire.

Before the meeting of the SWC, the War Cabinet, at the urging of Lloyd George, had decided to send Smuts to Egypt to confer with Allenby and a representative of Lieutenant General Sir William Marshall, who had taken control of the Mesopotamian force upon the death of Maude from cholera, as to the best method of coordinating British resources in order to eliminate Turkey from the war.[110] The prime minister distrusted the military's assessment and for that reason circumvented both the War Office and Allenby. By relying on the advice of Smuts, who had come around to his way of thinking, he had stacked the deck in his favor. It was clear to Colonel Walter Kirke, the Deputy DMO, who was a member of the mission sailing to Egypt, that Smuts was expected "to lend his bogus but considerable military prestige to supporting anything proposed by LG."[111]

Smuts left to undertake his mission early in February. The prime minister was pinning his hopes on achieving a cheap and easy victory over the Turks. Although he may not have understood all the implications, he would be taking a significant risk by providing Allenby with reinforcements at the expense of the western front. If anything went wrong, he would be vulnerable to the deadly charge of letting the army down, which in turn could bring down his government.

Chapter 13

BEFORE THE STORM

Although Lloyd George had stated publicly on many occasions that the war would not end until Germany surrendered unconditionally, he never really foreclosed the possibility of peace talks in order to avoid prolonging the horrendous slaughter. After the Kühlmann peace feeler had raised false hopes, Lloyd George told Riddell that "the time might come when they will offer terms we can consider."[1] His conditions for a stable peace included restitution of territory under Germany's occupation and democratization of its government. But the moment to engage in peace talks did not appear near in view of the Entente's dismal prospects.

In November 1917 President Wilson sent House overseas to urge the Allied leaders to enunciate moderate war aims so as to counteract Bolshevik propaganda and weaken public resolve in Germany. The mission arrived in London at the most inopportune moment. On November 28 the *Daily Telegraph* published a letter from Lord Lansdowne, a Conservative elder statesman, who made public the case for a negotiated settlement he had initially advanced in a memorandum to the Asquith cabinet a year earlier. Appalled that the flower of the country's manhood was being sacrificed in a conflict he believed was unwinnable, he pleaded with the government to revise its war aims, making it clear that the Allies did not intend to destroy Germany as a great power or ruin its commerce. Only by offering Germany acceptable terms, he asserted, would the war end by negotiation.[2]

The letter created a sensation, and its object, namely the futility of pursuing the war, emerged as a contentious political issue for the next few weeks. Lloyd George was livid with Lansdowne, whose action he felt had ruled out supporting the American call for an official statement of war aims. He informed Riddell that the letter was "ill-timed" because the Entente's current military situation would make it impossible to secure favorable terms.[3] In a public speech meant to answer Lansdowne's letter, he insisted that a premature peace would represent "a betrayal of the great trust with which my colleagues and I have been charged."[4] Bonar Law openly rebuked Lansdowne, calling his letter a "national misfortune" and emphasizing that a peace on the basis of the views expressed "would be nothing less than a defeat."[5] Still, Lansdowne's letter found a sympathetic audience not only with antiwar activists, but also with backbenchers of both major parties, labor leaders, prominent Liberals and even some cabinet ministers.[6]

As a consequence, Hankey, among others, urged Lloyd George to make a declaration of war aims "to try and get the people back to the old idealistic spirit of the early days of the war."[7] The prime minister, however, refused to do so, even though he was well aware of the growing sentiment for peace in the country. He may have recognized that a knockout blow against the Germans was improbable, but he preferred to continue the struggle until the Allies were in a position to negotiate for a better settlement. New developments, however, compelled him to change his mind.

In December, Smuts, accompanied by Philip Kerr, Lloyd George's secretary, journeyed to Switzerland to discuss the terms under which Austria and Turkey would leave the war. On December 18 and 19 Smuts held secret meetings with Count Albert Mensdorff, a former Austrian Ambassador to Britain, in a Geneva suburb. Smuts was instructed to discuss terms only for a separate peace and to assure Mensdorff that if Vienna broke with Berlin, the Allies would leave Austria intact. Mensdorff was grateful for the concession, which was preferable to the dismemberment of Austria in the interest of the subject nationalities, as the Entente had previously called for. But his orders were to insist on terms for a general peace, one that included Germany. Neither Smuts nor Mensdorff had any leeway to compromise. Smuts told the Austrian statesman that Britain's refusal to work for a general peace was based on the belief that an undefeated Germany would threaten the future political stability of Europe. Mensdorff was adamant that Austria, while anxious for peace, would not do anything as treacherous and dishonorable as to desert its ally. He argued that if Britain set forth reasonable terms, his government would exert great pressure on the Germans to consider a negotiated settlement.[8] Nothing definite resulted from the talks, but Smuts was optimistic that if the Entente could deal with the Austrians alone, he saw no insuperable difficulties in the way of a satisfactory arrangement. In the past, the Italians had stood in the way of a separate treaty with Austria by refusing to withdraw territorial claims guaranteed to them under the secret Treaty of London (signed on April 26, 1915).[9] But the British government was satisfied that Italy's recent humiliation at Caporetto made it more likely that it would adopt a sensible attitude, once "confronted with a concrete offer."[10]

Much as Lloyd George wanted to induce Austria to leave the war, he believed that the chances were greater that an arrangement could be struck with Turkey, since it was reportedly war weary and receiving little help from Germany.[11] Turkey, in fact, was hardly on the point of collapse and he was not being realistic if he expected Constantinople to accept the harsh terms the Entente was certain to lay down as a condition for peace. While ignoring the claims of France, Lloyd George told Haig on February 17 that Britain did not intend to give up "Mesopotamia or Palestine or Syria (if we took it)," but would be prepared to compensate Turkey monetarily "and to recognize her flag as supreme in those countries just as we did for many years in Egypt."[12]

Kerr had been deputed to probe Turkey's intentions through Dr. Humbert Parodi, an Egyptian middleman often used by the British to contact Turkish authorities. Parodi explained that the Committee of Union and Progress (CUP), which held the reins of power in Turkey, was divided into two factions, one favoring Germany and the other, the Entente. The Germanophiles dominated the CUP and remained confident that Germany would win the war. Parodi thought that the smaller pro-Entente faction might be able to seize control of the CUP if Turkey were offered terms along the following lines: Arabia, Syria, Palestine and Mesopotamia to be given autonomy under nominal Turkish suzerainty; the fate of Armenia to be decided by the Entente; the integrity of Turkey proper, including Constantinople, be assured. He requested that Britain state its peace terms in a way that would be clear and definite, so that there would be no misunderstanding. Kerr was not encouraged by the interview. Parodi did not represent the Ottoman government, and it was obvious from his remarks that the ruling faction in the CUP was not ready to negotiate on terms that either the British or its allies would have found acceptable.[13]

A more compelling factor was the fallout from the Bolshevik seizure of power in Russia. On November 22 Lenin and his associates published the texts of the secret Allied treaties so as to expose them as shameless predators, no better than the Central Powers.[14] Their next major diplomatic step, more harmful than embarrassing for the Allies, was to sign an armistice with the Central Powers on December 15, 1917. This was followed by their appeal to the Central Powers for a statement of peace terms preparatory to the opening of formal negotiations in the Polish town of Brest-Litovsk. The Central Powers obliged, giving a false impression that they were ready to negotiate on the Bolshevik formula of no annexations or indemnities. The moderate war aims enunciated by the spokesman of the Central Powers, Count Ottokar Czernin, coming on top of the publications of the secret treaties, appeared to call into question Allied claims that they were fighting to thwart Germany's imperialistic objectives.[15]

Hitherto, there had been no call for the Entente to give a wide-ranging definition of its war aims. Lloyd George had been vague in treating the matter in public, being specific only in demanding the withdrawal of Germany from occupied territory as a prerequisite for peace. Indeed, he had considered a definition of war aims to be counterproductive. To do so would reveal that

Britain and its allies had territorial ambitions – sometimes in conflict with one another – that were inconsistent with their professed idealism.

Lloyd George began to waver after learning of Mensdorff's suggestion that a redefinition of the Entente's war objectives, with the implied accent on moderation, might have "an important effect on Austrian and even German policy." Czernin's declaration proved decisive, leaving the Entente with little choice but to respond with its own declaration of liberal war aims.[16]

There are some historians who have gone beyond the traditional explanation. It has been suggested that Lloyd George's knowledge that US President Wilson intended to make a major statement on war aims may have played a part in spurring him to action. A case can be made for thinking along those lines. Lloyd George may have wanted to anticipate Wilson's declaration to steal some of his thunder or, as one historian put it, "to steer him along safe channels."[17] To what extent, if any, these considerations influenced Lloyd George's decision must remain a matter of conjecture.

At least Wilson's name did surface when the War Cabinet discussed issuing an independent statement on war aims on December 28 and again three days later. The members agreed that it was necessary to make an official and detailed reply to the challenge posed by the enemy. It was recognized that the best approach would be to issue a declaration of war aims to which all the Allied countries subscribed. However, experience had shown that a document of this nature was difficult to draft and was apt to lose its effectiveness and to "become merely a cumulative statement of every country's claims." Thus Lloyd George accepted Cecil's suggestion that the government follow Wilson's practice of issuing pronouncements solely on behalf of the United States, and declare war aims unilaterally. That settled, the War Cabinet agreed that the statement should be couched in moderate and reasonable terms in order to show both Allied and enemy countries that the war was not being prolonged for imperialistic or unreasonable war aims. The War Cabinet discussed key points that should be included in the draft, but left it to the prime minister, assisted by Cecil and Smuts, to work out the details.[18]

Lloyd George held little hope that Germany, in the hour of its great triumph in Russia, was genuinely interested in a broad peace.[19] On one of the rare occasions, he concurred with Robertson's observation that the Germans were not seeking a peace as much as a truce in order to sow dissention among the Allies, while rallying their people and husbanding their resources for another and more conclusive war at a later date.[20] Lloyd George's statement was not intended to make serious overtures to the enemy. Rather, its purpose was to stiffen resistance at home, counteract enemy propaganda and show the people of the Central Powers that it was not the Allies, but their own governments that stood in the way of peace.[21] Still, the prime minister was willing to leave the door open to the possibility of negotiating an end to the war and, to all appearances, at Russia's expense. He was bitter over Russia's defection and he seemed disposed to giving the Germans a free hand in the east in exchange for generous concessions to the Allies in the west.[22]

Although the Allies were faring poorly in the conflict, there was no defeatist talk among the policymakers in London. Lloyd George and his colleagues remained confident that with the vast potential supply of manpower in America, it was only a matter of time before the tide of war turned in the Entente's favor. They were much less certain, however, that the Allies would be able to inflict a defeat on Germany of such dimensions as to compel it to renounce militarism. They accepted Barnes' view that to insist that Germany embrace democracy would be a barrier to eventual peace negotiations.[23]

In the final draft, Lloyd George contributed some of the passages, but most of the work was done by others, particularly Smuts and Cecil.[24] It was approved by the War Cabinet after minor alterations. Before delivering his speech, Lloyd George consulted with leaders of the Liberal party and representatives of organized labor. In recent weeks, many Liberals had expressed sympathy with Lansdowne's sentiments. Lloyd George felt that it was important to obtain the endorsement of their leaders so that his peace proclamation would be on behalf of the whole nation. Never entirely politically secure, it may also be that he was worried that radicals and pacifists might convince Asquith that he should offer to head a peace ministry as an alternative to his own.[25] By associating Asquith with the government's terms, he was preempting such a possibility. Whatever the case, Lloyd George met with Asquith and Grey for breakfast on January 4, 1918. The gathering took place at Asquith's house and the atmosphere between former colleagues was cordial and relaxed. Lloyd George read them his prepared text and they approved it, suggesting only slight stylistic changes.[26]

Likewise, the prime minister arranged to confer with representatives of the Labour party. In mid-December a subcommittee of the parliamentary committee of the Trade Union Congress (TUC) and the National Executive of the Labour Party completed a memorandum setting down its own war aims (see ch. 3) and unequivocal opposition to selfish imperialist objectives. The program was accepted by a special Labour party conference held on December 28.[27] Lloyd George could not afford to alienate organized labor. On the contrary, he required the goodwill and cooperation of trade unions if his government hoped to obtain further army recruits from exempted workers. Lloyd George's discussion with labor leaders went off better than he expected. His task in gaining their support was made much easier because labor peace proposals did not differ significantly from those he intended to put forward.[28]

As parliament was not in session, Lloyd George chose to deliver his address before an audience of trade unionists on January 5 at Caxton Hall. To set the right tone, he dismissed Czernin's statement as vague and inconsistent, although his own program was hardly a model of clarity. He had to build layers of camouflage to conceal his true intent. He told Riddell that "we should have to secure some territory to compensate us for what we had expended – the greater part of the German Colonies, Palestine and Mesopotamia." He added that the Germans might be satisfied if they could expand at Russia's expense. As far as he was concerned, Russia had acted badly and should be left to face the consequences alone.[29]

Lloyd George told his audience that Britain had been driven into the war in defense of the public law of Europe, which had been ruthlessly violated by Germany's invasion of Belgium. He denied that Britain wanted to break up Germany or destroy its navy. Contrary to what he had said in the past, the removal of the militarists from office was no longer deemed essential. He declared that the establishment of democracy in Germany, while desirable to promote a lasting peace, was a matter for the German people alone to decide. He made no mention of Britain's desire to annex Germany's former colonies. Instead, he called for the colonies to be placed under governments acceptable to their inhabitants – the principle of self-determination was, of course, a mask to ensure that Britain retained the overseas territories. He demanded the restoration of Belgium, Serbia and Montenegro, as well as occupied parts of Romania, Italy and France. Beyond calling for a revival of an independent Poland, he ignored Germany's occupation of large stretches of Russian territory. He confined his remarks about Russia to warning the Bolsheviks that if they signed a separate peace, the Allies would "have no means of intervening to arrest the catastrophe" certain to befall their country. It was a signal to the Germans that given the weakness of Russia, they would be free to retain a large part of their eastern conquests.

Lloyd George made it clear that Britain would stand by France's demand for the return of Alsace–Lorraine. There were some ministers who questioned privately whether it was in Britain's interest to risk prolonging the war so that France could recover the lost provinces, but to have insisted otherwise would have shattered the alliance. On September 25, 1917 Painlevé pressured Lloyd George into agreeing that Britain would not lay down its arms until France recovered the territory that it had been forced to cede to Germany in 1871. Painlevé became suspicious about Britain's intentions when Balfour told him during an interview several weeks earlier that he fully supported France's desire to regain its lost provinces, but that he was speaking only for himself. Consequently, the French prime minister made it a point to obtain a public declaration from Britain that it would back France's claim to Alsace–Lorraine, a request Lloyd George felt he could not refuse.[30] The prime minister's attitude was different when it came to fulfilling Italy's aspirations. He pointed out that Britain would support only those territorial claims against Austria that were in accord with the principle of nationality.

Lloyd George also touched on issues that centered on the lesser enemy states. He denied that Britain planned to dismantle the Austrian Empire, but at the same time, required it to grant self-government on democratic principles to its subject nationalities. Similarly, Turkey was to retain its capital and "the rich and renowned lands of Asia Minor and Thrace," but not the rest of its Empire – Armenia, Mesopotamia, Palestine, Syria and Arabia. By applying the principle of self-determination, Britain would be assured of exercising control or influence over the territories it coveted. In another vital area of the Middle East, Lloyd George noted that the waterways linking the Mediterranean to the Black Sea – Bosphorus and the Dardanelles – should be internationalized.

There were two final points: the first was to indemnify British merchant seamen and others who were injured by nations acting in violation of international law; the second was the establishment of an international organization "to limit the burden of armaments and diminish the probability of war."[31]

All in all, the stated terms, as David French has noted, marked a sharp retreat from the maximum war aims list that "the British had agreed to with their allies between 1914 and 1916, or even from the more moderate, but still ambitious program they had transmitted to Wilson in January 1917."[32] Of course, the statement was delivered mostly for propaganda value and did not accurately reflect what the British hoped to gain from the war.[33] Interestingly enough, the War Cabinet, although expecting to acquire former German colonies and a large portion of the Ottoman Empire, never got around to defining a formal program of war aims because of the sudden end of the conflict.

The reaction to Lloyd George's speech at home was mixed, just as it was among Britain's allies. Henderson, now out of the government but still a dominant force in the Labour party, generally approved of Lloyd George's speech, but he found disconcerting the brusque treatment accorded to the Bolsheviks. J. L. Garvin, editor of the *Observer*, was convinced that if the Germans accepted Lloyd George's terms, they would be stronger than they had been in 1914 and he predicted that after a brief pause, a new war in which they would emerge triumphant. Churchill expressed similar sentiments. By contrast, Riddell believed that the speech was a tour de force and, as far as he could determine, had "met with almost universal approval."[34]

From France, Clemenceau gave a one-sentence public endorsement, but privately was rather lukewarm, telling Esher "that Germany can and should be beaten flat."[35] The Italian government was less than pleased that Dalmatia might elude its grip, as Lloyd George had confined his support of Italy's claims against the Austrian Empire only to those areas consistent with the principle of nationality. The Serbian Crown Prince, for his part, lamented that public morale had been undermined by Lloyd George's failure to recognize Serbia's aspirations.[36] President Wilson was of two minds about the speech. He was delighted that the British prime minister's views were similar to his own and that there would be no confrontation with London over war objectives. But he was peeved that Lloyd George had made his terms known publicly before he did. The President had already drafted a speech on the subject that he intended to deliver before Congress, and he feared that Lloyd George had irreparably blunted the impact of his message. His first thought was that his own address was no longer necessary, but House convinced him otherwise. He assured Wilson that his address "would so smother the Lloyd George speech that it would be forgotten and that he, the President, would once more become the spokesman for the Entente, and indeed ... for the liberals of the world."[37]

House's flattering prediction was borne out, but not necessarily because Wilson's blueprint for peace on January 8 had more merit than the one Lloyd George delivered three days earlier. Indeed, the two speeches were nearly akin in substance and neither man can be said to have had a commanding authority over the other. Why then, did Wilson's Fourteen Points have more impact on contemporary thinking and on posterity than Lloyd George's statement? His program was given wide publicity and translated into numerous languages and its style was appealing – a series of "placard" points giving the impression of clarity. Given that the United States was free from territorial ambitions and secret treaties, Wilson had more credibility than Lloyd George. His Fourteen Points were directed nearly as much to America's allies as to the Central Powers – in short, a peace without victory. Going beyond Lloyd George's vague and passing reference, Wilson was unequivocal in emphasizing the establishment of a world organization committed to disarmament and the preservation of the peace.

Wilson's address was enthusiastically received in the United States and in European liberal and radical circles. The response among Allied statesmen, however, was more circumspect. Lloyd George sent word through the Foreign Office that he was grateful that his and Wilson's peace policies were "so entirely in harmony."[38] The complimentary message was necessarily vague because, as the Foreign Office explained to its ambassador in Washington, Sir Cecil Spring-Rice, "there are certain obstacles to a more precise endorsement, and there are naturally some slight divergences between the two speeches." Much as Lloyd George wanted to stress that the President's program coincided in the main with his own, there were several important differences. Wilson's second point calling for absolute freedom of the seas was alien to Britain's interest and was an issue that would have to be resolved at a later date. The other major disagreement was over Russia. Lloyd George took a hard line towards the Bolsheviks, leaving no doubt that Britain would wash its hands of Russia if it persisted with the Brest-Litovsk negotiations. In case peace talks materialized, Lloyd George was prepared to offer concessions to Germany at Russia's expense. Wilson, on the other hand, insisted on German withdrawal from Russian territory and sought to establish a bridge between the Allies and the Bolshevik government. He hinted at the possibility of extending American aid to Russia, regardless of the character of its rulers and their apparent unwillingness to fight.

There was no immediate reaction from the enemy to either of the two speeches. Lloyd George wanted Smuts to again journey to Switzerland to reestablish contact with Count Mensdorff. The Foreign Office reasoned that Italy would feel betrayed if it discovered that Anglo–Austrian talks had been held behind its back. Foreign Office officials placed no faith in Mensdorff's overtures and worried that efforts at personal diplomacy would backfire, resulting in the departure of Italy, not Austria, from the war.[39] Smuts, who was aware of Foreign Office concerns, argued that renewal of his mission should be postponed until the effects of the prime minister's statement in enemy countries were known. The War Cabinet agreed with Smuts.[40] As Germany's rulers persisted in keeping silent, Lloyd George sought to draw them out by questioning their commitment to peace during a speech he made at the Trade Union Congress on January 18: "There has been no response from any man in any position in Germany that indicates a desire on the part of the ruling powers in that land to approach that problem in a spirit of equity."[41]

The long-awaited reply from Berlin came in the form of Chancellor Georg Hertling's address to the Central Committee of the Reichstag on January 24. Hertling did not mince his words in flatly rejecting the peace moves by Lloyd George and Wilson.[42] His answer may have disappointed the members of the War Cabinet, but it could hardly have come as a surprise. All along, Lloyd George and others had suspected that Czernin's statement was just a smokescreen. As it happened, the Germans were only interested in concluding a separate peace with Russia. With the strength of their army undiminished, they were confident of crushing the French and British on the battlefield and of establishing their hegemony in Europe.

The War Cabinet had barely redirected all of its attention on the war, when the long simmering feud between Lloyd George and Robertson burst into the open. It will be remembered that the prime minister had taken an indirect approach to undermine Robertson's influence by promoting the establishment of an inter-Allied Supreme War Council and appointing Henry Wilson as its British representative, followed by a successful maneuver at Versailles to place the General Reserve in the hands of the newly formed Executive War Board headed by Foch.

Lloyd George knew from previous experience that Robertson would use every expedient to rally the country to his side in preparation for the impending showdown. The prime minister had reason to fear the consequences of trying to dismiss Robertson if Derby and Haig were willing to stand or fall with him. On January 11 Lloyd George tried to separate Derby from the soldiers by offering him the embassy in Paris. Derby turned down the appointment, as he considered it his duty to protect the generals from the prime minister's wrath.[43] Lloyd George, however, was not easily discouraged. On February 3 he confided to Hankey that he intended to replace Balfour with Cecil at the Foreign Office, banish Derby to Paris, and send Milner to the War Office.[44]

Robertson assumed that with he, Derby and Haig presenting a united front, Lloyd George would have no option but to retreat or face a political storm, the consequences of which might topple his ministry. Although the CIGS considered Derby to be supportive and aboveboard, he was less certain that the secretary for war had sufficient mettle to stand up to Lloyd George. In an effort to stiffen Derby's backbone, Robertson wrote to him on February 2, asking him pointedly whether he was prepared to tolerate a system in which an officer, neither on the Army Council nor directly under the control of secretary of war, was invested with the authority to issue orders to a commander in charge of a two million-man army. In a postscript he added, "The Army, the Army Council, the C.I.G.S., the Commanders-in-Chief, will look to you, their Minister, to see that they are not placed in an impossible, unfair, and unpractical position."[45] This seemed to spur Derby into writing an uncharacteristically harsh note to the prime minister: "I might as well have been a dummy for all the advice I have been asked for. ... It is impossible for anybody in my position to accept such a situation."[46]

At the War Cabinet meeting on February 4, Derby was still in a combative mood and refused to cast a vote in favor of ratifying the prime minister's agreement with Britain's allies to establish a General Reserve. But Derby stood alone and the resolution passed. Subsequently, the prime minister voiced his hope that the Army Council would act in good faith and give practical effect to the Supreme War Council's decision without delay. To avoid revealing classified information, not to mention instigating what was certain to be a divisive national debate, it was also decided that the Press Bureau be instructed to prevent any reference to the formation or command of the Allied General Reserve in British newspapers.[47]

Lloyd George evidently did not understand army culture, because if he had, he would have realized that the chances were nil that the Army Council would render a verdict contrary to the wishes of Robertson and Derby. To the surprise of no one, except some ill-informed members of the War Cabinet, the Army Council objected to the proposed status of the Executive War Board. One reason given was that the new arrangement was unworkable as it placed Haig under two masters, Foch and the Army Council. Another, that it was unconstitutional, for it impinged on the province of the Army Council, "which was responsible for the safety and welfare of the British army."[48]

All that remained to cement Robertson's position was Haig's unqualified support. But on February 7 Derby breakfasted with Lloyd George, who told him that Haig had approved of the main principles of the Versailles agreements. Derby, who had expected Haig to be in Robertson's corner, was shaken by the revelation. Later in the morning, Derby wrote to Haig to request his confirmation:

> If it is really so that you agree with the principles ... then I should be justified in remaining in office, because it would then only be a question of Robertson opposing a scheme to which you had given your assent. If, on the other hand, you are in agreement with Robertson, and Robertson is got rid of because he won't agree to it, then, naturally I should have to go too.[49]

A troubled Robertson, having heard Lloyd George make the same statement about Haig's views, hoped to draw his old comrade firmly on his side:

> It would help me if you could incidentally drop a line to Derby and say what you think about the Reserve question, so far as concerns the proposal that the Executive Committee should issue orders to you on this subject – thus constituting two authorities. ... I ask this because LG states that you are quite agreeable and in fact [have] accepted it. The solution is, put me on the Versailles Committee, then all is well, I think.[50]

Haig had his own problems and had no wish to become embroiled in the escalating dispute between Robertson and the prime minister. But Derby had requested his presence in London and his only option was to indicate what day and time he would be arriving at Victoria Station. On the issue under discussion, he offered Robertson only token support. "I consider General Reserve desirable but do not concur in system set up for commanding it," was his reply to Derby.[51]

Lloyd George's plans were almost derailed when the *Morning Post* published a telegram from Colonel Repington in Paris on February 8. An able military correspondent, Repington had been fired by the *Times* and was currently working for the *Morning Post*. In the cable he declared that the recent decisions of the inter-Allied War Council were of so strange a character that "Parliament should demand the fullest details and a Parliamentary Committee should examine them at once and take the opinions of our General Staff and our commanders in the field concerning the new arrangements." In the evening, the pro-Unionist *Globe* reprinted the Repington telegram and added comments of its own. It trusted that Asquith would not stand idly by and allow the High Command to be broken to "gratify the whim of any individual, however important." The paper went on to say:

> It may also be hoped that the House of Commons ... will refuse to allow itself to be elbowed out of its proper functions, and that at least we may be allowed to know what is going on behind the scenes, as no arrangement can make for military efficiency that precipitates a crisis in our High Command on the eve of a new campaign. Is there or is there not a Generalissimo?

It was assumed in high political circles – inaccurately, it must be said – that Robertson had leaked classified information to Repington to serve his own purpose. Milner was especially indignant, telling Lloyd George bluntly that "the sooner we make a move the better." Milner thought that Haig would honor the Versailles agreement, but that if he proved intractable, he should be superseded as well. "It is no use having a great rumpus and getting rid of Robertson," he perceptively observed, "if the policy is to be sidetracked ... by Haig."[52] But Lloyd George was unwilling to take such extreme measures. He surmised that if he could drive a wedge between Haig and Robertson, he could achieve his purpose with the minimum of political difficulty.

Lloyd George had breakfast with Milner and Derby on February 9, at which time the decision was taken to relieve Robertson of his current responsibilities. The prime minister agreed to prepare a document defining the relations between the War Office, War Cabinet and Versailles. The meeting broke up and the prime minister immediately attended to his task. In the first draft he produced, Wilson would be appointed Deputy CIGS and a member of the Army Council in addition to retaining his seat at Versailles; orders regarding the handling of the General Reserve would be sent directly to Haig by the Deputy CIGS; and the powers of the new CIGS would be reduced to what they had been before Robertson went to the War Office – that is, the CIGS would continue to be the chief military adviser to the government, but he would no longer be responsible for issuing orders to the commanders in the field.

Lloyd George showed the draft to Derby and, after he left, called in Milner at 12:30 p.m. Milner objected on the grounds that Wilson's close association with the War Office would eradicate his independent position. Without missing a beat, the prime minister produced another plan in which Robertson and Wilson would exchange posts. Milner replied that the new scheme was not much of an improvement, but Lloyd George disagreed. If Robertson accepted the new formula he would be left to cool his heels at Versailles, while Wilson and Lloyd George controlled policy in London. On the other hand, if he turned down what appeared to be a good position, his support would erode, as he would no longer be seen as the wronged party. Lloyd George felt that either way he could not lose.[53]

The only potential stumbling block was Haig, as Lloyd George was uncertain how he would react to the proposed arrangement. Derby was on hand to greet Haig on his arrival at Victoria Station at 3:30 p.m. Derby was unaware of the counterproposal Lloyd George had revealed to Milner. By previous arrangement with the driver, the motorcar took a circuitous route to 10 Downing Street so that Derby would have time to talk with Haig. He announced that Robertson was going to be sacked and that this issue, having been settled, Haig's opinion was no longer sought. Haig was not happy that Wilson and Foch, both of whom he distrusted, would command so much authority.

When Haig sat down with Lloyd George, he voiced his concern, but not in personal terms: "I pointed out the tremendous powers now being given to Versailles that the Military Representatives there had full powers to commit the Government *possibly against my opinion* and take decisions which the British Government ought alone to take." Instead, he preferred the CIGS's proposal (made at Versailles) by which Robertson and Foch should issue orders jointly regarding the General Reserve.[54]

Having lured Haig into his den, Lloyd George sprang his trap. He remarked that he had similar concerns and suggested that Wilson and Robertson exchange posts, promising that the latter, as British military representative, would be "absolutely free and unfettered" in the "advice which he gives." Haig raised no objections to the scheme, except to say that Wilson was not trusted in the army. He deluded himself into thinking that Robertson, by being posted at Versailles, "might save us from defeat by opposing Lloyd George's desire to send troops to the East against the Turks."[55] Lloyd George's ingenious maneuver had succeeded in weaning Haig away from Robertson. As for Derby, who had anxiously been looking for a compromise that would satisfy all parties, Lloyd George's new proposal came as a pleasant surprise. Looking back a week later, he wrote, "I was quite ready to see Sir William Robertson accept Versailles as I felt that it was a post, not only of great importance at the present, but that as the Americans came into the field more and more work of coordination would have to be done there and I do not think it was in any way derogatory to Sir William Robertson to offer him the place."[56] It did not seem to have struck either

Haig or Derby that although Robertson would be completely free to offer advice from Versailles, the War Cabinet would be equally free to reject it. Or if they had thought about it, they simply did not care. Robertson's fate was all but sealed.

It has often been asked why Haig showed such ingratitude towards Robertson, who had been his unwavering champion against the politicians. We know that Haig had become miffed with Robertson because, as he told his wife, the CIGS had not resolutely adhered to the policy of concentration on the western front.[57] This was an unfair and inaccurate charge because, as we have seen time and time again, Robertson had put his career on the line, trying hard to prevent the diversion of resources to distant theaters as well as fighting Haig's battles in the War Cabinet. Indeed, he had incurred the prime minister's wrath because he had always marched with Haig, sometimes even against his better judgment. It is true that in recent months their relationship had cooled somewhat, not because of Robertson's lack of commitment to the western front, but because he worried about Britain's declining manpower and had expressed personal doubts to Haig about his strategy, particularly at Passchendaele. Did Haig honestly believe that Wilson would sweat more blood for him than Robertson? It may be that Haig genuinely believed that it was his duty to accept the government's wishes, irrespective of his personal feelings,- although one could argue that in the past he had resisted War Cabinet policies whenever they had threatened his own plans. A more likely explanation was that his foremost concern was the preservation of his own position, which had been weakened after Passchendaele and Cambrai, and that he was determined to avoid being dragged down with Robertson. No one can say for sure how Lloyd George would have reacted if Haig had stood by Robertson. But even John Terraine concedes that Haig should have done so.[58] In any case, it is sufficient to say that this was not Haig's finest hour.

It was Robertson's misfortune during this period that he was at Eastbourne recuperating from a severe attack of bronchitis. Alerted to what was happening, he rushed back to London where he was given his option: he could remain as the CIGS with reduced powers or accept the post in Versailles. Robertson found neither to his liking. He knew that whatever post he took, the prime minister would throw his weight behind the other one and pay him no heed. He was now concerned less with the command structure of the General Reserve than with preventing Wilson and Lloyd George from taking control of British strategy. Robertson bluntly told Derby that he would not accept Lloyd George's formula, using the familiar argument that it was impossible to direct the war effectively under a system of dual authority. He repeated his argument that as the officer "who is to give orders regarding the reserves" and who must be "in constant communication with the various departments of the War Office," it followed that whoever held the post of CIGS should also be the British representative at

Versailles. In reply, Derby disagreed that one man could combine both jobs. His reasoning was that, with the CIGS living in London, any delay in giving a decision during a crisis might prove fatal in France. He begged Robertson to reconsider his decision, emphasizing that he was not being asked to take an inferior post.[59] But Robertson would not budge an inch, even after Haig admonished him that "this was no time for anyone to question where his services were to be given."[60]

Determined to fight to the finish, Robertson could count on many powerful allies. The Army Council had met early on the morning of February 11, and while conceding that the constitutional issues had been resolved, continued to insist that the CIGS should also occupy the post at Versailles.[61] Later that day, Repington delivered another salvo at the prime minister in the *Morning Post*. He indiscreetly revealed the existence of a plan for an Allied Reserve Army, including that it was to be controlled by an Executive Board presided over by General Foch. He accused Lloyd George and the War Cabinet of occupying "themselves in teaching soldiers how and where to make war," and of placing British troops under a foreign general. What was worse, he described in detail future Allied plans, namely, to stand on the defensive on the western front and to use the General Reserve wherever it was needed to help blunt the impending German attack, while Allenby swept the Turks out of Palestine. He ended by calling on the Army Council to make a "firm and united stand" against the new arrangements and for parliament "to do its bit" as well.

By revealing state secrets, Repington and the *Morning Post* were in violation of the Defence of the Realm Act and subject to prosecution. Lloyd George wanted to indict them for high treason, but such a charge would have been impossible to prove in light of the assertion by the Director of Military Intelligence, General Macdonogh, that he would "find it very difficult to state on oath in a court of law that information had been given which was likely to be of any great use to the enemy."[62] The War Cabinet voted to shut down the paper, but Lloyd George suspended the decision after consulting, among others, the Home Secretary.[63] Apart from the legal objections, the prime minister recognized that attaching too much attention to this case would be tantamount to validating Repington's disclosures. Thus, Repington and the editor of the paper were charged with technical breach of the Defence of the Realm Act, found guilty, and each fined £100 plus court costs. Reflecting on the incident many years later, Lloyd George wrote, with his usual penchant for hyperbole, "I know nothing comparable to this betrayal in the whole of our history."[64] One cannot help but ask why Lloyd George did not show the same sense of outrage in May 1915 when Repington's dispatch, blaming the British failure at Aubers Ridge on a shortage of shells, was a key factor in bringing down the Liberal government.

Now that the cat was out of the bag, Lloyd George did not need to be told that he was in deep political trouble. In November, when the Supreme War Council was established, he had assured Parliament that the function of the inter-Allied General Staff would be advisory, not executive. He knew that there were many in parliament waiting to pummel him at the least pretext. Besides the Liberal Opposition headed by Asquith, there was the Unionist War Committee as well as prominent Tories such as Cecil, Walter Long (secretary of the colonies) and Austen Chamberlain, who had always championed the army. The prime minister dreaded the thought of having to face awkward questions in Parliament the next day and, to deepen his anxiety, he was bothered by a severe cold.

Milner sensed that the prime minister was beginning to wilt under pressure. On more than one occasion he had witnessed the prime minister back down at the eleventh hour, rather than force the issue, in confrontations with Robertson. He was angry with Robertson for challenging civilian authority and urged the prime minister to stay the course: "We are on absolutely strong ground," he insisted, "[and], if there is to be a fight, [which] I don't feel sure of, we can win. But let us at least make sure that at the end of the fight we are free men [and] not still saddled with our Old Man of the Sea."[65]

Not known for his steadiness, Derby was already set to retreat, less than twenty-four hours following his pledge to endorse Lloyd George's plan. He had been shaken by the growing support for Robertson outside the War Office and he feared the political consequences, not to mention that he did not wish to be portrayed in an unfavorable light after trumpeting himself a steadfast protector of the High Command. At the War Cabinet on February 12, Derby reported that he had met earlier with Robertson, who had flatly refused to reconsider his decision to turn down the Versailles post. He thought it would be a shame to lose a soldier of Robertson's caliber. Derby suggested that Robertson be retained as CIGS, though without the special powers conferred upon him in January 1916 as a result of his compact with Kitchener. Of the ministers present, only Lloyd George, Derby and Milner had been directly involved in the démarche against Robertson. With a crisis brewing, Balfour, Curzon and Bonar Law eagerly grasped Derby's solution, but Milner and, to a lesser extent, Barnes argued that the prime minister's arrangement should stand and that Robertson should either go to Versailles or be dismissed. Needless to say, the prime minister shared the views expressed by Milner and Barnes, but he refrained from acting decisively, preferring to wait until he had gauged parliament's pulse.[66]

In the afternoon, Lloyd George confronted a hostile parliament and handled himself badly. A brilliant speaker, Asquith was in good form, taking advantage of a rare opportunity to attack the government without appearing to be disloyal. He opened by eulogizing both Haig and Robertson and hinted that their authority would be circumcised by the new arrangements at Versailles. He pointed out that there was a huge difference between coordination and subordination, and the country's interests dictated that the commander-in-chief receive his orders from the CIGS and no one else. He asked what had prompted the government to depart from its pledge not to confer executive authority on the SWC and what the new functions and duties of that body would entail.

Lloyd George was deliberate and ill at ease when he rose to speak and implied that the probing of arrangements at Versailles was tantamount to asking for information that would materially assist the enemy. Asquith indignantly interrupted, protesting against the insinuation made and repeated his question, "In what respect have the functions of this council been permanently enlarged?" Lloyd George hastened to apologize, explaining what he meant was that it would be unwise to reveal the details about the decisions at Versailles. But he was not forthcoming, and his efforts to evade tough questions on security grounds only soured the mood of the parliamentarians. In the course of the debates, the prime minister was asked if Robertson and Haig had approved of the new arrangements. Aware that he would be savagely assailed if he acknowledged he had overruled the military authorities, he replied quite untruthfully that they had. He concluded what had been a rough session with an open challenge to his critics: "If the House of Commons and the country are not satisfied with the conduct of the War, and if they think there is any Government which can conduct it better, then it is their business, in God's name, to put that other Government in."[67]

Lloyd George's bravado, however, had not offset his poor showing and beaten look, and he knew that his standing with parliament and the press had been damaged. Sensing that his ministry was in danger, he began to wobble and considered trying to work out a compromise with Robertson. He justified his change of heart by telling Hankey that he could not sack Robertson because the Northcliffe press (whose owner was closely associated with the prime minister) had been attacking the CIGS with unbridled fury and if he was dismissed, the nation would say that it had been done at the press baron's dictation.[68]

Given the prime minister's indecision about Robertson's fate, Derby worked assiduously behind the scenes to effect a compromise. In what was an amended version of his earlier plan, he suggested that Robertson should remain at the War Office with diminished status, but given a seat on the Executive Board where Wilson would act as his deputy whenever he was unable to attend its sessions. "On being asked whether these arrangements were agreeable to me," Robertson wrote in his memoirs, "I at once accepted them without qualification of any kind." He went on to say that they left in the hands of the CIGS "unquestioned authority over the employment of the Army, and did not divide it between two officers as was done in the Prime Minister's Note."[69] The War Cabinet, however, was divided. Anxious to retain Robertson's services, Balfour and Curzon approved of the plan. Milner, Bonar Law and Barnes rejected it because it nullified Lloyd George's main objective of making the British military representative independent of the War Office. They were adamant that, as Robertson had refused the Versailles post, his employment should be terminated.[70] But the prime minister's political instincts would not permit him to risk such action, much as he would have wished. Milner reacted by strongly advising the prime minister against placing the British military representative under the orders of the CIGS: "If you put your foot down ... you will be on strong and unassailable ground and the thing will work, otherwise I foresee a fresh series of squabbles and misunderstandings."[71]

The king followed the events closely from the moment he learned of Robertson's likely dismissal. On February 13 he sent his private secretary, Lord Stamfordham, to 10 Downing Street to convey his concern. Stamfordham told the prime minister that the king deprecated the idea of Robertson's removal as CIGS, which he felt would have a devastating impact on the army, would be resented in the country and would damage the government. Lloyd George replied that he did not share the king's extremely favorable opinion of Robertson, who had never held a field command, had hardly ever visited the front and was not known by the rank and file. He insisted that Robertson had shown no capacity as a strategist and he could not think of a single instance when he had given a sound piece of advice. In fact, his forecasts had generally been wrong. Stamfordham pointed out that Robertson only asked to enjoy the same authority as Foch, who was both Chief of the General Staff and a member of the Executive Board. Lloyd George declared that no such analogy was possible. Foch was located in Paris, whereas Robertson was not on the spot to issue orders to the General Reserve at a moment's notice in case of an emergency.

After returning to Buckingham Palace, Stamfordham called Robertson and Derby to his room and the whole question was thrashed out and examined from all sides. Robertson stuck to his guns, adamant that the prime minister's scheme would spell disaster. Derby did not concur, saying that Haig had approved of it and thought it was workable. Derby added that if the prime minister submitted to Robertson's terms, Milner and Barnes would resign. On the other hand, if Robertson went, he would resign and so would Curzon, perhaps resulting in the collapse of the government. Stamfordham begged Robertson not to relinquish his post, adding that he should confine his protest to placing on record his disapproval of the system and his belief that it might cost the Entente the war. Nevertheless, he should stay on for the sake of king and country and do his best to work under the new arrangement. Robertson replied that he would think it over. He would have a better idea of what to expect after his scheduled breakfast with the prime minister the following morning.[72]

Robertson did not keep his rendezvous with the prime minister. Instead, he appeared before the War Cabinet to plead his case in a prepared statement. He pleaded for a quick resolution of the issue, as work was being neglected at the War Office, particularly in attending to campaign requirements in the west and in the east. He summarized the events of the past fortnight, beginning with the proceedings of the last SWC meeting and ending with the proposal that he should take up the post at Versailles or remain CIGS without the special powers he had been granted by an Order in Council in January 1916. Robertson never admitted it, but, from his action, it was evident that he was fighting to retain his ascendancy over British strategy. He maintained that he opposed not the idea of creating a General Reserve, but the prime minister's projected system that divided responsibility for military operations between two officers in violation of the basic principle of centralized authority. He was adamant that the only workable method, and one that was within the constitutional framework, was for the CIGS to be a member of the Executive Committee. The argument that he could not handle both jobs could be overcome by using the deputy CIGS to act for him in his absence at the Executive Board meetings.

At this point, the prime minister interrupted and asked Robertson whether he would be prepared to go to Versailles as the deputy CIGS if his system were adopted. Caught off guard and trying desperately to collect his thoughts, Robertson asked to postpone his answer until he had finished his statement. When he replied, he requested that, as a full general for nearly two years, he be spared from going to Versailles to work as deputy to Wilson, who was only a temporary general. Robertson's explanation is understandable, given army tradition, but to the politicians, he seemed to place the protection of his status ahead of the nation's interests.[73]

Once Robertson withdrew, the members engaged in a brief discussion and concurred with the prime minister that it was unwise for one man to hold both positions. It was further decided to send Balfour and Derby to see if they could break down Robertson's resistance.[74] The mission was a failure. Robertson remained unmovable, oblivious to all blandishments.[75] His intransigence exhausted the patience and goodwill of Balfour, altering the political balance in the War Cabinet. Lloyd George's delaying tactics were beginning to pay dividends, but he remained troubled at the possibility of stepping on a mine. For one thing, he was curious to know why Asquith was holding meetings with Lansdowne. Did he intend to lay the groundwork simply for mischief or for a bid to regain the premiership? Lloyd George did not think that Asquith could muster enough support in parliament to oust him from 10 Downing Street, but in the back of his mind, there was a lingering fear that opposition groups might combine to vote him out of office and a dark horse would emerge to become the new prime minister.

Uncertain of the ground ahead, Lloyd George paused to take stock. He knew that he could rely on Milner, Barnes and Bonar Law. Balfour had been won over as a result of his conversation with Robertson, and Curzon, while not tipping his hand, could be counted on to behave honorably in the last resort. Those backing the military party included Long and Cecil. These men did not carry the same weight as regular members of the War Cabinet, but they were buttressed by a powerful section of the press, as well as by many Liberals and Tory backbenchers in parliament. After careful consideration, Lloyd George decided to bite the bullet and move against Robertson.

Lloyd George's preferred candidate to replace Robertson was Wilson, but he was a notorious intriguer and distrusted both in the army and in parliament. There were obvious risks in selecting Wilson, not the least of which would make Robertson's supersession much more difficult. To forestall criticism, the prime minister offered Robertson's post to a highly reputable field officer, General Sir Herbert Plumer, then commanding the British forces in Italy. Plumer declined the appointment on February 15, apparently out of loyalty to Robertson.[76] Lloyd George was not unhappy with Plumer's refusal, which now opened the way for Wilson. On the same day, the prime minister received a note from Hankey, informing him of more good news. Esher had lunched with Lansdowne who shed light on his own position as well as that of Asquith. Both he and the former prime minister agreed that for want of an obvious successor, Lloyd George "must be kept in office."[77] The events on February 15 had reenergized the prime minister. Hankey, who drove down to Walton Heath in the evening, found him "full of fight," and declaring that he was "better than he had been for months." The prime minister had made up his mind to appoint Wilson as CIGS and, in the event Derby resigned, to put Milner in his place.[78]

The next day, Lloyd George went to Buckingham palace to see the king. Before his audience with His Majesty, he spoke briefly with Stamfordham. He told him that things had moved too far and that if the king insisted on retaining the services of Robertson, he would have no alternative but to resign. Stamfordham assured Lloyd George that the king would not do so. The interview was painful for the king. He indicated that he valued Robertson's talent and sincerely believed that his removal would be a serious loss to the army, but Lloyd George countered with arguments of his own. The king accepted the inevitable, for the consequences of overriding the prime minister, even though he disliked him personally, would have been too serious. Lloyd George showed himself to be forceful but not closed-minded. He proposed to give Robertson one last chance to remain as CIGS under the new conditions or go to Versailles. If Robertson should refuse, Wilson would be appointed CIGS and Haig would be consulted as to the most suitable officer to replace him at Versailles.[79]

At the War Cabinet, which assembled at 12:30 p.m., Lloyd George reported the results of his talk with the king. There were no objections to Lloyd George's proposals, which had received royal acquiescence. A minister raised the question of whether Haig should also be consulted about the relations between the CIGS and the British military representative. The prime minister, with the general assent of his colleagues, turned thumbs down. It was one thing for Haig to place his own man at Versailles, quite another to allow a question that had hamstrung the government for days to be reopened. Another inquiry centered on what would happen if Haig withdrew his previous consent to the new arrangements and pressed his objections to the point of putting his command on the line. In such an eventuality, the prime minister, with the full support of the cabinet, held that he would refuse to accept his resignation.[80]

Later in the afternoon, Lloyd George called in Robertson and again gave him the option of accepting one of the two aforementioned military positions. What else passed between the two is not known, except that Robertson asked for time to think the matter over. It took Robertson about an hour to decide to reject the government's offer, which he formally communicated in a letter to the prime minister.[81] On the previous day, Robertson had written to Haig, explaining why he could not agree to the terms laid down by the government. It would have been disgraceful for him to "accept a system as CIGS which I had already condemned as dangerous." On the other hand, he "would have been a useless fool at Versailles, with Wilson here as CIGS, who could always have scotched me." Robertson was right in surmising that "the whole thing is, in fact, a plot to get me out of here."[82] His letter of refusal was taken as his resignation and Wilson was then installed in his place. Lloyd George had one more major task before facing parliament – reach an accommodation with Haig.

Summoned by Derby, Haig arrived in London on February 17. Derby met him at the station and informed him that Robertson had been sacked. Robertson gave his side of the story when he visited Haig at 9:30 the next morning and warned that "H. Wilson as CIGS would get the country into difficulties." Haig maintained that he had never been asked whether he approved of Lloyd George's "new scheme of higher control," only whether he was satisfied with "the proposed arrangements for giving me orders." He observed that the constitutional objections he had raised had been met by making the military representative a member of the Army Council. He insisted, moreover, that he had never approved of the Executive War Board's plan to create and command the General Reserve.[83] It is doubtful that Robertson derived much comfort from Haig's remarks. He evidently hoped that the man he had shielded against the politicians for thirteen months, and, in the process, been beaten black and blue, would respond by offering more than perfunctory support. But Haig understood political realities and had no intentions of walking the plank with Robertson.

Haig repeated the substance of his statement when he visited Lloyd George at Walton Heath in the early afternoon.[84] When asked why he found the new proposals objectionable, Haig listed his reasons, but went on to say that he nevertheless felt it his duty to abide by the decision of the War Cabinet. Lloyd George raised the point whether Haig would react differently if he knew that Derby had submitted his resignation – out of loyalty to Robertson, it must be stated, not because of any disagreement with the line taken by the War Cabinet. The prime minister was surprised that, far from being disturbed, Haig "sniffed it aside with an expression of contempt." He had, the prime minister observed, "a poor opinion of Derby's stalwartness, and did not hesitate to show it."[85] Derby, whatever his faults, had done well by Haig. He had defended him for months on end and saved him from the guillotine on several occasions. He deserved Haig's gratitude and respect, instead of being the object of a hatchet job. But as we have already noted, Haig expected others to be absolutely loyal to him, but he had no compunction about deserting faithful supporters when it suited his purpose, and he did so without apology or excuse. Lloyd George was delighted that he could count on Haig's allegiance and he spent the evening relaxing and singing his favorite hymns.

On leaving 10 Downing Street, Haig returned to his house at Kingston and in the evening Henry Wilson paid him a visit. Their past relationship had been strained and it was understandable that Wilson would want to start their association on the right track. Haig was cordial and told Wilson "that all these quarrels had nothing to do with him" and assured him that he would do his best to carry out the policy of the War Cabinet. Wilson invited Haig to propose his successor at Versailles. Haig recommended General Henry Rawlinson, on whom he could rely to do his bidding. If Rawlinson went to Versailles, Wilson inquired, could Robertson have his post? Haig replied that the former CIGS was "quite unfitted to command troops."[86]

Everything came together for Lloyd George on February 18. He had telephoned Bonar Law on the previous day, asking him to try to persuade Derby to withdraw his resignation. Although under normal circumstances the prime minister would have been happy to rid himself of Derby, the time to do so, in his view, was not propitious. As he told Hankey, it was best that Derby stay, "for in his statement of the reason for resignation he must give away that Haig and Plumer disapproved of the Versailles arrangement."[87] Bonar Law's mission was successful and the other Unionists, who had threatened to go, came around one by one. Robertson had hoped that Asquith, with whom he was in contact, would spring to his defense as he had in the past. But Asquith had no stomach for a fight to the finish. The Liberal leader, as J. A. Spender, his close friend and editor of the *Westminster Gazette,* revealed to Esher, "has no desire to take office now."[88]

Asquith was astute enough to recognize that he did not command the requisite support in parliament to overthrow Lloyd George. The Tories had no use for Lloyd George, but preferred him to Asquith as a war leader. Henderson liked Asquith personally, more so than Lloyd George, but considered him ill-suited to lead the nation in wartime. Robertson saw the handwriting on the wall and, dependent as he was on his soldier's salary for his livelihood, swallowed his pride and accepted the Eastern Command in southeastern England. It was a brutal and humiliating demotion for a soldier of his caliber. As sad as it was to see him fall, he had no one but himself to blame. Too often he forgot that his first obligation was to present the government with impartial military advice, not serve as Haig's defense attorney. He was stubborn, inflexible and contemptuous of politicians, particularly Lloyd George. In the final showdown with Lloyd George, he was misled into believing that the large cross section of parliamentarians and the press rallying to his side was proof that his cause was just and that, in the end, he would prevail. Robertson never understood that most of the politicians and newspaper editors who were critical of the way he had been dismissed would hesitate to press home their attack, because they could not identify a consensus prime minister-in-waiting to replace the current occupant of 10 Downing Street. Much as they admired and respected Robertson, they had no doubt that he could be replaced. On the other hand, Asquith was the only possible alternative to Lloyd George, and he had already proven himself to be a poor war leader. In hindsight, Robertson recognized that his support had been broad but not deep. He told Repington that "he had found that he had more friends than he knew, but fewer on whom he could count than he expected."[89]

It only remained for Lloyd George to explain to the Commons the reason for Robertson's dismissal. As he stood before the parliamentarians on February 19, he was confident, in high spirits and in better health than he had been in some weeks. After reading from a prepared speech, he handled questions from the floor with his customary aplomb. He was lavish in his praise of Robertson and insisted that the government had done everything to retain his services, but to no avail. Lloyd George's premise, one that struck a responsive chord with parliamentarians, was unassailable, given Britain's long standing tradition that final authority must rest with civilian rather than military authority. Asquith went through the motion of replying to Lloyd George's statement, but his performance was uninspiring and showed that he had no desire to prolong the debate over a lost cause.[90] When he tried to make an issue of Lloyd George's liberty with the truth, he was jeered. The atmosphere in the House had changed since the previous week. It was time, as one MP remarked, to get on with the war.

It is ironic that the General Reserve, command of which had triggered Robertson's removal, never materialized. The Executive Board, on which Rawlinson had replaced Wilson, formulated a plan that called for a reserve of thirty divisions – 14 French, 9 British and 7 Italian. Conscious that his army was under strength in marked contrast to the enemy's growing concentration in the west, Haig was unwilling to contribute his quota. Concern for his front was undoubtedly his primary reason, but it is also conceivable that he was to some extent influenced by suspicions that Wilson "means to help Lloyd George to detach troops from my Command to fight against the Turks."[91] On February 25 Wilson visted GHQ to impress upon Haig the benefits that would accrue from the creation of the General Reserve. Haig bluntly told Wilson that he was short of reserves and, with an impending German assault, he would not run the risk of placing any of his divisions in the hands of another person. He threatened to resign if ordered to do so. Wilson pointed out that the contribution of British troops to the General Reserve did not mean that they were lost to Haig. If attacked, the British divisions would be handed back to him and he would have the advantage of being able to draw upon other units from the General Reserve in case of an emergency.[92]

Haig was aware that Pétain was jealous and suspicious of Foch and had refused to contribute any troops to the General Reserve. He and Pétain had concerted arrangements for mutual support in case the need arose, reasoning that a personal understanding between them, as in the matter of the extension of the British line, was preferable than surrendering control to an exterior authority. Clemenceau came down on the side of Pétain, the victor of Verdun. The Tiger told Haig of his support for Pétain and that he would arrange to gradually marginalize Foch.

Wilson discussed with Lloyd George the question of Haig's refusal to give any of his army divisions to the General Reserve on March 4. The prime minister thought it "was very stupid and shortsighted," but recognized that he "could not force Haig at this moment." Lloyd George was still licking his wounds from his bruising battle with Robertson. He was not anxious to confront Haig so soon and risk his resignation.[93] At a War Cabinet meeting on March 6, Wilson felt he had no option but to defend Haig's attitude, to the surprise of most of the ministers. His professed reasoning was that since Haig was faced with the possibility of an imminent attack, it would be a mistake to disrupt his arrangements with Pétain by allocating a portion of his reserves to the Allied General Reserve. The ministers hesitated to force Haig's hand, only agreeing that his position was not necessarily final and would be reviewed at the forthcoming SWC in London the following week.[94]

Haig crossed over to London to attend the meeting of the SWC set for March 14. Recent GHQ intelligence reports showing a massive enemy buildup on the western front should have given him pause for concern. These had identified 187 German divisions as of March 18.[95] The greater part of the enemy's strength, some 87 divisions in line plus 30 more in reserve, was arrayed against the British front, which was defended by a total of 57 divisions. Intelligence officials reported that a heavy enemy attack was about to begin, one that was likely to fall on the Third and Fifth Armies.[96] Haig was optimistic that he could inflict a crushing defeat on the Germans, notwithstanding the warning given by General Sir Hubert Gough, C-in-C of the Third Army, that his defenses were weak. Haig told his army commanders on March 2 that his only fear was that the "enemy would find our front so very strong that he will hesitate to commit his Army to the attack with the almost certainty of losing very heavily."[97]

Shortly after his arrival, Haig visited Wilson at the War Office and repeated what he had told him earlier. Wilson impressed on him that his failure to part with any of his divisions would spell the end of the General Reserve and "he would have to live on Pétain's charity, and he would find that very cold charity." But Haig stood firm. Wilson was reluctantly driven to the conclusion that "if we have to choose between a General Reserve and Haig, we must choose Haig, wrong as I believe him to be."[98] Wilson reckoned that if anyone could persuade Haig to change his mind, or at least agree to a compromise, it was the prime minister. Accordingly he arranged for Haig to see Lloyd George the next morning.

Milner was disturbed that Lloyd George was doing little to prevent the demise of the General Reserve before it could see the light of day. In the evening, he saw Wilson, who informed him of the result of his talk with Haig. Milner wanted Lloyd George to take a more active role in bringing to fruition an institution he had loudly proclaimed in the past to be essential. This was the gist of what was contained in a letter he sent him the next day. He reminded the prime minister that there was more at stake than the security of the Allied forces. If Haig succeeded in blocking the creation of the General Reserve, he stressed, "we shall have once more passed under the yoke of the generals."[99]

Whether the note reached Lloyd George before his meeting with Haig in mid-morning on March 14 is unknown. It would not have made a difference if it had. Haig has left an account of the hour-long interview. He claimed that the prime minister had tried alternately to frighten and flatter him into releasing certain divisions for the General Reserve. Refusing to budge, Haig insisted that "this was a military question of which I was the best judge." By contrast, "Versailles was too distant and not in touch with the actual military situation."

Lloyd George did not see any point in belaboring the issue. Standing against him was not only Haig, but Pétain and Clemenceau as well.[100] A realist above all, he knew when to fold his cards. He acknowledged defeat by saying that, with a large enemy assault expected soon, it was at any rate too late to upset current defense arrangements.[101]

To Haig's delight, Lloyd George adopted a similar line at the opening session of the SWC late on the morning of March 14. His proposal was that General Reserve should be maintained, but built up gradually, as the Americans came into the line and set free British and French units. Clemenceau said that he was in full agreement with the British prime minister. While there was no question of abandoning the principle of the General Reserve, it was impossible, for the present, to withdraw any divisions from the command of either Haig or Pétain because of the threatened attack against their front. Foch was the only dissenting voice, but he was cut off by Clemenceau, who became angry and rudely ordered him to "shut up."[102]

The preservation, in principle, of the General Reserve could not disguise the fact that the body, as one observer commented, was "dead as a doornail."[103] Thus, without the General Reserve, the security of the Anglo–French line rested solely on the personal agreement between Haig and Pétain for mutual support. Since the two field commanders were divided in their strategic outlook, with each expecting the main German blow to fall on his front, it stood to reason that only troops that could be spared over and above their defensive requirements would be available to assist the other. Only time would tell whether their defensive measures were adequate to meet the powerful German offensive that was about to be unleashed.

Chapter 14

CRISIS ON THE WESTERN FRONT

The new CIGS, Henry Wilson, was fifty-four years old and one of the most controversial officers of his era. Articulate, quick-witted, intellectually sharp and prone to expressing strong opinions on issues and individuals, he is remembered as much for his love of intrigue as for his accomplishments. He was tall, bald and thin as a reed, with a prominent nose and gothic features, and, by his own admission, was the "ugliest man in the British army." His strength was as an administrator, not as a field general.[1]

As head of the Imperial General Staff, Wilson had little in common with his predecessor. He was more popular with politicians than with his brother officers. He spoke French fluently, which was certainly a valuable asset in dealing with the nation's difficult ally. His expositions were lucidly expressed and he offered equally clear reasons as to why a course of action should be adopted or rejected. "It was a delight to hear him unravel and expound a military problem," Lloyd George has written. "For that reason he was specially helpful in a council of civilians."[2] Yet, also in contrast to Robertson, when faced with the need to make a firm decision, one in which he would be held responsible, his nerves failed him. As Lloyd George put it, he "shrank from the responsibility of the final word, even in advice." He concluded that Wilson was not the ideal man for the post, but still, in what was certainly a gross overstatement – given that Wilson had failed to enter Sandhurst twice and Woolwich three times and pursued the back-door route into the army through the militia – "much the best brain I had met in the upper ranks of our professional army."[3] In truth, Wilson did not possess Robertson's talent as a soldier, not to mention that his character was less than admirable. But he was a solid enough administrator, knew when to bend with the wind, got along well with Lloyd George and, on the whole, was more suited than Robertson to act as the chief military adviser to the current government.

Although a closet westerner, Wilson's conviction that German defenses could not be broken in 1918 made it easier for him to embrace Lloyd George's peripheral policy. As we have already seen, Smuts had been sent on a fact-finding mission to the Middle East early in February 1918. After consulting with Allenby and Major General W. Gillman, Chief of Staff (COS) of the Mesopotamian Expeditionary Force, he cabled home his assessment on February 15. Since British resources would not permit offensive action in Syria and Mesopotamia simultaneously, he reasoned that one of the two forces should assume a defensive role and supply reinforcements to the other. Smuts observed that the MEF, being farther from Aleppo, would require greater railroad construction; and beyond Mosul, its right flank would be exposed to danger. Consequently, he recommended that it should stand on the defensive and send two infantry divisions and one cavalry brigade to Palestine.[4]

Smuts' report was circulated and discussed briefly at a War Cabinet meeting on February 21. Lloyd George wanted his colleagues to look at the broader implications of a victory in Palestine. The long-term object was not so much to cover Britain's Asiatic position or force Turkey's surrender, but to preserve Britain as a great power. He did not want the British army to be bled white in further attritional battles in the west. Unless the Allies, led by the Americans who were expected to do most of the fighting and dying, succeeded in the next phase in breaking the stalemate, he saw no alternative but a compromise peace. In such an event, the French might be persuaded to accept less than the whole of Alsace–Lorraine in exchange for compensation in Syria.[5] A decision was postponed, pending Smuts' expected return at the end of the month. The discussion resumed on March 4 and continued two days later when approval was given to Allenby to advance "to the maximum extent possible, consistent with the safety of the force under his orders."[6]

One does not need the advantage of hindsight to question the War Cabinet's priorities. Instead of laying plans for a forward policy in the Middle East, it should have arranged to bring back some troops from that region as well as from German East Africa and further fortify defenses in the west. Lloyd George did not seem to understand that it was preferable for British troops in Palestine and Mesopotamia to go on the defensive than to risk a defeat in the west and lose the war. Unfortunately, the ministers were so dazzled by Lloyd George's rosy picture of the great benefits that would accrue from a victory in the Middle Eastern theaters, that they appeared to have lost sight of the frightful danger looming closer to home. No amount of success against the Turks would have counted if the Germans had effected a breakthrough in the west in the spring of 1918. No one tried to bring the talks down from the realm of fantasy to the solid earth of reality. Milner summed up the general attitude when he wrote to the prime minister on the eve of the enemy's violent attack:

> How right was the instinct, wh[ich] led you all along to attach so much importance to the Eastern campaigns & not to listen to our only strategists, who could see nothing but the western front. If it were not for the position

we have won in Mesopotamia and Palestine & the great strength we have developed on that side, the outlook would be black indeed.[7]

It surely will be argued by some historians that the War Cabinet had been lulled into thinking that a German attack, if and when it came, would not amount to much of a threat. Haig had made his views known in London that he expected a great attack in the spring, but his warning was not taken seriously. Haig's record of predicting the German army's intentions and assessing its capabilities was abysmal, as a result of which Lloyd George and most of his associates no longer had any faith in his judgment. Still, there was plenty of corroborating evidence pointing to the imminence of a heavy German assault. Even before the end of 1917, Robertson, Maurice and the General Staff had repeatedly warned the War Cabinet that the Germans were concentrating forces on the western front for an all-out assault with the object of gaining a victory before American aid became effective.[8] But Lloyd George chose to ignore the warnings of the impending peril, not only of the War Office military experts, but also of British and French intelligence reports showing that the Germans were increasing their strength week by week. By the middle of February it was known that they had 81 divisions facing Haig's 57 skeletonized divisions. There should not have been much doubt as to where the next blow would fall. Besides, common sense dictated that the Germans would try to crush the Anglo-French armies before the impact of American's potential military strength could be felt in the field. Yet, the War Cabinet, incredible as it may seem, was under the delusion that Germany would maintain an active-defense in the west and concentrate on expanding its position in Asia. At any rate, the planned offensive in Palestine was cancelled by the momentous events on the western front.

Shortly before 5:00 a.m. on March 21, as the pre-dawn fog was spreading over the countryside, the Germans unleashed a massive artillery bombardment, heralding the start of their long-awaited offensive.[9] Code-named "Michael," the attack was directed at a vulnerable part of the Anglo-French line, the point where the two sectors joined.[10] The de facto commander of the German army, General Erich Ludendorff, had chosen to throw most of his weight against the British, because he considered them more obstinate and tough than the French. Once the British were defeated, Ludendorff was confident that the French would not hold out for long.

The German army held a considerable numerical superiority over its adversaries on the western front. By the end of the third week in March there were 192 German divisions as against 169 Allied. The Germans had a further advantage in that they could concentrate greater forces in the sector of their choosing, because they knew precisely where they were going to attack.

A compact force of 76 German first-class divisions was deployed on a fifty-mile front from Arras to Laon in an attempt to drive a wedge between the British and French armies. German storm troops had been trained in the von Hutier tactics that had proven so successful at Caporetto and Riga in Russia.[11]

In the enemy's path lay Brigadier General Hubert Gough's Fifth Army in the southernmost sector of the BEF, consisting of only 14 divisions along a 42-mile front and, to the north, General Julian Byng's Third Army of 17 divisions, which defended 28 miles. To fill the ranks of the BEF depleted by the recent attritional battles, Haig had requested 334,000 reinforcements but had received a little over 174,000 by March 21. The pool of able young men in Britain was shrinking and a portion of these were required to work in the vital war industries. As a result of the manpower shortage, the government mandated that each British division reduce its battalions from 12 to 9. The prime minister had further handicapped Haig by agreeing to Pétain and Clemenceau's request that the BEF take over an additional 30 miles of trenches so as to free six French divisions. The decision meant that Gough's meager forces would be stretched even more thinly and, to make matters worse, the defenses in the old French line were, at best, rudimentary.

The Germans outnumbered the British along their 126-mile front six to four, but against Gough's crucial sector the advantage was five to one. Shielded by fog, the first waves of German infantry crossed no-man's-land and were not detected until they had practically reached the British front line. By nightfall, the Germans had overrun the forward zone on virtually all of the Fifth Army's front, though their advance was less impressive against Byng's Third Army, which had more defenders and better-prepared positions. Reinforcements were not immediately available because Haig, misjudging the direction of the main German attack, kept them too far north. Staring disaster in the face, Gough ordered his shattered units to fall back to the Somme on March 22. The Germans were now in a position to march on the railroad junction at Amiens, the capture of which would split the British and French sectors apart.

On learning of the German attack, Haig was delighted, since he was beginning to worry that his men might "become stale from expecting and preparing" for it "for so long." He was sanguine that "the enemy will get more than he anticipates." He had not changed his opinion at the end of the first day's fighting, describing the results as "highly credible to British troops." With Gough's men in full retreat on March 22, he remained buoyant: "All reports show that our men are in great spirits."[12] It was not until March 23 that Haig began to grasp the reality of what had happened and moved to his advanced headquarters at Dury.

In London, there was nothing in the initial reports of the battle that gave cause for anxiety.[13] Lloyd George told his wife on March 22 that the early German army's gains were no more than might have been expected,[14] but on the following day the extent of the German breakthrough become clearer. Lloyd George had spent the night at his home in Walton Heath and before leaving for London, announced to Riddell, who had just arrived for a visit, "I must go back to London at once. The news is very bad. I fear it means disaster."[15]

Lloyd George was imperturbable and at his best in a crisis. He cancelled a scheduled morning meeting of the War Cabinet and with characteristic energy, took charge of the War Office, coordinating all emergency measures that had to be taken. The prime minister recognized that eventually it would be necessary to pull troops out of secondary theaters – an issue that should have been addressed long before the German assault got under way – but Haig needed reinforcements immediately. The first priority was to determine how many men in uniform were ready to be rushed across the Channel. By diverting drafts for other theaters, sending boys eighteen-and-a-half into combat, instead of waiting until they had reached nineteen, and returning to their units the 88,000 men on leave, it was established that there was a total of 170,000 trained men in the country. Lloyd George's next move was to arrange for their transit as quickly as possible. In normal circumstances drafts were carried across the Channel at a rate of about 6,000 a day, but in discussions with Maclay, he found that enough transport shipping could be scrapped together to raise the number to 20,000 at once and gradually working up to 30,000.[16]

At 4:00 p.m. Lloyd George joined his War Cabinet colleagues for an update on the military situation. The deputy DMO at the War Office, Colonel Walter Kirke, who had just returned by airplane from Haig's Headquarters, presented a report that confirmed everyone's worst fears. He revealed that the Fifth Army's front had been shattered and that although the retreat was being carried out in good order, the casualties totaled about 40,000, and no fewer than 600 guns had been lost. Wilson added that the British army was badly outnumbered and, without saying so, seemed to imply that its survival was contingent on immediate and extensive French help. Discussion turned on whether Pétain would honor his arrangements with Haig. Kirke noted that Haig was scheduled to confer with Pétain this very day on the matter. The question was raised whether it would be necessary to send someone over to Paris to put pressure on the French government to render Haig the requisite assistance. The prime minister interjected to decry the absence of a General Reserve, which he claimed already would have thrown in enough reinforcements to restore the line, precluding the need to engage in a bargaining process with the French government. The consensus was that the French should not be approached until the results of Haig's interview with Pétain were known.[17]

The more Lloyd George thought about the War Cabinet's resolution, the more he became convinced that it would be a mistake to delay action. As he could not absent himself from London, he summoned Milner to act as his emissary. He asked him to go over to France to get a first hand look at what was happening and to try to set matters right before disaster supervened.[18] In the evening, Lloyd George drove to Walton Heath for the weekend.

Sunday, March 24 was an anxious day for all concerned, as more bad news emanated from the front. Late in the afternoon, it was reported that the Germans were less than 30 miles from Amiens, prompting Wilson to telephone Lloyd George to request that he return to London. At 7:00 p.m. Lloyd George held a conclave with Bonar Law, Smuts and Wilson at 10 Downing Street. While they were talking, Haig phoned to announce that the Third Army was falling back and to ask Wilson to come over. "We are very near a crash," Wilson noted in his diary.[19]

As bad as things looked, Lloyd George remained calm and cheerful, giving no hint that he feared an inevitable defeat. Wilson observed that Lloyd George "has on the whole been buoyant" in contrast to Bonar Law who was "most depressing."[20] Churchill, who dined with Lloyd George on March 24, commented that the "resolution of the Prime Minister was unshaken under his truly awful responsibilities."[21] Riddell saw Lloyd George later in the evening and was also struck by his composure: "Although very anxious and much worried, he did not fail to have a good laugh as usual. His courage is remarkable. His work and anxieties are always with him, but he mingles them with bright and amusing conversation, which lightens the burden."[22]

It is not surprising that Lloyd George slept very little that night. He rose earlier than usual and agonized over what more could be done until 11:00 a.m., when the War Cabinet assembled. The meeting was long and devoted mainly to exploring new sources of manpower. Derby stated that 106,000 men, of whom ninety percent were infantry, were available for immediate transfer to France, excluding the 88,000 men on leave who were part of the existing army in France. On April 20 an additional 18,000 draftees would be ready for service, bringing the total to 212,000. The pool of available recruits was just about dry and painful measures were required to further reinforce Haig. Various suggestions were advanced, not all of which were practical. Men were to be drawn from munitions plants, coal mines, port labor and the navy's Royal Marines. The standard of eyesight tests would be modified to bring in more recruits. The age limit for recruits was to be raised. As an indication of how desperate the ministers were, questions were raised about recalling some of the wounded who had been discharged, using conscientious objectors in a noncombative capacity, making clergymen liable for military service and even extending conscription to potentially rebellious Ireland, hitherto exempt.[23]

There were two notable absentees from the meeting, Milner and Wilson. The former had crossed the channel on the previous day and the latter had followed him the next morning. Milner headed straight for Paris, but Wilson stopped at Haig's regular Headquarters at Montreuil before noon (on March 25). Here Wilson learned of the results of the meeting between Haig and Pétain held on the previous evening. Haig maintained that Pétain was in a state of panic, or, as he put it, "almost unbalanced and most anxious," during the talks – a claim substantiated by French sources at the time.[24] He went on to say that his arrangements with Pétain had broken down. Pétain, it seemed, had no intention of sacrificing part of his reserves for an army he considered doomed. If, as he anticipated, the Germans continued to press forward, he proposed to break contact with the British and direct his reserves southwest towards Beauvais in order to cover Paris. Haig pointed out that such a move would allow the Germans to drive a wedge between the two Allied armies and defeat them in detail. But no amount of reasoning could deflect Pétain from his purpose.

Haig was calm, but, according to Wilson, was despondent and shaken by his recent setback – perfectly understandable since he was conscious that the fate of the Allies might depend on what immediately followed. It was not time for recriminations, but Wilson could not resist the temptation to remind Haig that it was he, with Clemenceau's assistance, who had scuttled the plan for the General Reserve; nor could the CIGS pass up the opportunity to remind Haig that, without a General Reserve, he had been told that he would be dependent on Pétain's cold charity. Wilson's answer to Haig's predicament was to call for unity of action and he suggested that Foch be empowered to coordinate the action of the two army commanders. A contrite Haig did not object, even though in the past he had always resisted the idea of coming under the orders of a French commander.[25]

Wilson, Milner and Haig conferred with a French delegation that included Poincaré, Clemenceau, Pétain and Foch, at Doullens on March 26. The British, having concluded that Pétain had lost his nerve, pressed for the selection of Foch to ensure greater Allied operational unity. Clemenceau drew up a resolution charging Foch with coordinating the operations of the Allies in front of Amiens.[26] Haig was of the opinion that Foch's mandate did not go far enough. He wanted to ensure that Foch would be able to overrule Pétain and direct French forces to his imperiled front, even if it meant his own subordination. He proposed instead that Foch be given authority to supervise the action of all the Allied armies on the western front.[27] There was no opposition to the amended resolution.

The formula devised at Doullens was a step in the right direction, but its importance should not be exaggerated. Foch was not given the authority of a supreme commander in the field like Eisenhower would enjoy in the Second World War. He did not have the machinery of an Allied supreme commander, such as an integrated staff to work out plans for him – and, it must be added, made no effort to build one up.[28] His functions were limited to the British and French armies and did not extend to the other forces in the west – American, Belgian and Italian. He could not prepare future military operations or impose his will on the British and French commanders who remained in control of their own national armies. In short, Foch had immense responsibilities placed on his shoulders, but without proportionate authority.

Back in London, the crisis kept Lloyd George in a peripatetic state. His government, straining every nerve and sinew for a maximum effort, planned to draft an additional 400,000 to 500,000 men at the expense of undermining the economy and agricultural production. But these men would require at least four months before they could be shipped to France. In the interim there would be a dangerous gap at the front that only the Americans could fill.[29]

The United States certainly had the capacity to provide the Allies with large-scale assistance, but owing to lack of preparation, the training of its army had been considerably delayed. The American program contemplated raising forty-five divisions, but in the opening weeks of 1918 there were only four in France – though each division was nearly twice the size of a regular British division. On arrival, each American division was given additional training to prepare the recruits for trench warfare. One fully trained American division was in a quiet sector of the French front, but the others had yet to be used in an active role.[30]

The commander of the American troops, General John Pershing, was a native of rural Missouri and a West Point graduate. His combat experience included serving with the cavalry in the west on campaigns against the Indians, in the Philippines against Moros tribesman, and in the Spanish–American War. Before sailing to France, Pershing received little guidance about the extent or manner of his cooperation with the Allies and was more or less left free to act as he chose. Pershing had definite ideas about asserting American power. He envisaged the Americans playing a leading role in defeating Germany in climatic battles in 1919.[31] To that end, he proposed to husband his resources and to establish an independent field army with its own sector.

Both Haig and Foch saw that it would take many months for a separate American army to assume a significant burden of the fighting. The Americans had manpower, but nothing else. They were short of weapons, equipment, staff, officers and commanders. On top of this, their infantry and commanders had no battle experience. The Allied leaders wanted to hasten the active participation of the Americans by incorporating their battalions into their own depleted divisions. But Pershing resisted their requests, determined as he was to keep his army together under his control.[32]

As dark clouds gathered slowly over the western front, Robertson, prodded by Lloyd George, had asked Pershing during the second week in January 1918 to delay creating a homogenous American army and suggested that 150,000 men be sent out ahead of the others. These would be amalgamated with British units until such time as they would be recalled to join their own divisions. Pershing thought that Robertson was exaggerating the imminence and possible consequences of the attack. He left Robertson speechless when he shrewdly observed that it was difficult to reconcile the British "request for assistance in defense of the western front with Mr. Lloyd George's desire to act offensively in Palestine."[33] Robertson concluded from the interview that American power to help defeat Germany in battle was "a very weak reed to lean upon at present."[34]

Robertson had good reason to advocate against relying on American help, at least for the near future. Pershing was so single-minded about establishing the American army as an independent unit that he gave his program priority over even the defeat of the Germans. As enemy pressure became intense, Foch again found Pershing unwilling to allow the incorporation of American forces into French units. An exasperated Foch asked Pershing if he was prepared to see the French armies forced back to the Loire. "Yes I'm willing to take the risk," replied Pershing. "Moreover, the time may come when the American Army will have to stand the brunt of this war, and it is not wise to fritter away our resources in this manner."[35] For Pershing, America's associate status meant that it could use its strength in its own way, not at the behest of the Allies. In the overheated atmosphere of 1918, Pershing's attitude was hardly calculated to endear him to his hard-pressed partners.

At the height of the military crisis, Lloyd George made a direct appeal to President Wilson (March 28), requesting that 120,000 combat troops a month be sent to Europe during the period between April and July – a total of 480,000 – to be brigaded with British and French divisions. The president, who had been horrified at the force of the German assault, promised to send troops over "as fast as we can make them ready."[36] The Secretary of State, Newton Baker, subsequently informed London that the president approved in principle the "employment of troops in manner desired but leaves details to military chiefs."[37] Even Wilson's qualified commitment pleased Lloyd George, who told Riddell the next day that "this was the biggest thing he had accomplished during the last week."[38]

The prime minister was no less encouraged by the news from the front. North of the Somme, the Third Amy's line resisted the German onslaught, thanks to its well-prepared defenses, so that the dilemma of protecting the Channel ports never had to be faced. South of the Somme, the pace of the German advance was slowing down owing to the exhaustion of the men, overextended supply lines and the difficulty of bringing artillery across the badly cratered Somme battlefield. British and French reinforcements filled the gap created in the initial assault, patching together the semblance of a new defensive line by April 1.

In the aftermath of the Doullens conference, Foch flitted from headquarters to headquarters, suggesting, or urging, one plan after another that the commanders were free to follow or ignore. The two Allied commanders had no qualms about allowing Foch to bear the responsibility, but they, in particular Pétain, were loath to part with any authority. Finding it difficult to coordinate action without the power to command, Foch urged Clemenceau to strengthen the terms of his appointment.[39] Accordingly, Clemenceau requested a meeting with Lloyd George to address Foch's complaint. The War Cabinet discussed the question of whether "it might not be desirable to extend General Foch's powers, so as to give him the right of issuing directions or orders, instead of being limited to coordination." Lloyd George favored broadening Foch's authority to enable him to react rapidly and forcibly in case of an emergency, or to plan offensive operations. Wilson, however, was adamant that Foch did not require any extension of powers beyond those already accorded to him.[40] The consensus was that the arrangement was working satisfactorily as far as the British command was concerned and that it had been well received by the general public. Presumably in deference to the prime minister's wishes, the War Cabinet, in the end, agreed to leave it to his discretion to take whatever action he deemed necessary after he had discussed the matter with Haig.[41]

On April 3 Lloyd George, in company with Wilson, started out early in the morning. Once across the Channel, they picked up Haig near Montreuil on their way to Beauvais, the site of the conference. Haig, to Wilson's delight, claimed to be perfectly content with the current arrangement and saw no need to give Foch additional powers. Outnumbered, Lloyd George knew when to retreat and said no more on the subject. As they approached the town, they passed by remnants of some of the battered battalions of the Fifth Army. The soldiers cheered on seeing the British prime minister, who noted with satisfaction that they showed "no trace of dejection or despair." Looking back, he would write that they were hardly his "picture of a defeated army."[42]

The three men arrived at Beauvais around 1:00 p.m. and drove straight to the Hôtel de Ville, where they were welcomed by Clemenceau, Foch and Pétain, as well as Pershing and Bliss. After lunch, Clemenceau took Lloyd George and Wilson aside and produced a formula that would allow Foch to prepare as well as to coordinate military operations, while leaving tactical direction in the hands of the commanders-in-chief. Wilson thought that the changes would cause confusion, maintaining, quite speciously, that it would be difficult to separate tactics from strategy. But Lloyd George expressed himself in favor of the new plan.[43]

As the host, Clemenceau opened the conference at 3:15 p.m. by welcoming the foreign delegations. He explained that a stage had been reached when it was necessary to define, with greater precision, Foch's authority so as to ensure that the coordination of the two armies was carried out smoothly and promptly. Invited to speak next, Foch pointed out why the Doullens arrangement was insufficient. In quiet times when there was no action, there was nothing to coordinate. Something more was required. Before he could coordinate, he required the power to create action. To do so, his authority must be broadened to include the right "for the infusion of an idea of action." Lloyd George insisted that what the Allies needed above all was unity of control. In his opinion, Foch should be given the authority that he requested, otherwise he "would prove worse than useless." Both Pershing and Bliss argued that success would depend on the Allies having a single command. Haig, perhaps swayed by previous speakers, agreed that there should be only one head in France and that it was incumbent on the commanders-in-chief to work wholeheartedly in the closest cooperation with Foch. Wilson was the only one who spoke out against extending more authority to Foch. Although he made no impression on his listeners, he did succeed in inserting a qualifying sentence in the resolution. The new agreement, signed by France, Britain and the United States, gave Foch "strategical direction of operations," but allowed the national commanders to retain control of the tactical action on their fronts and the right to appeal to their respective governments any decision they thought endangered the security of their forces.[44] The Belgians and the Italians did not sign the document though they approved of it in principle.[45]

Foch's title was settled by correspondence and on April 14 he became "Supreme Commander of the Allied Armies in France." Of course, he did not possess anywhere near the powers of a supreme commander. As he had no staff, his technique, as Terraine has correctly observed, was "an outdated reversion to the personal command of earlier centuries."[46] It worked because of his infectious spirit and energy, the force of his personality and his habit of relying on persuasion rather than coercion.

Lloyd George was very pleased with what he got out of the Beauvais conference. He anticipated that once the military crisis was over, American troops flowing to Europe would enter the trenches, allowing many British divisions to be transferred to remote theaters where the fighting was less bloody. Haig would naturally resist any efforts to divert British units from the western front, but he was no longer an independent commander. The scenario visualized by the prime minister presupposed that Foch's views were in harmony with his own. In fact, Foch was wedded to offensives on the western front to an even greater extent than Haig. He not only intended to retain all of Haig's troops, but planned to use American reinforcements in the French, rather than in the British, sector. As Lloyd George would soon discover, he had merely exchanged one villain for another.[47]

On April 5 Operation Michael ground to a halt. By the standards of World War I it was a brilliant tactical success, having advanced up to forty miles in eight days. In a strategic sense, however, it had accomplished nothing. The BEF had neither been destroyed nor separated from the French army. The Germans had captured 70,000 British prisoners, but their losses numbered around 240,000, approximately equal to those of the British and the French combined. The Germans could no longer bear the losses as well as the Allies, not to mention that most of their casualties had been sustained by highly trained shock units.

The temporary lull in German operations gave rise to recriminations and finger pointing in London for the disaster that had practically destroyed the Fifth Army. Haig never accepted to his dying day that he had done anything wrong. In truth, he had no reason to pat himself on the back. From the beginning, he deluded himself into thinking that the Germans had been seriously weakened by his operations in Flanders and no longer posed a serious threat. He anticipated that the German attack would occur in the direction of Calais and Boulogne and for that reason had concentrated most of his troops in the north. It is difficult to blame him for taking steps to ensure the security of Flanders and the Channel ports, but he was wrong to leave the Fifth Army in such a weakened state. After the start of the battle, moreover, he was slow to perceive the main point and dimensions of the enemy's penetration and the seriousness of the Fifth Army's plight.

Haig could not bring himself to believe that it was superior tactical skill that had permitted the Germans to achieve a breakthrough, a feat that had eluded him in 1916 and 1917. Instead, as he would tell the king (who was visiting GHQ), he attributed it to factors over which he had no control: the Germans had tripled their forces in his sector during the past twelve months; he had 100,000 fewer men than in the previous year, but he was now facing three times as many Germans; he had been forced, on the order of the prime minister, to extended his line recently by twenty percent. In other words, Haig blamed the government for starving him of men.[48]

How credible is Haig's claim? It is true that he had requested 334,000 conscripts and received only 174,000. It is equally true that the British general reserve of 120,000 men had been kept in Britain, rather than sent over to France. However, it was not Lloyd George, but Robertson who had held back the general reserve. His decision was based on the following considerations: that it would be easier to conceal the men from enemy intelligence; that it would be better for the morale of the nation, which was still suffering from the effects of Passchendaele, to keep the men at home as long as possible; that it would help the economy if the men spent their money at home instead of in a foreign country.[49] Haig may have unwittingly encouraged War Office policy by assurances that he could withstand any German attack for at least 18 days with his existing forces. In the final analysis, Haig is correct in claiming that he had an insufficient reservoir of manpower to guard his newly extended line, but how can he justify throwing the entire blame on the politicians for this, when he allowed 88,000 men to go on leave on the eve of the March attack?

Lloyd George was not above censure, either. There is no doubt that he and the War Cabinet had not provided Haig with the necessary forces in the months preceding the offensive of March 21. The prime minister grossly miscalculated two factors. He chose to disregard the potential threat posed by the enemy buildup. In the second place, he failed to consider that the additional length of front Haig had taken over from the French required to be manned. Indeed, Haig had about 70,000 fewer troops than in the previous year to defend a much longer front. The country had not yet reached the bottom of the manpower barrel and there were still a fair number of potential recruits available. Equally important as a source of manpower were the unnecessary British divisions scattered in various theaters overseas. There were some 26 British divisions dispersed in minor theaters, 11 in Palestine alone (7 infantry and 4 cavalry). In a letter to the *Daily Telegraph*, that appeared on July 20, 1936, a noted German authority, General von Gallwitz, was thankful that many of these forces had not been concentrated on the western front. He wrote, "We Germans were grateful that very strong English contingents ... were chained to other theatres of war, especially in the East. The battles there did not burden us anything like as much as a large-scale transfer of British divisions to the western front would have done."[50] There was no reason why a dozen or so British divisions should not have been recalled – that is, those in excess of what was needed for defensive purposes and others replaced by African and Indian units unsuited to fight on the western front.

Between March 21 and August 31 over half a million men were sent to France from Britain and the Dominions, plus another 100,000 from Italy, Salonica and Palestine. It is obvious that large numbers of men were available to enter the line in France before March 21 if the government had so wished. Lloyd George had good reason to want to avoid a repetition of Passchendaele, but his mistrust of Haig did not justify placing the Allied cause in such jeopardy. Reinforcements should have been sent to the western front in greater numbers early in 1918 and Haig given explicit instructions that he was not to engage in any offensive action.[51]

Lloyd George, not surprisingly, held Haig mostly responsible for the military setback. He insisted that preparations for defense were slipshod, despite the knowledge that an attack was coming; that Haig had improperly deployed his men, keeping too many in sectors unlikely to be seriously attacked; that he had not selected the right commander to hold a dangerous section of the line with a relatively weak army; that he had held the reserves too far from where the main attacks occurred. He also excoriated Haig for standing opposed like a rock to the creation of an Allied General Reserve, which he felt would have helped blunt the German drive.[52] Lloyd George has some valid points, but not when he insists that the General Reserve could have stemmed the enemy tide. First, the French ended up sending twenty divisions to support the British, six more than their contribution would have been to the General Reserve. Then, too, the Reserve would not have been available at the outset of the battle. It can be argued that by retaining the nine British divisions earmarked for the General Reserve, Haig prevented a more disastrous breakthrough than was the case. The best justification for a General Reserve was that countermeasures could have been taken more easily and perhaps the German offensive could have been halted before it actually was. On balance, the General Reserve would not have made a significant difference, one way or the other.

Lloyd George also railed, albeit to a lesser extent, against President Wilson, because he had failed to respond to the war with a sense of urgency. He claimed that twelve months after Washington's declaration of war, the nominal combat strength of its forces in France was 214,000, of whom only about 70,000 were available for the fighting line. He went on to say, "I ascertained that at the corresponding period of our entry into the War we had 942,507 men ... in the various theatres and our casualties were 312,075."[53] The prime minister had good cause to be upset. To be perfectly blunt, the United States had not done as much as could be reasonably expected from a country with its resources.

Gough was less culpable than either Haig or Lloyd George, but in the end it was his head that fell under the axe. Gough was not a brilliant officer and maybe he should not have been given so large and important a command as that of an Army. But from the start he had to cope with two insurmountable problems that were not of his own making. He had been given the longest and most vulnerable stretch of the British front, with too few troops to hold it. In the weeks prior to March 21 Gough had alerted General Headquarters that he expected to be attacked in the near future and giving his reasons why, but his warnings were ignored – Haig did not expect the attack to extend to the Fifth Army's front. On March 19 his request that two reserve divisions be moved to his front was denied on the grounds that it was premature to do so.[54]

An adequate defense might have partially made up for inferiority in numbers, but the trench system inherited from the French was in frightful condition and Gough lacked the labor force and engineers to put it into shape – and as it happened, this was precisely the sector that Ludendorff chose to launch his spring offensive. British defensive tactics were in the midst of a change and

Gough has often been criticized for his failure to fully grasp the three-tier system – forward, battle and reserve zones – based on the latest German model. The charge has merit. The new doctrine was not properly taught, and unit commanders, accustomed to holding ground as close to the enemy as possible, kept too many men in the forward area where they were exposed to German artillery. It did not help that Gough's request for additional labor was denied, so that when the Germans struck, the second line was inadequately prepared and the reserve zone was so little developed that it scarcely existed. Still, when the breakthrough occurred, Gough, by all accounts, remained calm and skillfully conducted the retreat.[55]

In London, rumors were circulating that the government had practically invited the German success by reinforcing secondary theaters at the expense of the western front. Questions were being asked in parliament for an explanation of the causes of the sudden military reverse. The press, for its part, blamed the prime minister in no uncertain terms. The *Globe*, among the prime minister's most virulent critics, claimed that hundreds of thousands of troops who might have produced a victory in France were squandered in eccentric expeditions of little strategic value. It concluded that the present predicament was the "inevitable result of our national folly in allowing the war to be managed by men who know nothing of war." The *Daily News* linked the downturn in the nation's military fortunes to the dismissal of Robertson. For the *Star*, the only way to restore public confidence was to install Robertson as secretary for war.[56]

The drumbeat of criticism that he was mismanaging the war added significantly to Lloyd George's anxiety. He feared that unless he could stop the hemorrhaging, his days as prime minister would be numbered. He instinctively aimed his salvos at Gough, who, because of his ill conduct of operations in 1916 and 1917, made a convenient scapegoat. In his memoirs, Lloyd George praised Gough's gallantry and soldierly qualities, though in reality, he doubted his capacity, and in another disingenuous statement, maintained that he personally had no part in his shabby treatment. Gough's dismissal, Lloyd George writes, "was ordered by Haig entirely on his own initiative, without any instruction from home."[57] In fact, Haig had interceded on Gough's behalf, though, contrary to his diary entries, he did not make great efforts to do so.[58] Recalled from Versailles, Rawlinson assumed command of the remnants of the Fifth Army, which was renamed the Fourth.

Haig also came under fire for the manner in which he had handled the battle and in response, offered to resign if that was the wish of the government. Haig's letter was read in the War Cabinet on April 8 but omitted from the official notes. The debate occurred after the meeting. Lloyd George thought that they "ought to take Haig at his word," but the majority concurred with Wilson that, as no better general had been found, it was best to leave him where he was.[59]

Given the circumstances, it was probably a wise decision. The Germans were far from finished and, as a rule, it is never a good idea to change horses in midstream. Besides, while Haig had made avoidable mistakes, there was no better defensive field general in the British army. Lloyd George evidently thought otherwise, for he never gave Haig credit for possessing any military ability. Additionally, he held Haig responsible for his latest political difficulties, which had stemmed from the German onslaught. Little did he realize that he was about to face an even greater threat to his ministry, and it was not related to any German action.

Chapter 15

THE MAURICE AFFAIR

Newspapers favorable to the army, such as the *Globe* and *Morning Post*, continued to be a thorn in the government's side, holding it, not the generals, responsible for the German breakthrough. The daily pummeling of Lloyd George by a section of the press had its echo in parliament. On April 9 Lloyd George addressed the House of Commons and in the course of rebutting charges that he had deliberately kept Haig short of reserves, made several incorrect statements. He declared that in spite of heavy casualties in 1917, the British army in France was "considerably stronger" on January 1, 1918 than it had been twelve months earlier. The allegation is misleading. It can be justified only if Lloyd George had included noncombatants such as labor battalions. The prime minister also denied that he had large British forces locked in secondary theaters, forces that would have been more useful fighting the Germans in France. He claimed that there was only one white division in Mesopotamia, and in Egypt and Palestine there were only three white divisions; the rest were either Indians or mixed, with a very small proportion of white troops.[1] Here, what Lloyd George said was clearly untrue. In Palestine alone, Allenby had eleven divisions, consisting of about 100,000 white and only 6,000 Indian soldiers.

On the same day, Lloyd George learned that Ludendorff had launched a second major offensive, this time against a sensitive part of the British line, in the north between La Bassée Canal and Armentières, with the obvious aim of breaking though to the Channel ports.[2] The brunt of the attack fell on an overextended Portuguese division (one of two under British control), which broke and ran, leaving a six-mile-wide gap in the line. The Germans poured through the breach, advancing three miles before they were slowed down by the Lys and flanking British units. The following day, the Germans struck against Plumer's Second Army north of the Lys, overrunning Armentières and capturing most of Messines. Haig was shaken. He had no more reserves to commit, and the Germans were heading for the railroad junction at Hazebrouck, the capture of which might have opened the way to the Channel ports. Only the French could provide him with immediate help. He turned to Foch, who had been collecting French reserves farther south.

Foch did not think that the situation was as serious as Haig claimed and refused his request for reinforcements. He had concluded that the German attack in Flanders was merely a feint to cover a more serious blow farther south.³ Foch gave as an excuse that the French army still required nursing and could not be relied upon to fight in a difficult battle in which the defenders were giving ground. It is more probable, however, that because he was confident that the British could hold on alone, he did not want to squander any of his reserves, for he was hoping to mount a counteroffensive in the near future.

In London, the anxiety that War Cabinet members felt on receipt of the gloomy reports from the front was exacerbated by fear that Foch might not commit his reserves in time to avert a catastrophe. With the new crisis requiring maximum and effective effort by all key ministers, Lloyd George saw no reason to retain Derby any longer at the War Office. Derby had been a political appointment at the time his government was formed, intended to appease Robertson and his supporters. He had contributed little in the inner councils of war beyond running interference for Robertson and Haig. Lloyd George had no love for Derby and in the past had considered replacing him, but had held back lest he give his opponents an excuse to stir up trouble. With Robertson gone and Derby's reputation in political and military circles in tatters, Lloyd George considered the time was ripe to ease him out gracefully. Although Derby spoke no French, Lloyd George packed him off to Paris as the new British ambassador, succeeding Lord Bertie who was due to retire. Lloyd George transferred Milner to the War Office and replaced him in the War Cabinet with Austen Chamberlain.⁴

The highest priority for the government was to rush men to France as rapidly as shipping permitted. The enormous losses suffered by the BEF in the German offensives could not be replaced instantly from home and overseas. This meant that Britain would have to rely on its allies for a while. Foch had moved troops north, but, husbanding them for a counterattack at a propitious moment, had hesitated to commit them to battle. He counted on the dogged resistance of the British to absorb the enemy's sledgehammer blows and reestablish the line with only a minimum of the reserves at his disposal.⁵

Thus far, Washington had continued to vacillate over the subject of amalgamation, notwithstanding President Wilson's stated approval of the concept and Lord Reading's (the new British ambassador) frequent visits to the White House, stressing that the Entente faced annihilation unless American troops moved into the line in sufficient numbers. The crux of the problem was that the secretary for war, Newton Baker, was reluctant to commit to Lloyd George's program to send over 450,000 infantry and machine-gun units by

July. On April 19 he drew up a memorandum, supposedly intended to clarify the American government's position, but in reality was "a masterpiece of studied ambiguity." Baker indicated that the President accepted the principle of brigading, but left the number of troops to be allocated to American military leadership.[6] For all of its protestations of willingness to cooperate, the American government had again refrained from making a firm commitment.

Pershing was not likely to concede anything that would delay the creation of an independent role for the American army. Oddly enough, he was unaware of the results of the Baker–Reading conversations when he attended a meeting with Wilson and Milner in London on April 24 to work out his own arrangements with the British. He was shaken when shown Baker's memorandum. Interpreting it rather liberally, he concluded that Washington had succumbed to the concept of amalgamation, and so felt compelled to make limited concessions. He would go no further than to temporarily allow combat units of the six divisions scheduled to arrive in May to train and, in case of an emergency, to be used in combat in the British sector.[7] The so-called London Agreement was the best that the British could hope for, but it fell short of what they had requested from the American President. By offering divisions, rather than battalions, Pershing had undercut Haig's plan to use American replacements to restore his shattered divisions. Moreover, there was no guarantee that Pershing would supply forces to the British, or for that matter to the French, after May.

The French authorities were outraged when they discovered that the British, whom they suspected, quite unfairly, of holding back a hidden army, would soon be the beneficiaries of six American divisions. Clemenceau and his colleagues, ready as always to believe the worst about the British, felt that their ally across the Channel had wrung concessions from the Americans behind their backs. At the Supreme War Council, held at Abbeville on May 1–2, the first item on the agenda was the question of the employment of American troops. Clemenceau, his anger apparent, drew attention to the Pershing–Milner agreement, which he maintained had evidently altered the previous arrangements made by the military representatives at Versailles. It had been understood at Versailles that with the arrival of 120,000 American troops a month, half would join the British and half the French army. Under the new accord, it appeared that the French would receive no American troops. Clemenceau resented that Foch, as the supreme commander, had not been consulted in the matter. If the British received 120,000 American troops in May, he insisted that the French must receive a similar number in June. Milner pointed out that his understanding with Pershing did not reverse a Supreme War Council decision. He indicated that no recommendation by the military representatives had any validity until it had been endorsed by the SWC. To the best of his recollection, he could not remember any discussion involving the allocation of American troops on arrival in France. Pershing confirmed Milner's observations. Outflanked, the raging Tiger shifted his attack. If nothing had occurred at Versailles, he roared, something definite had been decided in London. Foch, who was intimately concerned in this question, had been ignored. While he did not wish to disrupt the arrangements for the distribution of American troops in May, he wanted to know what would be done with those arriving in June.

Lloyd George tried to redirect the discussion so that the focus would be on what was in the best interest of the common cause. He stated that the British army had been the most heavily engaged and, as a result, had suffered the heaviest casualties. All available drafts in the depots in Britain had been dispatched to France and every single man who became available in May and June would be sent out as well, regardless of the number of American troops allotted to the British army. The problem was that ten British divisions had been so decimated that they could not be reconstituted. These divisions had to be replaced by other divisions, either French or American. He suggested that the decision to allot American troops in June should depend on which army would bear the brunt of the fighting, the British or the French. He requested that Pershing extend his May program into at least June. Pershing interjected to say that not all American troops in France were going to the British. There were already four American divisions in the French sector and another three would soon be ready to move there. Pershing reminded the Allied leaders that American troops were not to serve indefinitely as drafts for the French and British armies. He looked forward to a time when the United States would have its own army, homogenous, and under its own supreme command. He would extend his program only in case of an emergency, but he did not believe that he required to make a decision at the moment.

Lloyd George fully accepted the principle laid down by Pershing, as did Foch and Clemenceau. The British prime minister thought that the critical month would be in September or October and that, if an independent American army could come into the field then, it would suit everybody. But he requested that Pershing make a decision about possibly extending the program before the end of May, because the problem of tonnage had to be considered. Foch assured Pershing that any help he might render the Allies during a period of crisis was not incompatible with the creation of a separate American army at the earliest possible moment. Pershing held out at first, but when the Allies threatened to bypass him and appeal directly to Wilson, he reluctantly agreed to the extension into June, and not beyond it as Lloyd George had urged. It was decided that the British would provide the shipping to bring over 130,000 American troops in May to serve with Haig. The following month, the Royal

Navy would ferry 150,000 American soldiers across the Atlantic, allotted either to the British or the French. In exchange for these concessions, Pershing obtained a promise that an American army would be formed as quickly as possible. There were two other resolutions of note passed by the SWC. The first extended Foch's authority to the Italian front; the other dissolved the Executive Board, its functions transferred to Foch.[8]

While the Allied leaders sat in the SWC, they were unaware that the momentum of the German attack had broken down. The battle had followed a familiar pattern. After the initial surge, the German advance, handicapped by the difficulty of bringing forward artillery and reinforcements and encountering stiffening British resistance, slowly ground to a halt. The Germans had forced the British back 15 to 20 miles in places, but they had failed to break though to the Channel ports. The British, aided by such men as Foch provided, fought magnificently, but their units were left in tatters, gasping and spent. Their casualties were officially listed at 82,040.[9] German losses were not much less. The German High Command deferred further action until it could replace its casualties.

In May, as the BEF welcomed the temporary lull in the fighting, a bombshell exploded on the British political scene, threatening to blow apart the Lloyd George administration. During the debate on the first German offensive in the Commons on April 23, Bonar Law claimed that the BEF's extension of the front to Barisis had not been imposed by the War Cabinet or the Supreme War Council, but had been a military arrangement between Haig and Pétain.[10] Technically, the statement was correct, but it omitted the preliminary and vital part played by the government. Haig brought the matter up when Milner visited his headquarters on April 28, saying that while he did not want to embarrass the government, he must insist that "a true statement of the facts be filed in the War Office." Milner assured him that he would do so.[11]

Haig was not the only high-ranking British officer upset with the government's efforts to cast blame on him for making the BEF vulnerable. To Sir Frederick Maurice, the government's recent action was aimed at nothing less than to build a case for the recall of Haig. Maurice had been removed as DMO by Wilson and, although currently unemployed, was scheduled to report for duty in France on May 10. Maurice feared that Haig's departure during this crisis would be a disaster and result in the loss of the war. He did not believe that anyone could replace Haig as C-in-C in France or evoke greater confidence among the troops.[12] An officer who normally shrank from political involvement, Maurice felt it was incumbent on him, as one of the few people in possession of all the facts, to thwart Lloyd George's design. He wrote to Wilson on April 30, and drew attention to the government's misleading declarations and their effect on the army, but received no reply.

His only other recourse was to publicly challenge the government's statements in parliament, a step that violated the king's regulations and, in effect, would end his military career.[13] He turned for advice to Robertson, his mentor and former chief. Robertson ought to have restrained Maurice, knowing as he did the consequences of public criticism of official superiors. But, alas, he encouraged Maurice to move forward, his judgment undoubtedly impaired by his hatred of the man who drove him from office.[14] Maurice had also intended to talk to Asquith, whom he knew well, but changed his mind, deciding to take responsibility for his own action.

Maurice's ulterior motive has been questioned by some historians. A. J. P. Taylor sees Maurice as seeking revenge against an administration that ousted him from the War Office.[15] John Gooch concludes that Maurice was trying to draw attention to the failings of the government in the hope that it would lead to the creation of a more efficient system of conducting the global war.[16] The standard interpretation, and the one that I find the most convincing from the documentary evidence, is that he was attempting to provoke a national uproar that would inhibit the government from sacking Haig.

Whatever the case, Maurice's letter appeared in four London dailies, including the *Morning Post*, on May 7. In it he accused the government of misrepresenting facts about the strength of the British army in France at the beginning of 1918 as compared with a year earlier, the number of white divisions in the Egyptian Expeditionary Force, and the extension of Haig's front. The intent of the letter was to suggest that the government had given false information to conceal the fact that it had starved Haig of the men necessary to defend his front. Once he had dispatched his letter to the press, Maurice left for the country to deflect attention from himself and to avoid any charge of political intrigue.[17] It would have helped his cause immeasurably if he had remained in London and worked with Lloyd George's detractors.

The allegations, made by one with direct access to official information, naturally produced an immense sensation in the nation. They confirmed rumors circulating outside of parliament and shook the faith of many of the government's ardent supporters. The central issue was less about the government's veracity than about its competence to manage the war. To what extent had Lloyd George's ongoing clashes with Haig impaired the war effort? Had he forced Haig to extend his line? Had he deliberately kept the army short of men? Had he diverted resources to secondary theaters when there was ample evidence that an attack was impending on the western front? These and other questions were being asked in the press. Opposition newspapers struck with a vengeance, implying that Lloyd George was no longer fit to remain in office. *The Westminster Gazette*, the leading mouthpiece for the Asquithian Liberals, proclaimed that Lloyd George had lost the confidence of the country and urged a change in government. The *Morning Post* returned to the charge with a blunt declaration that since Lloyd George, in defiance of good sense, had chosen to drive "the chariot of war," he must abide by the consequences of failure. Ironically, the right-wing paper, once a virulent critic of Asquith, now wanted him to take over the reins of government and to reinstate Robertson as CIGS. Even papers normally in Lloyd George's camp, such as the *Times*, agreed that Maurice's charges were so serious that they could not be circumvented.[18]

Maurice had not acted in concert with anyone else, but given the highly charged atmosphere since March 21, it would have been understandable if Lloyd George had drawn the conclusion that the letter was part of a conspiracy orchestrated by the military party to topple his government. But in his memoirs, Lloyd George overreached himself when he maintained that powerful forces in the press and in parliament, supported by the higher ranks in the army, were aiming to create a military junta under Robertson for the rest of the war.[19] In view of Britain's long democratic tradition, it was absurd to suggest that either the press or parliament would have tolerated a military dictatorship, or that Robertson would have been interested in heading one. What was indisputable was that the survival of the government depended on its ability to refute Maurice's grave charges.[20]

At the morning session of the War Cabinet on May 7 the ministers' nerves were on edge, but their mood was defiant. The content of Maurice's letter was analyzed and discussed at length. Bonar Law was troubled by the allegations that impugned his personal honor as well as that of the prime minister. His chief concern was to prove that the statements in question had been honest, if not truthful. Lloyd George was confident that he could parry Maurice's charges. The question was how to do so in a manner satisfactory to parliament without revealing military secrets. It was eventually decided that Bonar Law should announce in the Commons that Maurice's breach of military discipline would be handled by the Army Council and that the government would ask two judges to act as a court of honor to inquire into the alleged misstatements.[21]

Bonar Law came under fire when he appeared in the Commons in the afternoon. Carson, now free of ministerial responsibilities, had a sharp exchange with Bonar Law. Asquith rejected the idea of a judicial inquiry and pressed instead for a select committee of the Commons. Bonar Law tried to allay Asquith's suspicions by offering to let him appoint the two judges. But Asquith demurred and insisted that the matter be discussed on the floor of the House. He invited the government to select a date for the debate.[22] Asquith made a terrible blunder by turning down Bonar Law's offer. The statements made by the leading government officials would have been carefully scrutinized by an impartial judicial court, unaffected by political expediency or heated rhetoric. Its report, in all likelihood, would have proven embarrassing to the government.

At the War Cabinet meeting on May 8, Lloyd George told his colleagues that he was absolutely opposed to the idea of a select committee because it would be constituted along party lines and its proceedings would be marked by political wrangling, not judicial investigation. Nor was he any longer in favor of a judicial inquiry. Churchill, it seems, had persuaded him that it would be inappropriate to ask judges to inquire into the integrity of ministers.[23] Lloyd George concluded that it would be better to meet the political threat with an open debate in the House, followed by a vote of confidence.[24] He was impatient to get the matter resolved and thought that he had a good case. But his best weapon was Asquith. The prime minister correctly sensed that, if it came down to a choice, parliament would not vote to bring back Asquith.

The ex-prime minister had not seen Maurice's letter in advance, but he had been informed on the previous day of its impending publication. Asquith hated Lloyd George with a passion, but Walter Runciman, a close friend and former colleague, intimated that he "was not anxious to resume the reins at the moment,"[25] for reasons one can only speculate – perhaps because of his diminished energy, he had lost the will to shoulder the awesome responsibilities of a war leader; or it may be that as a true patriot, he recognized it would not be in the interest of the country to undergo a change of ministry during the worst crisis of the war. But the fate of the government rested less on Asquith's attitude than on whether the Opposition (Asquithian Liberals, and Tories) would present a united front. Carson tried to mobilize the Unionist War Committee against Lloyd George on May 8, but his efforts were unsuccessful. He told Repington later in the day that, after a three-hour meeting with the Unionists, their hatred "of Asquith overrides all other considerations, and that they will not back him tomorrow in the Maurice debate."[26] The Opposition was further handicapped because Maurice was not in the city and there was no one else who could supply them with the real facts. To the uninformed, however, the outcome of the political storm could not be predicted.

As zero hour approached, the whips in both parties made sure that all their members would be in attendance. There was as much excitement throughout the country as in parliament. With the life of the government hanging in the balance, the anticipated political debate was a subject of conversation in pubs and other public meeting places.[27]

On May 9 a confident and smiling prime minister entered the House of Commons. The floor was crowded as were the galleries. Asquith opened with a motion that a select committee be appointed to look into the allegations of incorrectness in statements made by several ministers "to this House." He proceeded to give a long-winded speech, devoted chiefly to an irrelevant explanation of the reasons why he preferred a select committee to an investigation by a two-judge panel.[28] He was evidently unaware that the prospects of an inquiry no longer existed. He barely mentioned what was at the heart of the crisis, Maurice's charges against the government, possibly because he had taken no steps to ascertain their validity and his knowledge of the affair was essentially restricted to what he had gleaned from newspapers. All in all, it was a pitiful performance by one of the most brilliant parliamentarians of his day.

Lloyd George rose to deliver his brief, which had been superbly prepared by the ingenious Hankey and rehearsed in front of several ministers. His fighting instincts aroused, the prime minister held the audience spellbound with his rhetorical skill, bravura display of statistics and facts, and matchless verve. He explained that the government had opted to forgo an independent inquiry because it could not be done either objectively or quickly. It was best, he and his colleagues believed, to present the facts and to let the public be the judge.

Lloyd George's preliminary remarks dwelled on what he termed was the "inconsistent conduct of General Maurice." He noted that Maurice had never called attention to any inaccuracy in his speech of April 9 while he was still at the War Office. The general was in daily contact with him and had had plenty of opportunity to do so. Yet, he had not protested to him, or to the secretary for war, or to the CIGS about a matter that he considered so vital as to drive him to break the king's regulations. The inference was that Maurice was being used as a tool by the government's enemies. Lloyd George had made a telling point. Maurice subsequently explained in his published account that he was too preoccupied with his work to read Lloyd George's speech (of April 9) and was unaware of its contents until he visited General Headquarters on April 14.[29] The speech was widely reported and discussed in the press. Indeed, Maurice's diary on April 9 alludes to parts of Lloyd George's remarks, so that he was probably aware of his misstatements before going over to France.[30] What probably happened was that Maurice heard of the dismay at General Headquarters over the prime minister's speech and felt guilty for not speaking out while he was the DMO. That may account for his note to Wilson on April 30, shortly after his return.

As for the charges themselves, Lloyd George dealt first with the declaration he made that the fighting strength of the British army was stronger on January 1, 1918 than it had been on the first day of the previous year. He surprised his critics by maintaining that the figures upon which he had based his statement were supplied by Maurice's own department while he was still at the War Office. To still any lingering doubts, he produced the actual note sent over by the DMO's office and waved it in the air. Therefore, if the public had been misled, the fault lay with Maurice. But since then, his own investigation had revealed that the figures were quite accurate. Lloyd George's defense appeared ironclad, but it was dishonest. On May 8 the new DMO Major General Percy de B. Radcliffe, had sent over to Philip Kerr, Lloyd George's secretary, revised figures from the Adjutant General's Office that showed a decrease in rifle strength from the preceding year. Thus, Lloyd George had been given the corrected figures before he made his speech but chose to suppress them. An entry in Hankey's diary reads:

> While he [Lloyd George] had had figures from the DMO's Dept. showing that the fighting strength of the army had increased from 1 Jan to 1918, he had the Adjutant-General's figures saying the precise contrary, but was discreetly silent about them.[31]

Actually Lloyd George did not have to lie. He could have made a case that rifle count was not the only criterion to measure fighting strength. Labor units building entrenchments, roads and railways, and bringing supplies and armaments to the front, were not only often exposed to deadly fire, but released regular soldiers for combat duty.

Lloyd George then turned to defend the statement he made about the strength of British troops in the Middle East. It will be recalled that during his speech on April 9 he had indicated that there was one white division in Mesopotamia and three white divisions in the Egyptian Expeditionary Force and the other divisions were composed of either Indian or Indian mixed with a small number of British troops. He assumed that there was no dispute about the single division in Mesopotamia. On the other hand, the prime minister avowed that his statement about the three white divisions in Egypt and Palestine was based on information supplied by the CIGS at a War Cabinet meeting, which Maurice had attended. The DMO subsequently was given a copy of the minutes. He thus had an opportunity to correct the CIGS's error. Lloyd George admitted that when he spoke, there had been more than three white divisions in Allenby's army, but he attributed the error to a misunderstanding. Orders had already been given to substitute Indian forces for the units in Allenby's army being transferred to France, but he protested that he was unaware that the change had not been completed. But what he did not say was that Wilson (at the War Cabinet meeting on March 23) was referring to the white divisions only in Egypt, not in the entire EEF.[32] This explains why Maurice had not challenged the numbers.

Finally, Lloyd George dealt with the allegation that Haig had been pressured by the Supreme War Council to take over additional lengths of front against his will. Maurice had been careless in phrasing his charge. The SWC had not been involved. The prime minister was basically correct in insisting that the extension to Barisis had come out of an agreement between Haig and Pétain before the SWC had ever met. He conceded that Haig had been reluctant to extend his line, but that the pressure had come from the French, not the War Cabinet. This was not the full story. To be sure, the matter had initially been advanced by Painlevé in September 1917, but Robertson had been reluctant to make any firm commitment. Clemenceau pursued the matter more aggressively the next time the issue was brought up, and, under pressure, Lloyd George agreed in principle and did so without consulting Haig, who surely would have taken exception. The field marshal was understandably livid when he learned that so vital a decision had been made in his absence and yet, as a soldier, he had no option but to accede to political authority. From his headquarters in France, Haig's reaction to Lloyd George's speech was that it was a "clap-trap."[33]

As the speech neared its end, Lloyd George expressed regret that Asquith had acknowledged, but not seen fit to condemn, Maurice's breach of discipline. He made it clear that he considered Asquith's motion tantamount to a vote of censure, which if carried, would make it impossible for him to continue in office. In such an event, control of the government would pass into the hands of "the one who is responsible for the motion." He concluded by pleading that with the country facing a grave threat, it was time for everyone to come together and end the bickering: "I really beg and implore, for our common country, the fate of which is in the balance now and in the next few weeks, that there should be an end of this sniping."[34]

Lloyd George's speech, riddled though it was with distortions and bald-faced lies, had the desired effect. What followed was anticlimatic. The Opposition had no one to brief them about the true facts and could offer no credible rebuttal. When the motion was put to a vote, it was defeated by 293 to 106. Most of the Laborites abstained, and the Irish Nationalists were absent. Normally, a majority of almost three to one can be described as an overwhelming victory. In this instance, however, it was hardly impressive, since it was less a ringing endorsement of Lloyd George than an utter rejection of Asquith.[35]

Nevertheless, Lloyd George emerged from the Maurice affair stronger than ever and would be immune from further challenges for the rest of the war. There were other consequences that flowed from the incident. It finished once and for all Asquith's prospects as an alternate prime minister. It widened the split in the Liberal party, which never reemerged as a major force in British politics. Maurice, although not tried for military insubordination, was placed on half pay and dismissed from the army. He would enjoy a very successful career outside the army. To many officers in the military, Maurice would remain a selfless hero, a man who had sacrificed himself to expose the lies and policies of a government that had led to the disaster that had almost wrecked the BEF.

Haig also felt bad for Maurice, but thought his action inappropriate on the grounds that no soldier, whatever the reason, should meddle in politics.[36]

In the aftermath of the Maurice affair, Lloyd George, with nothing to fear from parliament, moved to tighten his grip over military policy. On May 14, using as a pretext the excessive workload of the War Cabinet, he set up a subcommittee, consisting of himself, Milner, Wilson and Hankey with Leo Amery taking the minutes, to deal with military questions and future strategy. Known as X Committee, it was supposed to report back to the War Cabinet as circumstances warranted. In reality, it was a device to bring Milner into the inner council of war and to avoid subjecting military policy to excessive scrutiny.[37]

Just like the War Cabinet, the SWC lost much of its *raison d'être* and was pushed into the background. Its most important functions were taken over by Foch and his personal staff when he became commander-in-chief of the Allied forces.[38] Henceforth, it would be chiefly preoccupied with military–political questions in secondary theaters, not the least of which was to pressure President Wilson into sanctioning and supporting an expedition to Russia.

Chapter 16

THE ORIGINS OF INTERVENTION IN RUSSIA

The Bolshevik seizure of power in Russia on November 7 came as no surprise to Lloyd George and his colleagues who in recent months had despaired over the inability of the Provisional Government, crippled by factionalism and inertia, to restore discipline in the army and order in the home administration. Lloyd George had no use for socialism, less so for the tyrannical form which Lenin, Trotsky and their associates represented. Yet, it is quite clear that British and Allied intervention in Russia was not the result of an intense hatred of the revolutionary nature of the Bolshevik regime. Had Lenin been willing to fight the Germans, the British would have embraced him regardless of his politics, just as they extended their hand to Joseph Stalin a quarter of a century later. It is equally apparent that the decision to intervene was neither deliberate nor premeditated, but came about imperceptibly, by small increments, the product of the march of events. What is uncertain is whether the Allies initially acted out of a desire to overthrow the Bolshevik regime or rebuild the eastern front to prevent the Germans from concentrating their full strength in the west. British policymakers in the beginning pursued a twisted and contradictory policy, namely, to maintain unofficial contacts with both the Bolsheviks and opposition forces.

The rule of the Bolsheviks created much fear and uncertainty in London. One concern was that Britain held much of Russia's debt (though by no means as large as France's). Another was the safety of its nationals in Russia as well as its diplomatic corps, which, contrary to convention, was not granted immunity.[1] Then, too, it was vital to prevent British war supplies for the Russian army, stockpiled in the ports of Murmansk and Archangel in the north and Vladivostok in the east, from falling into enemy hands. Similarly, it was essential to deny the Germans access to Russian grain and oil, control of which would allow them to break the blockade and extend the war indefinitely. British policy of relying on Russia to inhibit Germans and Turks from threatening India by advancing through Transcaucasia and Transcaspia to Bukhara and Afganistan was now up in the air.[2] Finally, without even an enfeebled Russia in the war, most of the German divisions in the east would be free to reinforce those on the western front. Thus, there were good reasons to avoid a rupture with the Bolsheviks.

In the days immediately following the Bolshevik coup, the War Cabinet had no clear idea of what was happening in Russia. What little news that dribbled in from local British representatives varied from day-to-day and was sometimes contradictory. All that was known was that there was anarchy in Petrograd and severe fighting in Moscow and Kiev. There was nothing in the messages to suggest that the Bolsheviks possessed the strength to rule over the entire country.[3] British political authorities would have preferred to wait until the situation clarified in Russia before deciding on a course of action, but, as the defeat of Germany occupied first place, a policy of inactivity was a luxury they could ill afford. At the War Cabinet on the morning of November 21, Balfour reported that he had received an important telegram from King Carol of Romania. The Romanians had entered the war in August 1916 on the high tide of the Brusilov offensive, but before the end of the year their army had been routed and their capital occupied. Carol had retreated with the remnant of his army to the mountainous northeastern part of the country and set up his headquarters in the town of Jassy near the Russian border. If the Russians bowed out of the war, the Romanians, given their predicament, were likely to follow suit.[4]

In the telegram, Carol maintained that if the Allies continued to give him support, he would try with some of his troops to force a passage through to southern Russia to link up with the Don Cossacks under General Alexei Kaledin, and ultimately, if circumstances permitted, with British forces in Mesopotamia. If, on the other hand, he could no longer count on Allied help, he might be forced to come to terms with Germany and Austria. Balfour urged that every effort should be made to keep Romania from signing a separate treaty with Germany. The most practical solution, it seemed, was to contact Kaledin in order to persuade him to cooperate with the Romanians.

The War Cabinet had very little information about Kaledin or the strength of his forces. All that its members knew about him was that he had proclaimed his opposition to the Bolsheviks. It was pointed out that the British were most unpopular in Russia and that it might be unwise to approach Kaledin directly, for he was only the leader of a faction. The prevailing view was that the British government should do nothing, "which appeared to take sides in the internal dispute now raging in Russia." The War Cabinet decided that an agent should be sent, either from Britain or Romania, to get in touch with Kaledin.[5] Its initial purpose, therefore, was not to interfere in Russia's internal affairs, but to get support for the Romanians.

In the afternoon, Lloyd George and Balfour raised the matter with Colonel House, who was in London for preliminary talks before attending an Allied

Conference in Paris later in the month. House did not think that it was a good idea to take any overt steps in support of Kaledin lest it strengthen the Bolsheviks' determination to make peace or be used by them to inflame anti-Allied feelings in Russia. The most the Allies could do would be to advise the Romanians to cooperate with whatever forces loyal to the Allies were closest to them without specifically naming any of them. Both Lloyd George and Balfour agreed with House's suggestion.[6]

The next day, it was announced in the War Cabinet that the Bolsheviks had issued a wireless message to the world announcing their intention to seek an immediate armistice. The discussion centered on the extent to which the Allies could take effective action in Russia against the Bolsheviks. Balfour noted that the Allies had not recognized the Bolsheviks as a government of Russia and would not accord such status to any group seeking a separate treaty with the enemy. The difficulty was that any overt action against Lenin and his associates might drive them into Germany's arms, "and so defeat the very object we are aiming at." Nor did they have sufficient knowledge that would justify them, at this juncture, either to back Kaledin or any other anti-Bolshevik group. Balfour reported the interview with House, explaining that he had expressed his opinion that the best move would be to let the Romanians appeal to Kaledin on purely military grounds, as the commander of the nearest effective army. This initiative would not constitute an intervention in Russia's internal affairs to the same extent as an appeal to Kaledin directly from the western Allies, and at the same time, it would afford an opportunity to ascertain what were the general's real strength and intentions. The War Cabinet modified the previous day's decision by directing the CIGS to wire Brigadier General C. R. Ballard (the British military attaché in Jassy), asking him, after consultation with the head of the French military mission, General H. R. Berthelot, "to advise as to the best procedure for approaching General Kaledin, or otherwise securing Russian help for Roumania."[7]

On November 26 Lloyd George, Balfour and Milner crossed the Channel to attend an Allied Conference in Paris set to begin on the last day of the month. They were therefore absent when the War Cabinet convened on November 29 to consider issues raised by the recent arrival of several telegrams. One, sent by Sir George Buchanan, the British ambassador in Petrograd, advised against giving encouragement to counterrevolutionary movements. Describing the state of affairs in the country as "desperate," he urged the government to release Russia from its obligations to the Allies (under the Pact of London) so that it could act as it chose, either purchasing peace on Germany's terms or fighting on with the Allies. This course, if adopted, would make it impossible for the Bolsheviks to reproach the Allies for driving Russian soldiers to slaughter for their imperialistic aims. The ministers discussed the alternate options – that is, following Buchanan's advice or waiting until the situation became clearer – but ultimately recognized that it was a matter that only the Allied conference could decide.

The other telegram came from Ballard who proposed that if Kaledin were found to be well disposed towards the Allies, a fully accredited Anglo–French mission should be dispatched to his headquarters with the authority to provide him financial support up to £10 million and be empowered to act on its own initiative. Once again, the War Cabinet was split between those who favored proceeding along the lines suggested by Ballard and those who preferred to wait until they had obtained more information. It was decided that Cecil, the acting head of the Foreign Office, should refer the telegrams to the British delegation in Paris and add that the members of the War Cabinet were divided as to what steps should be taken.[8]

In Paris, the Allied conference held at the Quai d'Orsay opened with a discussion of the events, such as they were known, in Russia. Lloyd George drew attention to Buchanan's telegram, advocating that the Allies release Russia from the 1914 treaty and allow it to decide whether it desired peace on Germany's terms. The French Foreign Minister, Stéphane Pichon, considered the British proposal dangerous and calculated to help the Bolsheviks. As far as was known, large sections of the Russian people, like the Cossacks and Ukranians, were hostile to the Bolshevik peace proposals. To make the declaration would be "to desert our friends, and perhaps throw them into the hands of the Bolsheviks." Balfour shared Pichon's views as did Sonnino. Lloyd George emphasized that Buchanan's proposal had the support of Major General Alfred Knox, Britain's military attaché in Petrograd, whose opinions throughout the war had proved correct, and required most careful examination. Before it was rejected, he would like to hear the views of the Russian ambassador in Paris, V. N. Malakoff (who was not present). Clemenceau maintained that nothing would induce him to let Russia off the hook. "If Russia made a separate peace she would betray us," the Tiger growled. "Let us keep the moral advantage of being betrayed. Let us keep our dignity."

The delegates turned to other business while word went out to invite Malakoff's attendance. When Malakoff arrived, Lloyd George explained Buchanan's suggestion and asked for his reaction to it. Malakoff thought that the British ambassador had gone too far if Lloyd George had interpreted his proposal correctly. What he thought Buchanan really meant was that the Allies should discuss their war aims with a loyal Russian government if one were formed. This is the course he would advise the Allies to follow. Lloyd George asked Malakoff if he favored an Allied declaration of their readiness to discuss war aims. Malakoff replied that he did not suggest that the declaration should be made by the conference. All he meant was that it should be made through some channel, like a statement in parliament or an interview in the press. The Bolsheviks were advancing the notion that the Allies wanted the Russians to fight in order to fulfill their own war aims. The Moderate party could offer no rebuttal against this line of argument. Therefore, he would like some declaration issued to give a platform to the Moderate party. Lloyd George asked Malakoff to draft a statement that he thought would carry more weight in Russia than if it were done by the Allies. House suggested that Malakoff prepare alternate drafts. Malakoff agreed to do so. On that note, the conference adjourned until 4:30 p.m. the following day.

When the Conference reconvened, Malakoff circulated four alternate draft statements from which he suggested one should be chosen and communicated to Russia. A long discussion followed, in the course of which other proposals were introduced. Balfour criticized all of them on the grounds that they "had the effect of saying that if there were a decent government in Russia we should be willing to discuss our war aims with it, which we had not really intended to do." They gave the impression, therefore, that the Allies "were being frightened into a discussion of our war aims." He thought it was impossible to draft an identical declaration to which all the governments could be a party. Even if it were possible to produce one, it would be faulty, leaving out everything that was vigorous and useful. It was best, in his view, for each government to send its own declaration to Russia.

Lloyd George interrupted the proceedings to announce that he had just learned from London that the Russians, who were seeking to engage in armistice talks, had asked the Germans for three days in order to communicate with their allies before moving forward. He added that four Russian armies had already accepted an armistice and that others would follow suit. It was evident that the Bolsheviks did, in fact, speak on behalf of the Russian armies and probably the Russian people so that their note would have to be answered. It was equally apparent to Lloyd George that the Moderate party had little public support and that Buchanan's earlier assessment had been correct.

The haggling over the various solutions advanced made it apparent that it would be impossible to agree on a joint declaration. Lloyd George said that the more he thought about the matter, the more he became convinced that the idea of a joint declaration should be abandoned. In the case of the British government, it would be counterproductive to make any announcement of its consent to discuss war aims after the publication of Lord Lansdowne's letter. Describing Lansdowne as an important Unionist leader and elder statesmen, the prime minister claimed that a public declaration by the government would be regarded as an endorsement of his views. He feared the consequences it would have on the nation's will to continue fighting. He suggested that each nation should tell its own ambassador in Russia to let it be known that the government he represented was ready to discuss war aims. Much profit could be derived from such a discussion. Take, for example, Russia's war aims. The Russians had aspired to control Constantinople, the Bosphorus and the Dardanelles, but whether possessions of these continued to hold their interest was a matter for them to decide. At present, Russia's war aims were a barrier to any separate peace with Turkey. He therefore was inclined to favor Balfour's proposal. There was general support for such action. But this really would have been an exercise in futility. The Allies could do nothing to induce Russia to stay the course. They did not understand that the Russian public and army as a whole were sick of the war and that the only way the Bolsheviks could survive was to conclude a peace treaty with the Germans.

At this point, the Japanese ambassadors in Paris (Matsui Keishiro) and London (Chinda Sutemi) were escorted into the conference room and introduced. Japan had joined the Entente late in August 1914, but thus far had confined its activities chiefly to the Far East. Chinda and Matsui had been invited to give their opinion about the possibility of further Japanese assistance, which the French had raised on the previous day. At the time, Lloyd George thought that the idea was impractical. Quite apart from the heavy price the Japanese would exact – there were rumors that they wanted Cochin China – the necessary transport would present a huge problem. The Allies were already short of ships to bring over American troops. He asked a rhetorical question: "Could anybody doubt that the cooperation of United States troops was infinitely more than that of [the] Japanese?" Pichon acknowledged the merit of Lloyd George's arguments, but he did not intend to ask the Japanese specifically for military help, only if they felt they had done as much as they could. House observed that the Americans had tried such an approach with them, but to no avail.

With the Japanese ambassadors listening attentively, Pichon took up from where he left off on the previous day. While he appreciated Japan's effort in the war (such as it was), he suggested that it would be useful to examine what more could be done, leaving it up to Tokyo to determine what form further cooperation should take. Matsui stressed that his government was doing all that it possibly could. It had sent warships to the Mediterranean and munitions to France and Russia. It had to be remembered that the Japanese army had been organized for home defense and that it lacked essential equipment for a distant expedition. Then, too, the Japanese did not possess the necessary tonnage to transport and supply a major force any great distance from home. Lastly, it would not be wise to embark on a distant operation unless there was general public support, a condition that could not be met. From what the ambassador said, it did not seem likely that further Japanese aid would be forthcoming.

During the later stages of the proceedings, General Berthelot asked that the various groupings in southern Russia be placed under his command. These would include Romanians, some Russians and Czechoslovakians – a corps formed from Czechs living in Russia before the war, together with Czech and Slovak prisoners and deserters from the Austrian army.[9] Balfour squashed the proposal by asking if the Allies placed Berthelot in charge of large Russian forces, how should they "stand towards a properly constituted Russian Government if one came into being." Lloyd George read Ballard's telegram in which he recommended that a combined French and British mission be sent to Kaledin's headquarters with full powers to guarantee him financial support of up to £10 million. After some discussion, Ballard's suggestion was approved.[10]

Lloyd George left Paris before the final session of the conference began and was back in London on December 2, the day that the Bolsheviks, under Leon Trotsky as Commissar for Foreign Affairs, opened armistice talks with the Germans. As a sign of desperation, the War Cabinet went beyond the decision taken at the Allied Conference and proposed to extend unlimited financial help, not only to the Cossacks, but also to the Ukrainians and other viable groups that would actively oppose the Bolsheviks.[11] The object in strengthening counterrevolutionaries was to deter the Bolsheviks from making peace; or at the very least, to keep southern Russia and unoccupied parts of Romania within the Allied camp. The War Cabinet had acted impulsively, before it had received reports from its investigative agents and without carefully weighing the impact on Britain's relations with the Bolsheviks.

In Petrograd, Knox and Buchanan, given their experience and with access to better intelligence, read with disbelief the War Cabinet's decision to aid anti-Bolshevik groups. Knox sent a strongly worded protest, claiming that Kaledin's strength was exaggerated and that Ukrainian forces amounted to only a few mutinous regiments in Kiev. He was adamant that neither the Cossacks nor the Ukrainians were willing to continue fighting any more than the people in the rest of Russia. Besides, Knox noted, to "ask us to intrigue while we are here in the power of the Rebel Government is merely to get our throats cut to no purpose." Buchanan expressed himself along similar lines.[12] An officer sent to the Don by Ballard to investigate matters essentially confirmed what Knox and Buchanan had reported, namely that the Cossacks were demoralized and unreliable and that Kaledin would not fight in areas outside his control.[13]

Before the one-sided advice from officials in Russia and Romania could be considered, the War Cabinet needed to establish a policy towards the Bolsheviks. The ministers had no love for the Bolsheviks, particularly after Lenin openly incited the Muslim population of India to revolt against their occupiers. There were two avenues opened to the British. They could recognize the Bolsheviks and make the best possible arrangements with them; or they could refuse to recognize them and take "open and energetic steps against them."[14]

The matter was debated at the War Cabinet meeting on December 10. Balfour was absent, but he had submitted a memo in which he made no mention of recognizing the Bolshevik regime, but urged that Britain avoid a breach with the usurpers as long as possible. A break with the Russian government, in his view, would have fatal consequences, not only endangering British subjects in Russia, but giving Lenin and his associates justification for "welcoming in their midst German officials and German soldiers as friends and deliverers." Undergoing a change of heart since the Paris Conference, Balfour concluded that large forces to succor the Romanians did not exist and that efforts to collaborate with Kaledin would be considered a hostile act by the Bolsheviks.[15]

Lloyd George shared Balfour's views, but there were others in the War Cabinet, not mentioned by name in the minutes, who did not. It was pointed out that efforts to placate the Bolsheviks would be inconsistent with British support for Kaledin in south Russia. The upshot was that the cabinet declined to make any change in its policy towards Russia, that is, maintain unofficial contacts with both the Bolsheviks and with opposition forces in the south.[16] According to Robertson, what "we are really trying to do is to keep up a state of chaos of some sort and not to drive the Bolshevists into the arms of the Germans."[17] The question one must ask is how did the British authorities expect to simultaneously woo both the Bolsheviks and their enemies?

Their rationale was obvious. If, as expected, the Bolsheviks remained in power only for a few months, it was best to appease them in the hope that they would keep Russia in the war. Alternatively, if the Bolsheviks were able to consolidate their power and reach an arrangement with the Germans, the British wanted to form a large bloc – consisting of the Don Cossacks, the Caucasus Cossacks, the Ukraine and unoccupied Romania – to resist the Germans from gaining access to food and other supplies in southern Russia. Neither option was realistic, because the Russians everywhere were sick of the war, in the south as much as in the north.

On seizing power, Lenin had called for a general peace, without annexations or indemnities and based on the right of self-determination of all ethnic groups living under foreign rule. When the western Allies did not respond, Lenin repudiated Russia's commitment not to make a separate peace and, as already mentioned, opened direct talks with Berlin (December 2). On December 15 the Bolsheviks and Germans signed an armistice at Brest-Litovsk, which called for a cessation of hostilities for a month. Formal peace negotiations were to begin in the same place as soon as possible. The chances of keeping Russia tied to the Allies were not entirely gone but, to all appearances, were diminishing rapidly.

A few days later, Lloyd George had an interview with Colonel William Boyce Thompson, a wealthy American financier and copper magnate, just back from Russia. Thompson gave him a somewhat different impression of affairs in the country than what was generally believed. He claimed that the Bolshevik regime was there to stay and that the Allies had not shown themselves sufficiently sympathetic to the Revolution. He observed that neither Lenin nor Trotsky were on Berlin's payroll or agents of German policy. He maintained that the Allies were not suitably represented in Petrograd and that they should form an Allied Council composed of specially selected men to conduct propaganda in Russia. He was adamant that the Russian army and people "were out of the war and that the Allies would have to choose between Russia as a friendly or a hostile neutral."[18]

Lloyd George reported his conversation with Thompson to the War Cabinet on December 19. By pressing for a definite policy towards the Bolsheviks, Thompson had raised an issue that the War Cabinet had been reluctant to face. The ministers proceeded to debate whether the Allies should change their policy and grant the Bolshevik government de facto recognition. The discussion continued over the next few days, interminable and unprofitable, complained Hankey, with much time wasted because Lloyd George had got it "into his head that we ought to support the Bolsheviks."[19]

With the approval of the War Cabinet, Lloyd George sought to establish contact with the Bolsheviks through an official agent. There could be no question of according de facto recognition to a regime dedicated to the subversion and overthrow of western governments and of dubious durability, but the dispatch of the prime minister's special emissary, it was hoped, would be seen as a friendly gesture. Lloyd George's purpose was to establish cordial ties with the Bolsheviks as the first step towards persuading them to get Russia back into the war. If he succeeded, he imagined that the Bolsheviks, given their single-mindedness and cohesiveness, might prove more effective than the late Provisional Government in inspiring a national stand against the Germans.[20] The man chosen to undertake this difficult mission was R. H. Bruce Lockhart.

A clean-cut Scot, looking younger than his 34 years, Lockhart had been attached to the British Consulate in Moscow from 1912 to 1917. Knowledgeable, energetic, and imaginative, his engaging personality and fluency in Russian enabled him to move freely in Russian social and political circles. Buchanan considered him the most able of his subordinates. He rose from junior vice-consul to acting consul-general by the summer of 1915, but his promising career was almost wrecked when he flouted the strict conventions of government service. Shortly before the Revolution, Buchanan, with much sorrow, sent Lockhart home, ostensibly on sick leave, but in reality because he was involved in an adulterous affair with a Russian woman. He was out of a job until brought to the notice of the prime minister, who gave him the opportunity to return to Russia. At the same time, the War Cabinet decided to recall Buchanan, whom the Bolsheviks viewed suspiciously because of his close association with the Cadet Party.[21]

Back in London, Lockhart was struck by the prevailing ignorance of British policy makers about the conditions in Russia. He wrote in his memoirs:

> I could not share the general belief, stimulated by the opinion of nearly all the Russian experts in London, that the Lenin régime could not last more than a few weeks and that then Russia would revert to Tsarism or a military dictatorship. Still less could I believe that the Russian peasant would return to the trenches. Russia was out of the war. Bolshevism would last – certainly as long as the war lasted. I deprecated as sheer folly our militaristic propaganda, because it took no account of the war-weariness which had raised the Bolsheviks to the supreme power. In my opinion we had to take the Bolshevik peace proposal seriously. Our policy should now aim at achieving an anti-German peace in Russia.[22]

Lockhart's pleadings with the many politicians he met were usually futile, but he had more success when he argued that it was essential to establish contact with the men who currently guided Russia's destiny. To what extent Lloyd George was aware of the differences between Lockhart and himself is unclear. When he summoned Lockhart to 10 Downing Street, he seemed to have done most of the talking. Lockhart has left a record of the interview:

> He [Lloyd George] asked me a few questions about Lenin and Trotsky. A fresh question followed almost before I had time to answer the previous one. I saw that his own mind was made up. He had been greatly impressed ... by an interview with Colonel Thompson ... who had just returned from Russia and who had denounced in blunt language the folly of the Allies in not opening up negotiations with the Bolsheviks. The questions ended, Mr. Lloyd George stood up, referred briefly to the chaotic conditions in Russia and to the necessity of getting in touch with Lenin and Trotsky, emphasized the need for tact, knowledge and understanding and finished up by stating that Mr. Lockhart was obviously a man whose right place at that moment was in St. Petersburg [pre-war name for Petrograd] and not in London.[23]

Before Lockhart left for Petrograd, Lloyd George delivered his war aims speech to a special trades union congress on January 5, 1918. In it, as already examined in detail, the prime minister sent a blunt message to the Bolsheviks, in effect telling them that because they initiated unilateral negotiations with the enemy, Britain no longer felt bound to fight in the interests of Russia. It was also an unmistakable hint to the Germans that they were at liberty to fulfill their annexationist aims at the expense of Russia. The speech had no impact on the Bolsheviks one way or the other.

In the weeks that followed, the War Cabinet periodically discussed whether Britain should accord recognition to the Bolshevik regime or break off relations with it altogether. Balfour felt that full recognition to the Bolsheviks could not be given until it was shown that they were representative of the Russian people. Cecil, the most hawkish of the British ministers, regarded Lenin and Trotsky as German agents. He felt that any dealing with the Bolsheviks was likely to discourage friendly elements in south Russia. But the consensus was that the British government should avoid a rupture as long as possible, as it appeared that the Bolsheviks were proving to be tougher bargainers than their main adversaries, the Social Revolutionaries, were likely to be. It was known that the Germans were transferring troops to the west to mount a great offensive. Anything that promised to delay enemy plans would be beneficial to the Allies.[24]

In Petrograd, Lockhart had been warmly received by the Bolsheviks, who were anxious to play off the Germans against the Allies. Buchanan had returned to Britain, but the rest of the embassy staff remained in the capital and many of them favored recognizing the Bolshevik regime, as did Lockhart. That prospect received a boost when Lockhart learned from G. V. Chicherin, a high Bolshevik official close to Lenin, that the talks at Brest-Litovsk "were going badly and that now was the great opportunity for England to make a friendly gesture towards Russia." Chicherin admitted that the Bolsheviks had no use for either German militarism or British capitalism, but at the moment they perceived the former as a greater menace.[25] Lockhart reported his every step to London.

On February 7 the War Cabinet considered a telegram from Lockhart requesting a more official status in dealing with Trotsky, so as to pave the way for a fuller understanding with the Bolshevik government. Balfour thought that Lockhart should be empowered to enter into direct relations with the de facto Bolshevik government. He was not in favor, however, of recognizing the Bolsheviks, first because they were not in control of the entire country, and second, because it would be incompatible with British support to the Ukraine and to the Don Cossacks. Cecil doubted that anything should be done to please or encourage a regime that behaved in such an irresponsible manner. Even the partial recognition that Balfour advocated might discourage anti-Bolshevik elements in south Russia and could prove helpful in the spread of Bolshevik propaganda, not only in Britain, but in France and Italy as well. Lockhart's wire, it seemed to him, was seeking wider authority than what the Foreign Secretary was recommending.

Lloyd George chimed in to say that it should not be their concern what socialist experiment or form of government the Bolsheviks were trying to establish in Russia. He thought that the Germans and the Austrians had more to fear from Bolshevism than Britain. He observed that granting Lockhart more authority might prove useful in obtaining from the Bolsheviks an agreement to refrain from interfering in the internal politics of Allied countries. He was most anxious that the War Cabinet accept the recommendations of the British representatives in Russia and he referred to several instances in the past where he thought errors had been made by ignoring their advice. The opinion he had formed of Lockhart was such as to cause him to hesitate before rejecting any advice he offered. Curzon favored taking a more cautious line. He thought that recognition of the Bolsheviks, when it appeared likely that they would sign a separate peace with Germany, would produce a very unfortunate effect in Britain and in the other Allied countries.[26]

The War Cabinet was split pretty much down the middle. The prime minister "was certain that further recognition of the Bolsheviks would affect matters in one way; his opponents were as certain that it would affect them in exactly the opposite direction."[27] Balfour stood between the two sides but closer to Lloyd George's position.

The War Cabinet resumed discussion of the subject the next day. The debate was animated, and at times heated. Both sides repeated their arguments.[28] Lloyd George felt that he was being pragmatic, but others considered him too sympathetic towards the Bolsheviks, and even Hankey, in a moment of exasperation, unfairly referred to him as half Bolshevik. He went on to say:

> Ll. G. ... seems to have forgotten that they [Bolsheviks] have shamefully broken Russia's solemn treaty with us, repudiated the enormous sums we have lent Russia, seized our property, allowed the guns we supplied to fall into the enemy's hands, and that they are engaged in a war against all civilized institutions.[29]

The War Cabinet, after making a few amendments, approved a draft Balfour had prepared in reply to Lockhart's telegram. Balfour's statement of policy was quite reasonable. He began by disabusing Lockhart of the notion that the government's disinclination to offer the Bolsheviks qualified recognition was influenced by anxiety that such a course might deal a crippling blow to bourgeois elements in Russia. He stated emphatically that the government was unconcerned with the internal affairs of Russia except insofar as it affected the war. If the people of Russia preferred Bolshevik rule, that was their choice, not Britain's, and it had nothing to do with the issue of diplomatic recognition. He pointed out that there was no significant difference over the form of recognition to be accorded between the views he (Lockhart) expressed and those the government held. Both agreed that, at the moment, it was impossible to grant the Bolsheviks complete recognition and undesirable to make a complete rupture. The solution was to opt for a middle course. Thus, he favored Lockhart's proposal that his status should be raised and that, in his semi-official dealings with the Bolsheviks, he should function as the British Embassy's acknowledged representative. Lockhart was urged to try to thwart a peace settlement between the Bolsheviks and the Germans, and, failing that, to delay it as long as possible. It was also suggested that in talks with Trotsky, he was to point out that, whatever differences existed between their respective governments, they were united in their desire to end German militarism.[30]

By the time that Lockhart received Balfour's memo, important developments had occurred at Brest-Litovsk. The Bolsheviks wanted a peace, with no annexations or indemnities, based on self-determination of all peoples. But the Germans had no intentions of surrendering lands they currently occupied. On February 10 Trotsky broke off negotiations because he considered Germany's terms too severe. He proposed to his colleagues that they should declare an end to the war and demobilize without signing any peace. Lenin disagreed, saying that peace, no matter how high the price, had to be made to save the Bolshevik revolution. The Bolshevik Central Committee, by a vote of nine to seven, voted to accept Trotsky's formula of "no peace, no war." The Germans responded by terminating the armistice with Russia and resuming their advance. As the Germans threatened the Russian capital itself, Bolshevik leaders came around to Lenin's view and formally accepted Germany's terms – which turned out to be harsher than those originally presented – on March 3, 1918.[31]

To the Allies, deserted in the midst of a life-and-death struggle, the Treaty of Brest-Litovsk was more than an act of betrayal. It would permit the Germans to release many of their divisions in the east for action against the weary Allied armies in the west. It also would enable them to escape from the strangling effects of the Allied blockade by drawing foodstuffs and raw materials from the areas that had passed under their control. There existed, moreover, the danger that the vast quantities of military stores, crammed in the ports of Archangel, Murmansk and Vladivostok, might fall into the enemy's hands.[32] Finally, the British feared that Germany and Russia might combine to threaten India and the Middle East. Direct intervention in Russian affairs might solve their dilemma. Immediately, two potential sites appeared opened to them, one an expedition to take control of the northern ports of Murmansk and Archangel, and the other an invasion of eastern Siberia with the object of seizing Vladivostok.

The number of friendly groups in the former tsarist empire they could count on to lead the fight was shrinking perceptibly. The Ukraine had made a separate peace with Germany. With the Bolsheviks closing in, Kaledin shot himself, leaving the Don Cossacks demoralized and in disarray. To make matters worse, the Romanian government in Jassy, feeling helpless after both the Ukraine and Russia exited from the war, sued for peace. Germany had now pacified the entire eastern front, from the Baltic Sea to the Black Sea.

The powerful German offensive in the west, which began on March 21, had ruled out any possibility that the British or French could assemble enough troops to intervene in Russia. The only members of the Allied coalition that could spare significant manpower for such a mission were Japan and the United States. Even before the Bolsheviks pulled out of the war, the French had wanted Japan to send forces to occupy Vladivostok, where huge stores lay unprotected, to take control of the Trans-Siberian railway and to open communications with south Russia. They applied pressure on the British who fell in step, quickly but unenthusiastically. Balfour and Lloyd George had misgivings about the idea but a majority in the War Cabinet, led by Milner and Cecil, were all for it. On February 25 the War Cabinet, with the prime minister absent, reaffirmed its decision to back Japanese intervention.[33] The prime minister rang up Hankey the next day and expressed his dissatisfaction with the War Cabinet's action.[34] He believed that an accommodation with the Bolsheviks would serve Allied interests better than opening Russia up to a large-scale Japanese invasion. It was no secret that the Russians, ever since the Russo–Japanese War, had been convinced that the Japanese wanted to establish a foothold in Siberia. Lloyd George feared that the presence of the Japanese in Siberia would force the Russians to seek help from the Germans in exchange for their active cooperation. It was a scenario that he was anxious to avoid, but for reasons about which one can only speculate, he made no attempt to reverse the War Cabinet's action.

The Japanese were reluctant to get involved in Russia, unless given a free hand, and then only with full and formal American approval. President Wilson, however, was stubbornly opposed to any military activity on Russian soil. His thoughts raced back to Mexico and the difficulties involved in intervening in another country's revolution. Moreover, he did not see Bolshevism as a serious threat in the early stages and believed that the Russian people should be left free to decide how they should be governed. An invasion of Russian territory would violate the principle of self-determination, one of his most cherished goals. He was distrustful of Japanese motives, suspecting that they might convert eastern Siberia into a Japanese colony at the end of the war. Lastly, he not only questioned the feasibility of a Japanese-led enterprise, but feared that it might create an anti-Allied backlash in Russia.[35]

After the treaty of Brest-Litovsk, the pressure on President Wilson to cooperate with the British and the French was intense and unremitting. The lobbying campaign was waged on two different diplomatic levels. In Washington, Lord Reading and his French counterpart, Jules Jusserand, beat a path to the White House to argue the case for intervention. From Versailles, the Supreme War Council, convinced of the need to interrupt the transfer of an estimated forty German divisions from east to west, bombarded the President (through Bliss) with equally importune appeals. Wilson resisted all pressure until July, when events forced him to change his mind.

Left without a role after Brest-Litovsk, the Czechoslovak Legion, as it came to be called, obtained the permission of the Bolshevik government to leave the country. A force of some 70,000 men, it had kept its discipline, cohesion and morale, as it made its way across Siberia to Vladivostok, where it expected that Allied ships would be waiting to take it to France to fight the Germans. The French were anxious to use the Czechoslovaks on the western front, but the British, who would have the task of transporting them, felt that they could play a more useful role if they remained in Siberia where they would be less likely than the Japanese to alienate Russian public opinion. Lloyd George thought that they could form the nucleus of a strong front against the Germans. There was a sense of urgency in the air. With the fighting in the west reaching a crescendo, the Entente's manpower disadvantage could not be redressed unless a sizeable part of the German army remained immobilized on the Russian front. Additionally, Lloyd George feared German exploitation of human and material resources in east Europe.

Early on the morning of May 17 Lloyd George gathered with the other members of the X Committee. At the start of the session, Wilson read a telegram from a reliable agent stating that the Central Powers were now receiving substantial aid from the Ukraine. An estimated 600 carloads of food were leaving for Austria, which was now getting four-sevenths of the total, with the remainder going to Germany. The cost of living had declined in Austria, food was plentiful and crop prospects were also good. The informant mentioned that 5,000 Austrian prisoners were coming back from Russia, and that half of the oil wells in Romania were now in working order.

Lloyd George reported that on the previous day he had a conversation with Leslie Urquhart, chairman of the Russo–Asiatic Corporation, who was positive that any force could go straight through Russia "like a hot knife through butter." Wilson mentioned that the War Office was sending to Russia Major General Frederick Poole, who was confident that he could raise a large army and organize active military operations there.[36]

Discussion on the subject continued at the War Cabinet meeting, which followed immediately. The prime minister wondered whether it was possible to proceed with intervention without the participation of Japan and the United States. With the Germans withdrawing troops from the Russian front, the British army was bearing the brunt of Ludendorff's assaults without any significant American military contribution. It thus seemed to him that "we had every justification for not allowing the Americans and the Japanese to block any attempts on our part to stultify these German withdrawals." If the Czechoslovaks possessed such good fighting qualities as had been reported, there was a possibility that, by adding Allied contingents, they could be used to great effect in Russia.

Balfour felt that the Czechoslovaks held the key to Japanese and American intervention. He was convinced that the Japanese would not consent to an enterprise into Siberia unless they could take a leading part. He thought that if the British proposed to act without them, it would force their hand and they would immediately wish to join up. Once the Japanese were involved, he maintained, American cooperation would almost certainly follow. Milner doubted that the scheme would work. In the first place, the French were very keen that the Czech force should be transported to the western front, and this had been confirmed by a telegram he had just received from Clemenceau. In the second place, all available information tended to show that the Czechoslovaks themselves were unwilling to become involved in Russia's internal strife. Their desire was to fight Germans, not Bolsheviks. Cecil contended that once definite steps had been taken towards intervention, the rest of the Allies would soon conform. The French government had always been pressing for intervention in Russia and, if it realized that the British meant business, it would consent to the use of the Czechs for this purpose. All agreed with Milner's statement that it was essential to obtain French cooperation before trying to use the Czech force.[37]

The French were certainly in favor of intervention, so long as it was not done at their expense. Therefore, Clemenceau reacted angrily to the British proposal:

> This is not the hour when English effectives are diminishing, when France has imposed upon herself the last sacrifices to maintain the numerical superiority of our armies, for you to think of depriving us of soldiers who are courageous, well trained, and profoundly devoted to our cause.[38]

The petty squabbling between Paris and London dragged on for weeks until events themselves caused a resolution. The original mission of the Czech Legion had been to fight the Germans, but difficulties and misunderstandings with Bolshevik officials en route, caused it to break with the radical regime. By early June, the Czechs were in control of a large stretch of the Trans-Siberian railroad. On June 7 Czech forces, aided by anti-Bolshevik Russians, attacked

Omsk, capital of Siberia, and Samara, on the Volga. Both towns fell without offering much resistance. At the end of the month, Czech forces seized Vladivostok, which was followed by an Allied announcement on July 6 placing the whole area under their temporary protection. The success of the Czechs heartened General Anton Denikin, leader of a Volunteer movement in south Russia, and led to the fusion of all anti-Bolshevik movements in Siberia, hitherto confined to isolated pockets of resistance.

In London, the British authorities had just about reached the end of their tether after trying unsuccessfully for months to induce President Wilson to agree to a policy of intervention. On May 29 an exasperated Milner inquired whether the Allies ought to let the attitude of the United States paralyze their action indefinitely. He suggested that the policy of Japanese intervention should be pursued even without the collaboration of the United States. The War Cabinet decided to raise the matter at the forthcoming meeting of the Supreme War Council in Versailles.[39]

At the Supreme War Council, which Lloyd George, Milner and Balfour attended, an agreement was reached on June 3 to invite the Japanese to undertake military action in Siberia subject to certain conditions: that Japan promise to respect the territorial integrity of Russia; that it would take no side in the internal politics of the country; and that it would advance as far west as possible with the object of engaging the Germans. If Japan accepted to intervene under these conditions, it was surmised that it would be easier to obtain the consent of President Wilson.[40]

In the War Cabinet, one member in particular, Cecil, was growing impatient at the slow pace of the negotiations between London, Washington and Tokyo. He suspected, and rightly so, that Lloyd George was doing his best to thwart Japanese intervention. It was vital that something be done. The Germans were within 37 miles of Paris. On June 6, as the War Cabinet discussed the results at Versailles, Cecil took the offensive and did not mince his words. He saw no prospect of a successful conclusion of the war unless a second front was re-created in the east. He was convinced that in the next year, unless something was done, the Germans would be able to induce the Russians to work, or perhaps even to fight for them, thus adding appreciably to their manpower and economic resources. He blamed the prime minister (whose leadership he did not hold in high regard) for the delay and was equally critical of the War Cabinet, accusing it of dragging its feet because it was not even certain that intervention was right. He thought that if a strong military case, supported by the SWC, was put before President Wilson there was a good chance that he might agree to go along.[41]

But a good deal of spadework needed to be done before a military plan could be drawn up. As it was, no study existed to investigate the transportation and logistical difficulties of a campaign in Siberia, or the number of troops that would be required, or the degree of help they were likely to receive from the population and groups opposed to the government. In truth it would have been impossible, in view of the size and chaotic conditions in Russia, to have completed such an extensive survey in a matter of a few months. The War Cabinet was uncertain of what to do, as Cecil had correctly stated, because it was operating in the dark. The prime minister, for his part, not only distrusted the Japanese, but also felt they were likely to do more harm than good.

Lloyd George faced a difficult challenge: how to protect Allied stores and check German influence in Asia without driving Russia into Germany's arms. Milner, at a meeting of the X Committee on June 19, urged action, convinced that Tokyo was ready to move with only slight encouragement. In view of the urgency, he recommended that President Wilson ought to be approached again. The prime minister voiced concern that the presence of Japanese on Russian soil might turn the Russian people against the Entente. This was one instance where a mistake could prove fatal. "If Germany got the gigantic manpower of Russia into her hands," he observed, "the Allies would be bankrupt." He felt that the Czechs ought to have been used "as a nucleus of a democratic anti-Bolshevist movement in Siberia, which could have formed a government, and then invited the Japanese in to help." What was needed to inspire and organize such a movement was someone like "Chinese" Gordon, "with a streak of genius in him."[42] Lloyd George may be excused for his poor analogy since history was no more his forte than details. There was a world of difference between the China of the 1860s and Russia in 1918. As John Grigg has written, "There was no scope for a man like Gordon, even if one had been available."[43]

A few days later, Lloyd George threw in the towel when it became evident that he could not prevail. From the beginning, the War Office had led the fight for intervention, convinced that, by transporting Japanese troops all the way to the Urals on the edge of European Russia, the Allies would gain control of Siberia, create a rallying point for pro Entente units and inhibit the Germans from either expanding into Asia or transferring troops to the west.[44] Although the soldiers had indulged in wishful thinking, as some may have suspected, their views could not be ignored. On top of this, the mood in the War Cabinet had swung unmistakably in favor of Japanese intervention. The new attitude was primarily due to two factors. There were encouraging reports suggesting that the Bolshevik regime was about to collapse. Perhaps of more concern to the policy makers were deep fears, fanned by the War Office, of the prospect of a further German advance into Russia that could extend all the way into Asia. As opinion for action hardened in London, Lloyd George "began to exert leadership."[45]

June 24 was a day in which Russia received much of the attention in London. In the morning the Japanese government, through its ambassador, replied to the SWC's note, reiterating an earlier position that it would not contemplate intervention without American assent. If it did intervene, however, it would honor the first two conditions, but not the third. It observed that there were practical difficulties to pushing as far west as was necessary to engage the enemy. The Japanese ambassador followed up his government's note with a visit to 10 Downing Street. He told Lloyd George that serious political obstacles stood in the way of Japanese intervention, quite apart from America's attitude. In an effort to explain Japan's hesitancy to take the initiative, he claimed that the government had to convince, in descending order, an inter-party committee, its elder statesmen and the emperor.[46]

After lunch, Lloyd George held a long interview with Alexander Kerensky, the deposed prime minister of the Provisional Government, who had come to seek support against the Bolsheviks. He was favorably impressed with Kerensky (as he would later tell Hankey, Riddell and the Imperial War Cabinet), but painted a less than flattering picture of him in his *War Memoirs*. Kerensky claimed that he had been authorized by all politically active Russian elements, save the reactionaries and Bolsheviks, to come to England to clear up relations with the Allies. He alleged that the executive committee of the constituent assembly, which represented most of the Russian people, had passed a resolution on May 18 repudiating the treaty of Brest-Litovsk. As expected, Kerensky was scathing in denouncing the Bolsheviks, describing Trotsky as pro-German and Lenin as living in the clouds. He asserted that the Russian people were disillusioned with the Bolsheviks and that the time was ripe for Russia to take up arms against Germany. He thought that with the help of the Allies, it would be possible to reconstruct the eastern front. He maintained that the Russian people would not oppose Japanese intervention if the Allies took part. Lloyd George put off Kerensky by explaining that Entente intervention would be an act of war against the de facto government and could not be contemplated – in fact, as has been described, it was being discussed seriously in the War Cabinet. He suspected that Kerensky's real objective was to gain Allied recognition for himself and his exiled friends as the legitimate government of Russia.

That evening Lloyd George met with the Committee of Prime Ministers, a subcommittee of the Imperial War Cabinet, and gave the gist of his conversation with Kerensky. At the end, the prime minister of New Zealand asked Lloyd George whether the western front would be weakened if some Allied troops went along with the Japanese army in the event it intervened in Siberia. The prime minister said that it would not. He expected that only a nucleus would be sent to give the appearance of Allied involvement. These troops would be drawn from the garrison at Hong Kong or from northern China.⁴⁷ The discussion continued two days later when the Committee of Prime Ministers convened again. Lloyd George read the Japanese note, which in his view meant that the Japanese, providing they had overall command and America gave its blessing, were ready to send a force to Siberia. He added that Japan would not commit itself to go beyond Central Asia as the Allies wished. Robert Borden, the prime minister of Canada, argued that the main objective was to unite the various Russian factions against Germany, though it was apparent to him that they would make no headway without Allied intervention. He thought that once the Japanese embarked on the expedition, they might be induced to go farther, but at any rate, even limited intervention was better than no intervention at all. The prime ministers of New Zealand and Australia generally concurred with Borden. The next issue raised was over the supreme command. Milner ended the exchange when he pointed out that, as the Japanese would be providing almost all the troops for the expedition, it would be impossible to deny them the command.⁴⁸

Nothing could be done, however, without the approval of Wilson. The obvious question was how to approach him after exhausting practically all the arguments to win him over. At the urging of Lloyd George, the Imperial War Cabinet agreed on June 27 to try once more. An appeal to the American president was to be made through the SWC, stressing that without a reconstitution of the eastern front, there was little likelihood that the Allies would be able to concentrate a force of sufficient superiority over the enemy as to ensure victory on the western front in 1919.⁴⁹ Before journeying to Versailles, Lloyd George received a piece of good news. Clemenceau had accepted that the Czech Legion, for logistical reasons, should remain in Siberia.

The SWC, which opened its proceedings on July 2, accepted the British proposal with only slight modification. The Allies presented their most forceful case in an effort to break down Wilson's resistance to Japanese intervention. To begin with, it was pointed out that the success of the Czech Legion proved that the bulk of the Siberian people were no longer sympathetic to the Bolsheviks. This removed the apprehension that Allied intervention would meet with such serious opposition from the local population in the east that it would make penetration to western Siberia very difficult. The latest information, however, indicated that the Czech Legion, in its movement eastward along the Trans-Siberian railway had clashed with Austrian and German ex-prisoners of war,⁵⁰ and was in danger of being cut off. As a result, its spokesmen had appealed for immediate military assistance. Intervention in Siberia, the Allies maintained, was therefore an urgent necessity, both to save the Czechs and to take advantage of gaining control of Siberia, an opportunity which might never return. Furthermore, it was becoming apparent to a vast majority of Russians that the Bolsheviks had not fulfilled their promises and that anarchy, disorder and starvation lay ahead under their rule. Practically all Russians now recognized that a foreign power would have to step in to end the anarchy and suffering. The reactionaries would naturally prefer the Germans, whereas liberal and democratic elements had asked for Allied assistance. Hence, intervention was urgently necessary to save Russia from the establishment of an autocracy, supported by German bayonets. Lastly, Allied intervention was essential to defeat the Germans. Unless the eastern front was reconstituted to tie down a large number of German divisions, there was practically no chance that the Allies would be able to win the war in 1919.

The Allied line of argument was reinforced by assurances that intervention as a practical policy was easier than it had ever been. The Japanese had agreed to send an expedition into Siberia, subject to the approval and active support of the United States. Although they would not commit themselves to go beyond Irkutsk, there was no reason to suppose that this would be the limit of their advance. It was also emphasized that the Japanese has accepted the conditions set by the SWC, promising not to interfere in Russia's internal politics and to evacuate Russian territory after the war. The Czech forces were already in occupation of western Siberia. The addition of American and British troops would create a force truly Allied in character and acceptable to the Russian people. Only the assent and cooperation of the United States was needed to set in motion a policy that promised success and that, if accomplished, was bound to have decisive results in the war.[51]

All along, President Wilson suspected that the British had an ulterior motive when they urged intervention in Russia. His suspicions were heightened when he learned that the British government was sending Knox to Vladivostok to try to organize pro-Entente elements into some sort of an army. Wilson concluded that Knox, who was known to be a fervent anti-Bolshevik, would gather around him former tsarist officers and lead a movement to reestablish the old regime.[52] Britain's aim, therefore, was not so much to defeat Germany as it was to crush a revolution.

Reading dispatched a letter to the Foreign Office, describing American misgivings about Knox and stressing the need to dispel the President's apprehension if he was to submit to American action in Russia. Balfour brought the matter before the War Cabinet on July 16. The question asked was whether Reading's warning should be ignored, or someone other than Knox selected. Cecil pointed out that the government's objective was to collect the friendly elements among the Russian troops and form them into an army. Knox, given his knowledge of the language, judgment and forecasts in the past, was more qualified to undertake the mission than any other Englishman he could name. The upshot was that the War Cabinet authorized Knox to proceed to Vladivostok at once.[53]

Lloyd George believed that it was not President Wilson's place to comment on an appointment made by the British government. Without notifying Balfour, he vented his anger in a long letter to Reading. He opened his remarks by trumpeting Knox's qualifications, observed that he had spent his whole career, not as a politician, but as a soldier, and that it was a mistake to identify him with the tsarist administration. The prime minister went on to deny the American charge that British policy was sympathetic to Russian reactionaries, insisting that his government favored the establishment of a liberal and progressive regime in Russia. Such a solution would not only benefit the Russian people, but would help maintain world peace and secure the frontier of India. By contrast, the return of the forces of reaction in Russia would work to the disadvantage of the British Empire. Since autocracy and militarism went hand in hand, it was conceivable that a tsarist Russia would become aggressive and ally itself with Germany. Britain's relations with the Bolsheviks since the beginning of 1918 were sufficient proof that its policy was not to foster reaction in Russia, but to allow the Russian people to determine their own form of government. Lloyd George concluded by asking Reading to assure Wilson that he was prepared to back him, providing his policy was aimed at establishing Allied control over the entire Siberian railway before winter set in. His fear, however, was that "we shall drift along until it is too late to save Russia from falling under German domination."[54]

Although much of what Lloyd George claimed was patently untrue, his letter had no effect on Wilson one way or the other. On the very day that it arrived in Washington, July 17, Wilson formally approved of American involvement in Siberia. The increasing pressure – anxiety over the fate of the Czechs, together with petitions from the SWC and continuing diplomatic appeals from London and Paris – was simply too much for Wilson to bear, particularly since there was a growing clamor for action from within his own government. Yielding to the Allies with trepidation, Wilson drew the line on the extent of intervention. The aim of the president's relief mission was to guard Allied stores, evacuate the Czech Legion, and keep an eye on the Japanese in eastern Siberia. He made it clear that the Allies were not to become involved in Russia's internal affairs or attempt to reconstitute the eastern front.[55]

The president's policy clashed with that of Japan and Britain. The Japanese planned to dominate eastern Siberia. The British wanted to keep the Czechs in Siberia to help them revive the eastern front and bring about a change of government in Moscow that would be sympathetic to Allied interests. Quite apart from divergent objectives, there were no unified military plans. The British and the French could not spare the men to send sizeable contingents to Russia. To make matters worse, intelligence was unreliable even when available and there was no clear understanding of domestic conditions in revolutionary Russia. In particular, Allied optimism that under a pro-Entente government Russia would reenter the war was a pipe dream. It is no wonder that the anti-Bolshevik policy failed.

As foolhardy as the Allied intervention in Russia appears in hindsight, it must be remembered that it was occasioned by the desperate military situation resulting from Russia's capitulation, the belief that the war would last at least until 1919 and that something needed to be done to prevent the extension of German influence in the east. Lloyd George held out for months against a purely military and mainly Japanese intervention, but ultimately was swayed by political pressure and long-term military considerations. It is ironic that at the very moment that Japanese troops began to disembark at Vladivostok on August 2, the premise upon which intervention had been based, as will be seen in the next chapter, was crumbling rapidly.

Chapter 17

THE GERMAN ADVANCE HALTED

The X Committee, previously described as a device Lloyd George created to plot future British strategy, held its first meeting on May 15, 1918. There was an awkward moment in the proceedings when Milner implied that Lloyd George should issue a statement, correcting the figures he had used about the combat strength of the British army during the Maurice debate. It had just come to the secretary of war's attention that the original figures supplied by the War Office were inaccurate and he wanted the prime minister to set the record straight. Lloyd George replied curtly that he could not be held responsible for an error made in Maurice's department and, as far as he was concerned, the matter was closed.[1] Milner was a man of high integrity – a rare virtue for a politician – and he was obviously dismayed by the prime minister's cynicism. But he should have known by now that for Lloyd George to admit publicly that he had made a mistake would have been out of character.[2] The relationship between the two men was never the same again and, in fact, went from bad to worse because of Milner's changed perspective as secretary for war.

Milner had been one of Lloyd George's most dependable allies in the War Cabinet, particularly in confrontations with soldiers over strategic policy, but his allegiance shifted when he assumed charge of the War Office. In a bid to wrest control of manpower statistics from the army – presumably so that he could juggle figures when politically convenient – Lloyd George proposed to place a civilian in charge of a new agency created by merging the departments of the adjutant general and quartermaster general. Milner successfully resisted the plan, which was bitterly resented by senior military officials. Another dispute arose over a replacement for Sir Nevil Macready, who had been eased out as adjutant general when he wrote a blistering memorandum blaming the government's past manpower policy for weakening and imperiling Haig's army. Lloyd George objected strenuously to the selection of Sir George Macdonogh, a close ally of Robertson, but yielded grudgingly after Milner again made it a question of confidence in his stewardship of the War Office. Milner's refusal to act as Lloyd George's puppet in the War Office would widen the gulf between them for the remainder of the war.[3]

In the late spring and summer the War Cabinet was absorbed mainly in discussing plans for 1919. Lloyd George and his colleagues saw that Russia's capitulation eliminated any prospect that the Allies would be able to end the war in 1918. The assumption that the war would extend into 1919, or even longer, prompted Henry Wilson to suggest that the time had come to replace Haig, whom he had strongly defended in the past. Wilson had learned from several sources that the BEF had lost confidence in the High Command.[4] It also seemed to him that Haig had done little to improve communications across the Somme below Amiens so that reserves could readily be moved up and used where needed.[5] The man he had in mind to replace Haig was Plumer, a proven field commander. He gave the following as his reasons: (1) the army had more confidence in Plumer; (2) Haig's position, owing to Foch's appointment, had decreased in importance; (3) Plumer was better at organizing rearward services, which were currently in disarray; (4) Haig had lost his grip.[6] But neither Lloyd George nor Milner believed that the moment was right. The prime minister had fought two bruising battles in the last months and he was not in the mood to tackle another one. Wilson had no more success when he brought the matter up again a fortnight later, lamenting that "I don't feel sufficiently strong or clear to really press it."[7]

Despite the ongoing threat to the western front, there remained much interest in reigniting operations in the eastern theaters, partly to secure British interests in the region and partly because there seemed to be no other place where the British could seize the strategic initiative, at least for the immediate future. A memorandum by Leo Amery on the subject drew the attention of the policy makers. He suggested that once the peril to the western front was over, the government ought to reinforce Allenby to permit him to carry out the offensive he had been forced to cancel some months earlier.[8] Amery was not the only minister to warn of German designs in the Middle East, but he was certainly among the most persistent.[9]

At the fourth meeting of the X Committee on May 27 Wilson appeared ready to endorse a concentration of effort in the east. He estimated that the Allies would face two months of "real anxiety," followed by two more of "serious, though diminishing, anxiety." By September, providing the Allies were able to fend off the enemy's onslaught, the threat to the security of the western front would have practically disappeared. Thereafter, the arrival of large-scale reinforcements from the United States would permit the Allies to build up their forces for an all-out attack against the enemy. But until the decisive moment arrived, the British should adopt a peripheral strategy. Playing the part of the devil's advocate, presumably for the benefit of the doubters, Lloyd George pointed out that the Germans could not afford to allow their allies to be knocked out of the war. Wilson agreed, saying that one of the objectives in striking in the outlying theaters would be to draw the enemy from the western front. Lloyd George thought that a peripheral policy would become more practical as soon as the demand on shipping eased. Wilson noted that the Indian government was raising 91 new battalions, which would facilitate the kind of operations he had in mind.[10]

In the midst of strategic planning talks, Lloyd George and Milner received unsettling reports through Foch that the Clemenceau government planned to amalgamate the British and French armies. It was Wilson who scented a plot to end the independence of the British army as a means for the French to assume the role of senior partner. Wilson no longer held Foch with the same boundless admiration as he once had. He felt that Foch was taking too much upon himself, and he was especially upset when five battered British divisions were moved to a quiet French sector on the Aisne to recuperate. "The French are shaping to take us over administratively as well as strategically," he wrote to Haig on May 16. "This will not do."[11] A day earlier, Wilson, with the backing of the Army Council, had warned Milner in a paper that the British army was disappearing with its units dispersed in the French line, ruling out any control by General Headquarters. Forwarding Wilson's memo to Lloyd George, Milner, in an attached minute, emphasized the need to make clear to the French at once that "when we agreed gladly to strategic unity of control, we never contemplated the *administrative unification* of the French & British Armies, & that it is quite impossible for us to agree to it."[12]

The matter was aired in the X Committee on May 16. Wilson did not object to Foch's policy of using British divisions to relieve tired French divisions in the front line. However, he insisted that the British divisions should be grouped together and not be dispersed among the French divisions. He feared that the British might lose control over their supply services if the French were allowed to have their way. To attend to the needs of the British troops scattered about in their line, the French were likely to insist on controlling the ports through which the supplies were brought, possibly even wanting to command the merchant ships carrying the cargoes. Another point Wilson made was that British troops sent to occupy part of the French trenches ought to be returned to the British army whenever their service was completed. He was adamant about preserving the British army as a separate entity. Milner strongly supported Wilson's arguments. On the other hand, Lloyd George did not take so drastic a view of the mixing of British and French divisions as Wilson and Milner. He felt that the first consideration was to win and that nothing must be done to handicap Foch in achieving that end. If Foch had reason to want to relieve a particular French division, it might be difficult for him to do so if he was prohibited from replacing it with a British division. He wanted the French army to be in a fit condition, hoping that it would take a large share in the next stage of the fighting. The prime minister "did not want the British army to be so reduced that next year we should find ourselves the third Military Power on the western front."[13]

Foch never pressed the issue of permanent amalgamation of the two armies, particularly after Haig sent a blunt message through the French liaison officer that it would never work and he should dismiss it from his mind at once.[14] Foch was more concerned with another matter. He was troubled over the manpower shortages in the BEF in view of rumors that the British government was withholding 1,400,000 men in khaki. He intended to issue a protest to London through his own government.[15]

Paris had good reason not to allow the matter to drift. On May 27 Ludendorff unleashed his third major offensive (code name Operation Blücher), this time against the French army along the Chemin des Dames. The Germans easily broke though the ill-prepared French lines and three days later reached the Marne, near Château-Thierry, and were within 55 miles of Paris. Once more the French capital seemed in danger.

Allied political and military officials gathering at Versailles on June 1 were understandably in a state of high anxiety. Even the normally optimistic Wilson feared the worst, confiding to his diary that "there is a possibility, perhaps a probability, of the French army being beaten."[16] Foch read from a memorandum he had prepared for a committee of the Supreme War Council, which was restricted to only French and British leaders. Foch pointed out that France, not withstanding a manpower shortage, had strained every nerve to maintain the number of its divisions in the field. He charged that, by contrast, the British were allowing their divisions to dwindle away, without making an effort to provide the necessary reinforcements from their manpower pool. Indeed, he went on to say that the British army was decreasing at a more rapid rate that the increase in the size of the American forces. The result was a decline in the total strength of the Allies.[17]

The French were undoubtedly making a larger contribution to the war on land than the British, but in fighting to defend their own territory, they also had a greater motive. What was tactless on their part was the implication that the British were not pulling their weight. They seemed to have forgotten that for the last year the British had done a disproportionate share of the fighting, that since March 21 they had lost three times as many soldiers as the French, that their operations in other theaters were tying down enemy forces and that their navy was used to bring over American troops as well as to blockade the coast of Germany and to keep the sea lanes open for Allied shipping. Amery was premature when he maintained at the start of 1917 that Britain "was in a position to dominate and control its allies," but such was not the case a year later when it would have been at least justified in taking the lead.[18] The French army was not the instrument it had been after the Nivelle debacle when no fewer than 54 of its 112 divisions were affected by the wave of mutinies. It is true that the French army recovered sufficiently by late August to launch a successful assault at Verdun and in October scored another triumph by gaining the crest of the Chemin des Dames. But these were limited affairs in the overall context of the fighting in France and Belgium. It may be that the impact of the mutinies has been overstated, as one recent study argues,[19] but what is undeniable is that from the summer of 1917 the forces under Haig had to shoulder the main responsibility for operations on the western front. Lloyd George never took full advantage of the British army's preeminent role and continued to allow the French to have a major, if not dominant, voice in determining strategy.

Foch's paper was bound to provoke a sharp reaction from the British delegation. Milner protested against Foch's figures, stating, "one would think we had sent no men at all." Milner asserted that 250,000 men had crossed the Channel since March 21, but it was the high casualties that were responsible for the reduction in the number of British divisions. Foch claimed that if the British could not maintain their 53 divisions, the Allies would lose the war. Clemenceau weighed in to emphasize that despite the loss of 2,000,000 men, France, with a smaller population than Britain, intended to maintain one hundred divisions. Lloyd George insisted that every able-bodied man up to 50 years old, not engaged in the navy, merchant marine or essential war industries, was being sent over. As he had nothing to hide, he suggested, somewhat foolishly, that a French expert come to London where he would be given access to the government's manpower figures. Clemenceau accepted the proposal and the heated discussion ended.[20]

The Supreme War Council, at which all the usual Allies were represented, opened its proceedings following the Anglo–French conference. The business, much of which related to Allied intervention in Russia, was completed by the afternoon of June 3. On the way home, Hankey remained gloomy about the ongoing battle. He penned his thoughts in his diary: "I do not like the outlook. The Germans are fighting better than the Allies and I cannot exclude the possibility of a disaster."[21] What neither he nor his colleagues realized then was that the German drive had stalled in the face of stiffening resistance. French troops, reinforced by Americans, blunted every German effort to cross the Marne, and on June 6 Ludendorff called off the offensive.

The removal of the threat to Paris did not halt the bickering between London and Paris. During the German assault, Foch had first withdrawn the French reserves in Haig's sector, then he directed that all the American divisions training with the BEF be sent south. On June 4 Foch made further demands, signaling Haig to place three British divisions astride the Somme immediately.²² Haig was certain that the Germans would open with a feint against a sector of the French line, but that their main assault would be delivered on his front. After all, he reasoned, why would the Germans waste their time and resources attacking the French in strength when they were confident that Paris would accept satisfactory peace terms once the British army was defeated.²³ Haig complied with Foch's order, but protested to his government that the removal of his reserves imperiled the British army.²⁴

Lloyd George and Wilson were equally alarmed over Foch's handling of the troops, for, like Haig, they doubted that the Germans would push their main attack against the French front. They suspected, rather unfairly, that Foch was behaving more like a French general taking orders from Clemenceau than an Allied supreme commander. An Anglo–French conference was hurriedly held in Clemenceau's office on June 7 to thrash the matter out. Haig complained that his front had been weakened by the withdrawal of eight French and five American divisions and now he was being asked to move three British divisions to the Somme sector. While he had no objection to the movement of troops from his front to support the French in case of necessity, he felt that he ought to have been consulted before the order was given. As it was, he considered that the proposed withdrawal of British troops would threaten the security of his front. Haig, however, did not dispute that as generalissimo, Foch had the authority to move troops of any nationality wherever he saw fit and at short notice. Milner and Clemenceau agreed that Foch exercised such powers but suggested that he and Haig ought to meet more frequently. In the end, Clemenceau forbade Foch from moving any troops from the British sector unless cleared by Haig beforehand. The British representatives were pleased with the meeting, which they felt had cleared the air.²⁵

Contrary to British expectations, the next German assault fell not on the BEF, but on the French again. On June 9 Ludendorff launched Operation Gneisenau in the direction of Compiègne, with the object of reducing the Allied bulge between his salients. If successful, it would shorten his front and conserve manpower. Foch had anticipated the impending attack, which was confirmed by German deserters, and had taken appropriate countermeasures. The Germans smashed the thinly held front lines and advanced nine miles. But two days later, French troops waiting in the rear areas of the deep defensive zone delivered a counterattack that brought the enemy drive to a shuddering halt.

Notwithstanding the results of Operations Blücher and Gneisenau, British political and military leaders feared that the French army was practically finished. Indeed, the War Office had gone so far as to lay preliminary plans for the possible evacuation of the BEF from France. In the event that France collapsed, Lloyd George had no intention of concluding a peace settlement at the expense of allowing the Germans to expand in the east. He would settle for nothing less than victory, which the British Empire could achieve by maintaining its position in Palestine and Mesopotamia and forging stronger ties with the United States. In the two recent engagements, the Americans had given a good account of themselves against battle-hardened German troops and Lloyd George felt that as soon as they arrived in sufficient numbers, they would be able to carry the main load in the west, while the British concentrated in the secondary theaters.[26]

Lloyd George took pains to enlist the support of the Dominion prime ministers for his eastern strategy, a move he knew was bound to provoke opposition from both Haig and the French. At a meeting of the Imperial War Cabinet on June 11 he tried to link his peripheral strategy to the security of Britain's Empire. He explained that in the event the western continental Allies (France and Belgium) were forced out of the war, only Britain and the United States would be left to fight against Germany's ambition to create an unbroken line of influence stretching from Holland to the Persian Gulf and Siberia. He argued that if the Germans managed to gain control of either Palestine or Mesopotamia, they would be beyond the reach of the Royal Navy and could attack Egypt or India by overland routes. Since there was no chance of a decisive victory in Europe at least until 1919, the best immediate prospects lay in defeating Austria and Turkey. It was imperative to prevent Germany from acquiring territory in the east that it could use as bargaining chips for concessions in the west. If that should occur, Germany would be in a position to renew the struggle to regain its colonies or fulfill its dream of acquiring an eastern empire. For Lloyd George there was no alternative to victory, for unless "Germany is beaten now, there would be another fight."[27]

In reviewing the course of the war since their last meeting in May 1917, Lloyd George gave a frank, if somewhat depressing, assessment of the military situation in the west, but he made no effort to explain the reasons for Germany's success. This troubled Borden, who summoned Lieutenant General Sir Arthur Currie, the brilliant Canadian corps commander, and requested his "unvarnished opinion" about the British High Command's conduct of the war. A civilian in the Canadian reserve army when the war broke out, Currie resented the brusque manner in which he was treated by pompous, high-ranking British officers, notwithstanding his proven talent. Although he may have had an axe to grind, his indictment of British military methods was not without merit. Holding nothing back, Currie's description of the Headquarters staff as obtuse and rigid confirmed what Borden had learned from other sources. The Canadian prime minister subsequently took Currie over to see Smuts so that he could repeat his charges. Smuts encouraged Borden to bring the whole question of British generalship into the open at the next meeting.[28]

On June 13, Borden prefaced his hour-long speech by saying that he intended to be perfectly frank in the hope that the disasters and mistakes of the past would be avoided. He then proceeded to excoriate the High Command, particularly for its offensive at Passchendaele, where "the almost indescribable confusion" had cost the lives of 16,000 Canadians for a "gain that was not worth a candle." He attributed setbacks to a want of foresight and preparation and to defects in the organization and leadership of the British army. He despaired at the conspicuous failure to weed out incompetents at the higher level of the army while refusing to promote talented nonprofessionals beyond the rank of brigadier general. Canada was prepared to fight to the end "but *for God's sake* let us get down to earnest endeavor until the Americans can come in and help us sustain it to the end." Borden was warmly congratulated on his lucid and somewhat emotional-laden oration by practically everyone present, including Lloyd George who described it as "a memorable speech." Milner, seated next to Borden, whispered that his concerns would be addressed.[29]

The prime minister of New Zealand, W. F. Massey, took a line similar to Borden, dwelling on Passchendaele where his countrymen had been "shot down like rabbits" when ordered to do the impossible. The Australian prime minister added his voice to the criticism of the British leadership when he arrived in London several days later. What the Dominion prime ministers were requesting was a greater voice in the decisions affecting the war.[30]

If there was one person whose loyalty to Lloyd George was unswerving, it was Smuts. Since his inclusion in the War Cabinet, the South African had never refused to take on tasks requested of him, however difficult. He rose to the occasion once more on June 14 when he delivered a statement before the Dominion prime ministers that was calculated to exonerate the War Cabinet for the slaughter at Passchendaele. He recalled that Lloyd George had pleaded, to no avail, for a defensive policy in the west in 1917 in order to concentrate on German's war-weary allies.[31] No one had the presence of mind to point out that ultimate responsibility for deciding policy rested with the civilian authorities, not the military.

In the days that followed, memos by Amery and Wilson, plus long speeches by Curzon and others, hammered home the importance of seizing the strategic initiative in the eastern theater while holding the line in France for the remainder of the year.[32] The deluge of eastern sentiment was bound to make an impression on the Dominion prime ministers, or at least most of them. According to Hankey, only Massey remained an out-and-out westerner.[33]

Lloyd George realized that he must address the Dominion prime ministers' fears, for implicit in their criticism of the High Command was a warning that no more troops would be forthcoming if there was a repetition of Passchendaele.

As a defensive maneuver, he circulated minutes of the War Policy Committee, drawing particular attention to his efforts to dissuade Haig from moving forward with his Flanders plan. Acting on Hankey's advice, Lloyd George followed up by announcing on June 20 that he proposed to establish a Committee of Prime Ministers to investigate the whole issue of Passchendaele and to suggest future strategic options.[34] Lloyd George expected to steer that body in the direction of his choosing, strengthening his hand in dealings with Haig and Foch.

Lloyd George would need all the support he could muster if he hoped to execute his plan of transferring the main British effort to the Middle East as soon as the line in the west was secure. Transported mostly in British ships, Americans were crossing the Atlantic in record numbers. By the start of June 1918, Americans troops in France approached nearly half a million, out of which 11 combat divisions had been formed, each 25,000 strong. Lloyd George wanted the Americans to take a stretch of line in Haig's sector, freeing British troops for operations in secondary theaters. But Foch was threatening to wreck his imperial policy. Under an agreement between Pershing and Milner, 10 American divisions had been allocated to train with the British, but Foch, whether intentionally or not, had placed most of these in the French sector. It is ironic that Lloyd George, the main force in bringing about unity of command in order to defang Haig, was now prepared to challenge Foch's authority.[35]

The fundamental differences between the British and the French over war policy surfaced at the SWC meeting at Versailles early in July. It had been an unpleasant trip and Lloyd George was not in the best of moods. The ship used for the crossing was described as "disgusting" and, on the way to Versailles, his motor car broke down and he had to wait for another vehicle to pick him up. It was a hot day, made more uncomfortable by the crowded conditions in the second car.[36] He had to listen to Wilson, who warned him, for the umpteenth time, that the "French, especially Clemenceau, were steadily taking over us."[37] He did not need much of an excuse to lash out at someone. His first victim was André Tardieu, the high commissioner for Franco–American affairs, who was taken to task for interfering in the shipment of American troops. As a means to accelerate the transportation of troops to France, Tardieu had held unilateral talks with Washington without consulting the British who had to provide the ships. Lloyd George told Tardieu bluntly that all questions relating to shipping concerned only the United States and Britain.

The next day Lloyd George was provoked into an even more violent outburst when he learned that the French government had given General Franchet d'Esperey, the new C-in-C in the Balkans, authority to launch an offensive, contravening a decision taken in December 1917 by the SWC. Lloyd George pointed out that if conditions had changed considerably since the ruling by the SWC, as justification for an offensive, then the Allies ought to have been consulted. As it was, the "instructions were issued purely as the orders of the French government to a French General." There would be trouble the moment it was perceived that Foch was a servant of the French government. At present the Allies trusted him, but that feeling of confidence would disappear if it became evident that he was inclined to promote French as distinct from Allied interests. Lloyd George added that this was not the first time that the French government had adopted measures without notifying its allies in advance. He drew attention to the fact that the recent appointment of General Franchet d'Esperey, as a replacement for Sarrail's successor, General Marie Louis Guillaumat,[38] had been made without consulting the Allies. It had never been intended that one government should have the authority to take separate action.[39] According to Hankey, Lloyd George handled Clemenceau, sitting uncomfortably in his chair, "very roughly."[40] The upshot was that a resolution was passed instructing the permanent military representatives to consider military plans for next year.

Although the French had always insisted on maximum concentration of Allied troops in the west, they had made an exception in the case of the Balkan front. Lloyd George found it curious that Clemenceau, who had long been an outspoken opponent of the Balkan sideshow, decrying it as a waste of manpower, had undergone a change in attitude. It confirmed his suspicion that France's ambition was to dominate the Balkans, politically and financially, in the postwar period. Actually, Clemenceau's change of heart had more to do with military reality than anything else. With the army drained by its losses and social tensions at an all-time high, France was close to the kind of breakdown that had forced Russia out of the war. The army was capable of one more effort, and Clemenceau did not want to risk rolling the dice until the odds were in his favor. Thus, the prudent course was to shift the focus of the war eastwards and wait until the Americans became a dominant factor.

The conference had been marred by a good deal of acrimony – "the angriest we have had," according to Wilson – but the proceeding might have gotten out of hand if the British had revealed in open council that they proposed to transfer British divisions in France to secondary theaters in the autumn. It was known that Foch, who had planned to launch an offensive in 1919, would strenuously oppose the reduction of any British military power in the west. In private, the British debated whether they should fight it out with Foch and Clemenceau now or later. Wilson wanted the British to lay down their cards immediately. He was overruled by Lloyd George and Milner, both of whom wanted to complete preparations for an operation in Palestine before notifying the French, in the autumn, of the British government's intention to withdraw a number of divisions from the western front.[41]

Still, there were other aspects of war policy that continued to bedevil Anglo–French relations. Wilson advised the War Cabinet on July 11 that the Germans had brought up a fresh number of divisions, presumably to launch a new offensive against the Allied line. In the event that the weight of the German attack should fall on the British front, it would take time for French reserves to move north. Smuts was equally concerned, pointing out that Foch, possibly in his endeavor to safeguard Paris, kept his reserves too far south. The War Cabinet decided that the prime minister should write a letter to Clemenceau, emphasizing that, in distributing reserves, Foch should act in the interests, not mainly of the French, but of the Allies as a whole.[42]

The prime minister would have felt a little more at ease about the security of the British line if Foch had not monopolized the American divisions. It seemed to him that Foch was doing Clemenceau's bidding. He suspected that the French retention of the American divisions was calculated not so much to ensure the safety of Paris as it was to force the British to fill their depleted ranks.[43] In his letter to Clemenceau, Lloyd George argued that the British were entitled to American divisions because most of them had been transported in British ships. He warned that if Foch's distribution of troops left the British too weak to fend off an all-out enemy assault, it would be fatal to the continuance of the arrangement of a generalissimo.[44]

The uncertainty of the direction of the next large-scale enemy attack heightened tensions between the two allies. Although the last German drive could not even be regarded as a tactical success, Ludendorff was still hopeful that elusive victory was within reach. He proposed to launch one more offensive against Reims, giving the impression of a direct threat to Paris, but his objective was to draw in British reserves from the north. If all went as planned, he would deliver his long-delayed war-winning offensive against the British in Flanders. Ludendorff had not shifted German reserves from the north so that Allied intelligence could not determine whether his next blow would fall in Champagne or in Flanders. Foch, suspecting that it would come against the French, requested that General Headquarters transfer four British divisions to Champagne and to hold an additional four in readiness to move in the same direction.[45]

On July 14 Lloyd George learned of Foch's order for moving British reserves, while staying with Riddell at Hurstpierpoint in Sussex. He became extremely agitated, as Wilson had convinced him that the brunt of the German attack would be directed against Haig's front.[46] He summoned Milner, Wilson, Smuts and Borden to Riddell's home for an emergency meeting. He was almost violent in denouncing the proposed withdrawal of the British divisions. He insisted that he would not allow any of the British divisions to go south unless given a guarantee by Haig that the Germans would not attack his front. He suspected that Clemenceau was using "unfair political influence on Foch to save the French army and Paris at all costs." As far as he was concerned, the British had a right to American divisions, regardless of whether the German attack came off in Champagne. Smuts and Borden agreed with the prime minister, but Milner and Wilson were inclined to defer to Foch, "as we had appointed him Allied Commander-in-Chief." The talks broke up at midnight when a decision was reached to wire Haig that if he thought the proposed order placed the British army in jeopardy or was motivated by political considerations, he had the right to appeal to his government under the Beauvais agreement. It was also agreed to send Smuts over to General Headquarters to confer with Haig.[47]

Smuts was back in London on July 16 with a reassuring statement from Haig that he was less anxious about the security of his army. Initially, Haig had been alarmed at the prospect of losing as many as eight divisions in view of reports that his front was about to be attacked. By the time he held an interview with Foch, the storm had burst and the Germans were attacking the French on a front of some 55 miles. As the Germans had declared their intention, Haig was in a more accommodating mood. He agreed to send the requested divisions south after Foch assured him that he would place them in an area where they could return quickly in case of a German attack. Haig told Smuts that it was unlikely he would be attacked in strength as recent intelligence had revealed that Crown Prince Rupprecht (the German commander opposite his front), had dispatched no fewer than nine divisions to reinforce the troops assaulting the French. Haig, furthermore, had no complaints about Foch's distribution of American troops. He noted that their presence had boosted the morale of the French army, which, in his opinion, had enabled it to recapture an offensive spirit.[48]

The prime minister, however, was not in a conciliatory spirit, even though he did not have any evidence that Foch was acting improperly or bending under the weight of political pressure. Yet, he was quite prepared to challenge Foch's authority, and if necessary, end the concept of unity of command. Haig's appreciation both of Rupprecht's strength and of Germany's real intentions was disputed in London. Wilson told the War Cabinet on July 17 that there was not enough information to determine what the enemy was doing. Personally, he added, "he was far from being persuaded that it was the big attack, having regard to the fact that up to now only 30 divisions had been identified." Macdonogh did nothing to diminish Wilson's concern when he observed that War Office calculations showed that Rupprecht had 33 divisions at his disposal, 10 more than estimates by General Headquarters.[49] Given the conflicting testimony, it is not surprising that Lloyd George placed more trust in Wilson's, rather than in Haig's, line of thinking. At an X Committee meeting on July 17 he expressed considerable doubt whether "this was really the big attack" and suggested that the transfer of nine Rupprecht divisions identified thus far might only have been a decoy. He thought that some action should be taken, "not only to get back our own divisions, but to press for more American divisions."[50] The next day, he pursued the same theme. He was inclined to believe that Foch had acted precipitously in bringing the British divisions behind his front. He was adamant that if it should turn out that Foch "had let us down ... it would wreck the unity of command."[51] Fortunately, the matter was never put to a test.

The Germans made spectacular progress on the first day of the attack because Pétain had applied the principles of elastic defense, placing relatively few troops in the forward position. The Germans crossed the Marne, but encountered such strong resistance from Pétain's second line, that Ludendorff saw no point in continuing the battle. Instead, he turned his attention to the north, calculating that his latest attack had served its purpose of drawing reserves from Haig's thinly held front. Ludendorff had no intentions of giving up, despite the horrendous casualties suffered by the German army (over 800,000) since March 21, the apparent loss of morale among the troops (reflected in the significant rise of deserters) and a recent outbreak of influenza that had taken a heavy toll on them physically. What ended Ludendorff's Flanders dream was a counterattack launched by Foch on July 18.[52] The French, reinforced by fresh American divisions, used a combination of tanks and infantry to surprise the Germans and drive them back across the Marne. The Allied victory, known as the Second Battle of the Marne, not only ended the threat to Paris, but also wrecked Germany's remaining hope of winning the war. The initiative had now passed irretrievably to the Allies.

Chapter 18

THE TURN OF THE TIDE

Despite the changes that had occurred in the upper military echelons in 1917 and 1918, the man commanding the BEF had somehow managed to survive. Lloyd George had plenty of cause to give Haig the boot, particularly after Cambrai, but as we have already noted, shrank from doing so for one reason or another. The issue emerged again in the second half of July, mainly because new leadership was desired in anticipation of the campaign for 1919. Lloyd George never had much use for Haig, was convinced that he was obstinate, used unimaginative tactics and showed little interest in avoiding heavy casualties. Other factors now came into play. The prime minister resented that Haig would not join him to induce Foch to place American divisions in his sector, thus freeing British troops to assist in his plan to protect and expand the empire in the east. This brought up a related point, namely, that Haig was certain to collaborate with Foch to prevent the removal of British troops from the western front.[1]

The prime minister felt that the scorching indictment of Haig by Borden and the other Dominion prime ministers provided him with enough justification to sack Haig. He raised the matter at the meeting of the X Committee on July 16. Milner, however, was reluctant to follow his lead. He argued that the possibility of a change in the High Command had been repeatedly discussed, but he was not convinced that a better substitute could be found. He suggested that Borden's perception had probably been colored by press rumors. This angered Lloyd George, who lashed out at Milner, observing that the Dominion prime ministers had formed their opinion of General Headquarters on the strength of, not newspaper editorials, but reports of their own soldiers.[2] After the meeting, he called Hankey into his drawing room and asked him to warn Milner that if he did not appreciate the seriousness of the charges against army leadership, he would find someone who did. As the habitual peacemaker, Hankey sought to smooth out the differences between Milner and the prime minister. He sent Amery to urge Milner to tell the prime minister that he wanted to delay recalling Haig until a suitable replacement could be identified.[3]

One officer Lloyd George contemplated putting in Haig's place was the Earl of Cavan, C-in-C of the British forces in Italy. Wilson had praised Cavan highly after visiting Italy in the latter part of June. He was particularly impressed with the role Cavan had played in improving the organization and morale of the Italian army since its crushing defeat at Caporetto.[4]

During the third week in July, Cavan arrived in London, ostensibly to discuss the prospects of dealing Austria a decisive blow, but in reality to allow Lloyd George to judge his leadership qualities.[5] On July 23 he appeared before the Committee of Prime Ministers and expressed himself in favor of an Allied offensive on the Italian front, but he was vague and uncertain about where it should take place. Cavan's stumbling performance, in which it was apparent that he had not given the matter deep thought, lowered his stock in the eyes of some of his listeners, including Lloyd George.[6] Any further initiative to replace Haig ended a fortnight later when the British won a spectacular victory at Amiens.

The fate of Haig having been resolved, discussion in the inner war councils during midsummer centered on the future course of the conflict. Lloyd George was rather perturbed with a plan for 1919 by the operations section of the War Office that had called for a huge Allied offensive, backed by a large number of tanks, to end the war. In questioning Major General Tim Harington, Deputy CIGS, the prime minister inquired whether operations in other theaters had been considered. What guarantee could the War Office give that the Germans would not adopt a defensive posture and divert troops to Russia or some other front? In such an event, was it the War Office's intention that the British army should continue to hammer away at the western front? Did it not make sense, he asked, to eliminate Austria or Turkey before concentrating on Germany itself? Harington was vague in his reply, saying that the War Office was considering all options.[7]

Wilson tried to move the War Office's position closer to the prime minister's views in a long, rambling memorandum he prepared on July 25. While he did not minimize the importance of the east, he clearly favored concentrating on the western front, where the war would be won or lost. He recommended a series of limited operations before the winter to seize strategic points preparatory to delivering the final and decisive blow against the Germans in July 1919, when the Allies would have a substantial numerical superiority.[8]

Lloyd George was bitterly disappointed with the memorandum's western slant, describing it simply as "Wully redivivus."[9] The last thing he expected was to see Wilson morph into another Robertson. On July 31 the prime minister placed Wilson's paper before the Committee of Prime Ministers. Milner, who spoke first, was convinced that the Allies would not have the requisite 3 to 2 manpower superiority over the Germans to end the war in 1919. He wanted the British to accept the fact that they could no longer play the leading role on the western front and that they should leave the Americans and the French to supply the bulk of the men there to defeat the Germans. Haig's army ought to be reduced to 35 divisions, thus creating a reserve that could operate in other parts of the world. Hughes pointed out that the power that had the largest army in the west would have the greatest influence on the terms of peace. For that reason it was undesirable to leave the Americans and the French to finish the war on the western front. Lloyd George disagreed with Hughes, saying that the power that had obtained a decision elsewhere might carry the most weight. No one challenged the prime minister's observation, which was relevant only if the war ended in a stalemate.

Smuts did not dispute that the western front was the decisive theater, but like Milner, felt it was unrealistic to think that the Allies had a sufficient margin of strength to defeat Germany in 1919. He took exception with Wilson's recommendation, arguing that it would be fatal, likely to lead to a repeat of the Flanders offensive. He stressed that the Allies should remain on the defensive in the west and build up their strength before attempting their next big offensive. In the meantime, the British should consider undertaking a major campaign in Italy in 1919. Hughes reminded his colleagues that when Cavan was asked if Austria could be beaten, he had not given "a very satisfactory answer." He was convinced that the war aims of the British Empire could not be fulfilled unless the military power of Germany was broken.

Lloyd George agreed with Hughes that the Allied position at the peace conference would be unsatisfactory unless preceded by a military victory. But he drew his colleagues' attention to two vital considerations: find a way to win, and do so without bleeding the British Empire armies white and leaving only the Americans with a powerful army. He claimed that if there were a battle on a gigantic scale the following year, Britain would be bound to assume a share of the fighting. Casualties were certain to be enormous. Britain had reached the bottom of the manpower pool and would not be able to replace its casualties. He did not believe that the Allies could obtain a decision in 1919. Even if they were able to batter the Germans and cause them to sue for peace, what would be the state of the British army, he asked rhetorically. By then the United States would have as many as 120 divisions, dwarfing the remaining number of French and British divisions. It would be the United States that would dictate the terms of peace, and it was well known that President Wilson's aims were far different from those of the British Empire. This factor ought to be carefully weighed, the prime minister emphasized, before it was decided to put the British Empire's army on the table in 1919 and risk getting it smashed to pieces.

Next, Lloyd George dealt with the issue of how to win the war. He shared Milner's opinion that it was unlikely that the war could be won through attacks on the western front. Since the start of the war, the High Command had never failed to make sanguine predictions; the last time was in regard to the Passchendaele offensive:

> We had been told that the German morale was falling, and that our troops were confident. At the end of the year it was the morale of our troops that had been, broken, while that of the enemy had been raised. Next year we should not have a superiority of 3 to 2, which we had in 1916 and 1917 without achieving success.

The prime minister could only see one development that would make a difference. If Russia recovered and again became a factor in the war, it would compel the Germans to transfer substantial forces to the east. It would take three or four months to determine whether this scenario was likely to occur. The question the prime minister posed was what should be done in the event Russia refused to reenter the conflict. The fundamental error in the war had always been to attack the enemy on the strongest, rather than on the weakest front. He echoed Smuts' preference for an attack on the Italian front, where an advance would likely cause Austria, reportedly in an extremely critical condition, to capitulate.[10]

The following day, the Committee was set to resume the discussion on future military policy, when Borden happened to mention that he had been told "in confidence and great secrecy" that the Canadian Corps was being moved forward to another region to participate in an offensive. An astonished Wilson indicated that he knew nothing about any forthcoming operation. Milner thought that if it was a minor operation to rectify the line, "that was within General Foch's responsibility." The prime minister demurred, insisting that the government ought to know what was intended. He worried that Foch was contemplating a big push, observing that while he was a good strategist, he had always been reckless of human life. He noted that the French general remained under the impression that Britain had a reserve of 2,000,000 men, overlooking the demands imposed by industry. The prime minister was adamant that the country could not afford to repeat the experience of either the Somme or Passchendaele. Before he assented to any offensive, he wanted an examination of how the country stood in regard to its manpower reserves, along with an estimate of the casualties and the probable strength of the British army next year.

Lloyd George then raised the obvious question of their constitutional position vis-à-vis Foch. It was pointed out that under the Beauvais agreement they were not entitled to interfere with a plan by Foch unless Haig had reported that it placed the British army in danger. On the other hand, Haig was obligated to inform London of any operation that would involve heavy casualties. The government would have the final responsibility of deciding whether it would sanction the operation. Lloyd George made it clear that he wanted to conserve British strength and limit any "strategy to our income." Turning to Wilson, Lloyd George asked if he really thought that the Allies could obtain a decision on the western front in 1919. Wilson replied that he would like to make preparations for an attack set for July 1, 1919 and, as time approached, decide whether there was a good chance of success. If not, the operation would be postponed. Lloyd George remarked that he had heard this same line repeated on many occasions in the past. But each time, as "the moment of the attack approached, the Cabinet would be told that all preparations had been made and that it would break the spirit of the Army if the attack was not launched."

Changing the focus of the discussion, Hughes asked how many men the Allies would need to achieve a decisive victory in Italy. Wilson observed that Cavan's estimate to reach Trent was eighteen divisions, thirteen more than the British and French currently had in Italy. Wilson hinted that quite apart from the fact that so many divisions could not be spared from the western front, the Germans would only need to send down moderate numbers to block the Allied advance in the mountains. From the two-day discussion it was apparent that Smuts, Milner and all the prime ministers, save Hughes, thought that the Germans could not be defeated in the west and that it was preferable to concentrate in some other theater. Hughes firmly believed that real peace was not possible unless the German army was beaten. Lloyd George brought the discussion to a close by directing the CIGS to ascertain the scope of any offensive contemplated by Foch in the immediate future and to report on the possibility of knocking Austria out of the war.[11]

Lloyd George was becoming increasingly unhappy with Wilson's fixation on the western front and he sent Hankey the next day to let him know. Hankey told Wilson pointedly that the prime minister was disappointed with his approach to the war and found him too much like Robertson. Wilson got the message loud and clear. He had no illusions that he served at the prime minister's pleasure. He justified his action to Hankey on the grounds that "he was dominated by the idea of not quarrelling with our allies and more especially with Foch," and trying hard to placate his benefactor, explained that he had a scheme "for concentrating twelve divisions this winter on the Italian Front."[12]

Wilson reported to the Committee of Prime Ministers on August 6 that from what he had been able to gather (mostly from Lieutenant General Sir John Du Cane, British representative at Foch's headquarters), Foch proposed to limit his operations to harassing the enemy.[13] Two days later, Wilson returned to brief the prime ministers about his investigation into the feasibility of action on the Italian front. He explained that it would take six or seven weeks to mount an attack against Austria, by which time the snow in the High Alps "would put a stop to operations." Thus, unless Foch was willing to transfer the required divisions from the western front in the next few weeks, it would not be possible to mount an effective campaign against Austria before the onset of snow. He admitted, more for Lloyd George's sake than out of conviction, that the Italian theater held much promise, but he was afraid that the time to do anything in the autumn had passed.[14]

On the same day that Wilson threw cold water on the Italian option, dramatic events were occurring on the western front. Haig had persuaded Foch to let him attack the salient south of the Somme with the object of eliminating the German threat to Amiens and the railroad linking that city to Paris. The task was assigned to Rawlinson's Fourth Army, which had been enlarged to fourteen infantry and three cavalry divisions of British, Canadian and Australian troops and backed by over 400 tanks. Since surprise was deemed essential, Rawlinson chose to dispense with the preliminary bombardment in favor of a rolling barrage that would commence as soon as his troops left the trenches. At 4:20 a.m. on August 8 Rawlinson's men went "over the top" and, shielded by a heavy ground fog, fell on the Germans before they knew exactly what was happening. The sudden appearance of the tanks, impervious to rifle and machine-gun fire, and the scale of the attack had a devastating psychological impact among the defenders, many of whom gave way with barely a struggle. By the end of the day, Empire forces, with comparatively little cost to themselves, had penetrated to a depth of seven miles along an eleven-mile front.[15] All in all, it had been a spectacular day.

As with past operations on the western front, the momentum of the initial thrust could not be maintained. When the offensive resumed the next day, progress was slow, owing to the availability of fewer tanks – only 146 were ready for action – and the hardening resistance of German reserves hurriedly brought up to seal the ruptured front. This trend continued for the next two days and Haig, with an eye to preserving his limited manpower, called off the attack.[16] That same day, the Committee of Prime Ministers instructed Wilson to send congratulations to Haig, and the troops under his command, "for the brilliant operation just completed."[17] Lloyd George's praise of Haig was less fulsome. In a speech at Newport, Monmouthshire, he gave Haig only partial credit for the victory, which he attributed mostly to unity of command. In his memoirs, Lloyd George was highly critical of Haig for his supposed failure "to press forward with relentless drive" to exploit the break-in, allowing the Germans "time to recover and reform their lines."[18] In the past, Lloyd George had inveighed against Haig for throwing away the lives of his men in offensives that had stalled. Now Haig, after he had shown the good sense to know when to stop the attack, was being pilloried for lack of dash and boldness. Even John Grigg was driven to say that "one can only marvel at the lengths to which he

[Lloyd George] was prepared to go to avoid an unqualified acknowledgement of Haig's personal success."[19]

The jubilation in London and at General Headquarters over the Allied tactical victory at Amiens was restrained. Churchill was among the few who recognized the significance of the Allied triumph on August 8. He wrote to Lloyd George after returning from a visit to the front:

> There is no doubt Haig has won a very great success which may well be the precursor of further extremely important events.... It seems to me this is the greatest British victory that has been won in the whole war, and the worst defeat that the German Army has yet sustained.[20]

Lloyd George did not share Churchill's optimistic view about the impact of Haig's victory. He told Hankey on August 13 that he was not very sanguine about Allied military prospects, despite the recent success.[21] The way he saw it, the Germans had only been pushed back a few miles and not seriously weakened. He could hardly forget that the Allies had recovered from more serious disasters earlier in the year. The Germans had reestablished a new line, they were in possession of a large area of Europe, and with an army of some 2,500,000 men, their offensive power was relatively intact.[22] While waiting for the Americans to play a leading role in the operations in 1919, his immediate objective was to husband Britain's resources and exploit opportunities in the outer theaters to strip Germany of its props at low cost and at the same time, advance Britain's imperial interests.

No one in the Imperial War Cabinet was as pessimistic as Smuts, who expressed doubt that even with an influx of Americans, the Allies would be able to force a decision in the west in 1919. The western front had always been a fatal theater to the attacking party. The defense had such enormous advantages that after four years of the bloodiest fighting in the history of mankind, neither side had been able to break the stalemate. He disputed the CIGS's recent appreciation that a large-scale offensive in the west in 1919 was likely to produce a decisive victory. He predicted bloody fighting ahead with the Germans adopting a defensive posture in the west in 1919 and, if need be, retiring slowly from nonvital strategic areas. Freed from heavy obligations in the west, he feared that they would turn their attention to the east where there was a danger that they would join hands with the Turks to threaten India. Smuts' concern was not only about Britain's interests in the east but also about its status as a great power. According to a War Office paper, the British army, which started 1918 with 62 divisions, would be reduced to some 31 divisions by the end of 1919. What would be the purpose, he asked, if by prolonging the war and ultimately smashing Germany, Britain "became a second or third-class Power, and the leadership, not only financially and militarily, but in every respect, will have passed on to America and to Japan?" Smuts, in short, was pleading for a compromise peace, as Lansdowne had two years earlier. He thought that by knocking out Austria or Turkey, Germany might be induced into accepting a negotiated settlement.[23]

Smuts' defeatist attitude provoked a sharp response from several of his colleagues at a meeting the following day. With the prime ministers in attendance, Curzon led the assault. He thought it curious that in a speech delivered in the Midlands six or eight months earlier when the war was much less advantageous to the Entente than at present, Smuts "told his audience in emphatic terms that the defeat of Germany was certain." Smuts interjected to say that everything ought to be weighed "when we are discussing things seriously" and for that reason he had stressed the other point of view. Curzon replied that he was glad he did. He considered the military position of the Entente and the morale of the British troops more favorable than at anytime during the last year. He expressed confidence in the British High Command and believed that the plan of hammering away at the Germans was the only way to beat them into submission and compel them to accept a dictated peace. He thought that Smuts exaggerated the danger to Britain's position in the east. While he did not dispute that the Germans might turn their attention to the east, he thought that the options opened to them were limited. In short, he did not contemplate, as Smuts appeared to do, "a condition of affairs when the whole military effort of the Allies will be sterilized in the West while a gigantic tide of invasion will roll successfully towards the East."

Lloyd George shared Smuts' military assessment that the German army could not be beaten in 1919, but at the same time, he was convinced that the country had no alternative but to fight on. He was adamant that the only way to ensure a lasting peace was to inflict a decisive defeat on the enemy. He had no doubts that the British public would support a continuation of the struggle, and he was equally certain that France, which had recovered militarily, would be willing to stay the course until 1920 if there was a reasonable chance of trouncing its hereditary and bitter foe. He foresaw a good deal of fighting in 1919. While he did not anticipate a breakthrough, he expected that the constant pounding by the Allies would sufficiently wear down the Germans so that by the following year, "it is quite within the limits of achievement that we should be able to beat the Germans and inflict upon them a defeat which they themselves will recognize to be a defeat – and that is what is important."[24]

At the request of Lloyd George on August 12, Hankey undertook to prepare a draft report summarizing the Imperial War Committee's investigation into past military failures and laying down the broad outlines of future strategy.[25] As Borden was due to leave in a few days, the prime minister wanted the report completed in a hurry. Already stretched to the breaking point, Hankey writes that he was not too upset with the new assignment, for being familiar with the ways of the prime minister, he had begun to work on the report on August 5.[26] Nearly forty pages long, the document was ready on August 14 and circulated to the prime ministers the following day.

On August 16 the Dominion prime ministers breakfasted with Lloyd George before discussing the draft report. Early talks focused on a section that dealt with the responsibility of the government in the debacle of March 21. Lloyd George observed that prior to that date, the former CIGS, Brigadier General Robertson, had tried to persuade Haig to remove three officers from their posts, in particular General Gough. Robertson, finding that Haig wanted to keep all the officers in question, had dismissed two, but left Gough undisturbed. The present CIGS had subsequently written to Haig, recommending that it would be better not to retain Gough in his command. But Haig had strongly resisted the change and the CIGS had advised the government not to press the matter for the time being.

Lloyd George deftly managed to shift the attention from the government to Haig, who then came under criticism for allowing his loyalty to a subordinate cloud his judgment. Lloyd George readily agreed that Haig's weak point was in his choice of men. He had a tendency to select men based less on professional qualifications than on friendship and compatibility. Borden remarked that he enjoyed excellent personal relations with Haig, but, nevertheless, if he had been in England after the Passchendaele offensive, he would have pressed for his dismissal. He did not think that this step should be taken at present.

Discussion turned to examine the report's recommended future military policy. There were slight amendments here and there, but no major changes. The imperial leaders tried to minimize Britain's involvement in the continental war, recognizing that they could not reduce their commitment beyond a certain point without seriously damaging the anti-German coalition. They opposed any major operation in the immediate future that involved heavy casualties, such as had occurred in Flanders the previous year. They proposed to reduce Haig's army to 36 divisions, including Dominion forces, on the grounds that Britain required to maintain its war industries and shipping, fight on other fronts, and form additional tank crews. They accepted the general principle enunciated by Wilson that an all-out effort should be made on the western front in 1919, but postponed the date for the start of the operation until the situation in Russia had come into sharper focus. Lloyd George believed that the bid for victory ought to be delayed until 1920, but he went along with the general sentiment because, in his view, the western front included Italy. Finally, there was disagreement about Wilson's contention that an Allied offensive in Italy was unfeasible because Allied reinforcements could not be spared from the western front early enough to take action. The matter was reserved for further consideration.[27]

All the hard work that went into preparing, discussing and amending the report turned out to be a waste of time. Hughes did not agree with all aspects of the document and, perhaps for that reason, Lloyd George never got around to signing it before it became outdated by the rapid course of events.[28] Borden returned to Canada on August 16. Massey left for New Zealand several days later, but Hughes remained in London until the end of the war.

In hindsight, it was fortuitous that the recommendations of the final report were never carried out. As the Americans were pouring into France in large numbers, Lloyd George and his colleagues retained a strong interest in limiting the nation's commitment in the west to 36 divisions, so as to free troops with which to reinforce secondary theaters. Such a policy would have put the Lloyd George administration on a collision course with the French and "might have destroyed the concept of generalissimo, if not the alliance."[29] Lloyd George's relations with Foch were already strained because of a dispute over the use of the American divisions. Matters heated up further during the second week in August when Pershing, with Foch's blessing, proposed to withdraw three of the five remaining American divisions from Haig and place them under his own command. It seemed to Lloyd George that the French were using a devious expedient to force the British to maintain their existing number of divisions in France, an initiative he was determined to resist. He conveyed his concern to the British ambassador in Washington:

> Clemenceau and Foch mean to compel us to keep up our numbers on the British front by refusing to take over the line. This policy would be fatal to the British Empire as we have no reserve of men here which would enable us to keep up anything approximating to the number of divisions we now maintain in the field, and if we endeavoured to keep up that number until the summer of next year we should be left with no army at all for the rest of the war. I cannot conceive of a more disastrous plan from the British point of view. I mean to fight it with every available resource. Shipping is one of those resources and until the French and Americans come to terms with us on the question of the line I do not propose to give any further assistance in the matter of shipping.[30]

Lloyd George had already lodged a formal protest to Paris and it was not in his nature to be tactful when he felt aggrieved. His note to Clemenceau contained the following excerpt:

> I did not ask for the transfer of American divisions to the British front. ... What I did ask was that some more of the American divisions recently arrived in France, and which are not available for the line until after some

training, should be sent to complete their training in rear of the British lines. My object was to provide a reserve which could be used in the great emergency of a break-through by the enemy on our front, to hold the gap in conjunction with our local reserves, until the arrival of Divisions from the general reserves of the Allied Armies on the western front. I pointed out that this was not a very excessive demand when it is remembered that the greater part of the American troops were brought to France in British shipping and that in view of the sacrifices made to provide this shipping our people had a right to expect that more than five of the twenty-eight American Divisions now in France should be retained behind our lines. We are advised that a serious attack on the British front is still by no means improbable. I do not wish to trouble you to give me detailed explanations, but, in the interests of the unity of command for which I have made such great efforts, I do again urge that my very modest request to our General in Chief shall receive your support.[31]

Clemenceau did not even pretend to address Lloyd George's complaint. His reply is summed up in his opening sentence: "Events seem to me to render more and more superfluous a detailed reply to your telegram relating to the transfer of American troops to the British front."[32] Actually, Pershing was more culpable than Foch for limiting the number of American divisions available to the British. His long struggle to create an independent American army had been achieved late in July when he won approval to form the First American Army. On August 10 he received formal orders that his new army was to eliminate the St. Mihiel salient as its first operation. As he began the process of concentrating the requisite troops, he went to Haig's advanced headquarters to request the return of at least three of the American divisions training with British forces. Haig pointed out that the British had trained and virtually equipped the American troops and "just as they had become useful, it was proposed to take them away." Pershing appreciated the Field Marshal's feelings, but reminded him that the American troops, placed behind the British lines for training, were to be used in battle only to meet an emergency. He was adamant that he required the troops for his impending operation. Haig had no option but to concede, although he did not hide his disappointment.[33]

The loss of American troops did not alter Haig's determination to keep the pressure on the enemy. Haig was convinced that a further attempt by Rawlinson's Fourth Army to attack the enemy's prepared position in the Somme sector, as Foch wanted, would fail with heavy casualties. Instead, he preferred to make his main thrust farther north, with General Julian Byng's Third Army, in the general direction of Bapaume. In the clash of wills that followed, Haig prevailed over Foch.[34] As part of a broad offensive, Byng launched his attack at dawn on August

21 with five divisions, supported by tanks. After a modest advance, Byng halted in accordance with the British strategic plan. The Germans, encouraged by what they considered was a defensive victory, counterattacked on August 22 from their main position. Haig had anticipated their move and had only used part of his force on the first day. The counterattack was beaten back with devastating German losses. The next day, Byng resumed his drive with greater vigor, assisted by Rawlinson's Fourth Army on his right. Between the 23rd and 25th the two British armies made rapid progress, and it was apparent by the large numbers of defenders laying down their arms on first contact, that the enemy's morale was sinking rapidly. On August 26 the First Army, commanded by General Henry Horne, entered the fray on Byng's left. Pressed hard and almost continuously, the Germans suffered heavy casualties as they fell back across the Upper Somme towards the Hindenburg Line.[35]

Away from the scene, there was less excitement in London over Haig's victories than one might have expected. Haig's gains in the past weeks, although impressive, were much less extensive than those the Germans had achieved earlier in 1918. Besides, casualties had been heavy (as they had been on the German side). But what policy makers did not appreciate was that the character of the war had changed.

At a meeting of the X Committee on August 31, the prime minister asked Wilson for an update on the fighting. The CIGS indicated that Haig had reported that Foch wanted him to "press on with the successful operations on the British front." Lloyd George, with Passchendaele still a vivid memory, worried that Haig would waste his reserves in a premature attack. He reminded Wilson of the losses the British army had sustained at Bellecourt in 1917.[36] He felt that allowing the Canadians to be sacrificed, as the Australians had in attacking that difficult region the previous year, would be sheer folly. He was adamant that a clear signal ought to be sent to Haig that the War Cabinet did not want a repetition of last year's experience. If the Americans suffered heavy casualties, it would be as bad as in the case of the Canadians, since Pershing would not send any more men to the British line. No one disagreed with the prime minister's observation. Instead of sending Haig a congratulatory telegram on his superbly conducted campaign, the War Cabinet instructed the CIGS to warn him on its behalf not to undertake any attacks against the Hindenburg Line that would incur heavy losses, "whether to British or American troops."[37] In his *War Memoirs*, Lloyd George disassociated himself from the telegram, saying that Wilson had acted on his own without his knowledge.[38] It was not as if it was a misstatement attributable to a lapse of memory. It was an outright prevarication. By his own admission, Lloyd George had carefully perused the minutes of the meeting before commenting on the episode.

Haig was disgusted by Wilson's telegram, which not only failed to commend him on his brilliant victories, but implied a want of confidence in his judgment. He interpreted it as a cowardly move intended to insulate the prime minister against any possible failure. While the War Cabinet was allowing him to proceed with his offensive, it was clear that it would not stand by him if things went awry. His bitterness was unmistakable as his diary shows:

> The Cabinet are ready to meddle and interfere in my plans in an underhanded way, but do not dare openly to say that they mean to take the responsibility for any failure though ready to take credit for any success! ... If my attack is successful I will remain on as C. in C. If we fail, or our losses are excessive, I can hope for no mercy![39]

Haig gave a piece of his mind to Wilson. He described the politicians in high places as "a wretched lot," pointing out with cynicism "how well they mean to support me." He was emphatic that he watched his drafts most carefully. He reminded Wilson that two weeks earlier, he had withstood pressure from Foch to continue operations at Amiens because of the risk of heavy casualties.[40]

Haig could not see beyond his own circumstances, but skepticism about his leadership in London was understandable. In the past, his deeds had rarely matched his promises and so he had little capital to fall back upon. It also helps explain why the War Cabinet preferred to look for decisive results elsewhere than on the western front.

Acting on behalf of the French government, General Guillaumat crossed the Channel on September 4, hoping to persuade the British to reactivate the Balkan front. Clemenceau took the initiative after the military representatives at Versailles had recommended that subject to the needs of the western front, an offensive should be mounted in the Balkans before October 1.[41] Guillaumat had plenty of experience in the region. At the end of December 1917 he had replaced Sarrail, but was recalled in July 1918 to assume command of the troops defending Paris. In his place, as we have already seen, Clemenceau had appointed Franchet d'Esperey (known as "desperate Frankie," to the British soldiers), an excellent officer.

At a conference at 10 Downing Street, Guillaumat gave a succinct and lucid presentation on the merits of an offensive in the Balkans, after which he fielded questions from Lloyd George and other members present. The British representatives withdrew into another room to consider Guillaumat's proposal. Lloyd George agreed with Cecil that Guillaumat had put together a strong case. Wilson was not nearly as enthusiastic as his two colleagues, but contrary to what has sometimes been reported, did not rule out the scheme.[42] Hankey was wrong when he wrote that Lloyd George, in a rare instance, had overruled his military adviser.[43] Hankey was not at the meeting and he relied on Lloyd George's self-serving account when he wrote his book.[44]

Returning to the conference room, Lloyd George gave his consent to the offensive in the Balkans. He recommended that the Italians should be urged to launch a simultaneous attack on their front in order to immobilize Austrian forces that otherwise might be used to reinforce the Bulgarians. He was equally insistent that the operation in the Balkans should not be delayed until Italian cooperation was assured.[45]

London did not have to wait long for the advantageous results of the action in the Balkans. On September 14 Franchet d'Esperey's delivered his main attack across a mountain chain that formed the boundary between Greece and Serbia. By now, the Bulgarian army, weary, ill-supplied and fed, was thoroughly demoralized and in no state to fend off the onslaught of Franchet d'Esperey's well-equipped and larger multinational force. After three days of fighting, the Bulgarian army was cut in half and its high command opted to withdraw along the whole front. The RAF joined the pursuit, harrying the retreating Bulgarian soldiers with bombs and machine-gun fire and playing a key role in reducing them to a disorganized rabble.[46]

No less spectacular was Allenby's simultaneous campaign against the Turks. Throughout the summer months, Allenby had evolved a strategic plan designed to end the stalemate in Palestine. The removal of nearly 60,000 well-seasoned white troops to meet the needs of the western front in the spring had been replaced by two Indian divisions of dubious quality from Mesopotamia. Still, he retained at least a 2 to 1 superiority against the Turks and an even higher ratio at the point of attack – 35,000 infantry and 9,000 cavalry opposite 8,000 unsuspecting and ill-equipped infantry. Allenby was acting on his own without instructions from London. He opened his attack on September 19 along the coastal plain north of Jaffa. The infantry broke through after a few hours of fighting, opening a corridor for the cavalry, encircled thousands of Turkish soldiers. When the battle of Megiddo was over, Allenby had destroyed the Turkish Army as an effective fighting force. There was nothing to stop him now from occupying Damascus.[47] With the Allies advancing rapidly on all fronts, the tide of war had turned decidedly in their favor.

Chapter 19

THE ROAD TO THE ARMISTICE

On the western front, the Allied plan in September was to continue to hammer away at the Germans. As previously noted, the War Cabinet had qualms about allowing the BEF to storm the heavily fortified Hindenburg Line. Since Lloyd George expected the war to extend at least into 1919, he did not want the British army to take the primary role in attempting to break through Germany's defenses. He was determined to ensure that when the fighting stopped, Britain would still retain sufficient military and economic strength to dictate peace terms to all the belligerents. But the matter was really out of his hands. Haig and Foch were of one mind about keeping the pressure on the Germans. The British government could hardly overrule Haig if he was acting under the orders of the generalissimo.

Haig journeyed to London on September 9 to persuade the government to allow him "to exploit our recent great success to the full." The next day he had an interview with Milner and tried to impress upon him that German morale was breaking down and that victory was within sight.[1] Milner had been subjected to that song and dance routine too many times in the past to fall prey to Haig's boundless enthusiasm. The British army had sustained 800,000 casualties since the start of the year and received only 700,000 drafts, leaving it 100,000 short. Even by conscripting eighteen-year-olds, only 170,000 would be available to fill army ranks in 1919. Milner, with some justification, was afraid that the "British might melt away by the end of 1918" before decisive results had been achieved.[2] Although he remained dubious, he left ultimate responsibility to Haig. A subsequent ten-day visit to the front, during which he visited the headquarters of both Haig and Foch, did not allay Milner's anxiety. He warned Haig that "if the British Army is used up now, there will be no men for next year."[3] On returning to London he told Wilson that Haig was "ridiculously optimistic," and worried that "he might be embarking on another Passchendaele." Wilson concurred, confiding to his diary that he required to watch closely the "stupidity of D.H."[4]

Unable to control the course of events on the western front, Lloyd George devoted his attention to thinking ahead to 1919 and particularly to the issue of manpower. He was very bitter at Foch for depriving Haig of large contingents of American troops, not withstanding that most of them had been conveyed in British ships. He considered it a scandal that the British army, which had borne the brunt of the fighting in 1918, should have only two American divisions on its front, out of a force of a million-and-a-half men. He wanted the Americans to take over a larger section of the line from the British so that he could reduce Haig's forces. By this policy, the government could use its surplus troops elsewhere as well as meet the demands of industry.[5] The prime minister had no compunction about using shipping as a weapon to induce the French to loosen their grip on the American troops.[6]

The showdown with Foch never occurred because of the rapidly changing military picture on the various battlefields. On September 29 Haig's men penetrated the southern part of the Hindenburg Line, accomplishing a superb feat of arms. That same day, the Bulgarian government, recognizing the hopeless position of its army, signed an armistice. In imposing terms on the Bulgarians, Franchet d'Esperey, on Clemenceau's orders, had deliberately excluded General Sir George Milne, the British commander, from the negotiations. Lloyd George was unaware of the conditions of the armistice until they were presented to him as a fait accompli.[7] Moreover, Wilson reported that Franchet d'Esperey intended to push an army up to the Danube and occupy strategic positions in Bulgaria. Clemenceau's underhanded maneuver, together with Franchet d'Esperey's proposed advance to the Danube, strengthened Lloyd George's long-held suspicion that the French meant to create a postwar empire in the Balkans.

If the French aimed to exploit the advantages they had gained in the Balkans, there was nothing to prevent the British from acting in a similar manner in the east. On October 1 Allenby captured Damascus, cutting off the remaining Turkish defenders in Syria. An excited Lloyd George was most anxious to hasten the defeat of the Ottoman Empire so that the spoils could be parceled out before President Wilson, with his known aversion to imperialism, could intervene. To that end, he wanted to place the British force in the Balkans under Allenby's command and set it, along with the army in Palestine, on a course to Constantinople.[8] Balfour, Milner and Hankey, coming together for lunch, disapproved of the idea, worried as they were about the possibility of an attack by the Austrians from the north. At the War Cabinet on October 1 Lloyd George agreed to reconsider, when the general opinion favored consulting Britain's allies before undertaking further operations.[9]

A War Cabinet meeting was held on October 3 to consider the line the prime minister should adopt at his forthcoming meeting with Clemenceau and Orlando. Lloyd George was strongly in favor of excluding President Wilson from negotiations with Turkey, which he expected would soon take place. He held that the United States was not at war with Turkey and thus, Wilson was not entitled to a say in the matter. In the course of the discussion it was pointed out that in any peace negotiation with Turkey, the French would bring up the Sykes-Picot Agreement. As previously seen, the treaty concluded in May 1916, among other things, gave the French Syria and a strip of land to the east of it that included Mosul. At the time, Kitchener, anticipating that Britain's rivalry with Russia would resume after the war, wanted to create a French zone extending from the Mediterranean coast in the west to Mosul in the east. Such an arrangement would allow the French to act as a buffer between the Russians in Armenia and the British in Mesopotamia.[10]

Curzon reproached the Foreign Office for its concession to the French ambassador, Paul Cambon, on the previous day that essentially validated the Sykes-Picot Agreement. It seemed that Cambon had paid a visit to Balfour and pointed out that Allenby had entered the French sphere of influence as defined in the Sykes-Picot Agreement and that arrangements to administer the region should be made. A conference between Cecil and Cambon subsequently took place at the Foreign Office and the finalized arrangements were based on the assumption that the Agreement was still in force. The prime minister thought that the whole matter ought to have been discussed in the War Cabinet before Cecil's interview with Cambon. Like Curzon, he was strongly in favor of finding the means to circumvent the Agreement. He stated that the treaty had been concluded more than two years earlier and was inapplicable to present circumstances. Lloyd George maintained that Turkey's impending collapse was due to British arms, not to the Allies who had contributed little to the result. He was particularly incensed that under the Agreement, the French would have control of the rich oil fields of Mosul. The last thing he wanted was to depend on French good will to supply the British navy of its postwar needs. Curzon pointed out that one ground for revising the treaty "was that Russia had been an important party to the agreement, and was not now in a position to fulfill her share of it." The prime minister indicated that he would raise the matter at the upcoming conference with Clemenceau and Orlando.[11]

On October 4 Lloyd George, with Hankey in tow, left for Versailles, where they were met by Henry Wilson who had preceded them a day or two earlier. On October 5 they heard that the Allies had broken through the last section of the Hindenburg Line and were in open country with no prepared lines of defense ahead. With the breach of the Hindenburg Line and German forces retreating along the entire front, the war in the west moved into its final stages.

Before the inter-Allied conference opened, Lloyd George, Clemenceau and Orlando held private talks at the French Ministry of War. The three devoted their attention to discussing the best means to eliminate Turkey from the war. There were differences between Lloyd George and Clemenceau over which proposal to adopt. The French had a complicated and roundabout scheme to isolate Turkey and cut it off from the Black Sea. The British, on the other hand, wanted an immediate advance on Constantinople, either directly or through the Dardanelles (after an operation had opened the water route). Clemenceau further objected to Lloyd George's suggestion that Allenby, rather than Franchet d'Esperey, should command the future operation against Constantinople.[12]

The first session of the Allied conference that followed covered much the same ground as the prime ministers' preliminary talks. Nothing of importance was settled. Clemenceau tried unsuccessfully to induce Foch to agree with him that Allenby and his army would render greater service on the western front than by remaining in the Middle East. He was further annoyed when Foch supported the British plan for an advance on Constantinople. By contrast, the generalissimo scored points with Lloyd George.[13]

In the midst of the discussions came news that the German government had sent a note to President Wilson asking for an armistice, to be followed by a peace based on his Fourteen Points. The OHL, however, wanted peace on its terms. While it was prepared to withdraw from occupied territory in the west, it hoped to retain some of its gains in the east. Ludendorff's objective was to pull his men back into secure positions and allow them to rest, so that he would be ready to resume the war if the proffered peace terms were unsatisfactory.[14] He must have momentarily slipped out of the realm of reality if he thought that the Allies were gullible enough to agree to an armistice that would make it possible for Germany to fight again.

On October 6, the second session of the conference began at 3:00 p.m. with a discussion of the German peace overtures. The delegates formulated general principles on which the conditions of an armistice should be based. These included, apart from the continuance of the Allied blockade, German withdrawal from Alsace–Lorraine and evacuation of all occupied territory; German retirement behind the Rhine and immediate cessation of submarine warfare. As the issue also involved military matters, it was decided to invite the input of the Allied military authorities.

During the second half of the meeting the delegates considered the terms for an armistice with Turkey. Lloyd George stated that earlier in the day he had received a telephone message from the Admiralty that a Turkish envoy was on his way to Athens to open negotiations with the British ambassador, Lord Grenville. He thought that the Turks would ask for a peace settlement, rather than an armistice. An appeal on the previous day to the British ambassador in Berne from a Turkish revolutionary group acting on behalf of the sultan indicated that what concerned him most was how much territory Turkey would be allowed to retain. Lloyd George was of the opinion that it would be easier for the British, French and Italian governments to settle the terms of peace by themselves than at a full conference. Pichon remarked that it would not be proper to discuss the conditions of peace with Turkey in the absence of President Wilson. Lloyd George cut him off by saying that if Wilson was not represented at their conferences it was his own fault. He had always ignored such gatherings. Clemenceau sided with Lloyd George. He recommended that they decide now "how much territory was to remain Turkish." Lloyd George had brought with him a draft of the conditions of an armistice with Turkey that Hankey had prepared. With minor amendments, it was accepted by Clemenceau and Sonnino. The revised draft called for Turkey to demobilize, open access to the Black Sea, surrender territory occupied by non-Turks and sever relations with the Central Powers.[15]

That evening the British delegation, augmented by the arrival of Bonar Law and Cecil, enjoyed a late dinner together. Afterwards there was an animated discussion about the future partition of the Ottoman Empire. There is the following entry in Hankey's diary:

> Ll. G. took a very *intransigent* attitude and wanted to go back on the Sykes-Picot agreement, so as to get Palestine for us and to bring Mosul into the British zone, and even to keep the French out of Syria. ... He was also very contemptuous of President Wilson and anxious to arrange the division of Turkey between France, Italy and G. B. before speaking to America. He also thought it would attract less attention to our enormous gain in this war, if we swallowed our share of Turkey now, and the German colonies later.[16]

Nothing of substance occurred at the third session on the morning of October 7, but before the conference reassembled in the afternoon, Lloyd George met privately with Clemenceau at the Ministry of War. He had just learned about Franchet d'Esperey's plan to divide Milne's army, proposing to include one division as part of an Allied force, under the command of a French general, to march on Constantinople while the remainder of the British troops were sent somewhere into Bulgaria. Lloyd George could not contain his anger. He thought it was outrageous that the British, who had carried out by far the greater part of the fighting against the Turks and in the process sustained very heavy losses, should be given a subsidiary role in the operation against Constantinople. He made it quite clear to Clemenceau that he would remove Milne from Franchet d'Espery's command and order him to advance on Constantinople. The interview was cut short because the conference was about to begin at the Quai d'Orsay.[17]

The heated debate continued in the conference with Clemenceau on the receiving end of Lloyd George's blows. The British prime minister asserted that Franchet d'Esperey, unlike Foch, was not behaving like an Allied commander-in-chief. In what was certainly an ironic statement, he accused the French general of basing his plan on political rather than military factors. Lloyd George observed that Franchet d'Esperey had appointed "a French general to command against Constantinople, a French general to command in Bulgaria, and a French general to command in Albania." It seemed to Lloyd George that the commander-in-chief "ought to be specially careful of the political susceptibilities of his Allies." How would the French Government react, he asked rhetorically, if the situation were reversed.

Clemenceau assured his British counterpart that he had not given Franchet d'Esperey any instructions or advice, only called for a plan. He was quite prepared to cancel the plan if it went against the wishes of the conference. Lloyd George was content to allow Franchet d'Esperey to continue to exercise control over the British army, rather than place it under Allenby, provided that Milne commanded the section ordered to march to Constantinople. Clemenceau accepted Lloyd George's proposal.

During the remainder of the session there was an attempt to set a time limit to an armistice with Germany. Lloyd George thought that there was a danger even in a brief armistice; once the weary Allied soldiers laid down their arms, he doubted that they could be induced to fight again. He suggested that the Allies should have an idea of what the Germans would accept before an armistice was declared. His solution was to refer the question to the military representatives at Versailles for further study. There were no dissenting voices.[18]

Business was light on October 8 as the delegates waited for the arrival of President Wilson's answer to the German approach. The first item on the agenda related to the negotiations with Turkey. Lloyd George pointed out that his government had received information from Athens that the Turkish emissaries had been sent by Rahmi Bey, the Vali of Smyrna, and not by the Turkish authorities. It appeared that Rahmi Bey was contemplating a revolution in Constantinople and wanted to know what terms the Allies would give him in such an event. He had suggested a number of conditions that Lloyd George deemed unacceptable. A reply to Grenville had been drafted, forbidding him to hold talks with persons other than representatives of the Turkish government. The conference agreed with the conditions set forth in the British reply.

The delegates then turned their attention to the other item, namely setting armistice terms with Germany. To that end two proposals were put forward, one by Foch and the other by the military representatives at Versailles.[19] Both wanted to impose drastic terms as a condition for an armistice. The military representatives differed from Foch to the extent that they favored disarming the Germany army before it evacuated the occupied territories. Bonar Law declared that it "amounted virtually to an unconditional capitulation." Lloyd

George expressed himself along similar lines. That seemed to be the consensus, but it was decided to put off a decision for further consideration.[20]

When the delegates gathered around the table on October 9, lying before them was a copy of the telegram Woodrow Wilson had sent to Berlin on the previous day. House had urged the president to consult the Allies before replying to the Germans. According to Wiseman, the president declined to do so because the delay would have been bad for the morale "of our troops and peoples generally," and in his opinion the note was "too vague to justify reference to the Allies."[21]

In his communication, the American president indicated that before replying to the German appeal, he required clarification of two issues so as to avoid any misunderstanding. Did the German government accept his Fourteen Points as a basis for peace or as a starting point for negotiations? Additionally, were the Germans prepared to withdraw from the conquered territories as a preliminary condition?[22]

Clemenceau was pleased with the document, stressing that it called for the German evacuation of France, Belgium, Italy and Luxemburg. Lloyd George, on the other hand, saw things differently. The British premier was incensed with President Wilson, first because neither he nor Clemenceau had been consulted; and secondly because the American president assumed that the Allies shared his vision as spelled out in his Fourteen Points. That certainly was not the case. British authorities had serious misgivings about several of Wilson's points, quite apart from wanting to include several matters of their own. The most objectionable of Wilson's program, in the eyes of Lloyd George and his colleagues, read as follows: "Absolute freedom of navigation upon the seas, outside territorial waters in peace and war, except as the seas may be closed in whole or in part by international action, for the enforcement of international covenant." This stipulation could be taken to mean that, if Britain found itself at war in the future, its navy could not impose a blockade or exert economic pressure on its enemy unless enforcing international covenants. In the past, British policymakers had not drawn attention to their differences in the interest of Anglo–American harmony, but now they could no longer afford to maintain their silence.

Lloyd George had no doubts that the German Chancellor, Prince Max of Baden, with Germany seemingly on the verge of defeat, would readily accept President Wilson's proposals without any alteration. He was adamant that if they raised no objections before Wilson's note was published, the Germans would be entitled to regard it as the Allied conditions for an armistice. He then read the draft of a telegram that he had prepared as an answer to Wilson. In it he observed that Wilson's demand that the Germans evacuate the occupied territories as a condition for an armistice did not go far enough. He maintained that the conditions should be drawn up by the Allied governments' military advisers and framed "as to preclude the enemy from obtaining any advantage by withdrawing unpursued to a shorter line, thus placing himself in a better posture of defense than he was at the time of the commencement of the armistice." Both Sonnino and Cecil agreed with Lloyd George that the Allies would be committed to the conditions of an armistice they disapproved of unless they spoke out at once. They, too, favored warning Wilson privately that the condition he had prescribed as a preliminary to the armistice was not sufficient by itself. Clemenceau came around to the same view.[23]

That afternoon a formal reply to the American president was drafted, setting out Allied views on the armistice terms. The document embodied mostly the suggestions of Foch and the permanent military representatives, signaling a hardening of attitude since the preliminary discussion on the previous day.[24] The Allies insisted that evacuation of all conquered territory, however essential, was insufficient. They claimed that there was nothing to prevent the Germans from taking advantage of the armistice to withdraw from their current military predicament, shorten their front and form up in new positions. They maintained that the "conditions of an armistice can only be fixed after consultation with the military experts and in accordance with the military situation at the actual moment when negotiations are entered on." A separate message was sent to President Wilson, pointing out that the time had come when decisions might have to be taken at short notice and urging him to send a trusted representative to Europe with whom they could confer when the occasion arose.[25]

Lloyd George was back in London on October 10. Two days later, he motored to his country retreat at Danny Park, near Hurstpierpoint in Sussex, which Riddell had placed at his disposal for the summer. The next day he learned that the German government had replied to Wilson's note, accepting the conditions laid down, but asking that a mixed commission be formed to supervise the arrangements for the evacuation. The request fed Lloyd George's suspicions that Berlin was trying to buy time to allow the German army to regroup and strengthen its defenses. He called at once for a meeting, which was held in the afternoon. In attendance, besides Lloyd George, were Balfour, Churchill, Wemyss, Reading, Kerr and Hankey. As expected, the Germans had assumed that evacuation of the occupied territories was to be the sole condition of the armistice. After much discussion it was decided to ask President Wilson to disabuse Berlin officials of that notion, and to impress upon him the necessity of setting terms that would prevent Germany from reopening the war in the event of a breakdown in the negotiations. It was also agreed to hint to him in another telegram that the British government would not accept all of the Fourteen Points.[26]

Wilson's second communication to the Germans on October 14, again sent without prior consultation with the Allies, struck a harsher tone than the first. He was under intense pressure from the Allies, as well as his domestic foes, who demanded more stringent terms. In all likelihood he was also influenced by the German army's wanton acts of brutality and destruction as it fell back across northern France, plus the sinking of yet another passenger ship by a U-boat. Thus, in his note he made it clear that the process of evacuation and conditions of the armistice would be based on the judgment of the military advisers of the United States and Allied governments. No arrangements would be accepted without absolute safeguards to maintain the present superiority of the armies of both the United States and Allies in the field. Wilson rebuked the Germans for their illegal and inhuman war practices on land and on sea and called for a change in the character of their government.[27]

On October 15 Lloyd George discussed Wilson's latest pronouncements with the CIGS, Reading, Milner and Hankey on the terrace of 10 Downing Street. According to Hankey, "All were very sarcastic about the note, which seems a complete *volte-face*, flying from excessive leniency to austere strictness."[28] Henry Wilson wanted the Allies to frame a reply to the American President to put "him in his proper place," but he was unable to elicit the support of the prime minister.[29] The matter received further attention at the ensuing War Cabinet meeting, but it was decided to take no action.[30]

On the same day, Curzon prepared a memorandum in which he stressed that the terms of an armistice ought to be jointly discussed and set by the Allies, not negotiated solely by the American president. It was his feeling that the conditions should contain some of the Fourteen Points, plus other items such as the surrender of the German fleet, reparations for the cost of the war and punishment for those responsible for the war. Curzon, in effect, called for Germany's unconditional surrender – an attitude shared by several of his colleagues.[31]

With Lloyd George absent from the War Cabinet session on October 18, several items on the agenda had to be postponed. After the conclusion of business, Curzon exploded, castigating the prime minister for failure to keep all the members abreast of important events and for the manner in which he had handled armistice talks, notably at Danny Park a few days earlier, when only a few of them had been present. Long followed in a similar vein, but Cecil and Bonar Law tended to treat the matter lightly, citing as justification the urgent need to reply to Wilson's note and the difficulty of assembling the full membership at short notice. Still Hankey had to admit that "the P. M. is assuming too much the role of a dictator and he is headed for very serious trouble."[32] Hankey described what had occurred in a confidential letter to the prime minister and pressed him to sooth the bruised feelings of his disgruntled colleagues at an upcoming War Cabinet meeting.[33] Lloyd George did not act on Hankey's recommendation.

The next day, at the X Committee meeting at 10 Downing Street, Haig, along with Beatty and Weymss, were in attendance to give their views on the conditions of an armistice with Germany. The naval representatives pushed for draconian terms, including the surrender of the greater part of the German High Seas Fleet and all submarines. The central figure in the discussion was Haig, who felt that if Britain's goals could be met without further fighting, there was no justification for sacrificing the lives of his troops simply to punish Germany or to advance French interests. He indicated at the outset that the nature of the terms depended on two questions: whether Germany was so beaten that it would accept any terms, and could the Allies press the Germans with sufficient vigor during the winter months to prevent them from destroying roads, bridges and railways on their way back to Germany. His answer to both was an unqualified "No." He thought that the German army was badly beaten but remained intact and was capable of retiring to its own frontiers and holding at bay equal or even superior forces. On the other hand, the French army was worn out and lately had not been fighting well. The American army was disorganized, ill-trained and ignorant of the conditions of modern war, with the result that it would take at least a year before it could be converted into a capable fighting force. Thus, neither the French nor the Americans were capable of undertaking a serious offensive at the present time. The British army was the most formidable fighting machine in the world, but it could not force a decision by itself. The most sensible course, it seemed to Haig, was to offer the Germans terms they would accept at once, namely, to evacuate Belgium and the occupied French territory and to surrender Alsace–Lorraine.

Henry Wilson considered the proposed terms inadequate, as did Bonar Law. On the basis of the evidence supplied by Haig, the prime minister did not think that the Germans were sufficiently defeated to acquiesce to stern terms. He pointed out the danger of losing a good bargain by asking too much. Milner questioned whether they could ignore the aspirations of the Poles and east European minorities. The prime minister replied, "we cannot expect the British to go on sacrificing their lives for the Poles."[34] He was guided, he insisted, by the need to ensure that Britain acquired its war aims – which had received a boost when President Wilson told Sir William Wiseman on October 16 that he had no objections if Britain retained Germany's captured colonies as long as they were administered as a trustee for the proposed League of Nations.[35]

Lloyd George had come to appreciate that Britain would benefit most by an early peace. He reasoned that if Britain could gain its ends through a negotiated settlement, there was no purpose to continue the war. The German High Command had the means to delay the Allied offensive, retreat behind the Rhine and fight a long defensive war. By leaving unnecessary stores behind, destroying bridges, roads and railways, and planting time fuses for mines and shells that could retard explosions for days or weeks, they could make good their escape. It would take many months before the Allies could resume their advance. If they took the war into Germany, moreover, they would suffer hundreds of thousands of casualties. Lloyd George had one more matter to consider. Since the British had done most of the recent hard fighting, they would enjoy a dominant voice during the peace negotiations if the war ended in 1918. But if the war extended into 1919, Haig's losses could not be replaced and the lead would pass to the rapidly growing American Expeditionary Force (AEF). With the AEF delivering the final blow against the German army, the extraordinary gains and performance by Haig's men in the last half of 1918 would be forgotten. Instead, the Americans would reap the glory and President Wilson would be in a position to take control of the peace negotiations and deprive Britain and its allies of the full fruits of victory.

Discussions continued in the War Cabinet and X Committee, at times in desultory fashion, in the ensuing days. For Lloyd George, the dilemma was to formulate terms that were severe enough to handcuff the Germans but not so unreasonable that they would prefer to fight to the finish rather than submit to them. During the War Cabinet meeting on October 21 a telegram was received announcing that the Turkish government wanted to open peace negotiations. Allenby's capture of Damascus, but more importantly, the surrender of Bulgaria, which opened the road to Constantinople, and the retreat of the German army had induced the Turkish authorities to throw in their hand when it might have been possible to hold out a little longer.[36] Lloyd George pointed out that if Turkey went out of the war, it would immeasurably assist Entente prospects on the western front the following year. Eventually, it was agreed to send a reply to the effect that the British government was prepared to negotiate with properly accredited Turkish agents, but that armistice conditions could only be set after consultations with its allies.[37] The matter was further complicated by a dispute with the French as to who should command the fleet that would proceed up the straits to receive Turkey's surrender in Constantinople. While Clemenceau had deferred grudgingly to Lloyd George's wish that Milne should lead an expedition against Constantinople, he refused to allow the British to command the naval operations as well. A sharp exchange of letters between the two prime ministers had not resolved their differences.[38]

The War Cabinet had barely reconvened after lunch when it was sidetracked by receipt of Berlin's reply to Wilson's second note. The German government agreed to all the conditions laid down by the American president.

It accepted that the terms of the armistice would be arranged by opposing military experts, but asked that no demand be made "that would be irreconcilable with the honor of the German people and with paving the way to a peace of justice." It further promised to evacuate occupied territories, to order U-boat commanders to spare passenger ships in the future, that the retreating armies would respect private property and to make constitutional changes that would end absolute rule and the military's influence in shaping the nation's policy.[39]

There followed a long discussion that ended with the decision to send Wilson a telegram, warning him against a possible German trap and asking him not to act without consulting the Allies.[40] Wilson, as usual, moved ahead on his own and forwarded his third note to Prince Max on October 23. He came close to asking for Germany's unconditional surrender and for the removal of the Kaiser. He reiterated that the terms would be set by the military advisers of the United States and its associates.[41] With the preliminary round over, Wilson was ready to act in concert with the Allies.

In the War Cabinet, Lloyd George welcomed the president's proposals, now that he had made it clear that the armistice terms would be framed in such a way as to prevent Germany from resuming hostilities. The prime minister supported the idea that the negotiations should be placed in the hands of Foch and the Allied commanders-in-chief (presumably he meant Pershing as well). He reasoned that if the talks broke down, it would be clear to the public that it was due not to the action of politicians, but to the unwillingness of the Germans to accept the terms laid down by the Allied military chiefs.[42]

On October 25 and 26 the War Cabinet discussed Wilson's program, which the Germans presumably expected would form the basis of a peace settlement. Balfour indicated that however drastic and stringent the terms of the armistice might be, it would be impossible, in imposing a peace settlement, to go beyond the Fourteen Points. The Germans would be entitled to say that they had accepted the restrictions that would make their army incapable of resuming the war on condition that the peace was based on the Fourteen Points. The prime minister agreed with Balfour. He was particularly troubled by Wilson's insistence on the freedom of the seas, which Admiralty experts warned would undermine British naval power and prestige.[43] He recommended that the British government ought to make a statement in opposition to this clause and others it found objectionable, otherwise the Germans would have a right to assume that the Fourteen Points were the worst conditions that could be imposed on them. There followed a long debate as to whether the best course would be to send a telegram to Wilson and Britain's principal allies, outlining the government's position, or to circulate a document on the subject shortly before the meeting of the Supreme War Council scheduled for the 29th of the month. The War Cabinet chose the latter option.

The other main topic addressed was whether the British government considered it desirable to agree to an armistice at present, or to demand such drastic terms as to invite certain rejection by the Germans, with the object of crushing them completely the following year and obtaining their unconditional surrender. Lloyd George claimed he was open-minded on the subject, but from his remarks he seemed inclined to favor the latter option. Since it was contrary to his previous statement, he may have been playing devil's advocate. At any rate, his rationale was as follows: The industrial part of France had been devastated by the war that Germany had caused. At the first moment that the Allies were in a position to smash the Germans, they had thrown their hands up. He questioned whether they ought not to continue lashing Germany as it had lashed France. Austin Chamberlain reminded the prime minister that the cost to exact vengeance would be high. Lloyd George replied that it "was not vengeance, but justice." Virtually all the other ministers came down against prolonging the war, even though Major General Harington, the deputy CIGS, claimed that the Germans could not last much longer because of the rapidly deteriorating state of their army and would be forced to accept whatever terms the Allies wanted to impose. There was a deep-rooted fear expressed by practically everyone at one time or another that continuing to fight into 1919 would so erode Britain's strength that it would lose its dominance in world affairs. The War Cabinet avoided calling for specific armistice terms, but to secure Britain's territorial and economic interests, it did endorse general guidelines for Lloyd George and Balfour to follow at the Allied Conference.[44]

During the last week in October, British policymakers were overwhelmed by the rapid march of events. President Wilson's last note had been received with consternation in Berlin, provoking an acrimonious debate between the civil and military authorities. Ludendorff had pulled himself together after losing his nerve (caused by the German army's defeats) and vowed to fight on rather than accept the humiliating armistice terms. His authority challenged, Prince Max approached the Kaiser and made it clear that he must choose between Ludendorff and himself. On October 26 the Emperor called in Ludendorff and forced him to resign.[45] That same day, the Reichstag completed a revision of the Imperial constitution, which reduced the near absolute authority of the Kaiser to the level of a democratic monarch.

Germany's remaining allies were ready to throw in the towel as well. On October 24 the Italian army, with extensive British and French help, initiated a push from the Piave that culminated five days later in the victory at Vittorio Veneto.[46] With the Austrian army in full retreat, Emperor Karl requested an armistice. Given that Allenby's victories in Palestine and the surrender of Bulgaria had placed the Turks in extreme difficulty, the War Office advised Lieutenant General Sir W. R. Marshall, in command of the Mesopotamian Expeditionary Force, to gain as much ground as possible up the Tigris in anticipation of a cessation of hostilities in the near future. Starting his advance on October 23, he forced the surrender of a Turkish force at Sharqat before occupying Mosul on November 4, five days after a cease-fire had been formally declared.[47]

Turkish envoys had arrived at Mudros on the island of Lemnos on October 26 to conduct armistice negotiations with Vice Admiral Sir S. A. Calthorpe, British naval commander in the Mediterranean. The discussions, from which the French naval commander was excluded, led to an armistice between Turkey and Britain alone on the evening of October 30.[48]

Lloyd George was in Paris attending an inter-Allied Conference while Anglo–Turkish negotiations were approaching a conclusion. On November 29 talks had been held at the Quai d'Orsay, with House joining the members of the three Allied delegations. As the first order of business, Clemenceau moved that the Allies should send a reply to President Wilson, setting the terms on which an armistice should be granted. Lloyd George pointed out that if the notes exchanged between Washington and Berlin were studied closely, it would seem that an armistice had been proposed on the assumption that it would be based on Wilson's Fourteen Points. He turned to House and asked if his interpretation was correct. House replied that it was. Lloyd George maintained that unless something was said to the contrary before the armistice, the Allies would be bound by Wilson's terms.

Clemenceau stated that as he had not been consulted, he did not consider France committed to them. Lloyd George echoed similar sentiments. At Clemenceau's request, Pichon began to read out the Fourteen Points, only to be interrupted by an outburst on the part of Lloyd George, who insisted that Britain would not accept the principle of freedom of the seas under any conditions. If that clause had been in operation, he fumed, the Entente would have been unable to apply a blockade. He contended that the effect of the blockade was no less responsible than the military operations for breaking Germany's will to extend the conflict. He was unsympathetic to the suggestion that the matter be referred to the League of Nations, particularly since no one could foretell what shape it would take or the extent of its influence in world politics. House was shaken by the pummeling of the US at the hands of Clemenceau and especially Lloyd George. He was never a good debater, accustomed as he was to operating behind the scenes, and he responded by unwisely trying to bluff his way out. He insisted that if the object was to take the Fourteen Points off the table, Wilson would have no option but to notify Berlin that the Allies would not accept his conditions. The question would then arise as to whether America would discuss issues of peace directly with Germany.

Clemenceau was uncertain that he had heard correctly. He asked House whether he meant to imply that the United States would make a separate peace with the enemy. Such a possibility existed, House answered, if the United States disagreed with the terms formulated by its associates. Lloyd George was unfazed by what he correctly perceived was a hollow threat. He remarked that if the United States went ahead and made a separate peace, it would be deeply regretted, but it would not deter the Allies from fighting on alone. Clemenceau weighed in with a simple "*Oui.*" Lloyd George went on to say that his government would never accept an armistice under Wilson's conditions. He explained that Britain was not really a military power and that its main defense was its fleet. To give up the right to use its fleet in war was the one thing Britain could not surrender. Clemenceau considered Wilson's clause absurd. How could there be war, he inquired, if there was freedom of the seas?

As the delegates moved on to examine other points, tempers on both sides cooled. Apart from the freedom of the seas clause, Lloyd George pointed out that there was nothing in Wilson's program about indemnifying aggrieved parties. He insisted that reparations needed to be extracted from Germany for its sinking of ships and wanton destruction of property in France and Belgium. Otherwise, he had no objections to the rest of the Fourteen Points. House, having regained his equanimity, asserted that the Fourteen Points should not be seen as etched in stone, but would require to be amended and qualified before put into practice. As for Lloyd George's other reservation, he pointed out that reparations had been implied in Wilson's speeches and in two of his clauses where it had been stated that the invaded countries must be evacuated and restored. The same principle would apply to illegal sinkings at sea. When the delegates parted at the end of the afternoon, they agreed to meet again the next day at the Quai d'Orsay.[49]

The next morning (October 30) Lloyd George, accompanied by Hankey and Kerr, motored to the French War Office for a meeting with Clemenceau and House. In the span of about twenty minutes, they agreed on the wording of a reply to Wilson. The note stated that subject to two qualifications, the Allied governments accepted the Fourteen Points as a basis of the peace negotiations. The first reservation, which involved freedom of the seas, was open to various interpretations, some of which the Allies found unacceptable. They therefore "reserve to themselves complete freedom on this subject when they enter the peace conference." The second objection was the absence of compensation, which, it was asserted, Germany must provide for damages to

Allied civilian population and property caused by its forces on land and sea, and from the air.

Reassembling at 3:00 p.m., the Conference quickly approved of the decisions embodied in the note and moved on to consider the terms of an armistice with Austria. Lloyd George drew attention to the great advantages of settling with Austria before dealing with Germany. He was well prepared for the discussion and advanced a set of proposals drawn up for him by Henry Wilson. The main points included (1) evacuation of all occupied territories, (2) reduction of the army to a level consistent with domestic safety, (3) Allied rights to occupy such strategic sites as they determine and to move freely over road, rail and waterways, (4) repatriation of prisoners and civilians.[50] Adopted in principle without dissent, they were referred to the military representatives who were expected to add propositions of their own. The Allied Naval Council, meeting coincidentally in Paris, had already submitted a draft of the naval terms. After examining them, Clemenceau commented that the Naval Council "had not asked for the Emperor's trousers, but that is about all."[51]

Thus far, agreement on the issues had not been terribly difficult, but Lloyd George's announcement that he had just received a message that Rear Admiral Calthorpe hoped to have terms of an armistice with Turkey signed that very evening brought the French to their feet. Pichon complained that the armistice negotiations had failed to involve Britain's allies. Lloyd George replied that Franchet d'Esperey had not consulted Milne in arranging an armistice with Bulgaria. The British had not complained because they understood that the business could best be transacted by a single person. For that reason, it was agreed by all that Foch, as the Supreme Allied Commander, should conduct the armistice negotiations with Germany. The case of Calthrope was the only instance where the British alone had conducted the negotiations. Besides, he stressed, this was only right, as Britain had done almost all the fighting against the Turks. Clemenceau maintained that there was an essential difference, in that Franchet d'Esperey was Milne's superior, while Calthorpe was under the orders of Admiral Gauchet (French Commander in the Mediterranean). Lloyd George disagreed, saying the British had always been in command in the north Aegean. When it has been a question of attacking the Dardanelles (in the spring of 1915), the French had been very willing to leave the command in British hands. Clemenceau thereupon switched tracks. He stated that he was concerned not so much by procedure as by national susceptibility, which could not be ignored. He had no objections to the terms, but recommended that instead of placing Calthrope in charge of an Allied task force proceeding up the Dardanelles, both British and French fleets should enter the waterway simultaneously. He further proposed that the British and French naval commanders should sign the armistice simultaneously, particularly since the former admiral had not received full powers from the two governments to conduct the negotiations.

Lloyd George's retort was swift and uncompromising. He declared that when questions of national dignity and susceptibility were raised, France was the last nation that ought to complain. He alluded to the 2,000,000 British soldiers on the western front under the command of a French general, a concession, he was quick to remind Clemenceau, that had entailed considerable political risks on his part. Similarly, at Salonica, although the British had a bigger army, they had allowed it to pass under a French general of dubious capacity (Sarrail). It would be well for the French to remember that the British and Italians also had their susceptibilities. Clemenceau admitted that France owed much to Lloyd George and Britain, but the question was not over the appointment of Foch as generalissimo on the western front, but who would sign the armistice with Turkey. He reiterated that Calthrope did not have the authority to do so on behalf of France. Lloyd George did not conceal the fact that he was dismayed "at the lack of generosity on the part of the French Government." He asserted that Britain had done all the fighting and its armies had taken thousands of casualties before Turkey had succumbed. Despite numerous appeals for assistance, France had only contributed a few black "policemen to see that we did not steal the Holy Sepulchre." The moment, however, "there was a question of signing an armistice, there was all this rush to take part." If the French wished to insist on signing the armistice with Turkey, he threatened to raise the matter in the presence of the other nations concerned at the Supreme War Council. There he would urge that this same principle be applied in the signature of all armistices. For example, in the case of the western front, the armistice terms would have to be signed, not just by Foch, but by the generals of all the nations represented in that theater.

Pichon, after conferring with Clemenceau for a few minutes, stated that he and his colleagues did not want to prolong the discussion. He pointed out that he harbored strong attachment to the British whose services to the Alliance could not be overestimated. In the spirit of conciliation, the French government would accept the matter as a fait accompli. On that note, the conference adjourned.[52]

Apart from private gatherings of the Allied and Associate leaders, the Supreme War Council held four sessions at Versailles between October 31 and November 4 before formally setting down the armistice terms with Austria and Germany. There was little disagreement among the Allies about deciding the conditions for Austria. It was a different matter when it came to imposing terms on Germany. The discussions were prolonged, partly because Lloyd George was concerned about safeguarding British interests and at the same time arguing against imposing excessively harsh terms on Germany. Thus the treaties of Brest-Litvosk and Bucharest were to be abrogated, forcing Germany back to its

1914 frontiers in the east and removing any possible threat to Britain's eastern Empire. Lloyd George, furthermore, protected Britain's maritime supremacy and succeeded in reserving for discussion at the peace conference such sensitive issues as freedom of the seas, reparations and the future of enemy colonies. Yet, he did not want to see terms imposed on Germany that were so draconian that they would result in their rejection or dramatically upset the balance of power in Europe. While he was satisfied that the German army could not resume fighting, he was opposed to marching it into captivity or reducing it to impotence. There were rumors of disturbances and increasing chaos in Germany, which aroused his fears and those of his colleagues that it might succumb to Bolshevism. The German army, it was felt, should be strong enough to maintain internal order and head off a possible Bolshevik takeover. As it turned out, the German army was not disarmed and was allowed to march back to Germany.[53]

Lloyd George dominated the proceedings that had led to the armistice terms with Austria and Germany and he could not have represented the interests of his country much better. Hankey would recall nearly half a century later:

> Never in my long association with Lloyd George did I see him rise to greater heights, nor express the national sentiments with greater vigour, dignity and authority than in those quiet conversations at the Quai d'Orsay and the Rue de l'Université [House's residence]."[54]

The work was all but finished when news came in on November 3 that Austria, to the delight of all the delegations, had signed the armistice. When Lloyd George left Paris the next day, further operations against Germany could not be excluded. On November 7 Foch presented armistice terms to a German delegation that included civilian as well as military personnel. By then Germany was in turmoil and Prince Max warned the Kaiser that unless he abdicated, the country would be torn apart by revolution. Wilhelm refused to listen, prepared as he was to use the army to suppress the growing insurgency. Hindenburg, when consulted, told Wilhelm that this was out of the question as the army would no longer obey the Emperor's orders and certainly would not fire on fellow citizens.[55] Abandoned by the military, Wilhelm wrote out his letter of abdication on the morning of November 9 and left for Holland. Later in the day, Prince Max resigned in favor of Frederick Ebert, leader of the Majority Socialists. The new German administration accepted the armistice terms and at 11:00 a.m. on November 11, the war came to an end.

CONCLUSION

Lloyd George emerged from the war with his prestige at an all-time high. All the political crises he had provoked through his inept deviousness were forgotten. He was hailed as the "man who won the war" (not the least by himself), a characterization that was patently untrue. For one thing, the war was not won by Britain alone but by a coalition of powers. For another, there were factors that probably weighed more than Lloyd George's leadership in the final victory: the strangling naval blockade that hastened Germany's capitulation; Kitchener, who built a formidable army, which became the mainstay of the Entente after the spring of 1917; American help; and Haig, who learned from past defeats, and adopted a formula in 1918 that would produce a string of brilliant victories.

Still, there are many modern day historians who consider that Lloyd George was the indispensable man in the First World War, just like Churchill would be in the Second. They argue that he brought talented men into government, cut through red tape to achieve his objective and conciliated the workers, and that he could withstand relentless pressure, maintain his composure in the face of adversity and possessed dogged determination, a fertile imagination, boundless energy and the ability to inspire those with whom he came into contact. In other words, there was no one else on the political scene better suited to cope with the myriad and complex problems stemming from the worldwide conflict.[1]

But are they correct in their lofty assessment of Lloyd George's handiwork during the period of his war premiership? In trying to answer this question, it is necessary to divorce popular myth from fact. Before proceeding, it is useful to keep in mind that the combination of industry, perseverance, imagination and nerves of steel, however admirable in a public servant with heavy responsibilities, is no substitute for meaningful results. Nor is it pertinent to ask if anyone could have done better, although I think there were other national politicians who could have taken Lloyd George's place. Had he fallen from grace, consensus undoubtedly would have formed quickly around a candidate, perhaps even one without a distinguished past, much as in 1940 when Churchill succeeded Chamberlain. Daily and weekly publications urging Lloyd George's removal in the fall of 1917 did not believe that he was irreplaceable. A case in point was the

Spectator, which wrote on November 17, 1917, "There are plenty of people to put in Mr. Lloyd George's place, and a week after he had left office the world would be asking how it had been possible to endure his levity for so many months." It went on to identify two candidates (Geddes and Cecil) as being better cast than Lloyd George to lead the nation. Another name bandied about was that of Milner who would not have been a bad choice if he had been able to form a ministry. At any rate, the absence of an obvious viable alternative is immaterial to assessing Lloyd George's work. It certainly has had no bearing in evaluating Haig's generalship and should not have any relevance in the case of Lloyd George. Thus, by stripping away extraneous factors we can focus on the legitimate criteria by which Lloyd George should be judged: how well he handled the three areas crucial to victory, namely, managing the home front, directing the war effort and sustaining the spirit and confidence of the nation.

Lloyd George enjoyed his greatest success on the home front where his political skills and experience came into play. Nevertheless, his performance was far from flawless. He had no clear idea of how to control manpower, and it was not until late in the war that a policy was adopted. When Lloyd George took over the reins of government, military conscription had become law, but retarding the development of a comprehensive and balanced manpower policy were the increasing requirements of industry, transportation, farms and mines, all of which competed openly with the army for the services of the remaining men. Because of the hostility of trade unions to industrial conscription, Neville Chamberlain was not given the authority to transfer labor to vital war work and instead was compelled to rely on volunteerism. When the appeal for volunteers proved to be a disappointing failure, Chamberlain unveiled a new blueprint based on the "clean cut." But facing resistance from every quarter and deserted by the prime minister, he resigned his post. Auckland Geddes, his successor, was given control over the whole field of manpower. His ministry thus combined the functions of supplying the army with recruits and redirecting labor to essential war production. The recognition by labor that the nation confronted a situation of the utmost gravity enabled Geddes to establish the principle of the "clean cut" so that essential industries would be obliged to release all fit males within a certain age group. The scheme went into effect just as the enemy was about to unleash its spring offensive. The government's tardiness in sanctioning a coherent war policy, however, prevented maximum efficient utilization of manpower.

Conversely, Lloyd George deserves high praise for his adept management of labor, made more complicated and difficult because of the extension of state intervention in British industry. This required a drastic change in the relationship between the state and organized labor. To meet the needs of war production, it was necessary for the government to take a softer line with labor and establish mutual good will. Accordingly, Lloyd George made it a point to identify and consult leaders of powerful unions as well as to bring popular Labour politicians into the government. He appealed to the patriotism of workers to head off strikes and isolated militants and divided them from trade union leadership. When disruptive strikes occurred, his policy was to ignore unauthorized representatives like shop stewards and negotiate only with formal trade union leadership. If there were stoppages in key industries, the state could not afford to wait out the strikers. In such instances, the government made generous concessions or, if the strikers proved unreasonable, exploited the widespread public support for the war to take a hard line. All in all, it is doubtful if any other major national political figure could have handled labor as skillfully as Lloyd George.

If manpower and labor were key factors impacting the issue of victory or defeat, shipping was another. J. A. Salter reminds us that control of shipping, as in the case of all state-controlled concerns during the war, was arrived at not by a conscious and deliberate policy, but by ad hoc and incremental measures.[2] As the conflict wore on, the demands on shipping mounted sharply owing to the need to supply the various theaters of war and Britain's allies, as well as to transport American troops across the Atlantic. At the same time, there was an alarming reduction in the quantity of shipping because of the depredations of the U-boats. It was left to Maclay to find an antidote to the shipping shortage. Lloyd George's trust in Maclay was not misplaced. Under Maclay, all merchant shipping was requisitioned, and space on board was allocated only to vital commodities. Nonessential imports were prohibited. The government purchased goods from the nearest sources, irrespective of costs. An ambitious shipbuilding program was initiated and orders were placed abroad for additional tonnage. A large body of servicemen joined dock workers to clear the congestion in home ports. Last but not least, the introduction of the convoy system, at a moment when the situation was almost desperate, had the effect of reducing shipping losses to tolerable levels. Collectively, these initiatives provided the right antidote. By the end of 1917 the shortage of shipping ceased to be a factor hampering the general war effort.

Still, the shipping shortage in 1916 and 1917 exacerbated the government's task to preserve the nation's food supply. Britain produced only part of its consumption of food in normal times and for the remainder relied on foreign purchases. During the first two years of the war, rural output in Britain, in fact, declined steadily on account of labor lost to industry and to the army, insufficient fertilizers and farm implements, requisitioning of horses by the military and poor harvests.

High on the Lloyd George government's priority list was to reduce the nation's dependence on imported food. Consequently, measures to increase home production were taken in hand: agricultural workers were exempted from military service; grassland and derelict areas were brought back into production; the state guaranteed minimum prices for certain commodities; higher wages were paid to agricultural laborers to encourage them to remain on the farm; large groups of women and boys assisted during the harvest period; and different chemicals, other than the prewar standard ones, were used to produce fertilizers. The government's food production policy was on the whole successful, resulting in a substantial increase in the stock of such commodities as cereals and potatoes, but, it must also be added, at the cost of a decrease in meat and dairy products.

Prices soared for articles in short supply and long lines in front of food stores became a common sight. The obvious solution would have been for the government to control prices and take charge of food distribution so as to spare the public hardship and avoid the resulting raging discontent. But the government was reluctant to embrace revolutionary change and preferred to rely on voluntary appeals. Lloyd George had expressed resentment towards Asquith for hesitating to take appropriate measures when necessary, and in the first weeks that he was in office, promised that he would bring a new dynamism in the management of the home front. But his rhetoric did not always translate into bold action. He pointed to working class prejudice against rationing to justify his cautious approach of "first exhausting the possibilities of voluntary control."[3] Those with an insider's knowledge, such as William Beveridge, did not agree with the prime minister's observation, insisting that the public would have accepted compulsory rationing at any time after 1916. He pointed out that once the rationing scheme went into effect in the early months of 1918, it operated smoothly and equitably, resulting in the disappearance of lines. Beveridge concludes as follows:

> The Ministry of Food ... accomplished what private enterprise in the War could never have accomplished. The British people were fed not only better and more cheaply ... than they could possibly have been fed in the War, but probably on the whole better than before the War, because wages were relatively high, work was regular and distribution fair.[4]

In grappling with the war, Lloyd George had more than his share of failures. It would be difficult to conceive of anything more destructive to the nation's interests in wartime than for a government and its High Command to be constantly at odds over the most effective way to fight the enemy. The time wasted by both sides in trying to outdo the other kept them from devoting their full energies to the pressing business of war, not to mention that it inhibited the development of a sound national strategy. A government has every right to replace a commander if it judges him to be ineffective, but at the same time is expected to fully support him as long as he is in charge of the nation's troops. Asquith had refrained from interfering in the execution of policy, but took steps to remove Sir John French once he finally determined that he was not up to the task. Churchill adopted the same approach with his generals during the Second World War. By contrast, Lloyd George kept the commander he inherited, but used every means he could think of to undermine him. He was contemptuous of Haig, viewing him as a second rate soldier without the necessary intelligence and flexibility to lead Britain's troops to victory.

Lloyd George maintained, with justification, that he could not have formed a ministry without agreeing to keep Haig in place. That being the case, the most sensible approach was to reach an accommodation with Haig and if he found him to be unacceptable after a reasonable trial, replace him when it was politically feasible to do so – like immediately after Cambrai. Had Lloyd George accepted the primacy of the western front, he would have won over Robertson and the two would have been able to induce Haig to abandon the hugely expensive attritional policy in favor of the Pétain tactics and to wait until the Americans became an effective ally before attempting to finish off Germany.

However, Lloyd George had made up his mind the moment he moved to 10 Downing Street, and as a result of his confrontational style, initiated the conflict with the generals. The crux of the problem was that Lloyd George believed that he could conduct the war effectively without the advice of his generals, but in reality he was a novice, as knowledgeable about strategy as he was about Russian literature. The prime minister's analogy that war, like politics, was uncomplicated and based on rules and common sense was plainly absurd. Nothing, or very little, is predictable in war. To apply strategy effectively is a difficult art and even carefully trained soldiers make errors. It certainly is beyond the grasp of amateurs, as Lloyd George proved repeatedly.

Lloyd George's peripheral strategy was designed to avoid the costly offensives on the western front and to defeat Germany by bringing down its weaker partners. He flitted from one half-baked scheme to another without seriously considering relevant factors such as logistics, terrain, interior versus exterior lines and probable enemy response. Even when operations were carried out successfully they were not worth the distraction and investment. While some benefits accrued, such as the effect on public morale and the security and expansion of the British Empire, they did not contribute to the destruction of the German army. The nature of the war on the western front precluded pursuing a policy of limited liability. There was no quick and cheap way to defeat the enemy. The German army could only be beaten on the western front, and even if Haig had employed more imaginative tactics in 1916 and 1917, the price of victory would have been tragically high.

As we have seen, there were dark periods in which Lloyd George, dubious about the chances of victory, appeared open to the idea of cutting a deal with the Germans. Going a step further, Professor Millman has argued that Lloyd George had sunk into gloom early on and under the right circumstances would have accepted a negotiated settlement. He adds that Lloyd George's new eastern strategy, where gains were expected at low costs, was designed to strengthen Britain's hand at the negotiating table.[5] It should be pointed out that Lloyd George frequently changed his mind and that not unlike the typical politician, sometimes said one thing and meant something else. I am therefore not convinced that Lloyd George had become a confirmed pessimist or that, when shove came to push, he would have settled for a draw. For one thing, he could not, without destroying his political career, renege on his promise to the British public to see the war through until victory was secured. But if Millman's scenario is accurate, can Lloyd George's eastern strategy be justified? Admittedly, it would have improve Britain's bargaining position, but to what end? Any compromise peace, even one that would have conceded to Britain its principal war aims in Europe and some of its territorial conquests elsewhere, would have left Germany dominant on the continent. Lloyd George and his colleagues fully understood that such an uneasy truce would have been broken sooner or later. All the British casualties (nearly 3,000,000 by November 1918) in the first war, in addition to the financial costs, would have been in vain. The second time around would have involved the two superpowers alone in a fight to the finish. Then, too, there is no guarantee that Britain would have triumphed in the second conflict. Thus, regardless from which direction Lloyd George's eastern policy is viewed, it was an expensive and faulty exercise.

Lloyd George's strategic misjudgments also extended to the western front. Because of his distrust of Haig, he sought to place the British army under the orders of an unproven French general. Had his original plan prevailed, the British army would have forfeited its independence and been compelled to fight at a time and in places that best suited French interests. It was only because Robertson and Haig strenuously resisted that the arrangement was not made permanent.

This brings up a related point that has been either overlooked or glossed over by historians of the period. Painlevé, the new French minister of war, had no confidence in Nivelle's contemplated offensive, but any justification he had to stop it vanished when Lloyd George threw his enthusiastic support behind it. The abysmal failure of Nivelle's offensive had profound consequences: it substantially reduced the effectiveness of the French army for a year, during which the BEF sustained massive casualties in carrying the fight to the Germans practically alone; and it may very well have prolonged the war.

CONCLUSION

No less lamentable was Lloyd George's role during the second phase of Passchendaele, which involved a quality of misery for the British army that is almost without parallel. To be sure, Haig must bear most of the responsibility. He chose the area of operations, and set goals that could not be achieved for want of necessary resources. When the offensive stalled, he elected to press on. He had given such lavish promises of success to the political leaders in London that it would have been undoubtedly embarrassing for him to call a halt and admit defeat. But he could not have proceeded without the acquiescence of the prime minister who refused to intervene, ignoring pleas by some members of the War Cabinet that he do so.

Perhaps the most damning indictment of Lloyd George was that he deliberately kept the British army short of recruits as a means to force Haig to change his methods. Although the prime minister had good cause to be wary of Haig, he lacked the moral courage to lay down policy, preferring to take a circuitous, rather than the direct, route. There was ample intelligence late in 1917 that the Germans were planning a massive assault in the spring before the concentration of Americans in the field gave the Entente overwhelming numerical superiority. In these circumstances, the most sensible approach for 1918 would have been to concentrate maximum resources on the western front, impose a defensive policy on Haig, and wait for the Americans to become a decisive factor before mounting an all-out offensive. But Lloyd George chose to play down intelligence reports as well as warnings by War Office military leaders, confident that the western front was "overinsured" and would have no difficulty in repelling any enemy assault. Considering what was at stake, it would have been immensely better to err on the side of caution. The manpower pool in the nation was shrinking rapidly by the end of 1917 and it is true that the army's large demands for drafts could not be met without disrupting war production and the economy. The government, however, could have supplemented the available drafts from home with the unnecessary number of British divisions overseas and replaced most of the remaining ones with units from India and Africa, and this move might have prevented, or at least minimized, the damage of the German breakthrough in the spring of 1918. The prime minister erred again when he coerced Haig into extending his front in order to release a French army of six divisions late in 1917. Before Haig could initiate the movement, he was ordered to send five divisions southwards to prop up the Italian army in the wake of Caporetto. Haig was guilty of exercising poor judgment prior to and during the early stages of the German onslaught, but it is equally true that he had less troops to defend a more extensive front. The upshot was that the British army came closer to total defeat than at any other period in the war.

There were occasional rays of light in Lloyd George's conduct of the war. He understood that coalition warfare imposed restrictions on Britain's freedom of action in the west. He showed himself to be a generous partner, deferring to the French, more often, perhaps, than he should have, considering that the BEF shouldered the brunt of the fighting after the spring of 1917 and that a good portion of British shipping was diverted to supply the nation's allies. He made great efforts to establish a Supreme War Council and to bring the Entente armies under a single command. Lloyd George may have been driven for selfish reasons, but both innovations aided in the march towards victory. It should also be pointed out that he collaborated with the French to help the Italian army stop the Austrian advance. By keeping Italy in the war, the Austrians were unable to shift some of their divisions to the western front to assist Ludendorff in the spring and summer of 1918.[6] Lastly, Lloyd George, in helping draft the terms of the armistice, fought hard to protect British interests.

Although a brilliant orator, Lloyd George fell considerably short of matching the heroic status Churchill would attain during the Second World War. Part of the reason was that his stirring speeches were not heard by a wide audience. They were usually delivered in a hall before a limited number of spectators and not over the radio – which was not readily accessible to the public at the time – when they could have struck a responsive chord with householders. Much of Lloyd George's image was shaped by the press. Universally welcomed as a man of action, dynamic energy and unsurpassed ability when he elbowed Asquith out of the premiership, his approval rating was high for the next eight or ten months, notwithstanding that the course of the war went from bad to worse with blood-draining losses in futile offensives on the western front, a submarine crisis that threatened to starve the British into submission, the French army crippled by a mutiny in many of its units and the impending loss of Russia. A section of the press began to turn against him towards the latter part of 1917 because of his duplicity, missteps and deepening struggle with the High Command over strategy. The faultfinding continued with increasing frequency and virulence until the tide turned in the summer of 1918. To what extent the steady drumbeat of criticism damaged Lloyd George's standing with the nation cannot be measured with any certainty. It is difficult to avoid the conclusion, however, that it could not have helped but reduce public confidence in his leadership. In fact, if there had been a prime-minister-in-waiting, it is doubtful that he would have survived the war.

One more angle needs to be covered. The late John Grigg reminds us that Lloyd George was in many respects a pioneer, facing "tasks and challenges that were without precedent."[7] That is certainly a consideration in appraising his work, but should not be given undue weight. After all, the same argument can be applied to Asquith during the first two years of the war and it need not be emphasized that contemporaries and practically all historians, including Grigg, have judged his stewardship inadequate.

After all that has been said and done, what are we to make of Lloyd George's legacy as a war leader? On the home front he achieved varied results in tackling difficult, and in some instances, unprecedented problems. It would be hard to have improved on his dealings with labor and the program to increase homegrown food, but in the sectors of manpower, price control and food distribution he adopted the same approach as his predecessor, taking action only in response to the changing nature of the conflict. In the vital area of national morale, while he did not have the technical advantages of Churchill, his personal conduct damaged his ability to do more to inspire the nation. All things considered, it is unlikely that any of his political contemporaries could have handled matters at home as effectively as he did, although it can be argued that if someone else had been in charge, the difference would not have been sufficient to change the final outcome. In his conduct of the war he did advance the cause of the Entente significantly in some ways, but in determining strategy, one of the most important tasks for which a prime minister must be responsible, he was undeniably a failure. To sum up, while Lloyd George's contributions outweighed his mistakes, the margin is too narrow, in my opinion, to include him in the pantheon of Britain's outstanding war leaders.

NOTES

Preface

1 Kenneth O. Morgan, *Lloyd George* (London: Weidenfeld and Nicolson, 1974), 10.
2 A. J. P. Taylor's introduction to Morgan, *Lloyd George*, 7.

1. Setting the Stage

1 John Grigg, *The Young Lloyd George* (London: Eyre Methuen, 1973), 32–33.
2 Peter Rowland, *Lloyd George* (London: Barrie and Jenkins, 1975), 41–42.
3 Grigg, *Young Lloyd George*, 45–46.
4 Bentley B. Gilbert, *David Lloyd George: Architect of Change, 1863–1912*, vol. 1 (Columbus: Ohio State University Press, 1978), 46–47.
5 Grigg, *Young Lloyd George*, 59.
6 Richard Lloyd George, *My Father Lloyd George* (New York: Crown, 1961), 53–58; Lady Olwen Carey Evans, *Lloyd George was my Father* (Llandysul: Gomer Press, 1985), 63–68.
7 Kenneth O. Morgan, ed., *Lloyd George: Family Letters, 1885–1936* (Cardiff and London: University of Wales Press/Oxford University Press, 1973), 14.
8 Don M. Cregier, *Bounder From Wales*, (Columbia: University of Missouri Press, 1976), 36.
9 Rowland, *Lloyd George*, chs. 4–6.
10 Cregier, *Bounder*, 72–74.
11 Unless otherwise stated the material for Lloyd George's political career between 1906 and 1916 is drawn from the following sources: Gilbert, *David Lloyd George*, vol. 1, and the sequel *David Lloyd George: The Organizer of Victory, 1912–1916*, vol. 2 (London: Batsford, 1990); Grigg, *The Young Lloyd George*, and the next two volumes *Lloyd George: the People's Champion, 1902–1911* (Berkley: University of California Press, 1978) and *Lloyd George: From Peace to War, 1912–1916* (Berkley: University of California Press, 1985); Cregier, *Bounder*; and Rowland, *Lloyd George*.
12 For the details of the affair, see Francis Donaldson, *The Marconi Scandal* (London: Hart-Davis, 1962).
13 Roy Jenkins, *Asquith* (London: Collins, rev. ed., 1978), 252–53.
14 Michael G. Fry, *Lloyd George and Foreign Policy*, vol. 1 (Montreal: McGill-Queen's University Press, 1977), 213.
15 David French, *British Strategy and War Aims, 1914–1916* (London: Allen and Unwin, 1986), ch. 1.
16 Morgan, *Family Letters*, 169.

17 The political crisis in May 1915 is described in detail in Lord Beaverbrook, *Politicians and the War, 1914–1916* (London: Oldbourne, 1960) bk. 1, ch. 8; Roy Jenkins, *Asquith*, 355–62; Robert Blake, *The Unknown Prime Minister* (London: Spottiswood, 1955), 242–47; R. J. Q. Adams, *Bonar Law* (Stanford: Stanford University Press, 1999), 181–88; Cameron Hazlehurst, *Politicians at War* (London: Jonathan Cape, 1971), pt. 3; George H. Cassar, *Asquith as War Leader* (London: Hambleton Press, 1994), ch. 6.

18 For a very favorable view of Lloyd George's stint at the Ministry of Munitions see R. J. Q. Adams, *Arms and the Wizard: Lloyd George and the Ministry of Munitions* (College Station, TX: Texas A and M University Press, 1978).

19 For an in-depth treatment on the origins of the Salonica campaign see Roy A. Prete, "Imbroglio Par Excellence: Mounting the Salonika Campaign, September–October 1915," *War and Society* 19 (2001), 47–70; George H. Cassar, *The French and the Dardanelles* (London: Allen and Unwin, 1971), ch. 8; Jan K. Tanenbaum, *General Maurice Sarrail, 1856–1929* (Chapel Hill: University of North Carolina Press, 1974), ch. 4.

20 The contentious issue of conscription is ably told by R. J. Q. Adams and Philip P. Poirier, *The Conscription Controversy in Great Britain, 1900–1918* (London: Macmillan, 1987) and Keith Grieves, *The Politics of Manpower, 1914–1918* (Manchester: Manchester University Press, 1988).

21 Cassar, *Asquith*, 149–64.

22 Cassar, *Asquith*, 186–88.

23 French, *British Strategy*, 228.

24 The text is reproduced in its entirety in Grigg, *Lloyd George: From Peace to War*, 424–28.

25 David Lloyd George, *The Great Crusade* (New York: Doran, 1918), 11–18.

26 Beaverbrook, *Politicians*, chs 26–41; Robert Blake, *The Unknown Prime Minister* (London: Eyre and Spottiswoode, 1955), chs 19 and 20; Trevor Wilson, *The Downfall of the Liberal Party, 1914–1935* (London: Collins, 1966), ch. 4 and appendix, and *The Myriad Faces of War* (Cambridge: Polity Press, 1986), 418–23; Jenkins, *Asquith*, chs 26–27; and Cassar, *Asquith*, ch. 12, are among the many books dealing with the rise of Lloyd George to the premiership.

27 See, for example, Philip Williamson, ed., *The Modernisation of Conservative Politics: The Diaries and Letters of William Bridgeman* (London: Historians' Press, 1988), 110. A prominent Conservative, Bridgeman served as the first Parliamentary Secretary of the Ministry of Labor.

28 Malcolm Thompson, *David Lloyd George* (London: Hutchinson, 1949), 20.

29 A. J. Sylvester, *The Real Lloyd George* (London: Cassell, 1947), 3.

30 Thompson, *David Lloyd George*, 18.

31 Lord Hankey, *Supreme Command, 1914–1918* (London: Allen and Unwin, 1961), vol. 2, 576.

32 Thomas Jones, *Lloyd George* (Cambridge University Press, 1951), 264–65.

33 Richard Lloyd George, *My Father, Lloyd George* (New York: Crown, 1961), passim; Lady Olwen Carey Evans, *Lloyd George Was My Father* (Llandysul: Gomer Press, 1985), also dwells upon her father's infidelities in ch. 5.

34 Lord Beaverbrook, *Men and Power, 1917–1918* (London: Hutchinson, 1956), xvii.

35 Alfred Gollin, *Proconsul in Politics* (London: Blond, 1964), 387.

36 John Maynard Keynes, *Essays in Biography* (New York: Harcourt, Brace and Co., 1933), 37.

37 Cited in Martin Gilbert, *Winston Churchill*, vol. 3 (Boston: Houghton Mifflin, 1971), 623.

38 Cited in David Marquand, *Ramsday MacDonald* (London: Jonathan Cape 1977), 527.

39 A. J. P. Taylor, *English History, 1914–1945* (Oxford: Oxford University Press, 1965), 74.

40 Thompson, *David Lloyd George*, 265.

NOTES

41 Jenkins, *Asquith*, 464–65.
42 David French, *The Strategy of the Lloyd George Coalition, 1916–1918* (Oxford Clarendon Press, 1995), 19.
43 Bertie to Hardinge, Bertie Papers, FO 800/191.
44 Beaverbrook, *Men and Power*, xvi; Grigg, *Lloyd George; From Peace to War*, 490.
45 French, *Lloyd George Coalition*, 19; Grigg, *Lloyd George: From Peace to War*, 483–85; Lloyd George, *War Memoirs*, vol. 1, 607–9.
46 H. A. L. Fisher, *An Unfinished Autobiography* (London: Oxford University Press, 1941), 91–92.
47 David Lloyd George, *War Memoirs*, vol. 1 (London: Odhams, 1938), 642.
48 Grigg, *Lloyd George: From Peace to War*, 492–94.
49 Lord Hankey, *Government Control in War* (Cambridge: Cambridge University Press, 1945), 40–44; John Ehrman, *Cabinet Government and War, 1890–1940* (Cambridge University Press, 1958), 71–76.
50 Paul Guinn, *British Strategy and Politics, 1914 to 1918* (Oxford: Clarendon Press, 1965), 191; Rowland, *Lloyd George*, 381; Stephen Roskill, *Hankey: Man of Secrets*, vol. 1 (London: Collins, 1970), 325; L. S. Amery, *My Political Life*, vol. 2 (London: Hutchinson: 1953), 97.
51 Blake, *Unknown Prime Minister*, 342–45; Adams, *Bonar Law*, 248–49; Rowland, *Lloyd George*, 373–74; Hankey, *Supreme Command*, vol. 2, 577–78; Lloyd George, *War Memoirs*, vol. 1, 609–615; Beaverbrook, *Men and Power*, xix–xx; Keynes, *Essays*, ch. 3.
52 David Gilmour, *Curzon* (New York: Farrar, Straus and Giroux, 2003), passim; Winston S. Churchill, *Great Contemporaries* (London: Odhams Press, 1949), 219; Beaverbrook, *Men and Power*, 322–23; Hankey, *Supreme Command*, vol. 2, 578; Frank Owen, *Tempestuous Journey* (New York: McGraw-Hill, 1955), 405–6; Jones, *Lloyd George*, 97.
53 P. A. Lockwood, "Milner's entry into the War Cabinet, December 1916," *Historical Journal* 7 (1964), 120–34; Hankey, *Supreme Command*, vol. 2, 578–79; Amery, *Political Life*, vol. 2, 98.
54 Fisher, *Unfinished Autobiography*, 135.
55 John Grigg, *Lloyd George: War Leader, 1916–1918* (London: Allen Lane, 2002), 13–14; A. J. Marder, *From the Dreadnought to Scapa Flow*, vol. 4 (London: Oxford University Press, 1969), 62; French, *Lloyd George Coalition*, Roskill, *Hankey*, vol. 1, passim.
56 John F. Naylor, "The Establishment of the Cabinet Secretariat," *Historical Journal* 4 (!971), 790–92.
57 The best account on this subject is John Turner, *Lloyd George's Secretariat* (Cambridge: Cambridge University Press, 1980).
58 Lloyd George, *War Memoirs*, vol. 1, 643.
59 Owen, *Tempestuous Journey*, 406–7.
60 Roskill, *Hankey*, vol. 1, 353–54.
61 John Turner, "Cabinets, Committees and Secretariats: The Higher Direction of War," in *War and the State*, ed. Kathleen Burke (London: Allen and Unwin, 1982), 57; John M. Bourne, *Britain and the Great War, 1914–1918* (London: Edward Arnold, 1989), 130.
62 Roskill, *Hankey*, vol. 1, 353.
63 Roskill, *Hankey*, vol. 1, 370–71.
64 Turner, "Cabinet, Committees and Secretariats," 64–67.
65 John Ehrman, "Lloyd George and Churchill as War Ministers," in *Transactions of the Royal Historical Society*, ser. 5, vol. 11 (London: Royal Historical Society, 1961), 105–6.

2. The Search for a Manpower Policy

1. Keith Grieves, *The Politics of Manpower, 1914–1918* (Manchester: Manchester University, 1988), 1–5.
2. P. E. Dewey, "Military Recruiting and the British Labour Force during the First World War," *Historical Journal* 27 (1984), 199–223; David French, *British Strategy and War Aims, 1914–1916* (London: Allen and Unwin, 1986), 15, 25–26.
3. Humbert Wolfe, *Labour Supply and Regulation* (Oxford: Clarendon Press, 1923), 20–35.
4. Dewey, "Military Recruiting and the British Labour Force," 215.
5. Grieves, *Politics of Manpower*, 31–37; Wolfe, *Labour Supply*, 40; Chris Wrigley, *David Lloyd George and the British Labour Movement* (New York: Barnes and Noble Books, 1976), 168; R. J. Q. Adams and Philip P. Poirier, *The Conscription Controversy in Great Britain, 1900–1918* (Columbus: Ohio State University Press, 1987), 177–78.
6. James Hinton, *The First Shop Stewards' Movement* (London: Allen and Unwin, 1973), 38–39; Adams and Poirier, *Conscription Controversy*, 179–81; Wolfe, *Labour Supply*, 44–45.
7. French, *British Strategy*, 225–27; Grieves, *Politics of Manpower*, 36–37, 68, 75–76; Adams and Poirier, *Conscription Controversy*, 190–91.
8. A. Geddes, "General Review, Manpower Position," December 12, 1916, A. Chamberlain papers, AC 16/1/24.
9. Minutes of the War Cabinet, December 14, 1916, CAB 23/1.
10. Minutes of the War Cabinet, December 19, 1916, CAB 23/1.
11. Keith Feiling, *The Life of Neville Chamberlain* (London: Macmillan, 1946), 64; Sir Charles Petrie, *The Life and Letters of Rt. Hon. Sir Austen Chamberlain*, vol. 2 (London: Cassell, 1940), 63–64.
12. David Dilks, *Neville Chamberlain*, vol. 1 (Cambridge: Cambridge University Press, 1984), 200.
13. David Lloyd George, *War Memoirs*, vol. 1 (London: Odham Press, 1938), 642.
14. Grieves, *Politics of Manpower*, passim; John Grigg, *Lloyd George: War Leader 1916–1918* (London: Allen Lane, 2002), 212–13.
15. Dilks, *Chamberlain*, 202.
16. Parliamentary Debates, *House of Commons*, December 19, 1916, vol. 88, cols. 1333–1358.
17. Proceedings at a Conference held on January 12, 1917, annexed to the minutes of the War Cabinet for the same day, CAB 23/1, Appendix IV.
18. "Report by the Director-General of National Service to the War Cabinet." The paper is annexed to the minutes of the War Cabinet for January 19, 1917, CAB 23/1.
19. Minutes of the War Cabinet, January 19, 1917, CAB 23/1.
20. Field Marshal Sir William Robertson, *Soldiers and Statesmen, 1914–1918*, vol. 1 (London: Cassell, 1926), 308.
21. "Memorandum by the Army Council Regarding the Supply of Men for the Army," February 2, 1917, annexed to the minutes of the War Cabinet for February 5, 1917, CAB 23/1.
22. N. Chamberlain, "Second Report of the Director-General of National Service," February 3, 1917, annexed to the minutes of the War Cabinet for February 5, 1917, CAB 23/1.
23. Charles à Court Repington, *The First World War*, vol. 1 (Boston: Houghton Mifflin, 1921), 454–55.
24. Dilks, *Chamberlain*, vol. 1, 219–20; Grieves, *Politics of Manpower*, 109–10.
25. Grieves, *Politics of Manpower*, 112.
26. Lloyd George to N. Chamberlain, February 20, 1917, N. Chamberlain papers, NC 8/5/2/19; Lloyd George to Derby, January 22, 1917, Lloyd George papers, F/14/4/16.

27 Minutes of the War Cabinet, March 1, 1917, CAB 23/2.
28 Dilks, *Chamberlain*, vol. 1, 223.
29 Robert Self, ed., *The Neville Chamberlain Diary Letters*, vol. 1 (Aldershot: Ashgate, 2000), 367.
30 Rhondda, "Military Service Exemptions," March 21, 1917, CAB 24/8/GT244.
31 Minutes of the War Cabinet, March 23, 1917, CAB 23/2.
32 Robertson, *Soldiers and Statesmen*, vol. 1, 311.
33 Derby to Lloyd George, May 19, 1917, Lloyd George papers, F/14/4/44.
34 Robertson to Haig, May 26, 1917, Robertson papers, 7/7/27.
35 "Memorandum by the Adjutant–General Regarding the Position and Prospects of Recruiting," May 31, 1917, Robertson papers, 4/2/10.
36 N. Chamberlain, Tenth Report, June 22, 1917, N. Chamberlain papers, NC 8/5/4/12.
37 N. Chamberlain to Lloyd George, June 29, 1917, Lloyd George papers, F/7/1/8.
38 Lloyd George to N. Chamberlain, July 3, 1917, N. Chamberlain papers, NC 8/5/2/25.
39 N. Chamberlain to Lloyd George, July 4, 1917, N. Chamberlain papers, NC 8/5/2/26.
40 Self, ed., *Neville Chamberlain*, 209.
41 Memorandum by N. Chamberlain et al, "Manpower," July 18, 1917, CAB 24/20/1445.
42 N. Chamberlain to Lloyd George, July 19, 1917, Lloyd George papers, F/7/1/11.
43 Lloyd George to N. Chamberlain, July 20, 1917, N. Chamberlain papers, 8/5/2/28.
44 N. Chamberlain to Lloyd George, July 21, 1917, N. Chamberlain papers, NC 8/5/2/29.
45 A. Geddes, "The Theory and Practice of Recruiting," July 23, 1917, CAB 24/20/GT1481.
46 Grieves, *Politics of Manpower*, 134.
47 Dilks, *Chamberlain*, vol. 1, 243–44; Grieves, *Politics of Manpower*, 135.
48 N. Chamberlain to Lloyd George, August 8, 1917, N. Chamberlain papers, NC 8/5/2/31.
Chamberlain, diary of the events between August 7 and 9, 1917, N. Chamberlain papers, NC 8/5/4/17.
49 Lloyd George to N. Chamberlain, August 10, 1917, N. Chamberlain papers, NC 8/5/2/32.
50 Adams and Poirier, *Conscription Controversy*, 212.
51 Grieves, *Politics of Manpower*, 138–39.
52 A. Geddes to Lloyd George, August 13, 1917, Lloyd George papers, F/38/2/17.
53 Grieves, *Politics of Manpower*, 139.
54 Lloyd George, *War Memoirs*, vol. 1, 812–13.
55 A. Geddes, "Recruiting Position. The Problem and Prospects," October 13, 1917, CAB 24/28/GT2295.
56 Minutes of the War Cabinet, November 26, 1917, CAB 23/13.
57 A. Geddes, "Memorandum on Man-Power," November 17, 1917, CAB 24/4/G174.
58 Minutes of the War Cabinet, December 3 and 6, 1917, CAB 23/4.
59 Grieves, *Politics of Manpower*, 114.
60 Minutes of the War Cabinet, December 10, 1917, CAB 23/4.
61 Chris Wrigley, *David Lloyd George*, 224.
62 Grieves, *Politics of Manpower*, 182–83.
63 Minutes of the War Cabinet, March 23–25, 1918, CAB 23/5.
64 A. Geddes, "Amendment of Military Service Acts," March 26, 1918, CAB 24/46/GT4036.
65 Barnes to Lloyd George, March 26, 1918, Lloyd George papers, F/4/2/26.

66 Alan J. Ward, "Lloyd George and the 1918 Irish Conscription Crisis," *Historical Journal* 17 (1974): 111; Minutes of the War Cabinet, March 29, 1918, CAB 23/5.
67 Minutes of the War Cabinet, March 27, 1918, CAB 23/5; Lloyd George, *War Memoirs*, vol. 2, 1598–99.
68 French to Lloyd George, March 5, 1918, Lloyd George papers, F/48/6/5; Minutes of the War Cabinet, March 25, 1918, CAB 23/5.
69 Malcolm Thomson, *David Lloyd George* (London: Hutchinson, 1948), 292.
70 Ward, "Lloyd George and the 1918 Irish Conscription Crisis," 127.
71 Minutes of the War Cabinet, March 29, 1918, CAB 23/5.
72 "Draft of a Bill," April 3, 1918, CAB 24/47/GT4124.
73 John Turner, *British Politics and the Great War* (New Haven: Yale University Press, 1992), 289.
74 Ward, "Lloyd George and the 1918 Irish Conscription Crisis," 114.
75 Devised by Asquith in the fall of 1915 as a means to delay compulsion, the scheme was named after the Earl of Derby, then the Director of Recruiting and the man responsible for administering it. Under the plan, males between the ages of 18 and 41 were invited to pledge their willingness to serve if summoned, with the assurance that married men would not be called up until all the bachelors had joined the colors.
76 Adams and Poirier, *Conscription Controversy*, 238.
77 Ward, "Lloyd George and the 1918 Irish Conscription Crisis," 126.
78 Grieves, *Politics of Manpower*, 196.

3. The Challenge of Labor

1 David Lloyd George, *War Memoirs*, vol. 2 (London: Odhams, 1938), 1141.
2 The material for the paragraph was drawn from the second report of a committee that Winston Churchill, then Minister of Munitions, set up after the strike at Coventry in July 1918 (about which more will be said later in this chapter) to investigate the causes of the industrial unrest. Of the two reports, the second one was more comprehensive and was submitted in December 1918, a month after the armistice. See Humbert Wolfe, *Labour Supply and Regulation* (Oxford: Clarendon Press, 1923), 143–47.
3 Chris Wrigley, *David Lloyd George and the British Labour Movement* (Hassocks: Harvester Press, 1976), 76.
4 Trevor Wilson, *The Myriad Faces of War* (Cambridge: Polity Press, 1986), 221–27; John Grigg, Lloyd George: From Peace to War, 1912–1916 (Berkeley: University of California Press, 1985), 218–20, 265–67; Pelling, *A History of British Trade Unionism* (London: Macmillan, 1987), 150–53.
5 Grigg, *Lloyd George: From Peace to War*, 218.
6 Mary Davis, *Comerade or Brother: A History of the British Labour Movement, 1789–1951* (London: Pluto Press, 1993), 116ff; Chris Wrigley, "Trade Unions and Politics in the First World War," in *Trade Unions in British Politics*, ed. Ben Pimlott and Chris Cook (London: Longman, 1982), 81–82; Branco Pribićević, *The Shop Steward's Movement and Worker's Control, 1910–1922* (Oxford: Basil Blackwell, 1959), passim; Walter Kendall, *Revolutionary Movement in Britain, 1900–1921* (London; Weidenfeld and Nicolson, 1969), 149–69.
7 Wrigley, *David Lloyd George*, 177–78.
8 Wrigley, *David Lloyd George*, passim.
9 Passed in 1914 and 1915, the three Defence of the Realm Acts (DORA) gave the government broad powers to take whatever measures it deemed necessary for the public safety and defense of the country, including restricting civil liberties and requisitioning factories and controlling production.

10 Minutes of the War Cabinet, April 2, 1917, CAB 23/2.
11 Lloyd George, *War Memoirs*, vol. 2, 1149.
12 James Hinton, *The First Shop Stewards' Movement* (London: Allen and Unwin, 1973), 198–99.
13 Keith Middlemas, *Politics in Industrial Society* (London: André Deutsch, 1979), 101–2.
14 Lloyd George, *War Memoirs*, vol. 2, 1149–50.
15 Earlier in the war (during Asquith's tenure), Lloyd George had toyed with the idea of bypassing union officials and attempting to strike a deal with the shop stewards, but was dissuaded from following through. See Middlemas, *Politics*, 81.
16 Christopher Addison, *Four and a Half Years*, vol. 2 (London: Hutchinson, 1934), 382.
17 Minutes of the War Cabinet, May 16, 1918, CAB 23/2.
18 Hinton, *Shop Stewards' Movement*, 205–6.
19 Addison, *Four and a Half Years*, 382–83; Hinton, *Shop Stewards' Movement*, 206; Wrigley, *David Lloyd George*, 195–96.
20 Addison, *Four and a Half Years*, 383–86.
21 Addison, *Four and a Half Years*, 386.
22 John Grigg, *Lloyd George: War Leader, 1916–1918* (London: Allen Lane, 2002), 113.
23 Kenneth and Jane Morgan, *Portrait of a Progressive: The Political Career of Christopher, Viscount Addison* (Oxford: Clarendon Press, 1980), 65. The events leading to his resignation and break with Lloyd George are examined in detail in ch. 5.
24 Lloyd George, *War Memoirs*, vol. 2, 1152.
25 Wrigley, *David Lloyd George*, 198–204.
26 Lloyd George, *War Memoirs*, vol. 2, 1153–54.
27 Minutes of the War Cabinet, May 25, 1917, CAB 23/2.
28 Lloyd George, *War Memoirs*, vol. 2, 1154.
29 Accounts of the conference are available in Stephen R. Graubard, *British Labour and the Russian Revolution, 1917–1914* (Cambridge: Harvard University Press, 1956), 36–40; Ralph Miliband, *Parliamentary Socialism* (London: Merlin Press, 1973), 55–57; Kendall, *Revolutionary Movement*, 174–76.
30 Cited in Wilson, *Myriad Faces*, 522.
31 Wrigley, *David Lloyd George*, 206; Carl F. Brand, *The British Labour Party* (Stanford: Stanford University Press, 1964), 45–46;
32 Minutes of the War Cabinet, May 11, 1917, CAB 23/2.
33 From the moment of its inception, the Provisional Government was challenged by the more radical Petrograd Soviet, a self-appointed council of workers and soldiers. Similar councils sprang up in other cities, but the one in Petrograd maintained its preeminence because of its location in the capital where power had traditionally been concentrated. Organized principally by Social Revolutionaries and Mensheviks, the new Soviets had their own program, which included land reform, worker democracy and a speedy end to the war against Germany.
34 Lloyd George, *War Memoirs*, vol. 2, 1119–20.
35 F. L. Carsten, *War Against War: British and German Radical Movements in the First World War* (Berkeley: University of California Press, 1982), 98.
36 Lloyd George, *War Memoirs*, vol. 2, 1120.
37 Minutes of the War Cabinet, May 16, 1917, CAB 23/2.
38 Minutes of the War Cabinet, May 21, 1917, CAB 23/2.
39 Minutes of the War Cabinet, May 23, 1917, CAB 23/2.
40 Lloyd George, *War Memoirs*, vol. 2, 1124.
41 J. M. Winter, "Arthur Henderson, the Russian Revolution, and the Reconstruction of the Labour Party," *Historical Journal* 15 (1972), 766–67.

42 Wrigley, *David Lloyd George*, 211; Chris Wrigley, *Arthur Henderson* (Cardiff: GPC Books, 1990), 117.
43 Trevor Wilson, ed., *The Political Diaries of C. P. Scot, 1911–1928* (Ithaca: Cornell University Press, 1969), 297. Scott recorded his entries after talks with Curzon and Lloyd George; Wrigley, *David Lloyd George*, 211–12.
44 Minutes of the War Cabinet, June 26, 1917, CAB 23/3.
45 Lloyd George, *War Memoirs*, vol. 2, 1127.
46 Lloyd George, *War Memoirs*, vol. 2, 1128–29.
47 Minutes of the War Cabinet, August 1, 1917, CAB 23/3.
48 Minutes of the War Cabinet, August 1, 1917, CAB 23/13.
49 Milner to Curzon, August 2, 1917, Curzon papers, EUR F 112/113.
50 Carson to Lloyd George, August 4, 1917, Lloyd George papers, F/6/2/42.
51 Carson to Lloyd George, August 7, 1917, Lloyd George papers, F/6/2/43. Carson submitted a third note on August 8. It can also be found in the Lloyd George papers, F/6/2/44.
52 Amery to Lloyd George August 7, 1917, and a memorandum, "The Stockholm Conference," Lloyd George papers, F/2/1/5.
53 Wrigley, *David Lloyd George*, 214–15.
54 Wrigley, *Arthur Henderson*, 118.
55 Minutes of the War Cabinet, August 8, 1917, CAB 23/3.
56 F. M. Leventhal, *Arthur Henderson* (Manchester: Manchester University Press, 1989), 68.
57 Leventhal, *Arthur Henderson*, 69.
58 Wrigley, *Arthur Henderson*, 120.
59 The Labour party and the Trades Union Congress, "Memorandum on War Aims", December 28, 1917, CAB 24/37/GT3167.
60 Minutes of the War Cabinet, December 31, 1917, CAB 23/4.
61 Hinton, *Shop Stewards' Movement*, 259.
62 Wrigley, *David Lloyd George*, 227–29.
63 Minutes of the War Cabinet, July 24, 1918, CAB 23/7.
64 The statement of July 26 can be found in the Lloyd George papers, F/79/4/31.

4. Controlling Shipping and Food

1 C. Ernest Fayle, *The War and the Shipping Industry* (London: Oxford University Press, 1927), passim; and *Seaborne Trade*, vols 2 and 3 (London: John Murray, 1923–1924), passim; Sidney Pollard, *The Development of the British Economy, 1914–1950* (London: Edward Arnold, 1962), 48; David Lloyd George, *War Memoirs*, vol. 1 (London: Odhams, 1938), 718–21.
2 Fayle, *War and the Shipping Industry*, 161–62, 192–93; and *Seaborne Trade*, vol. 3, 5–6; J. A. Salter, *Allied Shipping Control* (Oxford: Clarendon Press, 1921), 64–66; Lloyd George, *War Memoirs*, vol. 1, 1938), 722–26; Minutes of the War Committee, November 13, 1916, CAB 42/24/5; L. Margaret Barnett, *British Food Policy During the First World War* (London: Allen and Unwin, 1985), 73–74.
3 Fayle, *Seaborne Trade*, vol. 3, 1–8.
4 Lloyd George, *War Memoirs*, vol. 1, 726.
5 Fayle, *Seaborne Trade*, vol. 2, 380–81.
6 Lloyd George, *War Memoirs*, vol. 1, 726–27
7 Parliamentary Debates, *House of Commons*, December 19, 1916, vol. 88, col. 1345.

8. John Grigg, *Lloyd George: War Leader: 1916–1918* (London: Allen Lane, 2002), 47–48.
9. Lloyd George, *War Memoirs*, vol. 1, 731.
10. Parliamentary Debates, *House of Commons*, December 19, 1916, vol. 88, col. 1345–46.
11. Maclay to Lloyd George, February 2, 1917, in Lloyd George, *War Memoirs*, vol. 1, 731–32; Maclay, "Nationalization of Shipping ," annexed to the minutes of the War Cabinet, January 26, 1917, CAB 23/1.
12. Minutes of the War Cabinet, February 12, 1917, CAB 23/1.
13. Minutes of the War Cabinet, April 10 and 17, 1917, CAB 23/2.
14. A. J. Marder, *From the Dreadnought to Scapa Flow*, vol. 4 (London: Oxford University Press, 1969), 102.
15. David French, *The Strategy of the Lloyd George Coalition, 1916–1918* (Oxford: Clarendon Press, 1995), 74.
16. French, *Lloyd George Coalition*, 74; Minutes of the War Cabinet, March 2 and April 4, 1917, CAB 23/2. Maclay, "Building of Merchant Ships at Home and Abroad," February 28, 1917, annexed to the minutes of the War Cabinet of March 2.
17. John Terraine, *Business in Great Waters: The U-Boat Wars, 1916–1945* (London: Leo Cooper, 1989), 766.
18. Jellicoe, "Total Number of Vessels and Estimated Tonnage Under Construction," May 31, 1917, CAB 24/16/GT1071; Ministry of Shipping, "Notes on the Tonnage Position and the Necessity for a Greatly Extended Building Programme," May 31, 1917, CAB 24/15/GT982.
19. E. Geddes, "Report on Shipping Sitiation," July 5, 1917, CAB 24/19/GT1312.
20. French, *Lloyd George Coalition*, 76.
21. Terraine, *Business in Great Waters*, 766.
22. Keith Grieves, *Sir Eric Geddes* (Manchester: Manchester University Press, 1989), 42–43.
23. Money, "Proposal to Secure Absolutely the National Safety by Concentrating Shipping in the Atlantic," May 4, 1917, CAB 24/12/GT660; Money, "Shipping Strategy and the Submarine Attack," May 7, 1917, CAB 24/12/GT698; Money, "Shipping Strategy and the Atlantic," May 11,1917, CAB 24/13/GT711.
24. Minutes of the War Cabinet, May 14 and 30, 1917, CAB 23/2.
25. As reported by Marder, *From the Dreadnought*, vol. 4, 69.
26. Marder, *From the Dreadnought*, vol. 4, 66–68.
27. Lloyd George, *War Memoirs*, vol. 1, 750–54.
28. Thomas H. Middleton, *Food Production in War* (Oxford: Clarendon Press, 1923), 160–61; Lloyd George, *War Memoirs*, vol. 1, 757.
29. See his speech on December 19, 1916, in House of Commons, *Parliamentary Debates*, vol. 88, cols. 1346–47.
30. C. S. Orwin, article on Prothero in *Dictionary of National Biography, 1931–1940*.
31. Lord Ernle, *Whippingham: The Reminiscenes of Lord Ernle* (London: John Murray, 1938), 285.
32. Ernle, *Whippingham*, 290–91.
33. P. E. Dewey, *British Agriculture in the First World War* (London: Routledge, 1989), 92–93.
34. Ernle, *Whippingham*, 292–93; Middleton, *Food Production*, 168–69. The work of the County Executive Committees is described in detail in Dewey, *British Agriculture*, ch. 12.
35. Middleton, *Food Production*, 166.
36. Ernle, *Whippingham*, 309–10.
37. Grigg, *Lloyd George: War Leader*, 131.
38. Minutes of the War Cabinet, December 13, 1916, and January 12, 1917, CAB 23/1.
39. Dewey, *British Agriculture*, 93–95.
40. Dewey, *British Agriculture*, 96.

41 Lloyd George to Derby, January 22, 1917, Lloyd George papers, F/14/4/16.
42 Barnett, *British Food Policy*, 201; Ernle, *Whippingham*, 297–98.
43 Dewey, *British Agriculture*, 106–7.
44 Lloyd George, *War Memoirs*, vol. 1, 780–81.
45 See especially Dewey, *British Agriculture*, Ch. 9.
46 Barnett, *British Food Policy*, 199; Alan Clark, ed., *"A Good Innings": the Private Papers of Viscount Lee of Fareham* (London: John Murray, 1974), 166–67.
47 Barnett, *British Food Policy*, 201.
48 Lloyd George, Speech at Guildhall, April 27, 1918, Lloyd George papers, F/232.
49 Middleton, *Food Production in War*, 210–11; Lee, "Memorandum on Steps taken with Reference to the Program for the 1918 Harvest," August 16, 1917, Lloyd George papers, F/70/20/12.
50 Dewey, *British Agriculture*, 99.
51 Lee to Lloyd George, April 22, 1918, Lloyd George papers, F/31/2/9; Middleton, "The food production campaign and the supply of breadstuffs in the cereal year 1918–1919," May 18, 1918, Lloyd George papers, F/70/33/3.
52 P. E. Dewey, "Food Production and Policy in the United Kingdom, 1914–1918," in *Transactions of the Royal Historical Society*, Fifth Series, vol. 30 (London: Royal Historical Society, 1980), 84.
53 Barnett, *British Food Policy*, 205.
54 J. D. Ritchie, article on Devonport in *Dictionary of National Biography, 1931–1940*.
55 Lloyd George, *War Memoirs*, vol. 1, 641–42.
56 Barnett, *British Food Policy*, 94.
57 *Times*, December 9, 1917; *Observer*, December 10, 1917.
58 Frank. H. Coller, *A State Trading Adventure* (London: Oxford University Press, 1925), 37–38; José Harris, *William Beveridge: A Biography* (Oxford: Oxford University Press, 1977), 235–36. Beveridge did not mask his dislike of Devonport in 1917 but in his official history, *British Food Control* (London: Oxford University Press, 1928), he was more restrained in his criticism.
59 José Harris, "Bureaucrats and Businessmen in British Food Control, 1914–1919," in *War and the State*, ed. Kathleen Burk (London: Allen and Unwin, 1982), 140; Beveridge, *British Food Control*, 35–37; Harris, *Beveridge*, 235–37.
60 Harris, *Beveridge*, 35.
61 Lloyd George, *War Memoirs*, vol. 1, 788.
62 Beveridge, *British Food Control*, 45–46.
63 Barnett, *British Food Policy*, 98.
64 *Punch*, April 11, 1917, 235.
65 Sir Stephen Tallents, *Man and Boy* (London: Faber and Faber, 1943), 237.
66 Robert Smillie, *My Life for Labour* (London: Mills and Boon, 1924), ch. 15.
67 Christopher Addison, *Politics From Within*, vol. 2 (London: Hutchinson, 1934), 59–61.
68 Rhondda to Lloyd George, June 14, 1917, Lloyd George papers, F/43/5/21.
69 Sir Thomas G. Jones, *The Unbroken Front: Ministry of Food, 1916–1944* (London: Everybody's Books,1944), 11–12; Harris, *Beveridge*, 238–39; Barnett, *British Food Policy*, 125–26; Beveridge, *British Food Control*, 68–69; Viscountess Rhondda, "A Character Sketch," in *D.A. Thomas, Viscount Rhondda*, ed. Viscountess Rhondda et al. (London: Longmans, Green and Co., 1921).
70 Cited in Barnett, *British Food Policy*, 134.
71 For Rhondda's methods see especially Sir E.C.K. Gonner, "Lord Rhondda at the Ministry of Food," in *D. A. Thomas, Viscount Rhondda*, ed. Viscountess Rhondda et al.

72 Beveridge, *British Food Control*, 117.
73 Beveridge, *British Food Control*, 57–58.
74 Beveridge, *British Food Control*, 108–9.
75 Beveridge, *British Food Control*, 163–64.
76 Jones, *Unbroken Front*, 10.
77 Minutes of the War Cabinet, May 7, 1917, CAB 23/2.
78 Minutes of the War Cabinet, May 30, 1917, CAB 23/2.
79 Coller, *State Trading*, 63; Talents, *Man and Boy*, 232.
80 Beveridge, *British Food Control*, 195–96.
81 J. R. Clynes, *Memoirs, 1869–1924* (London: Hutchinson, 1937), 235.
82 Coller, *State Trading*, 115.
83 Barnett, *British Food Policy*, 143.
84 Clynes, *Memoirs*, vol. 1, 235–36.
85 Tallents, *Man and Boy*, 243.
86 Keith Middlemas, ed., *Thomas Jones: Whitehall Diary*, vol. 1 (London: Oxford University Press, 1969), 54; Lloyd George to Rhondda, February 8, 1918, Lloyd George papers, F/43/5/55.
87 Grigg, *Lloyd George: War Leader*, 399–400.
88 Hankey diary, February 24, 1918, Hankey papers.
89 Barnett, *British Food Policy*, 144–45.
90 Barnett, *British Food Policy*, 146.
91 Beveridge, *British Food Control*, 207–08.
92 Beveridge, *British Food Control.*, 230–31.
93 Parliamentary Debates, *House of Commons*, December 20, 1915, vol. 77, col. 121.

5. The First Attempt at a Unified Command

1 A. Temple Patterson, ed., *The Jellicoe Papers*, vol. 2 (London: Navy Records Society, 1968), 68.
2 McKenna, "Our Financal Position in America", October 18, 1916, CAB 37/157/40.
3 The idea was to strike suddenly to break off a limited section of the German line, fortify it and, after the enemy had exhausted itself in counterattacks, begin the process again.
4 Major General Thomas D'Oyly Snow, then commander of the 27th Division, recorded the following after a visit from Balfour: "I was very much struck by the knowledge Mr. Balfour showed in the matter of explosives and indeed in military matters generally." Snow, Narrative of the 27th Division, 27, WO 95/2254.
5 Balfour to Cecil, September 12, 1917, Cecil papers, ADD 51071; John Ehrman, "Lloyd George and Churchill as War Leaders," in *Transactions of the Royal Historical Society*, ser. 5, vol. 11 (London: Royal Historical Society, 1961), 102–3.
6 Victor Bonham-Carter, *Soldier True: The Life and Times of Field Marshal Sir William Robertson* (London, Frederick Muller, 1963), passim; David R. Woodward, *Field Marshal Sir William Robertson: Chief of the Imperial General Staff in the Great War* (Westport, CN: Praeger, 1998), passim ; B. H. Liddell Hart, *Through the Fog of War* (New York; Random House, 1938), 104–10: E. L. Spears, *Prelude to Victory* (London: Jonathan Cape, 1939), 33–35.
7 David Woodward, "Sir William Robertson and Sir Douglas Haig," in *Haig: A Reappraisal 70 Years On*, ed. Brian Bond and Nigel Cave (London: Leo Cooper, 1999), 65.
8 Woodward, "Sir William Robertson and Sir Douglas Haig," 65–66.

9. On Haig, see especially John Terraine, *Douglas Haig: The Educated Soldier* (London: Hutchinson, 1963); Gerard J. De Groot, *Douglas Haig, 1862–1928* (London: Unwin Hyman, 1988); Tim Travers, "A Particular Style of Command: Haig and GHQ, 1916–1918," *Journal of Strategic Studies* 10 (1987), 363–76; Denis Winter, *Haig's Command* (London: Viking, 1991); the various articles in *Haig*, ed. Bond and Cave; and the most recent biography, Walter Reid, *Architect of Victory: Douglas Haig* (Edinburgh: Birlinn, 2006).
10. German note, December 12, 1916, communicated by the American ambassador, annexed to the minutes of the War Cabinet, December 18, 1916, CAB 23/1.
11. On Britain's war aims, see V. H. Rothwell, *British War Aims and Peace Diplomacy, 1914–1918* (Oxford: Clarendon Press, 1971), and Kenneth J. Calder, *Britain and the Origins of the New Europe, 1914–1918* (Cambridge: Cambridge University Press, 1976).
12. For example, there was his famous "knockout" blow interview with Roy Howard already alluded to.
13. Minutes of the War Committee, February 22, 1916, CAB 42/9/3; Hankey, "Most Secret Addendum to the Proceedings of the War Committee on March 21, 1916," CAB 42/11/6; John Grigg, *Lloyd George: From Peace to War, 1912–1916* (Berkeley: University of California Press, 1985), 430–31; Field Marshal Sir William Robertson, *Soldiers and Statesmen, 1914–1918*, vol. 1 (London: Cassell, 1926), 280–83.
14. David Lloyd George, *War Memoirs*, vol. 1 (London: Odhams, 1938*)*, 631
15. Parliamentary Debates, *House of Commons*, December 19, 1916, vol. 87, cols. 1333–38.
16. Minutes of the War Cabinet, December 18, 1916, CAB 23/1.
17. Wilson note, communicated by the United States ambassador, December 20, 1916, annexed to the minutes of the War Cabinet, December 21, 1916, CAB 23/1.
18. Foreign Office, "Note on the German Offer of Peace," December 15, 1916, annexed to the minutes of the War Cabinet, December 18, 1916, CAB 23/1.
19. The Allied reply to the German and American notes are annexed to the conclusions of the Anglo–French conference held at 10 Downing Street on December 26–28, 1916, CAB 28/2. For a full treatment of the episode see Sterling Kernek, "The British Government's Reactions to President Wilson's 'Peace Note' of December 1916," *Historical Journal* 13 (1970): 721–66.
20. Cyril Falls, *Military Operations: France and Belgium, 1917*, vol. 1 (London: Macmillan, 1940), 1–11.
21. Lord Riddell, *War Diary, 1914–1918* (London: Nicholson and Watson, 1933), 265.
22. Robertson, *Soldiers and Statesmen*, vol. 2, 87–88.
23. Minutes of the War Cabinet, December 9, 1916, CAB 23/1; Robertson, Memoranda, December 23 and 27, 1916. The former memo is annexed to the minutes of the War Cabinet on December 26 and the latter to the minutes on December 27, CAB 23/1.
24. Minutes of the Anglo–French Conference, December 27 and 28, 1917, CAB 28/2.
25. George H. Cassar, *The Forgotten Front: The British Campaign in Italy, 1917–1918* (London: Hambledon Press, 1998), 13–14.
26. Brigadier General Sir James E. Edmonds, *Military Operations: Italy, 1915–1919* (London: HMSO, 1949), 10–11.
27. The battles along the Isonzo River are meticulously described in John R. Schindler, *Isonzo: The Forgotten Sacrifice of the Great War* (Westport, CN: Praeger, 2001).
28. Lloyd George, *War Memoirs*, vol. 1, 836–37.
29. Minutes of the War Cabinet, December 30, 1916, CAB 23/1.
30. "Memorandum Circulated by the Prime Minister to the Delegates," undated, annexed to the minutes of the Allied Conference, January 5–7, 1917, CAB 28/2.

31 Lord Hankey, *Supreme Command, 1914–1918*, vol. 2, (London: Allen and Unwin, 1961), 607–8.
32 Minutes of the Allied Conference, January 6, 1917, CAB 28/2; Hankey, *Supreme Command*, vol. 2, 610–11.
33 Lloyd George, *War Memoirs*, vol. 1, 847.
34 Minutes of the Allied Conference, January 6, 1917, CAB 28/2.
35 David R. Woodward, ed., *The Military Correspondence of Field Marshal Sir William Robertson, Chief of the Imperial General Staff, December 1915–February 1918* (London: Bodley Head for Army Records Society, 1989), 136.
36 Lloyd George, *War Memoirs*, vol. 1, 846–47; Hankey diary, January 7, 1917, Hankey papers.
37 A. J. P. Taylor, ed., *Lloyd George: A Diary by Frances Stevenson* (New York: Harper and Row, 1971), 137.
38 Minutes of the Allied Conference, January 7, 1917, CAB 28/2.
39 Hankey, *Supreme Command*, vol. 2, 613.
40 Randolph S. Churchill, *Lord Derby: King of Lancashire* (New York: G. P. Putnam's Sons, 1960), 246–47; Woodward, *Sir William Robertson*, 87–88; Hankey, *Supreme Command*, vol. 2, 614; Minutes of the War Cabinet, January 15 and 16, 1917, CAB 23/1; Falls: *France and Belgium, 1917*, vol. 1, 28–29.
41 Robertson to Esher, February 6, 1917, Robertson papers, 8/2/12.
42 Robert A. Doughty, *Pyrrhic Victory* (Cambridge: Harvard University Press, 2005), 323–24.
43 David R. Woodward, *Lloyd George and the Generals* (Newark, DE: University of Delaware Press, 1986), 142–43.
44 Robert Blake, ed, *The Private Papers of Douglas Haig, 1914–1919* (London: Eyre and Spottiswoode, 1952), 192.
45 Terraine, *Douglas Haig*, 255–57.
46 Robertson, "Note on the Forthcoming Operations on the western front," January 24, 1917, WO 106/311; General Staff, "A General Review of the Situation in all Theatres of War," March 20, 1917, WO 106/311.
47 Paul Painlevé, *Comment J'ai nommé Foch et Pétain* (Paris: Félix Alcan, 1923), 32–34; André Maurois, *Lyautey* (New York: Appleton, 1931), trans. by Hamish Miles, 303–4; See also Emile Herbillon, *Souvenirs d'un Officier de Liaison pendant la Guerre Mondiale*, vol. 2 (Paris: Jules Tallandier, 1930), 22, 25. Herbillon points out that a number of French generals were equally hostile to Nivelle's plan.
48 Woodward, *Lloyd George*, 143; Minutes of the War Cabinet, January 17, 1917, CAB 23/1.
49 Hankey diary, January 17, 1917, Hankey papers.
50 Minutes of the War Cabinet, January, 17, 1917, CAB 23/1.
51 Woodward, *Lloyd George*, 144.
52 *Evening Standard*, February 14, 1917.
53 Charles à Court Repington, *The First World War*, vol. 1(London: Constable, 1920), 460–61, 464; De Groot. *Haig*, 295–98.
54 Woodward, *Lloyd George*, 144.
55 Spears, *Prelude*, 546 (Appendix IX).
56 Minutes of the War Cabinet, February 24, 1917, CAB 23/1.
57 Hankey diary, February 24, 1917, Hankey papers.
58 David R. Woodward, *Lloyd George*, 146–47; Minutes of the War Cabinet, February 24, 1917, CAB 23/1; Memorandum on a conversation between Lord Curzon and Lord Stamfordham, March 4, 1917, Royal Archives, RA GV Q1079/6.

59 Peter Rowland, *Lloyd George* (London: Barrie and Jenkins, 1974), 390.
60 Elizabeth Greenhalgh, *Victory Through Coalition* (Cambridge: Cambridge University Press, 2005), 142.
61 "Notes of an Anglo-French Conference held at the Hotel Terminus, Calais," Second Session, February 26, 1917, CAB 28/2; Blake, ed., *PPDH*, 200; Gary Sheffield and John Bourne, eds., *Douglas Haig: War Diaries and Letters, 1914–1918* (London: Weidenfeld and Nicolson, 2005), 270–71.
62 "Projet d'organization de l'unité de commandement sur le front occidental," February 26, 1917; annexed to minutes of the meeting on February 27, 1917, CAB 28/2.
63 Stephen Roskill, *Hankey: Man of Secrets*, vol. 1 (London: Collins, 1970), 362–63.
64 Spears, *Prelude*, 143.
65 Spears, *Prelude*, 143.
66 Spears, *Prelude, 145–46;* Roskill, *Hankey*, vol. 1, 363; Blake, ed., *PPDH*, 200–1.
67 "Agreement signed at Anglo-French Conference held at Calais," February 26 and 27, 1917, annexed to the minutes of the Anglo-French Conference, February 27, 1917, CAB 28/2; Hankey, *Supreme Command*, vol. 2, 616–17.
68 Minutes of the War Cabinet, February 28, 1917, CAB 23/1; Robertson to Haig, February 28, 1917, Woodward, ed, *MCWR*, 155.
69 Hankey Diary, March 2, 1917, Hankey papers.
70 Derby to Lloyd George, March 6, 1917, Lloyd George papers, F/14/4/24; Derby to Stamfordham, March 4, 1917, RA GV Q1079/18; See also Long to Curzon, March ? 1917, Curzon papers, EUR. F 112/113.
71 It was common knowledge that Lloyd George had no use for the monarchy and, in that spirit, made no effort to pay proper observances to the king. In particular, he discontinued his predecessors' habit of sending the king a handwritten summary of cabinet proceedings. Stamfordham complained to Balfour that "His Majesty is deeply pained at what he regards as not only a want of respect, but as ignoring his very observances." Stamfordham to Balfour, April 6, 1917, FO 800/199.
72 An unsigned, memorandum, March 12, 1917, RA GV Q1079/35.
73 Minutes of the War Cabinet, February 28, 1917, CAB 23/1; Robertson to Haig, February 28, 1917, Woodward, ed., *MCWR*, 155.
74 Blake, ed., *PPDH*, 203.
75 Woodward, *Sir William Robertson*, 100.
76 Terraine, *Douglas Haig*, 278–79.
77 Nivelle to Haig, March 6, 1917, 2/3/70, Spears papers.
78 The note, dated March 7, 1917, is unsigned but almost certainly it was written by Nivelle. It was handed to Hankey, probably by Bertier de Sauvigny, for transmission to the prime minister. Lloyd George papers, F/3/2/14; Hankey diary, March 10, 1917, Hankey papers.
79 Eric Drummond (Balfour's private secretary) to Lloyd George, March 7, 1917, with the enclosed French note, Lloyd George papers, F/3/2/14.
80 Spears, *Prelude*, 177.
81 Robertson, Memorandum, March 2, 1917, CAB 24/6/GT93.
82 Robertson to Haig, March 6, 1917, Woodward, ed., *MCWR*, 157–58.
83 Woodward, *Lloyd George*, 151.
84 Hankey to Lloyd George, March 7, 1917, CAB 63/19.
85 Minutes of the War Cabinet, March 8 and 9, 1917, CAB 23/2.
86 "Notes of an Anglo-French Conference held at 10 Downing Street," March 12 and 13, 1917, CAB 28/2.

87 Hankey, *Supreme Command*, vol. 2, 623.
88 Cassar, *Forgotten Front*, 22–23.
89 Spears, *Prelude*, 201–2.
90 Painlevé, *Comment j'ai nommé Foch et Pétain*, 44–46.
91 Anthony Clayton, "Robert Nivelle and the French Spring Offensive of 1917," in *Fallen Stars*, ed. Brian Bond (London: Brassesy's, 1991), 57.
92 Minutes of the War Cabinet, May 3, 1917, CAB 23/2.
93 On the Nivelle offensive and its immediate aftermath see, Robert A. Doughty, *Pyrrhic Victory* (Cambridge: Harvard University Press, 2005).

6. Facing the Submarine Menace

1 David French, *British Strategy and War Aims, 1914–1916* (London: Allen and Unwin, 1986), 27.
2 Dwight R. Messimer, *Find and Destroy: Anti-Submarine Warfare in World War I* (Annapolis: Naval Institute Press, 2001), passim; Richard Hough, *The Great War at Sea, 1914–1918* (Oxford: Oxford University Press, 1988), 303–4; Paul G. Halpern, *A Naval History of World War I* (Annapolis: Naval Institute Press, 1994), 343ff; A. J. Marder, *From the Dreadnought to Scapa Flow*, vol. 4 (London: Oxford University Press, 1969), 63–93.
3 French, *British Strategy*, 224.
4 Minutes of the War Committee, November 9, 1916, CAB 42/23/11.
5 Lord Hankey, *The Supreme Command, 1914–1918*, vol. 2 (London: Allen and Unwin, 1961), 554.
6 Hough, *Great War at Sea*, 59–60; A. J. Marder, *From the Dreadnought to Scapa Flow*, vol. 2 (London: Oxford University Press, 1965), 10–11, and vol. 4, 56–58; Correlli Barnett, *The Sword Bearers* (London: Eyre and Spottiswoode, 1963), 109, 112, 116, 119, 127; A Temple Patterson, *Jellicoe* (London: Macmillan, 1969), passim.
7 Minutes of War Committee, November 2, 1916, CAB 22/62/3.
8 David Lloyd George, *War Memoirs*, vol. 1 (London: Odhams, 1938), 677.
9 Marder, *From the Dreadnought*, vol. 4, 116–17.
10 Patterson, *Jellicoe*, 165–66; Marder, *From the Dreadnought*, vol. 4, 119–21.
11 Admiral Reinard Scheer, *Germany's High Sea Fleet in the World War* (London: Cassell, 1920), 248–52; Halpern, *Naval History*, 336–38.
12 C. Ernest Fayle, *Seaborne Trade*, vol. 3 (London: John Murray, 1924), 465; Lloyd George, *War Memoirs*, vol. 1, 690; Halpern, *Naval History*, 341.
13 The Canadian-born Sims was an old friend of Jellicoe, whom he had first met in China in 1901. Besides his reputation for being an Anglophile, he had a temperament suited to working well with officers of different nationalities.
14 William S. Sims, *The Victory at Sea* (London: John Murray, 1920), 6–7.
15 Cited in H. Montgomery Hyde, *Carson* (London: Constable, 1987), 416.
16 Hyde, *Carson*, 420.
17 Lloyd George, *War Memoirs*, vol. 1, 684.
18 Cited in Lord Beaverbrook, *Men and Power*, (London: Hutchinson, 1956), 151.
19 Hankey, *Supreme Command*, vol. 2, 640.
20 Stephen Roskill, *Hankey*, vol. 1 (London: Collins, 1970), 357–58.
21 Henry Newbolt, *Naval Operations*, vol. 5 (London: Longmans, Green and Co., 1931), 10–15; Hankey, *Supreme Command*, vol. 2, 647–48.
22 Lloyd George, *War Memoirs*, vol. 1, 687; Marder, *From the Dreadnough*, vol. 4, 157.

23 Lloyd George, *War Memoirs*, vol. 1, 688–89.
24 Hankey, *Supreme Command*, vol. 2, 648.
25 John Grigg, *Lloyd George: War Leader, 1916–1918* (London: Allen Lane, 2002), 52.
26 Marder, *From the Dreadnought*, vol. 4, 118–19.
27 Hankey, *Supreme Command*, vol. 2, 648.
28 Hankey, *Supreme Command*, vol. 2, 649.
29 Minutes of the War Cabinet, April 20, 1917, CAB 23/2.
30 Robertson to Curzon, April 20, 1917, Curzon papers, EUR F 112/120.
31 Milner wanted Curzon to join him in pressing this point on the prime minister but events over the course of the next few days rendered a meeting unnecessary. Milner to Curzon, April 26, 1917, Curzon papers, EUR F 112/113.
32 Jellicoe, "The Submarine Menace and Food Supply," April 22, 1917, annexed to the minutes of the War Cabinet, April 23, 1917, CAB 23/2.
33 Marder, *From the Dreadnought*, vol. 4, 153–55.
34 J. A. Salter, *Allied Shipping Control* (Oxford: Clarendon Press, 1921), 123; Newbolt, *Naval Operations*, vol. 5, 18.
35 Minutes of the War Cabinet, April 23, 1917, CAB 23/2.
36 Lloyd George, *War Memoirs*, vol. 2, see chapter 40, "The Peril of the Submarines."
37 Minutes of the War Cabinet, April 25, 1917, CAB 23/2.
38 Hankey diary, April 30, 1917, Hankey papers.
39 Newbolt, *Naval Operations*, vol. 5, 19–20.
40 Newbolt, *Naval Operations*, vol. 5, 21–24.
41 Lloyd George, *War Memoirs*, vol. 1, 691–92.
42 Carson interview in the *Morning Post*, September 24, 1934.
43 Marder, *From the Dreadnought*, vol. 4, 162–63.

7. Prelude to Catastrophe

1 David Woodward, *Trial By Friendship: Anglo-American Relations, 1917–1918* (Lexington: University Press of Kentucky, 1993), 44–45.
2 Brock Millman, *Pessimism and British Policy, 1916–1918* (London: Frank Cass, 2001), 12.
3 Gerald J. De Groot, *Douglas Haig, 1861–1928* (London: Unwin-Hyman, 1988), 317–20; Trevor Wilson, *The Myriad Faces of War* (Cambridge: Polity Press, 1986), 458–60.
4 Brigadier General John Charteris, *At GHQ* (London: Cassell, 1931), 217–19.
5 Haig to Robertson, April 29 and 30, 1917, Robertson papers, 7/7/25 and 4/4/82.
6 David Woodward, *Field Marshal Sir William Robertson* (Westport, CN: Praeger, 1998), 128–31.
7 David Woodward, *Lloyd George and the Generals*, (Newark, DE: University of Delaware Press, 1983), 160.
8 The letter was published in full in David Lloyd George, *War Memoirs*, vol. 2 (London: Odhams, 1938), 1182–84.
9 Georges de Manteyer, ed., *Austria's Peace Offer 1916–1917* (London: Constable, 1921), chs. 1 and 2; Wilfred Fest, *Peace or Partition: The Hapsburg Monarchy and British Policy 1914–1918* (London: George Prior, 1978), 66–67; A. Ribot, ed., *Journal de Alexandre Ribot* (Paris: Plon, 1936), 67; Lloyd George, *War Memoirs*, vol. 2, 1184–85; A. J. P. Taylor, ed., *Lloyd George: A Diary by Frances Stevenson* (New York: Harper and Row, 1971), 150.
10 Lord Hankey, *The Supreme Command, 1914–1918*, vol. 2 (London: Allen and Unwin, 1961), 735.

11 Manteyer, ed., *Austria's Peace Offer*, 113–117; Lloyd George, *War Memoirs*, vol. 2, 1186.
12 "Memorandum on the Anglo-French-Italian Conference, April 19, 1917," CAB 28/2; Lloyd George, *War Memoirs*, vol. 2, 1187–88; Hankey diary, April 19, 1917, Hankey papers.
13 Manteyer, ed., *Austria's Peace Offer*, 118–21; Lloyd George, *War Memoirs*, vol. 2, 1189–90.
14 V. H. Rothwell, *British War Aims and Peace Diplomacy, 1914–1918* (Oxford: Oxford University Press, 1971), 110–11; Manteyer, ed., *Austria's Peace Offer*, 166–72.
15 Roskill, *Hankey*, vol. 1, 379.
16 Smuts, "The General and Military Situation and Particularly that on the western front," April 29, 1917, CAB 24/11/GT597; Smuts to Robertson, April 29, 1917, Robertson papers, 7/5/65.
17 Robertson, "Operations on the West Front," April 30, 1917, CAB 24/11/GT599.
18 Minutes of the War Cabinet, May 1, 1917, CAB 23/13.
19 Haig diary, May 3, 1917, Haig papers.
20 Statement by Robertson to the Anglo-French Conference, May 5, 1917, annexed to the minutes of the meeting, CAB 28/2.
21 "Summary of the Proceedings of the Anglo-French Conference Held at Paris," May 4 and 5, 1917, CAB 28/2.
22 Woodward, *Lloyd George*, 165–66.
23 Keith Neilson, *Strategy and Supply: The Anglo-Russian Alliance, 1914–1917* (London: Allen and Unwin, 1984), 254; Robertson to Monro, April 19, 1917, in David R. Woodward, ed., *The Military Correspondence of Field Marshal Sir William Robertson, Chief of the Imperial General Staff, December 1915–February 1918* (London: Bodley Head for Army Records Society, 1989), 177.
24 Wilson diary, May 1, 1917, Wilson papers.
25 Derby to Haig, May 27, 1917, WO 256/18.
26 Minutes of the War Cabinet, May 1 and 9, 1917, CAB 23/13.
27 Robertson, "Military Effect of Russia Seceding from the Entente," May 9, 1917, CAB 24/12/ GT678.
28 Woodward, *Lloyd George*, 166–67.
29 Esher to Robertson, May 11, 1917, enclosed along with Robertson's letter to Lloyd George, May 13, 1917, Lloyd George papers, F/44/3/12; Robertson to Haig, May 14, 1917, Haig papers, no. 113.
30 Wilson diary, May 20, 1917, Wilson papers.
31 Wilson diary, June 2, 1917, Wilson papers.
32 "Résumé de l'entrevue du 2 juin à Bavincourt entre le Major-General et le Maréchal Haig," Benson papers, B1/107; Robert Blake, ed., *PPDH* (London: Eyre and Spottiswoode, 1952), 234, 236.
33 Wilson diary, June 4, 1917, Wilson papers.
34 Robin Prior and Trevor Wilson, *Passchendaele: The Untold Story* (New Haven: Yale University Press, 1996), ch. 6.
35 Spiers to Maurice, June 4 and 5, 1917, Spears papers, M I/13/1; Minutes of the War Cabinet June 6, 1917, CAB 23/3.
36 Spiers to Maurice, June 6, 1917, Spears papers, MI/13/1.
37 Minutes of the War Cabinet, June 8, 1917, CAB 23/16.
38 "Note by Milner," June 7, 1917, annexed to minutes of the War Cabinet, June 8, 1917, CAB 23/16.
39 Hankey, *Supreme Command*, vol. 2, 672–73. Hankey misdated the period in which the meetings occurred.

40 Minutes of the War Policy Committee, June 19, 20 and 21, 1917, CAB 27/6; Haig dairy for the same June dates, in 1917, Haig papers.
41 Haig diary, June 9, 1917, Haig papers.
42 Minutes of the War Policy Committee, June 19, 20, and 21, 1917, CAB 27/6.
43 Minutes of the War Policy Committee, June 19, 20, and 21, 1917, CAB 27/6; Lloyd George *War Memoirs*, vol. 2, ch. 63, part 1 and 2.
44 Jellicoe "Remarks on the occupation of the North Coast of Belgium by the Germans," June 18, 1917, CAB 27/7; Minutes of the War Policy Committee, June 20, 1917, CAB 27/6.
45 Minutes of the War Policy Committee, June 21, 1917, CAB 27/6.
46 "Note by the C.I.G.S. on the Prime Minister's Memorandum regarding future Military Policy," June 23, 1917, CAB 27/7.
47 Minutes of the War Policy Committee, June 21, 1917, CAB 27/6.
48 Minutes of the War Policy Committee, June 25, 1917, CAB 27/7; Haig diary, June 25, 1917, Haig papers; Haig, Memorandum, June 22, 1917, CAB 27/7; "Note by the CIGS on the Prime Minister's Memorandum regarding future Military Policy," June 23, 1917, CAB 27/7.
49 Hankey, *Supreme Command*, vol. 2, 683.
50 Woodward, *Lloyd George*, 186.
51 Gary Sheffield and John Bourne, eds., *Douglas Haig: War Diaries and Letters, 1914–1918* (London: Weidenfeld and Nicolson, 2005), 301.
52 Blake, ed., *PPDH*, 242; Lloyd George, *War Memoirs*, vol. 1, 699.
53 Blake, ed., *PPDH*, 242.
54 For further details see Roskill, *Hankey*, vol. 1, 404–5.
55 Milner to Lloyd George, June 26, 1917, Lloyd George papers, F/38/2/10; A. M. Gollin, *Proconsul in Politics* (London: Anthony Blond, 1964), 437–38.
56 Lord Beaverbrook, *Men and Power, 1917–1918* (London: Hutchinson, 1956), 172–74.
57 Beaverbrook, *Men and Power*, 174.
58 Milner to Lloyd George, July 7, 1917, Lloyd George papers, F/38/2/11.
59 Milner to Lloyd George, July 16, 1917, Lloyd George papers, F/38/2/12.
60 Beaverbrook, *Men and Power*, 175–76.
61 The Mesopotamia Commission was set up by Asquith to investigate the events leading to Major General Townshend's surrender at Kut-el-Amara on April 29, 1916. The report turned into a damning indictment of the manner in which the operations were conducted, with the victims of criticism having been given no chance to defend themselves.
62 Report of the Cabinet Committee on War Policy, August 10, 1917, CAB 27/6.
63 David French, "Who Knew What and When? The French Army Mutinies and the British Decision to Launch the Third Battle of Ypres," in *War, Strategy and International Politics*, ed. Lawrence Freedman, Paul Hayes and Robert O'Neil (Oxford: Clarendon Press, 1992), 151–52.
64 Report of the Cabinet Committee on War Policy, August 10, 1917, CAB 27/6; Hankey, *Supreme Command*, vol. 2, 683–84.
65 Woodward, *Lloyd George*, 183.
66 Report of the Cabinet Committee on War Policy, August 19, 1917, CAB 27/6.

8. The Horror of Passchendaele

1 Hankey diary, July 23, 1917, Hankey papers.
2 After the March revolution, the Russians made one last military effort, pulling together 200,000 men to attack the Austrians in Galicia. Significant gains were made initially,

but the Russian army had neither the weapons nor the morale to sustain a long campaign. A German counterattack drove back the Russian army in panic and many of its units disintegrated. On July 16–17, antiwar demonstrations erupted in Petrograd.
3. Report of the Military Conference, July 26, 1917, annexed to the minutes of the inter-Allied Conference, July 25–26, 1917, CAB 28/2.
4. Field Marshal Sir William Robertson, *Soldiers and Statesmen, 1914–1918*, vol. 2 (London: Cassell, 1926), 250.
5. Notes of an Allied Conference Held at the Foreign Office, Paris, July 26, 1917, CAB 28/2.
6. Minutes of the War Cabinet, July 31, 1917, CAB 23/13; Smuts, Memorandum, July 31, 1917, CAB 24/21; Roskill, *Hankey*, vol. 1, 418.
7. The new concept relied on a zigzag series of pillboxes with interlocking fields of fire. The forward line was lightly manned, with most of the defenders concentrated further back. Consequently, casualties resulting from preliminary bombardment would be kept to a minimum and counterattacks could be organized wherever they were needed.
8. There are many books on Passchendaele, but the best, in my view, is Prior and Wilson, *Passchendaele: The Untold Story* (New Haven, CT: Yale University Press, 1998).
9. Haig to Robertson, "Report on the battle of 31st July, 1917, and its results," August 4, 1917, CAB 24/22/GT1621.
10. Robertson to Kiggell, August 2, 1917, Kiggell papers, 3/8.
11. Wilson diary, August 2 and 7, 1917, Wilson papers; David R. Woodward, *Lloyd George and the Generals* (Newark, DE: University of Delaware, 1983), 192–93.
12. "Notes of an Inter-Ally Conference Held at 10 Downing Street," August 7, 1917, CAB 28/2.
13. Report of the Military Conference, August 7, 1917, annexed to minutes of the Inter-Ally Conference, August 7, 1917, CAB 28/2.
14. "Process-vèrbal of a meeting between representatives of the British, French, and Italian Governments, at 10 Downing Street," August 8, 1917, CAB 28/2.
15. Woodward, *Lloyd George*, 193.
16. Robertson to Haig, August 9, 1917, Haig papers, no. 116. Robertson wrote in a similar vein to Kiggell on August 9 (Kiggell papers, 3/9) and referred to the prime minister as "an under-bred swine."
17. As reported by the CIGS or the DMO to the War Cabinet, August 17, 20, and 30, 1917, CAB 23/3.
18. Robertson to Haig, September 15, 1917, in David R. Woodward, *The Military Correspondence of Field Marshal Sir William Robertson, Chief of the Imperial General Staff, December 1915–February 1918* (London: Bodley Head for Army Records Society, 1989), 223.
19. See for example David Lloyd George, *War Memoirs*, vol. 2 (London: Odhams, 1938), 1382.
20. Lord Hankey, *The Supreme Command, 1914–1918*, vol. 2 (London: Allen and Unwin, 1961), 693.
21. Milner to Curzon, June 18, 1918, EUR F 112/122, Curzon papers.
22. Lloyd George, *War Memoirs*, vol. 2, 1382.
23. Woodward, *Lloyd George*, 195.
24. Lloyd George, *War Memoirs*, vol. 2, 1371.
25. Major General Sir C. E. Callwell, *Field-Marshal Sir Henry Wilson*, vol. 2 (London: Cassell, 1927), 3.
26. Wilson diary, August 17, 1917, Wilson papers.
27. Wilson diary, August 23, 1917, Wilson papers.
28. Lord Riddell, *War Diary, 1914–1918* (London: Nicholson and Watson, 1933), 266.

29 Wilson diary, August 24, 25 and 27, 1917, Wilson papers.
30 Hankey, *Supreme Command*, vol. 2, 693–94.
31 Lloyd George, *War Memoirs*, vol. 2, 1385–86.
32 Riddell, *War Diary*, 267.
33 Lloyd George, *War Memoirs*, vol. 2, 1386–87.
34 Cecil to Balfour, August 29, 1917, Balfour papers, ADD 49738; Minutes of the War Cabinet, August 28, 1917, CAB 23/13.
35 Cecil to Balfour, August 29, 1917, Balfour papers, ADD 49738.
36 David R. Woodward, *Field Marshal Sir William Robertson, Chief of the Imperial General Staff in the Great War* (Westport, CN: Praeger, 1998), 145.
37 Riddell, *War Diary*, 269–70.
38 Hankey, *Supreme Command*, vol. 2, 694–95; Riddell, *War Diary*, 269–70; Telegram to Rennell Rodd , August 29, 1917, Lloyd George papers, F/56/1/48.
39 Robertson to Maurice, August 31, 1917, Robertson papers, 7/9/4.
40 Hankey, *Supreme Command*, vol. 2, 695–96.
41 Hankey diary, September 4 ,1917, Hankey papers.
42 Robert Blake, ed., *The Private Papers of Douglas Haig, 1914–1919 (London: Eyre and Spottiswoode, 1952)*, 252–53.
43 Blake, ed., *PPDH*, 253.
44 Gary Sheffield and John Bourne, eds., *Douglas Haig; War Diaries and Letters, 1914–1918* (London: Weidenfeld and Nicolson, 2005), 321–22; Minutes of the War Cabinet, September 4, 1917, CAB 23/13; Hankey diary, September 4, 1917, Hankey papers.
45 Hankey diary, September 4, 1917, Hankey papers.
46 Hardinge to Bertie, September 11, 1917, FO 800/175 (Misc 17/20).
47 Notes of an Anglo-French Conference held at 10 Downing Street, September 4, 1917, CAB 28/2.
48 Blake, ed., *PPDH*, 253.
49 George H. Cassar. *The Forgotten Front: The British Campaign in Italy, 1917–1918* (London: Hambledon Press, 1998), 56–57.
50 Prior and Wilson, *Passchendaele*, 171–81.
51 Brigadier General Sir James Edmonds, *Military Operations: France and Belgium, 1917*, vol. 2 (London: HMSO, 1948) , 360–61.
52 Woodward, *Sir William Robertson*, 148–49.

9. The Peripheral War

1 Germany's colonies in Africa had fallen by 1916, save for German East Africa, where the fighting was arduous, if not relentless, and lasted beyond the end of the war. With an army that never exceeded 15,000 men, the highly gifted and resolute German commander, Major General Paul Lettow-Vorbeck, abandoned set-piece battles early in 1915 and instead employed guerilla tactics. For over two years he eluded British efforts to encircle and destroy his small force, but was eventually driven back into the southeast corner of the colony. In October 1917 he slipped into the Portuguese colony of Mozambique, captured a number of outposts and maintained himself on captured supplies. He crossed back into German East Africa and from there invaded Northern Rhodesia on November 2, 1918. It was not until November 25, nearly two weeks after the armistice, that he finally surrendered. By his remarkable exploits, he had tied down 130,000 Allied troops for a period of more than four years.

2   David R. Woodward, *Field Marshal Sir William Robertson, Chief of the Imperial General Staff in the Great War* (Westport, CN: Praeger, 1998), 117–18.
3   A. J. Barker, *The Bastard War: The Mesopotamian Campaign of 1914–1918* (New York: Dial Press 1967), chs. 15 and 16.
4   Field Marshal Sir William Robertson, *Soldiers and Statesmen, 1914–1918*, vol. 2 (London: Cassell, 1926), 75–76.
5   The Straits Agreement in March 1915 promised Russia Constantinople, the Straits and eastern Turkey. This was followed a year later by the Sykes-Picot Agreement under which the British and the French divided Turkey's Arab lands among themselves.
6   Robertson, *Soldiers and Statesmen*, vol. 2, 76–77: David Lloyd George, *War Memoirs*, vol. 2 (London: Odhams, 1938), 1078–79; Brigadier General F. J. Moberly, *The Campaign in Mesopotamia, 1914–1918*, vol. 3 (London: HMSO, 1925), 204.
7   Minutes of the War Cabinet, February 28, 1917, CAB 23/1.
8   Sir Arnold T. Wilson, *Loyalties: Mesopotamia, 1914–1917*, vol. 1 (Oxford: Oxford University Press, 1936), 225.
9   Barker, *Bastard War*, ch. 17.
10 Moberly, *Campaign in Mesopotamia*, vol. 3, 302.
11 Jan K. Tanenbaum, *General Maurice Sarrail, 1856–1929: The French Army and Left Wing Politics* (Chapel Hill: University of North Carolina Press, 1974), 149–50.
12 Notes of an Anglo–French Conference held at Calais, February 27, 1917, CAB 28/2.
13 Paul G. Halpern, *A Naval History of World War I* (Annapolis: Naval Institute Press, 1994), 391.
14 Minutes of the War Cabinet, March 30, 1917, CAB 23/2.
15 Painlevé had replaced Lyautey as minister of war in the new cabinet headed by the elderly Alexandre Ribot.
16 Halpern, *Naval History*, 391.
17 "Anglo-French-Italian Conference, " April 19, 1917, CAB 28/2; Minutes of the War Cabinet, April 23, 1917, CAB 23/2; Hankey diary, April 18 and 19, 1917, Hankey papers.
18 David Woodward, ed., *Military Correspondence of Field Marshal Sir William Robertson, Chief of the Imperial General Staff, December 1915–February 1918* (London: Bodley Head, 1989), 176–77.
19 Minutes of the War Cabinet, May 1, 1917, CAB 23/2.
20 Summary of the Proceedings of the Anglo–French Conference, May 4 and 5, 1917, CAB 28/2.
21 For details of the offensive see Alan Palmer, *Gardners of Salonika*, (New York: Simon and Schuster, 1965), ch. 7.
22 Matthew Hughes, *Allenby and British Strategy in the Middle East, 1917–1919* (London: Frank Cass, 1999), 31.
23 Cited in Hughes, *Allenby*, 31.
24 Minutes of the War Cabinet, May 23, 1917, CAB 23/2.
25 Minutes of the War Cabinet, May 23, 1917, CAB 23/2.
26 Robertson, "Note on a Proposal to Occupy Larissa," April 13, 1917, CAB 24/10/GT430; Robertson, "Withdrawal of the British Troops from Salonica," May 1, 1917, CAB 24/12/GT606; Robertson, "French Proposal for the Occupation of Greece," May 25, 1917, CAB 24/14/GT840.
27 A. J. P. Taylor, ed., *Lloyd George: A Diary by Frances Stevenson* (New York: Harper and Row, 1971), 161.

28 Notes of an Anglo–French Conference held at 10 Downing Street, May 28, 1917, at noon, CAB 28/2.
29 Cecil, "British Memorandum on Greek Policy," n.d., annexed to the notes of the Anglo–French conference for May 28, 1917, CAB 28/2.
30 Minutes of the War Cabinet, May 28, 1917, CAB 23/2.
31 Minutes of the War Cabinet, May 28 and 29, 1917, CAB 23/2.
32 Notes of an Anglo–French Conference held at 10 Downing Street, May 29, 1917 at 11:00 a.m., CAB 28/2.
33 Taylor, ed., *Lloyd George*, 161.
34 Tanenbaum, *Sarrail*, 163.
35 Minutes of the War Cabinet, June 5, 1917, CAB 23/3.
36 Lloyd George to Ribot, June 6, 1917, letter is annexed to the minutes of the War Cabinet for June 6, CAB 23/3.
37 Raymond Poincaré, *Au Service de la France*, vol. 9 (Paris: Plon, 1932), 158–59.
38 David Dutton, *The Politics of Diplomacy: Britain and France in the Balkans in the First World War* (London: Tauris, 1998), 131.
39 Tanenbaum, *Sarrail*, 174.
40 Dutton, *Politics of Diplomacy*, 131.
41 Minutes of the War Cabinet, June 11, 1917, CAB 23/3.
42 Minutes of the War Cabinet, June 11, 1917, CAB 23/3.
43 David Dutton, "The Deposition of King Constantine of Greece, June 1917: An Episode in Anglo-French Diplomacy," *Canadian Journal of History* 12 (1977–78), 343–44.
44 Minutes of the War Cabinet, June 26, 1917, CAB 23/3.
45 Lord Hankey, *The Supreme Command, 1914–1918*, vol. 2 (London: Allen and Unwin, 1961), 684.
46 Robertson to Curzon, July 4, 1917, Curzon papers, EUR F112/120.
47 Draft Report of the War Policy Committee, July 19, 1917, CAB 27/7.
48 Minutes of the War Cabinet, July 20, 1917, CAB 23/13.
49 Notes on an Allied Conference held in Paris, July 25 and 26, 1917, CAB 28/2.
50 Notes of an Allied Conference held at 10 Downing Street, on August 7 and 8, 1917, CAB 28/2.
51 Robertson, *Soldiers and Statesmen*, vol. 2, 143.
52 For details about the campaign in Palestine, see Lieutenant General Sir George MacMunn and Cyril Falls, *Military Operations: Egypt and Palestine*, 2 vols. (London: HMSO, 1928 and 1930); David R. Woodward, *Hell in the Holy Land: World War I in the Middle East* (Lexington: University Press of Kentucky, 2006); Anthony Bruce, *The Last Crusade* (London: John Murray, 2002); John D. Grainger, *The Battle for Palestine 1917* (Woodbridge; Boydell Press, 2006.
53 Charles à Court Repington, *The First World War*, vol. 1 (Boston: Houghton Mifflin, 1920), 420.
54 Robertson, *Soldiers and Statesmen*, vol. 2, 147–48.
55 All the telegrams exchanged between Robertson and Murray, cited in the text for December 1916, can be found in MacMunn and Falls, *Egypt and Palestine*, vol. 1, 259–61.
56 MacMunn and Falls, *Egypt and Palestine*, vol. 1, 251–58.
57 Robertson, *Soldiers and Statesmen*, vol. 2, 165–66.
58 MacMunn and Falls, *Egypt and Palestine*, vol. 1, 272.
59 Robertson, *Soldiers and Statesmen*, vol. 2, 167; Minutes of the War Cabinet, January 30, 1917, CAB 23/1.
60 MacMunn and Falls, *Egypt and Palestine*, vol. 1, ch. 16. An excerpt of Murray's report can be found on p. 319.

61 Minutes of the War Cabinet, March 30 and April 2, 1917, CAB 23/2.
62 MacMunn and Falls, *Egypt and Palestine*, vol. 1, 322–23.
63 Woodward, *Sir William Robertson*, 123.
64 Minutes of the War Cabinet, April 5, 1917, CAB 23/13.
65 Smuts to Lloyd George, May 26, 1917, Robertson papers, 8/2/50; and Smuts to Lloyd George, May 31, 1917, Lloyd George papers, F/45/9/4.
66 Lawrence James, *Imperial Warrior: The Life and Times of Field-Marshal Viscount Allenby, 1861–1936* (London, Weidenfeld and Nicolson, 1993), 106.
67 David Lloyd George, *War Memoirs*, vol. 2 (London: Odhams Press, 1938), 1089.
68 Field Marshal Viscount Wavell, *Allenby: Soldier and Statesman* (London: White Lion, 1974), 154.
69 Lloyd George, *War Memoirs*, vol. 2, 1089–90; Robertson, *Soldiers and Statesmen*, vol. 2, 172–73; Minutes of the War Cabinet, June 5, 1917, CAB 23/3.
70 Hankey, *Supreme Command*, vol. 2, 637.
71 Minutes of the War Cabinet, May 1, 1917, CAB 23/13.
72 Minutes of the War Cabinet, May 9, 1917, CAB 23/13.

10. The Quest for a Negotiated Peace

1 Stephen Roskill, *Hankey: Man of Secrets*, vol. 1(London: Collins, 1976), 348.
2 L. S. Amery, *My Political Life*, vol. 2 (London: Hutchinson, 1953), 105–08; Lord Hankey, *The Supreme Command, 1914–1918*, vol. 2 (London: Allen and Unwin, 1961), 660–61; David Lloyd George, *War Memoirs*, vol. 1 (London: Odhams, 1938), 1027–34.
3 Minutes of the Imperial War Cabinet, March 20, 1917, CAB 23/40.
4 For records of the Curzon committee see CAB 21/77 and CAB 29/1.
5 The materials related to the Milner committee are in CAB 21/71. A summary of the report can be found in Lloyd George, *War Memoirs*, vol. 1, 1066–67.
6 Lloyd George, *War Memoirs*, vol. 1, 1037–38.
7 Minutes of the Imperial War Cabinet, April 26 and May 1, 1917, CAB 23/40. Hankey, *Supreme Command*, vol. 2, 662.
8 Brock Millman, "A Council of Despair: British Strategy and War Aims," *Journal of Contemporary History* 36 (2001), 241–70.
9 Cited in David R. Woodward, *Trial by Friendship: Anglo-American Relations, 1917–1918* (Lexington: University Press of Kentucky, 1993), 59–60.
10 Arthur S. Link, *Woodrow Wilson: Revolution, War, and Peace* (Arlington Hights, IL: AHM Publishing Corp., 1979), 79–80.
11 Woodward, *Trial by Friendship*, 60.
12 British war aims in Mesopotamia are fully described in V. H. Rothwell, "Mesopotamia in British War Aims, 1914–1918," *Historical Journal* 13 (1970): 273–94.
13 Bertie to Hardinge, April 20, 1917, Bertie papers, FO 800/191.
14 Notes of a Conference held at 10 Downing Street, April 3, 1917, CAB 24/9/GT372.
15 Minutes of the War Cabinet April 25, 1917, CAB 23/2.
16 Smuts, "Mesopotamian Campaign," July 29, 1917, CAB 24/21/GT1547.
17 A Unionist MP with a substantial private income, he had traveled widely, especially in the Middle East, and spoke Turkish fluently. With the blessing of the Foreign Office, he went to Switzerland to explore if the Turks would be interested in discussing the terms of a peace settlement.
18 V. H. Rothwell, *British War Aims and Peace Diplomacy, 1914–1918* (Oxford: Oxford University Press, 1971), 134–37.

19. Rothwell, *British War Aims*, 137.
20. Smuts, "Note on our Prospects," July 31, 1917, CAB 24/21/GT1573.
21. Minutes of the War Cabinet, July 31, 1917, CAB 23/13; Robertson, "The Present Military Situation in Russia and its Effects on Our Future Plans," July 29, 1917, CAB 24/21/GT1549.
22. The note is quoted in full in James B. Scott, ed., *Official Statement of War Aims and Peace Proposals, December 1916 to November 1918* (Washington, DC: Carnegie Endowment For International Peace, 1921), 129–31.
23. Minutes of the War Cabinet, August 20 and 21, 1917, CAB 23/3.
24. Rothwell, *British War Aims*, 103.
25. The treaty, signed in 1802, provided only a year's truce in the worldwide struggle between France and Britain.
26. Lloyd George, *War Memoirs*, vol. 2, 1218–19.
27. Minutes of the War Cabinet, August 20 and 21, 1917, CAB 23/3; Fritz Fischer, *Germany's Aims in the First World War* (New York: Norton, 1967), 419; Hans W. Gatzke, *Germany's Drive to the West* (Baltimore: John Hopkins Press, 1950), 222–24; L. L. Farrar, *Divide and Conquer* (New York: Columbia University Press, 1978), 90–93.
28. Fischer, *Germany's Aims*, 426.
29. Balfour, "Peace Negotiations," September 20, 1917, CAB 1/25.
30. The letter, addressed to Lloyd George, was passed on to Balfour on September 21; Lloyd George papers, F/160/1/8.
31. A. Ribot, ed., *Journal d'Alexandre Ribot*, (Paris: Plon, 1936), ch. 9; Farrar, *Divide and Conquer*, 94.
32. Minutes of the War Cabinet, September 24, 1917, CAB 23/16.
33. David R. Woodward, "David Lloyd George, a Negotiated Peace with Germany, and the Kühlmann Peace Kite of September, 1917," *Canadian Journal of History* 6 (1971), 86.
34. Minutes of the War Cabinet, September 27, 1917, CAB 23/16.
35. Brock Millman, *Pessimism and British War Policy, 1916–1918* (London: Frank Cass, 2001), 118.
36. Hankey's notes of a conference held at Haig's headquarters, September 26, 1917, CAB 1/25/16; Lloyd George, *War Memoirs*, vol. 2, 1242.
37. Haig's memorandum is discussed in the next chapter.
38. *Times*, September 27, 1917.
39. Trevor Wilson, ed., *The Political Diaries of C. P. Scott, 1911–1928* (Ithaca: Cornell University Press, 1970), 303–4.
40. David R. Woodward, *Lloyd George and the Generals* (Newark, DE: University of Delaware Press, 1983), 203; Lord Riddell, *War Diary, 1914–1918* (London: Ivor Nicolson and Watson, 1933), 285.
41. Woodward, *Lloyd George*, 203; Rothwell, *British War Aims*, 107.
42. Ribot, ed., *Journal*, 216n; Rothwell, *British War Aims*, 107.
43. Minutes of the War Cabinet, September 27, 1917, CAB 23/16.
44. Cited in Woodwood, *Lloyd George*, 204.
45. Balfour to Lloyd George, September 24, 1917, Lloyd George papers, F/3/2/30; Balfour, "Peace Negotiations," September 20, 1917, Balfour papers, ADD 49699.
46. Foreign Office to William Wiseman, October 4, 1917, FO 800/201; Balfour, "Memorandum Circulated to the King and War Cabinet," October 8, 1917, CAB 23/16.
47. Gatzke, *Germany's Drive*, 226ff; Fischer, *Germany's Aims*, 420–28; Farrar, *Divide and Conquer*, 94–95.
48. Scott, ed., *Official Statement of War Aims*, 157–61.

49 Pétain was certainly not the first soldier to advocate the concept of attacks with limited objectives. Lloyd George may not have known it, but Kitchener had tried unsuccessfully to persuade both the French and British High Commands to adopt such tactics as early as the spring of 1915. See Cassar, *Kitchener's War: British Strategy from 1914 to 1916* (Washington, DC: Brassey's, 2004), 163, and ch. 11.
50 Hankey, *Supreme Command*, vol. 2, 662.

11. The Creation of the Supreme War Council

1 Robert Blake, *The Unkown Prime Minister* (London: Eyre and Spottiswoode, 1955), 290.
2 George H. Cassar, *Kitchener's War: British Strategy from 1914 to 1916* (Washington: Brassey's, 2004), 120, 124, 128–29.
3 George H. Cassar, *Asquith as War Leader* (London: Hambledon Press, 1994), 135; Lord Hankey, *The Supreme Command, 1914–1918*, vol. 2 (London: Allen and Unwin, 1961), 449–50.
4 Robertson to Curzon, July 6, 1917, Robertson papers, 8/5/20; Matthew Hughes, *Allenby and British Strategy in the Middle East, 1917–1919* (London: Frank Cass, 1999), 32–33; Cyril Falls, *Military Operations: Egypt and Palestine*, vol. 1, pt. 2 (London: HMSO, 1930), 27.
5 Minutes of the War Policy Committee, September 24, 1917, CAB 27/6.
6 Procès-verbal of an Anglo–French conference, held at Boulogne, September 25, 1917, CAB 28/2.
7 For details of the treaty see Roger Adelson, *Mark Sykes: Portrait of an Amateur* (London: Jonathan Cape, 1975), 199–201; Jukka Nevakivi, *Britain, France and the Arab Middle East, 1914–1920* (London: Athlone Press, 1969), 35–42; David Fromkin, *A Peace to End All Peace* (New York: Henry Holt, 1989), 189–96; Isaiah Friedman, *The Question of Palestine, 1914–1918* (London: Routledge and Kegan Paul, 1973), 107–112; and Elie Kedourie, *Into the Anglo-Arab Labyrinth* (Cambridge: Cambridge University Press, 1976), 123–24, to cite only a few sources.
8 Fromkin, *A Peace*, 288.
9 Fromkin, *A Peace*, 271.
10 John Grigg, *Lloyd George: From Peace to War, 1912–1916* (Berkley: University of California Press, 1985), 349–50.
11 Cassar, *Asquith*, 71–75.
12 David Lloyd George, *War Memoirs*, vol. 1 (London: Odhams, 1938), 349.
13 Jehuda Reinharz, *Chaim Weizmann* (Oxford: Oxford University Press, 1993), 67–68.
14 There is no dearth of published material describing the events leading up to the Balfour Declaration. There are, of course, the memoirs and biographies of the men involved, such as Lloyd George, Balfour, Sykes and Weizmann. Among the better general studies are Fromkin, *A Peace*; Friedman, *Question of Palestine*; David Vital, *Zionism: The Crucial Phase* (Oxford: Clarendon Press, 1987); and Leonard Stein, *The Balfour Declaration* (London: Valentine, Mitchell and Co., 1961), still useful, even if a bit outdated.
15 Vital, *Zionism:* 220.
16 Friedman, *Question of Palestine*, 175.
17 Adelson, *Mark Sykes*, 227–28, 234; .Vital, *Zionism*, passim; Christopher M. Andrew and A. S. Kanya-Forstner, *France Overseas: The Great War and the Climax of French Imperial Expansion* (London: Thames and Hudson, 1981), 126–30.
18 Montagu, "Zionism," October 9, 1917, CAB 24/28/GT2263.

19 David Lloyd George, *Memoirs of the Peace Conference*, vol. 2 (New Haven: Yale University Press, 1939), 733.
20 Curzon, "The Future of Palestine," October 26, 1917, CAB 24/30/GT2406; David Gilmour, *Curzon* (New York: Farrar, Straus and Giroux, 1994), 481.
21 Minutes of the War Cabinet, October 4 and 25, 1917, CAB 23/4.
22 Minutes of the War Cabinet, October 31, 1917, CAB 23/4.
23 Minutes of the War Policy Committee, October 3, 1917, CAB 27/6.
24 Hankey diary, October 6, 1917, Hankey papers.
25 Procès-verbal of an Anglo–French Conference held at Boulogne, September 25, 1917, CAB 28/2.
26 Gary Sheffield and John Bourne, ed., *Douglas Haig: War Diaries and Letters, 1914–1918* (London: Weidenfeld and Nicolson, 2005), 331–32.
27 Robert Blake, ed., *Private Papers of Douglas Haig, 1914–1919* (London: Eyre and Spottiswoode, 1952), 259.
28 Jellicoe, "Future Naval Policy," October 9, 1917, CAB 27/8/GT2250.
29 Haig, "Role of the British Forces Should Russia Fall Out of the War," October 8, 1917, CAB 27/8/GT2243.
30 Milner minute on Haig's memorandum of October 8, 1917, Milner papers, dep. 360/304.
31 Lloyd George, *War Memoirs*, vol. 2, 1243.
32 Robertson to Haig, October 9, 1917, in David R. Woodward, ed., *The Military Correspondence of Field Marshal Sir William Robertson, Chief of the Imperial General Staff, December 1915–February 1918* (London: Bodley Head for Army Records Society, 1989), 234.
33 Minutes of the War Policy Committee, October 8, 1917, CAB 27/6.
34 Robertson, "Future Military Policy," October 9, 1917, CAB 27/8/GT2242.
35 Robertson, "Occupation of Jaffa-Jerusalem Line," October 9, 1917, CAB 27/8/GT2243.
36 David R. Woodward, *Field Marshal Sir William Robertson: Chief of the Imperial Staff in the Great War* (Westport, CN: Praeger, 1998), 161.
37 Paul Painlevé, *Comment j'ai nommé Foch et Pétain*, (Paris: Félix Alcan, 1923), 244–45.
38 The Council of War had been convened to decide whether to ratify or reject the General Staff's prewar military arrangements with the French army.
39 Minutes of the War Cabinet, October 10, 1917, CAB 23/13.
40 Hankey, *Supreme Command*, vol. 2, 712–13.
41 Allenby had maintained that prospects of success against the Turks would be good if he enjoyed a superiority in manpower of two to one. Lloyd George applied his remarks to the western front.
42 Minutes of the War Cabinet, October 11, 1917, CAB 23/13.
43 Secretary's notes of a conversation at Chequers Court, October 14, 1917, CAB 28/2; Hankey, *Supreme Command*, vol. 2, 713–14.
44 Hankey, *Supreme Command*, vol. 2, 714.
45 Hankey, *Supreme Command*, vol. 2, 714–15.
46 French, "The Present State of the War, the Future Prospects, and Future Action to be Taken," October 20, 1917, CAB 27/8/WP60.
47 Wilson, "The Present State of the War, the Future Prospects, and Future Action to be Taken," October 20, 1917, CAB 27/8/WP 61.
48 Memorandum by Robertson, October 26, 1917, CAB 27/8/WP62.
49 Hankey, *Supreme Command*, vol. 2, 716.
50 Mario A. Morselli, *Caporetto 1917: Victory or Defeat* (London: Frank Cass, 2001) is the most recent account of the battle.

51 Hankey, *Supreme Command*, vol. 2, 716–717.
52 Hankey, *Supreme Command*, vol. 2, 718.
53 At a military conference in April 1917 Foch suspected that the Central Powers would launch their next attack from the Trentino and for that reason wanted any Anglo–French troops sent to Italy deployed in the area around Vicenza and Padua and not on the Izonzo front where they risked being cut off. See Morcelli, *Caporetto*, 107.
54 George H. Cassar, *The Forgotten Front: The British Campaign in Italy, 1917–1918* (London: Hambledon Press, 1998), 69–70, 221–22.
55 Cassar, *Forgotten Front*, 70; Field Marshal Sir William Robertson, *From Private to Field Marshal*, (Boston: Houghton Mifflin, 1921), 313; Lloyd George, *War Memoirs*, vol. 2, 1394.
56 Hankey diary, October 29, 1917, Hankey papers.
57 Minutes of the War Cabinet, October 30, 1917, CAB 23/13.
58 Hankey diary, October 31, 1917, Hankey papers.
59 Lloyd George to Painlevé, October 30, 1917, annexed to the minutes of the War Cabinet for the same day, CAB 23/13; Minutes of the War Cabinet, October 31, 1917, CAB 23/13.
60 Minutes of the War Cabinet, November 1, 1917, CAB 23/4.
61 Hankey diary, November 2, 1917, Hankey papers; Minutes of the War Cabinet, November 2, 1917, CAB 23/4.
62 Minutes of the War Cabinet, November 2, 1917, CAB 23/4.
63 Lloyd George, *War Memoirs*, vol. 2, 1438–39.
64 Hankey diary, November 5, 1917, Hankey papers.
65 H. James Burgwyn, *The Legend of the Mutilated Victory: Italy, the Great War, and the Paris Peace Conference, 1915–1919* (Westport, CT: Greenwood Press, 1993), 109–11.
66 "Meeting of Representatives of the British and French Governments, held at the 'New Casino Hotel,' Rapollo," November 5, 1917, CAB 28/2.
67 "Scheme of Organization of an Inter-Allied War Council," November 7, 1917, annexed to the minutes of the Conference, CAB 28/2.
68 Procès-Verbal of a Conference of the British, French, and Italian Governments, held at Rapallo, November 6, 1917, CAB 28/2.
69 "Scheme of Organization of a Supreme War Council," November 7, 1917, annexed to the minutes of the Conference, CAB 28/2.
70 Procès-Verbal of the Conference, November 6 and 7, 1917, CAB 28/2; Painlevé. *Comment j'ai nommé*, 265–66; Lloyd George, *War Memoirs*, vol. 2, 1440.
71 Hankey diary, November 7, 1917, Hankey papers.
72 Field Marshal Sir William Robertson, *From Private to Field Marshal*, (Boston: Houghton Mifflin, 1921), 328.
73 Procès-Verbal of the First Session of the Supreme War Council Held at 4:00 p.m., November 7, 1917, CAB 28/2.

12. The Plans for 1918

1 Hankey diary, November 8, 1917, Hankey papers.
2 John R. Schindler, *Isonzo* (Westport, CT: Prager, 2001), 261–62.
3 Lord Hankey, *The Supreme Command 1914–1918*, vol. 2 (London: Allen and Unwin, 1961), 725–26.
4 *Times*, November 13, 1917.
5 David Lloyd George, *War Memoirs*, vol. 2 (London: Odhams, 1938), 1441.

6 David R. Woodward, *Lloyd George and the Generals* (Newark, DE: University of Delaware Press, 1983), 225.
7 J. M. McEwen, "Northcliffe and Lloyd George at War, 1914–1918," *Historical Journal* 24 (1981), 668; and "Brass-Hats and the British Press," *Canadian Journal of History* 18 (1983), 60–61; Woodward, *Lloyd George*, 223–24; *Nation*, November, 22, 1917; *Daily News*, November 14, 1917; *Spectator*, November 17, 1917.
8 Proceedings of the Army Council, November 12, 1917, annexed to the minutes of the War Cabinet of November 16, 1917, CAB 23/4; Lord Riddell, *War Diary, 1914–1918* (London: Nicholson and and Watson, 1933), 293–94;
9 Minutes of the War Cabinet, November 16, 1917, CAB 23/4.
10 Riddell, *War Diary*, 293–94.
11 Curzon to Lloyd George, November 18, 1917, Lloyd George papers, F/11/8/18.
12 Derby to Lloyd George, November 18, 1918, Lloyd George papers, F14/4/77. The most important part of the letter can be seen in Woodward, *Lloyd George*, 227.
13 Derby to Haig, November 26, 1917, Derby papers, 920 DER (17).
14 Charles Seymour, ed., *The Intimate Papers of Colonel House*, vol. 3 (Boston: Houghton and Mifflin, 1928), 218.
15 David R. Woodward, *Trial By Friendship: Anglo-American Relations, 1917–1918* (Lexington: University Press of Kentucky, 1993), 92–93.
16 Arthur S. Link, ed., *The Papers of Woodrow Wilson*, vol. 44 (Princeton: Princeton University Press, 1983), 125–130.
17 As Woodward has cogently written, American leaders "viewed their country's expansion from coast to coast and overseas in the Philippines and elsewhere as the fulfillment of America's civilizing mission rather than conquest." *Trial By Friendship*, 93.
18 Cited in Woodward, *Trial By Friendship*, 92.
19 Mary R. Kihl, "A Failure of Ambassadorial Diplomacy," *Journal of American History* 57 (1970), 648–51.
20 W. B. Fowler, *British-American Relations, 1917–1918: The Role of Sir William Wiseman* (Princeton: Princeton University Press, 1969), ch. 4.
21 Link, ed., *Papers of Woodrow Wilson*, vol. 44, 373–75.
22 Link, ed., *Papers of Woodrow Wilson*, vol. 45, 69; Seymour, ed., *Papers of Colonel House*, vol. 3, 219.
23 Seymour, ed., *Papers of Colonel House*, vol. 3, 220.
24 Lloyd George, *War Memoirs*, vol. 2, 1446.
25 Paul Painlevé, *Comment j'ai nommé Foch et Pétain* (Paris: Félix Alcan, 1923), 241. Lloyd George had urged Painlevé to be patient to allow him time to prepare British public opinion.
26 Parliamentary Debates, *House of Commons*, November 19, 1917, cols. 883–906.
27 Robertson to Haig, November 22, 1917, Robertson papers, 7/7/67.
28 Randolph S. Churchill, *Lord Derby: King of Lancashire*, (New York: G. P. Putnam's Sons, 1959), 291–92.
29 Minutes of the War Cabinet, November 21, 1917, CAB 23/4.
30 General Sir James Marshall-Cornwall, *Haig as Military Commander* (London: Batsford, 1973), 252, 254; John Terraine, *Douglas Haig: The Educated Soldier* (London: Hutchinson, 1963), 382–83.
31 Walter Reid, *Douglas Haig* (Edinburgh: Birlinn, 2006), 397–98.
32 Minutes of the War Cabinet, December 5, 1917, CAB 23/4.
33 Robert Blake, ed., *Private Papers of Douglas Haig, 1914–1919* (London: Eyre and Spottiswoode, 1952), 270.

34 Cabinet Committee on Man-Power, December 10, 1917, CAB 27/14; General Staff, "Estimated Strength of Opposing Forces," December 8, 1917, CAB 27/14/MPC5.
35 Lloyd George to Robertson, December 11, 1917, Lloyd George papers, F/44/3/38.
36 David R. Woodward, *Field Marshal Sir William Robertson: Chief of the Imperial General Staff in the Great War* (Westport, CT: Praeger, 1998), 163.
37 *Times*, December 12, 1917.
38 Churchill, *Lord Derby*, 297–302; De Groot, *Douglas Haig*, 353–55, 359–60; Blake, ed., *PPDH*, 272–73; Woodward, *Lloyd George*, 231–32; David French, *The Strategy of the Lloyd George Coalition, 1916–1918* (Oxford: Clarendon Press, 1995), 167–68; Marshall-Cornwall, *Haig*, 255–57.
39 Stephen Roskill, "The Dismissal of Admiral Jellicoe." *Journal of Contemporary History* 1 (1966), 70–71.
40 A. J. Marder, *From the Dreadnought to Scapa Flow*, vol. 4 (London: Oxford University Press, 1969), 323–27.
41 Lloyd George, *War Memoirs*, vol. 1, 700.
42 For the details of Geddes' earlier professional activities see Keith Grieves, *Sir Eric Geddes* (Manchester: Manchester University Press, 1989), chs. 1–3.
43 Marder, *From the Dreadnought*, vol. 4, 213–15, 221–22; Hankey, *Supreme Command*, vol. 2, 655.
44 Lady Wester Wemyss, *The Life and Letters of Lord Wester Wemyss* (London: Eyre and Spottiswoode, 1935), 364; Marder, *From the Dreadnought*, vol. 4, 339.
45 Hankey diary, October 26, 1917, Hankey papers.
46 Hankey diary, October 21, 1917, Hankey papers.
47 Marder, *From the Dreadnought*, vol. 4, 299–303, 335–38.
48 A. Temple Patterson, *Jellicoe* (London: Macmillan, 1969), 203–4: Roskill, "The Dismissal of Admiral Jellicoe," 72.
49 Lord Beaverbrook, *Men and Power, 1917–1918* (London: Hutchinson, 1956), 181.
50 Vincent Baddeley, "Rosslyn E. Wemyss," *Dictionary of National Biography, 1931–1940*.
51 John Grigg, *Lloyd George: War Leader, 1916–1918* (London: Allen Lane, 2002), 373–74.
52 Riddell, *War Diary*, 301.
53 War Office, *Statistics of the Military Effort of the British Empire during the Great War, 1914–1920* (London: London Stamp Exchange, 1992), 260–64.
54 French, *Lloyd George Coalition*, 171.
55 Robertson, "Future Military Policy," November 19, 1917, Robertson papers, 4/6/5.
56 Minutes of the War Cabinet, November 26, 1917, CAB 23/13.
57 Jean-Baptiste Duroselle, *Clemenceau* (Paris; Fayard, 1988), 624.
58 Lloyd George has an interesting piece on Clemenceau, which includes his views of, and relations with him, in *War Memoirs*, vol. 2, 1602–9.
59 Derby to Balfour, April 25, April 29, July 14, and August 3, 1918, Balfour papers, ADD 49743.
60 Major General Sir Edward Spears, "An Appreciation " in Nancy Maurice, ed., *The Maurice Case: From the Papers of Major-General Sir Frederick Maurice* (Hamden, CN: Archon Books, 1972), 49.
61 Minutes of the War Cabinet, November 19, 1917, CAB 23/4; Robertson, "Situation in Macedonia," November 14, 1917, CAB 24/32/GT2615.
62 Foch was replying to a question by Herbert Lawrence, Haig's Chief of Staff, as to his working relationship with Weygand. The answer was passed on to Liddell Hart who noted it on September 23, 1929, and can be found among his papers, 2/1929/15.

63 Procès-verbal of the Second Session of the Supreme War Council, December 1, 1917, CAB 28/3.
64 John Turner, *British Politics and the Great War* (New Haven: Yale University Press, 1992), 261–62.
65 Hankey, *Supreme Command*, vol. 2, 740.
66 Draft Report of Cabinet Committee on Manpower, March 1, 1918, CAB 27/14.
67 Hankey diary, December 6, 1917, Hankey papers.
68 Draft Report of the Cabinet Committee on Man-Power, March 1, 1918, CAB 27/14; Hankey, *Supreme Command*, vol. 2, 740–42; R. J. Q. Adams and Philip P. Poirier, The Conscription Controversy in Great Britain, 1900–1918 (London: Macmillan, 1987), 221–22; Macready, "Summary of the Requirements of the Army in men in order to maintain fighting efficiency of the Expeditionary Forces," December 10, 1917, CAB 27/14/MPC4; Brigadier General Sir James E. Edmonds, *Military Operations: France and Belgium, 1918*, vol. 1 (London: Macmillan, 1935), 51.
69 "Memorandum by the Military Members of the Army Council on the draft report of the War Cabinet Committee on Man-Power," January 7, 1918, CAB 24/38/GT3265.
70 Minutes of the War Cabinet, January 7, 1918, CAB 23/13.
71 Field Marshal Sir William Robertson, *Soldiers and Statesmen, 1914–1918*, vol. 1 (London: Cassell, 1926), 320–22.
72 Haig to Robertson, January 7, 1918 (memo sent to Hankey on January 9), CAB 24/38/GT3268; Robertson, *Soldiers and Statesmen*, vol. 1, 322–24.
73 Robertson to Edmonds, December 1, 1932, CAB 45/193.
74 Lloyd George to Robertson, December 11, 1917, in David R. Woodward, ed., *The Military Correspondence of Field Marshal Sir William Robertson, Chief of the Imperial General Staff, December 1915–February 1918* (London: Bodley Head for Army Records Society, 1989), 267.
75 Minutes of the War Cabinet, December 12, 1917, CAB 23/4.
76 Matthew Hughes, *Allenby and British Strategy in the Middle East 1917–1919* (London: Frank Cass, 1999), 64–65.
77 Minutes of the War Cabinet, December 12, 13, and 18, 1917, CAB 23/4; War Office to GOC in Egypt, December 12, 1917; GOC in Egypt to Robertson, December, 14, 1917; Robertson to GOC in Egypt, December 18, 1917; all in CAB 24/37/GT3112.
78 GOC in Egypt to Robertson, December 20, 1817, CAB 24/37/GT3112.
79 Woodward, *Sir William Robertson*, 164.
80 Lloyd George, *War Memoirs*, vol. 2, 1092–93.
81 Permanent Military Representatives, Joint Note No. 12: 1918 campaign, January 21, 1918, CAB 25/120/SWC57.
82 Robertson, "Future Operations in Palestine," December 26, 1917, CAB 24/37/GT3112.
83 Hughes, *Allenby*, 64–65.
84 Wilson's diary, December 30, 1917, Wilson papers.
85 Minutes of the War Cabinet, December 19, 1917, CAB 23/4.
86 Blake, ed., *PPDH*, 277–78.
87 Hankey diary, January 18, 1918, Hankey papers.
88 Haig diary, January 21, 1918, Haig papers.
89 Woodward, *Lloyd George*, 246.
90 Liddell Hart talk with Lloyd George, September 2, 1932, Liddell Hart papers, 11/1932/42.

91 Robertson to Gwynne, January 22, 1918, in Woodward, ed., *MCWR*, 273–74. See also Stamfordham, Memorandum, February 13–18, 1918, RA GV F1259/32.
92 Maurice to his wife, February 6, 1918, Maurice papers, 3/1/4.
93 Hankey diary, January 31, 1917, Hankey papers.
94 Robertson to Derby, February 2, 1918, Derby papers, 920 DER (17).
95 Procès-verbal of the morning session of the Supreme War Council, February 1, 1918, CAB 28/3.
96 Admiral Sir John Fisher (then First Sea Lord) had, despite serious misgivings, offered no opinion during the discussion that led to the Dardanelles campaign in January 1915.
97 Hankey diary, February 2, 1918, Hankey papers.
98 On July 20, 1916, the Asquith cabinet had appointed a Royal Commission to inquire into the origin and conduct of the ill-fated Dardanelles campaign.
99 Robertson, *Soldiers and Statesmen*, vol. 2, 287–88.
100 Procès-verbal of the afternoon session of the Supreme War Council, February 1, 1918, CAB 28/3.
101 Robertson to Lloyd George, February 1, 1918, Robertson papers, 7/8/5. Most of letter was reproduced in Victor Bonham-Carter, *Soldier True: The Life and Times of Field Marshal Sir William Robertson*, (London: Frederick Muller, 1963), 329, and Woodward, *Lloyd Geiorge*, 259.
102 Woodward, *Lloyd George*, 259.
103 Hankey, *Supreme Command*, vol. 2, 769.
104 Procès-verbal of the Supreme War Council, February 2, 1918, CAB 28/3; Blake, ed., *PPDH*, 282.
105 Peter E. Wright, *At the Supreme War Council* (London: Eveleigh Nash, 1921), 62.
106 Terraine, *Douglas Haig*, 403.
107 Hankey, *Supreme Command*, vol. 2, 752–54; Edmonds, *France and Belgium, 1918*, vol. 1, 46–47. Lloyd George, *War Memoirs*, vol. 2, 1656–61.
108 Procès-verbal of the Supreme War Council, February 2, 1918, CAB 28/3.
109 Gary Sheffield and John Bourne, *Douglas Haig: War Diaries and Letters, 1914–1918* (London: Weidenfeld and Nicolson, 2005), 378.
110 Minutes of the War Cabinet, January 28, 1918, CAB 23/5.
111 Cited in Hughes, *Allenby*, 68.

13. Before the Storm

1 Lord Riddell, *War Diary, 1914–1918* (London: Ivor Nicholson and Watson, 1933), 283.
2 The Lansdowne memorandum of November 13, 1917 can be found, among other places, in CAB 37/159/32.
3 Riddell, *War Diary*, 296; Minutes of the War Cabinet, December 4, 1917, CAB 23/13.
4 *Times*, December 15, 1917.
5 Frank Owen, *Tempestuous Journey* (New York: McGraw-Hill, 1955), 441–42.
6 Cecil to Lloyd George, December 5, 1917, Lloyd George Papers, 5/6/5/10; Barnes, "Notes on the War," December 30, 1917, CAB 1/25/28; Riddell, *War Diary*, 297–98; Peter Rowland, *Lloyd George* (London: Barrie and Jenkins, 1975), 427; John Turner, *British Politics and the Great War* (New Haven: Yale University Press, 1992), 249–52.
7 Stephen Roskill, *Hankey*, vol. 1 (London: Collins, 1970), 471. Barnes was another who gave similar advice. See his letter to Lloyd George, December 30, 1917, CAB 1/25/28.

8. Smuts, Report of General Smuts Mission, Part 1, December 18 and 19, 1917, CAB 1/25/27. The text is printed in full in David Lloyd George, *War Memoirs*, vol. 2 (London: Odhams, 1938), 1478–89.
9. In return for intervention against Austria, Italy was promised, among other things, the Trentino, South Tyrol, the entire Istrian peninsula to the outskirts of Fiume and a share of Ottoman territory.
10. Wilfried Fest, *Peace or Partition: The Hapsburg Monarchy and British Policy, 1914–1918* (London: George Prior, 1978), 162.
11. V. H. Rothwell, *British War Aims and Peace Diplomacy, 1914–1918* (Oxford: Clarendon Press, 1971), 171–72.
12. Gary Sheffield and John Bourne, eds., *Douglas Haig: War Diaries and Letters, 1914–1918* (London: Weidenfeld and Nicolson, 2005), 382.
13. Kerr, "Note of interview with Dr. Parodi, Head of the Mission Scolaire Égyptienne," December 19, 1917, CAB 1/25/27.
14. Arno J. Mayer, *Political Origins of the New Diplomacy, 1917–1918* (New Haven: Yale University Press, 1959), 278.
15. David R. Woodward, "The Origins and Intent of David Lloyd George's January 5 War Aims Speech," *Historian* 29, (1971). Czernin's statement is in James B. Scott, ed., *Official Statement of War Aims and Peace Proposals, December 1916 to November 1918* (Washington: Carnegie Endowment, 1921), 221–23.
16. Rothwell, *British War Aims*, 147.
17. Victor S. Mamatey, *The United States and East Central Europe, 1914–1918* (Port Washington, NY: Kennikat Press, 1972), 175.
18. No minutes for the meeting on December 28 were taken on orders of the Prime Minister. However a record for the proceedings on December 31 does exist and can be found in CAB 23/13.
19. Minutes of the War Cabinet, January 3, 1918, CAB 23/5.
20. Robertson, "Present Military Situation with Reference to the Peace Proposals by the Central Powers," December 29, 1917, CAB 24/37/GT3145.
21. Minutes of the War Cabinet, January 3, 1918, CAB 23/5.
22. Minutes of the War Cabinet, January 3 and 4, 1918, CAB 23/5; J. L. Hammond, *C. P. Scott of the Manchester Guardian* (London: Harcourt, Brace and Co., 1934), 232.
23. David French, *The Strategy of Lloyd George Coalition, 1916–1918* (Oxford: Clarendon Press, 1995), 202–03; Barnes, "Notes on the War," December 30, 1917, CAB 1/25/28.
24. Smuts, "War Aims," January 3, 1918, CAB 24/37/GT3180; Cecil, "War Aims," January 3, 1918, CAB 24/37/3181.
25. It appears that Kerr sent a memorandum to Lloyd George on December 4, 1917, containing a warning that Asquith's supporters were urging him to publicly endorse Landsdowne's position. The note was unsigned and may not have been written by Kerr. Lloyd George papers, F/89/1/9.
26. Stephen Koss, *Asquith* (London: Allen Lane, 1976), 231–32; Trevor Wilson, ed., *The Political Diaries of C. P. Scott, 1911–1928* (Ithaca, NY: Cornell University Press, 1970), 327–28; Lloyd George, *War Memoirs*, vol. 2, 1492.
27. "The Labour Party and the TUC, Memorandum on War Aims," December 28, 1917, CAB 24/37/GT3167; Keith Robbins, *The Abolition of War: The Peace Movement in Britain, 1914–1918* (Cardiff: University of Wales Press, 1976), 152–53; Mayer, *Political Origins*, 315–21.
28. Lloyd George, *War Memoirs*, vol. 2, 1491
29. J. M. McEwen, ed., *The Riddell Diaries, 1908–1923* (London: Athlone Press, 1986), 210.

30 Paul Painlevé, *Comment j'ai nommé Foch et Pétain* (Paris: Félix Alcan, 1921), 249–51.
31 The text is printed in full in Lloyd George, *War Memoirs*, vol. 2, 1510–17.
32 French, *Lloyd George Coalition*, 205.
33 Lloyd George told Riddell that "the speech was a counter-offensive against the German peace terms with a view to appealing to the German people and detaching the Austrians." Riddell, *War Diaries*, 304.
34 Riddell, *War Diaries*, 304–5.
35 Esher to Hankey, January 13, 1918, Lloyd George papers, F/23/2/9.
36 French, *Lloyd George Coalition*, 205.
37 Arthur S. Link, ed., *The Papers of Woodrow Wilson*, vol. 45 (Princeton: Princeton University Press, 1984), 556–57.
38 Drummond to Spring Rice, January 12, 1918, FO 800/209.
39 Rothwell, *British War Aims*, 164–65.
40 Minutes of the War Cabinet, January 8, 1918, CAB 23/16.
41 *Times*, January 19, 1918.
42 Fritz Fischer, *Germany's Aims in the First World War* (New York: Norton, 1967), 614–17.
43 Derby to Lloyd George, January 11, 1918, Lloyd George papers, F/14/5/2.
44 Hankey diary, February 3, 1918, Hankey papers.
45 Robertson to Derby, February 2, 1918, in David R. Woodward, ed., *The Military Correspondence of Field Marshal Sir William Robertson, Chief of the Imperial General Staff, December 1915–February 1918* (London: Bodley Head for Army Records Society, 1989), 281.
46 Derby memorandum (to Lloyd George), February 4, 1918, Derby papers, 920 DER (17).
47 Minutes of the War Cabinet, February 4, 1918, CAB 23/5.
48 Minutes of the Army Council, February 4–6, 1918, WO 163/23.
49 Derby to Haig, February 7, 1918, Haig papers, no. 123.
50 Robertson to Haig, February 7, 1918, Haig papers, no. 123.
51 Haig to Derby, February 8, 1918, Derby papers, 920 DER (17).
52 Milner to Lloyd George, February 8, 1917, Milner papers, dep. 669/39.
53 Milner Memorandum, February 14, 1917, Milner papers, dep. 374/54. This is the most detailed documentary record of the events leading to Robertson's dismissal. See also the excellent account in David R. Woodward, *Lloyd George and the Generals* (Newark, NJ: University of Delaware Press, 1983), 262–72.
54 Robert Blake, ed., *The Private Papers of Douglas Haig, 1914–1919* (London: Eyre and Spottiswoode, 1952), 283–84.
55 Blake, ed., *PPDH*, 284–85; Lloyd George to Milner, February 9, 1918, Milner papers, dep. 355/23.
56 Randolph S. Churchill, *Lord Derby: King of Lancashire*, (New York: G.P. Putnam's Sons, 1960), 310.
57 Haig to Lady Haig, February 5, 1918, Haig papers, no. 149.
58 John Terraine, *Douglas Haig* (London: Hutchinson, 1963), 407.
59 "Note from the Prime Minister to the Secretary of State for War," n.d.; "Minute from C.I.G.S. to Secretary of State for War," February 11, 1918; "Minute from Secretary of State for War to C.I.G.S., February 11, 1911, all annexed to the minutes of the War Cabinet, February 12, 1918, CAB 23/13.
60 Blake, ed., *PPDH*, 284.
61 "Minute by the Army Council," February 11, 1918, annexed to the minutes of the War Cabinet, February 12, 1918, CAB 23/13.
62 Minutes of the War Cabinet, February 11, 1918, CAB 23/5.
63 Minutes of the War Cabinet, February 11, 1918, CAB 23/5.

64 Lloyd George, *War Memoirs*, vol. 2, 1676.
65 Milner to Lloyd George, February 11, 1918, Lloyd George papers, F/38/3/12.
66 Minutes of the War Cabinet, February 11, 1918, CAB 23/13; Hankey diary, February 12, 1918, Hankey papers; Milner memorandum, February 14, 1918, Milner papers, dept. 374; Woodward, *Lloyd George*, 267.
67 Parliamentary Debates, *House of Commons*, February 12, 1918, vol. 103, cols. 14–30.
68 Hankey diary, February 13, 1918, Hankey papers.
69 Field Marshal Sir William Robertson, *Soldiers and Statesmen*, vol. 1 (London: Cassell, 1926), 235.
70 Churchill, *Lord Derby*, 322.
71 Milner to Lloyd George, February 13, 1918, Lloyd George papers, F/38/3/13.
72 Stamfordham memorandum, Royal Archives, RV GV F1239/32. An objective account of the crisis between February 13 and February 16, 1918.
73 "Statement by General Sir William Robertson," February 14, 1918, annexed to the minutes of the War Cabinet, February 14, 1918, CAB 23/13.
74 Minutes of the War Cabinet, February 14, 1918, CAB 23/13.
75 Balfour's notes of a conversation with Robertson, February 14, 1918, Balfour papers, ADD 49726.
76 Hankey diary, February 15, 1918, Hankey papers; Minutes of the War Cabinet, February 16, 1918, CAB 23/13.
77 Roskill, *Hankey*, vol. 1, 497; Esher War Journals, February 15, 1918, Esher papers.
78 Lord Hankey, *The Supreme Command, 1914–1918*, vol. 2 (London: Allen and Unwin, 1961), 778.
79 Stamfordham memorandum, Royal Archives, RA GV F1239/32; Minutes of the War Cabinet, February 16, 1918, CAB 23/13.
80 Minutes of the War Cabinet, February 16, 1918, CAB 23/13.
81 Robertson, *Soldiers and Statesmen*, vol. 1, 236–37.
82 Robertson to Haig, February 12, 1918, in Woodward, ed., *MCWR*, 303.
83 Blake, ed., *PPDH*, 286.
84 Blake, ed., *PPDH*, 286.
85 Lloyd George, *War Memoirs*, vol. 2, 1689.
86 Wilson diary, February 17, 1918, Wilson papers.
87 Hankey diary, February 17, 1918, Hankey papers.
88 Esher War Journals, February 18, 1918, Esher papers.
89 Charles à Court Repington, *The First World War*, vol. 2 (Boston: Houghton Mifflin, 1921), 246.
90 Parliamentary Debates, *House of Commons*, February 19, 1918, vol 103, cols. 633–54.
91 Blake, ed., *PPDH*, 290.
92 Diaries of Wilson and Haig for February 25, 1918.
93 Wilson's diary, March 4, 1918, Wilson papers.
94 Minutes of the War Cabinet, March 6, 1918, CAB 23/13.
95 Terraine, *Haig*, 408.
96 Blake, ed., *PPDH*, 291.
97 Blake, ed., *PPDH*, 291.
98 Wilson diary, March 13, 1918, Wilson papers.
99 Milner to Lloyd George, March 14, 1918, Lloyd George papers, F/38/3/19.
100 In *War Memoirs*, vol. 2, 1720, Lloyd George falsely claimed that he did not know until the Supreme War Council met on the morning of March 14 that Clemenceau had encouraged both Haig and Pétain to retain all the divisions under their command.

Wilson had known about it since February 26, and discussed it with him and other members of the War Cabinet.
101 Blake, ed., *PPDH*, 292.
102 Minutes of the Superior War Council, first session held at 10 Downing Street, March 14, 1918, at 11.30 a.m., 28/3; Haig diary, March 14, 1918, Haig papers; Lloyd George, *War Memoirs*, vol. 2, 1720.
103 Cited in Woodward, *Lloyd George*, 277.

14. Crisis on the Western Front

1 There are four major biographies on Wilson: Bernard Ash, *The Lost Dictator: A Biography of Field Marshal Sir Henry Wilson* (London: Cassell, 1968); Basil Collier, *Brasshat: A Biography of Field Marshal Sir Henry Wilson, 1864–1922* (London: Secker and Warburg, 1961); Major General Sir C. E. Callwell, *Field Marshal Sir Henry Wilson*, 2 vols. (London: Cassell, 1927); and Keith Jeffrey, *Field Marshal Sir Henry Wilson* (Oxford: Oxford University Press, 2006).
2 David Lloyd George, *War Memoirs*, vol. 2 (London: Odhams Press, 1938), 1688.
3 Lloyd George, *War Memoirs*, vol. 2, 1688.
4 Cyril Falls, *Military Operations: Egypt and Palestine*, vol. 2, pt. 1 (London: HMSO, 1930), 298.
5 Minutes of the War Cabinet, February 21, 1918, CAB 21/13.
6 Minutes of the War Cabinet, March 4 and 6, 1918, CAB 21/13; David R. Woodward, *Lloyd George and the Generals*, (Newark, DE: University of Delaware Press, 1983), 283.
7 Milner to Lloyd George, March 20, 1918, Lloyd George papers, F/38/3/20.
8 See for example Robertson, "Future Military Policy," November 19, 1917, Robertson papers, 4/6/5; Maurice to Lloyd George, December 18, 1917, Lloyd George papers, F/44/3/40; Minutes of the War Cabinet, December 19, CAB 23/4.
9 On the German offensives in 1918 see Martin Kitchen, *The German Offensives of 1918* (Stroud: Tempus, 2001).
10 Erich von Ludendorff, *Ludendorff's Own Story*, vol. 2 (New York: Harper and Bros., 1919), 221.
11 Rather than advance along the whole front with massed ranks of infantrymen, the idea was to infiltrate weak spots in the line with small and well-equipped infantry groups. Moving speedily ahead, the leading assault units would bypass pockets of resistance, leaving them to be mopped up by forces following behind. Such tactics allowed the attackers, at the risk of leaving their flanks unguarded, to isolate enemy units, disrupt communications and reach rear areas before reserves could be brought up. For an in-depth look at the von Hutier tactics and their evolution see Bruce I. Gudmundsson, *Stormtroop Tactics: Innovation in the German Army, 1914–1918* (New York: Praeger, 1989); T. Lupfer, *The Dynamics of Doctrine: The Changes in German Tactical Doctrine during the First World War* (Fort Leavenworth, KS: Combat Studies Institute, 1981).
12 Haig diary, March 21 and 22, 1918, Haig papers; Gerald J. De Groot, *Douglas Haig, 1861–1928* (London: Unwin Hyman, 1988), 371–72.
13 Minutes of the War Cabinet, March 21 and 22, 1918, CAB 23/5.
14 Lloyd George to his wife, March 22, 1918, in Kenneth O. Morgan, *Lloyd George: Family Letters, 1885–1936* (Cardiff and London: University of Wales Press/Oxford University Press, 1973), 186.
15 Lord Riddell, *War Diary*, (London: Ivor Nicholson and Watson, 1933), 319.
16 Lloyd George, *War Memoirs*, vol. 2, 1727–28.

17 Minutes of the War Cabinet, March 24, 1918, CAB 23/5.
18 Lloyd George, *War Memoirs*, vol. 2, 1730–31.
19 Wilson diary, March 24, 1918, Wilson papers.
20 Wilson diary, March 24, 1918, Wilson papers.
21 Winston, S. Churchill, *The World Crisis*, vol. 4 (New York: Charles Scribner's Sons, rep. 1955), 144.
22 Riddell, *War Diary*, 321.
23 Minutes of the War Cabinet, March 25, 1918, CAB 23/5.
24 Robert Blake, ed., *The Private Papers of Douglas Haig, 1914–1919* (London: Eyre and Spottiswoode, 1952), 297; Clive diary, March 24, 1918, Clive papers. In Haig's original handwritten version there is no mention of Pétain's state of mind. The typescript, produced after the war, contained many amendments, mostly minor. Still, in view of the unflattering manner in which French contemporary sources described Pétain's comportment at the time, Haig's observation, even if it was recorded a few years later, was probably correct.
25 Wilson diary, March 25, 1918, Wilson papers.
26 Milner, "Memorandum ... on his visit to France, including the conference at Doullens, March 26, 1918," CAB 28/3; Wilson diary, March 26, 1918, Wilson papers, Haig diary, March 26, 1918, Haig papers; Raymond Poincaré, *Au Service de la France*, vol. 10 (Paris: Plon, 1933), 89–90.
27 Haig diary, March 26, 1918, Haig papers.
28 John Terraine, *Douglas Haig: The Educated Soldier* (London: Hutchinson, 1963), 426.
29 Lloyd George, *War Memoirs*, vol. 2, 1817.
30 Lloyd George, *War Memoirs*, vol. 2, 1792–93.
31 David F. Trask, *The United States in the Supreme War Council* (Middletown, CN: Wesleyan University Press, 1961), 74.
32 Trask, *Supreme War Council*, 72.
33 Field Marshal Sir William Robertson, *Soldiers and Statesmen*, vol. 1 (London: Cassell, 1926), 327–30.
34 Robertson, "American Battalions for British Divisions," January 12, 1918, Robertson papers, 4/6/6.
35 Cited in Donald Smythe, *Pershing*, (Bloomington: Indiana University Press), 115.
36 Daniel R. Beaver, *Newton D. Baker and the American War Effort, 1917–1919* (Lincoln: University of Newbraska Press, 1966), 134–36.
37 Reading to Lloyd George, April 7, 1918, WO 106/475. The cable was included with another one sent a week later.
38 Riddell, *War Diary*, 322.
39 B. H. Liddell Hart, *Foch*, (Boston: Little, Brown and Co., 1932), 285–86.
40 David Woodward has argued that Wilson's action was motivated by self-interest in that he recognized that increasing Foch's power would undercut his own authority. See *Lloyd George*, 289.
41 Minutes of the War Cabinet, April 2, 1918, CAB 23/5.
42 Lloyd George, *War Memoirs*, vol. 2, 1745.
43 Wilson diary, April 3, 1918, Wilson papers.
44 Procès-verbal of a Conference held at the Hôtel de Ville, Beauvais, April 3, 1918, CAB 28/3; Wilson diary, April 3, 1918, Wilson papers; Haig diary, April 3, 1918, Haig papers; Lord Hankey, *The Supreme Command, 1914–1918*, vol. 2 (London: Allen and Unwin, 1961), 791–92.
45 At the fifth session of the Supreme War Council on May 2, Vittorio Orlando, the Italian Prime Minister, proposed a compromise in response to Clemenceau's insistence that

Foch's authority be extended to cover the Italian front. He would allow Foch to coordinate the movements of the Italian army but refused to grant him full powers unless Allied forces in Italy fought under the same conditions as those in France. Failing that (as was virtually certain), the Italian front would be subject to Foch's coordinating authority as defined in the Doullens agreement of March 26. In other words, Foch's authority in Italy was to be merely advisory, not executive. The Belgians, for their part, held out against accepting Foch's directions until the final autumn offensive.

46 Terraine, *Haig*, 426
47 Trevor Wilson, *The Myriad Faces of War* (Oxford: Polity Press, 1986), 568.
48 Haig diary, March 31, 1918, Haig papers.
49 Woodward, *Lloyd George*, 238; and his article "Did Lloyd George Starve the British Army of Men Prior to the German Offensive of March 21, 1918?" *Historical Journal* 27 (1984): 241–52.
50 Quoted in Brigadier General Sir James E. Edmonds, *Military Operations: France and Belgium, 1918*, vol. 2 (London, Macmillan, 1937), 468n.
51 Edmonds, *France and Belgium, 1918*, vol. 2, 470.
52 Lloyd George, *War Memoirs*, vol. 2, 1709–10, 1715–16, 2019.
53 Lloyd George, *War Memoirs*, vol. 2, 1820.
54 General Sir Hubert Gough, *The Fifth Army* (London: Hodder and Stoughton, 1931), 229ff.
55 See especially Edmonds, *France and Belgium, 1918*, vol. 2, 119–20.
56 Woodward, *Lloyd George*, 292.
57 Lloyd George, *War Memoirs*, vol. 2, 1741–42.
58 Blake, ed., *PPDH*, 301; De Groot, *Douglas Haig*, 375–76.
59 Wilson diary, April 8, 1918, Wilson papers; Hankey diary, April 8, 1918, Hankey papers.

15. The Maurice Affair

1 Parliamentary Debates, *House of Commons*, April 9, 1918, vol. 104, cols. 1337–51.
2 Minutes of the War Cabinet, April 9, 1918, CAB 23/6.
3 B. H. Liddell Hart, *Foch* (Boston: Little, Brown and Co., 1932), 299.
4 Randolph S. Churchill, *Lord Derby: King of Lancashire* (New York: G. P. Putnum's Sons), 341ff; John Turner, *British Politics and the Great War* (New Haven: Yale University Press, 1992), 294; A. M. Gollin, *Proconsul in Politics*, (London: Anthony Blond, 1964), 508–9.
5 Minutes of the War Cabinet, April 17, 1918, CAB 23/6.
6 Daniel R. Beaver, *Newton D. Baker and the American War Effort, 1917–1918* (Lincoln: University of Newbraska Press, 1966), 140.
7 John J. Pershing, *My Experiences in the World War*, vol. 2 (New York: Frederick Stokes, 1931), 5–7; Donald Smythe, *Pershing*, (Bloomington: Indiana University Press, 1986), 109–10; David R. Woodward, *Trial By Friendship: Anglo-American Relations, 1917–1918* (Lexington: University Press of Kentucky, 1993), 160.
8 Procès-verbal of the Supreme War Council, May 1–2, 1918, CAB 28/3.
9 Brigadier General Sir James E. Edmonds, *Military Operations: France and Belgium: 1918*, vol 2, (London: Macmillan, 1937), 488–90. The total British losses for the two battles, that is, between March 21 and April 30, were placed at 236,300. The French, who played a smaller role, lost about 92,000 men. German losses amounted to 348,000, slightly higher than the Allied total.
10 Parliamentary Debates, *House of Commons*, April 23, 1918, vol. 105, col. 851–52.
11 Robert Blake, ed., *The Private Papers of Douglas Haig, 1914–1919* (London: Eyre and Spottiswoode, 1955), 306.

12 Major General Sir Frederick Maurice, *Intrigues of the War* (London: Loxley Bros., 1922), 34–35.
13 Maurice wrote a letter to his children telling them about his article that was about to be published in the press, his reasons for doing so, and the consequences that awaited him. The letter (4/5/5), dated May 5, 1918, can be found in his collection.
14 David R. Woodward, *Field Marshal Sir William Robertson: Chief of the Imperial General Staff in the Great War*,(Westport, CN: Praeger, 1998), 209.
15 A. J. P. Taylor, *English History, 1914–1945* (Oxford University Press, 1965), 104.
16 John Gooch, "The Maurice Debate," *Journal of Contemporary History* 3 (1968), 218.
17 Maurice, *Intrigues*, 35.
18 David R. Woodward, *Lloyd George and the Generals (Newark, DE: University of Deleware Press, 1983)*, 299–300.
19 David Lloyd George, *War Memoirs*, vol. 2 (London: Odhams, 1938), 1673.
20 Lord Beaverbrook, *Men and Power, 1917–1918* (London: Hutchinson, 1956), 252.
21 Minutes of the War Cabinet, May 7, 1918, CAB 23/6.
22 Parliamentary Debates, *House of Commons*, vol. 105, May 7, 1918, cols. 1981–84.
23 Beaverbrook, *Men and Power*, 253–54.
24 Minutes of the War Cabinet, May 8, 1918.
25 Cited in Turner, *British Politics*, 299.
26 Charles à Court Repington, *The First World War*, vol. 2, (Boston: Houghton Mifflin, 1921), 298.
27 Beaverbrook, *Men and Power*, 255.
28 Parliamentary Debates, *House of Commons*, May 9, 1918, cols. 2347–54.
29 Maurice, *Intrigues*, 34.
30 Nancy Maurice, ed., *The Maurice Case* (Hamden, CN: Archon Books, 1972), 80.
31 Hankey diary, May 9, 1918, Hankey papers. In October 1934 J. T. Davies (private secretary to Lloyd George, 1915–1922, and for many years after, a valued confidant) and Frances Stevenson were sorting out official papers when they came across a document written by Radcliffe dated May 8, 1918, in which he corrected the first figures sent out by the Adjutant General's Office. Davies crumbled the document and threw it in the fire, remarking, "Only you and I, Frances, know of the existence of this paper." He was wrong, thanks to Hankey and, ironically, Frances Stevenson, who noted the incident in her diary eighteen years later.
32 Minutes of the War Cabinet, March 23, 1918, CAB 23/5.
33 Blake, ed., *PPDH*, 309.
34 Parliamentary Debates, *House of Commons*, May 9, 1918, vol. 105, col. 2373.
35 Turner, *British Politics*, 299–300.
36 Blake, ed., *PPDH*, 308–9.
37 Minutes of the War Cabinet, May 14, 1918, CAB 23/6; L. S. Amery, *My Political Life*, vol. 2 (London: Hutchinson, 1953), 157–58 ; David French, *The Strategy of the Lloyd George Coalition*, (Oxford: Clarendon Press, 1995), 232–33; Woodward, *Lloyd George*, 304.
38 David F. Trask, *The United States in the Supreme War Council* (Middletown, CN: Wesleyan University Press, 1961), 65.

16. The Origins of Intervention in Russia

1 The Bolsheviks were unwilling to extend diplomatic privileges to officials in the various foreign embassies unless their governments granted the same rights to Russian agents. The idea that governments would allow within their borders agents who would plot their overthrow was plainly absurd and a demand that the British were reluctant to meet.

2 David French, *Strategy of the Lloyd George Coalition, 1916–1918* (Oxford: Clarendon Press, 1995), 176–77.
3 Michael Kettle, *The Allies and the Russian Collapse, 1917–1918*, vol. 1 (London: André Deutsch., 1981), 117–18.
4 Kettle, *Allies and the Russian Collapse*, vol. 1, 132.
5 Minutes of the War Cabinet, November 21, 1917, CAB 23/4.
6 Charles Seymour, *The Intimate Papers of Colonel House*, vol. 3 (Boston: Houghton Mifflin, 1928), 236–37.
7 Minutes of the War Cabinet, November 22, 1917, CAB 23/4.
8 Minutes of the War Cabinet, November 29, 1917, CAB 23/4.
9 Kettle, *Allies and the Russian Collapse*, 132.
10 "Notes of a Conversation Held at the Ministry of Foreign Affairs, Paris, on November 30 and December 1, 1917," CAB 28/3.
11 Minutes of the War Cabinet, December 3, 1917, CAB 23/4.
12 Richard H. Ullman, *Anglo-Soviet Relations, 1917–1921*, vol. 1 (Princeton: Princeton University Press, 1961), 46–49.
13 Ullman, *Anglo-Soviet Relations*, vol. 1, 49.
14 Minutes of the War Cabinet, December 7, 1917, CAB 23/4.
15 Balfour, "Notes on the Present Russian Situation," December 9, 1917. The memorandum is annexed to the minutes of the War Cabinet for December 10, CAB 23/4.
16 Minutes of the War Cabinet, December 10, 1917, CAB 23/4.
17 Robertson to Plumer, December 10, 1917, Robertson papers, 8/3/41.
18 Minutes of the War Cabinet December 19, 1917, CAB 23/4.
19 Hankey diary, December 23, 1917, Hankey papers.
20 John Grigg, *Lloyd George: War Leader, 1916–1918* (London: Allen Lane, 2002), 432.
21 Formed in 1903, the Cadet (Constitutional Democratic) Party was liberal in outlook and favored a parliamentary system on the west European model.
22 R.H. Bruce Lockhart, *Memoirs of a British Agent* (London: repr. Pan Books, 2002), 196–97.
23 Lockhart, *Memoirs*, 199–200.
24 Minutes of the War Cabinet, January 17 and 22, 1918, CAB 23/5.
25 Lockhart, *Memoirs*, 221–23.
26 Minutes of the War Cabinet, February 9, 1918, CAB 23/5.
27 Kettle, *Allies and the Russian Collapse*, vol. 1, 224.
28 Minutes of the War Cabinet, February 8, 1918, CAB 23/5; Additional information is provided in Keith Middlemas, ed., Thomas Jones, *Whitehall Diary, 1916–1925*, vol. 1 (London: Oxford University Press, 1969), 48–52. Jones was Assistant Secretary of the War Cabinet.
29 Hankey diary, February 8, 1918, Hankey papers.
30 Balfour's memorandum is published in its entirety in David Lloyd George, *War Memoirs*, vol. 2 (London: Odhams, 1938), 1555–57.
31 The provisions of the treaty can be found in any text on Russian history.
32 David Lloyd George, *War Memoirs*, vol. 2, (London: Odhams, 1938), 1888.
33 Minutes of the War Cabinet, February 25, 1918, CAB23/5.
34 Stephen Roskill, *Hankey: Man of Secrets*, vol. 1 (London: Collins, 1970), 501–2.
35 Series of notes sent by Wiseman to Drummond during March 1918; Reading to Balfour, March 29, 1917, all in Balfour papers, ADD 49741; David R. Woodward, "The British Government and Japanese Intervention in Russia During World War I," *Journal of Modern History* 46 (1974), 663–71; Eugene P. Trani, "Woodrow Wilson and the Decision to Intervene in Russia: A Reconsideration," *Journal of Modern History* 48 (1976),

441–45; French, *Lloyd George Coalition*, 240–1; Kettle, *Allies and the Russian Collapse*, vol. 1, 250–51, 253.
36 Minutes of the X Committee, May 17, 1918, CAB 23/17.
37 Minutes of the War Cabinet, May 17, 1918, CAB 23/6.
38 Cited in Ullman, *Anglo-Soviet Relations*, vol. 1, 171.
39 Minutes of the War Cabinet, May 29, 1918, CAB 23/6.
40 Procès-verbal of the third meeting of the Supreme War Council, June 3, 1918, CAB 28/4.
41 Minutes of the War Cabinet, June 6, 1918, CAB 23/6.
42 Minutes of the X Committee, June 19, 1918, CAB 23/17.
43 Grigg, *Lloyd George: War Leader*, 567.
44 For further details see David R. Woodward, "British Intervention in Russia during the First World War," *Military Affairs* 41 (1977), 171–75.
45 Woodward, "British Government and Japanese Intervention," 679–80.
46 Minutes of the X Committee, June 24, 1918, CAB 23/17.
47 Notes of an interview between the Prime Minister and M. Kerensky, at 10 Downing Street, June 24, 1918, CAB 24/55/GT4948; Minutes of the Committee of Prime Ministers, June 24, 1918, CAB 23/44; Lord Hankey, *The Supreme Command, 1914–1918*, vol. 2 (London: Allen and Unwin, 1961), 819; Lloyd George, *War Memoirs*, vol. 2, 1904–6; Lord Riddell, *War Diary, 1914–1918* (London: Ivor Nicholson and Watson, 1933), 335.
48 Minutes of the Committee of Prime Ministers, June 26, 1918, CAB 23/44.
49 Minutes of the Imperial War Cabinet, June 27, 1918, CAB 23/41.
50 After the treaty of Brest-Litovsk, some 800,000 German and Austrian prisoners were released east of the Urals.
51 Procès-verbaux of the Supreme War Council, July 2–4, 1918, CAB 28/4. The British proposal is annexed to the minutes of the meeting.
52 Lloyd George, *War Memoirs*, vol. 2, 1906.
53 Minutes of the War Cabinet, July 16, 1918, CAB 23/7.
54 Ullman, *Anglo-Soviet Relations*, vol. 1, 221–22; Lloyd George *War Memoirs*, vol. 2, 1906–7.
55 The aide-memoire is published in full in George F. Kennan, *The Decision to Intervene*, vol. 2 (New York: Atheneum, 1967), 482–85.

17. The German Advance Halted

1 Minutes of the X Committee, May 15, 1918, CAB 23/17.
2 Stephen Roskill, *Hankey: Man of Secrets*, vol. 1 (London: Collins, 1970), 551–52.
3 David R. Woodward, *Lloyd George and the Generals* (Newark, DE: University of Delaware Press, 1983), 311–12.
4 Brock Millman, *Pessimism and British War Policy, 1916–1918* (London: Frank Cass, 2001), 253.
5 Major General Sir C. E. Callwell, *Field Marshal Sir Henry Wilson*, vol. 2 (London: Cassell, 1927), 87.
6 Wilson diary, May 11 and 13, 1918, Wilson papers.
7 Wilson diary, May 28, 1918, Wilson papers.
8 Amery, "Future Military Policy," May 22, 1918, Wilson papers, HHW 2/8/12.
9 See, for example, his memoranda, "Germany and the Middle East," March 12, 1918, Wilson papers, HHW 12/3/18; and "Unity of Operations in the East," March 20, 1918, Wilson papers, HHW 2/8/9.

10 Minutes of the X Committee, May 27, 1918, CAB 23/17.
11 Cited in John Terraine, *Douglas Haig: The Educated Soldier* (London: Hutchinson, 1963), 438.
12 Milner to Lloyd George, May 15, 1918, Lloyd George papers, F/38/3/32.
13 Minutes of the X Committee, May 16, 1918, CAB 23/17; Milner to Lloyd George, May 15, 1918, Lloyd George papers, F/38/3/32.
14 Robert Blake, ed., *The Private Papers of Douglas Haig, 1914–1919* (London: Eyre and Spottiswoode, 1952), 304.
15 Haig diary, May 16, 1918, Haig papers.
16 Callwell, *Field Marshal Sir Henry Wilson*, vol. 2, 103.
17 "Memorandum by General Foch," June 1, 1918, annexed to the secretary's notes of the Anglo–French conference for the same date, CAB 28/3.
18 Amery, "Unity of Control," January 17, 1917, Wilson papers, HHW 2/8/1a.
19 Robert A. Doughty, *Pyrrhic Victory* (Cambridge: Harvard University Press, 2005), see especially 377–79.
20 Minutes of the Anglo–French Conference, June 1 1918, CAB 28/3; Hankey diary, June 1, 1918, Hankey papers; Haig diary, June 1, 1918, Haig papers; Wilson diary, June 1, 1918, Wilson papers.
21 Lord Hankey, *The Supreme Command 1914–1918*, vol. 2 (London: Allen and Unwin, 1961), 813.
22 Gary Sheffield and John Bourne, eds., *Douglas Haig: War Diaries and Letters, 1914–1918* (London: Weidenfeld and Nicolson, 2005), 419; Callwell, *Sir Henry Wilson*, vol. 2, 105.
23 Haig diary, May 27, 1917, Haig papers.
24 Minutes of the X Committee, June 5, 1918, CAB 23/17.
25 Haig diary, June 7, 1918, Haig papers; Wilson diary, June 7, 1918, Wilson papers; General Jean Mordacq, *Le Ministère Clemenceau*, vol. 2 (Paris: Plon, 1930), 66–67.
26 Woodward, *Lloyd George*, 314–15; "Arrangements for evacuation from France," June 25, 1918, Milner papers, dep. 374; Wilson diary, June 8, 1918, Wilson papers.
27 Minutes of the Imperial War Cabinet, June 11, 1918, CAB 23/43.
28 Henry Borden, ed., *Robert Laird Borden: His Memoirs*, vol. 2 (Toronto: Macmillan, 1938), 813.
29 Borden ed., *Memoirs*, vol. 2, 814.
30 Minutes of the Imperial War Cabinet, June 13, 1918, CAB 23/43.
31 Minutes of the Imperial War Cabinet, June 14, 1918, CAB 23/43.
32 Amery, "War Aims and Military Policy," June 15, 1918, Lloyd George papers, F/2/1/25; Minutes of the Imperial War Cabinet, June 18 and 25, 1918, CAB 23/43; Wilson, "British Military Policy, 1918–1919," WO 106/315; Benjamin Schwarz, "Divided Attention: Britain's Perception of a German Threat to her Eastern Position in 1918," *Journal of Contemporary History* 28 (1993): 111–15.
33 Hankey diary, June 21, 1918, Hankey papers.
34 Minutes of the Imperial War Cabinet, June 20, 1918, CAB 23/40; Hankey, *Supreme Command*, vol. 2, 816.
35 Woodward, *Lloyd George*, 318.
36 Hankey diary, July 1, 1918, Hankey papers.
37 Wilson diary, July 2, 1918, Wilson papers.
38 At the end of 1917 the French Government sent General Guillaumat to replace Sarrail, who had spent more time intriguing in Greek politics than in fighting the Germans. Clemenceau recalled Guillaumat in June 1918 and appointed Franchet d'Esperey in his place.
39 Procès-verbaux of the Supreme War Council, July 2–4, 1918, CAB 28/4.

40 Hankey diary, July 3, 1918, Hankey papers.
41 Hankey, *Supreme Command*, vol. 2, 821; Wilson diary, July 3, 1918, Wilson papers.
42 Minutes of the War Cabinet, July 11, 1918, CAB 23/14.
43 Minutes of the X Committee, July 12, 1915, CAB 23/17.
44 Lloyd George to Clemenceau, July 13, 1918, Lloyd George papers, F/50/3/7.
45 Terraine, *Haig*, 443–44.
46 Hankey, *Supreme Command*, vol. 2, 826.
47 Wilson diary, July 14, 1918, Wilson papers; Hankey, *Supreme Command*, vol. 2, 826–27.
48 Minutes of the Committee of Prime Ministers, July 16, 1918, CAB 23/44.
49 Minutes of the War Cabinet, July 17, 1918, CAB 23/7.
50 Minutes of the X Committee, July 17, 1918, CAB 23/17.
51 Minutes of the X Committee, July 18, 1918, CAB 23/17.
52 B. H. Liddle Hart, *Foch* (Boston: Little, Brown and Co., 1932), 336–38.

18. The Turn of the Tide

1 David R. Woodward, *Lloyd George and the Generals* (Newark, DE: University of Delaware Press, 1983), 322.
2 Minutes of the X Committee, July 16, 1916, CAB 23/17.
3 Hankey diary, July 16, 1918, Hankey papers.
4 George H. Cassar, The *Forgotten Front: The British Campaign in Italy, 1917–1918* (London: Hambledon, 1998), 168–69.
5 Hankey diary, July 23, 1918, Hankey papers.
6 Cassar, *Forgotten Front*, 171–72: Lord Hankey, *The Supreme Command, 1914–1918*, vol. 2, (London: Allen and Unwin, 1961), 829.
7 Minutes of the X Committee, July 1, 1918, CAB 23/17.
8 Wilson, "British Military Policy, 1918–1919," July 25, 1918, CAB 27/8/WP70.
9 Stephen Roskill, *Hankey: Man of Secret*, vol. 1 (London: Collins, 1970), 584.
10 Minutes of the Committee of Prime Ministers, July 31, 1918, CAB 23/44.
11 Minutes of the Committee of Prime Ministers, August 1, 1918, CAB 23/44; Wilson diary, August 1, 1918, Wilson papers.
12 Hankey, *Supreme Command*, vol. 2, 831.
13 Minutes of the Committee of Prime Ministers, August 6, 1918, CAB 23/44.
14 Minutes of the Committee of Prime Ministers, August 8, 1918, CAB 23/44.
15 Robin Prior and Trevor Wilson, *Command on the western front: The Military Career of Sir Henry Rawlinson, 1914–1918* (London: Pen and Sword, 2004), ch. 28; John Terraine, *Douglas Haig: The Educated Soldier* (London: Hutchinson, 1963), 451–57; Brigadier General Sir James E. Edmonds, *Military Operations: France and Belgium, 1918*, vol. 4 (London: HMSO, 1947), chs 2–5.
16 Terraine, *Haig*, 458–60.
17 Minutes of the Committee of Prime Ministers, August 12, 1918, CAB 23/44.
18 David Lloyd George, *War Memoirs*, vol. 2 (London: Odhams, 1938), 1869.
19 John Grigg, *Lloyd George: War Leader, 1916–1918* (London: Allen Lane, 2002), 560.
20 Churchill to Lloyd George, August 10, 1918, Lloyd George papers, F/8/2/30. See also Woodward, *Lloyd George*, 327–28.
21 Roskill, *Hankey*, vol. 1, 589.
22 Woodward, *Lloyd George*, 328.
23 Minutes of the Imperial War Cabinet, August 14, 1918, CAB 23/43.

24 Minutes of the Imperial War Cabinet, August 15, 1918, CAB 23/43.
25 Hankey, "Report of the Committee of Prime Ministers: Preliminary Draft as a Basis for Consideration," August 14, 1918, CAB 23/44.
26 Hankey, *Supreme Command*, vol. 2, 831.
27 Minutes of the Committee of Prime Ministers, August 16, 1918, CAB 23/44.
28 Hankey, *Supreme Command*, vol. 2, 832.
29 Woodward, *Lloyd George*, 330.
30 Lloyd George to Reading, August 26, 1918, Lloyd George papers, F/43/1/15.
31 Lloyd George to Clemenceau, August 2, 1918, Lloyd George papers, F/50/3/10.
32 Clemenceau to Lloyd George, n.d., Lloyd George papers, F/50/3/11.
33 John J. Pershing, *My Experiences in the World War*, vol. 2 (New York: Frederick A. Stokes, 1931), 216–17; Gary Sheffield and John Bourne, eds., *Douglas Haig: War Diaries and Letters, 1914–1918* (London: Weidenfeld and Nicolson, 2005), 443.
34 Haig diary, August 15, 1918, Haig papers.
35 Jeffrey Williams, *Byng of Vimy: General and Governor General* (London: Leo Cooper/Secker and Warburg, 1983), 242–45; Edmonds, *France and Belgium, 1918*, vol. 4, chs 10–16; Walter Reid, Douglas Haig (Edinburgh: Birlinn, 2006), ch. 22.
36 The Australians resented the way they had been handled during the fighting at Bellecourt (which formed part of the wider Arras offensive), in which they had suffered heavy casualties.
37 Minutes of the X Committee, August 31, 1918, CAB 23/17.
38 Lloyd George, *War Memoirs*, vol. 2, 2030.
39 Haig diary, September 1, 1918, Haig papers.
40 Terraine, *Haig*, 463.
41 Cyril Falls, *Military Operations: Macedonia*, vol. 2, (London: HMSO, 1935), 110.
42 Wilson diary, September 4, 1918, Wilson papers.
43 Hankey, *Supreme Command*, vol. 2, 837.
44 Lloyd George, *War Memoirs*, vol. 2, 1918–19.
45 Minutes of the Anglo-French Conference, September 4, 1918, CAB 28/5.
46 Alan Palmer, *The Gardeners of Salonika* (New York: Simon and Schuster, 1965), ch. 12.
47 Anthony Bruce, *The Last Crusade* (London: John Murray, 2002), ch. 9.

19. The Road to the Armistice

1 Haig diary, September 10, 1918, Haig papers.
2 David R. Woodward, *Lloyd George and the Generals*, (Newark, DE: University of Delaware Press, 1983), 332–33.
3 Haig diary, September 21, 1918, Haig papers.
4 Wilson diary, September 23, 1918, Wilson papers.
5 Woodward, *Lloyd George*, 333.
6 Lloyd George to Maclay, September 29, 1918, Lloyd George papers, F/35/2/84. See also Lloyd George to Milner, September 29, 1918, Lloyd George papers, F/38/4/20.
7 David French, *The Strategy* of the *Lloyd George Coalition, 1916–1918* (Oxford: Clarendon Press, 1995), 261–62.
8 Hankey diary, October 1, 1918, Hankey papers.
9 Minutes of the War Cabinet, October 1, 1918 CAB 23/8.
10 George H. Cassar, *Kitchener's War; British Strategy from 1914 to 1916* (Washington, DC: Brassey's, 2004), 276; French, *Lloyd George Coalition*, 266.

11 Minutes of the War Cabinet, October 3, 1918, CAB, 23/14.
12 Hankey diary, October 5, 1918, Hankey papers.
13 Procès-verbal of a Conference held at Versailles, October 5, 1918, CAB 28/5.
14 Robert B. Aspery, *German High Command at War* (New York: William Morrow, 1991), 467–73; Fritz Fischer, *Germany's Aims in the First World War* (New York: Norton, 1967), 634–35.
15 Procès-verbal of a Conference held at the Quai d'Orsay, October 6, 1918, CAB 28/5.
16 Hankey diary, October 6, 1918, Hankey papers.
17 Hankey diary, October 7, 1918, Hankey papers.
18 Procès-verbal of a Conference held at the Quai d'Orsay, October 7, 1918, CAB 28/5.
19 Copies of the two notes are annexed to the process-verbal of the conference on October 8.
20 Procès-verbal of a Conference held at the Quai d'Orsay, October 8, 1918, CAB 28/5.
21 Wiseman to Reading, October 9, 1918, Reading papers, F/118/90; "A memorandum by Sir William Wiseman," October 16, 1918, in Arthur S. Link, ed., *The Papers of Woodrow Wilson*, vol. 51 (Princeton: Princeton University Press, 1985), 350.
22 A copy of Wison's note is annexed to the minutes of the conference on October 9, 1918. It can also be seen in Link, ed., *PWW*, 264–65.
23 Procès-verbal of a Conference held at the Quai d'Orsay, October 9, 1918, CAB 28/5.
24 Lord Hankey, *The Supreme Command, 1914–1918*, vol. 2 (London: Unwin and Allen, 1961), 855.
25 Copies of both notes are annexed to the procès-verbal on October 9, 1918, and are also reprinted in David Lloyd George, *War Memoirs*, vol. 2 (London: Odhams, 1938), 1958–59.
26 Hankey diary, October 13, 1918, Hankey papers; Minutes of the War Cabinet, October 14, 1918, CAB 23/8.
27 Link, ed., *PWW*, vol. 51, 333–34.
28 Hankey diary, October 15, 1918, Hankey papers.
29 Wilson diary, October 15, 1918, Wilson papers.
30 Minutes of the War Cabinet, October 15, 1918, CAB 23/8.
31 Curzon, "Conditions of Armistice," October 15, 1918, CAB 23/67/GT6015.
32 Hankey diary, October 18, 1918, Hankey papers.
33 Hankey to Lloyd George, October 18, 1918, Lloyd George papers, F/23/3/17.
34 Minutes of the X Committee, October 19, 1918, CAB 23/17.
35 "A memorandum by Sir William Wiseman," October 16, 1918 in Link, ed., *PWW*, vol. 51, 350.
36 Cyril Falls, *Military Operations: Egypt and Palestine*, vol. 2 (London: HMSO, 1930), 633.
37 Minutes of the War Cabinet, October 21, 1918, CAB 23/14.
38 Minutes of the War Cabinet, October 21, 1918, CAB 23/14; Lloyd George, *War Memoirs*, vol. 2, 1974–75.
39 Link, ed., *PWW*, vol. 51, 417–18.
40 Minutes of the War Cabinet, October 21, 1918, CAB 23/14.
41 Link, ed., *PWW*, vol. 51, 417–19.
42 Minutes of the War Cabinet, October 24, 1918, CAB 23/8.
43 French, *Lloyd George Coalition*, 274.
44 Minutes of the War Cabinet, October 25 and 26, 1918, CAB 23/14.
45 Correlli Barnett, *The Sword Bearers* (London: Eyre and Spottiswoude, 1963), 356–57.
46 George H. Cassar, *The Forgotten Front: The British Campaign in Italy, 1917–1918* (London: Hambledon Press, 1998), ch. 9.

47 Brigadier General F. J. Moberly, *The Campaign in Mesopotamia*, vol. 4 (London: HMSO, 1927), chs. 44–45.
48 Cyril Falls, *Macedonia*, vol 2, 265–66.
49 Notes of a conference at the Quai d'Orsay, October 29, 1918, CAB 28/5; Hankey diary, October 31, 1918, Hankey papers.
50 Wilson diary, October 30, 1918, Wilson papers.
51 Hankey diary, October 30, 1918, Hankey papers.
52 Notes of a Conversation at the Quai d'Orsay, October 30, 1918, CAB 28/5.
53 Procès-verbal of the four sessions of the Superior War Council, October 31–November 4, 1918; Notes of Conversation at House's residence, November 1, 3, and 4, 1918; Notes of a Conversation at the Ministry of War, November 2, 1918; Notes of a conversation in Clemenceau's Private Room, November 2, 1918, all in CAB 28/5; French, *Lloyd George Coalition*, 279–80; Lorna S. Jaffe, *The Decision to Disarm Germany* (London: Allen and Unwin, 1985), 106–7.
54 Hankey, *The Supreme Command*, vol. 2, 863.
55 Aspery, *German High Command*, 485–87.

Conclusion

1 Peter Rowland, in a biography of Lloyd George, has entitled the chapter on his war premiership, "THE MAN WHO WON THE WAR." Kenneth O. Morgan in *David Lloyd George* (Cardiff: University of Wales Press, 1963), 85, as well as in his other publications covering the period of the war, has no qualms about claiming that Lloyd George was the real architect of victory. A. J. P. Taylor, in a lecture delivered on the campus of the University of New Brunswick in 1961, considered Lloyd George to have been a greater war leader than Churchill. Taylor made similar remarks in his writings. See for example, *English History, 1914–1945* (Oxford: Oxford University Press, 1965), 87 and 192; and his introduction to Kenneth O. Morgan's biography of his hero, *Lloyd George* (London: Weidenfeld and Nicolson, 1974). I know from my personal contact with John Grigg, not to mention his inferences in his last study, which he nearly completed before his death, that he considered Lloyd George no less the equal of Churchill.
2 J. A. Salter, *Allied Shipping Control* (Oxford: Clarendon Press, 1921), 62
3 David Lloyd George, *War Memoirs*, vol. 1 (London: Odhams, 1938), 788
4 Sir William H. Beveridge, *British Food Control* (London: Oxford University Press, 1928), 338
5 Brock Millman, *Pessimism and British War Policy, 1916–1918* (London: Frank Cass, 2001), See especially ch. 5
6 George H. Cassar, *The Forgotten Front: The British Campaign in Italy, 1917–1918* (London: Hambledon Press, 1998), 221–22
7 John Grigg, "Churchill and Lloyd George," in *Churchill*, ed. Robert Blake and Wm. Roger Louis (Oxford University Press: 1993), 109.

BIBLIOGRAPHY

Manuscript Sources

Departmental records

National Archives (formerly Public Record Office), London

Cabinet files:
    Cabinet memoranda
    Committee of Prime Ministers
    Imperial War Cabinet
    Manpower Committee
    War Cabinet
    War Policy Committee
    "X" Committee

Foreign Office files

War Office files

Private collections (The location is London unless otherwise indicated)
    Addison papers: Bodleian Library, Oxford.
    Balfour papers: British Library.
    Benson papers: Liddell Hart Centre for Military Archives, King's College.
    Bertie papers: National Archives
    Bonar Law papers: Parliamentary Archives (formerly House of Lords Record Office).
    Cecil papers: British Library.
    Chamberlain (Austen) papers: Birmingham University Library.
    Chamberlain (Neville) papers: Birmingham University Library.
    Clive papers: Liddell Hart Centre for Military Archives, King's College.
    Curzon papers: India Office Library.
    Derby papers: Liverpool Record Office, Liverpool City Library.
    Esher papers: Churchill College Library, Cambridge.
    George V papers: Royal Archives, Windsor.
    Haig papers: National Library of Scotland, Edinburgh.
    Hankey papers: Churchill College Library, Cambridge.
    Kiggell papers: Liddell Hart Centre for Military Archives, King's College.
    Liddell Hart papers: Liddell Hart Centre for Military Archives, King's College.
    Lloyd George papers: Parliamentary Archives.
    Lothian (Kerr) papers: Scottish Record Office, Edinburgh.
    Maurice papers: Liddell Hart Centre for Military Archives, King's College.

Milner papers: Bodleian Library, Oxford.
Rawlinson papers: Churchill College Library, Cambridge.
Reading papers: India Office Library.
Robertson papers: Liddell Hart Centre for Military Archives, King's College.
Spears papers: Liddell Hart Centre for Military Archives, King's College.
Wilson papers: Imperial War Museum.

Official Publications

Beveridge, Sir William H. *British Food Control.* New Haven: Yale University Press, 1928.
Edmonds, Brigadier General Sir James E. *Military Operations: France and Belgium.* vols. for 1917–1918. The series was published in London by Macmillan and HMSO.
Edmonds, Brigadier General Sir James E. and Major General H. R. Davies. *Military Operations: Italy, 1915–1919.* London: HMSO, 1949.
Falls, Cyril. *Military Operations: Macedonia.* 2 vols. London: HMSO, 1933–35.
Fayle, C. Ernest. *Seaborne Trade.* vols. 2 and 3. London: John Murray, 1923–1924.
Macmunn, Lieutenant General Sir George and Cyril Falls. *Military Operations: Egypt and Palestine.* vols. 1 and 2. London: HMSO, 1928–30.
Moberly, Brigadier General F. J. *The Campaign in Mesopotamia, 1914–1918.* vols 3 and 4. London: HMSO, 1925–1927.
Newbolt, Henry. *Naval Operations.* vol. 5. London: Longmans, Green and Co., 1931.
Parliamentary Debates. *House of Commons* for 1916–1918.
War Office. *Statistics of the Military Effort of the British Empire during the Great War, 1914–1920.* London: London Stamp Exchange, 1992.

Published Sources

Adams, R. J. Q. *Arms and the Wizard: Lloyd George and the Ministry of Munitions.* College Station, TX: Texas A and M University Press, 1978.
_____. *Bonar Law.* Stanford: Stanford University Press, 1999.
Adams, R. J. Q. and Philip P. Poirier. *The Conscription Controversy in Great Britain, 1900–1918.* London: Macmillan, 1987.
Addison, Christopher. *Four and a Half Years.* vol. 2. London: Hutchinson, 1934.
Adelson, Roger. *Mark Sykes: Portrait of an Amateur.* London: Jonathan Cape, 1975.
Amery, L. S. *My Political Life.* vol. 2. London: Hutchinson, 1953.
Andrew, Christopher M. and A. S. Kanya-Forstner. *France Overseas: The Great War and the Climax of French Imperial Expansion.* London: Thames and Hudson, 1981.
Ash, Bernard. *The Lost Dictator: Field Marshal Sir Henry Wilson.* London: Cassell, 1968.
Aspery, Robert B. *The German High Command at War.* New York: William Morrow, 1991.
Barker, A. J. *The Bastard War: The Mesopotamian Campaign of 1914–1918.* New York: Dial Press, 1967.
Barnett, Correlli. *The Sword Bearers.* London: Eyre and Spottiswoode, 1963.
Barnett, L. Margaret. *British Food Policy During the First World War.* London: Allen and Unwin, 1985.
Beaver, Daniel R. *Newton D. Baker and the American War Effort, 1917–1918.* Lincoln: University of Nebraska Press, 1966.
Beaverbrook, Lord. *Men and Power, 1917–1918.* London: Hutchinson, 1956.

———. *Politicians and the War, 1914–1916*. London: Oldbourne, 1960.
Blake, Robert. *The Unknown Prime Minister*. London and Spottiswoode, 1955.
Blake, Robert, ed. *The Private Papers of Douglas Haig, 1914–1919*. London: Eyre and Spottiswoode, 1952.
Bonham-Carter, Victor. *Soldier True: The Life and Times of Field Marshal Sir William Robertson*. London: Frederick Muller, 1963.
Borden, Henry, ed. *Robert Laird Borden: His Memoirs*. vol. 2. Toronto: Macmillan, 1938.
Bourne, John M. *Britain and the Great War, 1914–1918*. London: Edward Arnold, 1989.
Brand, Carl F. *The British Labour Party*. Stanford: Stanford University Press, 1964.
Bruce, Anthony. *The Last Crusade*. London: John Murray, 2002.
Burgwyn, James H. *The Legend of the Mutilated Victory: Italy, the Great War and the Paris Peace Conference*. Westport, CT: Greenwood Press, 1993.
Calder, Kenneth J. *Britain and the Origins of the New Europe, 1914–1918*. Cambridge: Cambridge University Press, 1976.
Callwell, Major General Sir C. E. Callwell. *Field Marshal Sir Henry Wilson*. 2 vols. London: Cassell, 1927.
Cassar, George H. *Asquith as War Leader*. London: Hambledon Press, 1994.
———. *The Forgotten Front: The British Campaign in Italy, 1917–1918*. London: Hambledon Press, 1998.
———. *Kitchener's War: British Strategy from 1914 to 1916*. Washington, DC: Brassey's, 2004.
Charteris, Brigadier General John. *At GHQ*. London: Cassell, 1931.
Churchill, Randolph S. *Lord Derby: King of Lancashire*. New York: G. P. Putnam's Sons, 1960.
Churchill, Winston S. *Great Contemporaries*. London: Odhams, 1949.
———. *The World Crisis*. vol. 3. New York: Charles Scribner's Sons, 1955.
Clark, Alan, ed. *"A Good Inning": the Private Papers of Viscount Lee of Fareham*. London: John Murray, 1974.
Clemenceau, Georges. *Grandeur and Misery of Victory*. London: George Harrap, 1930.
Clynes, J. R. *Memoirs, 1869–1924*. London: Hutchinson, 1937.
Coller, Frank H. *A State Trading Adventure*. London: Oxford University Press, 1925.
Cregier, Don M. *Bounder from Wales*. Columbia: University of Missouri Press, 1976.
Davis, Mary. *Comerade or Brother: A History of the British Labour Movement, 1789–1951*. London: Pluto Press, 1993.
De Groot, Gerald J. *Douglas Haig, 1861–1928*. London: Unwin Hyman, 1988.
De Manteyer, G., ed. *Austria's Peace Offer 1916–1917*. London: Constable, 1921.
Dewey, P. E. *British Agriculture in the First World War*. London: Routledge, 1989.
Dilks, David. *Neville Chamberlain*. vol. 1. Cambridge: Cambridge University Press, 1984.
Doughty, Robert A. *Pyrrhic Victory*. Cambridge: Harvard University Press, 2005.
Duroselle, Jean-Baptiste. *Clemenceau*. Paris: Fayard, 1988.
Dutton, David. *The Politics of Diplomacy: Britain and France in the Balkans in the First World War*. London: Tauris, 1998.
Ernle, Lord. *Whippingham: The Reminiscenes of Lord Ernle*. London: John Murray, 1938.
Evans, Lady Olwen Carey. *Lloyd George was my Father*. Landysul: Gomer Press, 1985.
Farrar, L. L. *Divide and Conquer*. New York: Columbia University Press, 1978.
Farrar-Hockley, Anthony. *Goughie*. London: Hart-Davis, MacGibbon, 1975.
Fayle, C. Ernest. *The War and the Shipping Industry*. London: Oxford University, 1927.
Feiling, Keith. *The Life of Neville Chamberlain*. London: Macmillan, 1946.
Fest, Wilfred. *Peace or Partition: The Hapsburg Monarchy and British Policy 1914–1918*. London: George Prior, 1978.

Fischer, Fritz. *Germany's Aims in the First World War*. New York: Norton, 1967.
Fisher, H. A. L. *An Unfinished Autobiography*. London: Oxford University Press, 1941.
French, David. *British Strategy and War Aims, 1914–1916*. London: Allen and Unwin, 1986.
―――――. *The Strategy of the Lloyd George Coalition, 1916–1918*. Oxford: Clarendon Press, 1995.
Friedman, Isaiah. *The Question of Palestine, 1914–1918*. New York: Schocken Books, 1973.
Fromkin, David. *A Peace to End All Peace*. New York: Avon Books, 1990.
Fry, Michael G. *Lloyd George and Foreign Policy*. vol. 1. Montreal: McGill-Queen's University Press, 1977.
Gatzke, Hans W. *Germany's Drive to the West*. Baltimore: John Hopkins Press, 1950.
Geddes, Auckland. *The Forging of a Family*. London: Faber and Faber, 1952.
Gilbert, Bentley B. *David Lloyd George: The Architect of Change, 1863–1912*. Columbus: Ohio University Press, 1978.
―――――. *David Lloyd George: Organizer of Victory, 1912–1916*. Columbus: Ohio University Press, 1992.
Gilbert, Martin. *Winston Churchill: The Challenge of War, 1914–1916*. Boston: Houghton Mifflin, 1971.
Gilmour, David. *Curzon*. New York: Farrar, Straus and Giroux, 2003.
Golin, Alfred. *Proconsul in Politics*. London: Blond, 1964.
Graubard, Stephen. *British Labour and the Russian Revolution*. Cambridge: HarvardUniversity Press, 1956.
Greenhalgh, Elizabeth. *Victory Through Coalition*. Cambridge: Cambridge University Press, 2005.
Grieves, Keith. *The Politics of Manpower, 1914–1918*. Manchester: Manchester University Press, 1988.
Grigg, John. *Lloyd George: From Peace to War, 1912–1916*. Berkeley: University of California Press, 1985.
―――――. *Lloyd George: The People's Champion*. Berkley: University of California Press, 1978.
―――――. *Lloyd George: War Leader, 1916–1918*. London: Allen Lane, 2002.
―――――. *The Young Lloyd George*. London: Eyre Methuen, 1973.
Halpern, Paul G. *A Naval History of World War I*. Annapolis: Naval Institute Press, 1994.
Hankey, Lord. *The Supreme Command, 1914–1918*. 2 vols. London: Allen and Unwin, 1961.
Harris, José. *William Beveridge: A Biography*. Oxford: Oxford University Press, 1977.
Herbillon, Colonel Emile. *Sovenirs d'un Officier de Liaison pendant la Guerre Mondaile*. vol. 2. Paris: Jules Tallandier, 1930.
Hinton, James. *The First Shop Stewards' Movement*. London: Allen and Unwin, 1973.
Hough, Richard. *The Great War at Sea, 1914–1918*. London: Oxford University Press, 1983.
Hughes, Matthew. *Allenby and British Strategy in the Middle East, 1917–1919*. London: Frank Cass, 1999.
Hyde, H. Montgomery. *Carson*. London: Constable, 1987.
Jaffe, Lorna S. *The Decision to Disarm Germany*. London: Allen and Unwin, 1985.
James, Lawrence. *Imperial Warrior: The Life and Times of Field Marshal Viscount Allenby, 1861–1939*. London: Weidenfeld and Nicolson, 1993.
Jeffrey, Keith. *Field Marshal Sir Henry Wilson*. Oxford: Oxford University Press, 2006.
Jellicoe, Earl. *The Submarine Peril*. London: Cassell, 1934.
Jenkins, Roy. *Asquith*. London: Collins, 1978.

Jones, Thomas. *Lloyd George*. Cambridge: Harvard University Press, 1951.
Jones, Thomas G. *The Unbroken Front: Ministry of Food, 1916–1944*. London: Everybody's Books, 1944.
Kendall, Walter. *Revolutionary Movement in Britain*. London: Weidenfeld and Nicolson, 1969.
Kennan, George F. *Russia Leaves the War*. New York: Atheneum, 1967.
———. *The Decision to Intervene*. New York: Atheneum, 1967.
Kettle, Michael. *The Allies and the Russian Collapse*. vol. 1. London: André Deutsch, 1981.
Keynes, John Maynard. *Essays in Biography*. New York: Harcout, Brace and Co., 1933.
Kitchen, Martin. *The German Offensives of 1918*. Charleston, SC: Tempus, 2001.
Leventhal, F. M. *Arthur Henderson*. Manchester: Manchester University Press, 1989.
Liddell Hart, B. H. *Foch*. Boston: Little, Brown and Co., 1932.
———. *Through the Fog of War*. New York: Random House, 1938.
Link, Arthur S., ed. *The Papers of Woodrow Wilson*. vols. 44–51. Princeton: Princeton University Press, 1983–85.
———. *Woodrow Wilson: Revolution, War, and Peace*. Arlington Heights, Il: AHM, 1979.
Lloyd George, David. *Memoirs of the Peace Conference*. vol. 2. New Haven: Yale University Press, 1939.
———. *The Great Crusade*. New York: Doran, 1918.
———. *War Memoirs*. 2 vols. London: Odhams, 1938.
Lloyd George, Richard. *My Father Lloyd George*. New York: Crown, 1961.
Lockhart, R. H. Bruce. *Memoirs of a British Agent*. London: repr. Pan Books, 2002.
Ludendorff, Erich von. *Ludendorff's Own Story*. New York: Harper and Brothers, 1919.
Mamatey, Victor S. *The United States and East Central Europe, 1914–1918*. Port Washington, NY: Kennikat Press, 1972.
Marder, A. J. *From the Dreadnought to Scapa Flow*. vols. 2 and 4. London: Oxford University Press, 1965 and 1969.
Marshall-Cornwall, General Sir James. *Haig as Military Commander*. London: Bataford, 1973.
Maurice, Major General Sir Frederick. *Intrigues of the War*. London: Loxley Bros., 1922.
Maurice, Nancy, ed. *The Maurice Case: From the Papers of Major-General Sir Frederick Maurice*. Hamden, CN: Archon Books, 1972.
Maurois, André. *Lyautey*. New York: Appleton, 1931.
Mayer, Arno J. *Political Origins of the New Diplomacy, 1917–1918*. New Haven, Yale University Press, 1959.
Messimer, Dwight R. *Find and Destroy: Anti-Submarine Warfare in World War I*. Annapolis: Naval Institute Press, 2001.
Middlemas, Keith. *Politics in Industrial Society*. London: André Deutsch, 1979.
Middlemas, Keith, ed. *Thomas Jones: Whitehall Diary, 1916–1925*. vol. 1. London: Oxford University Press, 1969.
Middleton, Thomas H. *Food Production in War*. Oxford: Clarendon Press, 1923.
Miliband, Ralph. *Parliamentary Socialism*. London: Merlin Press, 1973.
Millman, Brock. *Pessimism and British War Policy, 1916–1918*. London: Frank Cass, 2001.
Mordacq, General Jean. *Le Ministère Clemenceau.*, vol. 2. Paris: Plon, 1930.
Morgan, Kenneth O. *Lloyd George*. London: Weidenfeld and Nicolson, 1974.
Morgan, Kenneth O, ed. *Lloyd George: Family Letters, 1885–1936*. Cardiff and Oxford: University of Wales Press/Oxford University Press, 1973.
Morgan, Kenneth and Jane. *Portrait of a Progressive: The Political Career of Christopher, Viscount Addison*. Oxford: Clarendon Press, 1980.

Neilson, Keith. *Strategy and Supply: The Anglo-Russian Alliance, 1914–1917*. London: Allen and Unwin, 1984.
Owen, Frank. *Tempestuous Journey*. New York: McGraw-Hill, 1955.
Painlevé, Paul. *Comment j'ai nommé Foch et Pétain*. Paris: Alcan, 1923.
Palmer, Alan. *The Gardeners of Salonika*. New York: Simon and Schuster, 1965.
Patterson, A. Temple. *Jellicoe*. London: Macmillan, 1969.
Pelling, Henry. *A History of British Trade Unionism*. London: Macmillan, 1987.
Pershing, John J. *My Experiences in the World War*. 2 vols. New York: Frederick Stokes, 1931.
Philpott, William J. *Anglo-French Relations and Strategy on the Western Front, 1914–1918*. New York: St. Martin's Press, 1996.
Poincaré, Raymond. *Au Service de la France*. vols. 9 and 10. Paris: Plon, 1932–1933.
Powell, Geoffrey. *Plumer: The Soldier's General*. London: Leo Cooper, 1990.
Prior, Robin and Trevor Wilson. *Command on the Western Front: The Military Career of Sir Henry Rawlinson 1914–1918*. London: Pen and Sword, 1992.
———. *Passchendaele: The Untold Story*. New Haven: Yale University Press, 1996.
Reid, Walter. *Architect of Victory: Douglas Haig*. Edinburgh: Birlinn, 2006.
Reinharz, Jehuda. *Chaim Weizmann*. Oxford: Oxford University Press, 1993.
Repington, Charles à Court. *The First World War*. 2 vols. Boston: Houghton Mifflin, 1921.
Ribot, A., ed. *Journal de Alexandre Ribot*. Paris: Plon, 1936.
Riddell, Lord. *War Diary, 1914–1918*. London: Nicholson and Watson, 1993.
Robbins, Keith. *The Abolition of War: The Peace Movement in Britain, 1914–1918*. Cardiff: University of Wales Press, 1976.
Robbins, Simon. *British Generalship on the Western Front 1914–1918*. London: Frank Cass, 2005.
Robertson, Field Marshal Sir William. *From Private to Field Marshal*. Boston: Houghton Mifflin, 1921.
———. *Soldiers and Statesmen, 1914–1918*. 2 vols. London: Cassell, 1926.
Roskill, Stephen. *Admiral of the Fleet Earl Beatty: The Last Naval Hero – An Intimate Biography*. New York: Atheneum, 1981.
———. *Hankey: Man of Secrets*. vol. 1. London: Collins, 1970.
Rothwell, V. H. *British War Aims and Peace Diplomacy, 1914–1918*. Oxford: Oxford University Press, 1971.
Rowland, Peter. *Lloyd George*. London: Barrie and Jenkins, 1975.
Salter, J. A. *Allied Shipping Control*. Oxford: Clarendon Press, 1921.
Schindler, John R. *Isonzo*. Westport, CT: Prager, 2001.
Scott, James B., ed. *Official Statement of War Aims and Peace Proposals, December 1916 to November 1918*. Washington, DC: Carnegie Endowment for International Peace, 1921.
Self, Robert, ed. *The Neville Chamberlain Diary Letters*. vol. 1. Aldershot: Ashgate, 2000.
Seymour, Charles, ed. *The Intimate Papers of Colonel House*. vol. 4. Boston: Houghton Mifflin, 1928.
Shakespeare, Sir Geoffrey. *Let Candles Be Brought In*. London: Macdonald, 1949.
Sheffield, Gary and John Bourne, ed. *Douglas Haig: War Diaries and Letters, 1914–1918*. London: Weidenfeld and Nicolson, 2005.
Sheffy, Yigal. *British Military Intelligence in the Palestine Campaign, 1914–1918*. London: Frank Cass, 1998.
Silverlight, John. *The Victor's Dilemma*. New York: Weybright and Talley, 1970.
Sims, William S. *The Victory at Sea*. London: John Murray, 1920.
Smillie, Robert. *My Life for Labour*. London: Mills and Boon, 1921.

Smith, Gene. *Until the Last Trumpet Sounds:The Life of General of the Armies John J. Pershing*. New York: John Wiley and Sons, 1998. Smythe, Donald. *Pershing*. Bloomington: Indiana University Press, 1986.
Spears, E. L. *Prelude to Victory*. London: Jonathan Cape, 1939.
Stein, Leonard. *The Balfour Declaration*. London: Valentine, Mitchell and Co., 1961.
Sylvester, A. J. *The Real Lloyd George*. London: Cassell, 1947.
Tallents, Sir Stephen. *Man and Boy*. London: Faber and Faber, 1943.
Tanenbaum, Jan K. *General Maurice Sarrail, 1856–1929*. Chapel Hill: University of North Carolina Press, 1974.
Taylor, A. J. P. *English History, 1914–1945*. Oxford: Oxford University Press, 1965.
Taylor, A. J. P., ed. *Lloyd George: A Diary by Frances Stevenson*. New York: Harper and Row, 1971.
Terraine, John. *Douglas Haig: The Educated Soldier*. London: Hutchinson, 1963.
Thompson, Malcolm. *David Lloyd George: the Official Biography*. London: Hutchinson, 1949.
Trask, David F. *The United States in the Supreme War Council*. Middletown, CT: Wesleyan University Press, 1961.
Travers, Tim. *The Killing Ground: The British Army, the Western Front and the Emergence of Modern Warfare, 1900–1918*. London: Allen and Unwin, 1987.
Turner, John. *British Politics and the Great War*. New Haven: Yale University Press, 1992.
———. *Lloyd George's Secretariat*. Cambridge: Cambridge University Press, 1980.
Ullman, Richard H. *Anglo-Soviet Relations, 1917–1921*, vol. 1. Princeton: Princeton University Press, 1961.
Vital, David. *Zionism: The Crucial Phase*. Oxford: Clarendon Press, 1987.
Williams, Jeffrey. *Byng of Vimy: General and Governor General*. London: Leo Cooper/Secker and Warburg, 1983.
Williamson, Philip, ed. *The Modernisation of Conservative Politics: The Diaries and Letters of William Bridgeman 1904–1935*. London: Historians' Press, 1988.
Wilson, Sir Arnold T. *Loyalties: Mesopotamia, 1914–1917*, vol. 1. Oxford: Oxford University Press, 1936.
Wilson, Trevor. *The Myraid Faces of War*. Cambridge: Polity Press, 1986.
Wilson, Trevor, ed. *The Political Diaries of C. P. Scott, 1911–1928*. Ithaca: Cornell University Press, 1970.
Winter, Denis. *Haig's Command*. London: Viking, 1991.
Wolfe, Humbert. *Labour Supply and Regulation*. Oxford: Clarendon Press, 1923.
Woodward, David R. *Field Marshal Sir William Robertson: Chief of the Imperial General Staff in the Great War*. Westport, CT: Praeger, 1998.
———. *Hell in the Holy Land: World War I in the Middle East*. Lexington: University Press of Kentucky, 2006.
———. *Lloyd George and the Generals*. Newark, DE: University of Delaware Press, 1983.
———. *Trial By Friendship: Anglo-American Relations, 1917–1918*. Lexington: University Press of Kentucky, 1993.
Woodward, David R., ed. *The Military Correspondence of Field Marshal Sir William Robertson, Chief of the Imperial General Staff, December 1915–February 1918*. London: Bodley Head for Army Records Society, 1989.
Woodward, Sir Llewellyn. *Great Britain and the War of 1914–1918*. London: Methuen, 1967.
Wright, Peter E. *At the Supreme War Council*. London: Eveleigh Nash, 1921.
Wrigley, Chris. *Arthur Henderson*. Cardiff: GPC Books, 1990.
———. *David Lloyd George and the British Labour Movement*. Hassocks: Harvester Press, 1976.
———. *Lloyd George*. Oxford: Blackwell, 1992.

Articles

Adams, W. S. "Lloyd George and the Labour Movement." *Past and Present* (February, 1953): 55–64.

Cassar, George H. "Political Leaders in Wartime: Lloyd George and Churchill," in *The Great War 1914–1945*, vol. 1, ed. Peter Liddle, John Bourne and Ian Whitehead. London: HarperCollins, 2000.

Clayton, Anthony. "Robert Nivelle and the French Spring Offensive of 1917," in *Fallen Stars*, ed. Brian Bond. London: Brassey's, 1991.

Dewey, P. E. "Food Production and Policy in the United Kingdom, 1914–1918," in *Transactions of the Royal Historical Society*, ser. 5, vol. 30. London: Royal Historical Society, 1980.

———. "Military Recruiting and the British Labour Force during the First World War." *Historical Journal* 27 (1984): 199–223.

Dutton, David. "The Deposition of King Constantine of Greece, June 1917: An Episode in Anglo-French Diplomacy." *Canadian Journal of History* 12 (1977–1978): 325–45.

Ehrman, John. "Lloyd George and Churchill as War Leaders," in *Transactions of the Royal Historical Society*, ser. 5, vol. 11. London: Royal Historical Society, 1961.

French, David. "Who Knew What and When? The French Army Mutinies and the British Decision to Launch the Third Battle of Ypres," in *War, Strategy, and International Politics*," ed. Lawrence Freedman, Paul Hayes and Robert O'Neill, Cambridge: Cambridge University Press, 1992.

Gonner, E. C. K. "Lord Rhondda at the Ministry of Food," in. *D A. Thomas, Viscount Rhondda*, ed. Viscountess Rhondda et al. London: Longmans, Green and Co., 1921.

Grigg, John. "Churchill and Lloyd George", in *Churchill*, ed. Robert Blake and Wm. Louis Roger. Oxford: Oxford University Press, 1993.

Harris, José. "Bureaucrats and Businessmen in British Food Control, 1914–1919 in *War and State*, ed. Kathleen Burk. London: Allen and Unwin, 1982.

Hussey, John. "Portrait of a Commander-in Chief," in *Haig: A Reappraisal 70 Years On*, ed. Brian Bond and Nigel Cave. London: Leo Cooper, 1999.

Kernek, Sterling. "The British Government's Reaction to President Wilson's 'Peace Note' of December 1916." *Historical Journal* 13 (1970): 721–66.

Kihl, Mary R. "A Failure of Ambassadorial Diplomacy." *Journal of American History* 57 (1970): 636–53.

Levene, Mark. "The Balfour Declaration: A Case of Mistaken Identity." *English Historical Review* 107 (1992): 54–77.

Lockwood, P. A. "Milner's entry into the War Cabinet." *Historical Journal* 7 (1964): 120–34.

McEwen, J. M. "Brass-Hats and the British Press." *Canadian Journal of History* 18 (1983): 43–67.

———. "Northcliffe and Lloyd George at War, 1914–1918." *Historical Journal* 24 (1981): 651–72.

Milliman, Brock. "Counsel of Despair: British Strategy and War Aims, 1917–1918." *Journal of Contemporary History* 36 (2001): 241–70.

Naylor, John F. "The Establishment of the Cabinet Secretariat." *Historical Journal* 14 (1971): 783–803.

Rhondda, Viscountess. "A Character Sketch," in *D. A. Thomas, Viscount Rhondda*, ed. Viscountess Rhondda et al. London: Longmans, Green and Co., 1921.

Roskill, Stephen. "The Dismissal of Admiral Jellicoe." *Journal of Contemporary History* 1 (1966): 69–93.

Rothwell, V. H. "Mesopotamia in British War Aims, 1914–1918." *Historical Journal* 13 (1970): 273–94.
Schwarz, Benjamin. "Divided Attention: Britain's Perception of a German Threat to Her Eastern Position in 1918," *Journal of Contemporary History* 28 (1993): 103–22.
Stevenson, David. "The Failure of Peace Negotiations." *Historical Journal* 34 (1991): 65–86.
Trani, Eugene P. "Woodrow Wilson and the Decision to Intervene in Russia: A Reconsideration." *Journal of Modern History* 48 (1976): 440–61.
Travers, Tim. "A Particular Style of Command: Haig and GHQ, 1916–1918." *Journal of Strategic Studies* 10 (1987): 363–76.
Turner, John. "Cabinets, Committees and Secretariats: the Higher Direction of War," in *War and the State*, ed. Kathleen Burk. London: Allen and Unwin, 1982.
Ward, Alan J. "Lloyd George and the 1918 Irish Conscription Crisis." *Historical Journal* 17 (1974): 107–129.
Winter, J. M. "Arthur Henderson, the Russian Revolution, and the Reconstruction of the Labour Party." *Historical Journal* 15 (1972): 753–773.
Woodward, David R. "The British Government and Japanese Intervention in Russia during World War I." *Journal of Modern History* 46 (1974): 663–685.
———. "British Intervention in Russia during the First World War," *Military Affairs* 41 (1977): 171–75.
———. "David Lloyd George, a Negotiated Peace with Germany, and the Kühlmann Peace Kite of September 1917." *Canadian Journal of History* 6 (1971): 75–93.
———. "Did Lloyd George Starve the British Army of Men Prior to the German Offensive of March 21 1918?" *Historical Journal* 27 (1984): 241–52.
———. "Sir William Robertson and Sir Douglas Haig," in *Haig: A Reappraisal 70 Years On*, ed. Brian Bond and Nigel Cave. London: Leo Cooper, 1999.
———. "The Origins and Intent of David Lloyd George's January 5 War Aims Speech." *Historian* 34 (1971): 22–39.
Wrigley, Chris. "Trade Unions and Politics in the First World War," in *Trade Unions in British Politics*, ed. Ben Pimlott and Chris Cook. London: Longman, 1982.

Serial Publications

Daily Chronicle
Daily News
Daily Telegraph
Evening Press
Globe
Manchester Guardian
Morning Post
Nation
Observer
Times
Spectator
Westminster Gazette

INDEX

Adams, W.G.S., 16
Addison, Christopher, 42; and Lloyd George, 44–45; settles strike, 43–44
Alexandretta, 172
Allenby, General Sir Edmund, 328, 338; advised to advance slowly, 177–78; appointed commander of EEF, 152; approval given to advance, 246; captures Damascus, 326; captures Jerusalem, 207; consulted by LG, 245; destroys Turkish army at Megiddo, 324; drives Turks from Gaza-Beersheba line, 192; requests thirteen additional divisions, 199
Amalgamated Society of Engineers (ASE), 34, 42–44
Amery, Leo, 304, 311; memo suggesting Allenby be reinforced, 298; opposed to sending delegation to Stockholm conference, 51–52
Aosta, Duke of, 191
Army Council, 239, 299; appalled over government's proposed manpower policy, 34, 207; concedes that constitutional issue has been resolved, 233; objected to the proposed status of Executive Board, 228–29; requests more recruits for army, 25–26; wants military representative to be subject to orders of, 193
Arras, battle of, 98
Asquith, H.H., 44, 78, 230, 350; agrees to formation of first coalition government, 6; appoints Kitchener secretary of state for war; 5; attacks LG's leadership, 196; avoids defining war aims, 80; confident in free play of private enterprise, 63; critical of SWC, 234–35; defends Lloyd George during Marconi scandal, 4; discusses war aims with LG, 223; fall of government of, 9–10, 21–22; holds meeting with Lansdowne, 237; and Ireland, 4–5, 8; lacks support in Commons to overthrow LG, 241; Leeds speech, 166–67; as leader of the opposition, 12; and Maurice affair, 267–70, 271; reluctant to introduce conscription, 7–8; replies to LG's statements in Commons, 234–35; sets up Manpower Distribution Board, 22; succeeds Campbell-Bannerman, 3; ultimately removes John French, 347; unwilling to overrule Board of Trade in November 1916, 57

Bacon, Admiral Sir Reginald, 201
Baden, Prince Max of, 331, 336–337, 342
Baghdad, 139–140, 142, 151, 159–160
Baker, Newton, 263–64
Balfour, Arthur, 332; appointed Foreign Secretary, 5; approves of Derby's compromise plan, 236; and armistice negotiations and terms; 336; character and work habits, 13; considers Lloyd George a novice on strategy, 78; fervently committed to promoting Zionist interests, 176; on German peace proposal, 163–65, 167–168; grasps Derby's solution, 234; on intervention in Russia, 274–76, 279–280, 283–86, 288

Balfour, Arthur, (*Continued*)
289; LG considers making a change at FO, 228; mission to Washington, 159; replies to Pope, 162–63, unable to sway Robertson, 237; withdraws support of Robertson, 237–238
Balfour Declaration, 176–77
Ballard, Brigadier General C. R., 275–276, 279
Barnes, George, 14, 41, 165, 205, 223, 234, 238; opposed to extending conscription to Ireland, 35; replaces Henderson in War Cabinet; rejects Derby's compromise plan, 236
Beatty, Admiral Sir David, 105, 107, 334
Beaverbrook, Lord, on Lloyd George, xix, 12
Beck, Cecil, 29–30
Below, General Otto von, 184
Benedict XV, Pope, offers to mediate a settlement, 162
Berthelot, General H. R., 275, 279
Bertie, Sir Francis Bertie, 13, 160
Bertier de Sauvigny, Commandant, 91
Beveridge, William, 68–69, 346
Bey, Rahmi, 330
Bliss, General Tasker H., 193, 195, 205, 254
Bonar Law, Andrew, 50, 73, 134, 191, 250; and armistice negotiations and terms, 330, 334; asks Haig's opinion on chances of German assault in 1918, 207; character, 15; claims time not propitious for consideration of Jewish homeland, 176; declines offer to form government; 10; forces creation of first coalition government, 6; grasps Derby's solution, 234; and Ireland, 8; and Maurice affair, 265, 267; member of War Cabinet, 14; openly rebukes Lansdowne, 219; opposes compromise settlement, 165; persuades Derby to withdraw resignation, 240; recommends appointment of Maclay, 58; recommends using convoy system; 101; rejects Derby's compromise plan, 236; suggests French should be consulted, 164; supports LG, 123, 238
Borden, Robert, 292; critical of British generalship, 303–04, 307, 314, 320
Boselli, Paolo, 187
Brandeis, Louis D., 175
Brest-Litovsk, 221, 280; treaty of, 285, 287, 341
Briand, Aristide, 191; at Allied and Anglo-French conferences, 87, 93–95, 141–42; contacted by German agent to discuss peace possibilities, 163; resignation of, 97; urges British to support aggressive policy in Balkans, 84, 141–42
Brownlie, J.T., 43
Buchanan, Sir George, 48, 175, 275–76, 277, 279, 281–282
Bucharest, Treaty of, 341
Byng, General Julian, 248, 321–22

Cadorna, General Luigi, 86, 127–28, 136; launches attack, 134; promised help, 135; removed from command, 188–189, 191; not strong enough to make much progress, 129–30
Caillaux, Joseph, 143
Calthorpe, Vice Admiral Sir S.A., 338, 340–41
Cambon, Jules, 84
Cambon, Paul, 163, 167, 327
Cambrai, battle of, 197–98, 232
Campbell-Bannerman, Sir Henry, 3
Caporetto, battle of, 185, 187, 192, 202, 220
Carol, King of Romania, 274
Carson, Sir Edward, 134, 167; appointed First Lord of the Admiralty; asks LG to take position regarding Stockholm conference, 51; calls LG a liar, 109; excluded from War Cabinet, 14; and Ireland, 5, 8; gives LG lukewarm support, 167; joins War Cabinet, 124–25, 200; member of Manpower Committee, 205; probably would leave post if Robertson resigns, 180; and submarine crisis, 103–04, 107, 109;

INDEX 411

supports Haig, 135; tries to mobilize Unionist War Committee, 268
Cavan, Earl of, 312
Cave, Sir George, 36–37
Cecil, Robert, 136; appointed Minister of Blockade, 13; and armistice negotiations, 332; backs Robertson, 134, 180, 238; defeatist attitude noted by Wilson, 116; on future strategy, 323; hatches plan to starve Athens into submission, 145; identified as possible replacement for LG, 192, 344; LG contemplates sending him to FO, 228; meeting with Cambon, 327; on Russian intervention, 283, 286, 288–289, 293; and Stockholm conference, 47–48; works on draft of LG's war aims speech, 222–23
Chamberlain, Austen, 23, 193, 234, 262, 337
Chamberlain, Joseph, 3
Chamberlain, Neville, 14, 343; characteristics and attitude of, 24; as Director of National Service, 24–31, 344, relations with Lloyd George, 28–31
Chantilly, Allied Conference at, 82, 86, 88
Charteris, Brigadier General John, 112, 118, 197, 199
Chicherin, G.V., 283
Churchill, Clementine, on Lloyd George, 12
Churchill, Winston, 332, 343, 347, 350–351; dines with LG, 250; opposed to a judicial inquiry, 268; role in ending serious strike, 54–55; sees potential significance in Haig's victory, 317
Clemenceau, Georges, 302; armistice negotiations and terms, 329, 331–2, 338–41; changes mind about Balkan front, 306; does not address LG's complaint, 321; on employment of American troops, 263–64; on future operations against Turkey, 327–330, 335; and General Reserve, 244, 251; relations with Lloyd George, 203–04; and intervention in Russia, 288, 292–93; at SWC, 213; unenthusiastic about LG's war aims speech, 225–25; visits front after becoming prime minister, 78; wishes to extend Foch's authority, 254
Committee of Prime Ministers, 291, 312–15
Committee on Manpower (chaired by Milner during Asquith's Administration), 30–31
Constantine I, King of Greece, 83, 142, 144, 145–46, abdicates in favor of son, 148
Council of War, 180–81
Cowans, Sir John, 73
Currie, Lieutenant General Sir Arthur, 303
Curzon, Lord, 117, 148, 162; appointed to War Cabinet, 15; approves of Derby's compromise plan, 236; and armistice negotiations, 333; character, 15; cool to prospect of Jewish state, 176; critical of LG's failure to keep War Cabinet informed, 333; delivers long speeches in Imperial War Cabinet, 304; endorses Derby's solution, 234; favors taking a more cautious line, 284; finds fault with Smuts' pessimism, 318; on Manpower Committee, 205; recommends drive into Mesopotamia be delayed, 177; report of committee on territorial aims, 156; report of Shipping Control Committee, 57; reproaches FO for concessions to the French, 327; states case for War Cabinet's support of Nivelle, 92; suggests setting up subcommittee, 33; thinks Haig should be allowed to go ahead, 123; urges LG to come to terms with Robertson, 193; wants submarine issue brought to attention of LG, 106; warns of

Curzon, Lord, (*Continued*)
consequences of Robertson's resignation, 180–81
Czernin, Count Ottokar, 221, 227

Daily Chronicle, 192
Daily Mail, 211
Daily News, 192, 259
Daily Telegraph, 198, 219, 257
Dardanelles campaign, 7, 172
Davenport, Lord, 14, 63, 70; character and outlook, 67–68; as Food Controller, 68–69, 72
Defence of the Realm Acts (DORA), 42, 233, 358n9; new regulations added to, 64
Denikin, General Anton, 289
Derby, Earl of, 92, 136, 197, 213; appointed Secretary of State for War, 13; becomes British ambassador in Paris, 262; character and attitude, 13, 29–30; conversation with Ribot and Painlevé, 144–45; excluded from War Cabinet; 14; and Haig, 117, 239, 207, 229, 231, 239; and Lloyd George, 95; objects to LG's formula to replace Haig and Robertson, 199; refuses to accept Robertson's resignation, 180; reports on troops available for immediate transfer to France, 250; sympathetic to Robertson , 187, 228–3; wants to call up 30,000 agricultural workers for army, 65; withdraws resignation, 240; works out arrangement with LG, 193
Derby scheme, 37, 358n75
Diaz, General Armando, 191
Douglas, Sir Charles, 180
Drummond, Sir Eric, 167, 195
Duff, Admiral Sir Alexander, 104, 108–109
Duke, H.E., 36

Ebert, Frederick, 342
El-Arish, 149
Esher, Lord, 118, 241
Evening Standard, 91

Executive War Board, 216, 229, 233, 236–237, 239, 334

Fayle, C. Ernest, 62
Fisher, H.A.L., 13
Fisher, William Hayes, 30
Foch, General Ferdinand, 182, 189, 236, 251, 299; appointed to head Executive Board, 216; believes Turks cannot be forced out of the war, 128; chosen to coordinate Anglo-French armies, 251, 254; no confidence in Flanders operation, 118; lukewarm towards Alexandretta scheme, 173; prefers selection of Duke of Aosta,191; reads statement regarding policy on Russia, 128; as supreme commander, 255, 261–62, 264–65, 299–302, 307–08, 321–22; wants Anglo-French army to concentrate on defeating Germany, 129–30; on Weygand, 204; on withdrawal of French guns, 135–36
Franchet, d'Esperey, General Louis, 98, 340; and future operations against Turkey, 328–29; imposes terms on Bulgaria, 326; Lloyd George on, 329–30; receives authority to launch an offensive in Balkans, 305
Franklin-Bouillon, Henri, 182, 187–188
Fraser, Lovat, 211
French, David, 225
French, Sir John, 182; believes that conscription is feasible in Ireland, 36; conversation with LG,133; at Council of War meeting, 181; submits report on future strategy, 183
Fry, Michael, 5

Gallwitz, General von, 257
Garvin, J.L., 225
Gaza, first and second battle of, 151
Geddes, Auckland, drafts Military Service Bill, 35; as head of Ministry of National Service, 31–35, 344; submits memorandum on availability of manpower for army,

22; suggests different basis for recruiting, 30
Geddes, Eric, 91, 123–124, 192; as controller at Admiralty, 61; dismisses Jellicoe, 200–203; identified as possible replacement for LG, 192, 344; replaces Carson at Admiralty, 125
General Reserve, 214–15, 230–231, 237, 240, 242–244
George, Elizabeth, 1
George, William, 1
George V, King, 166, 366n71; pained at the prospect of Robertson's imminent departure, 238
Gillman, Major General W., 246
Globe, 192, 230, 259, 261
Gooch, John, 266
Gordon, Charles "Chinese," 290
Gough, Brigadier General Hubert, 248, 319; blamed for German breakthrough, 258–59
Grenville, 328
Grey, Sir Edward, 174, 195; discusses war aims with LG, 223
Grigg, John, xix–xx, 58–59, 105, 202, 290, 316–17, 350
Guillaumat, General Marie Louis, 306, 323
Gwynne, H.A., 211

Haig, Sir Douglas, 136, 179, 203, 221, 263–264; on armistice negotiations and terms, 334; assuaged by Robertson, 178; attack in Arras sector, 98; attends military conference at War Office, 135; battle of Cambrai, 197–98; battle of Paschendaele, 129, 131–132, 137, 244; battles in 1918, 316, 320–21, 326; character, 79; conceals from London state of French army, 118; confident of beating back imminent German attack, 243; considers Jellicoe weak and vacillating, 124; criticized by French, 183; on defensive strategy, 179, 203; on Derby, 240; distrusts Wilson, 133; on extension of British front, 182, 216–17, 256, 265–266, 270–71; fails to grasp lessons of the Somme, 137; favors extending Foch's authority, 255; favors policy of attrition on western front, 79, 112; and Flanders operation , 89, 112, 116, 120–23, 125, 305; generalship during Operation Michael, 256–258; gives interview to French journalists, 91; incensed by War Cabinet's want of confidence, 323; and Lloyd George, 80, 89, 91, 94–95, 98–99; makes little effort to support Robertson, 229, 231–32, 239–40; and manpower, 32–33, 37, 205–06, 256; and Nivelle, 89, 95; offer to resign not accepted, 259–60; ordered to send two divisions to Italy, 185; on possibility of a German assault in 1918, 207, 210; Pershing to withdraw three divisions under British command, 320; pressured into making staff changes, 199; compromise with Lloyd George over guns to Italy, 135; reaction to Maurice's letter, 272; refuses to give up divisions to General Reserve, 242–243; response to massive German offensive, 248, 251–252, 261, 301–02, 308; told not to embark on another Passchendale, 325; visited at GHQ by Asquith, 167; visited by H. Wilson in London, 240
Hankey, Lieutenant Colonel Maurice, 73, 124, 304, 306, 332; acts as peacemaker between LG and Milner, 311; absent from War Cabinet, 178; at Anglo-French and Allied conferences, 86, 93–94; appointed Secretary of War Cabinet, 16; and armistice negotiations, 333; carries out assignments for LG, 311, 315; compiles report of Imperial War Committee's work, 319; critical of LG, 135–36; Curzon warns of

Hankey, Lieutenant Colonel Maurice, *(Continued)* consequences of Robertson's resignation, 180–81; diary entry that LG would like to get rid of Haig, 90; errs in assertion of LG's role, 323–24; finds LG optimistic, 134; informs LG of disaster at Caporetto, 185; on LG's army figures, 270; on LG's conduct of armistice negotiations and terms, 342; LG confides in, 113; LG justifies working out compromise with Robertson, 235; maintains LG assuming too much the role of dictator, 333–34; and manpower, 205–06; prepares speech for LG; LG not optimistic about Haig's victory, 317; notes that LG said it was best that Derby stay, 240; reaction to creation of Imperial War Cabinet, 155–56; records LG's determination to go back on Sykes-Picot Agreement, 329; refers to LG as half Bolshevik, 284; reports on inspection of western front, 211; sparse diary entry of War Cabinet meeting, 92; and submarine crisis, 104–06, 108–109; thinks LG is taking a gamble, 182–82; urges LG to make a declaration of war aims, 220; visited by LG in office, 91; worries about a military disaster, 301; on X Committee, 272

Hardinge, Lord, 136

Harington, Major General Tim, 312, 337

Henderson, Arthur, 22, 28, 41, 43, 72; appointed to War Cabinet, 14; drafts program of war aims for Labour party, 53; reaction to LG's war aim speech, 225; regarded as lightweight in War Cabinet, 14–15; resigns from government, 53; and Stockholm conference, 47–53; visits Russia 48–49

Henderson, Commander R.G., 106–07

Herbert, Aubrey, 161

Hertling, George, 227

Herzl, Dr. Thedore, 174

Hindenburg, General Paul von, 168, 342

Hinderburg line, 95, 197, 327

Hodge, John, 14, 23, 41, 43

House, Colonel Edward, 159, 193; and armistice negotiations and terms, 338–39; consulted about policy for Russia, 274–75; on Lloyd George, 195, 219, 226–277

Howard, Roy, 8

Hughes, William, 313, 315, 320

Imperial War Cabinet, 155–57, 291,

Issacs, Rufus, see Lord Reading

Izonzo, 185; eleventh battle of, 134

Jacob, General Claude, 211

Jellico, Sir John, 125, 145, 178; character and outlook, dismissed from Admiralty, 200–202; 101; pleads for a reduction of commitment in distant theaters, 62, 142; supports Flanders operation, 122; and submarine crisis, 102–104, 106, 108, 109

Jerusalem, 151, 159, 179, 192, 199, 207

Jones, Kennedy, 28

Jusserand, Jules, 287

Kaledin, General Alexie, 274–275, 279–280, 286

Karl, Emperor of Austria, 112–13, 337–38

Keishiro, Matsui, 278

Kerensky, Alexander, 291

Kerr, Philip, 16, 220, 227, 270, 332; holds meeting with Parodi, 221

Keynes, John Maynard, on Lloyd George, 12

Kiggell, Sir Lancelot, 129, 132, 199

Kirke, Colonel Walter, 217, 249

Kitchener, Lord, 5, 7, 21, 180, 196, 327, 343

Knox, General Alfred, 276, 293

Kornilov, General L.G., 164

Kühlmann, Richard von, 163, 168, 219

Lancken, Oscar von der, 163

Lansdowne, Lord, 219, 223, 237, 277

INDEX 415

Lee, Arthur, 64, 66–67, 182
Lenin, Vladimir, 202, 221, 274–275, 279–280, 283
Leslie, Norman, 107–108
Link, Arthur S., 159
Lloyd, Richard, character and attitude, 1; as foster father to George children, 1
Lloyd George, David, 101; and Addison, 44–45; at Allied and Anglo-French conferences, 86–88, 93–95, 113–14, 116, 127–28, 129–31, 141–43, 145–46, 172–73, 188–89, 254–55, 275–79; and armistice negotiations and terms, 328 *et seq*; arrangement with Robertson breaks down, 135; assessment as war leader, 343–51; attempts to forge closer ties with Washington, 193–94; attracted to idea of military triumvirate, 133; believes the French mean to create postwar empire in Balkans, 326; and Boer War, 2–3; on Chamberlain (Neville), 23–24, 27; as Chancellor of the Exchequer, 3 *et seq*; character and attitude, 10–12; claims Haig's weakness is in choice of subordinates, 319; committed to creation of Jewish homeland, 174–77; considers giving Wilson more authority, 210; creates War Cabinet, 14–15; on Derby, 13, 240, 262; discontent with Asquith, 9–10; early years and training, 1–2; at fault for starving Haig of men, 257, 258; favors extending Foch's authority, 254–55; furious that earlier plan to send troops to Italy was thwarted, 185–86; hesitant about supporting Britain's entry in war in 1914, 5; and Haig, 80, 86, 89, 91, 94–99, 116, 135, 166, 178, 242–43; 259–60, 298, 316; and Henderson, 50–53; hostile reaction in London to Paris speech, 192; ignorant on military matters, 78; ignores warnings of impending German attack, 247; and Imperial War Cabinet, 155–57; on intervention in Russia, 274–295; and Ireland, 4–5, 8, 35–37; on Jellicoe, 103, 107, 200; keeps up nation's morale, 171; key in creation of first Coalition, 7; and labor, 39–55; learns of Italian defeat at Caporetto; livid at being deceived by Robertson, 198–99, 207; on Maclay, 58; maneuvers Robertson out of War Office, 227–39; and manpower, 7–8, 21–37, 205–07; Marconi scandal, 4; marriage, 2; and Maurice affair, 265–71, 297; meeting with French delegation at New Casino Hotel, 188; meeting with Sarrail, 87; as member of parliament, 1890–1905, 2–3; as Minister of Munitions, 6–7; on the monarchy, 366n71; orchestrates removal of Jellicoe, 200–202; partially at fault for bloodletting at Passchendaele, 138; pays high tribute to John French, 133; peripheral war, 139–153; personal secretariat, 16–17; pessimistic, 117, 153, 161, 318; on possibility of a negotiated settlement, 80–82, 112–113, 117, 160–67; president of Board of Trade, 1906–1908, 3; and the press,192, 211, 229–30, 259, 261, 266–67; proposes to anoint Nivelle commander of British army, 92 *et seq*; reaction to Wilson's Fourteen Points, 226–27; realizes it is too late to upset current defensive arrangements, 242; relations with Clemenceau, 191, 203–04, 213, 307–08; replaces Asquith as prime minister, 10; requests the recall of Sarrail,147; response to German attacks in 1918, 249–50; 252–54; 302, 308–09, and Robertson, 78–79, 89, 94, 96, 178, 184, 209, 199, 213–15, 222; and Russia,117, 121, 128, 164–65, 202, 221; sanctions Flanders operation, 125;

Lloyd George, David, (*Continued*)
  Secretary of State for War, 8–9;
  selects cabinet, 12–14; shipping and
  food crisis, 57–74; social reformer,
  3–4; speeches in House of
  Commons, 24–25, 196, 235, 241,
  261, 269–271, and Stockholm
  conference, 47–53; strained
  relations with the French, 320–21,
  325–26; strategy, 6–7, 77–78,
  82–86, 89–90, 111–12, 115,
  127–28, 134, 168–69, 171–72, 177,
  202–03, 206–07, 246, 302–06,
  312–15, 319, 323–24, 326–29;
  and submarine crisis, 103–09;
  summons Council of War, 180–81;
  and SWC, 180, 182, 186, 188–89,
  212–14, 244, 263–64, 305–06;
  upset over Asquith's speech at
  Leeds, 166–67; urged to come to
  terms with Robertson, 193; wants
  to remove, Haig, 90, 199, 211,
  310–11; wants to revise Sykes-Picot
  Agreement, 144, 159–60, 173, 327,
  329; war aims, 54, 144, 156,
  159–60, 219–25; and *War Memoirs*,
  39, 50, 59, 85, 104, 108, 291, 322;
  and War Policy Committee,
  120–23, 172, 148; and Woodrow
  Wilson, 158–59, 253, 258, 326–27,
  331; work habits, 17–18
Lloyd George, Margaret Owen, marriage
  to L G, 2
Lockhart, R.H. Bruce, mission to Russia,
  281–285
Long, Walter, 30, 234, 238, 333
Ludendorff, Erich von, 301, 307, 350;
  forced to resign, 337; launches
  attacks in 1918, 247, 261, 300,
  302, 307; will not renounce
  Belgian hinterland,168
Lyautey, General Hubert, 90, 141–42
Lynden-Bell, Major General Arthur,
  179

MacDonald, Ramsay, 50, 53; on Lloyd
  George, 12; and Stockholm
  conference, 47

Macdonogh, Lieutenant General Sir
  George, 33, 177, 233, 297
Maclay, Sir Joseph, 104; appointed to
  head Ministry of Shipping, 14, 58;
  character and outlook, 58; as
  Minister of Shipping, 59–62, 345
Macready, Lieutenant General Sir Neville,
  29, 35, 297
Mahon, General Sir Byrne, 36
Malakoff, V.N., 276–77
Manchester Guardian, 192
Manpower Committee (set up by Lloyd
  George), 33–34, 205–07
Marder, A.J., 109
Marshall, Lieutenant General Sir
  William, 217, 338
Massey, W.F., 304, 320
Maude, General Sir Stanley, 139–41, 142,
  151, 178
Maurice, General Sir Frederick, 134–135,
  247; accuses LG of lying, 265–69;
  on constitution for SWC, 186–87;
  dismissed from army, 271–72;
  observation on LG and Robertson,
  212
Maxwell, General R.C., 199
Mensdorff, Albert, 220, 222
Messines, battle of, 119
Michaelis, Georg, 163
Middleton, T.H., 64, 66
Military Service Act, 34; amended by
  Cave Committee, 36–37
Millman, Brock, 158, 348
Milne, General Sir George, 329, 340;
  excluded from negotiations with
  Bulgaria, 326;
Milner, Lord, 63, 134, 228, 265, 298;
  applauds LG's peripheral strategy,
  246–47; appointed to War Cabinet,
  15; ardent Imperialist, 117; and
  armistice negotiations and terms,
  333–34; asks LG to set record
  straight, 297; begs Lloyd George to
  intervene at Passchendaele, 133;
  character, 15–16; clashes with Foch,
  301; critical of Lloyd George, 51;
  disagrees with LG, 306–07; does
  not consider moment right to recall

Haig, 298; favors Jewish homeland, 176; on Foch, 302, 314; and food committee, 63–64; on future strategy,119, 313; on intervention in Russia, 275, 286, 288–290, 292; and manpower, 28, 30–31; member of X Committee, 272; opposes mixing British and French divisions, 299; overrules Wilson, 306; on peace talks, 164–65, 177; recommends changes at Admiralty and War Cabinet, 124–25; report of committee on non-territorial issues, 156; supports LG, 123; understanding with Pershing, 263–64; undertakes mission to France, 250–51; unmoved by Haig's assurances, 178; unsympathetic to Robertson, 230–31, 234–37; wants LG to consider more anti-submarine measures, 106; warns Haig to conserve men, 325; will comply with Haig's request, 265

Money, Sir Leo Chiozza, 62–63

Montagu, Edwin, 22–23, 176

Morley, Lord, 176

Morning Post, 9–10, 167–68, 192, 211, 229–30, 233, 261, 266

Munitions of War Act, 40–41, 45, 54

Murray, General Archibald, 149–52, 160, 179

Nation, 192

Nivelle, General Robert, 97, 111–12, 150; arrives in London to sell plan, 88–90, and Haig, 95; proposal to put him in charge of British army, 92 *et seq*; failure of attack of, 98

Northcliffe, Lord, 10, 69

Observer, 67, 192, 225

Orlando, Vittorio, 187, 214–15; agrees to relieve Cadorna of command, 188

Pact of London, 80, 158, 275

Painlevé, Paul, 167, 182, 196; and Balkan front, 142, 144; defends Sarrail, 147; falls from power, 203–04; on German peace talks, 165; lacks confidence in Nivelle's plan, 97–98, 348; at Rapallo Conference, 188–89; supports idea of Supreme War Council, 180, 186; turns down LG's suggestion to appoint Thomas war minister, 191

Passchendale, see Third Battle of Ypres

Pershing, General John, 254; on creation of an American army, 252, 265, 321; intends to withdraw three American divisions from Haig, 320; on subject of amalgamation of American troops, 252–53, 263–64,

Pétain, General Philippe, 265; agreement with Haig for mutual support, 244; agrees to limit extension of Haig's front, 216–17; alleged to be in state of panic, 251; no confidence in Flanders operation, 118; refuses to contribute troops to General Reserve, 242; replaces Nivelle, 98; on sending guns to Italy, 135–36; under impression Italian army no longer exists, 187

Petrograd Soviet, 47–48, 359 n33

Pichon, Stéphane, and armistice negotiations, 328–29, 341; considers British proposal dangerous, 276; would like Japan to do more, 278

Picot, Georges, 175

Plumer, General Herbert, 119, 240, 298; rejects offer to succeed Robertson, 238

Poole, Major General Frederick, 287

Prothero, R.E., 13; character and outlook, 63–64; as president of Board of Agriculture, 63–66

Punch, 69

Radcliffe, Major General Percy de, 270

Rawlinson, General Sir Henry, 240, 242, 259, 316

Reading, Lord, 4, 262, 287, 293–94, 332–33 Redmond, John, 8

Rennell Rodd, Sir James, 134

Repington, Charles à Court, 26–27, 22–30, 229–30, 233, 241, 268
Rhondda, Lord, 13, 30, asked to investigate manpower issue, 27; character and attitude, 69–70; findings of committee, 28; as Food Controller, 70–72; threatened with dismissal, 73, rationing plan ultimately a success, 74.
Ribot, Alexandre, 84, 204; against superseding Sarrail,147; appears to be wavering,116; appointed minister of war, 97; and Balkans, 142, 144, 149; likely to oppose British protectorate over Palestine,160; objects to bringing Italy into the negotiations, 113
Richmond, Captain Herbert, 106
Riddell, Lord, 133, 219, 225, 250, 291, 307
Roberts, G.H., 55
Robertson, Sir William, 116, 133, 136, 181, 187, 193; adamant that British resources should be concentrated in France, 62, 78–79, 115, 117, 179, 203; on Alexandretta, 172; and Allenby, 177–79, at Allied conference in Rome, 86–87; asked to investigate consequences of Russia's collapse, 164; assessment as CIGS, 137–38, 241; and Balkans, 83–84, 141–43, 145–47, 148; believes Germans are trying to sow dissension among Allies, 222; character, 79; comparison with Henry Wilson, 245; confers with LG, 29; doubts that Germany can be beaten without Russia, 166–67; ejected from War Office after losing fight to retain authority, 228–39; encourages Maurice, 266; favors making political concessions to detach Germany's allies, 162; favors removal of Sarrail,147; and Haig, 79, 112, 117, 120–21, 178, 185, 197–98, 207, 229, 239–40; holds back general reserve, 257; informed of what LG had done, 187; leaves for Italy on fact-finding mission, 184–85; and Lloyd George, 78–79, 89, 94–95, 98–99, 178, 184, 186, 196–97, 211–15; and Mesopotamia, 139–40; misleads LG and War Cabinet, 92, 129, 132, 198–99; note from Esher about the French; 118; objects to sideshow, 83, 122–23, 139; and Palestine, 149–52, 160, 177–78, 208–10, 213; on policy with Bolsheviks, 280; possible replacement for Carson, 124; at Rapollo Conference, 188–89; recommends appointment of Allenby, 152; replies to French and Wilson's criticism, 184; resents decision to summon Council of War, 180; struggles to establish control over military representative, 193; at SWC, 213–14; unable to persuade Pershing to delay creating homogenous army, 251–52; unimpressed by Nivelle's plan, 89–90; visits Lloyd George at Hurstpierpoint, 134–35; warns government of impending German assault, 247; worries about submarine threat, 106
Runciman, Walter, 101, 268
Rupprecht, Crown Prince, 308
Russian Provisional Government, 47–48, 173–75, 291

Salter, J.A., 345
Samuel, Herbert, 174
Sarrail, General Maurice, 142, 146; failure of spring operation of, 143–44; favors an offensive in Balkans, 83; meeting with Lloyd George, 87; to be recalled home, 204; removal contemplated, 147–48; submits plans for operation in Balkans, 141
Scott, C.P., 167
Shortt, Edward, 31
Seaman's Union, 48
Shipping Control Committee, 57
Sims, Rear Admiral William S., 103, 107
Sixte, Prince, 112–14

Smillie, Robert, 69
Smuts, General Jan. C., 135, 227, 250; ardent Imperialist, 117; believes Haig should be allowed to move forward, 123; declines command of EEF, 152; equates defeat with compromised settlement, 161; critical of Foch's dispositions, 307; on future strategy, 313–14, 317; holds meeting with Mensdorff in Switzerland, 220; invited to Chequers, 182; LG relies on advice of, 217; loyal to LG, 304; report on fact-finding mission to Middle East, 245–46; report on general military situation, 114–15; report on inspection of western front; 211; supports Jewish homeland, 176; visits Haig, 308; works on draft of SWC, 188; works on draft of LG's war aims speech, 222–23
Sonnino, Baron Sidney, 187, 276; admits not qualified to state opinion,128; and armistice negotiations, 332; raises possibility of attack on Italian front, 129–30; stands in way of separate peace with Austria, 113–14
Spectator, 192, 344
Spender, J.A, 241; reports that Asquith has no desire to assume office, 241
Spiers, Lieutenant Colonel Edward, 94, 119
Spring-Rice, Sir Cecil, 195
Stalin, Joseph, 273
Stamfordham, Lord, 92; begs Robertson not to relinquish post, 236
Stanley, Albert, 13,
Star, 259
Stevenson, Frances, 11, 145
Stockholm peace conference, 47
Supreme War Council, 188–89, 205, 209, 212–13, 244, 263–64, 272, 289, 292–93, 301, 305–06
Sutemi, Chinda, 278
Sutherland, William, 44–45
Sykes, Mark, 160, 175

Sykes-Picot Agreement, 144, 159–61, 173, 327, 329
Sylvester, A.J., on Lloyd George, 11

Tardieu, André, 305
Taylor, A.J.P., on Lloyd George, 12, 266
Terraine, John, 232
Thomas, Albert, 48, 84, 128, 135, 191
Thompson, Malcolm, 36
Thompson, William Boyce, 281
Thursby, Admiral C.F., 105
Times, 8, 26, 67, 192, 229, 267,
Trade Card Agreement, 22, 28, 43
Trade Union Advisory Committee, 55
Trade Union Congress (TUC), 39, 46, 72, 223
Treasury Agreement, 40
Trotsky, Leon, 273, 283, 285

Unionist War Committee, 211, 268
Urquhart, Leslie, 287

Venizelos, Eleutherios, 83, 144, 148
Victor Emmanuel III, King, 191
Villalobar, Marquis de, 163

Walsh, Stephen, 30
War Cabinet, accepts Maclay's recommendations, 59; agrees to establishment of SWC, 186; armistice negotiations and terms, 336–37; and Balkans, 84; debates fate of Robertson, 239; decides to offer post of Director of National Service to Montagu, 23; discusses Smuts' Middle East report, 246; extension of British front, 216–17; favors North Atlantic shipping route, 62; hopes to avoid general rationing blasted, 72–73; on intervention in Russia, 274–75, 279–281, 283–84, 286, 289–90; and labor, 43, 46; and manpower, 25–37; membership, 14–16; and military policy, 111, 115, 125, 129–30, 135, 140, 145, 153, 161–62, 210, 298, 307; and Nivelle, 88–90, 92–93; on peace

War Cabinet, (*Continued*)
negotiations, 80–81, 160, 164–65;
Robertson pleads case before, 237;
and Stockholm conference, 47–52;
and submarine crisis, 106, 107;
successor to War Committee,
17–18; votes to subsidize bread, 71;
on war aims, 160, 222–23, 327;
will not force Haig's hand, 242
War Policy Committee, approves of
Flanders operation, 125; considers
whether Haig should undertake
Flanders operation, 120–23;
discusses future strategy, 177–79;
membership, 120; recommends
withdrawal of British divisions from
Balkans, 148
Webb, Sidney, 53
Weizmann, Chaim, 144, 174–75
Wemyss, Admiral Sir Rosslyn, 105, 332,
334; appointed First Sea Lord,
201–02
Westminster Gazette, 192, 241, 266–67
Weygand, General Maxime, 204
William II, Kaiser, 336, 337; forced to
abdicate, 342
Wilson, Sir Henry, 182, 263, 265; and
armistice negotiations and terms,
333–34, 340; conversation with LG
and other members of War
Cabinet, 133–34; at Beauvais
conference, 254–55; character and
outlook, 245; comments on
defeatist attitude of some ministers,
116–17; at Council of War
meeting, 181; crosses over to
France, 250–51; designated
representative on SWC's general
staff, 187, 189; enjoys confidence of
LG, 209; expected to act
independently of WO general staff,
205; fears the French might make
peace, 119; feels Haig must be
watched closely, 325; on Foch, 299,
314; on future strategy, 183–84,
298–99, 306, 312, 315–16, 323;
and German spring attacks in 1918,
251, 307–08; gives update on
Haig's gains, 322; on matters
relating to appointment as CIGS;
235, 237–38; meets British
delegation at Versailles, 327; memo
on strategic initiative in eastern
theater, 304; reports on Franchet
d'Esperey's proposed march, 326;
sees merit in General Reserve,
242–43; suggests removal of
Haig, 298; at SWC, 215; visits
Haig in London, 240; wants
British to be forthcoming with the
French, 306
Wilson, Woodrow, 8, 193, 222, 264;
armistice negotiations and terms,
326, 328–29, 331–38; differences
with Lloyd George, 158, 195;
distaste of imperialism, 158, 175;
on intervention in Russia, 286–87,
289, 292–94; mounts peace
initiative, 81–82; no objection to
Britain's retention of German
colonies, 334; promises to send over
reinforcements, 253; supports idea
of Jewish homeland, 176, on war
aims, 158, 219, 226
Wimborne, Lord, 36
Wiseman, Sir William, 331, 334; forms
close personal relationship with
House, 195
Woodward, David, 123, 211

X Committee, 287–88, 290, 297–99,
308–09, 311, 322, 334–45;
membership, 272

Ypres, third battle of, 129, 131–32, 137,
199, 232, 304–05

Zionism, 174–77

www.ingramcontent.com/pod-product-compliance
Lightning Source LLC
Chambersburg PA
CBHW021813300426
44114CB00009BA/160